A HISTORY OF THE UNITED STATES
SINCE THE CIVIL WAR

A HISTORY

OF

THE UNITED STATES

SINCE THE CIVIL WAR

BY

ELLIS PAXSON OBERHOLTZER

IN FIVE VOLUMES

VOLUME II: 1868-72

NEGRO UNIVERSITIES PRESS
NEW YORK

Originally published in 1917-37
by The Macmillan Company, New York

Reprinted 1969 by
Negro Universities Press
A DIVISION OF GREENWOOD PUBLISHING CORP.
NEW YORK

SBN 8371-2643-6

PRINTED IN UNITED STATES OF AMERICA

CONTENTS

CHAPTER IX

RECONSTRUCTING THE SOUTH

CHAPTER X

IMPEACHMENT AND TRIAL OF ANDREW JOHNSON

CHAPTER XI

The Campaign of 1868

CHAPTER XII

GRANT AS PRESIDENT

CHAPTER XV

To the Pacific and Beyond

CHAPTER XVI

The End of the Orgy

CONTENTS

A HISTORY OF THE UNITED STATES SINCE THE CIVIL WAR

CHAPTER IX

RECONSTRUCTING THE SOUTH

THE progress of the South in the re-establishment of its industries and the recuperation of its commercial strength was slow. The pique and despair of the people during the first months following the surrender had yielded various plans of escape from the full measure of its consequences. One made way for another. The emigration to Mexico, as we have seen, had ended in fiasco even before the downfall of Maximilian. Other men had turned their eyes toward Brazil, Venezuela and Honduras, schemes which soon ran a similar course. General de Goicouria, who had been appointed a special agent by the Emperor Dom Pedro, opened an office in New Orleans and advertised for colonists in the newspapers of Louisiana, Texas, Mississippi and Tennessee.[1] Ships bound out from New Orleans and Mobile were carrying parties of dispirited men and women to their new homes.[2] They were "utterly sick at heart"; a "more sorrowful emigration," said the New Orleans Picayune, was "not recorded in history."[3]

From the first the movement had been discountenanced by the sensible leaders and the responsible press of the South. Brazil was 4,000 miles away. The colonists would pass from plenty to destitution, from ease to misery.[4] Nearly every letter from those who had gone out brought back pitiful ac-

[1] New Orleans Picayune, April 8, 1867.
[2] Cf. New Orleans Times, July 28, 1867; New Orleans Picayune, May 14, 1867.
[3] Issue of April 16, 1867.
[4] New Orleans Picayune, May 14, 1867.

1

counts of the adventure. They spoke of the "stunning disappointment" which they had suffered upon their arrival in the new land.[1] Many were advanced in years and never had done as much as a day's work in their lives. They could not speak or understand Portuguese, the language which was in use among the people around them. Their slaves ran off, and they knew not how to recover them.[2] They were without food and they had no means of producing it. They had no flour, no butter, no milk; there was not even water to drink. There were no wagons or carts, no oxen to draw vehicles, and no roads. The manner in which the Southern people had been deceived was "worse than criminal," said a former citizen of New Orleans who wrote home from Para.[3] Some were impressed into the Brazilian army for the war on Paraguay.[4] Only in one case was there a different story. At Rio Dolce in the province of Espirito Santo, grouped around a fresh water lake, fifty miles from the ocean, on land grants made to Colonel Gunter, of Alabama, there were some settlers who were said to be prosperous.[5] Starving in the interior, they sought refuge in the cities. Though it hurt the pride of these Confederate exiles to carry the accounts of their tribulations to our consular officers they did so, and the agents of a government, whose rigors the colonists had fled to escape, collected money to feed them and otherwise aid them in their distress. Our consul at Rio, James Monroe, wrote to Secretary Seward in their behalf. In a little while Secretary Welles addressed the commanders of all homeward bound American ships of war, asking them to take on board as many destitute Southerners as could be accommodated. Thus were numbers of unfortunate people returned to the South.[6]

[1] New Orleans Picayune, Feb. 12, 1868.
[2] James Monroe, Lectures, Addresses and Essays, p. 198.
[3] N. Y. Tribune, Nov. 16, 1867, quoting New Orleans Times.
[4] N. Y. Herald, Jan. 27, 1868.
[5] N. Y. Freeman's Journal, quoted in New Orleans Picayune, April 10, 1868.
[6] James Monroe, op. cit., pp. 198-204. A settlement dating back to this period 100 miles north of Sao Paulo, called Villa Americana, still survives.—N. Y. Evening Post, April 26, 1921.

The difficulty of using negro labor, now that the blacks had been freed, continued to call for immigration from the Northern and Western states, and Europe. Louisiana with its harbor at New Orleans, where shipping was being resumed, with lines to Hamburg, Liverpool, St. Nazaire and other foreign ports,[1] looked to a future in which negroes would be replaced by white colonists willing to work in Southern households and till the plantations. The newspapers were filled with advertisements for white cooks, porters, gardeners, nurses. "Intelligent white labor" was urgently required on the plantations and a few Germans who came in on ships from Hamburg, trained to agriculture and with "contented and happy dispositions," were welcomed by people and press.[2]

Bureaus of immigration were established in nearly all the Southern states to advertise their soil, climate and productions. Depots to welcome emigrants and labor exchanges were established. Private associations for the encouragement of immigration were chartered by the legislatures.[3] Conventions met in several Southern cities to promote similar ends. Delegates who assembled in Charleston demanded direct steamer communication with Europe and presented plans for attracting to South Carolina colonists who had already settled in the West and Northwest.[4] A convention in Montgomery bade colonists a hearty and honest welcome to Alabama. It issued an address, directing the attention of the people of the United States and Europe to the agricultural and mineral wealth of the state, and the commercial advantages which were to be enjoyed by those who might come to dwell there.[5] Georgia[6] and Virginia[7] sent commissioners to Europe. At one time Virginia had 300 agents in Germany and 250 in

[1] Cf. New Orleans Picayune, Oct. 24, 1867.
[2] Ibid., Oct. 26, 1867.
[3] For acts relating to this subject see Laws of Louisiana for 1869, p. 106; Laws of Texas for 1871, p. 127; Acts of Virginia for 1872-3, p. 272; Acts of Arkansas for 1868, pp. 61, 124; Laws of Mississippi for 1866-7, p. 654; Laws of Georgia for 1869, p. 26; ibid. for 1872, p. 318.
[4] American Annual Cyclopedia for 1870, p. 683.
[5] Ibid. for 1869, p. 10.
[6] Ibid. for 1870, p. 342.
[7] Ibid., p. 749.

England, distributing pamphlets and laboring otherwise to bring the state's attractions to the notice of the people. But in three months preceding June, 1870, only 130 foreign colonists settled in the state and the superintendent in charge of the work was unable to collect his expenses from the legislature.[1] Not anywhere was there response to the South's appeals except in Arkansas and Texas, whose climate and situation caused them to share in the general development and expansion of the West.[2]

Many Southern planters looked with favor upon the plan for the importation of Chinese coolies which were being used with success not only on the Pacific coast in the construction of the transcontinental railroad, but also in Cuba and South America.[3] The Irish and other white laborers threw heavier spadefuls but at the end of the day it was found that the Chinese had removed more earth.[4] In Louisiana in November, 1867, they were being bound to work from dawn until dark, with two hours for breakfast and dinner, standing watch at night during the sugar making and on Sundays, for $14 a month in greenbacks.[5] South Carolina sought them for work in the river bottoms where rice and long cotton were raised. Here in a sickly climate where white men could not live, it was said that they would enjoy "almost perfect health." They could be engaged for a five year period at $125 a head and a hire price of fifty cents a day.[6]

A strong impulse was lent to the movement at a Chinese immigration convention which met in Memphis on July 13, 1869. The hotels of the city were crowded with planters from Tennessee, Arkansas, Mississippi and other states and the meetings continued for two or three days. Ex-Governor Harris of Tennessee presided. A resolution was adopted—

[1] American Annual Cyclopedia for 1870, p. 749.
[2] For Arkansas see Powell Clayton, Aftermath of the Civil War, pp. 207 et seq.
[3] New Orleans Picayune, Sep. 22, 1867.
[4] Phila. Ledger, July 13, 1869.
[5] New Orleans Picayune, Nov. 16, 1867.
[6] American Annual Cyclopedia for 1870, p. 683.

"the best interests of the South" required that "all legitimate inducements" should be offered at once "to encourage the immigration of Chinese laborers in large numbers direct from China to supply the great demand now existing for steady and reliable labor." [1] A Hollander named Koopmanschap, engaged for many years in the China trade in California, who had brought to this country half of the Chinese on the Pacific coast, was present with offers to collect and import any desired number of cheap Asiatic workmen. [2]

The subject attracted widespread attention. The newspapers, North as well as South, opened their columns to a discussion of the question. Only 11 Chinese had come to the United States between the years 1820 and 1840, only 35 between 1840 and 1850, but for the ten years ending with 1860 the arrivals numbered 41,396. [3] From the first of January, 1862, to September 30, 1870, according to the records of the port of San Francisco, no less than 51,000 had reached that city. [4]

But at the very moment when the question of bringing the Chinese into the South was being discussed at Memphis the white laborers in California were giving the world strange exhibitions of their jealous rage. They clubbed the little yellow men and pelted them with stones in the streets of San Francisco without legal hindrance, or as much, indeed, as protest from bystanders. [5] "Anti-Coolie Leagues" were formed by workingmen in all parts of the North, and petitions were sent to the President urging him to action which would "ever be remembered by a grateful and Christian people." [6] Less prejudice could not be looked for in the South. Already Radical politicians and newspapers were engaged in an effort to make the negroes believe that this was another part of the premeditated scheme of the old white master class

[1] N. Y. Tribune, July 6, 1869.
[2] Phila. Ledger, July 17, 1869; N. Y. Tribune, July 21 and Nov. 12, 1869.
[3] Phila. Ledger, Nov. 22, 1870.
[4] Ibid., Dec. 15, 1870.
[5] Ibid., July 13, 1869.
[6] Ibid., Nov. 7, 1870.

to deprive them of their rights.[1] It was but another form of slavery. The plan to revive the coolie trade under the plea of a want of labor at the South, the New York Tribune said, was "monstrous"; it should meet "the stern and uncompromising opposition of conscientious men."[2]

The Radical Congress expressed similar views. The trade had been prohibited by a law of 1862 in so far as Chinese should be dragooned and brought into the country against their will. It was an "odious and abhorrent" traffic. The government would give effect to the "moral sentiment of the nation" and prevent the "further introduction of coolies into this hemisphere or the adjacent islands," and Secretary Seward had issued a circular on the subject.[3] A brig laden with Chinamen which came into the Mississippi from Havana for a planter living near Donaldsonville, La., was not permitted to land. The United States district attorney seized the ship's papers and the consignee was obliged to feed the men at his own expense while it lay at anchor in the river.[4]

Secretary Boutwell when he was appealed to for a ruling on the subject made it clear that the government would interfere only if the Chinese had been coerced into leaving their homes; if their immigration was a voluntary act on their part there was no contravention of the law and Koopmanschap and Co. were enabled to continue their trade very much as before.[5] But the prohibition of the making of contracts in China increased the price of this labor and put it out of the reach of the planters of the South, whose hope had been to introduce the apprentice system which was in use in Cuba. Now that it was made to appear that a Chinaman would cost twice and perhaps three times as much as a negro hand their interest in the subject waned.[6]

Nevertheless some hundreds, perhaps a few thousands, of

[1] N. Y. Tribune, July 27, 1869; Powell Clayton, Aftermath of the Civil War in Arkansas, pp. 208, 214.
[2] Issue of Aug. 9, 1869.
[3] Senate Ex. Doc., 40th Cong. 2nd sess., No. 80.
[4] New Orleans Times, Aug. 7, 1867.
[5] Phila. Ledger, July 27, and Sep. 29, 1869; Pub. Miss. Hist. Soc., vol. ii, p. 380.
[6] Phila. Ledger, Aug. 20, 1869.

coolies did find their way into the South. They came from San Francisco on contracts made with them after they had reached that city. They were seen at work on sugar plantations near New Orleans,[1] and in Arkansas.[2] Some, too, were employed in gangs on the Southern railroads.[3] Robert Somers, an English traveller, found 600 living in tents and working side by side with negro laborers on the line of the new "Alabama and Chattanooga." [4] "Pig tails" could be seen any day on the streets of New Orleans.[5] But all the experiments proved disastrous and soon came to an end. The wiser Southern leaders anyhow discouraged this as well as other movements to replace the negroes, whether with white or Chinese labor, just as they discountenanced the schemes for their own people to emigrate to Mexico and Brazil.[6]

The immediate outlook was dark enough, but if all else failed the Southern whites could work their way out of their difficulties by the use of their own hands. And this was sage counsel, the wisest which came to them from any side. "Our people," said the New Orleans Picayune, "need to be thrown entirely upon their own resources and the heavier the shock, the more complete the overthrow of the past system of negro and other vicarious labor . . . the more likely are they to begin where their fathers began without the negro." Let them give up the cook and the laundress who carried out of the house more than their work came to, the farm hand who stole the crops and the cattle.[7] The South would card its own wool and spin its own cotton. It could weave on hand looms and in "dog power" factories.[8] At Augusta and Columbus in

[1] Ku Klux Report, vol. xiii, p. i; cf. Phila. Ledger, Oct. 13, 1869, and Nov. 29, 1870.
[2] Powell Clayton, Aftermath of the Civil War in Arkansas, pp. 207 et seq.
[3] Phila. Ledger, Dec. 13, 1870.
[4] Robert Somers, Southern States After the War, pp. 163-4.
[5] Ibid., p. 225.
[6] Cf. opinion of General Gordon in Ku Klux Report, Georgia Testimony, pp. 307-8.
[7] New Orleans Picayune, Dec. 29, 1867.
[8] Ibid., Dec. 25, 1867, quoting Lexington, Miss., Advertiser; cf. proceedings of Charleston convention in May, 1870, American Annual Cyclopedia for 1870, p. 684.

Georgia water power was being used to turn the machinery of cotton mills.[1] More than 70 small but successful cotton factories erected since the war were in operation in that state;[2] 13, employing 900 persons and representing an investment, it was said, of one million dollars, were at work in Tennessee.[3] Several fine new mills for the manufacture of sheetings and shirtings were seen and admired by travellers through the state of Alabama.[4]

Many men were building railroads. Others were exploring the mineral wealth of Alabama and Tennessee. Deposits of marl and phosphate were being put to commercial use. The seed of the cotton which had been held to be without value was beginning to be crushed in mills where the oil was expressed from it and the fibre was converted into guano. Timber was being felled and sawed into lumber. Quarries were yielding valuable marble and granite. Commercial conventions assembled in several cities of the South to discuss the advancement of trade. Everywhere there were agricultural fairs for the competitive display of farm products.[5] A growing interest was manifested in the improvement of the soil. In 1870 Georgia expended $10,000,000 for commercial manures, one fifth as much, so it was said, as was being laid out in a year for the fertilization of the land in Great Britain.[6]

But progress in all directions was obstructed by political agitation and social disturbance. Outside capital which was needed for development would come sparingly, immigrants would settle reluctantly in a country which was in the midst of such an uproar as attended reconstruction.

This work, in accordance with the plans of Congress, proceeded under the direction of the generals appointed to com-

[1] Ku Klux Report, Georgia Testimony, p. 830; C. M. Thompson, Recon. in Ga., p. 307.

[2] Phila. Ledger, June 17, 1867.

[3] Ibid., June 19, 1867.

[4] Montgomery Advertiser, quoted in Phila. Ledger, Aug. 14, 1868; Somers, Southern States After the War, pp. 136-8.

[5] Somers, Southern States After the War, pp. 23-4, 57; N. Y. Tribune, Nov. 27, 1869.

[6] Ku Klux Report, Georgia Testimony, p. 829.

mand the five military districts—Schofield in Virginia, Sickles in the Carolinas, Pope in Georgia, Alabama and Florida, Ord in Mississippi and Arkansas, and Sheridan in Louisiana and Texas. The act of March 2, 1867, "to provide for the more efficient government of the rebel states," with its supplements of March 23 and July 19, contemplated absolute military domination over such civil magistrates as had been designated by the people, with the assistance of President Johnson, until "loyal and republican" state governments could be established by Congress. The male citizens more than twenty-one years of age, whether white or colored, in each district were to be registered by officers appointed by the general in command who, before assuming their duties, should take the "iron clad" test oath of 1862.[1] All applicants for registration were to be barred if, by their participation in the rebellion, they had violated an oath to support the Constitution of the United States, or had given "aid or comfort" to those engaged in the war against the Union. Thereupon, after thirty days notice, the commanding general should order an election, at which time those who had been properly registered were to choose by ballot a number of delegates equal to the membership in the lower house of the legislature of the state in 1860.

At the same election they were to determine whether or not a convention should meet. If a majority of those qualified to vote should vote upon the subject, and a majority of this majority should favor a convention, the delegates were authorized to come together within sixty days and to frame a constitution. If this constitution guaranteed the franchise to blacks and whites alike, and it should be ratified by the registered voters, upon its submission to them at the polls, by a similar majority of the majority, it should be sent to the President for transmission to Congress. If Congress found it to be a satisfactory form of government for the state and approved it, and the state, meanwhile, should adopt the Fourteenth Amendment, and that amendment should be ratified

[1] McPherson, Hist. of Recon., p. 193.

by a number of states large enough to make it effective as a part of the Constitution of the United States, its senators and representatives might take their seats in Congress, military control would cease and it could resume self government.

The carrying out of such a program, in view of the condition of the public mind, both North and South, was attended, in the nature of the case, with the gravest difficulties. Questions large and small as to jurisdiction and right, which would have called for the talent of the ablest constitutional lawyers, came up for determination. Who were the officers of the United States and of the individual states that, having taken an oath to support the Constitution, had, nevertheless, engaged in insurrection or rebellion, and, on this account, were to be barred from the franchise? In what did giving aid and comfort to the Confederacy consist? How were the delegates to be apportioned? Reference of questions to General Grant often met with a request that the commander who was on the ground should exercise his personal discretion. Tact and capacity of a kind, which in the military service had not been called out before, were demanded of men who, in many cases, did not possess these qualities.

The work of registering the voters was begun immediately in all of the five districts. But of necessity it proceeded slowly because of the difficulties which attended travel from place to place, the inexperience of the registrars, and the complete ignorance of many of those who were to be sworn and qualified for the casting of the ballot. Great swamps and trackless expanses of woodland separated the polling places where the boards were to sit for service. The officers must make long and roundabout journeys upon horseback. Thirty miles must be traversed to reach a place distant but six. Travel could not proceed at night because of the condition of the roads, and weeks elapsed before the returns could be received, compiled and revised and the lists were ready for the elections.

Men suitable to serve as registrars were not easily found. General Schofield placed Union army officers, Freedmen's Bureau agents, honorably discharged officers of the army and loyal citizens upon the boards in Virginia. Commanders in other districts drew upon the same sources, though negroes were pressed into the service by Pope, Sickles and Sheridan. In support of his plan to place one black man upon each board of three members in Georgia, Alabama and Florida Pope said that it was "surely better to have an incompetent but loyal man in office than to have a rebel of whatever ability." [1]

At first there was a disposition on the part of the Southern whites to acquiesce in the plans of Congress for the reconstruction of the states. Generals Lee, Johnston, Beauregard, Harden, Hood, Wade Hampton and Longstreet; ex-Governors of Southern states, Magrath and Aiken of South Carolina and Joseph E. Brown of Georgia among them, were urging the people to submit as promptly and with as much grace as possible. The spirit in which this acquiescence was given was naturally not very cordial or sincere. It was expressed with candor by ex-Senator A. G. Brown of Mississippi when he said that it was a nauseating and odious dose, but it should be taken without "grimaces" which could serve only to increase the pleasure of their enemies. "Thad" Stevens was "drunk with rage," he continued, changing his metaphor, and "wants to run his engine over us." He will not "run over me." "I will not be the little bull to try to butt the thing off. I would rather step aside and see him grit and gnash his teeth at his disappointment." [2]

Governor Humphreys asked the people of Mississippi "to offer no resistance to any steps" which might be taken toward reorganization in that state.[3] In the Third District the governors of Alabama and Florida tendered Pope friendly assistance.[4] On the other hand Governor Jenkins of Georgia was outspoken in his opposition and the commander was on the point of removing him from office. The people, said ex-

[1] Report of Sec. of War for 1867, vol. i, p. 351.
[2] Speech at Holly Springs, quoted in N. Y. Herald, Sep. 3, 1867; cf. Garner, Recon. in Miss., p. 179, for opinion of other Mississippi leaders.
[3] New Orleans Picayune, April 9, 1867.
[4] For Alabama cf. Fleming, Recon. in Ala., pp. 503-4.

Governor Johnson, never would "approve of or consent to
or accept" the "poisoned chalice" offered to their lips.[1] Benjamin H. Hill, Herschel V. Johnson and other Georgians of
influence made no concealment of their hostility. Sheridan
had dismissed the governors of Louisiana and Texas for ob-
structing his course in those states.

Everywhere the blacks were being brought under the influence of agents of the Northern Republican party. Southern Republican leaders like John Minor Botts in Virginia
had expressed the fear that if the negroes were enfranchised
they would vote with their old masters.[2] They might have
done so but for a determination on the part of the Radicals
in the North that nothing of this kind should come to pass.
Many speakers and political managers, both white and black,
were sent into the South in the spring and summer of 1867,
to be aided by Freedmen's Bureau agents,[3] Federal office
holders, such as United States marshals, internal revenue col-
lectors and mail agents, settled in the country, and the flot-
sam and jetsam left by the disbanding Union armies—camp
followers, chaplains, quartermasters, sutlers, teachers—which
were found in every Southern state. These were re-enforced
by Southern white men who stood ready to embrace so advantageous a political opportunity, though it cost them their
reputations in the communities in which they dwelt, and also,
not rarely, by mean and desperate fellows who perhaps cherished some grudge against their neighbors and saw in the occasion a favorable chance for revenge.

As a means to the end in view the blacks were gathered
into lodges and clubs, an outgrowth of the Union League
clubs which had been formed in various Northern cities during the war. The idea had spread into neighborhoods where
the predominant sentiment was sympathetic with the Confederacy, in the "Border states" as well as farther South. Here

[1] Augusta, Ga., corr. N. Y. Tribune, July 17, 1867.

[2] Richmond Enquirer, July 8, 1867, quoted in Eckenrode, Political
Recon. of Va. (Johns Hopkins Series, vol. 22), p. 54.

[3] For the part played in reconstruction by the Freedmen's Bureau
cf. Paul S. Peirce, The Freedmen's Bureau (Univ. of Iowa Studies),
chap. ix.

the clubs took on a secret character. Their object was to create opinion favorable to the Union which could be turned to political use. In some places, as in North Carolina, they were known as "Heroes of America" and "Red Strings," and again in Florida as the "Lincoln Brotherhood." [1]

In 1865 and 1866 all these bodies, whatever their names, were consolidated into a national organization called the Union, or Loyal League. At first the members had been white men. Few yet dreamed of universal suffrage, but, when it was seen that the negroes were to vote, they were invited to join the lodges and the native white element retired.[2] Trim, black dandies from New York, Philadelphia, Boston and other Northern cities passed from cabin to cabin to beguile the simple minded people. Initiations, passwords, and rituals, all calculated to put terror into ignorant heads, were devised.[3] Videttes and pickets were posted outside of meeting places to halt passers-by and keep away any but members of the organization.[4] The League soon came to embrace practically the entire black population of the South. Meetings were held at midnight in churches and school houses, in deserted barns, in half-burnt buildings, or, perhaps, in the woods around brush fires, where by incantation and recourse to African fetichism the negroes became ready victims of the Radical leaders.[5]

Many had flocked into the towns. Those who remained in the country would be seen idly standing in the fence corners or at the doors of their cabins.[6] When their old masters would ask them of a morning where they had

---

[1] Fleming, Doc. Hist. of Recon., vol. ii, pp. 20-21; Davis, Recon. in Fla., p. 471; John Wallace, Carpet Bag Rule in Fla., p. 42; Hamilton, Recon. in N. C., pp. 63-4, 244, 281, 456.

[2] Cf. Fleming, Recon. in Ala., pp. 514, 558.

[3] Fleming, Doc. Hist. of Recon., vol. ii, pp. 3-21; and Recon. in Ala., pp. 559-61.

[4] New Orleans Picayune, Oct. 24, 1867, quoting Liberty, Miss., Herald.

[5] Richmond corr. N. Y. Herald, Sep. 29 and Oct. 6, 1867; Petersburg corr. N. Y. Herald, Oct. 1, 1867; cf. Eckenrode, Pol. Recon. of Va., pp. 61, 67; Pub. Miss. Hist. Soc., vol. ii, pp. 377-80; ibid., vol. iv, pp. 114-8.

[6] They would say, as they looked around them at the fertile lands— "De cullud people'll soon hab all dese yere plantations." Helena corr. Memphis Avalanche, quoted in N. O. Picayune, May 17, 1867.

been during the night the reply was at some meeting or
muster. Women now would not pick cotton in the fields;
they were ladies and would stay in the house.[1] Everywhere
labor had become an entirely secondary interest in life. The
entire black race had put work out of view and preferred to
pursue "the chimerical idea of perfect liberty and equality
to anything so degrading." [2] Sums of money, which they
could ill afford to part with, were wrung from them in membership dues. Oaths carrying obligations, with threat of
punishment in case of disobedience of the rules of the order,
were imposed upon those who joined it. Some were bucked and
gagged, flogged, slain, indeed, for breaches of discipline.[3] Such
methods kept the negro mind at a high pitch of excitement.[4]

In the campaigns to elect delegates to the constitutional
conventions and to establish Radical state governments in the
South the full strength of the managers of the League was
exerted upon the black phalanx. Every likely method was
employed to awaken a feeling of distrust for and antagonism
to the old Southern master class who, the negroes were told
by the cunning Radical emissaries, were their dangerous
enemies.[5]

In pursuit of the general design of their leaders the negroes
were armed. They were assembled for military drill. In-
toxicated with liquor, distributed among them to win their
favor, they by day and night frequently moved over the roads,
in squads,[6] shouting and firing off their guns as they marched
along, and this little more than savage race, whose weaknesses
were being played upon for selfish objects by incendiaries
and demagogues, became a most disturbing influence in every
Southern state.

Many of those who at first had recommended acquiescence

[1] Ku Klux Report, Georgia Testimony, p. 829.
[2] New Orleans Picayune, Oct. 26, 1867.
[3] Fleming, Recon. in Ala., p. 565.
[4] Cf. Fleming, Doc. Hist. of Recon., vol. ii, pp. 22-9, and authorities
cited in that place.
[5] Ku Klux Report, North Carolina Testimony, pp. 309-12; Wallace,
Carpet Bag Rule in Fla.. p. 46
[6] Fleming, Recon. in Ala., p. 562.

in the policies of Congress now recanted. All who could take the oath prescribed by the registration officers were urgently asked to appear before the boards and enroll their names upon the voting lists. Promptness in doing so, said the New Orleans Picayune, would convince the North "that we mean to take care of our own affairs."[1] That negroes are to vote, this newspaper continued, addressing the white men of Louisiana, "does not degrade you, nor diminish your influence, unless you purposely abandon the field to them."[2] Georgia expected every man to do his duty, said the Savannah News, and to register without delay to show his reverence for his "noble commonwealth."[3] That you should register, the Charleston Courier said to the whites of South Carolina, is an imperative duty which each man owes to himself, to his community and to his state.[4]

But the whites came forward slowly, while the jubilant negroes, urged on by their guides and mentors in the Loyal Leagues, pressed around the precincts. In New Orleans, when the offices were opened in April, four-fifths of all who came in were black men. Forty or fifty were in line at sunset, so many that they were asked to return on the following day.[5] Another time, at seven in the morning, at the opening of the office, 200 negroes were waiting for the opportunity to register.[6] The city was full of "cullud gemmen" from the pine woods who were seeking the "francise."[7] The whites were holding back, so it was said, until the "black rush" was over.[8]

Similar conditions prevailed in Alabama. The negroes came in crowds, while "appalling apathy" was noted among the whites.[9] The same attitude was displayed in South Carolina.[10] Torchlight processions passed through the streets of

[1] New Orleans Picayune, April 11, 1867.
[2] Ibid., April 14, 1867.
[3] Quoted in C. M. Thompson, Recon. in Ga., p. 187.
[4] Charleston Courier, quoted in N. Y. Tribune, Aug. 16, 1867.
[5] New Orleans Picayune, April 16, 1867.
[6] Ibid., May 2, 1867.
[7] Ibid., April 17, 1867.
[8] Ibid., April 20, 1867.
[9] Montgomery corr. N. Y. Herald, July 20 and Aug. 5, 1867.
[10] Charleston corr. N. Y. Herald, Aug. 17, 1867.

Charleston. Agents of the Republican managers, both white
and black, moved from plantation to plantation to arouse the
negroes, who soon filled the roads, and haunted the precincts,
to the neglect of their tasks in the fields for days and weeks
together. They outnumbered the whites three to one at the
registration offices in Charleston; [1] two to one in North Carolina.[2]

In Florida it was only in the towns that the whites evidenced any interest in the result.[3] At the end of the first week
in August the ratio of blacks to whites who had registered in
Jackson county was twelve to one, in Leon county eleven to
one, in Jefferson county ten to one.[4] Many white men seemed
to be preoccupied with the serious business of making a living for themselves and their families; others resented the disfranchisement of the South's best citizens and in protest would
withdraw from any part in political life; all were disinclined
to meet and touch shoulders with "niggers" in the registration offices, or to appear before boards composed in whole
or in part of blacks.

The misgivings of the leaders in Louisiana, because of the
indifference of the old and patrician Creole classes in the
French quarter and other elements of value in New Orleans,
were unconcealed. Vainly day after day they were appealed
to in the gazettes and at "rallies" in wards and districts. It
was "suicidal folly," said the Picayune, to surrender the state
to the negroes. If white men did not become citizens under
the constitution as surely as they lived they never would do
so except "by revolution." [5] If you do not vote, said the
Picayune again, you will "put all the authority in the hands
of the strangers and renegades who have made loyalty their
trade and peddle it out among the freedmen." Thus would
the state fall into "alien hands." Not to register and not
to vote was "to vote against the South." [6] Should the white

[1] Charleston corr. N. Y. Herald, Aug. 19, 1867.
[2] Washington corr. N. Y. Tribune, Aug. 29, 1867.
[3] Jacksonville corr. N. Y. Tribune, Aug. 26, 1867.
[4] Davis, Recon. in Fla., p. 488.
[5] New Orleans Picayune, May 15, 1867.
[6] Ibid., April 21, 1867.

men of Louisiana be unwilling to perform their political duties and do their parts "to rescue her from the blighting and foul domination of the Puritan and the African"[1] they might better go to Brazil or Mexico at once.[2] It was not a "party matter," but one of "individual interest." In no other way could they expect to secure "a fair, impartial and just constitution," and rout the "emissaries of evil."[3] Up to April 30 in New Orleans 8687 negroes and only 2012 white men had registered. The white vote before the war had never been more than 11,000 or 12,000; the black vote now would exceed that total. In Iberville parish in Plaquemine, the county town, out of 700 registrants only 60 were white men.[4] Where, "in the name of Heaven," asked the alarmed people of New Orleans, was "the ship of state drifting to?" Plainly "to Africa."[5]

The ignorance of the blacks was dense. Never before in the history of democracy had it been proposed to make voters of a body of men in so benighted an intellectual condition. Thousands had been born in Africa and were in but a little better moral and mental state than they had been at home.[6] Multitudes, when asked, could not give the names of the counties and beats in which they lived. Other multitudes could not tell their ages; it was mere conjecture. Boys as young as sixteen were registered in all parts of the South. Many did not know their own names; indeed they had none. Bob,

[1] New Orleans Picayune, Feb. 12, 1868.
[2] Ibid., April 14, 1867.
[3] Ibid., May 3, 1867. One reason for the reluctance of the whites to register was found in their rather confident opinion, which was shared by President Johnson and his Cabinet officers, that the hand of Congress would be stayed by the Supreme Court in the Georgia and Mississippi test cases. They were like ostriches in Mississippi, said the New Orleans Picayune,—sticking their heads into the sand of the Supreme Court while their tails were being pulled by the Radicals. (Issue of May 9, 1867; cf. issue of May 19, 1867.) These cases were decided on April 15, and May 15, 1867.—State of Miss. v. Johnson, 4 Wallace, p. 475, and State of Georgia v. Stanton, 6 Wallace, p. 50.
[4] New Orleans Picayune, May 18, 1867.
[5] Ibid., May 2, 1867.
[6] In Florida the point was made before some of the boards that the negroes were aliens and were disqualified from voting on that account, until they should be naturalized.

Tom, Cæsar, Scipio, Pompey, Sam, Jack, Quash, Christmas, and Friday, from the "big house" and the plantation, gave for "de odder name" whatever came into their heads. Some must be supplied with family patronymics by the registration officers. In Charleston it was said that the voting lists contained 63 Abraham Lincolns, 46 George Washingtons and thirty odd Andrew Jacksons. The negroes would not remain within their own districts. Many roamed about and seemed to have no homes. They registered promiscuously, often three, four or more times at different places, at the direction of scoundrels whose purposes were made plain on election day.

A registrar in South Carolina said that in many cases the negroes in that state had not even a remote understanding of what registration meant. Some had brought bags and baskets "to put it in." They had rushed to the towns for fear there would not be "enough to go round." That it was something to eat or wear, or the confiscated land under a new name about which they so long had heard was in many minds.[1]

[1] One of the new voters, after he had been sworn at a precinct in Charleston, was heard to say, when asked to give an account of his experience:—"De gemman wid de big whisker make me swar to deport [support] de laws ob United Souf Ca'lina." (N. Y. Herald, Sep. 24, 1867.) The following colloquy at one of the registration offices in New Orleans was transcribed for his newspaper by the New Orleans correspondent of the Louisville Courier (quoted in New Orleans Picayune, April 29, 1867):

Registrar—"What is your name?"

Colored Citizen—"My name is Cæsar, boss."

R.—"What is your other name?"

C. C.—"Well, boss, dey diden gib me no odder name, but ol' massa's name was Grandison, an I spose I mus' hab his name now."

R.—"Did you ever hold any office under the United States or under the state of Louisiana?"

C. C.—"Yah, yah. Well, yas, boss, I sweeps out an assurance office in a lawyer's office."

R.—"Did you ever give aid or comfort to the Confederate states?"

C. C.—"Diden gib nuffin, kase I diden hab nuffin ter gib."

R.—"Did you ever serve in the Federal or the Rebel army?"

C. C.—"Well, boss, I diden serb in neifer, but de Yankees want ter teck me ter make brefworks for um, an so I went ter cook for de rebs."

R.—"Then you gave them aid and comfort, didn't you?"

C. C.—"Why, no, boss, dey gib me all de aid an comfort, for if it wusn't fur dem I'd bin dead nigger long 'go."

R.—"Swear him in."

While charity was carried to the greatest length by the registrars in the work of qualifying the negroes for the exercise of the voting privilege white men, on the other hand, were refused registration by the Radical officers upon the slightest pretext. A man who once had been a commissioner of election;[1] another who, as a boy, had been a clerk in a notary's office;[2] another who, before the war, had served on a police jury and had been an officer of militia and who, during the war, had subscribed money to feed hungry Confederate soldiers,[3] were not allowed to register in Louisiana. Men who had been overseers of the public roads were barred in Texas and Arkansas.[4] Those who had subscribed to Confederate loans or hired horses to the Confederate government could not register in North Carolina.[5] One day in that state when three ex-governors, a former justice of the Supreme Court, several ex-members of Congress and other distinguished men were dining together, the only person present who could vote was the negro who served them the meal.[6] The New Orleans Times said that at least one third of the white voters presenting themselves for registration in Louisiana were rejected.[7]

In Virginia about 120,000 white men and 106,000 negroes were registered. There were white majorities in 52·and colored majorities in 50 counties of the state.[8] The registrars in North Carolina placed 106,000 white and 73,000 colored men on the voting lists, giving the state a white majority, therefore, of 33,000. In Georgia Pope's registration boards returned a white majority of 1200 in a total enrollment of about 191,000. When the unsettled spaces in Texas could be reached and organized there was found to be a white majority

[1] New Orleans Picayune, May 2, 1867.
[2] Ibid., May 3, 1867.
[3] New Orleans Times, June 19, 1867.
[4] Report of Sec. of War for 1868, vol. i, p. 243; ibid., p. 564.
[5] Hamilton, Recon. in N. C., p. 236.
[6] Raleigh Standard, June 9, 1868.
[7] Issue of July 9, 1867.
[8] Senate Ex. Doc., 40th Cong. 2nd sess., p. 2; Report of Sec. of War for 1867, pp. 22-3, 240-42, 294-95, 396-97.

of about 10,000 in that state. In Mississippi the negroes were in a large majority, probably 20,000, although General Ord made no separate record of their number. In Alabama they outnumbered the whites by 43,000, in Louisiana by 39,-000, in South Carolina by 33,000, in Florida by 4,000.

The number of white voters in the parish of Orleans was found to be 14,845, while there were 14,825 black voters, a total of 29,670. The population of the parish in 1860 had been 174,491, composed of 149,068 whites, 14,484 slaves and 10,583 free colored people. A few more than 25,000 blacks, therefore, had been invested with a political power equal to that of nearly 150,000 whites. Not one in ten white persons had registered, while the names of black men were inscribed upon the voting lists equal to more than a half of the entire number of colored men, women and children in the parish. More negroes were registered in 1867 than the total number of black males of all ages resident in Orleans in 1860. It was "an awful story of registration swindling," said the Picayune. In Louisiana, as a whole, one in four and a quarter colored persons had been made into a voter by the Radical registrars, while only one out of seven white persons in New York exercised the franchise.[1]

In Barbour county, Alabama, only 773 white men out of 2,867 were registered; in Dallas county only 775 out of 2,520; in Mobile county only 2,682 out of 13,292.[2] Over 5,000 more negroes were registered in Charleston than had ever resided in the city.[3]

Most, if not all of the states, had been gerrymandered. Pope had so apportioned the representation in the convention in Georgia that 94,303 white men had only 65 delegates, while 93,417 negroes could elect 102 delegates. Twenty-two out of 65 counties in Alabama had black majorities; these were given 52 delegates in the convention of 100 members.[4] In Mississippi where the negro population was entitled to 56½ and

[1] New Orleans Picayune, Nov. 12, 1867; cf. ibid., Aug. 2, 1867.
[2] Montgomery corr. N. Y. Herald, Aug. 5, 1867.
[3] Charleston corr. N. Y. Herald, Nov. 7, 1867.
[4] Fleming, Recon. in Ala., p. 514.

the white population to 43½ delegates, the blacks had been given 70½, leaving the whites but 29½.[1] One black county with 901 votes had two delegates, as many as were apportioned to a white county with 3,273.[2]

The conservatives were not idle, but their situation on its face in the states in which the negroes were in a majority seemed hopeless; it was almost so in Virginia and North Carolina, where many for a time, however, expressed faith in a favorable outcome. The newspapers were filled with urgent counsel. Up to the last day the people were asked to throw off their indifference and face the crisis which confronted them. Better it would have been, said the New Orleans Picayune, if the Southern people had enfranchised the negroes immediately after the surrender, so that they might have been attached in gratitude to the Southern side instead of to the Radicals, who were now to reap the fruits of the policy. They were working "for us in the fields; why should they not do so at the polls?"[3] If the negroes were properly directed, said General Beauregard, the South could defeat its adversaries "with their own weapons." They were Southern born and they could be made to "side with the whites."[4] United States Senator-elect Burnett of Texas addressed a letter to the people of that state. "Teach these ill-informed and lately inducted politicians that their best interests are identical with ours," he said, "that they are Southerners by birth, by residence, in person, in property and in territorial prosperity."[5] In Alabama the conservatives went so far as to ask the negroes to sit in a convention beside the whites, to the end that "Alabamans should rule Alabama." The mothers who had given them birth had been nursed by the whites; they had played in infancy and childhood with the whites. For the welfare of their families, that they might have employment and continue to gain their daily bread,

[1] Vicksburg Times, quoted in N. Y. Tribune, Nov. 11, 1867.
[2] Garner, Recon. in Miss., p. 187.
[3] New Orleans Picayune, April 14, 1867.
[4] Ficklen, Hist. of Recon. in La., p. 185.
[5] New Orleans Picayune, April 13, 1867.

they should put their trust in the men whom they had always known.[1]

But the conservatives had waited too long.[2] In May and June it was thought that a majority of the white people of the South were ready to accept the Congressional plan of reconstruction, but in September travellers said it was seldom they met a man that paid taxes and was able to write his own name, who did not speak of it with open, if not violent disapprobation. The change had been brought about by the arbitrary administrations of Sheridan, Sickles and Pope, and by the odious activity of the Loyal Leagues and the imported managers of the Republican party, who were massing the negroes for a political program altogether at variance with the interests of the white population.[3] There was "utter paralysis," said an old leader in South Carolina, because of the prospect of "negro supremacy." Soon conditions would become "intolerable." The negroes had been welded into a solid political organization against which their old masters were powerless.[4] "What shall be done with the nigger?" had given place to a new question—"What will the nigger do with us?"[5] "We ask not to govern or control others," said the New Orleans Picayune, "but we do ask to govern and control ourselves," to be the masters of "our own household."[6] One-fourth of the population was to rule the other three-fourths, declared the New Orleans Times with irony, because the one-fourth were colored and five years ago were slaves.[7] "The majorities of an intelligent, educated and enlightened race, who have enjoyed the blessings of freedom, civilization and Christianity for two thousand years," said the Times again, "are to be nullified and overruled by the majorities of a race whose ancestors two hundred years ago were roam-

[1] Montgomery Mail, quoted in N. Y. Tribune, July 29, 1867.
[2] Montgomery corr. N. Y. Herald, Aug. 5, 1867.
[3] Columbus, Ga., corr. N. Y. Herald, under date of Sep. 23, 1867.
[4] N. Y. Herald, Sep. 10, 1867.
[5] Vicksburg corr. N. Y. Herald, Sep. 29, 1867.
[6] New Orleans Picayune, Sep. 29, 1867.
[7] New Orleans Times, Aug. 22, 1867.

ing savages and cannibals, and who themselves have just emerged from slavery." [1]

Better military rule, in the opinion of Wade Hampton, than what was promised the South by the Radicals. Better no representatives in Congress than such as would be sent there under such a system of government. It was recommended as a means to peace. Let men look at Tennessee to see the kind of peace which was in store for the rest of the Southern states. With Patrick Henry they could cry "Peace! Peace! but there is no peace." [2] To give "these ignorant stupid sans culotte" the right to vote, said the Memphis Appeal, was "a union of villainy and absurdity so despicable" that it would wreathe the "countenance of Beelzebub" with "a sardonic smile." [3] Let us continue under one despot, said Governor Sharkey of Mississippi; this were preferable to life under the control of many. [4]

"In the name of humanity to both races, in the name of citizenship under the Constitution, in the name of a common history in the past, in the name of our Anglo-Saxon race and blood, in the name of the civilization of the nineteenth century," the Conservative Democratic party of South Carolina in an address to the people of the state protested against such a policy as "destructive to the peace of society, the prosperity of the country and the greatness and grandeur of our common future." [5]

"We are to feed the vulture that tears our flesh," said Benjamin H. Hill in a speech in Georgia in September, "to enrich the robber who takes our property, to strengthen the hand that deals our stripes and to pet the monster that crushes our life." [6] What reason, what pretext, what excuse had the triumphant party for that which it was about to do to the

---

[1] New Orleans Times, Nov. 17, 1867. Herschel V. Johnson expressed a similar opinion—cf. C. M. Thompson, Recon. in Ga., p. 188.
[2] Letter of Wade Hampton to citizens of Columbia, S. C., reprinted in N. Y. Herald, Aug. 31, 1867.
[3] Quoted in Cong Globe, 40th Con., 2nd sess., p. 3303.
[4] N. Y. Herald, Oct. 1, 1867; cf. ibid., Oct. 19, 1867.
[5] Hollis, Early Period of Reconstruction in S. C., p. 81.
[6] N. Y. Herald, Oct. 1, 1867.

Southern people, asked the New Orleans Times. "Is it their weakness, their utter helplessness, their silent despair which provokes further violence and inflames that hate which the oppressor always feels towards those whom he has wronged?" [1]

At ground the incensed feeling of the people was not aimed at the negro but the "political drill masters," to use the descriptive words of Herschel V. Johnson, who were teaching him that he had "injuries to avenge against the whites." [2] By incendiary word and dishonest act these men who came from the North were at work upon their great plan to "Africanize" the country. All were "doing little but the meanest mischief." [3] The wealth of New Orleans attracted "gangs of itinerant adventurers," [4] "vagrant interlopers," who were "too dissolute, depraved, dishonest and degraded to get the lowest of places in the states they had just left." [5] They were "hungry political hacks" who at home could not get a policeman's office. [6] These vagrants in Louisiana came to be called "carpetbaggers," [7] a name which, serving a need, soon made its way into general use. They were the "carpet sack gentlemen," transients who had come South with only a piece of hand luggage, and were "ringing in with the negroes." [8]

But viler yet were the blatant, vindictive, unprincipled characters gathered up from the South itself who, cloaking themselves in a pretense of "loyalty" to the Union, took up the task of winning office in the reorganized states by base and hypocritical appeals to the new negro voters. For the most part these men were turncoats. They had been small slave holders, and secessionists. But, failing on the rebel side to gain the prominence they craved, they had gone North to sell their tongues to the Republicans, while the war still had not come to an end, or, if not this, were now ready to do

[1] New Orleans Times, July 9, 1867.
[2] N. Y. Tribune, Aug. 12, 1867.
[3] New Orleans Picayune, Nov. 21, 1867.
[4] Ibid., May 28, 1868.
[5] Ibid., April 16, 1868.
[6] New Orleans corr. N. Y. Herald, Nov. 22, 1867.
[7] At first known as "squatters" in North Carolina.—Hamilton, Recon. in N. C., p. 253.
[8] General Clanton in Ku Klux Report, Alabama Testimony, p. 233.

so. Such men soon came to be known to the Southern people as "scalawags."[1]

A more conspicuous example of this type of Southern Radical than James W. Hunnicutt of Virginia could not have been found. He was a native of South Carolina. Like many of the rough fanatics who came forward during this period he had been a preacher, which enabled him in speech to quote the Scriptures with some freedom and authority. Before the war he had edited a paper in Fredericksburg called the Christian Banner. In its columns he had said that negroes should not be permitted to gather together in separate churches, lest they organize uprisings to overthrow the institutions of the South. He had voted for the ordinance of secession and in 1861 had presented a plan for the capture of Fortress Monroe. In due time he went North to write a book, to lecture and to make stump speeches for the Republican party. At the war's end he returned to Virginia and settled in Richmond where he began to publish another paper which he called the New Nation. With such a firebrand neither Governor Peirpoint nor John Minor Botts, more moderate Republican leaders, could cope.[2] He harangued crowds of negroes in Richmond and at other places in the state, urging them in the most violent language to lay burdensome taxes on and to disfranchise the whites. For counselling the young freedmen to bear arms, the older ones and the boys and girls to apply torches to buildings and crops he was put under arrest.[3] The Southern conservatives spoke of importing white labor from Europe. Hunnicutt would meet this movement

[1] A word, said Wade Hampton in a speech in South Carolina, used by drovers to describe "the mean, lousy and filthy kine that are not fit for butchers or dogs." (N. Y. Nation, Aug. 27, 1866.) It was a term, according to Eckenrode, applied to the "scaly, scabby runts in a herd of cattle." (Political Reconstruction in Va., p. 105.) "The name originated," said General Clanton, "in a fellow being kicked by a sheep so that he died. He said he didn't mind being killed but he hated the idea of being kicked to death by the meanest wether in the whole flock—the scaly sheep. We mean by scalawag a meaner man than a carpetbagger."—Ku Klux Report, Alabama Testimony, p. 233.
[2] Debates of Virginia Convention pp. 328 et seq.; Eckenrode, Political Recon. of Va., p. 67.
[3] N Y. Herald, Nov. 29, 1867.

with black immigration. He would "overturn Africa right into América," if so much were necessary to secure negro ascendency.[1]

Little better than the carpetbaggers and the scalawags were the mulattoes and quadroons who, perhaps, were free born. Before the war they had been the most exacting of masters, the most cruel of overseers. More intelligent than men of darker skin, and embittered by the fate which had thrown them into a social class with the negroes, they now in self interest eagerly played their part in arraying the black against the white race.[2]

All of these forces conspiring together for the attainment of their ends awakened the greatest resentment throughout the South. The whites could not hope to outvote the negroes. But as a majority of all those who were registered must declare themselves either for or against the proposal to call a convention they could, perhaps, defeat the Radical scheme by themselves declining to participate in the elections and by persuading as many negroes as possible to remain away from the polls. Newspapers and popular leaders in Georgia, Alabama, Texas and some other states were practically unanimous in advising that this course be pursued,[3] except in districts in which the whites were in a majority and were running conservative candidates, when they were enjoined, while abstaining from expressing themselves on the question of calling a convention, to vote for delegates.[4]

Such appeals were effective. The elections were held in September, October and November, 1867, in all of the ten states except Texas, where the lists were not ready until the

---

[1] Petersburg corr. N. Y. Herald, Oct. 1, and Oct. 11, 1867.

[2] New Orleans Picayune, May 5, 1867; Shreveport, La., Southwestern, April 15, 1868.

[3] For days the Augusta Chronicle and Sentinel kept this appeal at the head of its editorial columns:—"Let every man in the state, white and black, who is opposed to the infamous designs of the Radicals to place the intelligence, virtue and respectability of the South under the domination of scalawags, traitors, Yankee emissaries and negroes be sure not to vote either for or against a convention."

[4] N. Y. Tribune, Nov. 21, 1867; C. M. Thompson, Recon. in Ga., p. 188; cf. Ramsdell, Recon. in Texas, p. 194.

next February. Only 1,400 out of 11,000 or 12,000 registered white men voted in Florida; only 2,000 out of 44,000 in South Carolina; only 36,000 out of 96,000 in Georgia. In Alabama 24,000 went to the polls; 37,000 remained at home. In Texas 18,000 cast their ballots, while 41,000 did not participate in the election. In Mobile county, Ala., with a population of 80,000 only 100 whites voted; in Montgomery county, with 50,000, only 100; in Russell county only two; in Lowndes county only three; in Dallas county only six and in Lee county none at all.[1] In two days at Macon no white men came to the polls to vote, at Savannah two, at Columbus 25.[2] At Milledgeville and Americus no white votes were polled.[3] In Vicksburg there were eight, whom it seemed to be impossible to identify for public reproach, though a newspaper of the city had offered one dollar each for the names of "the interesting sneaks."[4]

By one method or another 24,000 negroes were dissuaded from visiting the election places in Georgia; 32,000 in Alabama and 14,000 in South Carolina. Voters, both white and black, to the number of 63,000 out of 139,000, did not take part in the election in Mississippi; 70,000 out of 166,000 did not visit the polls in Alabama.[5]

In not one state, however, did the plan to defeat the arrangements of Congress succeed. The large black vote, in spite of such efforts as could be put forth to reduce it, was sufficient for the purposes of the reconstructionists. In every state a majority of the votes polled was favorable to the meeting of a convention, and in every state the total vote polled on the question was a majority of the total number of registered voters. The margin had been small, for as many as 42 per cent had not cast their votes in Alabama, 44 per cent

[1] Montgomery corr. N. Y. Herald, Nov. 10, 1867.
[2] Despatches from Georgia to N. Y. Tribune, Oct. 31, 1867.
[3] Augusta, Ga., corr. N. Y. Tribune, Nov. 2, 1867; cf. C. M. Thompson, Recon. in Ga., p. 189.
[4] Garner, Recon. in Miss., p. 181.
[5] Senate Ex. Doc., 40th Cong., 2nd sess., no. 53, and Reports of Sec. of War for 1867 and 1868.

in South Carolina and Georgia, and 46 per cent in Florida
and Mississippi.

Recrimination followed everywhere. Educated white men
had been defeated for seats in the conventions by negroes
who were unable to read and write, and by white criminals
from other states. Indubitably the elections were marked
by much irregularity. Without a question negro boys not yet
of age voted in large numbers. Blacks who three months before had given their names to the registration officers now
could not remember what they were. They voted promiscuously in whatever precincts they chose,[1] and in many cases
in more than one place. At Augusta crowds of South Carolina negroes crossed the river to swell the vote in Georgia.[2]
Often they came up to the polls under leaders in military
organization. Many flourished knives and bore fire arms.[3]
For days large numbers of negroes were encamped outside
of Montgomery waiting for the election. Three thousand
were massed in the courthouse square in Clayton, Ala.[4] Other
thousands arrived to the sound of beating drums and broke
ranks in the square at Eufaula in the same state.[5] Radical
agents gave them the tickets which had been prepared for
them and they were pushed up to the polling windows as
animals advance to the processes of a packing house. Conservative ballots found in their hands were seized and torn
up. They had been enfranchised by the Republican party;

[1] The average black in Alabama, so it was alleged, voted once for
himself and once "for Jim who couldn't come." (Fleming, Recon. in
Ala., p. 515.) Darkies coming from a polling place would be asked if
they had voted. They said "No." "Didn't you go up to a little box
and put a piece of paper in it?" "Yes, Uncle Dick marched us 'roun'
and gib us a piece of paper an tole us ter put it in de box." They
said they did not know that this was voting. (Ku Klux Report, South
Carolina Testimony, p. 124.) In Tennessee when they were told to
put their ballots in the letter boxes attached to the lamp posts on the
streets in Memphis they did so and believed that they were exercising
the franchise.—Phila. Ledger, Oct. 1, 1867.

[2] N. Y. Tribune, Nov. 2, 1867.

[3] Eufaula corr. N. Y. Herald, Oct. 13, 1867; Petersburg corr. N. Y.
Herald, Oct. 31, 1867.

[4] Fleming, Recon. in Ala., pp. 54-5.

[5] Eufaula corr. N. Y. Herald, Oct. 13, 1867.

hereafter, they were told, loyal blacks would govern disloyal whites. If they did not vote for the party of Abraham Lincoln their wives could wear hoopskirts no longer and they would be made to work on the roads. The whole race would be returned to slavery. The moon would turn red and the stars would fall.[1] Multitudes had come upon promises that they would receive land. Some bore halters to lead their mules away. Now and again they refused to return to their homes until the pledges made to them by the scoundrels who had brought them to town had been fulfilled, and they became a charge upon the neighborhood.[2]

In Virginia the incendiary leadership of Hunnicutt had for its inevitable result a consolidation of the entire white race against the Republican ticket. All of the white Republicans in Richmond and two-thirds of all in the state who might have supported the party candidates, it was complained by discerning Radicals in the North, were compelled in self defense to act with the conservatives.[3] No scheme of reconstruction could succeed, said the New York Nation, "with the white race at the South unanimously opposed to it." Under such management "it must inevitably fail."[4] Led by "pestilent and insolent whites," said the Richmond Whig, in commenting upon the result, the negroes had "driven a deep blood-red line between themselves and the whites." They had proven that principles were nothing to them and color everything. There was no choice but "to regard them henceforward as enemies."[5] The whites must accept the issue; there was no escape, said the Richmond Enquirer and Examiner. They must treat the negroes "with defensive severity, differing not indeed in the spirit but only in the measure, from the treatment

[1] Fleming, Recon. in Ala., p. 514.
[2] Cf. Fleming, Recon. in Ala., p. 515; Arkansas corr. Cincinnati Enquirer, quoted in N. Y. Herald, Nov. 30, 1867; N. Y. Nation, Nov. 21 and 28, and Dec. 12, 1867.
[3] N. Y. Nation, Oct. 31, 1867.
[4] Ibid.; cf. N. Y. Tribune, April 12, 1867; Eckenrode, Political Recon. in Va., p. 69.
[5] Richmond Whig, Oct. 26 and 28, 1867.

which our English friends used towards the Sepoys in India."[1]
Drilled in the manner of an army, manœuvred as such, obeying an order from a central league, the negroes, said the
Charlottesville Chronicle, had delivered their votes "like a
concentrated broadside." They had "set their seal to their
doom." No longer could there be peace. The question now
was who—whether the whites or the blacks—should occupy
and rule the territory lying between 40 and 32 degrees north
latitude.[2] It was "war to the knife."[3]

The white carpetbaggers and scalawags, and the mulattoes,
griffes[4] and quadroons leading the negroes, complained that
their voters were being intimidated by threats of dismissal
from employment now, and refusal to engage them for work
in the future, if they should support the Radical candidates.[5] They were to be set adrift unhesitatingly and to be
"shunned as enemies."[6] "Let no man sleep under your roof,
break your bread, drink of your cup who has spoken at the
polls in favor of that party which would despoil your house,
embitter your crust with slavery and fill your cup with the
poison of humiliation."[7] They were deprived of their lease-
holds by landlords, thrust off of lands they had planted with
crops. They were turned out of the shanties which served
them for homes. One hundred and fifty negroes had been
discharged from work at the Wythe iron mines for voting the
Radical ticket.[8] White men who controlled mills told blacks
that they would not grind their corn or saw their lumber.[9]
They would not be treated by doctors when they fell sick.

---

[1] Oct. 26, 1867.
[2] Quoted in N. Y. Herald, Oct. 29, 1867.
[3] Richmond corr. N. Y. Herald, Oct. 30, 1867.
[4] A griffe in Louisiana was understood to be a person one-fourth
white and three-fourths negro, a child, therefore, of a mulatto and a
pure African.
[5] Protests of citizens of Richmond and Schofield's reply in Report of
Sec. of War for 1867, vol. i, pp. 189-95.
[6] Petersburg, Va., Index.
[7] Ibid., quoted in Cong. Globe, 40th Cong., 2nd sess., p. 3303.
[8] Lynchburg News, quoted in N. Y. Herald, Oct. 29, 1867.
[9] Cf. Louisiana Contested Elections, House Mis. Doc., 41st Cong., 2nd
sess., no. 154, pt. 1, p. 218.

Hunnicutt in Virginia advocated state aid for "gentlemen" who had been punished for exercising the "right that is the inalienable privilege of every American freeman." For voting the Republican ticket they had been thrown upon "the cold charities of a heartless world." They had been set out "to starve and freeze and die" in violation of the laws of "our high and holy Christianity." [1] "Don't employ them," said the Augusta Chronicle and Sentinel. "We advise the Southern people to refuse employment, support, aid or patronage to those negroes who have arrayed themselves in a position of hostility to the Southern whites." [2]

The next step was the selection by the military commanders of a time and a place in each state for the delegates to meet to devise and prepare the new constitutions. Alabama's 100 delegates assembled in Montgomery on November 5; Louisiana's 98 in New Orleans on November 23; Virginia's 105 in Richmond on December 3; Georgia's 169 in Atlanta on December 9, 1867. The Mississippi, Arkansas, South Carolina, North Carolina and Florida conventions met in January, 1868.

Thus far Congress had been going forward with a free hand. But the President still had a partial and indirect check upon the course of events through his choice of military commanders. Over this subject his control was not complete, first because of Stanton's recalcitrancy, then because of the protests of Grant, and later, after the impeachment proceedings were begun, because of the mad pressure of Radical opinion. Conservative criticism in the South was so hotly directed at three of the generals—Sheridan in New Orleans, Sickles at Charleston and Pope in Georgia, Alabama and Florida, and particularly at Sheridan who so lately had dismissed the civil governors of Louisiana and Texas—that, through the President's influence, as we have seen, they were removed. It was in August, 1867, while the work of registration was still in progress, that Grant most reluctantly and under open protest

[1] Debates and Proceedings of Virginia Convention, pp. 43, 44, 73.
[2] Issue of Nov. 1, 1867.

ordered to the Indian country his distinguished captain of cavalry, whose Radical sympathies were so well known, and established Hancock, a Democrat, in the place.

The new commander's arrival was anxiously awaited in Louisiana. Owing to the prevalence of yellow fever he did not reach New Orleans until the end of November, 1867. The constitutional convention had just begun its sessions and excitement ran high. Upon hearing that the steamer bearing him and his family was at the levee a crowd rushed to the landing. Amid huzzas he was escorted to the St. Charles Hotel, soon to proceed to the fine residence recently vacated by Sheridan. He was acclaimed by the newspapers as a "gallant soldier, a gentleman and an honest man." [1] He had "the culture, manners and habits to make him welcome as an agreeable member of society." [2] A proclamation which he issued met with warm approval. His dependence, he said, would be in the existing civil authorities; he would support the regularly constituted civil tribunals in the execution of the laws. [3] The editor of the Picayune had never read "a more wise, considerate, statesmanlike, just and well-poised declaration of sentiments and intentions." [4] Sheridan had admitted negroes to the jury box, which had "almost stopped the administration of law" in Louisiana, and had led to the resignation of judges of courts in some of the other Southern states.[5] Hancock repealed the order.[6] His coming brought an "irrepressible feeling of relief." He was cheered as he sat in his box at the opera, so that he must rise and bow repeatedly while the band played "Hail Columbia." Former commanders had treated the people of Louisiana as "a body of outlaws." Hancock revived in their hearts "sympathy for and remembrances of the old union." [7]

[1] New Orleans Times, Nov. 22, 1867.
[2] New Orleans Picayune, Nov. 7, 1867.
[3] Report of Sec. of War for 1868-9, vol. i, p. 210.
[4] Issue of Nov. 30.
[5] Report of Sec. of War for 1867-8, vol. i, pp. 305-7, 332-3, 348-50; ibid., for 1868-9, vol. i, p. 338.
[6] New Orleans Picayune, Dec. 3, 1867, and Report of Sec. of War for 1868-9, vol. i, p. 214.
[7] New Orleans Picayune, Dec. 9, 1867.

On New Year's Day he again assured the people of his desire to perform his duties without the exercise of "an arbitrary authority." [1] His name was received with applause at Democratic mass meetings.[2] The Radicals, persuaded that no aid was to be expected from him in the prosecution of their schemes, prepared petitions to be carried to Grant and Congress, urging that he be relieved from further duty in the district.[3] War began. In March, 1868, the new commander removed nine Radical members of the New Orleans city council, two white men and seven negroes, and nine others, chosen "without regard to their political sentiments," the "best men" he could find for the places, were appointed in their stead.[4] Grant telegraphed him to suspend his order. Hancock replied that it would be difficult to do so and retain his "self respect." Should his action be disapproved he must ask to be relieved from command.[5] It was "disapproved and revoked"; he was reprimanded for sending to Washington by telegraph communications of such length, and soon his relations with the War Department were severely strained.[6]

In Texas, on the ground that the rights of negroes were involved, the Freedmen's Bureau agents were arresting citizens, holding courts, trying cases, imposing fines and taking fees for their services. They were without jurisdiction. Hancock announced that he would confine these officers "within their legitimate authority." [7] His order removing a street commissioner in New Orleans whom he declared to be corrupt and unfit, was revoked by General Grant as in the case of the nine aldermen. The Radicals now called this distinguished Union soldier a "rebel" and a "Copperhead," [8] and on March 28, 1868, he was transferred to the Military Division of the Atlantic with headquarters at Washington, the Fifth District coming under the command of General J. J.

[1] Report of Sec. of War for 1868-9, vol. i, p. 218.
[2] New Orleans Picayune, Feb. 16, 1868.
[3] Ibid., Jan. 21, 1868.
[4] Report of Sec. of War for 1868-9, pp. 225-6, 228.
[5] Ibid., pp. 227-8.
[6] Ibid., p. 232.
[7] Ibid., p. 260.
[8] Ramsdell, Recon. in Texas, p. 192.

Reynolds, and in a little while of General R. C. Buchanan.[1]

Sickles was displaced in the Carolinas at about the time Sheridan was relieved in New Orleans. The control which he exercised over civil officers and his interferences in behalf of the freedmen caused him to be regarded as a dictatorial man by a population especially unfriendly to Northern control.[2] "No fanatical Puritan could have been dug out of the recesses of New England," said the New Orleans Times, "with half the vindictiveness, injustice and cynical spite."[3] Urgent demands that this "Persian satrap"[4] be removed reached the President. An opinion from an assistant Attorney General named Binckley, who was in charge in Mr. Stanbery's absence, in which it was stated that Sickles had interfered with the course of the courts,[5] furnished an excuse to Johnson for ordering him North in August, 1867, and Canby took his place.[6] Since this general was a native of Kentucky and had taken no very active part in the war he was warmly welcomed in the district, of which action many repented as soon as he issued his order introducing negroes to the jury box.[7]

Pope's undoing followed at the end of the year 1867. He had threatened Jenkins, the governor of Georgia, with a fate which had come to Wells in Louisiana and Throckmorton in Texas.[8] The governor had addressed the people, saying that the reconstruction act was "grievously oppressive" and "palpably unconstitutional." He used, said Pope, "the entire machinery of the provisional government to defeat the execution of the very law by whose sufferance alone it has any existence at all."[9] The commander was denounced in his district in the most bitter terms and in retaliation he withdrew official advertising from the newspapers. Even this measure was with-

[1] Ramsdell, Recon. in Texas, p. 208.
[2] Hollis, Early Period of Recon. in S. C., pp. 69-70.
[3] New Orleans Times, Nov. 29, 1867.
[4] F. A. Porcher, The Last Chapter in the Hist. of Recon. in S. C., Southern Hist. Soc. Papers, vol. xii, p. 174.
[5] Opinion printed in Philadelphia Press, Sep. 2, 1867.
[6] Hamilton, Recon. in N. C., p. 232.
[7] Hollis, Early Period of Recon. in S. C., pp. 71-3.
[8] Senate Ex. Doc., 40th Cong. 2nd sess., no. 30, pp. 2-3.
[9] Report of Sec. of War for 1867-8, p. 323.

out effect, and criticism and abuse continued to be showered upon him to such an extent that in a little while few who were eligible to civil office could be persuaded to accept it at his hands because of the personal degradation they would suffer in the eyes of the population by doing so. His downfall was the occasion of much rejoicing in the South. Meade came to take his place early in January, 1868, to be welcomed as a courteous gentleman and a fine soldier,[1] as Hancock had been a few weeks before in New Orleans.

But such illusions as may have been entertained regarding the course he would pursue were short-lived, for he almost at once dismissed Governor Jenkins and also the comptroller who had removed the public records and emptied the state treasury. They were using their places, he said, to obstruct the work of the constitutional convention and he installed army officers in their stead.[2]

Ord also was superseded at the end of the year, and on January 9, 1868, General Gillem, a native of Tennessee and a friend of President Johnson, a happy introduction to the South,[3] took command in the Fourth District. He became almost a favorite with the people. The Radicals concluded that he was of "no more service in supporting the reconstruction plan than Jeff Davis."[4] There was, they said, "no greater enemy" to reconstruction in Mississippi than he,[5] and they began to intrigue for his overthrow.

Of the five commanders originally appointed to the districts only Schofield in Virginia was considered to have taken a course marked by fairness to the South, and consequently only he enjoyed the confidence of Johnson and the President's advisers at Washington. He adopted the rule of interfering with the civil government which he found in the state "only when it was believed to be necessary." Up to October,

[1] N. Y. Nation, Jan. 23, 1868.
[2] Meade's Life and Letters, vol. ii, pp. 291-2; Report of Sec. of War for 1868-9, vol. i, p. 75.
[3] Garner, Recon. in Miss., p. 182.
[4] House Mis. Doc., 40th Cong. 3rd sess., no. 53, p. 259.
[5] Ibid., p. 272.

1867, he had removed only five officers,[1] and throughout his administration, until he was made Secretary of War, and he was superseded by General Stoneman, in June, 1868, his appointments to vacancies created by death, resignations and removals, nearly all of a minor character, numbered only 532.[2] He referred the question of admitting negroes to jury service to the constitutional convention, and aroused no popular enmity on this subject. It is true that he paid no heed to the charges which were made concerning the frauds at the election for delegates in October, and declined to interfere to the disadvantage of Hunnicutt and the men who were using the negroes in Virginia for selfish ends,[3] but he continued to retain the good opinion of the community.[4] The "wisdom" of his policy seemed to be "demonstrated by the result" and clashes were "exceedingly rare."[5]

The reconstruction law itself rendered it difficult to put men of intelligence and efficiency into civil office. Section 9 of the act provided an oath to which few but negroes and carpetbaggers could subscribe. Several commanders asked that it be repealed. Citizens of worth and usefulness desired to cooperate in the work of reconstruction in Louisiana, Hancock declared, but they were barred from service. Stoneman, when he arrived in Virginia, said that Schofield who had preceded him, though that officer had made only the most necessary changes, had "very nearly exhausted the available material." In some cases it was "absolutely impossible to find any person upon whom an appointment could be conferred."[6] General Gillem was confronted by similar difficulties in Mississippi when he reached that state.[7]

But Congress was far from wishing to aid the military commanders along these lines and proposed to amend the recon-

---

[1] Report of Sec. of War for 1867-8, vol. i, p. 241.
[2] Ibid. for 1868-9, vol. i, p. 320.
[3] Ibid. for 1867-8, vol. i, pp. 391-5.
[4] Eckenrode, Pol. Recon. in Va., p. 106.
[5] Report of Sec. of War for 1867-8, vol. i, p. 240.
[6] Ibid. for 1868-9, vol. i, p. 320; cf. Eckenrode, Political Recon. in Va., p. 106.
[7] Report of Sec. of War for 1868-9, vol. i, p. 603.

struction act in a very different sense. Johnson's removal of
Pope, and Hancock's reactionary course in New Orleans
brought forward a plan to abolish the separate commands and
to include the whole South in one military district, responsive
to the direction of General Grant. He should have absolute
power to detail officers to and remove them from duty.[1] The
bill to make the general of the army "supreme dictator over
the ten Southern states," [2] passed the House in January, 1868,[3]
and was sent to the Senate, to be lost, however, in the excitement which attended the impeachment of the President.[4]

The first constitution to be completed was Alabama's. The
convention in that state was in session for only thirty days.
Arkansas, Florida, Louisiana, Georgia, North Carolina and
South Carolina followed, all before the end of March. The
sessions in Virginia continued until April, in Mississippi until
May, 1868. The Texas convention did not meet until June,
1868, prolonging its discussions amid stormy scenes until 1869.

The various assemblies had much in common. It was said
of them truly by a conservative in Louisiana that they were
agrarian and revolutionary. Our own and the French Revo-
lutions had not yielded more prolific discussion of the subjects of freedom and equality, the "inherent right of suffrage"
under a republican form of government, the "God-given and
sacred right" to vote, the "halo of liberty" which, henceforward, would surround every human head, especially if it belonged to a poor and ignorant man.

The conventions arrogated to themselves much which did
not properly fall within the range of their authority. They
held themselves to be legislatures, governors and courts in
the several states, as soon as they came together, on the principle that they possessed that sovereign power which is attributed to such bodies, although in truth they were but the
creatures of the army and of Congress which had called them
into life. Several, as Alabama's and North Carolina's, em-

[1] Cong. Globe, 40th Cong. 2nd sess., p. 476.
[2] Words of Representative Brooks, ibid., p. 511.
[3] Ibid., p. 664.
[4] N. Y. Nation, Jan. 16 and 23 and Feb. 6, 1868.

ployed themselves with the divorce of unhappily married couples. In Mississippi counties named for "rebels" were renamed for loyal men. In Texas new counties were established and on the strength of the action of the convention court houses were built.[1] Poverty and distress, of which much still was seen and heard, called for remedy. Rains, cold weather and insects had ruined the cotton crop. Federal taxation oppressed the industry. Congress was to be asked for loans to assist the helpless people. Money must be expended for the improvement of Southern rivers so that the produce of the plantations could be sent to market. In North Carolina for a year no grain was to be used in the manufacture of intoxicating liquors; it must be saved for bread. Stay laws were passed; debts were to be scaled and repudiated. Everywhere there were plans for setting aside and giving land to the poor. In Alabama it was proposed that negroes should collect from their old masters $10 for every month of service from January 1, 1863, when they were emancipated, until the end of the war.[2] A resolution appeared in the Mississippi convention requesting the commanding general of the district to furnish the negroes with money enough to carry them back to their homes or their places of birth.[3]

Always and everywhere the question of the intermarriage of the races was in mind. Negroes must enjoy their civil rights on railroads and boats, in theatres, churches, schools and hotels. They must be treated respectfully in the press. Newspaper reporters were expelled from the convention in Mississippi for calling the delegates "colored" and for failing to prefix "Mr." to their names.[4] Ordinances were passed to incorporate and extend aid to railroad, canal and steamboat companies, and to amend the charters of cities. Resolutions were adopted commending "the ruling majority in Congress" and supporting the impeachment of the President. A chaplain in

[1] Ramsdell, Recon. in Texas, p. 251.
[2] Fleming, Recon. in Ala., p. 521.
[3] Publications of Miss. Hist. Society, vol. i, p. 365.
[4] Garner, Recon. in Miss., p. 202.

Louisiana prayed that Johnson would "pause in his career of
vice and folly," that he would "cease from doing evil" and
"learn to do right." [1]   Another in Alabama invoked the blessings of God on "Unioners and cusses on rebels." [2]   The names
of negroes were brought forward for election to the presidency
and vice presidency of the United States.

Now for the first time "the bottom rail had got to the top." [3]
Each convention contained a block of negroes, many of them
from the plantations with the blackest of faces, strange, new
figures in a constituent assembly.   Sambo and Cuffee had
entered the halls of government.   On the first day more
than thirty "unquestionably colored members," and many
others considerably tinged in complexion, appeared in the convention in Louisiana. [4]   The yellow fever had driven large
numbers of white men from the state and even those who had
been goaded by the press into registering for the election failed,
therefore, to participate in the choice of delegates.   The negroes had a majority of ten in the convention. [5]   A "coal black"
member was made temporary chairman of the body.   He
was "on'd by de s'lection ob de convention."   In putting a motion he asked those who favored it "to rise an stan on der
feet," and "all you contrairy men to rise." [6]   In South Carolina there were 76 colored and only 48 white delegates. [7]   There
were 18 negroes in the convention of Alabama, [8] 17 in Mississippi, 25 in Virginia, 18 in Florida, 13 in North Carolina, 37
in Georgia, 9 in Texas and 8 in Arkansas. [9]   "Gentlemen of
the convention" were either "colored" or "plain," an irony of

[1] Journal of the Proceedings of Louisiana Convention, p. 315.
[2] Fleming, Recon. in Ala., p. 519.
[3] A negro proverb—"De bottom rail is on de top," they were frequently heard to say, "and wese gwine ter keep it dar."
[4] New Orleans Picayune, Nov. 24, 1867.
[5] N. Y. Nation, March 26, 1868.
[6] New Orleans corr. N. Y. Herald, Nov. 29, 1867.
[7] Reynolds, Recon. in S. C., pp. 78-9.
[8] Fleming, Recon. in Ala., p. 518.
[9] Cf. N. Y. Nation, March 26, 1868; Garner, Recon. in Miss., p. 187;
Ramsdell, Recon. in Texas, p. 201; Thompson, Recon. in Ga., p. 189.
The figures vary because of the difficulty of classifying the quadroons
and other members in whom there was but a faint trace of African
blood.

conservative origin at which men laughed in all parts of the country.

Some of the negro members were teachers and preachers and displayed unexpected talent in debate. They spoke frequently and at length. Whenever it was alleged that the freedmen were illiterate the Northern Radicals had retorted that the Southern whites, barring a few, were enveloped in like ignorance. T. W. Conway said that of 200 white voters in one county in North Carolina only 30 could write their names; in another with a similar number of registered whites but 40 could do so.[1] Now the South could hear this from the negroes themselves. Grey, the eloquent young colored clergyman in the Arkansas convention, declared that for every illiterate black voter registered in that state he could produce a white voter who could neither read nor write.[2]

White delegates in the conventions viewed with horror the possibility of the marriage of the races, whereupon these clever colored orators could return with unanswerable force that they, too, were opposed to an intermingling of blood. But, if marriage were to be prohibited, cohabitation should be also. Children born in wedlock to white men and black mothers were not a worse catastrophe for civilization than the multitude of natural children of planters whose yellow skins were seen over all the South. The proud men who now held their noses while negroes rose to speak about law and politics had been not too proud to be suckled in their infancy at black breasts. It was disrespectful to call "gentlemen of the convention" negroes. But a black delegate in Arkansas said that they could call him what they liked. His was a race which had built the Pyramids where slept the bones of those whose learning had taught Solon and Lycurgus to frame the systems of their laws, and to which a later age was indebted for much of its art and knowledge.[3]

Whatever may have been the direct effect of the negroes

[1] N. Y. Tribune, Nov. 8, 1867.
[2] Debates and Proceedings of Ark. Convention, p. 93.
[3] Ibid., p. 89.

sitting in the conventions upon the form the constitutions finally assumed, their presence served to remind the white Radicals in control of those bodies of the vast potentiality of the great new enfranchised class from which these leaders had sprung. Colored men like Jonathan Gibbs, a preacher, in Florida; Grey in Arkansas; Cardozo, a preacher and teacher, and Whipper, Cain and Nash in South Carolina; Pinchback, a successful business man, in Louisiana;[1] Bayne and Hodges in Virginia; and Lynch, a mulatto preacher in Mississippi, of remarkable oratorical powers,[2] delighted the hearts of the old Northern Abolitionists who for so long had discerned a nearly god-like power in the African race.

The white Radicals included the two well known types—the carpetbaggers, much the more numerous class, and the scalawags. In some of the states not a third or a quarter of the delegates were native citizens; scores were of Northern birth and just now were seen for the first time in the states whose public affairs they were ready to direct. In many cases they had never resided in the counties to which they were assigned on the convention rolls. At least one member in Alabama did not know the whereabouts of the district he had been elected to represent.[3] Of the 45 white Radicals in the Virginia convention only 14 were natives of the state; 13 came from New York and 6 from the British Islands and Canada.[4]

The members of the convention of South Carolina, all taken together, it was said, paid only $879 in taxes. Of this sum one man's share was $508, the shares of three others $210, so that the rest contributed but $160 annually to the support of the state, and executions had been issued to secure the collection of $77 of this amount. The names of 56 negro delegates and 23 white delegates did not appear upon the assessors' lists at

[1] For his career see House Mis. Doc., 41st Cong. 2nd sess., no. 154, pt. 1, p. 286.
[2] Publications of Miss. Hist. Soc., vol. iv, p. 126.
[3] Fleming, Recon. in Ala., pp. 517-8. The New York Herald correspondent at Montgomery thought that at least two thirds of the members of the Alabama convention were Northern men settled in the state since the rebellion had come to an end.—N. Y. Herald, Nov. 29, 1867
[4] Eckenrode, Political Recon. of Va., p. 87.

all.[1] The whole negro population of fifteen counties in Virginia, it was said, owned but $139.09 worth of taxable property. They seldom paid their poll taxes.[2]

In all of the conventions except South Carolina's, in which state the whites had taken no part in the elections, there were small groups of conservatives. Such men as the Gibsons in Virginia, Semple and Speed in Alabama, Cypert in Arkansas, Durham in North Carolina, Judge Crawford in Louisiana, Waddell in Georgia indomitably led the opposition to negro suffrage and the other revolutionary proposals of the majority. Many foolish and dangerous suggestions of the carpetbag-scalawag-negro party were excluded from the constitutions through the vigilance and ability of these leaders. A few were expelled when they lost their tempers but the most of them kept at their posts until the end.

Guarantees that the negroes should vote Congress had demanded, though the subject was angrily debated in the conventions before this end was achieved. Even in South Carolina, where the native conservative population was without representation, it was proposed that each young man coming of age after 1875, or 1878, or 1890 (all three dates were suggested) should be entitled to exercise the franchise only if he were able to read and write. While all at present were to have the suffrage the ignorant must educate themselves, if they should continue to enjoy this privilege.[3] Two members of the committee on suffrage in North Carolina denied the power of Congress to determine who should and who should not vote in a state. The "great mass" of the negroes were "too

[1] Cong. Globe, 40th Cong. 2nd sess., p. 2448; Ku Klux Report, South Carolina Testimony, pp. 1241-44; Reynolds, Recon. in S. C., p. 79. Similar conditions prevailed in Alabama. When the members of the convention in that state objected to receiving their per diem in scrip they were reminded that it could be used to pay their taxes. "Oh, d——n the taxes!" one exclaimed. "We haven't got any to pay."— Fleming, Recon. in Ala., p. 521.

[2] Eckenrode, Political Recon. of Va., p. 98, quoting Richmond Enquirer.

[3] Proposed by the Suffrage Committee but defeated by a vote of 107 to 2 with 10 absentees.—Proceedings of the Convention, pp. 834-5.

ignorant and prejudiced" for suffrage.[1] They were "totally incapable of self government," said a conservative delegate in Arkansas.[2] They were to be enfranchised in Virginia for no purpose but to outvote the whites and beat the Democratic party.[3] To such views, however, expressed as they were only here and there and by a few, the conventions gave no heed. Delegates in Arkansas, South Carolina and Virginia in their sentimental zeal went so far as to record a wish that suffrage be conferred upon women, on the principle that "sooner or later everything in the shape of tyranny must yield."[4]

New officers, such as lieutenant governors and attorney generals, were provided to satisfy the cravings of the adventurers who were to ride into power upon the shoulders of the black voters. In most cases for the accommodation of the carpetbaggers a very brief period of residence within a state was made to suffice as a qualification for office. Judges were made elective by the people, a principle new and offensive to the old leaders in the South. Executive officers, who, usually, before the war, had been elected by the legislature, were now to be chosen by popular vote. In Florida and Mississippi, on the other hand, it was complained that too much power in the matter of appointment to office was made to rest with the governor.[5] Local judges in Louisiana need not be "learned in the law," a provision designed, it was believed, to place negroes on the bench. Town and other local forms of government, suggested by the experience of New England, were introduced in states where the conditions were not adapted to the system. Men with property were to be taxed to educate the children of the poor. A poll tax for the support of schools would have laid a part of the burden upon the shoulders of the negroes. Blacks and whites were to serve together in militia companies; their children were to attend the same

[1] Journal of the N. C. Convention, pp. 235-8.
[2] Debates and Proceedings of Convention in Ark., p. 668.
[3] Ibid., Va. Convention, p. 504.
[4] Ibid., S. C. Convention, p. 838.
[5] Cf. Garner, Recon. in Miss., p. 212.

schools. The states were gerrymandered; white counties were joined to black counties to form the greatest possible number of Republican districts. Everywhere the whites were trammelled with oaths looking to their disfranchisement, to satisfy the conditions of Congress and in answer to the vindictive demand of the Radical leaders in the various states, who, suddenly come to power, were seeking the means of intrenching themselves in this position for a long time to come.

Except in Florida and Texas the proceedings, for the most part, were orderly. But now and again the lie was passed. The words "scoundrel" and "base scoundrel" were flung across the halls. Conservative members were brought up to the bar of the house to be reprimanded. The Radicals usually went free, though clever leaders on the opposite side, aided by the newspapers, laid bare the record of many a scamp without crossing the proper bounds of parliamentary usage. Not a few of the members were accused of specific crimes which led to retorts on the floor and to demands for retraction outside of the chamber. Most of the delegates were armed.[1] Personal altercations, resulting in fisticuffs, horsewhippings and shooting affrays, were not infrequent.[2] It was discovered that a black incendiary, named Aaron Alpeoria Bradley of Savannah, who had had himself elected to the Georgia convention, had served two years in prison for seducing a woman in New York, and subsequently had been disbarred as a lawyer in Massachusetts. He was about to be "whitewashed" by the Radical majority when he grossly charged the presiding officer with similar immorality which led to his summary expulsion from the body.

Several Republican newspapers, under white or negro management, had been established in the South. There were two of these in New Orleans and two in Richmond. They were eager for the contracts for printing the proceedings of the conventions and for public advertising. Such gazettes found the delegates to be sagacious and representative citizens. The

[1] Cf. Garner, Recon. in Miss., p. 201.
[2] Publications Miss. Hist. Soc., vol. i, p. 365; N. Y. Nation, Feb. 13, 1868.

old newspapers were unanimously of a different mind. They
spoke day by day for the conservative interests of the South.
In South Carolina and Arkansas it was the "ring-streaked
and striped negro convention," the "ring-streaked and speckled
convention," the "black and tan convention," the "piebald
convention," a "mongrel menagerie";[1] in Virginia "a mass of
black ignorance and Hunnicutt beastliness and incendiar-
ism";[2] in Louisiana the "unconstitutional convention," the
"bones and banjo convention," the "miscegenation convention";[3] in Alabama the "black crook convention."[4] The constitution of Alabama had been formed by "strangers, deserters,
bushwhackers and perjured men."[5] The delegates had overlooked but one thing—changing the name of the state to Lo-
ango, or Angola, or Congo, or Dahomey, or Senegambia, or
Ashantee. Since so much had not been done in Alabama the
idea was commended to the convention in New Orleans, which
was "hammering out a constitution on the African pattern for
what used to be the state of Louisiana."[6] In Georgia it was
the "bogus convention"[7] and the "mongrel convention", it
held itself up "to the disgust and scorn of all honest men."[8]

A constitution was being given to Arkansas by "ring-tailed
coons," "apostles from distant lands" and "can't stay-at-
homes elsewhere";[9] to North Carolina by "baboons, monkeys,
mules and jackasses";[10] to Virginia by "New England squatters";[11] to Alabama by a "herd of adventuring scoundrels
and ignorant negroes,"[12] by "outlaws and ragamuffins and a
gang of jailbirds." The convention could have met with

[1] Cf. Proceedings of South Carolina Convention, p. 30; Debates and
Proceedings of Arkansas Convention, pp. 100-1, 365-6; New Orleans
Times, July 30, 1867.
[2] Richmond Whig, Oct. 26 and 28, 1867.
[3] New Orleans Times, Nov. 21, 1867; N. Y. Herald, Nov. 29, 1867.
[4] Fleming, Recon. in Ala., p. 519.
[5] Words used by a member, quoted in ibid., p. 536.
[6] New Orleans Picayune, Dec. 8, 1867.
[7] Journal of Georgia Convention, p. 179.
[8] New Orleans Picayune, Dec. 12, 1867.
[9] Debates and Proceedings of Ark. Convention, pp. 88, 369, 649.
[10] The North Carolinian, quoted by Hamilton, Recon. in N. C., p. 257.
[11] Richmond Enquirer, March 9, 1868.
[12] Mobile Advertiser in Cong. Globe, 40th Cong. 2nd sess., p. 3303.

more propriety in the penitentiary at Wetumpka than at the state house in Montgomery. If they were "turned loose in the Zoological Gardens" the members "would set the very giraffes and hippopotami to laughing." [1] In Louisiana they were "renegade rebels and alien political adventurers," [2] "highwaymen" who had come "to plunder the whites and work the blacks for their own sole use and behoof, and then return North to enjoy their spoils," [3] "Simon Suggs' and worse than cyphers" who were here "because they were intolerable elsewhere." [4] They were "infernal outside meddlers." The cotton worm was a blessing compared to these "greedy cormorants." [5] The "sable sons of Ham" trained to affairs of state "at the plowtail" were better than the "mean whites" with whom they were associated. "All the political prostitutes that ever disgraced" Louisiana, "all the hungry office wolves, all the despised dregs of society that have been boiled to the top by the stormy current of events" were to organize a government for a people who held them "in abhorrence." [6]

While Congress had found the money to pay for the registration of the voters and the election of the delegates the states themselves must support the conventions. The members were poor men and their needs were immediate. Many had come to the meeting places on horses and mules over mountain and through wood. Others, as in Arkansas and Florida, had walked for days through the brush with knapsacks on their backs. Some were five, six, even eight days on the way. They had brought with them not enough money to pay for their bed and board. [7] Each convention, therefore, faced a financial problem of some difficulty and of urgent interest to everyone. Loans were to be negotiated with bankers, scrip was to be is-

[1] Mobile Tribune, Nov. 6, 1867.
[2] New Orleans Picayune, May 9, 1867.
[3] Ibid., April 9, 1868.
[4] Ibid., March 21, 1868.
[5] Planters' Banner, quoted in House Mis. Doc., 41st Cong. 2nd sess., no. 154, pt. 1, p. 546.
[6] New Orleans Times, Nov. 21, 1867.
[7] Not one in ten in Alabama, said the New York Herald correspondent at Montgomery, could pay a week's board in advance.

sued and other provisional measures must be adopted to meet the state's temporary needs.

In view of such conditions the opportunities for thievery and pillage, which later became the distinguishing marks of legislative assemblies in the reconstructed South, were not large. Nevertheless nearly $30,000 were paid to newly established Republican newspapers in Mississippi for printing the proceedings of the convention in that state,[1] exclusive of the cost of the publication of the journal, and the constitution and the ordinances. Hunnicutt unblushingly seized the printing contracts in Virginia, and favorite Radical presses were the recipients of similar favors at exorbitant rates of remuneration in other states.

In Louisiana it was complained that $20 were paid for a Worcester's Dictionary which sold for but $11 in a store in New Orleans, $10 for a ream of paper, $2.50 for a box of pens and $1 for a bottle of ink, and that there had been free and careless buying for the use of delegates of matches, paper weights, penholders, calendars, arm rests, thermometers and brooms at 50 per cent. and in some cases 100 per cent. above the current retail prices of those articles.[2] Writing materials were purchased for those who could not write and newspapers for those who could not read.[3] Each member in Mississippi received five daily papers.[4] In Texas for 90 delegates the legislature subscribed for 2000 copies daily of one paper, for 500 copies of another and 400 copies of a third.[5] Wood to heat the hall in North Carolina was furnished at $6 a cord when the market price was $4.75.[6] Useless Radical henchmen, white and black, were added to the pay rolls as clerks, secretaries, pages and doorkeepers. The mileage rate in North Carolina was fixed at 20 cents. A white member who lived only 30 miles from Raleigh charged the state for 262 miles each way.[7]

[1] Garner, Recon. in Miss., p. 203.
[2] Journal of Proceedings of Louisiana Convention, p. 160.
[3] Cf. Garner, Recon. in Miss., pp. 190, 203-4.
[4] McNeily, Publications Miss. Hist. Soc., vol. i, p. 356.
[5] Ramsdell, Hist. of Recon. of Texas, p. 205.
[6] Journal of N. C. Convention, p. 425.
[7] Hamilton, Recon. in N. C., p. 259.

A negro whose home was 60 miles distant from the capital was paid for 260.[1] Mileage was computed at the rate of 40 cents a mile in Alabama and Mississippi.[2] The whole cost of the convention in Mississippi to the taxpayers of that state was not less than $300,000.[3]

Unusual scenes marked the progress of the work of preparing a constitution for Florida. The convention was a body of 46 members, 18 of whom were negroes. Only 41 attended at Tallahassee upon the meeting day and these immediately divided into two camps. Three or four carpetbaggers, none of whom had arrived in the state in time to become a registered voter, including a Canadian who had never been naturalized, seized the convention [4] and by a vote of 21 to 20 organized it under the presidency of a man named Richards. They assigned 30 of their friends to lucrative offices, and boisterous and disorderly scenes ensued. To a New York Tribune correspondent who was present the hall seemed "more like a gladiatorial arena" than a convention met to form a constitution for a state.[5] Losing hope of control the minority withdrew to a place called Monticello, some 30 miles away, to watch the course of events.

The faction which still remained in Tallahassee declared their number a "legal quorum," hastily adopted a ready-made constitution which seems to have been written in Chicago,[6] and transmitted it to General Meade in command of the district. On February 8 they adjourned for a week, whereupon the seceding faction returned to Tallahassee, broke into the state house at midnight, with the assistance of militiamen, and it would seem, too, of Federal soldiers, swore in enough new delegates to form a majority of the membership, elected their officers and proceeded to frame another consti-

[1] Hamilton, Recon. in N. C., p. 259.
[2] Fleming, Recon. in Ala., p. 520; Garner, Recon. in Miss., p. 189.
[3] Publications, Miss. Hist. Soc., vol. i, p. 369.
[4] The division in Florida was "caused by the unwillingness of the minority to recognize the right of unnaturalized persons and persons not resident of Florida to sit in the convention."—N. Y. Nation, Feb. 13, 1868. Cf. Davis, Recon. in Fla., pp. 493-9.
[5] N. Y. Tribune, Feb. 8, 1868.
[6] Davis, Recon. in Fla., p. 509.

tution. When Richards and his adherents returned they found the doors of the hall barred. At many times, while the excitement was at its height, bloodshed was imminent. The Monticello party were branded by Richards as "rebels," although at least thirteen of them appear to have been ex-United States army officers. They had tried to corrupt the negroes. Whiskey had "flowed as free as water," and money had been used in a manner to "disgrace any other part of Christendom," if not Florida.

To all of this the other side responded that Richards and his associates were not registered citizens. They were mere "political adventurers," who, when they were "disappointed in obtaining office in one state," were "ready to fly to another"; that anyhow what they had done was illegal for want of a quorum of delegates. They were cooperating with a ring which hoped to steal the railroads, and had issued scrip on the public credit, redeemable in the first moneys received by the state, to pay their mileage at the rate of 40 cents a mile and their per diem of $10 a day, which was computed not only for their period of service but also for 23 days preceding the date of the meeting of the convention. Moreover the scrip, so it was charged, had been overissued and somebody had filled his pockets with a quantity of it and had disappeared.

In the interest of peace General Meade visited Tallahassee in person. He persuaded Richards to retire in case General Horatio Jenkins, Jr., the presiding officer elected by the Monticello party, would do likewise. Colonel Sprague, in command in Florida, then took the chair and organized the convention. Jenkins's friends being in the majority, they reelected him. Richards and the non-residents were declared to be ineligible and were expelled from the house. In a few days another constitution was adopted. Eight members signed it under protest and nine flatly refused to append their names to the finished instrument of government, until it was made clear to them by the majority that if they did not do so they would not be paid for their services.[1]

[1] This account is made up from the statements of the opposing parties.

In Texas somewhat similar scenes were enacted. The convention of that state, consisting of 90 delegates, met in Houston on June 1, 1866, and the delegates divided into two factions, both Radical, as in Florida, though here as there, for its own purposes, one side professed a loyalty to the Union not possessed by the other. General A. J. Hamilton, a leader in the "Torch and Turpentine Brigade" of Loyalists, who had followed Andrew Johnson in his "swing around the circle" in 1867, had now in 1868 obtained a judgeship in the state and was a "conservative." Earlier the object of most malignant attacks by the secessionist element in Texas they now regarded him as a "patriot, firm, tried and true."[1] He led one party while his brother, Morgan C. Hamilton, and General Edmund J. Davis stood at the head of the other. A few Democrats, representing the predominant feeling of the South, held the balance of power. There was embittered discussion of plans to dismember the state and to disfranchise the "rebels." At one time a considerable number of delegates withdrew and formed a convention of their own, returning, however, before August,[2] by which time the convention had expended $100,000 and, failing to obtain more from the commanding general, was ready to adjourn until December.

Upon re-assembling angry disputation proceeded until February, 1869. The two Republican factions had come to hate each other·intensely. Oratorical invective marked the speech of the delegates; personal encounters were frequent. After some of the records had been seized and carried away by members and clerks the military took possession of the hall and brought together the proposals for submission to the people, though not before Davis and five others had secured $1,000 each for a mission to Washington to present their case to Congress. A. J. Hamilton and some of his friends followed

one by Richards, the other by Gleason, financial agent, and Alden, a delegate in the convention, in House Mis. Doc., 40th Cong. 2nd sess., nos. 109 and 144. Also Davis, Recon. in Fla., chap. 19, and American Annual Cyclopedia for 1868 in article on Florida.

[1] Ramsdell, Recon. in Texas, p. 255.
[2] Ibid., pp. 209-10.

and the subject was fought over, within the hearing of the President and the Radical leaders of the country, for many months. The two sessions of the convention, the net result of which was five months of wrangling, unprecedented, perhaps, in any parliamentary body in America, had cost the state more than $200,000.[1]

Six members of the Louisiana convention voted against the completed constitution;[2] 10 did so in North Carolina;[3] 21 in Arkansas;[4] 13 in Georgia;[5] 26 in Virginia;[6] 10 in Alabama.[7] In most cases, too, there were several absentees whose antagonism to the proposed new governments was unconcealed. Twelve left the convention in Mississippi immediately upon the adoption of the franchise article and two more followed the next day.[8] Twenty-three delegates in Virginia voted against a resolution to thank the president and the other officers of the convention.[9] Only in South Carolina was the constitution adopted by a unanimous vote. Here the delegates rose and broke out into cheers. In North Carolina while the constitution was being signed the state house bell was rung.

The completed instruments of government were immediately sent to the people for ratification. The conservative delegates issued individual or general protests which were intended for audiences larger than those assembled in the convention halls. In Alabama it was declared that the negro members had moved as subserviently, at the beck of foreign political adventurers, with no interest in the fate of the South, as ever slaves did at the command of their masters.

The whole black race had been flattered until it was filled with a "jealous hate of the white people of the state." [10]

[1] American Annual Cyclopedia for 1868 and 1869 in articles on Texas; Ramsdell, Recon. in Texas, chap. ix.
[2] Journal of Proceedings, p. 275. [3] Journal, p. 479.
[4] Debates and Proceedings, p. 657. [5] Journal, p. 535.
[6] Journal, p. 389. [7] N. Y. Herald, Dec. 6, 1867.
[8] Garner, Recon. in Miss., p. 201; Pub. Miss. Hist. Soc., vol. i, p. 366.
[9] Many had gone out of the hall when Benjamin F. Butler came in to avoid hearing him speak. One refused to serve with a negro on a committee which was to visit a hotel in Richmond to convey the respects of the convention to General Grant.
[10] N. Y. Tribune, Dec. 12, 1867.

The constitution of Arkansas, said one of the members of the conservative minority in that state, was a "monstrosity." Any man who would put it on exhibition throughout the United States would make a fortune from it "as the rarest specimen of human production ever known or heard of in all Christendom." It was a "damnable instrument of ruin" designed to crush the white race, an insult to the unfortunate people who were to live under it and an insult to Heaven.[1] It had been "concocted in secret," pressed through the convention upon its first reading, after midnight, and would surrender political control "to stolid and brutish ignorance."[2] Only "newcomers" had sat upon the committees. No "old Arkansan" had had a hand in the work.[3] A delegate said that the constitution of Louisiana would "drive many good citizens from and prevent emigration to the state." It would "blight her prosperity and destroy her peace and happiness."[4] The conditions imposed upon the people were "unjust, illiberal, ungenerous, humiliating" and unworthy of "emanating from an American head and an American heart."[5] The constitution of Georgia had not originated with the people of Georgia, but in Washington. It had been framed by adventurers from New England, convicts from penitentiaries and ignorant negroes from the corn fields.[6]

Organized protest might be unavailing, but some expression of feeling at such a time was inevitable. Nothing was left to the South but

"—the loud cry of trampled Hindostan."

The newspapers had urged the white men of the South to come out of their apathy before the elections for delegates. All of it was in vain. Now conventions were adopting "nigger constitutions" and the people must "move like a sea by the wind."[7] They might fail but they must make an effort "to save themselves and their posterity." The governments of

---

[1] Debates and Proceedings of Ark. Convention, pp. 660-61.
[2] Ibid., pp. 665, 668.   [3] Ibid., p. 642.
[4] Journal, p. 277.   [5] Ibid., p. 292.
[6] Quoted in Thompson, Recon. in Ga., p. 203.
[7] Charlottesville Chronicle, quoted in N. Y. Tribune, Nov. 16, 1867.

the Southern states must not be permitted to pass "unchallenged into the hands of Yankee emissaries, scalawags and debauched and ignorant negroes." [1]   Conservative conventions were called to meet in all the states. In Macon, in Richmond, in Charleston, in Raleigh, in Montgomery, in Jackson, in Little Rock, in Houston, Texas, men representing the intelligent, property-holding classes assembled to discuss their common plight. In Alabama it was resolved to set aside a day of fasting and prayer to Almighty God for the deliverance of the people of the state "from the horrors of negro domination." [2] Clubs must be formed. The people were asked to hold county and local conventions. For a while they must leave their plows and devote themselves to politics. The voters must be addressed at barbecues and on other occasions as in the days before the war. Let the negroes be brought together, if possible, into Democratic clubs, and not a few were found who, weary of the unfulfilled promises about mules and lands, declared themselves ready to abandon the Loyal Leagues and the Radical party. [3]

The conservative convention in Richmond found the "rule of a race just emerged from slavery" to be "abhorrent to the civilization of mankind." [4]   The Macon convention said that to force negro rule upon the South was "a crime against our people, against the continuance of free government, against peace and security, against the purity of the ballot box and against the dignity and character of representative institutions." [5]   The convention in Jackson called the "nefarious de-

[1] Augusta Chronicle, Nov. 24, 1867.
[2] N. Y. Herald, Jan. 17, 1868.
[3] One old negro in Louisiana expressed the disgust of many when he said: "I hab strained dese yere ol' eyes er mine nigh out lookin' down de road foh de drove er mules." (House Mis. Doc., 41st Cong. 2nd sess., no. 154, pt. 1, pp. 292-3.) Another, a preacher, said in his church when he was asked to describe the difference between a carpetbagger and a scalawag—"a carpetbagger is a man who come down here from some place and stole enough to fill his carpet bag full; but the scalawag knew the woods and swamps better then the carpetbagger did and he stole the carpetbagger's bag and ran off with it."—House Reports, 42nd Cong. 2nd sess., no. 92, p. 28.
[4] Eckenrode, Pol. Recon. of Va., p. 86.
[5] Macon corr. N. Y. Tribune, Dec. 7, 1867.

sign" to "degrade the Caucasian race to be the inferiors of the African race" a "crime against the civilization of the age, which needs only to be mentioned to be scorned by all intelligent minds." [1]

A group of white conservatives in Alabama said that the new constitution of that state was "hideous"; it was "totally incompatible with the prosperity and liberty of the people." [2] A mass meeting in New Orleans on February 15, 1868, presided over by Judge Lea, was attended by representatives of "all the worth and honor and truth and virtue and respectability" of the city. Crowds were turned away from the hall because of insufficiency of space to seat them. Resolutions were adopted protesting against the "consummation of a policy involving the degradation and ruin of the people, promising the destruction of their material interests, intending the overthrow of all constitutional safeguards, aiming at the perversion of every social, educational and governmental institution and obliterating every vestige of American civilization in this state." [3]

The first constitution to be submitted to a vote of the people was Alabama's early in February. Here, as in other states, the conspiracy to defeat the convention by remaining away from the polls had almost succeeded. Again it was required that a majority of all those who were registered, instead of a majority of those voting, should approve and a stupendous effort was put forth by the old conservative elements to prevent the attainment of this result. The whites, almost to a man, except the carpetbaggers and scalawags, resolved not to vote themselves and to employ every device to keep the negroes from doing so. [4] They preferred a "decent military government by white men to any government by negroes under the manipulation of the skirmishers, camp followers and political colporteurs of the Radical party." [5] Continue your "own rule by the sword," if you will, they said, "but do not, we implore you, abdicate your own rule over us by transferring us to the

[1] Garner, Recon. in Miss., p. 209.
[2] N. Y. Tribune, Dec. 23, 1867.
[3] New Orleans Picayune, Feb. 16, 1868.
[4] Fleming, Recon. in Ala., p. 537.
[5] Cong. Globe, 40th Cong. 2nd sess., p. 2194.

blighting, brutalizing and unnatural dominion of an alien and inferior race." [1]

As if to assist the conservatives the weather was cold and the rain fell in torrents to swell the streams and make the roads well nigh impassable. The registrars, judges and clerks had not been paid for their services in connection with the election in October. They were without enthusiasm for new tasks and would not man the polls.[2] In many precincts "rebels" were in complete control of the machinery. The election extended over several days. Watchers, pencils in hand, stood at the windows preparing "black lists," the newspapers inscribed the names of whites who came forward to vote on a "roll of infamy." [3] The Conservative Club of Montgomery passed resolutions declaring that those who voted for the constitution would be regarded as "enemies" of the white race. Posses terrorized men on the roads. Threatening speeches were made by employers of labor near the polling places.[4] Challenges, curses, jeers were uttered by armed men gathered around the ballot boxes. In many counties not a third, or a fourth, or a fifth of the registered whites appeared. Only 23 out of 1,400 of those on the lists voted in Chambers county, 20 out of 1,500 in Tallapoosa county, 3 out of 1,400 in Butler county, 4 out of 800 in Macon county.[5]

As for the negroes, though on their side in many parts of the state there were repeating and fraud of great variety,[6] it was declared under oath that it was as much as their lives were worth to come near the polls. Hundreds, so illiterate that they could make only their marks in lieu of signatures, swore that they had been dismissed from employment immediately after the election for voting for the constitution.[7]

---

[1] Petition read by Doolittle in Senate of the U. S., Cong. Globe, 40th Cong. 2nd sess., p. 2869.
[2] Meade to Grant in House Mis. Doc., 40th Cong. 2nd sess., no. 123.
[3] Cong. Globe, 40th Cong. 2nd sess., pp. 2058, 3303.
[4] Ibid., p. 1745.
[5] House Ex. Doc., 40th Cong. 2nd sess., no. 303.
[6] Fleming, Recon. in Ala., pp. 540-41.
[7] Such action on the part of employers was commended by Alabama newspapers. Cf. quotations in Cong. Globe, 40th Cong. 2nd sess., p. 3303.

Many, so Congress was told, were turned out of doors to freeze and starve. Some Republican judges went home for fear of their lives. A Freedmen's Bureau agent who had taken an active part in the election was brutally waylaid.[1] In some cases there was but one place in a county at which men could vote. Polling places which it had been announced would be open were kept closed. False dates were given to the negroes. Many did not vote in Mobile, so it was said, because they were told by designing Democrats that if they did so they would be drafted into the army which was to be sent to Mexico.[2] A correspondent of the Cincinnati Commercial found one conservative voter who had paired with as many as 15 radicals.[3] Tickets were mutilated and destroyed; ballot boxes were stuffed.[4] The result was that 13,000 or 14,000 less than one half of the number of registered voters cast their ballots either for or against the constitution and the whole proceeding was null.[5]

The obvious course was to change the law to avoid in other states a similar miscarriage of the plans of the Radicals. Southern conventions still in session prayed Congress to act at once to defeat "the declared and well known wish and purpose of the opponents of reconstruction."[6] Before Christmas Thaddeus Stevens had foreseen what would come to pass, and he was ready with a bill to amend the Reconstruction Act in this regard. It passed the House but received no attention in the Senate,[7] and now the subject must be attacked anew. No time was lost. Hereafter "a majority of the votes actually cast" would determine the question. At the same time it was stipulated that voters on the constitution might present their

---

[1] House Mis. Doc., 40th Cong. 2nd sess., no. 111.
[2] Phila. Ledger, Oct. 14, 1867.
[3] Quoted in N. Y. Nation, Feb. 20, 1868.
[4] Cf. Cong. Globe, 40th Cong. 2nd sess., p. 2138.
[5] The registered voters in Alabama numbered 170,631, a majority of which would have been 85,316. The vote cast for the constitution was 70,812. The vote cast against the constitution was 1005.—Meade to Grant, Report of Sec. of War for 1869, vol. i, p. 97; Cong. Globe, 40th Cong. 2nd sess., pp. 1934, 2858.
[6] As in Louisiana Journal of the Convention, pp. 27-8.
[7] N. Y. Nation, Feb. 20, 1868.

ballots at any polling place within the state; they need not vote within the districts in which they had been registered. And separate elections on the constitution and for the choice of Congressmen and state officers would not be necessary; both elections might be held at the same time.[1]

The elections in the other states followed fast,—Arkansas in March, Louisiana, Georgia, South Carolina and North Carolina in April, Florida in May and Mississippi in June. In Virginia Peirpoint had been removed from the governorship and the commander of the First District had appointed Henry H. Wells to the place. The new governor visited Washington to seek from Congress funds which could not be obtained at home to defray the cost of submitting the constitution to the people, but nothing was gained by his journey and the state remained under military rule.[2] In each state a majority was secured for the constitutions except in Mississippi, where great organized effort was put forth to defeat the scheme of government prepared by the convention and it went down to defeat.[3]

The action of Congress in making a majority of those voting sufficient to determine the question of the adoption of the constitution rendered obstruction by remaining away from the polls and intimidating others, so that they would not attend, no longer feasible. But other events testified to the unfriendly temper of the people. In Georgia many sheriffs were resigning so that there would be no officers of the peace. Meade, unable to fill their places, refused to accept their resignations. He threatened them with punishment if they did not remain at their posts and perform their duties.[4] The majority for the constitution in Georgia was about 18,000; Florida, 5,000; North Carolina, 21,000; South Carolina, 43,000; Louisiana,

[1] Act passed the Senate on Feb. 25 and the House, Feb. 26, 1868. It became a law without the President's signature on March 10, 1868. App. Cong. Globe, 40th Cong. 2nd sess., p. 500.
[2] Eckenrode, Political Recon. in Va., pp. 107-9.
[3] Garner, Recon. in Miss., p. 213. For the constitution, 56,231; against it, 63,860. There were 155,351 registered voters.—Report of Sec. of War for 1868-9, vol. i, p. 602.
[4] N. Y. Nation, April 23, 1868.

18,000.[1] The vote in Arkansas was close. The means of communication were so slow and imperfect that it was more than a month before the commander could report the returns to Washington.[2] Then General Gillem advised Grant that there was a majority of 1,316 for the constitution.[3] There were general charges of dishonesty in the hope of affecting the result. One called the frauds "stupendous."[4] Another said they were "shameless and enormous," and had "no parallel in all history."[5]

It appeared that the total vote in one county exceeded the total registration by 1,195; in another by 730. Ballots continued to be received in Little Rock for 17 or 18 days, so long, indeed, as there were voters to present them to the poll keepers.[6] All the old charges were repeated. Minors voted, so it was said. Women dressed as men presented ballots to the election officers. Negroes travelled from polling place to polling place voting as often as they liked. White men had been disfranchised without any kind of reason. Road overseers, offering to register, bailiffs for grand juries, clerks of elections, councilmen in towns and men at whose houses "rebels" had eaten during the war had been rejected. On the other side radicals accused the conservatives of driving the negroes from the polls, of intercepting them in the roads, of threatening them with loss of employment and bodily harm. They would be evicted from their homes; they would receive no further rations of meat and corn. Those who voted for the constitution would be "spotted" and hereafter could expect no favors or benefits in the communities in which they dwelt.[7]

But, as if to express complete contempt for the whole catalogue of charges upon which a contest could be based, the

[1] Cf. Cong. Globe, 40th Cong. 2nd sess., p. 2446.
[2] House Ex. Doc., 40th Cong. 2nd sess., no. 278, p. 3.
[3] Debates and Proceedings of the Convention, p. 808; 27,913 votes were cast for the constitution and 26,597 against it.
[4] House Ex. Doc., 40th Cong. 2nd sess., no. 278, p. 40.
[5] Ibid., p. 28.
[6] Cong. Globe, 40th Cong. 2nd sess., p. 2697.
[7] House Ex. Doc., 40th Cong. 2nd sess., no. 278, passim.

House, on May 8, voted to re-admit the state to representation in Congress. The Senate soon followed. On June 22 the bill became a law, despite the President's veto,[1] and the next day the senators and representatives of Arkansas took their seats in Congress.[2]

The other states were to be returned to the Union at one time with one movement in an "Omnibus Bill." Let all of them be taken together. Then there would be only one veto message and one discussion of this message.[3] But there were dissenting views in regard to Alabama and Florida. The New York Tribune was in favor of re-admitting Alabama in spite of the fact that a majority of the registered voters had not attended the polls and that she had not met the requirements of the law. Other Radical newspapers recommended a similar course. John Sherman and Henry Wilson in the Senate, and Bingham, Stevens and Farnsworth in the House, introduced bills or resolutions with this end in view.[4] The New York Nation discoursed on *ex post facto* laws. Such action with regard to Alabama, it said, would render elections in other states "a mere farce."[5] The constitution should be sent back to the people and a new election should be held. In March such a plan was approved by the House to be laid aside in the Senate.[6] The fate of the state was still undecided when the Committee on Reconstruction through Thaddeus Stevens, on May 11, reported the "Omnibus Bill" which was made to cover the cases of North Carolina, South Carolina, Louisiana, Georgia and Alabama.[7] It passed the House three days later and, going to the Senate, was referred to the Committee on the Judiciary of which Lyman Trumbull was the chairman. He reported it back on June 2 with an amendment, striking out the name of Alabama and inserting Florida's instead.[8]

[1] Cong. Globe, 40th Cong. 2nd sess., pp. 3330-31, 3361-63.
[2] Ibid., pp. 3389, 3341.   [3] Ibid., p. 2863.
[4] Ibid., pp. 1117, 1217, 1257, 1790. Cf. N. Y. Nation, Feb. 20, 1868.
[5] N. Y. Nation, Feb. 27, 1868.
[6] Cong. Globe, 40th Cong. 2nd sess., pp. 2217, 3213, 3366.
[7] Ibid., p. 2412.   [8] Ibid., p. 2858.

But there was some misunderstanding among the committeemen. The plan to include Florida in the bill also met with
opposition and the whole subject came before the Senate. On
June 5 Wilson of Massachusetts rose in behalf of Alabama.
His motion was adopted but only by the barest majority, 22
to 21, several Republican senators, including Trumbull, Fessenden, Howard, Morrill of Vermont, Frelinghuysen and Howe
voting against it.[1] Trumbull and others made themselves
heard at later points in the progress of the debate, but they
were voices in the wind. Senators and representatives on the
Radical side could show that negroes, in some cases the old and
the sick, had travelled hither and thither on foot a distance of
20 or 40 miles to reach the polling places. Words could "hardly
describe their sufferings." They had swum swift and flooded
rivers. They had gone without food for days in their holy
zeal for the Republican party.

Moreover, without good or legal cause, "rebel" election officers had rejected thousands of ballots. Many men had died
or left the state since the date of registration. Radical members of Congress pretended to have informants who had seen
crowds of people emigrating from Alabama to Tennessee.
Thus the majority which it was necessary to secure was made
fictitiously great.

It was a mere accident that the law in the first place had
not been phrased differently. "I do not think," said Senator
Wilson, "that we ought to take advantage of our own mistake, not to say blunder."[2] To Senator Sherman the provision was a "barren technicality." "If 5,000 more votes had
been cast for this constitution or against it at the election,"
he said, "your law would have been literally complied with."[3]

[1] Cong. Globe, 40th Cong. 2nd sess., p. 2965. "I am as anxious for the
early recognition of these states," said Senator Trumbull, "as any member upon this floor; but I cannot consent to violate fundamental principles; I cannot consent to force upon the people of any state by a minority vote a fundamental law; I cannot consent to break the faith of
this nation for the purpose of bringing Alabama into this bill."—Ibid.,
p. 2931.
[2] Ibid., p. 2859.   [3] Ibid., pp. 2860, 2861.

Here were tried and true friends of the Union who were being intimidated, proscribed and persecuted by men whose hands were still dripping with the blood of rebellion.[1] The negro's only refuge was the Republican party acting through the Congress of the United States.

Farnsworth in the House and a few other Radicals opposed the plan to re-admit Florida to representation in Congress, espousing the cause of the discredited faction which Meade had outwitted at Tallahassee. The state constitution established a "little oligarchy," since the governor had the power to appoint nearly all the state officers. It was not "republican" in form within the meaning of the Constitution of the United States.[2] But all obstruction was soon swept aside. The Fourteenth Amendment was yet to be ratified. Democratic legislatures in Ohio and New Jersey had revoked action on the subject which had been taken by previous Republican legislatures. Without them only 22 states, including Arkansas, had signified their approval; six more were needed and these would be at hand if Alabama and Florida were named in the "Omnibus Bill."[3] So it was passed a few days after the Arkansas bill, to be vetoed by President Johnson as a matter of course, and shortly to be re-passed over his veto. Only one unusual condition was imposed upon any of the six states.[4] In Georgia the constitution had provided for a repudiation of debts contracted prior to June 1, 1865; Congress demanded that this provision be nullified "by solemn public act" before she should be restored to "representation in Congress as a state of the Union."

Soon only Virginia, Texas and Mississippi remained in the hands of the military governors, and the districts in the South were promptly abolished or reorganized. General Canby remitted all authority to the new civil officers of North Carolina and South Carolina on July 24, 1868; Meade retired from Georgia, Florida and Alabama and he was given command of the new Department of the South (the old Second and

[1] Cong. Globe, 40th Cong. 2nd sess., p. 2058.
[2] Ibid., pp. 3090, 3091.   [3] Ibid., pp. 2691, 2862.
[4] Ibid., appendix, p. 510.

Third Districts). Canby followed Reynolds in command of the Fifth District, which now, since Louisiana had resumed civil government, comprised only Texas. Louisiana and Arkansas were joined to form the new Department of Louisiana, commanded by General Rousseau. Gillem remained in Mississippi after the withdrawal of Arkansas from the Fourth District and continued there until the end of President Johnson's administration. The troops were so distributed in the reorganized states that, at need, they could cooperate with and sustain the state authorities.[1]

Congress at the same time provided for the withdrawal from the South of the agents of the Freedmen's Bureau. With the coming into force of the new state constitutions the opportunity to bring its activities to an end was at hand. Most of the functions of this body, which had been defending the interests of the negroes amid so much antagonism, were to cease on January 1, 1869.[2]

[1] Report of Sec. of War for 1869, vol. i, p. xiii.
[2] McPherson, Hist. of Recon., p. 376; Paul S. Peirce, The Freedmen's Bureau, State Univ. of Iowa Studies, pp. 71-2; Laws of U. S., app. Cong. Globe, 40th Cong. 2nd sess., p. 513. The bill was received by the President on June 24 and became a law without his signature. Legally the Bureau continued until June 30, 1872; its existence was finally ended by act of June 10, 1872. The force employed in 1870 had been reduced to 87 persons.—Peirce, op. cit., p. 74.

CHAPTER X

A REPRESENTATIVE in Congress, James M. Ashley of Ohio, introduced his resolution to impeach President Johnson and the House referred it to the Judiciary Committee for an inquiry on January 7, 1867, in the first days of the second session of the 39th Congress. The life of this Congress soon came to an end and the committee was instructed to continue its investigation into the grounds for the grave charges in the period covered by the brief and fitful sessions of the new 40th Congress. Beginning on Wednesday, February 6, when General Lafayette C. Baker, head of the band of detectives which Stanton supported as an arm of the secret service in the War Department, was called before the committee, the examination of witnesses proceeded until Saturday, November 23, when Ashley was interrogated to discover what else he might have in hand to support his accusations and make good his case.

The range of the inquiry was wide; the evidence inconclusive to the last degree. No one at this day can study the mass of testimony and attach the least value to the information which was extracted by the inquisitors with reference to the President's honor, either as a public servant or a private man. Secretary of State Seward, Secretary of the Treasury McCulloch, Secretary of War Stanton, Attorney General Stanbery, Postmaster General Randall, General Grant, Chief Justice Chase, ex-Secretary Harlan, Montgomery Blair, General J. S. Fullerton, General O. O. Howard, General Canby, Horace Greeley, Judge Advocate General Holt, the President's private secretaries and many others were questioned and cross-questioned in an effort to adduce proof as

to Mr. Johnson's treason. The "scavenger," Ashley, meanwhile occupied himself in circulating stories as to the President's complicity in Lincoln's assassination,[1] in interviewing
this or that man in search of the evidence which he desired to
substantiate his dastardly charges, and in despatching hither
and thither and paying the expenses of sub-scavengers that
no garbage pail might escape. Baker and his detectives were
called and re-called. Men who had been present when Booth
was shot and captured were investigated, especially in reference to the assassin's diary which, so it was diligently advertised, had had leaves torn from it after it had fallen into
the custody of the government. What could these missing
sheets contain but evidence incriminating Andrew Johnson
in the plot against Lincoln's life? Ashley himself secretly
visited and talked with a convicted felon named Dunham or
Conover, in jail in Washington.[2] With this infamous man
Ashley consorted, sometimes late at night, to extract proof
which he was said to possess of the President's connection
with Booth. Mrs. Dunham or Conover travelled about on
Ashley's missions in search of letters and papers, while he in
return promised, if she came back with what he desired, to
use his offices to secure her husband's release from the prison
house.[3]

Stories about women who sold pardons to "rebels" and who
were not more or less than prostitutes, with access to Johnson's private apartments by back stairways at the White
House, were solemnly investigated.[4] An ignorant female
named Perry who had formed a lucrative business partnership,
conditioned upon a secret arrangement with Johnson concern-

[1] In spite of the patent fact that only two years since the military
commission which tried Lincoln's assassins found that President Johnson was an "intended victim of the wide-branched plot and condemned
a poor wretch for lying in wait to murder him."—Dewitt, Impeachment
and Trial of Andrew Johnson, p. 147.
[2] Sentenced to the penitentiary for ten years for perjury in connection with Judge Holt's attempt to fasten the assassination of Lincoln
upon Jefferson Davis.—Dewitt, p. 142.
[3] Ibid., pp. 154-5.
[4] Further amplified in General Baker's book, History of the United
States Secret Service.

ing the custom house administration in New York, was the subject of testimony.[1] Michael Burns, a sympathizer with the rebellion in Tennessee, and other men were called to show that Johnson had reaped profits corruptly through his relations with certain railroads in that state; the cashier of Jay Cooke's national bank in Washington to ascertain what money the President had on deposit and how it had come there; Provisional Governors Parsons and Sharkey to prove that the President had endeavored to prevent the South from ratifying the Fourteenth Amendment; gentlemen from Colorado who might be ready to testify that he had vetoed their statehood bill because they would not enter into a bargain to support his policy in regard to the admission to Congress of the Southern senators and representatives; other men respecting fraud and thievery in connection with the return to the people of the South of cotton, lands and other classes of abandoned and confiscated property; General Burton to ascertain if he knew anything to the disparagement of the President in respect of the custody and release of Jefferson Davis at Fortress Monroe; Chief Detective Baker to make certain where he had buried the dead body of Booth, that he had not as some pretended to believe tied stones to it and sunk it at sea, that he had not beheaded it, that he had not removed the heart from it and so on; Mrs. Surratt's daughter to see if she might know anything about nobody knew what.

Such a hotchpotch of calumnious and irrelevant triviality as the examination revealed it would be hard for the normal mind to conceive. But for months men and women continued to be sworn and to answer questions put to them by the members of the committee with no gain of knowledge of any sort. Nothing was divulged except what was clear before—that Johnson had suffered a sea change as to the policies to be pursued with reference to the South; that he had removed from office, as other Presidents before him had done, men who

[1] Many letters from this woman are preserved in the Johnson Papers. On one in Johnson's hand is a direction to his secretaries to file it with other attempts at "blackmail."

were not in sympathy with his course; that he had pardoned some "rebels" and restored their property to them; that some revenue officers and postmasters had been serving in the South without first taking the iron-clad test oath; that he in general was hostile to Congress on the whole subject of the reconstruction of the late Confederate states.[1]

Finally, on November 23, 1867, Ashley was brought before the committee to be asked if he had produced "all the testimony" which he had in hand to sustain his charges. "Substantially all," he replied.[2] "Have you stated to members of the House of Representatives," asked a member of the Committee, "that you had evidence which satisfied you that Mr. Johnson was connected with, or implicated in the assassination of Mr. Lincoln?" "Yes, certainly I have," Ashley answered. "Then," continued Mr. Eldridge, who was cross-questioning the witness, "why did you not produce this evidence to the committee?" "Because," Ashley continued, "it was not of that legal character which would have justified me in presenting it. It satisfied me from my standpoint, and that is what I meant." "Then," persisted Eldridge, "what do you mean by saying that you had no evidence in your possession which you considered valid?" "It was not that kind of evidence," the witness replied, "which would satisfy the great mass of men, especially the men who do not concur with me in my theory about this matter." He explained that in his opinion President William Henry Harrison, President Zachary Taylor and President Buchanan were "poisoned for the express purpose of putting the Vice President in the President's office." Mr. Lincoln had been assassinated with a like end in view.[3]

In reply to further requests for "evidence or fact" which would tend "in any degree to fasten the assassination" on Mr. Johnson Ashley said that he knew of none "at present."[4] "I have had numbers of men brought to me, or coming to me vol-

[1] House Reports, 40th Cong., 1st sess., no. 7.
[2] Ibid., Testimony, p. 1195.
[3] Ibid., pp. 1198-99. [4] Ibid., p. 1201.

untarily," he continued, "who thought they knew important
matters and when they made their statement it was worth-
less." [1]

Ashley had had the aid while the investigation proceeded
of a special "Assassination Committee" of the House, with
Benjamin F. Butler at its head, appointed ostensibly to examine and consider "all the facts and circumstances" attending Lincoln's death, though really with a view to involving
Johnson in the conspiracy.[2] A "drag net" was put out "to
catch every malicious whisper." The chief of the detective
police, Baker, stationed his spies within the very walls of the
White House.[3] Butler, like Ashley, had wrought with Conover.[4] But neither of the cunning blackguards found a scrap
of evidence of the kind which they sought to set before the
world.

In a word the entire accusatory scheme of the impeachers
had broken down, and Ashley was now compelled to acknowledge before the committee the total failure of his laborious
and much advertised attempts to lay murder or any lesser
crime at the President's door.

Yet, resting their case upon this highly ridiculous body
of testimony, for the most part without direct bearing upon
the question at issue, the Judiciary Committee, after some
reference to the history of the subject in English and American
law, recommended the impeachment of the President for his
high crimes and misdemeanors. The members had stood five
to four against preferring the charges until lately, when the
"Judas," Churchill, had joined Mr. Boutwell, Mr. Lawrence,
Mr. Thomas and Mr. Williams. Now there were but two of
the Republicans in opposition—Mr. Wilson, the chairman of
the committee, and Mr. Woodbridge, with whom the two
Democrats, Eldridge and Marshall, still cooperated.

Boutwell and his four associates found Johnson guilty on

[1] House Reports, 40th Cong., 1st sess., no. 7, Testimony, p. 1205.
[2] In response to a resolution of the House passed July 8, 1867.—
Cong. Globe, 40th Cong. 1st sess., pp. 515-7.
[3] House Reports, 40th Cong., 1st sess., no. 7, p. 110.
[4] Ibid., Testimony, pp. 1194-1208.

twenty-seven separate counts involving, they averred, "undoubted usurpation of power and repeated violations of law." He had "retarded the public prosperity, lessened the public revenues, disordered the business and finances of the country, encouraged insubordination in the people of the states recently in rebellion, fostered sentiments of hostility between different classes of citizens, revived and kept alive the spirit of rebellion, humiliated the nation, dishonored republican institutions, obstructed the restoration of said states to the Union and delayed and postponed the peaceful and fraternal reorganization of the government of the United States." [1]

Chairman Wilson and Mr. Woodbridge dissented from the conclusions of Boutwell and his colleagues; they disapproved of the temper and spirit of the majority. The committee, said these two clear-minded men, had brought forward "not a particle of evidence which would be received by any court in the land." They, like the majority, appealed to the history of impeachment as a constitutional proceeding in England and America. The President, they agreed, had "disappointed the hopes and expectations of those who placed him in power." He had "betrayed their confidence and joined hands with their enemies," and while they, Mr. Wilson and Mr. Woodbridge, would "acquit him of impeachable crimes" they must "pronounce him guilty of many wrongs." His "contest with Congress" had "delayed reconstruction and inflicted vast injury upon the people of the rebel states." He had been "blind to the necessities of the times and to the demands of a progressive civilization. . . . Incapable of appreciating the grand changes which the past six years have wrought he seeks to measure the great events which surround him by the narrow rules which adjusted public affairs before the rebellion and its legitimate consequences had destroyed and established others." [2]

The Democrats, Eldridge and Marshall, while at one with the two Republicans in the view that the President had been

[1] House Reports, 40th Cong. 1st sess., no. 7, pp. 1-59.
[2] Ibid., pp. 59-105.

guilty of no impeachable offense, were for withholding criticism of his course, since it was no duty of the committee, said they, to do more than determine whether he should or should not be impeached. The evidence, they continued with partisan hyperbole, would be received "with one universal burst of indignation of the American people." The President, surviving this attempt to load him with "disgrace and infamy," would "have and retain all over the land to a greater extent than ever before the respect and confidence of his countrymen." [1]

Boutwell represented the majority in the Judiciary Committee in stating the case to the House when it met in November, 1867. Wilson led the speaking for the other side and on December 7 the scheme to bring Johnson to the bar of the Senate was defeated by a vote of 108 to 57. The majority was made up of 67 Republicans and 41 Democrats; on the Republican side of the House, therefore, impeachment was opposed by ten more than favored it. [2]

But now, though three months were not gone, other things had come to pass. Johnson had asked Stanton to resign. The Secretary of War had refused. A week later, on the 12th, he was suspended and Grant, at the wish of the President, entered the office as Secretary *ad interim*. The Senate was not in session. When it did resume its meetings it received a statement from the President explanatory of his action in the case, and on January 13, 1868, by a vote of 35 to 6 it non-concurred. Thereupon Grant, choosing to consider that his duties were at an end, locked the office, and the keys fell into the hands of Stanton, who pretended to resume his functions. The verbal and epistolary colloquy between the President and Grant which ensued took on a significance as wide as the nation. Party feeling became intense. The minds of men from Maine to California were filled with wars and rumors of wars. That military force would be invoked by Stanton against the President and by the Presi-

- House Reports, 40th Cong. 1st sess., no. 7, pp. 105-11.
[2] Cf. vol. i of this History, pp. 461-3, 483-4.

dent against Stanton was implicitly believed. The situation stood thus when, on February 21, 1868, Johnson converted Stanton's suspension of August 12 into a removal, designating for the office, after divers attempts had been made to induce others to accept it, the Adjutant-General, Lorenzo Thomas. To this pliant, if not foolish man,[1] willing to do the President's bidding in unpleasant service at an excited time, Stanton was directed to transfer "all records, books, papers and other public property" in his "custody and charge." Then an unseemly wrangle ensued, Stanton holding his ground under advice and with the support of militant Radical friends, while Thomas, too tactlessly and too boastfully, attempted to take possession of the office.

The Senate on this same day (February 21), having read the communication from the White House announcing the event, passed into executive session wherein there was turbulent debate. Edmunds of Vermont offered a resolution expressive of the body's disapproval of the President's course. Dixon, Drake, Chandler, Wilson, Yates proposed amendments. Dixon, as Johnson's friend, urged that they content themselves, for the moment at any rate, with an inquiry—they could ask the President as to his authority in law for the removal. Yates on the other hand was in favor of a statement that the President's action was in "resistance of law" and "revolutionary." At length the resolution took the following form:

"Whereas, the Senate have received and considered the communication of the President of the United States, stating that he had removed Edwin M. Stanton, Secretary of War, and had designated the Adjutant-General of the Army to act as Secretary of War *ad interim*,

[1] "Of all the army," said Boutwell, "but one man has been found to obey his [the President's] will, and he old and impotent and weak. (Cong. Globe, 40th Cong. 2nd sess., app., p. 161.) W. B. Allison of Iowa called Thomas "a weak, irresolute old man." (Ibid., p. 203.) For what the President's own friends thought of Thomas see, e.g., Welles, who said that he was "weak and foolish," talking "openly and loudly" and "like a boy." He at once proved himself "unfit for the place." (Diary, vol. iii, pp. 289-90.)

"Resolved, by the Senate of the United States, that, under the Constitution and laws of the United States, the President has no power to remove the Secretary of War and designate any other officer to perform the duties of that office *ad interim.*" [1]

Twenty-eight Senators voted for the resolution and six (Buckalew, Davis, Doolittle, Hendricks, Patterson of Tennessee and Edmunds) against it, while 20, including Chandler, Dixon, Fessenden, Fowler, Frelinghuysen, Grimes, Henderson, Morgan and Sherman, did not vote at all.

In the House like despatch marked the course of the Radical leaders. When the impeachment proceedings, which had received the long and labored care of the Judiciary Committee, came to nothing in the previous December the question had been passed over to Thaddeus Stevens's Reconstruction Committee, famous for its intolerant and arbitrary management of whatever subject fell into its hands. As a beginning, on January 27, 1868, upon the motion of Spalding of Ohio, this committee was authorized to inquire "what combinations have been made or attempted to be made to obstruct the execution of the laws." [2] Two weeks later, on February 10, the testimony taken by the Judiciary Committee on the subject of Mr. Johnson, at Stevens's desire, was referred to his Reconstruction Committee.[3] The following day, the 11th, the Grant-Johnson correspondence was sent to the same committee,[4] and on February 13 its members by a vote of six (Beaman, Bingham, Hulburd and Paine, Republicans, and Beck and Brooks, Democrats) to three (Stevens, Boutwell and Farnsworth) disapproved a resolution which had been offered by Stevens to impeach the President.[5]

Now, on February 21, Stanton, further playing his part in the great game to set the President out of his office and take away his good name, forwarded a communication to

[1] McPherson, History of Reconstruction, pp. 262-3.
[2] Cong. Globe, 40th Cong. 2nd sess., p. 784.
[3] Ibid., p. 1087.   [4] Ibid., p. 1109.
[5] McPherson, Hist. of Recon., p. 265.

Speaker Colfax enclosing a copy of Johnson's order to Thomas which Mr. Colfax was asked to lay before the House of Representatives. Upon motion of Elihu B. Washburne of Illinois it, too, was sent to Stevens's Committee on Reconstruction.[1] An hour or two later on this eventful day John Covode, a Republican leader from Pennsylvania, offered a resolution "that Andrew Johnson, President of the United States, be impeached of high crimes and misdemeanors," which followed the familiar path into Stevens's committee room.[2]

Those who before had wavered now, in their own despite, were swept into the vortex of unthinking partisan fury. But a few hours sufficed to herd the madmen and drive them, as before the wind, at the President's head. It mattered little how he had offended. They would have voted to condemn him if some one had accused him of stepping on a dog's tail, said Mr. Welles.[3] As readily would they have voted to hang him in front of the White House as to impeach him in the Capitol.[4]

It was the anniversary of the birth of Washington. The day's significance for political proceedings was nearly as obvious as the 4th of July's. As a time to behead tyrants, to strike shackles from the necks of slaves, to restore dead liberties there was not a better in the American calendar. It was a Saturday, and its 24 hours were not long enough for the chieftains of radicalism to do all that they would in forging their thunderbolts for the destruction of Andrew Johnson. It was 11.59 o'clock on the following Monday morning before they were ready to allow this memorable day to reach its end.

Eldridge had endeavored to secure a reading of the Farewell Address which he would have followed with adjournment. But in vain. The galleries were crowded and the Speaker was compelled to call in the Capitol police to preserve order. Thaddeus Stevens gained the floor. His committee had con-

---

[1] Cong. Globe, 40th Cong. 2nd sess., pp. 1326-7.
[2] Ibid., pp. 1329-30. [3] Diary, vol. iii, p. 299. [4] Ibid., p. 300.

sidered the various resolutions which had been referred to it. In addition to what else might be at hand from which to frame an indictment against the President, he had yesterday "signed and issued a commission or letter of authority to one Lorenzo Thomas, directing and authorizing said Thomas to act as Secretary of War *ad interim*," etc. "In virtue of the powers" with which they had been "invested by the House" they, as a result of the collection of evidence, were ready to recommend the adoption of a resolution "that Andrew Johnson, President of the United States, be impeached of high crimes and misdemeanors in office." The report was signed by Stevens, Boutwell, Bingham, Hulburd, Farnsworth, Beaman and Paine,[1] four of whom, it was said, had opposed impeachment but nine days before. The old Radical from Pennsylvania, in characteristic vein, presumed that such a question would require no debate. He would say nothing as to a course so obviously natural and just, "unless gentlemen on the other side" should desire to discuss it. "The fact," said he, "of removing a man from office, while the Senate was in session, without the consent of the Senate, if there were nothing else, is of itself, and always has been considered a high crime and misdemeanor."[2]

One of the "gentlemen on the other side," James Brooks, a member of the Reconstruction Committee, at once rose to say that he had wished to prepare and offer a minority report. But the committee, after a meeting "hardly an hour in length," had rushed to its task. It had violated a well known rule of the House by sitting while the House was in general session and suddenly, "upon a very partial submission of facts," in a "partial Congress," still "representing but a section of a portion of the people" they were summoned to enter upon the "august proceeding of impeaching the chief executive officer of the government." He complained that he was "utterly unable" on this day of patriotic memories to do his duty to the people and to express himself "with that deep solemnity" which he felt "in rising to resist this untoward, this unholy,

[1] Cong. Globe, 40th Cong. 2nd sess., p. 1336.   [2] Ibid.

this unconstitutional proceeding." "Go on, go on, if you choose," he said, addressing the Radicals. "You may strip him of his office, but you will canonize him among those heroic defenders of constitutional law and liberty, in whose ranks it is the highest glory of human ambition to shine. . . . Suppose you succeed, suppose you make the President of the Senate President of the United States, you settle that hereafter a party, having a sufficient majority in the House and the Senate, can depose the President of the United States." The curse of all other countries, the curse of France, the curse of the South American republics had been that they had followed such a precedent as 'Congress now was asked to establish here, "the overthrow of their executive, not by law, not by Constitution, but by the irregular and arbitrary and revolutionary exercise of power in order merely to obtain a temporary possession of the government." [1]

Beck, Brooks's Democratic associate on the Reconstruction Committee, Holman, Eldridge, Woodward, Boyer, Wood and other Democrats spoke in a like strain. It was an attempt "to niggerize the republic," said one, "to Mexicanize it." [2] Where was the fury which aforetime had been expended upon Jefferson Davis? asked Mungen of Ohio. The President of the Southern Confederacy was running at large while the President of the United States who had performed "soldier's duty in the war for the country" was about to be impeached —and for what? a mere honest difference of opinion about the constitutionality of a law. [3] Briefly stated, said Phelps of Maryland, the issue is "whether white men or negroes shall control ten states and through them the nation." [4] One Radical followed another with malignant and vindictive assaults upon the President. To read the discourses, and the colloquies with which they were interrupted one could think himself listening to stump speeches in a village in the midst of an angry campaign rather than in a national legislative assembly de-

[1] Cong. Globe, 40th Cong. 2nd sess., pp. 1336-9.
[2] Ibid., app., p. 210.　　　　[3] Ibid., p. 213.　　　　[4] Ibid., p. 247.

termining the fate, under the Constitution and the laws, of an exalted public magistrate.

Spalding, Bingham, Farnsworth, Kelley, Logan, Ashley, E. B. Washburne, Julian, Thomas Williams, Boutwell and many others addressed the House. Wilson and Woodbridge of the Judiciary Committee, who had resisted tyrannical party influences before, were now whipped into line and came out in definite declarations in favor of impeachment. "He shall have his day in court," said Wilson, "and be taught for his own good and that of his successors in office that the President of the United States, clothed with all the great powers of his high official station, is as completely subordinate to the law of the Republic as is the humblest of its citizens." Awed into "a strict observance" of his "duty," Wilson would vote for the resolution "to the end that the law may be vindicated by the removal of an unworthy public servant from an official position, which he has dishonored by his perverse disregard of duty and his unjustifiable contempt for the supremacy of the law."[1]

Similarly Woodbridge publicly cast away the doubts he had earlier felt and expressed. The President, "assuming an unauthorized power," had "knowingly and wilfully and wickedly disregarded and violated the law of the land." The House must do its "duty" and impeach him, no matter what the cost.[2]

Other men proceeded in their own ways. John A. Bingham of Ohio denounced the President as a "usurper of authority and criminal violator of public trusts";[3] Farnsworth of Illinois, as an "ungrateful, despicable, besotted, traitorous man,"[4] —he was "an incubus and a disgrace to the great and glorious nation."[5] To W. D. Kelley of Philadelphia he was "the great

---

[1] Cong. Globe, 40th Cong. 2nd sess., p. 1387.
[2] Ibid., p. 1388. For Woodbridge's personal feelings which were still unchanged—he deprecated impeachment—see Welles, who says that "it would have been death for him to have resisted."—Diary, vol. iii, p. 295.
[3] Cong. Globe, 40th Cong. 2nd sess., p. 1341.
[4] Ibid., p. 1344.   [5] Ibid., p. 1347.

criminal of our age and country," who for two years had
been plotting "with deliberate and bloody purpose" the overthrow of the national institutions [1]—the "bloody and untilled
fields of the ten unreconstructed states" and the "unsheeted
ghosts" of unnumbered thousands of murdered negroes cried
out for the punishment of Andrew Johnson.[2] He reiterated
the old charge that somehow the President had been a party
to the assassination of Lincoln.[3] John A. Logan of Illinois
said that Johnson had dragged the robes of his office "in the
purlieus and filth of treason," and had committed "every
act" which could be "enumerated in the English language"
to obstruct the prosperity and harmony of the nation, every
act a man could conceive of "to degrade himself" and "to
destroy the rights of the American people." [4] Ashley declared that he was "a more faithful representative and a more
formidable ally of 'the lost cause' " than "any general of the
late rebel armies" would have been in his place.[5] His purpose was to dominate the government, usurp all political
authority and, if he were resisted, "to inaugurate a civil
war." He, Ashley, had seen this from the first day. He
was amazed at the blindness of others. By defending such
a man they would go down into history "as a party to his
crime." [6]

Julian of Indiana was glad to think that Johnson would be
hurled from the White House and consigned "once more to
the fond embrace of his rebel confederates in the South and
their faithful allies in the North." [7] E. B. Washburne of Illinois, declared that the President was "surrounded by red-
handed rebels" and that he was "advised and counselled by
the worst men that ever crawled like filthy reptiles at the
footstool of power." His "personal and official character"
had made him "the opprobrium of both hemispheres and
brought ineffable disgrace on the American name." [8] Stokes

[1] Cong. Globe, 40th Cong. 2nd sess., p. 1347. [2] Ibid., p. 1348.
[3] Ibid., p. 1347. [4] Ibid., p. 1353. [5] Ibid., p. 1362.
[6] Ibid., p. 1361. [7] Ibid., p. 1386. [8] Ibid., p. 1369.

of Tennessee said that the President had "wicked and hellish purposes." He was "the worst tyrant and usurper that history was ever called on to record." [1] Pile of Missouri spoke "in the name of the half million brave men whose ghastly corpses" lay "beneath the greensward of the South," the "armless and limbless men" who went "maimed and halting to the tomb"; the widows and orphans and desolated hearthstones of the war, demanded the impeachment and removal of the man who sought "to betray into the hands of its enemies the country for which they fought and died." [2] Newcomb of Missouri said that Johnson's place in history would be in the company of Nero, Torquemada and George Jeffreys; [3] Loughridge of Iowa that the President's full purpose was to capture the army, seize the Capitol, disperse Congress and consign the people's representatives to the dungeon and the scaffold; [4] Price of Iowa that "every vile traitor and bloody-handed rebel of the South," hidden away in dens and caves had "crawled into daylight," and now were "uncoiling themselves" under the warmth of Johnson's smiles; [5] Ben Butler that "for a tithe" of his "usurpation, lawlessness and tyranny our fathers dissolved their connection with the government of King George, for less than this King James lost his throne and King Charles lost his head." [6]

The words "tyrant," "criminal," "usurper," "incubus" and "apostate" were heard again and again; a half dozen alleged or implied that the President was a drunkard and two that he had had a hand in killing Lincoln. But now in the main the back stairs tattle and blackguardly allusion which had characterized the proceedings when the President's fate was in the hands of the Committee on the Judiciary were put aside. It was a single direct new issue, to wit: that Johnson had removed, or had attempted to remove Stanton as Secretary of War in violation of the terms of the Tenure of Office

---

[1] Cong. Globe, 40th Cong. 2nd sess., p. 1396.　[3] Ibid., app., p. 157.
[2] Ibid., p. 191.　[4] Ibid., p. 206.
[5] Ibid., p. 222.　　[6] Cong. Globe, 40th Cong. 2nd sess., p. 1393.

act of March 2, 1867, and that an *ad interim* appointment
had been made to fill the vacancy in further violation of law.
For this reason was the President a criminal, on this account
should he be impeached, tried, convicted and turned out of
office at the first good day.

The Tenure of Office act was an arbitrary, a vindictive and,
as many believed, an unconstitutional law, contrived to entrap the President, amid remonstrances from him and from
every member of his Cabinet, including Stanton, but upon an
alleged infraction of this law the Republican party was resting
its case. They were awkward facts, but no matter of that,
which were stated by the Democrats when they alleged that
Johnson had never appointed Stanton, who held a commission
from Lincoln which specified that he should continue in office
as Secretary of War only "during the pleasure of the President of the United States for the time being"; [1] that when
the Tenure of Office act was passed in February, 1867, and
the provision concerning the members of the Cabinet, about
which the Senate and the House had disagreed, was under
discussion it was distinctly stated by Senator Williams and
Senator Sherman that this part of the bill did not apply to
the "present President." It was all "quite an immaterial
matter" since, said Williams, "any Cabinet minister who has
a particle of self respect—and we can hardly suppose that
any man would occupy so responsible an office without having
that feeling—would decline to remain in the Cabinet after
the President had signified to him that his presence was no
longer needed"; or, as the same thought was expressed by
Sherman—"No gentleman, no man with any sense of honor
would hold a position as a Cabinet officer after his chief desired his removal, and the slightest intimation on the part
of the President would always secure the resignation of a
Cabinet officer." [2]

Finally all who were under an obligation to make speeches

[1] As, e. g., Mr. Golladay, Cong. Globe, 40th Cong. 2nd sess., app., p.
199.
[2] As, e. g., Brooks, Cong. Globe, 40th Cong. 2nd sess., p. 1339; Beck,
ibid., pp. 1350-5; Boyer, ibid., p. 1363; Golladay, ibid., app., p. 197;

to be printed and sent home to their constituents for a reading in the approaching campaign had done so, and as the hour of five o'clock on Monday afternoon, February 24, drew nigh Thaddeus Stevens rose to close the debate in the grandiloquent manner which he so well knew how to summon for such an occasion. The charges, "if falsely made," said he, would work a "cruel wrong" upon the President. "If on the other hand, the usurpations and misdemeanors charged against him are true he is guilty of as atrocious attempts to usurp the liberty and destroy the happiness of this nation as were ever perpetrated by the most detestable tyrant who ever oppressed his fellow men." He then would discuss "these questions in no partisan spirit but with legal accuracy and impartial justice." So he proceeded with a fling at Johnson's intoxication on the day he took the oath as Vice President. The founders of this government, he continued, were not willing to "rely for safety upon the avenging dagger of a Brutus, but provided peaceful remedies" in the form of processes of impeachment. The case by a few swift strokes was soon made out. The House could prove on trial that Johnson had been guilty of "misprision of bribery," and "highhanded usurpation of power" with a "wicked determination to subvert the laws of his country." He would be lucky if he escaped "with bare removal from office"; for such atrocities he could be "fined and incarcerated in the penitentiary afterward under criminal proceedings." The old advocate of "impartial justice" invoked "the God of our fathers" in dealing with this "first great political malefactor." What should now be done would "endure in its consequence until this whole continent shall be filled with a free and untram-

Getz, ibid., p. 270; cf. Cong. Globe, 39th Cong. 2nd sess., pp. 1515-17. But hear Hendricks who when the matter was under discussion said in reply to Williams and Sherman: "The very person who ought to be turned out is the very person who will stay in. A gentleman of course would not but a man who would have purposes to accomplish independent of the good of the country would stay." And again—"A decent man, a gentleman would not wait till he was turned out; but a dirty fellow who had no respect for himself or the high office could hold on under this bill."—Cong. Globe, 39th Cong. 2nd sess., pp. 1515, 1516.

melled people or shall be a nest of shrinking, cowardly slaves." [1]

The Speaker asked the clerk to read the resolution; Stevens called for the yeas and nays; 126 members voted for and 47 against impeachment—17 did not vote at all. [2] "The occupant of the chair," said Speaker Colfax, "cannot consent that his constituents should be silent on so grave a question." Therefore he also voted aye.

The Republican party presented a united front upon the issue. Not one member dared to vote with the Democrats, who were as unanimously arrayed on the other side. Only one Democrat failed to vote; he was paired with an absent Republican. [3]

The resolution having been approved Stevens moved that a committee of two be appointed to proceed to the Senate and at the bar, "in the name of the House of Representatives and of all the people of the United States," impeach the President of high crimes and misdemeanors in office, and announce that they in due time would "exhibit particular articles of impeachment against him and make good the same"; also that a committee of seven should be appointed to prepare and report articles of impeachment. After various dilatory motions of the Democrats had been disposed of these resolutions were adopted by a vote of 124 to 45. [4] To serve on the committee to communicate to the Senate the action of the House the Speaker named Thaddeus Stevens of Pennsylvania and John A. Bingham of Ohio; on the committee to prepare articles of impeachment, George S. Boutwell of Massachusetts, Thaddeus Stevens of Pennsylvania, John A. Bingham of Ohio, James F. Wilson of Iowa, John A. Logan of Illinois, George W. Julian of Indiana and Hamilton Ward of New York. [5]

Men in the Senate and the House were omniscient as to most subjects affecting the course of human affairs but they

---

[1] Cong. Globe, 40th Cong. 2nd sess., pp. 1399-1400.
[2] Ibid., p. 1400.
[3] McPherson, History of Reconstruction, p. 266.
[4] Cong. Globe, 40th Cong. 2nd sess., pp. 1400-2.
[5] Ibid., p. 1402.

were hard pressed to determine the proper course of procedure in this emergency. But Stevens and Bingham on Tuesday, the day following their appointment, appeared as they were directed to do, at the bar of the Senate and delivered their message. Wade presiding said, "The Senate will take order in the premises"; the committee withdrew, and, upon motion of Howard of Michigan, the subject was referred to a select committee of seven, composed of the maker of the motion, Trumbull of Illinois, Conkling of New York, Edmunds of Vermont, Oliver P. Morton of Indiana, Pomeroy of Kansas and Reverdy Johnson of Maryland. Stevens and Bingham, returning to the House, made a report of what they had done and, upon motion of Washburne of Illinois, it was resolved that, after the committee to prepare the articles of impeachment had finished its work, the debate upon them should continue not beyond four o'clock on the afternoon of the second legislative day, when, if they were agreed to, the House should by ballot elect seven managers to conduct the proceedings in the Senate.

It was Saturday, February 29, when Boutwell rose in the House and reported ten articles which had been prepared by his committee "in maintenance and support" of the impeachment against the President and the discussion began. Nine of the articles had to do with one or another phase of the President's alleged offense in removing Stanton and appointing Lorenzo Thomas to temporary incumbency of the office in his stead, while the tenth recited that the President had called before him General William H. Emory, in command in Washington City, and had instructed this officer not to obey the orders of the General of the Army but only such as came from the commander-in-chief under the terms of the Constitution of the United States, in violation of the terms of the Army Appropriation act of March 2, 1867. Boutwell opened the argument in a characteristic speech, Stevens closed it with allusions to the great lenity, the mercy, the fairness of the committee representing the "people," who had treated this "great malefactor" so gently, "unwilling" as they were "to blot the records of their country by mingling his crimes with their shame." The President's "bastard policy" of seducing men with offers of office, if they would abandon their "honest principles" and adopt his, "was a crime more heinous than that which brought many ancient agitators to the block." With all the arts of the king of bullies Stevens threatened and stormed. "Let me see the recreant," said he, "who would vote to let such a criminal escape. Point me to one who will dare do it and I will show you one who will dare the infamy of posterity." "Unfortunate man," Stevens went on as he addressed himself to the President, "thus surrounded, hampered, tangled in the meshes of his own wickedness—unfortunate, unhappy man, behold your doom!"

Neither Republican nor Democrat added aught to the discussion by their speeches of Saturday, the last day of February, or of Monday the 2nd of March by which time the ten articles had been consolidated and made into nine. The first which accused the President of removing Stanton in defiance of the terms of the Tenure of Office act of March 2, 1867, might have been called "the Stanton article." [1] The second, third and eighth articles were "the Thomas articles." [2] In them it was declared that the President's designation of Lorenzo Thomas to perform the duties of Secretary of War *ad interim* was in violation of law. The fourth, fifth, sixth and seventh articles were generally known as "the conspiracy articles," because they declared that some kind of a conspiracy had been entered into between the President and Thomas to set Stanton out and to gain possession of the War Office. In the fourth and sixth articles it was stated that the two men had violated the provisions of a certain act which had been passed on July 31, 1861, to prevent treasonable gatherings and plots during the war. In the eighth article reference was made to some supposed attempt on the President's part to control the disbursement of moneys appropriated for the military service. But underneath the verbiage in which

[1] Cf. Buckalew, in Trial, vol. iii, p. 218.
[2] Ibid., p. 223.

the charges of the impeachers had been concealed there were in the whole first eight articles but two facts, which were well known to every one—that the President had attempted to remove Stanton from the office of Secretary of War, and that he had appointed "one Lorenzo Thomas" to act as Secretary of War *ad interim*. The original tenth' article, "the Emory article," had become the ninth.

The first article was passed by a vote of 126 to 41, 22 members not voting; the second and third articles, each by a vote of 122 to 40; the fourth, by 116 to 39; the fifth, sixth, seventh and eighth, by 126 to 41; the ninth, which concerned the President's relations with General Emory, built upon the flimsiest foundations, by 107 to 40, 20 or more Republicans, who had supported the other articles failing to vote for this one.[1]

The House specifically reserved to itself the right to make further accusations against the President, and seven members were nominated and elected by ballot as managers to conduct the proceedings at the bar of the Senate: Thaddeus Stevens of Pennsylvania, Benjamin F. Butler of Massachusetts, John A. Bingham of Ohio, George S. Boutwell of Massachusetts, James F. Wilson of Iowa, Thomas Williams of Pennsylvania and John A. Logan of Illinois. The Democrats abstained from voting. Bingham received the largest number of votes, 114, Stevens the fewest, 105.[2]

Material for further articles had been offered in the closing hours of the debate on Monday, but time was not at hand for a full consideration of them and they were not adopted until the following day, March 3. The tenth article was invented and sponsored by Butler, the eleventh had been contrived by the cunning hand of Stevens but it was presented by Bingham. Butler's article recited at length statements from the President's speeches, including that one in Washington made "in a loud voice" on August 18, 1866, after the return of the delegates from the Philadelphia Convention, wherein he had

[1] Cong. Globe, 40th Cong. 2nd sess., pp. 1616-8.
[2] Ibid., p. 1619.

called Congress a body "hanging on the verge of the government," and those delivered in Cleveland and St. Louis during the "swing around the circle." Johnson had attempted on these occasions, so Butler averred, "to bring into disgrace, ridicule, hatred, contempt and reproach the Congress of the United States and the several branches thereof." He was "then and there guilty of a high misdemeanor."

Butler in presenting this article did not speak for the entire board of managers, for Mr. Wilson dissented and was ready to argue the matter on the floor of the House, where he was supported by Woodbridge, his old associate in opposition to impeachment in 1867. But Butler cared not for this and, pressing forward rough-shod, the article was adopted by a vote of 87 to 43. Numbered with the Democrats in the minority with Wilson and Woodbridge were ten other Republicans who had been held in line on the first nine articles on the preceding day, while 59 members, many of them Republicans, did not vote.[1]

The managers were unanimous in urging the adoption of the Stevens article. It was an *omnium gatherum* compounded out of the materials which had been worked up into the other ten.[2] It marked a return, with verbal variations, to the declaration that the President had attempted to remove Stanton, with allusions to the charge in the ninth article as to his alleged efforts to tamper with the integrity of General Emory, and the accusation in the tenth article in reference to indecorous and threatening speeches, with some vague new references to efforts to obstruct the restoration of government at the South under the terms of the Military Reconstruction Bill.

The eleventh article, a "concession," as Senator Buckalew said, to the "pertinacity" of Stevens,[3] was promptly passed by a vote of 108 to 32.[4] Still another article offered by Mr. Jenckes of Rhode Island, casting the Stanton-Thomas matter

[1] Cong. Globe, 40th Cong. 2nd sess., pp. 1638-42.
[2] Cf. Sumner's opinion, Trial, vol. iii, p. 279, and Curtis's argument, Trial, vol. i, p. 414.
[3] Trial, vol. iii, p. 228.
[4] Cong. Globe, 40th Cong. 2nd sess., p. 1642.

into a rather different mould, was referred to the managers, but they were in haste to be off to present their case to the Senate and it was not heard of again.[1]

Meantime the Senate was busily employed in framing and adopting rules of procedure to be followed in the trial. First Garrett Davis of Kentucky must make, at some length, the familiar argument that with the absence of the representatives from the Southern states the Senate was no more a constitutional and valid body for trying impeachments than as a house of legislature.[1] But such dilatory tactics were unavailing and soon 25 rules were drafted and adopted for the government of the court.[2]

On March 3 the Senate informed the House that it was ready to proceed and on the following day, March 4, at one o'clock the House, as a committee of the whole, preceded by Mr. Dawes of Massachusetts, in the absence of the senior member, Mr. Washburne of Illinois, supported by the clerk and the doorkeeper, followed the seven managers in procession to the Senate chamber on the grave business of removing the President of the United States and of putting Benjamin F. Wade in his place, because he had asked Edwin M. Stanton to vacate the War Office. That was the solemn issue, while the rumbling of the political conventions of 1868 was heard up and down the land, and the Republican party was shouting the name of Grant.

Seats were prepared in front of the rostrum for the managers. After their presence had been announced by the sergeant-at-arms they advanced within the bar and took their places. "Mr. Manager Bingham" rose to say that they had come to present articles of impeachment, whereupon the Senate's presiding officer, Wade, bade the sergeant-at-arms make proclamation. This officer cried "Hear ye! Hear ye! Hear ye! All persons are commanded to keep silence on pain of imprisonment while the House of Representatives is exhibiting to the Senate of the United States articles of impeachment

[1] Cong. Globe, 40th Cong. 2nd sess., pp. 1643-1661.
[2] Ibid., pp. 1516-17.　　　　[3] Trial, vol. i, pp. 13-15.

against Andrew Johnson, President of the United States." All the managers stood up, except Thaddeus Stevens, in whom age had weakened everything except his bitter spirit and acrid tongue, while Bingham read the eleven articles of impeachment. At the conclusion of this ceremony Wade said that the Senate would "take due order upon the subject of impeachment," giving "proper notice" to the House.

The managers withdrew, accompanied by the members who had escorted them to the Senate chamber, whereupon the senators fixed one o'clock on the following afternoon as the time for beginning the proceedings, and designated Pomeroy of Kansas, Wilson of Massachusetts and Buckalew of Pennsylvania a committee to wait upon the Chief Justice to notify him that he would be expected to meet the Senate at that hour.

When that hour arrived Chief Justice Chase, accompanied by Mr. Justice Nelson, the senior associate justice of the Supreme Court, was escorted by the three senators into the chamber. He took the chair and said: "Senators, I attend the Senate in obedience to your notice for the purpose of joining with you in forming a court of impeachment for the trial of the President of the United States, and I am now ready to take the oath." Justice Nelson administered it. Mr. Chase swore to "do impartial justice according to the Constitution and the laws." The senators who since the entrance of the Chief Justice had been standing now resumed their seats, the secretary called the roll and Chase administered the oath to 44 of them successively from Anthony to Van Winkle in alphabetical order.

When Wade's name was called objection was entered by Senator Hendricks, Democrat, on the ground that the senator from Ohio was a person in interest. Wade's rights in the matter were defended by Sherman, Sumner, Howard and others; the opposite side of the case was presented by Reverdy Johnson, Bayard, Garrett Davis, Buckalew, Dixon and Hendricks. A protracted and at times ardent debate ensued, which was continued for the rest of that day and a part of the following day,[1] when Mr. Hendricks withdrew the point he had raised and Wade, Willey, Williams, Wilson and Yates were sworn, as their names were respectively called. Other senators who had been absent on the 5th took the oath now, or at later dates when they appeared, until all were qualified members of the court. The Senate being organized for the trial the managers of the impeachment on the part of the House were sent for. They came and formally asked for process to be taken against the President, that he might "answer at the bar of the Senate upon the articles of impeachment," whereupon a 'summons" was issued to Andrew Johnson "returnable" that day one week—on Friday, the 13th of March at one o'clock in the afternoon.

It was the madly hostile Sumner who had asked the question whether after the trial had begun the Senate should "continue to transact legislative and executive business." Should it "hold its customary relations with the President arraigned at our bar in the name of the people of the United States," or should it adopt "a system of non-intercourse until the trial is brought to a close?"[2] But Rule 12 stated that the Senate should proceed in its regular way when it was not acting as a court, and both the Senate and the House continued their legislative sessions, except as the engagements of the members and the excitement of the hour prevented it, until the end of the trial. Now, for a week, the senators could discuss the funding of the public debt, pensions for Union soldiers, reconstruction in Alabama, consular and diplomatic expenditures and other familiar questions of state.

It was necessary to provide for seating the crowds which should apply for space in the Senate chamber while the trial was in progress. Tickets, not above 1,000 in number, were printed. Forty tickets were placed in the hands of Baron Gerolt, minister of Prussia, for distribution to the foreign legations; four were given to each senator, two to each member of the House, four to the Chief Justice, four to Speaker Col-

[1] Trial, vol. iii, pp. 360-401.
[2] Cong. Globe, 40th Cong. 2nd sess., p. 1535.

fax, two to each associate justice of the Supreme Court, two
to each Cabinet officer, two to General Grant, twenty to the
private secretary of the President "for the use of the President," sixty to the reporters of the press and so forth.[1] Men
in all parts of the country left their homes for Washington to
attend the trial. Senator Anthony's lodgings were besieged
before he was up in the morning. He made his way by back
streets to the Capitol only to find his committee room filled
with importunate applicants for tickets whom he turned over
to the sergeant-at-arms.[2]

At the hour of one o'clock, on Friday, the 13th day of
March, the Chief Justice re-appeared in the Senate hall, and
took the chair. The House of Representatives was informed
"that the Senate is in its chamber and ready to proceed with
the trial of Andrew Johnson, President of the United States,
and that seats are provided for the accommodation of the
members," whereupon, advancing as before in committee
of the whole, with E. B. Washburne at their head, the representatives crossed the Capitol to the scene of the trial, the
seven managers resuming their places inside the bar. The
return to the writ of summons was at hand. The sergeant-at-
arms had served the paper on the "said Andrew Johnson" at
the Executive Mansion, "the usual place of abode of the said
Andrew Johnson," and he now cried: "Andrew Johnson, President of the United States! Andrew Johnson, President of the
United States! appear and answer the articles of impeachment
exhibited against you by the House of Representatives of the
United States."

On the President's side preparations for the defence were
begun immediately upon receipt of knowledge that his enemies
were about to close in around him for this final test of their
strength. Friends wrote fortifying him for the ordeal. He
would be defended by "a Spartan band of brethren" from a
persecution, "conceived in malice, prompted through the iniquity of usurpers." The "miserably frivolous charges" of
the "black Radicals" would fall to the ground in the "farcical

[1] Trial, vol. i, p. 10.
[2] Cong. Globe, 40th Cong. 2nd sess., p. 1843.

court." Meetings were held, resolutions were passed, men offered him their property and lives. An admirer in New York state put $25,000 at his disposal and authorized him to draw upon the sum at sight.[1] He would come out of the test "as pure as gold seven times refined." He was laying up for the future "a crown of fadeless renown." Women prayed for his deliverance. The militant bade him be a Jackson or a Cromwell. They again tendered him companies of volunteers.[2]

He very naturally placed his case in the hands of his Attorney General. But other lawyers of eminence must be procured that there might be no want of alert and able counsel. It was urged on the first day that Benjamin Robbins Curtis[3] of Boston should be chosen to assist Mr. Stanbery.[4] Now nearly sixty years of age, he represented the best traditions of the older American bar. Learned, honorable, with a calm, judicial temper, cultivated by several years of service on the bench of the Supreme Court of the United States to which he was appointed by President Fillmore, through the influence of Daniel Webster, and from which he had resigned in 1857,[5] he was by common consent one of the country's foremost jurists. To his friends his sympathy with Mr. Johnson in the contest with Congress was well known.[6] "There is not a decent pre-

---

[1] Some of the money offered so freely before the trial was begun would have been welcome a few months later. As Johnson's term was ending in March, 1869, just before his return to Tennessee, O. Wendell wrote to say that a debt of $10,000, which he had assumed on account of the President's defence, was still unpaid. Only Postmaster-General Randall had given him aid in raising it and the "most strenuous" efforts, despite "repeated promises" of the President's friends, had met with the feeblest response.—Johnson Papers.

[2] Various letters in Johnson Papers.

[3] Brother of George Ticknor Curtis.

[4] Welles, vol. iii, p. 294.

[5] He had forcibly dissented from Taney in the Dred Scott decision. More lately he had been counsel for the state of Virginia in the case against West Virginia and had presented that matter in the Supreme Court (Va. v. West Va., 11 Wall., 39). Regarded as a radical in the Dred Scott case he was now, because of his connection with the Virginia litigation, looked upon as a conservative.—New Orleans Picayune, May 10, 1868.

[6] He had publicly expressed his sympathy with the objects of the Philadelphia convention of 1866.—Memoir of B. R. Curtis, vol. i, p. 389.

tense," he wrote when he was still not yet deep in the case, "that the President has committed an impeachable offense."[1] It was the unanimous view that he should be engaged and he consented to serve.[2]

Charles O'Conor was suggested, but he had defended Jefferson Davis, and thought of calling upon him must be abandoned.[3] Objection was made to the name of David Dudley Field by Seward and Stanbery.[4] Welles brought forward the name of Samuel Glover of St. Louis; Seward, Leonard Swett, the friend and intimate of Lincoln.[5] But they met with no general favor. It was desired that one Democrat should be included in the group and all turned to Jeremiah S. Black, who was in the intimacy and confidence of the President, and had been offering him much advice, to the point of writing some of his messages to Congress.[6] For this reason, possibly, and on other accounts, his choice might be ungrateful to some of the Republican senators before whom he should appear. But, after discussing the names of Thurman of Ohio and others,[7] Johnson put his weight in the scale and Black was selected.

The President expressed his desire for the assistance of an old friend, Thomas A. R. Nelson, who had practised law for thirty years in his own town of Greenville in Tennessee.[8] He, therefore, was retained. From the first day the name of William M. Evarts was in mind. The son of a Massachusetts editor and missionary, he had graduated from Yale and, now, at fifty, was a leader at the New York bar. His learning was widely acknowledged and his oratory was of a fine order. The leader of the New York delegation, in an alluring speech he

[1] Memoir of B. R. Curtis, vol. i, p. 416.
[2] Ibid., p. 408; Welles, vol. iii, pp. 298, 302.
[3] Welles, vol. iii, p. 298.
[4] Seward called Field "the greatest small man" (great in the sense of his being large in physical bulk) he had ever known.—Ibid., pp. 303, 308.
[5] Ibid., pp. 306, 307.
[6] Cf. House Reports, 40th Cong. 1st sess., no. 7, pp. 271-3.
[7] Welles, vol. iii, pp. 304-5.
[8] Nelson had been a member of Congress at the outbreak of the war, affirming his Unionism after the state had seceded.

had nominated Seward in the Chicago convention of 1860,[1] and had been employed by the administration as special counsel in the performance of difficult tasks for the government.[2] His name was brought forward by Seward. But it was averred that he had gone over to the Radicals, a statement which was but very partially true.[3] The group now was complete— Stanbery, Black, Curtis, Evarts and Nelson—and barring one of the number they were men of great strength.

Stanbery, a "chivalric gentleman,"[4] took up the cause with more than the loyalty of an Attorney General; he pledged to the President his personal talents and his honor as a friend in the great emergency.[5] That he might be entirely free for the service he resigned from the Cabinet forthwith.[6]

The entire Cabinet gave the President unmistakable evidences of their sympathy. Emissaries who came from the Radical camp to estrange Mr. Seward, promising him that if he would go with them he would not be disturbed in the State Department, received emphatic reproof. "I will see you damned first," said he. "The impeachment of the President is the impeachment of his Cabinet."[7] The President on his side exhibited a similar loyalty. Suggestions that he dismiss one or all of the heads of his departments to secure his own salvation were met with honest indignation.[8]

Should the President appear in person to answer the charges of his enemies and make a Roman holiday? This they cor-

[1] Arguments and Speeches of Wm. M. Evarts, vol. ii, pp. 488-9.
[2] As for instance for the prosecution of Jefferson Davis. He had been in attendance at Richmond when Davis was released on bail. Cf. Evarts's testimony before the Judiciary Committee, House Reports, 40th Cong. 1st sess., pp. 644-60.
[3] Welles seems to have opposed Evarts's choice more strongly than any other, though admitting that he was "unsurpassed as a lawyer."— Welles, vol. iii, pp. 298, 307-8.
[4] S. S. Cox, who also speaks of his "surpassing beauty of person and emphasis of presence."—Three Decades of Federal Legislation, p. 587.
[5] If he could keep well for the trial he told the President he would be willing to be sick for the remainder of his life.—W. G. Moore, Notes in American Hist. Review, Oct., 1913, p. 124.
[6] Welles, vol. iii, pp. 299, 303-4, 308, 311.
[7] W. G. Moore, Notes, loc. cit., p. 123.
[8] Ibid., pp. 125-6.

dially desired.[1] He himself seemed to favor it[2] and some
of his friends advocated his going to the Senate either alone
or supported by the Cabinet.[3] But such advice was overruled
and the plan was abandoned.

By what manner of men were Stanbery and his associates
opposed? The counsel would face the seven managers, who,
not content to be regarded as the delegates of the House of
Representatives, were free to say that, through that body,
they were the vicegerents of the "people of the United States."
They knew their Macaulay. They were to be the Burkes and
Sheridans in this trial of another Warren Hastings. But not
all of the seven were equal masters of the roaring thunder
which it was necessary to summon to blast such a miscreant
as Andrew Johnson, so by common understanding they assigned their rights and powers in large measure to one of their
number, and most of the little which six men may have hoped
to reserve to themselves was soon seized and appropriated by
their chosen agent, who became in a moment almost, if not
quite, the sole prosecuting attorney of the case.

Thaddeus Stevens, a year or two years ago, might have been
this, but he now was barely able to drag himself to his seat in
the House. Logan was a wild horse, distinguished by nothing
so much as an unruly temper and a mad hatred of the Democrats, from whose number he had recently sprung. Boutwell
had presented the cause for five of the nine members of the
Judiciary Committee in December and was looked upon as
one of the "original impeachers." He naturally was marked
out as a manager because of his supposed familiarity with
the charges against the President. He, moreover, was a stump
orator whose powers had been tried and his love of notoriety
made him eager for any prominence he could gain. But he
must stand aside when a better man for the emergency was
at hand. James F. Wilson was welcomed to the ranks of the
managers simply because he had opposed Boutwell's efforts

[1] Butler would have insisted upon it, but his associates, he complained,
were "too weak in the knees or back."—Butler's Book, p. 929.

[2] Moore, Notes, loc. cit., p. 127.

[3] Welles, vol. iii, p. 302.

at impeachment in the Judiciary Committee. He was a sinner come to repentance. A saner man than any other of the seven, he could not have been trusted, if he had been willing to assume the leadership. Thomas Williams, who, with Boutwell, had taken a laboring oar in the Judiciary Committee was heavy and slow. Bingham, the senior next to Stevens in length of service in Congress, had received the largest number of votes in the House. He was named as chairman in recognition of his position in the party, and as a facile and successful lawyer.[1]

Benjamin F. Butler was marked out in nearly all ways for the chieftaincy in such a service. The other six men had been members of Congress for from five to fourteen years. Butler had been elected for a Massachusetts district only in the autumn of 1866 and was serving his first term. Yet his character was such that he seemed from the standpoint of the President's enemies to be the man of the hour. He was a criminal lawyer with a widely notorious practice. His career as a military officer, to which pursuit he came through the doors of civil life, was unsoldierly and conspicuous only for its incompetency. His order in New Orleans that the ladies of the city, should they leave their homes while he commanded the garrison, would be treated as women of the street caused him to be known as "Beast" Butler, and the story that he had stolen spoons from some house which he had occupied for headquarters during the war was told and re-told until his last day. His whole person breathed contention and effrontery.[2] But this was the man who would open the argument for the managers, who would examine and cross-examine witnesses, who, in fine, would conduct the case against the President. The managers represented the House of Representatives, which, in turn, asserted its right to represent the people of the United States, and by this process Ben Butler, as he was known even to the boy in the street, became the

[1] "A shrewd, sinuous, tricky lawyer."—Welles, vol. iii, p. 274.
[2] Cf. G. F. Hoar, Autobiography, vol. i, chap. xxiv. Butler's military career was such, said Hoar, that in any other country he would have been cashiered and probably shot.—Ibid., p. 340.

spokesman of the American people in a most remarkable proceeding.

When the President's name was called in the Senate chamber by the sergeant-at-arms that officer, under instructions from the Chief Justice, proceeded to the President's room attached to the Senate wing·of the Capitol, to notify his counsel who had assembled there. Presently Mr. Stanbery, Mr. Curtis and Mr. Nelson came in. "Gentlemen," said the Chief Justice, when they were seated, "the Senate is now sitting for the trial of articles of impeachment. The President of the United States appears by counsel. The court will now hear you." Mr. Stanbery rose to say that he and his "brothers Curtis and Nelson" had the President's authority "to enter his appearance," which he proceeded to read:

"Mr. Chief Justice, I, Andrew Johnson, President of the United States, having been served with a summons to appear before this honorable court, sitting as a court of impeachment, to answer certain articles of impeachment, found and presented against me by the honorable, the House of Representatives of the United States, do hereby enter my appearance by my counsel, Henry Stanbery, Benjamin R. Curtis, Jeremiah S. Black, William M. Evarts and Thomas A: R. Nelson, who have my warrant and authority therefor, and who are instructed by me to ask of this honorable court a reasonable time for the preparation of my answer to said articles. After a careful examination of the articles of impeachment and consultation with my counsel I am satisfied that at least forty days will be necessary for the preparation of my answer and I respectfully ask that it be allowed. Andrew Johnson."

Counsel in their own behalf presented a separate statement. The articles, they said, involved "many questions of law and fact." There yet had been no opportunity to confer with Mr. Black and Mr. Evarts regarding the case which was one of great magnitude and entirely "out of the ordinary range of professional experience." The President was not a lawyer with the training which would enable him to prepare his own answer to his accusers. "Step by step" his counsel must consult with him and opportunity could be had only "at such intervals" as were allowed him "from the usual hours that must be devoted to his high official duties." Ample and respectable periods of time had been granted Judge Chase in 1805 and Judge Peck in 1831 when they were brought before the bar of the Senate on charges preferred against them by the House of Representatives.

The managers objected, Butler in a coarse stump speech in which he called the President a "criminal," while Stanbery reproved them, stating that it was their design to dispose of the case with "railroad speed," as if it were a proceeding in a police court. The senators finally agreed to retire with the Chief Justice into the reception room to discuss the subject, and, after more than two hours, re-appeared with an order that the respondent file his answer "on the 23rd day of March instant." The court thereupon adjourned for ten days and the senators returned as before to their accustomed constitutional tasks.[1]

Before this time came Black, as a result of occurrences little to his credit, had withdrawn as one of the counsel for the President. For some time he had been the attorney of claimants for damages on account of the Dominican Republic's seizure of a guano island called Alta Vela off the coast of Hayti.[2] Black chose now in the midst of the President's difficulties to take advantage of his needs and urged that an armed vessel of the United States should be sent to the scene. Black might have been on the right side in the controversy. Of that, however, the President could not be assured and he would not be moved by so improper a conjunction of circumstances, seeming on its face to imply a threat before which he had yielded.[3] He said to Welles that if Black had "for one moment deceived himself by supposing that he [the President] would deviate a hair's breadth from his duty in order to retain his [Black's] services, or prevent conviction even, he

[1] Trial, vol. i, pp. 17-34.
[2] Welles, vol. iii, p. 305.
[3] Ibid., pp. 316, 317-8, 319, 322-3; cf. W. G. Moore, Notes, loc. cit., pp. 127-128.

was a sadly deceived man."[1] He would rather be put to death than submit to such humiliation.[2]

William S. Groesbeck, who for some time had been in mind for the service,[3] now joined the counsel in Black's stead. He was an able young lawyer who before the war had sat in Congress for a term as a Democrat. He had been a delegate to the Philadelphia convention of 1866 and was still firmly on the President's side in his contest with the Radicals.

On the appointed day, March 23, answers to all nine of the articles were presented, as a result of "incessant and exhaustive" effort, to cite the words of Mr. Stanbery, to the exclusion of "all other engagements," in "every hour ordinarily devoted to labor," and "many required for necessary rest and recreation," covering two Sabbath days, up to a point only fifteen minutes prior to the time set for the meeting of the court. Mr. Curtis began the reading of the statement; it was continued by Mr. Stanbery and Mr. Evarts. The declaration on all the issues involved in the articles was careful, logical, dignified and complete. The law as well as the fact, lying behind the removal of Stanton and the appointment of Lorenzo Thomas, was stated with precision. Much of what was contained in the answer to the first article was referred to by way of reply to the other articles, except the ninth and the tenth, since all were essentially but one charge presented in variant forms. As for the ninth article, which involved questions of fact as to the content and purpose of a conversation with General Emory, there were explanation and denial. Respecting Article 10 counsel alleged that the extracts from the reports of Johnson's speeches in Washington, Cleveland and St. Louis, which Butler had used as the basis for his "specifications," were garbled and untrue and that these speeches were delivered by Mr. Johnson not as President of the United States but as an American citizen, "in his personal right and capacity," sharing with other

---

[1] Welles, vol. iii, pp. 322-3. Nelson's authorized explanation of the matter is in Trial, vol. ii, pp. 144-7; cf. Senate Ex. Doc., 40th Cong. 2nd sess., no. 38.

[2] W. G. Moore, Notes, loc. cit., p. 128.

[3] Ibid., p. 110; Welles, vol. iii, pp. 302, 308.

citizens his "right of freedom of opinion and of freedom of speech." [1]

The answer was received and ordered to be filed, whereupon Boutwell rose and said that he and his associate managers would be able to present "a fit replication" on the following day. A contest ensued, led by Mr. Evarts for the counsel, over the date of opening the trial. They would ask for thirty days, a request which was promptly and vigorously objected to by the impeachers, as represented by the managers and a considerable body of the members of the Senate. They were for going on at once. It was no matter from their point of view if the President and his lawyers should not be ready to proceed. After a battle of legal artifice the end of the day found a motion of Reverdy Johnson before the court, allowing the President's counsel ten days after the filing of the replication of the House in which to prepare themselves to defend the case.

This answer consisted of few more than 150 words and was signed by Speaker Colfax in behalf of the House. The carefully studied statement of Mr. Stanbery, Mr. Evarts and their associates was swept aside with an arbitrary hand. "Each and every averment," which denied or traversed "the acts, intents, crimes or misdemeanors" charged against the President was in turn denied. For replication the managers said merely that he was "guilty of the high crimes and misdemeanors mentioned in said articles and that the House of Representatives are ready to prove the same." [2] When it was a question of fixing a time for the trial to begin the senators again retired to an ante-chamber for consultation. This was a Tuesday, March 24. They came back with an order naming the following Monday, the 30th day of March.[3]

That day came and "the gentlemen managers of the House of Representatives" were bidden by the Chief Justice to proceed "in support of the articles of impeachment." Butler had

[1] Trial, vol. i, pp. 37-53.
[2] Ibid., p. 84.
[3] Ibid., p. 86.

put himself forward for the opening argument. But three days for preparation were at hand and the other managers were content to confide the case to his care. It was, he afterward recalled, the hardest labor of his life. In the seventy-two hours he slept but nine and received no aid from his associates.[1] William Lawrence of Ohio had prepared a brief of the authorities upon the law of impeachable crimes and misdemeanors which was referred to at points in Butler's discourse and was presented for filing. When the orator had proceeded for two hours a recess of ten minutes was taken that he might recover his energies, at the end of which time he resumed his argument and continued for an hour longer. However much pains it may have cost the author the speech was but a hectic mingling of the hyperbolical party campaign harangue with quarter sessions billingsgate.[2] It had been reduced to writing, but it was delivered with such vehemence, auditors said, that it made the impression of being extemporaneous.

Butler was followed by Manager Wilson who read the documents composing the testimony which the House proposed to use to "make good" its case, beginning with Johnson's oath of office and ending with the letters and other papers called out by the removal of Stanton. As the day was not long enough to complete this work adjournment was taken and the reading was resumed and brought to an end on the 31st, at which time the first witness was called, William J. McDonald of Washington. He swore that the evidence he should give "in the case now depending between the United States and Andrew Johnson" should be "the truth, the whole truth and

---

[1] Butler's Book, p. 928.

[2] It was "a dozen columns of sophistries, innuendoes, venom and arrogance," said the New Orleans Picayune (April 14, 1868). As might have been expected the speech was very much admired by Stanton, who wrote to Butler from his entrenched position in the War Department. "The world to all time is enriched by it," he said. "As an American citizen and as your friend," he continued, "I rejoice at the mighty blow you struck against the great enemy of the nation."— Private and Official Correspondence of General B. F. Butler, vol. v, p. 721, under date of March 31, 1868.

nothing but the truth, so help you God" and proved to be the
chief clerk of the Senate. Through him the prosecution would
establish the genuineness of a certain paper, bearing upon the
course of the case, which he had signed. Other government
employees were brought forward to testify on like points, and
before the day was done the managers were ready to hear
Burt Van Horn, a Republican representative from New York,
one of a number of Radical politicians, who had been with
Stanton when Thomas came to the War Office to demand the
custody of the records. He was examined by the managers
and cross-examined by counsel for the President, as was
General J. Kennedy Moorhead of Pennsylvania, another
member of the House, who had been at the War Department
when Thomas had attempted to gain possession of it. But
the court soon began to wrangle about its rules of procedure
and retired for consultation from which it did not emerge for
three hours.

The examination of the witnesses for the prosecution and the
disputation of the lawyers regarding the form in which the
evidence should be presented continued until April 4, when
Butler declared the case to be closed. All the testimony which
the managers felt it incumbent upon them to present was offered in five days. In that time they had called three or four
very minor employees in government departments in Washington to prove the authenticity of documents; three or four
men who by pre-arrangement were in the War Office when
Thomas came to eject Stanton and who could say only that
the scene had been much less violent than they had supposed
it would be, in view of the expectations which had been raised
by rumor in the streets and by the newspapers; a journalist
who had had some conversations with Thomas about the great
matter; six or seven stenographers who had made shorthand
notes of Johnson's speeches in Washington, Cleveland and St.
Louis; Colonel Moore, the President's private secretary, who
had corrected and expurgated one or more of the speeches for
the press; a certain man, who like Thomas was a citizen of
Delaware, and who, while this contest for the War Office

was on, had said to Thomas, "General, the eyes of Delaware
are on you," eliciting the reply that he (Thomas) would "kick
that fellow [Stanton] out"; a telegraph operator who had
transmitted the despatches which had passed between Johnson
and ex-Governor Parsons about the adoption of the Fourteenth
Amendment in Alabama; ex-Assistant Secretary of the Treasury William E. Chandler, who was to prove that Johnson had
some kind of a design upon the Treasury Department and was
full of a purpose to control the purse as well as the sword;
and the venerable chief clerk of the State Department who
was asked about the forms which, before the Tenure of Office
act was passed, had been and were now used in commissions.
In all 25 witnesses were sworn and heard. To unseat and destroy Andrew Johnson the House relied upon the testimony
of this small number of inconspicuous men whose knowledge
extended for the most part to entirely trifling subjects, aided
by the glib swagger and arrogance of the presiding manager,
Butler.

As the prosecution closed, on the afternoon of the fifth day,
Saturday the 4th of April, a new dispute arose as to the time
to be given the President's counsel for beginning the defence,
which resulted finally in adjournment until the following
Thursday, April 9. Then two unimportant witnesses for
the prosecution who had just arrived in town from the South
were put upon the stand for a few moments without advancing the case, whereupon Butler again announced that he had
"closed." "Gentlemen of counsel for the President," said the
Chief Justice, "you will proceed with the defence."

This was the signal for Mr. Curtis to rise and deliver the
opening speech for the President. Many distinguished men
were seated in the audience room in anticipation of the enjoyment of listening to his address.[1] He spoke from notes and
referred from time to time to tomes and documents lying at
his hand. In chaste word and learned phrase, with calmness,
moderation and dignity he presented the cause. "Here," the
eminent advocate began, "party spirit, political schemes, fore-

[1] Washington corr. N. Y. World, April 10, 1868.

gone conclusions, outrageous biases can have no fit operation."
The Constitution required that there should be a "trial." "The
only appeal which I can make in behalf of the President," he
continued, "is an appeal to the conscience and the reason of
each judge who sits before me." The argument was strictly
legal in matter as in form. It involved a close discussion of
the charges. The law which it was alleged that the President
had broken must be found; if it existed it must be construed
and applied to the case. The senators must show the President's criminal intent wilfully to break the laws before the
impeachment articles could be "supported." [1]

To this line of reasoning Mr. Curtis gave his attention. He
reviewed the various aspects of the subject with reference to
the Constitution, to the law of 1789 governing removal from
office prior to 1867, to the Tenure of Office act of 1867. Did
the Stanton case fall within the terms of this law of 1867?
Stanton had been appointed by Mr. Lincoln, not by Mr. Johnson. The possibility of such an *impasse* as the present one
had been in mind when the Tenure of Office bill was enacted.
The question of applicability had been raised, and it was stated
with appearance of authority, supported by the letter and the
spirit of the clause of the Constitution whereunder the Cabinet
was created, that the President's power with reference to the
removal of Mr. Stanton hereafter would be not less than
hitherto.

Anyhow, even if it could be established that the President's
action in the matter was in violation of the provisions of the
new law, it was plain that he could entertain an honest opinion
that this law was unconstitutional. His thought, as well as
his utterance, might tend in this direction, and, to arrive at
the truth, he might, without being accounted guilty of a high
crime and misdemeanor as charged in the articles, cherish a
desire to bring the issue before the only competent determining
body, the Supreme Court of the United States. It was the
President's right, the right of the nation, to know which party
to the dispute stood on solid ground, and accordingly he had

[1] Trial, vol. i, p. 411.

adopted such means as, in his belief, would bring the question to a speedy decision.

As for the conspiracy articles—the fourth, fifth, sixth and seventh—only two, the fourth and the sixth, were framed in conformity to any act of Congress which it was alleged that the President had violated. Here the impeachers had rested their case on an act of July 31, 1861, designed to punish "two or more persons" who should "conspire together to overthrow, or to put down, or to destroy by force the government of the United States," oppose the execution of the laws, seize public property, or, by intimidation, prevent others from accepting or holding public office. The attempt "to wrest this law to any bearing whatsoever upon this prosecution" Mr. Curtis found to be "extraordinary." He pursued this matter to a conclusion.

The ninth article, charging an effort on the President's part in an interview at the White House to seduce General Emory from his allegiance to the laws and the Constitution of the country, had been "disproved" by the witness, General Emory, while the tenth article which accused the President of indiscreet speech was, on the statement of Manager Butler himself, referable to no provision of law. He would not seek precedents which were made in the times of the Plantagenets, the Tudors and the Stuarts. Bills of attainder were prohibited by the Constitution. But here a doctrine was advanced that one branch of Congress, the House of Representatives, by a majority, could by vote to impeach send an article to the Senate, which by a two-thirds vote could work an attainder. Such, in effect, would a conviction be under this article. More than this, liberty of speech was involved, and laws infringing such a liberty were inhibited by the Constitution. Here then was a case not only where there was no law made prior to the act to punish the act, but also a case where Congress is expressly forbidden to legislate upon the subject under any circumstance.

The eleventh article, being but a summary and a bringing together of the other ten, contained "nothing new," said Mr.

Curtis, needing "any notice" from him. "It must be apparent
to every one in any way connected with or concerned in this
trial," he said as he brought his remarkable discourse to an
end, "that this is and will be the most conspicuous instance,
which ever has been or can ever be expected to be found, of
American justice or injustice—of that justice which Mr. Burke
says is the great standing policy of all civilized states, or of
that injustice which is sure to be discovered, and which makes
even the wise man mad, and which in the fixed and immutable
order of God's providence is certain to return to plague its in-
ventors."

Mr. Curtis's courtliness and grace seemed to belong to some
other time and place. He had arrived at a point in his argument "when, if it be within the pleasure of the Senate to allow
me to suspend it," said he, "it will be a boon to me to do so.
I am unaccustomed to speak in so large a room and it is
fatiguing to me. Still I would not trespass at all upon the
wishes of the Senate, if they desire me to proceed further."
His satire, when he indulged in it, which was but rarely, was
gentle. It would be a reference to the intimation of the President, that it would be impossible to allow Mr. Stanton to continue to hold office as one of his advisers, which had not
produced "the effect which, according to the general judgment
of well informed men, such intimations usually produce"; or
an allusion to Butler as the "learned manager," or again to
the House of Representatives, which, taking offense at remarks
made by the President, had "erected itself into a school of
manners, selecting from its ranks those gentlemen whom it
deems most competent by precept and example to teach de-
corum of speech."

When on Thursday Mr. Curtis had spoken for more than
an hour a recess of fifteen minutes was taken. After the Senate had re-assembled he continued for another hour. On Friday he spoke for two hours more and closed his argument.[1]
He made "an immense impression" upon his auditors.[2] But-

[1] Trial, vol. i, pp. 377-414.
[2] Washington corr. N. Y. World, April 10, 1868.

ler himself thought the presentation of the case so complete that, though "much else" was said, "nothing more" was added in the President's behalf in the whole course of the trial.[1]

When Mr. Curtis had finished, the defence proceeded to call its witnesses, beginning with General Lorenzo Thomas, to prove the circumstances under which he had been delegated by the President to take charge of the War Office. Mr. Stanbery conducted the examination, assisted by the alert and able mind of Mr. Evarts, who at need interposed a word or a speech to turn the current in a favorable direction. Thomas was on the stand for several hours on Friday and Saturday, April 10 and 11. Not before, at any time during the trial, had Butler's attitude been so offensive as now toward this witness. His insolent wit and pettifogging interruptions should have filled every auditor with revulsion. His were the arts on this occasion, said the New York Nation, that made him "feared in criminal courts and not greatly respected or admired elsewhere." If there were to be "a lack of decency on either side," the Nation writer continued, it ought rather "to have appeared on the side of the defendant; the more particularly as the case against him is largely made up of a charge of bad language and rowdy behavior." [2] Butler was playing to sixty writers in the press gallery and through them to the country at large before which he strutted day by day.

When the witness had been humiliated enough to please Butler's taste, and the cross examination was at an end General Sherman was brought forward by Mr. Stanbery to prove that nothing like a conspiracy had been entered into between the President and General Thomas on the subject of the War Office. Twice, so recently as on January 27 and 30, Mr. Johnson had offered to make Sherman Secretary of War *ad interim,* and it was desired to introduce testimony as to these facts. But the battle over the rules of receiving evidence was waged for hours with the greatest acrimony. It was for the "honorable manager," as the counsel for the President called

[1] Butler's Book, p. 930.
[2] Issue of April 16, 1868.

Butler, a mere trial in the Old Bailey. His analogies were to cases of men held for theft or assault in some police court. The President was entitled to no more consideration when he was on trial as a lawbreaker than "the humblest citizen in the land." Decency was not thought of as a rule for his own action in his extraordinary place of responsibility, and justice was still farther from his mind. Like some Jacobin in France he had got his hands on an enemy and this enemy, being obviously and certainly guilty, was to be convicted and punished.[1]

The President's counsel, representing as they did the highest traditions and standards of the American bar, held their ground in the contest with the unprincipled man by whom they were opposed. They were aided materially at one point by Reverdy Johnson, from his seat in the Senate, and thus were enabled, though the tide seemed to be nearly always against them when the votes were taken upon questions as to the admissibility of evidence, to introduce some of the more material parts of the testimony which they desired to set forth through General Sherman. It was made clear, in any event, either by witnesses or counsel, that not more than three weeks before Lorenzo Thomas appeared in Stanton's office asking him in the name of the President to vacate it, Sherman had been invited to undertake the same service, but had declined it; that the President, when there had been a discussion of the subject, had expressed the opinion that Stanton would not offer resistance because he was "cowardly";[2] that the principal purpose of the manœuvre, if Stanton could not be retired which was desired, was to "make up a case" and bring the subject of the relative rights of the co-ordinate executive and legislative departments of the government into the Supreme Court for arbitration. It was shown, too, that the President almost immediately had nominated Thomas Ewing, Sr., of Ohio to be Secretary of War in the room of Mr. Stanton, so that Thomas's

---

[1] His associates, it appears, made efforts to restrain him. But he told them that he would try the President held on high state charges in the same manner he would try a "horse case."—Butler's Book, p. 929.

[2] Trial, vol. i, p. 529.

incumbency never was intended to cover more than a few hours or days at the longest, and a great variety of documentary evidence was presented, touching appointments and removals and tenure of office from the beginning of the history of the government up to date.

A number of newspaper men brought on from Cleveland and St. Louis to testify about the President's speeches in those cities were made the butts of Butler's ribald gibes. Frederick W. Seward, Assistant Secretary of State, was examined concerning the forms of commissions issued to men appointed to Federal office. Secretary of the Navy Welles was interrogated as to the President's conversation with General Emory, to be handled very roughly by Butler, though he found but a poor victim and was tartly replied to at many points in the course of the colloquy. Through Mr. Welles, counsel for the President made repeated efforts to introduce the fact that all the members of the Cabinet in meeting assembled had expressed the view that the Tenure of Office bill was unconstitutional and that Stanton himself had drawn up the message vetoing the measure. Other members of the Cabinet were ready to testify along the same line. But Butler opposed the movement with his accustomed cunning and agility and after the Senate, distinctly against the advice of the Chief Justice,[1] had voted the evidence inadmissible, and Postmaster General Randall was heard in reference to an irrelevant matter concerning the appointment of a postmaster in Georgia, which had been introduced by the managers, nothing remained but to close the case.

Mr. Stanbery was taken ill on April 13, in the very midst of the work of submitting the proofs for the defence, and the

[1] Trial, vol. i, p. 693. Also to his great disappointment. (See his letter to Gerrit Smith, April 19, 1868, in Schuckers' Life of Chase, pp. 577-8, and Warden, p. 684.) "There is reason to believe that these questionable decisions not only increased the popular reprehension of the impeachment but actually contributed to the acquittal of the President." (Dewitt, p. 447; cf. Trial, vol. iii, p. 304.) This also was Chase's opinion. He wrote to Alexander Long on April 19: "The Senate in my opinion made its greatest and most injurious mistake yesterday when it refused to receive the testimony of the heads of the Departments."—Warden, p. 687.

burden was later to be borne alone by Mr. Evarts and Mr. Curtis. The requests for brief postponements because of this circumstance were treated by Butler with his accustomed brutality, and led on the 16th to a tirade from his tongue, perhaps the most distasteful and unfitting which ever was delivered in a court of justice. It alone, without other facts, should brand for history the impeachment and trial of Andrew Johnson with the mark of its true character. It was, in general, as Mr. Curtis had said of the conduct of a particular part of the trial, "a spectacle for gods and men." [1]

"Why stand ye here idle?" Butler raged. The President and his advocates had been seeking delays from the first day. It was no time for "exhibitions of courtesy." "Larger, higher, greater interests" were at stake. The whole country awaited the termination of the trial. Every hour was precious. In the South "our fellow citizens" were being "murdered day by day," and not a man in the Senate chamber who did not know that the moment "justice" was done "this great criminal" these murders would "cease." Moreover the President's friend, McGinnis, who had been appointed minister to Sweden, but whom the Senate would not confirm, was selling gold in New York for the government—"your gold," and we were to wait "day by day" while he put into his "pocket from the Treasury of the country money by the thousands." "In the name of Heaven" and of all that was "dear to any man and patriot" the trial must proceed, "all this corruption and all these murders" must stop. His mail was filled with the assassin's threats —"Butler, prepare to meet your God," "Hell is your portion," "The avenger is abroad on your track." But he was a free man. It was the threatened dog that lived the longest, and much more in a similar strain. [2] For twenty minutes he continued his "harangue," [3] as Mr. Evarts briefly characterized it in directing the Senate's attention to the interruptions of this and of other managers, who, he averred, opened their mouths

---

[1] Trial, vol. i, p. 394.   [2] Ibid., pp. 627-31.
[3] "A violent, indecent party harangue which disgraced the senators who failed to call him to order."—Welles, vol. iii, p. 333.

simply for the purpose of getting their names and opinions into the newspapers.

An opportunity was afforded the managers to present rebutting evidence. It was April 20 when both sides finally closed and the senators were ready to hear the argument, which began on the 22nd. Logan, who for some time, had let it be known that he wished to file a statement of his views for publication was allowed to do so. It was written for his constituents in Illinois, fills 52 pages of the report of the proceedings and is notable only for the evidence it affords of the partisan bigotry and animosity of its author.[1]

Boutwell was chosen to open the oral argument for the House of Representatives. He had presented the cause for five of the nine members of the Judiciary Committee in December, and was looked upon as one of the "original impeachers." His advocacy of the scheme to accuse, try, convict and remove Andrew Johnson, dated from a time little subsequent to Ashley's, and he had been as irrational and persistent in the pursuit of the idea. He continued to talk, except for a brief recess, throughout the afternoon, and resumed his speech the next morning.

Logan was "penetrated and overwhelmed with emotion" as he contemplated the man who had been "false to the people who took him from obscurity and conferred on him splendor . . . filled with all vanity, lust and pride, substituting with the most disgusting self-complacency and ignorance his own coarse, brutalized will for the will of the people," and so on.[2] Boutwell, on his side, exhibited more restraint. His presentation of the case was devoted in considerable degree to the charges and the evidence. He was plainly a violent partisan in a bitter hour, but his personal abuse knew some boundaries. It is true that Johnson's drunkenness in the Senate chamber on March 4, 1865, his "denunciatory, blasphemous declarations" in public speeches, and the murders, one upon another, for which he had been responsible in the South were not over-

[1] Trial, vol. ii, pp. 14-67.   [2] Ibid., p. 66.

looked. He would take his place with the "criminals" of history who had become "the scourge of communities and nations." [1] But, in the main, the Senate was asked to find the respondent guilty because he had "disregarded and violated the laws and the Constitution." It was an attempt on the part of "an usurping executive to break down the securities for liberty provided by the Constitution," which the Senate was asked not to punish—for adequate punishment for such offending was not in the hands of human tribunals—but to judge with a view to securing justice for the people in the weeks and months to come. [2]

As for the defence much still depended upon the outcome of Mr. Stanbery's illness. It had been contemplated from the first that he should sum up and make the principal argument for the President, but it was still doubtful whether the state of his health would permit him to do so. The opening speech fell to the President's friend, Mr. Nelson, who, with Mr. Groesbeck, by pre-arrangement had remained in the background hitherto. At first it had not been intended that he should address the Senate. [3] While such an intellect might do credit to the bar in a small county town, it was not the peer of that of many men now seated before him. His eloquence was of the kind which characterized many second rate barristers and politicians at that day. Moreover it had some of the manner which was commonly called Southern—florid, ornamented now and again with poetical quotations and classical allusions, all more or less familiar, which had served orators in rustic neighborhoods for many generations. The appeal was to emotion rather than reason. In a word it was a friend's defence of a friend—it was such a speech, somewhat embellished and amplified, as a village lawyer would address to a jury to sway it to the side of the accused, awaiting at the bar the determination of his fate on a charge of burglary or manslaughter.

Nelson's allusions to his own career, [4] his declaration that

[1] Trial, vol. ii, p. 116.   [2] Ibid., p. 118.
[3] Ibid., p. 9.   [4] Ibid., p. 118.

he had come forward to speak at such a time in no "spirit of idle vanity,"[1] and the flatteries directed at the Senate when he called it "the most exalted judicial tribunal now upon earth,"[2] can have laid no strong foundations for favor. When it came to questions of law he spoke, in large degree, at random. His statements were general, his references and analogies commonplace, from the standpoint of educated men. Tricks of phrase and a sounding manner were relied upon to convince wavering senators, and to reverse the judgments of any in whom opinions adverse to the President may have been formed. He occupied that part of the day which remained, after Boutwell had concluded, and continued his discourse throughout the next day. If the determination of the President's cause had depended upon such a display of unsupported eloquence it would have been fairly lost.

On the following day, Saturday, April 25, the second speaker for the President, Mr. Groesbeck, whose voice had not yet been heard, rose to address the Senate. He began with a statement as to the condition of his health, which led Mr. Fessenden, after a half hour, to suggest an adjournment, but he labored on with a carefully prepared, cogent argument which deserved and received constant attention. It was the discourse of a well trained lawyer with a clear mind, uninfluenced by an egotism making for a display of oratory, or a passionate friendship for the person of the President, or bias for the party principles which he upheld. Unconsciously the speaker seemed to sense the character of the occasion. If it were a grave matter, as the House managers iterated and reiterated, with the frenzy of some band of religious zealots or social revolutionists, it should be treated gravely, and this consideration it was now to receive.

As Mr. Groesbeck closed, having gone over the law and the

----

[1] Trial, vol. ii, p. 9.   [2] Ibid., vol. i, p. 28.
[3] It bore, said the New York Nation, "a striking resemblance to several orations on Andrew Johnson's life and services delivered by Andrew Johnson himself."—Issue of April 30, 1868; cf. Washington corr. Phila. Press, April 27, 1868.

evidence as to the entire eleven articles in turn, it was not without some allusions personal to the President: "What shall I say of this man? He is no theorist; he is no reformer. I have looked over his life. He has ever walked in beaten paths and by the light of the Constitution. The mariner, tempest-tossed in mid-sea, does not more certainly turn to his star for guidance than does this man in trial and difficulty to the star of the Constitution. He loves the Constitution. It has been the study of his life. He is not learned and scholarly like many of you; he is not a man of many ideas or of much spec-ulation; by a law of the mind he is only the truer to that he does know. He is a patriot, second to no one of you in the measure of his patriotism. He loves his country. He may be full of error; I will not canvass now his views; but he loves his country. He has the courage to defend it and I believe to die for it, if need be. His courage and his patriotism are not without illustration," and Mr. Groesbeck at this point al-luded to the services the President had performed during the conflict between the sections which had repeatedly been the subject of the compliments and the praises of grateful men, many of them those "who dwelt at the North, safely distant from the collisions and strife of the war," and who "knew but little of its actual trying dangers." He "went into the very furnace of the war and there served his country long and well." "Who of you have done more?" asked Mr. Groesbeck. "Not one . . . and it seems hard, it seems cruel, Senators, that he should be dragged here as a criminal, or that any one who served his country, and bore himself well and bravely through that trying ordeal, should be condemned upon miserable tech-nicalities." [1]

By its brevity and simplicity the speech was a *tour de force*. When Mr. Groesbeck had concluded Butler and the other managers as well as his own colleagues pressed around him to congratulate him.[2] For two days the Senate had listened to Boutwell's reading, for two days more to Nelson's ex-

[1] Trial, vol. ii, pp. 2, 16-17.
[2] Washington corr. Phila. Press, April 27, 1868.

temporaneous rambling. It was a fortuitous hour [1] for Groesbeck, and it was generally agreed by friend and foe that he had presented the ablest argument yet advanced on either side of the question.[2]

It was again the turn for the prosecution and on Monday, April 27, the "gentlemen managers on the part of the House of Representatives" were asked by the Chief Justice "to proceed with the argument." Thaddeus Stevens rose and began to read a speech, but after a few minutes he resumed his seat, from which position he continued his discourse. In a half hour, his voice being too low to be heard, Butler took the manuscript and concluded it. In but a few months his embittered soul was to take its flight into another world. He was surrounded now by a brood of his own children, wild, unforgiving, infuriated men, the best of them with only a small part of his ability, though he had implanted his spirit in them all.

He began in his familiar olden way. He would discuss the charges "in no mean spirit of malignity or vituperation." There was allusion to the intoxicating cup on the day of Johnson's inauguration as Vice President [3]—"the fatal day which inflicted him upon the people of the United States." Now he was President, "this offspring of assassination." How could he escape "the just vengeance of the law? Wretched man standing at bay, surrounded by a cordon of living men each with the axe of an executioner uplifted for his just punishment." The senator who should vote for acquittal would be "tortured on the gibbet of everlasting obloquy—How long and dark would be the track of infamy which must mark his name and that of his posterity." [4]

Another Pennsylvanian, drawn from the ranks of the managers, Thomas Williams, one of Boutwell's coadjutors in advancing the original scheme to impeach the President, followed Stevens, and in the same spirit in similar manner pursued the

[1] N. Y. World, April 27, 1868.
[2] Washington corr. Phila. Press, April 27 and April 29, 1868.
[3] Trial, vol. ii, p. 226.   [4] Ibid., p. 227.

argument. He exhausted the afternoon and took the floor again on the following day. To acquit the President, said Mr. Williams, in his ponderous and solemn oration, would be to "stir the heart of rebellion with joy"; the dead soldiers of the Union would "turn uneasily in their graves," while the victory would be celebrated by "the exultant ascent of Andrew Johnson to the Capitol, like the conqueror in a Roman triumph dragging, not captive kings, but a captive Senate, at his chariot wheels." [1] Would senators shrink from the consequences? Would they be moved by the appeals in his behalf, because of his charity and mercy for the South? "Mercy to whom? To the murdered Dostie and his fellows, to the loyal men whose carcasses were piled in carts like those of swine with the gore dripping from the wheels in that holocaust of blood, that carnival of murder which was enacted at New Orleans? To those who perished in that St. Bartholomew at Memphis?" and so on, at length. [2]

When Williams resumed his seat a personal altercation 'ensued between Butler and Nelson. Boutwell, in his opening argument for the managers, had referred to Black's retirement from the President's counsel because of the Alta Vela matter. [3] Nelson had replied in some detail, explaining the facts in the case and justifying the President. [4] As Butler's name had entered into the controversy the occasion was now at hand for this eminent ruffian to enter the discussion. Nelson was called "the veriest tyro in the law in the most benighted portion of the Southern country." [5] He was accused of "deliberate falsehood." [6] Nelson, nearly as expert a rowdy as Butler, was not wanting in language for an answer. He hurled back such imputations "with indignation and scorn." "So far as any question that the gentleman desires to make of a personal character with me is concerned, this is not the place to make it," Nelson continued. "Let him make it elsewhere, if he desires to do it." At this point Senator Yates of Illinois

[1] Trial, vol. ii, p. 261.   [2] Ibid., p. 262.   [3] Ibid., p. 82.
[4] Ibid., pp. 143-7.   [5] Ibid., p. 263.   [6] Ibid., p. 265.

called Nelson to order, but he with an apology proceeded suavely with his statement, until he offered to put in evidence some letters, which led Butler to express a hope that they had not been "mutilated." Disorder again seemed imminent, when Mr. Edmunds observed that the whole matter had nothing to do with any question before the Senate, and several gentlemen asked that the argument should proceed.[1]

The next day Sumner, choosing to construe Nelson's retort to Butler as provocative to a duel, "contrary to law and good morals," offered a resolution stating that Johnson's friend from Greenville "justly deserved the disapprobation of the Senate." There was a general hub-bub of men rising to their feet, and of interrupted speeches. Nelson was finally able to say that he was not a "duelist by profession," that he had meant "no offence to the Senate" in remarks made "under the heat" of what he had considered "great provocation."[2] When Sumner's order came to a vote it was found that but 10 senators supported it, while 35 opposed it, so it was laid upon the table and the incident was closed.[3]

The disturbance extended to the House when the representatives returned to their chamber. Such intemperate abuse of one member by another concerning the Alta Vela case, coupled with a personal altercation, staged at the same time by E. B. Washburne and Ignatius Donnelly, led rather aptly to the presentation of a resolution ordering the managers to withdraw the tenth article. A body providing such scenes of rowdyism could with ill grace prosecute President Johnson for improper speech.[4]

The time now had come for the address of William M. Evarts. The trial here reached its intellectual zenith. So valuable a document, either as a constitutional exposition or as an argument at the bar, scarce exists elsewhere in the records of the republic. It will hold a permanent place among state papers of the first rank in America. The orator's knowl-

[1] Trial, vol. ii, p. 268.   [2] Ibid., p. 281.   [3] Ibid., p. 307.
[4] Cong. Globe, 40th Cong. 2nd sess., p. 2367.

edge of legal and constitutional questions carried him so far
above the plane on which the House managers stood, as they
beat the air in their fury and passion, that to listen to him
was to pass into another realm. Here was an address, a series
of addresses, which sprang from a mind capable of compassing
the whole length and breadth of the controversy. It was an
emergency, a veritable crisis in our history, and Mr. Evarts
stood a bulwark of our institutions against the nation's disgrace. He raised the question from the level of politics into
the higher atmosphere of statesmanship and for four days,
in spirit and in letter, with thought and with word, directed
the attention of the Senate, the galleries and the country at
large, to which what he said soon was passed, to a great
constitutional discussion of impeachment in general, and
of this case made up against and aimed at Andrew Johnson
in particular.

One sophism after another of Boutwell and the other prosecutors was demolished. The absurd and trifling testimony
on which the charges were based was assigned to its rightful
place. Principles, which it was alleged that the President had
violated, were examined and his action was brought to wear
a favorable face. Law and precedent were summoned in his
defence. The entire fabric of charges was resolved into its
elements and it was seen for what it was—mere partisan rage
of persecutors eager to lay hands on and to punish one with
whose opinions they had come to disagree. The extraordinary
character of such a proceeding, the impropriety and danger of
adopting the course proposed by the leaders of the House,
were averred, with analogy and illustration, and at the end it
was but a man open to no kind of reason, with a mind fully
fixed, fearful of the judgments of the wild crowd outside of
the Senate to which the question was soon to be taken in the
elections, who could remain deaf to the fact and logic of his
argument.

Literary allusions punctuated the discourse at many points.
They were dignified and choice, the product of reading and the
outgiving of an intellect which knew how to use them for the

adornment of speech. The task which lay before Mr. Evarts was of the most difficult character, but his movements were deft. His criticism was so courteous that it gave no offense. That which stung most deeply often evoked the heartiest laughter. The audience for the most part was unwilling to be convinced, and would remain opposed to the conclusions of his argument, whatever he might say, yet he commanded its closest attention.

He could have found no better answer to the tenth article had he reviewed the whole history of the right of freedom of speech than the pages of the Congressional Globe. The President had said that Congress was "hanging on the verge of the government," and he had been impeached for it. But Sumner, a part of Congress, had earlier said in the Senate chamber that the President was "the enemy of his country," [1] and when he had been called to order Mr. Anthony presiding had declared that these words did not exceed "the usual latitude of debate," while the "honorable senator from Ohio," Mr. Sherman, had added that they were clearly in order; he had heard "similar remarks fifty times without any question of order being raised." [2] And in the House, volume and page being given, one of the "honorable managers" of this cause, Mr. Bingham, had said of another of the "honorable managers," Mr. Butler (earlier a Democrat), that he had "recorded his vote fifty times for Jefferson Davis, the arch traitor in this rebellion as his candidate for President of the United States." [3] Some remark concerning Bingham which Butler had made was repelled with "scorn and contempt," though he should be the "hero of Fort Fisher." Butler's response to this thrust was that "the gentleman from Ohio" had viewed the war from safe places, and, that "the only victim" of the gentleman's prowess, of whom he knew anything, was "an innocent woman hung upon the scaffold, one Mrs. Surratt," an allusion to Bingham's part in that affair. To this there was

[1] Trial, vol. ii, p. 327.   [2] Ibid.
[3] In the Charleston convention of 1860 when he had been instructed by the Massachusetts constituency which sent him there to vote for Douglas.—Cf. G. F. Hoar, Autobiography, vol. i, p. 332.

reply that what had just been said was only fit to come from a man who lives in a bottle and is fed with a spoon, of which words Mr. Evarts pretended not to know the meaning, but which were understood by everyone else to refer to Grant's averment that Butler had been in a "bottle" at Bermuda Hundred, and to the sorry old slander about his stealing Southern ladies' spoons and other silverware for shipment to his home in Massachusetts.

"To be serious," asked Mr. Evarts in a little while, when he had done with the "honorable managers" who were furnishing "for the purpose of this trial" a standard of "propriety of speech," what man "in a free republic will tolerate this fanfaronade about speech making? *Quis tulerit Gracchos de seditione querentes.*" [1]

His estimate of Andrew Johnson was akin to Mr. Groesbeck's. "I ask you to notice," said Mr. Evarts, "that bred in a school of Tennessee democratic politics he had always learned to believe that the Constitution must and should be preserved. . . . He is no rhetorician and no theorist, no sophist and no philosopher. The Constitution is to him the only political book that he reads. The Constitution is to him the only great authority which he obeys. His mind may not expand," Mr. Evarts continued with delightful humor, "his views may not be so plastic as those of many of his countrymen; he may not think we have outlived the Constitution and he may not be able to embrace the Declaration of Independence as superior and predominant to it. But to the Constitution he adheres. For it and under it he has served the state from boyhood up— labored for it, loved it. For it he has stood in arms against the rebellious forces of the enemy; and to it he has bowed three times a day with a more than Eastern devotion." [2] Mr. Evarts closed with allusions to the "great experiences and trials" of

[1] Trial, vol. ii, p. 329. Explanations of such allusions to Butler may be found in Butler's Book; Butler's speech upon the campaign before Richmond delivered at Lowell, Mass., Jan. 29, 1865 (a pamphlet); Life and Public Services of B. F. Butler by M. M. Pomeroy; Geo. F. Hoar, Autobiography, vol. i, chap. xxiv.
[2] Trial, vol. ii, p. 357.

the nation in its recent history. "Can we summon now," he said, "resources enough of civil prudence and of restraint of passion to carry us through this trial, so that whatever result may follow, in whatever form, the people may feel that the Constitution has received no wound?" He implored the senators to carry themselves back in mind "to the spirit and the purpose and the wisdom and the courage of the framers of the government," whose names had been made so familiar to everyone in the course of the trial. "How safe," then, would the issue be "in your hands! How safe is it now in your hands, for you who have entered into their labors will see to it that the structure of your work comports in durability and excellence with theirs." [1]

The argument of Mr. Evarts was a masterly and complete reduction of the case to absurdity. It was the afternoon of the 28th when he began to speak. He continued through the 29th and the 30th and concluded on May 1, a period in all of about 14 hours. It was complained that he had been "long-winded" [2] because of the "immense length of the radius" of his course. [3] But even the enemy was compelled to admire the great capacity of the orator and to fear the weight of his influence. [4] If he had failed "to exercise that electric power over his hearers" which had been Groesbeck's service to the President, there was a "tender pathos" in his closing passages which "touched the heart." [5]

By this time Mr. Stanbery had so far recovered from his malady as to be able to appear to close the argument. He had come to the Senate chamber only with difficulty. Physicians and friends had urged him not to attempt so much in the state of his health, but his condition served to give a dramatic touch to the proceedings. He was a "feeble champion of the right." The race was "not always to the swift nor the battle to the strong," and "in a just cause a single pebble from the brook was enough in the sling of the young shepherd." His manifest

---

[1] Trial, vol. ii, pp. 358-9.
[2] N. Y. Nation, May 7, 1868.
[3] Washington corr. Phila. Press, May 2, 1868.
[4] Ibid., April 29, 1868.
[5] Washington corr. N. Y. Herald, May 2, 1868.

difficulty in attempting the labor of the case, his courage in
coming forward to do so and the personal testimony which he
so cheerfully bore as to the President's good intentions should
have had, indeed, must have had some influence in determining the result. It was a compact, straightforward, lawyer-
like summing up of the case. If Evarts had not preceded him
Mr. Stanbery's argument would have seemed a greater achievement. But Evarts had covered nearly every phase and aspect
of the matter. With so much learning, and so much ability in
setting it forth, with so much sincerity and common sense, with
so much humor and force had the word been spoken for the
President before Stanbery came to the task that more seemed
in a way redundant, if not anti-climax. He continued through
the afternoon of May 1 and resumed on May 2, turning over
his manuscript for a considerable period to be read by a young
man at his side, and taking it again that he might in person
finish the work.

Here at the end he gave himself to the President unsparingly.
"Never were good intentions and honest motives more thoroughly proved" than in this case. Mr. Stanbery had been a
daily associate of the President. He declared himself whole-
heartedly and unreservedly on the side of the persecuted man.
He had come to Washington almost a stranger to Andrew
Johnson, unknown, too, to members of the Cabinet except to
Mr. Stanton, who had been a friend for many years. From
the moment that he had entered upon the performance of the
duties of his office "not a step was taken," said Mr. Stanbery,
that did not come under his observation, not a word was said
that escaped his attention. The President was surrounded by
"evil counsellors"; he was "tempted with bad advice." His
course was observed "with the most intense anxiety." "But
never," Mr. Stanbery continued, "in word, in deed, in thought,
in action did I discover in that man anything but loyalty to the
Constitution and the laws. He stood firm as a rock against
all temptation to abuse his own powers and to exercise those
which were not conferred upon him. . . . I have seen him endure day after day provocations such as few men have ever
been called upon to meet. No man could have met them with

more sublime patience." It had been said, "with almost official sanction, that the votes of the senators had been canvassed' and that the doom of the President was sealed." "Let that judgment not be pronounced in this Senate chamber," said Stanbery as he reached the end of his argument; "not here where our Camillus in the hour of our greatest peril single-handed met and baffled the enemies of the republic; not here where he stood faithful among the faithless; not here where he fought the good fight for the Union and the Constitution; not in this chamber whose walls echo with that clarion voice that in the days of our greatest danger carried hope and comfort to many a desponding heart, strong as an army with banners." [1]

On Monday, May 4, Tuesday, May 5, and Wednesday, May 6, the prosecution contributed the last words in the case. The chamber was jammed; aisles, doorways, steps on stairways were filled. To Bingham was assigned the task of making for the managers the concluding argument against the President and of fastening the lid, as it were, upon this unflinching and dangerous enemy of the Republican party. Bingham was a lawyer of experience in many causes. He could address a jury with vehemence. He could debate a legislative question fearlessly. As a stump speaker his temper had been tried; his voice had been heard in many a party emergency. Now by his oratorical powers he in some final declarations was to bring about the conviction of the President. Statement and denial, invective and vituperation, dogmatic assurance and grand solemnity developed as he proceeded from brief written notes,[2] and carried him to a peroration on the third day of his forensic effort which one must believe would have condemned to the gallows any murderer in the sight of any twelve men in any court house in Ohio. But his law was partisanship, his logic unbridled political passion and his history came from the grammar school.[3]

[1] Trial, vol. ii, pp. 387-9.
[2] Washington corr. Phila. Press, May 5, 1868.
[3] His rhetoric was so "rank and luxuriant," said the New York Nation, that to follow the argument in it was like threading "a trail through a tropical jungle."—Issue of May 7, 1868.

When Bingham was done a claque in the galleries broke out into applause and cheered. He, and not Evarts or Stanbery, had voiced popular feeling. Public sympathy in the Senate chamber, as well as outside of it—in the Northern part of the country generally—was with him and not with them.

In disproof of the descriptions of him by his enemies the President during the progress of the trial, as in most other emergencies, was reserved and calm. So much a part of his character was silence, even under the greatest provocation, that men standing in the closest relations to him, like Mr. Welles, and other members of his Cabinet, were constantly commenting upon this quality with disfavor.[1] Once he remarked that he thought many of those who had voted to impeach him felt more uncomfortable than he. He had made an issue which was demanded by his self respect. If he could not be President in fact he would not be so in name. "I have taken a step," said he in the hearing of his secretary, Colonel Moore, "which I believe to be right and I intend to abide by it. I do not want to see this government relapse into a despotism. I have ever battled for the rights and liberties of the people, and I am now endeavoring to defend them from arbitrary power."[2] "They have impeached me for a violation of the Constitution and the laws," he declared again. "Have I not been struggling ever since I occupied this chair to uphold the Constitution which they are trampling under foot?" Some one suggested that he use the patronage of his office to forestall a judgment against him. "I will do nothing of the kind," he replied; "if acquitted I will not owe it to bribery. I would rather be convicted than buy acquittal."[3]

At first in the President's circle it seemed to be assumed that conviction was a "foregone conclusion."[4] As Butler's bulldozing methods developed without reproof from the Senate, indeed with its emphatic endorsement, whenever the votes were taken on the subject of introducing testimony which it

[1] E.g., Welles, vol. iii, pp. 288, 289.
[2] Notes of W. G. Moore, American Hist. Review, Oct., 1913, p. 122.
[3] Ibid., pp. 123, 129.   [4] Welles, vol. iii, pp. 313, 324.

was expected would be favorable to the President, fear was expressed concerning the wisdom of the choice of counsel. To Welles, Stanbery seemed "sensitive and timid." He was "too courteous, gentlemanly and dignified" to meet and rebuke the insolence and audacity of the managers.[1] Men of "different metal" should have been employed for this important service.[2]

Yet despite the fortitude so much remarked by his friends the President had his unquiet moods.[3] Once he said that if the case were not conducted by his counsel according to his own ideas he would appear before the Senate in person and defend himself.[4] Another time he broke all reserve and spoke to the newspaper reporters. Seward's clerks had sought through the records of the State Department and had found a precedent for Stanton's removal in the action of John Adams with reference to Timothy Pickering in 1800.[5] Counsel wished to study the case and introduce it in the trial at the proper time, but the President gave out the facts to a Washington correspondent of the New York World. It was necessary for Stanbery to say to Mr. Johnson that he was now in the hands of his lawyers and that all "talks" to newspaper men must cease. Browning and other members of the Cabinet followed in the same sense, to the President's displeasure, but with the result that the indiscretion was not repeated.[6]

As the trial progressed the President and his friends gained confidence. Seward, Randall and McCulloch alleged that they were in possession of news which betokened acquittal. Stanbery and Evarts expressed assurance concerning the result. On May 5, before Bingham was yet done with his speech, Seward speaking to Browning at a Cabinet meeting, was ready to wager a basket of champagne that enough senators would escape the toils of the Radical leaders to free the President.[7]

Meantime Stanton held his ground in the War Office. Like some besieged garrison in a fort he and his friends maintained

[1] Welles, vol. iii, pp. 308-9.   [3] Ibid., p. 332.
[2] Ibid., pp. 313, 315, 316.   [4] Amer. Hist. Review, Oct., 1913, p. 123.
[5] Welles, vol. iii, p. 303.   [6] Ibid., pp. 291, 311.   [7] Ibid., p. 345.

a watch day and night against old General Thomas. Soldiers surrounded and filled the building lest an armed uprising to dispossess him and put the records of the government, as well as the control of the army, in the hands of "rebels" eager to undo the work of the war should be attempted.[1]

It had been called a "high court of impeachment," an "exalted tribunal" and much else in praise, but it was clear that the 54 judges were but weak mortal vessels. If it had been a fair and honest trial on the evidence, with reference to the law, the senators must have acquitted the President without delay. But they were the same senators who had been at variance with him at every stage of this slowly developing difference of feeling and mind which lay at the root of the controversy. They, in general, were in agreement with the prosecuting majority of the House—all taken together they controlled and directed the fortunes of the Republican party which was to be served by the conviction and removal of the President, all were urged forward by the party press and by the intolerant opinion of large bodies of the people.[2] Therefore, the judges, two from each Northern and Western state, displayed signs of the greatest agitation. Two-thirds of the number, 36, must vote for conviction else this scoundrel, one of the worst of all time, as they so frequently declared him to be, would go free.

The hour drew nigh. Senators whose course remained in doubt were to be addressed and intimidated, if they could be; the brand of traitor, as Thaddeus Stevens from the beginning had so openly counselled, was to be set upon their foreheads, if they should betray the party which had "saved the Union" and freed the black slave, and which sustained them, the mere agents of which they were.[3] Senators in excitement rose

[1] Welles, vol. iii, pp. 297, 309; Gorham, Edwin M. Stanton, vol. ii, pp. 443-4.

[2] The N. Y. Herald, with some truth, called the court "a party caucus for the removal of Andrew Johnson."—Issue of May 1, 1868.

[3] Said that excellent jurist Reverdy Johnson of these threats—"No more dishonoring efforts were ever made to corrupt a judicial tribunal. They are disgraceful to the parties resorting to them and should they be successful, as I am sure they will not, they would forever destroy the heretofore unblemished honor of this body."—Trial, vol. iii, p. 58.

and interrupted one another about the business of clearing
the galleries, of turning out the reporters of the press, of
re-opening the galleries, as to orders and rules and methods
of procedure, now that the time had come for a test of strength
to determine the President's fate.

It had been agreed on May 7 that the articles should be
taken up in order from number one to number eleven, and
that they should be disposed of separately,[1] and also that
each senator should be "permitted" to file a "written opinion"
to be printed with the proceedings.[2]   On Monday, May 11,
the doors were closed that the senators, somewhat as a jury,
which they were held to be, might discuss the matter among
themselves—the vote was to be taken on the following day at
noon.

In the privacy of the Senate's closed chamber it was made
clear that some of the members who would agree to convict
the President on some counts would not do so on others. A
dozen, such as Simon Cameron of Pennsylvania, Pomeroy of
Kansas, Drake of Missouri, Cattell of New Jersey, Thayer
and Tipton of Nebraska,[3] Chandler and Howard of Michigan,
Conness of California, Conkling of New York were openly
hostile to the President in a manner unfitting them to be
judges in the case. They had proven their bias on every
division when votes were taken as to the introduction of evidence during the course of the trial. Several of the number
held caucuses at Pomeroy's to discipline and strengthen one
another as the trial proceeded.[4]

Sumner on decisive divisions had been voting fitfully, torn
between the egotism which fed a desire to be separate from
other men and his fanatical hatred of Johnson and the old

[1] Trial, vol. ii, p. 478.   [2] Ibid.
[3] Of "approved and superabundant loyalty," from a state whose principal reason for its organization and admission to the Union at this
time was the fact that two senators would be gained for the impeachment and trial of the President.—Dewitt, Trial and Impeachment, p.
174. By how narrow a margin the Colorado bill failed in 1867 and two
senators of the same type to swell the ranks of the Radicals were kept
out of the "high court of impeachment" is told in ibid., p. 179.
[4] Welles, vol. iii, pp. 334, 346.

slave masters of the South, for whom in his mind the President
stood. He again drew upon his peculiar store of erudition
and again made it accessible to his colleagues in a long opinion, plentifully sprinkled with italicized words, wherein he
found "the enormous criminal" guilty of all the charges and
"infinitely more."[1] Others, as Fessenden, Grimes of Iowa,
Henderson of Missouri and Trumbull of Illinois, were so
uniformly voting with the Democratic minority it could have
been suspected they would not be numbered among the two-
thirds which the impeachers in every manner now were striving to muster against the President.

But no assurance of this was at hand. Johnson's friends
canvassed the subject constantly, as did the Radicals, and the
Republican senators who contemplated voting for acquittal,
were wise in giving their confidence to none. A week before
the day set for the balloting men like Welles and McCulloch
spoke rather certainly of Fessenden and Trumbull.[2] It was
believed that Grimes who was tied to Fessenden by the warmest of friendships would not vote to convict.[3] Secretary Mc-
Culloch had faith in Morton of Indiana.[4] Others believed
that Frelinghuysen of New Jersey, the two Morrills, Corbett
of Oregon, Cole of California, Fowler of Tennessee, Van
Winkle and Willey of West Virginia, Anthony of Rhode Island
and Ross of Kansas would vote "Not Guilty." Hope for
Henderson was entertained because of his contemplated marriage to a lady who was known to be unfriendly to impeachment; for Sprague of Rhode Island because of the influence of
his wife, who was a daughter of Chief Justice Chase.[5]

The defections, as they were noted, during the progress of
the Senate star chamber discussions were duly conveyed to the

[1] Trial, vol. iii, p. 278.
[2] Welles, vol. iii, pp. 345-6, 350.
[3] See e.g., Salter, Life of Grimes, p. 264. The Radical crowd in the
galleries at the end of the trial on the day Bingham spoke had hissed
the senator from Iowa and sang—
       "Old Grimes is dead, that bad old man,
        We ne'er shall see him more."
                    —Washington corr. Phila. Press, May 7, 1868.
[4] Welles, vol. iii, p. 346.   [5] Ibid., p. 349.

anxious world outside. The afternoon and evening of the 11th were filled with excitement. The news of what this or that senator had said to his colleagues was carried to the President. McCulloch and Welles who had gone to congratulate him found that the information which they bore had preceded them. Groesbeck now was convinced of success and Postmaster General Randall said that the vote would be 22 to 32, and "likely better than that." [1]

The party newspapers gave it up. The New York Tribune denounced the "infamy" of Fessenden, Trumbull, Grimes and Henderson. Three more "apostates" must be found, but conviction had become "very, very doubtful." [2] The Philadelphia Press said that the republic had been "betrayed in the house of its friends." Senators had refused to confer with those who had sent them to Washington. They were deaf to the voice of their constituents and they would vote for the acquittal of "the great patricide." Hope rested with the common people who had given their money and lives and hearts and sons to the country, and who now would not "willingly or unavenged see their great sacrifice made naught." [3]

When the alarming facts became known to the Radicals they found on the following day, the 12th, which had been fixed for the vote, that one of their leaders, Senator Howard, was sick. For him to come into the Senate chamber, his friends said, would imperil his life. It was a fortunate occurrence. Upon motion of his colleague, Zachariah Chandler, although no delay was to be thought of when the principal counsel of the President, Mr. Stanbery, was taken ill,[4] the court now would postpone the trial of strength by adjournment, until the following Saturday, May 16, at noon. The rest of the week could be employed by the impeachers in repairing the breaches in their lines. It was in effect, said the Philadelphia Press, "an appeal to the people." [5]

---

[1] Welles, vol. iii, pp. 351-2.
[2] Washington corr. N. Y. Tribune, May 12, 1868.
[3] Phila. Press, May 12, 1868. Cf. Cincinnati Gazette, May 12, 1868.
[4] Welles, vol. iii, p. 352.   [5] May 13.

Seldom has such tyranny been seen in party management; never fortunately elsewhere has it intruded in like manner to corrupt the judgments of a judicial body. From the earliest days of the trial legislatures, conventions, party mass meetings and other assemblages addressed by men with wild tongues had been exerting pressure in this way or that upon the senators.[1] Now there was a general outburst of passion. Radical newspapers called Grimes, Fessenden and others, who had dared to say that they would not vote to convict the President, "recreants," "apostates," "Judases," etc.[2] A party cabal in Washington, the "Union Congressional Committee," with Representative Robert C. Schenck at its head,[3] sent to individuals, clubs and other bodies for letters and telegrams which were to be despatched immediately to doubtful senators.[4] They came in "a fearful avalanche" from "every section of the country."[5] Those who were tempted to recreancy must "stay the lasting disgrace" which they would bring down upon themselves and their posterity, and "listen to the voice of their constituents, if not to the will of the great loyal masses, North and South."[6]

Members of the House visited the wavering to argue with them and to overbear and intimidate them. Witnesses were summoned by the managers to testify as to the views and opinions of senators. A veritable inquisition was begun.[7] All public business in the departments came to a standstill. Caucuses were held every few hours at Pomeroy's and elsewhere. Radicals from many parts of the Union hurried to Washington to badger men who might be suspected of the courage to vote as their own consciences should dictate. Theodore Tilton of New York was at hand to play the despot for the Radicals. Bishop Simpson, a sectarian politician of the Methodist Church, brought clerical influences to bear upon the doubtful Willey of West Virginia, through ex-Secretary

[1] Welles, vol. iii, pp. 320, 344.
[2] Dewitt, p. 529.
[3] Ibid., p. 353.
[4] Welles, vol. iii, pp. 354, 357.
[5] Washington corr. Phila. Press, May 14, 1868.
[6] Ibid.
[7] Welles, vol. iii, pp. 354, 355.

Harlan, a Methodist, returned after leaving Johnson's Cabinet to his place as a senator from Iowa.[1] The General Conference of the Methodist Episcopal Church in session in Chicago, with Willey as well as other possible apostates in mind, representing, so it was said, more than eleven hundred thousand members, appointed an hour of prayer for the safe deliverance of the country from the "corrupt influences" which were being exerted upon the senators to turn them from the path of duty with reference to Andrew Johnson. The African Methodists, meeting in Washington, prayed to the same end.[2] Henderson, pressed by the Radical representatives in Congress from his own state for assurances as to what he would do in the great case offered to resign. He would telegraph to the governor of Missouri, who might appoint a successor ready to do their will.[3] Ross of Kansas, a member of the Senate since July, 1866, when he took the place of General Lane, was so mercilessly dragged this way and that by both sides that at the end he seemed scarce to know whether he had opinions of his own.[4] His redoubtable Radical colleague, Pomeroy, badgered him. D. R. Anthony "and one thousand others" telegraphed him that Kansas, having "heard the evidence," demanded the conviction of the President.[5] Night and day the man was hunted as if he were a fox.

It was practically certain that there could be no conviction on the ninth article, the so-called "Emory article," since senators who were lawyers, and whose sense of justice and propriety was not wholly dethroned must agree that the charges made on this head had not been proven. Probably still more would not vote for the tenth article, which popularly bore the name of Mr. Butler. But it had been made clear in the star chamber on the 11th that Sherman of Ohio and Howe of Wis-

[1] Welles, vol. iii, p. 358; cf. Washington corr. N. Y. World, May 18, 1868. Harlan's denial is in Cong. Globe, 40th Cong. 2nd sess., p. 2514.
[2] Dewitt, pp. 530-31.
[3] Ibid., pp. 525-8; House Reports, 40th Cong. 2nd sess., no. 75, p. 15.
[4] "Like the bridge at Arcola, now trodden upon by one army and now trampled by the other."—Wash. corr. N. Y. Tribune, May 18, 1868.
[5] Dewitt, pp. 537-45.

consin would not vote to convict the President under the first article. Repeatedly it had been recalled that, when the final touches were being put upon the Tenure of Office act in Congress, Stanton and the other Lincoln appointees in Johnson's Cabinet were expressly declared in the Senate to be excepted from the provisions of the law. The Democrats in the House, beginning with Brooks, in resisting the impeachment resolution, had made this point clear. Counsel for the President brought out the fact in their arguments to the manifest embarrassment of the prosecution.

Sherman had been prominently named as one of the conferees and his words stood upon the pages of the Globe. He could not properly and did not seek to disavow his declarations. "Can I who made it and declared it to you, and still believe it to be the true and legal interpretation of those words—can I pronounce the President guilty of crime and by that vote aid to remove him from his high office for doing what I declared and still believe he had a legal right to do? God forbid!" [1] But having exculpated himself with reference to the record and declaring his intention to vote against the first, fourth, fifth and sixth articles on these grounds he turned to the second, third, seventh and eighth articles and by a peculiar course of reasoning found himself in agreement with the Republican majority in condemning the President for appointing General Thomas Secretary of War *ad interim*. In other words, said Senator Sherman, Stanton could be removed, but the President could not appoint Thomas to perform the duties of the office *ad interim* while the Senate was in session. His

[1] Trial, vol. iii, p. 11. Williams of Oregon, however, another of the Senate's conferees, whose statements had been as plain as Sherman's, took no account of his record and would have convicted the President, not only on the first, but, so far as appears, on all the other counts. He had been "sorrowfully and reluctantly brought to the conclusion" that Andrew Johnson was "a bad man." (Trial, vol. ii, pp. 347-53.) Nor was Sherman expected to remember what he had said and done with reference to the Tenure of Office act. (Welles, vol. iii, p. 258; cf. J. G. Blaine, Twenty Years of Congress, vol. ii, pp. 352-4.) Conferees on the part of the House pretended to have had a different understanding of the meaning of the compromise. This subject is discussed fully in Rhodes, vol. vi, pp. 129-32.

offense consisted in not sending to the Senate the name of an
acceptable man as a new Secretary of War, which he did in a
few hours—that of Thomas Ewing, Sr., to whom Sherman
would have found it difficult to object—instead of filling the
post temporarily. Here he had violated the Constitution and
the laws and for this high crime he should be convicted and unseated and "glorious Ben" Wade should be put in his place.
For Articles 9 and 10 Sherman could not vote but he
would support that cunningly contrived compound of all that
had gone before of Thaddeus Stevens, known as Article 11.[1]

Howe was moved by considerations similar to those animat-
ing Sherman as to Article 1. He believed that the good faith
of the Senate was at stake in view of what had been done
when the Tenure of Office bill had been passed, and that to
charge the President with crime in removing Stanton, whom
he had full right to remove, was absurd and without any kind
of basis in law.[2] Therefore, on Saturday, when Howard was
ready to return to the Senate, the disaffection of Sherman and
Howe as to the first article being known by the leaders, it
was determined to abandon the original order and first to take
the question upon the eleventh article.[3] In the days of agitation which had intervened since the adjournment the impeachers had regained confidence, but already the lines were
fixed. Those who would vote against conviction voted now
against the plan for a change of order in which the articles
were to be submitted to the senators.[4] Wade, the heir to
Johnson's place, if the President should be convicted was commended for his reticence and the general propriety of his conduct thus far. He had not spoken nor had he voted.[5] But on
this division he was numbered with the Radicals, and it was

[1] Trial, vol. iii, pp. 12-6.
[2] Ibid., vol. ii, pp. 68-9. Howe also demurred as to Article 9, but he
was ready to vote for conviction on Articles 2, 8, 10 and 11.—Ibid.
vol. iii, p. 81.
[3] Ibid., vol. ii, p. 484.
[4] Except Grimes, who still was in the ante-chamber and did not vote.
—Ibid., p. 485.
[5] Cf. N. Y. World, April 28, 1868.

known what his course would be henceforth. If he had twenty votes, he said now, they would be cast against Johnson.[1]

The managers and the members of the House were in their accustomed places. Senator Howard was in his seat and the President's enemies were relieved of anxiety on his account. But on the other side there was grave concern as to Senator Grimes, a sensitive man, who, most malignantly attacked by his old party associates for his out-spoken opposition to conviction on Monday, had suffered on Wednesday a stroke of paralysis.[2] There was still doubt whether he could appear. Mr. Fessenden asked for him. Reverdy Johnson said that he was down stairs, and in a moment was able to announce his arrival, supported by friends.[3] The secretary read the eleventh article and the chief clerk called the roll. "Indescribable anxiety," says Representative Julian, "was written on every face." Members of the House "grew pale and sick under the burden of suspense." Such stillness prevailed that the breathing in the galleries could be heard on the floor.[4] The clerk began with Anthony of Rhode Island. "Mr. Senator Anthony, how say you?" asked the Chief Justice. "Is the respondent, Andrew Johnson, President of the United States, guilty or not guilty of a high misdemeanor as charged in this article?" Mr. Anthony responded "Guilty." Bayard, Buckalew, Davis, Dixon and Doolittle answered "Not Guilty," as it was known that they would. Mr. Fessenden answered "Not Guilty." Mr. Fowler answered "Not Guilty." Mr. Grimes's name was called. The Chief Justice said that he might remain seated but friends helped him to his feet, and he also pronounced the President "Not Guilty." So, too, did Mr. Henderson;[5] Ross of Kansas, at whom the impeachers

---

[1] Washington corr. Hartford Courant, quoted in National Intelligencer, May 16, 1868.

[2] Cf. Welles, vol. iii, p. 353.

[3] "Disabled and shattered but nerved by the demand of high duty." —National Intelligencer, May 18, 1868.

[4] George W. Julian, Political Recollections, p. 316.

[5] Now bravely over the weakness which had led him to offer to resign and ready to fulfil the obligations of his oath.—Letter to Missouri delegation in National Intelligencer, May 16, 1868.

had stormed until he had led them to believe that he was on their side; Trumbull of Illinois; Van Winkle of West Virginia, and the Radicals were defeated. A motion to adjourn for ten days, until May 26, was immediately made. But first the vote must be announced officially. The chief clerk read the list of names whereupon the Chief Justice said: "Upon this article 35 senators vote guilty and 19 senators vote not guilty. Two-thirds not having pronounced guilty the President is, therefore, acquitted upon this article." [1] The motion to adjourn until the 26th was renewed and it was adopted.

Seven Republican senators had voted with the Democrats.[2] They had exhibited a temerity in the face of the sound, fury and threat which filled the air around them quite incomprehensible to their colleagues, to the Republican members of the House and to a great part of the people of the North, temporarily lost to reason. That such action had aught to do with a judicial temperament or a quick conscience, that there was statesmanship apart from partisan politics, or a heroism of character in the midst of tumult, and a governance of present action with respect for the judgments of history was beyond most men's power to understand. One senator had failed the conspirators, Fessenden, or Fowler, or Grimes, or Henderson, or Ross, or Trumbull, or Van Winkle, and, not knowing upon whom to expend their fury, all seven, as well as the Chief Justice, who for long had been charged with partiality for the President's side, were the objects of immediate and continuing recrimination.

So vilely pursued were some of the number that they were compelled to leave their lodgings in Washington and take refuge in a "Copperhead hotel" in Georgetown.[3] Trumbull

[1] Trial, vol. ii, p. 487.
[2] It seems certain that one or two more of the moderates would have done so, if such action had been necessary to prevent conviction. Cf. W. A. Dunning, Reconstruction Political and Economic, p. 107, based upon the author's conversations with Senator Henderson in 1901; also Century Magazine, Jan., 1913. Sprague, Willey and Morgan, it is said, stood ready to vote "Not Guilty." Cf. Horace White, Life of Trumbull, p. 321, and allusions to the same subject in the Johnson Papers.
[3] N. Y. Tribune, May 18, 1868.

was told that he was in danger of being hanged to the nearest lamp post if he should be seen on the streets of Chicago.[1] It was predicted that not one of the septemvirate would be able ever again to hold up his head in the society of his fellow men, though Ross was the special object of the Radical savagery. It was the irony of fate that the Republican party should so be served by a "Kansas man." None had thought, Sumner said, that "a Kansas man could quibble against his country."[2] He had played the part of Stanley on Bosworth field, promising fidelity almost up to the moment when he had broken faith. His had been "shameless treachery." It was sorrow to think that the case had been lost through the vote of such "a miserable poltroon and traitor."[3] Ross complained that he was passed in the streets and in the halls of Congress "like a leper, with averted face and every indication of hatred and disgust." Association with him was deemed "disreputable and scandalous."[4] Having telegraphed back to Anthony and "one thousand others" in Kansas, who had ordered him to vote for the conviction of Johnson, that he did not recognize their right to control his conscience, they rejoined that Kansas repudiated him as she did "all perjurers and skunks."[5] All seven had "sorely disappointed the country and disgraced themselves," said the Philadelphia Inquirer. They furnished another argument to those who declared that there was "no such thing as honesty in a public man."[6] The people would "sternly look on and award the punishment." For the "traitors" there could be "no allowance and no clemency." They had "tried, convicted and sentenced themselves."[7]

The suspicion under which the Chief Justice stood was founded upon his habit of rather primly and austerely lectur-

---

[1] N. Y. Evening Post, quoted in Horace White, Life of Trumbull, p. 315.
[2] House Reports, 40th Cong. 2nd sess., no. 75, p. 30.
[3] N. Y. Tribune, May 18, 1868.
[4] Cong. Globe, 40th Cong. 2nd sess., p. 4515.
[5] Dewitt, pp. 544-5; N. Y. Tribune, May 28, 1868.
[6] Phila. Inquirer, May 18, 1868.
[7] Ibid., May 16, 1868.

ing other men. Before the Senate yet had sent for him in the
premises he had addressed that body a letter, laying down the
law in the case and admonishing it for having received the
articles of impeachment and adopting rules of procedure for
the court before it was organized as a court.[1]

But the principal ground for the distrust of Mr. Chase was
the general knowledge of his own ambition to occupy the
highest office in the land and of his old rivalry in Ohio with
Wade, a very different kind of man,[2] who if the proceedings
were successful would now reach the Presidency. It had
begun to be noised about that if Chase could not be the Republican candidate, as he would not be, for all signs indicated
the unopposed selection of Grant, he would accept a nomination at the hands of the Democrats. Theodore Tilton in April
had written an article for the Independent, saying as much,
to Chase's great discomfiture.[3] Other gazettes dwelt upon the
same topic in the same spirit. What could be easier than to
connect the Chief Justice's ambitions with his want of ardor
for the impeachment proceedings? The very evening of the
day the articles were presented to the senators the President
had been a guest at a reception at Mr. Chase's residence in
Washington. Immediately the alarm of the Radicals was
great,[4] and, despite the Chief Justice's tactfulness, clashes were
unavoidable as the trial progressed. Should the presiding officer have a vote in case of a tie?[5] What were his rights in
making decisions, and how might these decisions be reversed?
His opinions were watched with unfriendly eyes to discover
if he were not indulging some favoritism for the President.

[1] Cong. Globe, 40th Cong. 2nd sess., p. 1644. Several senators, as
Grimes, shared the Chief Justice's views on this subject.—Salter, Life
of Grimes, pp. 336-7.

[2] It was clear enough, as the London Saturday Review observed, that
one influential reason for the acquittal of the President was the antipathy of some of the senators of the better class to "the unpolished
demagogue who would have succeeded to the vacant office." (Issue of
May 30, 1868.) If Johnson were deposed for addressing mobs in ribald
language he would be succeeded "by another orator of precisely the
same class in the person of Mr. Wade."—Ibid., April 18, 1868.

[3] Schuckers, pp. 579-80.
[4] Dewitt, p. 389.
[5] Trial, vol. i, pp. 185-8. For Sumner's opinion see Trial, vol. iii, pp.
281-95. For Chase's see Schuckers, pp. 576-7.

Doubtful senators dined at his home as the trial neared its end.[1] Instantly every Radical tongue began to wag and he was accused of attempts to interfere with the fair course of justice. Not only his son-in-law, Sprague, but also Anthony, Van Winkle, Grimes and Henderson might be turned from the path of patriotic duty by his influences.

The trial at an end the New York Tribune blamed him for what had come to pass; he had done "more than all others" to save Johnson from the fate which he so abundantly deserved.[2] His ambition had been "whetted by visions of a throne," said the Philadelphia Press. He had made himself a "fit crowning piece for a temple of Janus."[3] He had been "guilty of complicity in the most unscrupulous and shameless intrigue," said the Pittsburgh Gazette.[4] Such statements Mr. Chase properly repelled with vigor. He had not been favorable to impeachment from the first day, though he had confided in few, and throughout the trial, in a difficult position, he had conducted himself in a manner entirely above just reproach.[5] In his sight it was simply an effort to convict and sentence an offender on a charge of "general cussedness."[6] He had not sought to sway the mind of any senator and was "entirely uncertain" of the result up to the end.[7]

Republican newspapers, such as the New York Evening Post, the Springfield Republican, the Chicago Tribune, the Hartford Courant, the Cincinnati Commercial and the Providence Journal which approved of the President's acquittal were denounced in similar terms by the Radicals.[8]

There had been "corruption of the basest sort," said For-

[1] Dewitt, pp. 521, 524, 531; cf. Salter, Life of Grimes, p. 359.
[2] Issue of May 18, 1868.   [3] Issue of May 18, 1868.
[4] Cited in N. Y. Tribune, May 19, 1868.
[5] A. B. Hart, Life of Chase, p. 360. Concerning the charges against Chase, Evarts afterward said that they had amounted only to this— "that he had brought into the Senate under his judicial robes no concealed weapons of party warfare, and that he had not plucked from the Bible on which he took and administered the judicial oath the commandment for its observance."—Arguments and Speeches of Wm. M. Evarts, vol. i, p. 345.
[6] Chase to a friend, May 16, 1868, in Warden, pp. 694-5; cf. F. W. Seward, Seward at Washington, vol. ii, p. 377.
[7] Warden, p. 693.   [8] Phila. Press, May 18, 1868.

ney's Philadelphia Press, "ambition and jealousy of the vilest." Those who had voted for conviction had "covered themselves with imperishable honor and won for themselves a fame which every year their children and children's children will more dearly appreciate." The seven who had failed the impeachers had "plunged from a precipice of fame into the grovelling depths of infamy and death." They were "a new batch of rebellious chiefs." Better for them if they had "perished in the pangs of birth." They "doubly dying" would go down

> "To the vile earth from whence they sprung
> Unwept, unhonor'd and unsung."

In Chase, said the Press, "justice" had been "prostituted to ambition"; in Trumbull "statesmanship had drivelled into selfishness"; in Fessenden "conservatism" had "turned to cowardice"; in Henderson "confidence" had been "abused by treachery"; in Ross "littleness" had "simply borne its legitimate fruit"; in Grimes "vigor" had been "supplanted by impotence and idiocy"; in Fowler "treason simply waited for an opportunity to speak"; in Van Winkle "the cloak of fair protestation" had been "dyed in infamy." [1] Evarts, whose services in the President's behalf had been so pre-eminent, did not escape the fury of the outburst. His conduct had been "unpatriotic and base," said the New York Independent. He was called a "hireling counsel," though it was authoritatively averred that he had been promised and received no fee for his work, and that he had surrendered more than thrice the annual income of any ordinary lawyer by taking part in the proceedings. [2]

The President had never desponded. [3] There was in him, though he took little credit for it to himself, some of the faith of the martyr. He knew that he was right by all the law and history of the Constitution, as he understood the law and history of that instrument. [4] To a considerable extent he had

---

[1] Phila. Press, May 18, 1868.
[2] N. Y. Nation, May 21, 1868.
[3] Welles, vol. iii, p. 344.
[4] He was "honest, right-minded and narrow-minded," said Mr. Curtis

begun the contest with Stanton and, through Stanton, with Congress in order to obtain a judgment from the Supreme Court which would re-establish the balance of the government. For that reason was Lorenzo Thomas's arrest welcomed at the White House—the question would pass to the judiciary where it belonged. But that affair had been bungled to the President's disadvantage.[1] Two or three previous attempts to secure judicial intervention had failed; there was still hope of an opinion in the McCardle case. Congress, as we have seen, had interfered to take this resource from the President and now, in the midst of the impeachment trial, to his great chagrin, the court was glad to consider that it was without jurisdiction over the subject, and evaded the invitation to enter the controversy.[2] All, indeed, seemed lost— to the outer limits of his horizon, but his friends who saw him in these days unite in noting his courage and dignity.[3]

The news was received in the country at large with a good deal of equanimity.[4] As the trial proceeded the conviction grew that the impeachment was "politics." For many days men had been betting on the result. The event had been "degraded to the level of a horse race, or a fight between two bruisers for a champion's belt."[5] Nevertheless, in the large cities crowds gathered before the windows of newspaper offices seeking early word of the verdict. When it came "indignation meetings" were held in all parts of the North. Grimes was burned in effigy. The result was pleasing only to the "unterrified and the unwashed," the "rebels" of the South and the Democrats everywhere, said the New York Tribune,[6] which strove for so many years to bring dirt, drink, disloyalty and Democracy into some indissoluble alliance. "Every gambling

of his counsel, who had come from Boston to join with so much distinction in the defence. His "few ideas" were "right and true" and "he could suffer death sooner than yield up or violate one of them."— Memoir of B. R. Curtis, vol. i, p. 417.

[1] Welles, vol. iii, pp. 286, 294.
[2] Ibid., pp. 314, 320; Dewitt, p. 403. [3] Cf. Dewitt, pp. 555-7.
[4] Phila. Ledger, May 18, 1868.   [5] Ibid., May 13.
[6] Issue of May 18, 1868.

hell" in Washington on the night of the day the vote was
taken, said the Philadelphia Press correspondent, "every
policy shop, the saloons and the brothels" had "vomited out
their inmates to join in the saturnalia."[1] Democrats were
parading with bands of music in New Brunswick, N. J. They
fired a salute of 100 guns on Boston Common, in Philadelphia,
Hartford, Conn., and Springfield, Mass.[2] Bonfires burned at
Bridgeport, Conn., and in Lexington, Ky.[3] Telegrams poured
into the White House, rejoicing over the "glorious victory" for
the "Constitution and its dauntless defender." Letters came
from many sides. The President was congratulated on his deliverance from "the gigantic and unparallelled outrage" which
would "blacken our history to the end of time."

> "Sound the loud timbrels o'er Egypt's dark sea,
> Jehovah hath triumphed, his people are free."[4]

Competent onlookers, such as the editor of the New York
Nation, did not fail to view the event in its right light. It
should be dramatized, said he. The trial would "furnish the
materials for what the play bills call a side-splitting farce."
That Butler had damaged the managers' cause was plainly
seen and stated. His "want of manners or rather want of
decency throughout the case gave the President a constant
advantage which increased up to the very last day." From
the beginning the managers had been "overmatched in learning and ability."[5] As for the "traitors" they were the party's
"most trusted, longest tried leaders and counsellors." No men
in it had "given such guarantees of honor and purity and zeal."
The gratitude of the whole country was due the seven, "not
for voting for Johnson's acquittal but for vindicating, we presume nobody knows but themselves at what cost, the dignity
and purity of the court of which they formed a part and the
sacred rights of individual conscience. They have afforded

[1] Issue of May 18, 1868.
[2] Phila. Press and N. Y. Herald, May 17 and 18, 1868, and Johnson
Papers.
[3] N. Y. Herald, May 19, 1868.   [4] Johnson Papers.
[5] N. Y. Nation, May 21, 1868.

American young men an example such as no politicians have ever afforded them in the whole course of American history." [1]

"To denounce as corrupt" senators who might vote against the articles, said the Chicago Tribune, "to assail them with contumely and upbraid them with treachery" was "folly," to call it by its "mildest" name. It would be "revolting" to the people and "fatal" to the Republican party.[2] "When the heat of party passion" should pass away, said the New York Times, sober and reflecting men would wonder "how they could have been betrayed into such a violation of common sense and common decency." The nation had escaped a "black and lasting stain" on its reputation, and it was "one of the narrowest escapes any nation has ever made from one of the greatest dangers which any nation has ever encountered." [3] The seven senators who had saved the republic, said the National Intelligencer, could not be "too highly honored or too much commended for their courage, their fidelity to honest conviction and their noble stand against arrogant party dictation." [4]

Public opinion abroad had been "nearly unanimous" and news of the result was received in Europe with "unfeigned satisfaction" as a further proof of the ability of popular institutions in America "to sustain themselves under the severest trials." [5] "Foreign ill will," said the London Saturday Review, "would be incapable of libelling the national institutions with the ungenerous aptitude of patriots of the order of Mr. Stevens and Mr. Butler." Those who in America were vindicating the "judicial character of the impeachment" and defending the "right of senators to exercise an unbiassed judgment on the evidence" were deserving of the highest praise.[6] If the President had been convicted, said the London Times, it would have brought to an end that balance of powers con-

---

[1] N. Y. Nation, May 21, 1866.
[2] Chicago Tribune, May 14, 1868.
[3] Issue of May 18, 1868.
[4] Issue of May 18, 1868.
[5] General Dix, then in Paris, to Johnson, May 17, in Johnson Papers.
[6] Issue of May 30, 1868.

templated by the founders of the government. It was much
more than the President, it was the Constitution of the United
States which was on trial before the Senate.[1] That the impeachment had failed was "a matter of intense gratification to
every well wisher of the American republic." [2]

Whatever others thought of and said about his course Fessenden was quite clear that it was "the one act in his life
for which he deserved the most credit, putting at hazard,"
as he had, all his "own honor and interest from an imperative
sense of duty." [3] Upon taking the oath as a member of the
court, said Grimes, "I became a judge acting on my own responsibility and accountable only to my own conscience and
my Maker: and no power could force me to decide on such a
case contrary to my convictions, whether that party was composed of my friends or my enemies." [4]

This was well. But how different from judges were many
of the senators, how far removed from the character of fair
prosecuting litigants, ready to take the decision of the court
and abide by it, were many of the representatives became clear
at once. Senator Wilson had declared that if there were
doubts to vex him in the process of reaching a conclusion his
country should have the benefit of those doubts rather than
the President.[5] On the 18th in the Senate Sumner, as one of
the judges, though the President had been acquitted in legal
form on one charge, and awaited the further determination of
the court as to his guilt under the other articles, said that there
had been a "moral judgment against him." [6] He was "utterly
unprincipled and wicked." [7] There had been "great, manifold
and deep damnation," said Stevens, in the House, who still
called Johnson "the great criminal." [8]

[1] Issue of May 18, 1868.   [2] Ibid., May 27, 1868.
[3] Private letter of Fessenden, published in N. Y. Sun, and quoted in
National Intelligencer, May 27, 1868.
[4] Chicago Tribune, May 28, 1868, quoted in Salter, Life of Grimes,
pp. 359-60.
[5] Quoted in Horace White, Life of Trumbull, p. 315.
[6] Cong. Globe, 40th Cong. 2nd sess., p. 2495.
[7] Ibid., p. 2520.   [8] Ibid., p. 2530.

The managers, having returned from the scene of their galling defeat, immediately went into a hurried secret conference, from which they emerged with a resolution authorizing them to send for papers and examine witnesses, to discover whether "improper and corrupt means" had been used to gain the result.[1] Of course one, or several, or all of the seven recusants had been bought for Johnson. They had been false once; now they would be so browbeaten that the President should not escape the net of the managers in reference to the other articles. Bingham declared that senators as well as presidents might be impeached by the House of Representatives in the name of the omnipotent sovereign American people.[2] If there were to be an inquiry minority leaders vainly contended for the appointment of a committee, so that they might have a hand in the proceedings, but the managers would listen to no such suggestion. The Democrats had been placed on important committees before, said Butler. Secrets of state were not safe in their hands. "Whoever heard of the friends and defenders of a supposed criminal being put on a grand jury to aid in investigating his crimes?" It was as "impudent" a request as for Ali Baba, if he were before a grand jury, to ask to have some of his Forty Thieves put on that grand jury.[3]

A committee was charged with an investigation of the case of Senator Henderson with reference to a letter addressed to him by the Radical representatives from Missouri. The Democrats in the House first made the demand for this inquiry; the action was authorized by the Republicans.[4]

In their extraordinary work the managers, under Butler's direction, were inconceivably active and insolent. Instantly the telegraph offices in Washington and Baltimore were ransacked by their agents and all dispatches sent in or out for several days prior to the taking of the vote in the Senate were seized. Officers of banks were constrained to reveal the con-

[1] Cong. Globe, 40th Cong. 2nd sess., p. 2503.
[2] Ibid., p. 2503.　　　　　　　　[3] Ibid., pp. 2675-6.
[4] Ibid., pp. 2471, 2495, 2497, 2548.

dition of the accounts of their depositors. Desks were opened
and private letters were read. Many men were brought in to
be examined as to their intimate personal affairs. A Ken-
tuckian named Woolley who lived in Cincinnati and was
known in Washington as a lawyer, in alliance with the "Whisky Ring," given to betting on horse races and speculation in
Wall Street, refused to answer all the questions Butler propounded to him. The sergeant-at-arms was sent to arrest him
and for several days, until he could "purge himself of his contempt," he was confined in a "coal hole" in the crypt of the
Capitol, which proved to be a room in which Miss Vinnie
Ream, a sculptress, was modelling a statue of Lincoln to stand
in the rotunda of that edifice.

In this movement two purposes were simultaneously sub-
served. Miss Ream had received her lucrative commission
from Congress. But she was a friend of Senator Ross of
Kansas, who lodged with her mother and called at her studio,
and she had been engaged, so it was alleged, in influencing
that man to vote against the conviction of the President. Representative George W. Julian had gone to her before the vote
was taken, to convince her of the error of her ways,[1] presumably, as it appeared, without effect. For this she was to be
punished by making her room into a prison cell, while the
"recusant witness," for having been impertinent to Butler, was
to be punished by brooding for a term of days beside her unfinished clay model.[2] Thurlow Weed, as a friend of Seward,
was brought before the managers. Even senators were summoned and examined for signs of their base bargaining.
Henderson, who had been asked to appear before the committee, put his case to his colleagues. He said that the resolution
of the House and the course of the managers, acting under it,
was a "direct insult to the Senate as a body." To take "a
judge and a juror" out of the court prior to the conclusion of
a trial, and subject him to a "secret inquisition," not before
any authorized body but a number of persons acting as

[1] Cong. Globe, 40th Cong. 2nd sess., pp. 2674-5.
[2] National Intelligencer, May 30, 1868.

prosecutors for the accused, was an outrageous proceeding. Such methods recalled the "harsh and cruel" tortures "which in past days sought the blood of the heretic and dissenter." [1] Pomeroy, Sumner and some others eagerly embraced the opportunity to testify and extend their statements about Johnson and such senators as had voted for his acquittal.

Further coercion of the "traitors" would be applied by the party machinery at the national convention in Chicago. There it would be made plain what fate would befall senators who had defied, and who might in the later course of the trial continue to defy the general will.

Those who had gone West to attend the convention trailed home and on May 26 the court, after a ten days' recess, re-assembled. Much wrangling ensued as to further proposed adjournments, but it was determined to try the President's strength under the second and third articles. Ross, still inscrutable, set upon with greater fury than before, might yet serve the purpose of the Radicals. But he, amid the complete stillness which prevailed in the chamber, as everyone hung upon his words, twice said "Not Guilty." On both articles, therefore, the President was acquitted by precisely the same vote as had been cast on the eleventh article,[2] whereupon, despairing of any other result, the impeachers, in uncontrollable wrath, were willing to adjourn *sine die.* "Without friends, save those bought by gold or bound by the comradeship of crime, and without a future," Forney's Philadelphia Press dismissed Andrew Johnson "without a word or further thought" and left him "to himself and history." [3]

Impeachment was "laid out for dead and buried with all the honors of war." Again seven senators had refused to follow despotic party leadership and had preserved "the fame of the nation in the eye of Christendom." [4] All the members

---

[1] Cong. Globe, 40th Cong. 2nd sess., p. 2549.
[2] Dewitt, vol. ii, pp. 496-7.
[3] Issue of May 27.
[4] National Intelligencer, May 27, 1868.

of the Cabinet were in the White House when the news was carried to the President. His "countenance lighted up," says his friend Welles, "and showed a pleasant and satisfied smile, but the same quiet composure remained." [1]

Foreign ministers, officers of the government, civil and military, in large numbers, and citizens crowded into the Executive Mansion. Johnson met his callers with a "God's will be done." It was a victory, not for him, but for the country and the Constitution. [2]

Congratulations were renewed in the press. "Let the people sing songs of joy," said the Baltimore Times; "let a grateful people return thanks. The President is vindicated; his enemies are confounded; the nation is saved." [3] Mr. Curtis who had returned to Boston before the trial had come to an end wrote to the President: "I have not esteemed this proceeding of very great personal importance to you. But to the country it was of such importance that it would be difficult to overstate it." And Mr. Groesbeck said in a letter from Cincinnati that "a judgment of conviction and the seizure of your office upon so miserable a case would have been little better than taking possession of it in the first instance with a file of soldiers. They tried to destroy you," he continued; "they have but exalted you the more highly." [4]

Butler's "smelling committee" had failed of its purposes. But he was yet to publish his report. In it he suppressed the testimony, or used only such parts as would serve his ends. He had found several "corrupt rascals" whom he called the "Astor House conspirators," since, when they were in New York, they met in a room in that hotel, though in Washington they were traced to a certain "Parlor Number 6" at Willard's. He connected Woolley, Sheridan Shook, an internal revenue collector in New York; Samuel Ward and Ralph W. Newton, speculators and operators in the Gold Room; E. D. Webster, a custom house officer in New York; J. B. Craig, a New York lawyer; Perry Fuller, an Indian contractor; the President's

[1] Welles, vol. iii, p. 368.   [3] National Intelligencer, May 27, 1868.
[2] Issue of May 27, 1868.   [4] Johnson Papers.

late private secretary, Edmund Cooper, and several others with some confused scheme which he said spelled monstrous dishonesty.[1]

A few of the number manifestly were betting, or guiding others in the placing of bets on the result of the trial, either directly or through the New York stock exchange, and were following the course of events on this account. Others, identified with the "Whisky Ring," were acting in some way, as they believed, in the interest of that corrupt organization. Others were concerned with the outcome of the nominating conventions, and were in Washington to see what might be done to forward the candidacies of Chief Justice Chase or George H. Pendleton. Still others, led by Collector of the Port Henry A. Smythe of New York, were collecting a purse of $100,000 to be given to President Johnson, if he should be convicted and dismissed from office, or $50,000 in case of his acquittal to pay the fees of his counsel.

Nothing of any kind was proven, even in regard to these matters. No definite word of suspicion was spoken regarding any one of the seven Republican senators who had voted against conviction. The only members whose honor the testimony even vaguely touched, Nye, Tipton, Wilson, Thayer, Anthony, Sprague, Morton and Pomeroy (who to the managers' and his own surprise gained a quite unenviable prominence)[2] had voted for conviction. But these facts Butler waved aside since they were "gentlemen of the highest honor," his inference being plain that, if bribes could be offered to any, money must have passed between the "Whisky Ring," or some friend or friends of Johnson, and the seven senators, who

---

[1] For Butler's preliminary report see Cong. Globe, 40th Cong. 2nd sess., pp. 2575-8; the final report is in House Committee Reports, 40th Cong. 2nd sess., no. 75.

[2] This leader of the "impeachmentites," as Grimes called them, had not scrupled to propose a bargain with Johnson in March covering a complete change in the Cabinet, which would provide him personally, it is presumed, with a high office. In return for this the charges against the President were to be withdrawn.—On the authority of President Johnson's secretary, Colonel Moore, in American Hist. Review, Oct., 1913, pp. 125-6.

were not men of honor.[1] The "logic" of such a line of reasoning, Senator Henderson said truly, was "as vicious and
corrupt as the motives prompting the proceeding." [2]

Nothing remained but the statements in the closing hours
of the session of such of the senators who had been so vilely
assailed in Butler's report as chose to notice it. Henderson
and Fowler who had been brought into the affair in a particularly exasperating manner, and Ross who now, after he
had found where he stood, was pleased by the prominence he
had gained, retorted in the obvious way by reviewing the pic-
turesquely unpleasant chapters in Butler's civil and military
life. The investigation, Henderson said, was simply "a work
of vengeance." Butler alone signed the report; the other
managers had washed their hands of the entire proceeding. It
was not meant to "vindicate truth" but to serve the "selfish
and malicious purposes" of its "contemptible author," [3] who in
response in the House dismissed Henderson with pity as Uncle
Toby did the fly, which after it had buzzed about his head
he had caught and let out of his hand at the window with a
"Go, poor devil! there is room enough in the world for both
thee and me." [4]

Fowler, partially to even his scores with such a man, called
him "a being bloated by his own corrupt and dishonorable
passions," a "wicked man who had sought to convert the
Senate of the United States into a political guillotine." [5] Ross,
not to be outdone by rivals in this kind of rejoinder, attributed
to Butler's "inefficiency and cowardice the bleaching bones
of many of the patriotic dead of the war." His "well known
grovelling instincts and proneness to slime and uncleanness"
had led "the public to insult the brute creation by dubbing
him 'the beast.' " [6]

In the Senate a committee was appointed, upon the motion

[1] House Reports, 40th Cong. 2nd sess., no. 75, p. 33.
[2] Cong. Globe, 40th Cong. 2nd sess., p. 4465.
[3] Ibid., pp. 4463-5.
[4] Appendix to Cong. Globe, 40th Cong. 2nd sess., p. 472.
[5] Cong. Globe, 40th Cong. 2nd sess., p. 4513.
[6] Ibid., pp. 4516-7.

of Davis and Ross, to ascertain what constraint and intimidation there had been with a view to influencing the result. Its members were Buckalew, Morrill of Maine, Chandler, Stewart and Thayer.[1] But it held only two meetings, made no report and at the end of the next session in March, 1869, declared that it would render none.[2]

Democrats during the course of the trial, as for example Robinson of New York, recalling Benton's indomitable efforts to clear the name of Andrew Jackson, which were rewarded at length with success, proposed to expunge the impeachment resolution. The journals should be marked "Expunged by order of the House," and the record of the action was to be engrossed, framed and hung in the Capitol, copies of it being forwarded to Andrew Johnson, to his various living lineal descendants and to each public library and reading room in the United States.[3] The expungers continued their efforts intermittently afterward, but, without a party to espouse his cause, Johnson was not to have a vindication except as it has come to him through the judgment of history at this calmer day.

Attempts to pack the Senate with enemies of the President procéeded while the result of the trial still depended. Nebraska, as has been noted, had sent two men to the scene for the task of bringing about his conviction, and the Radicals were barely prevented from executing their design to make a state out of the territory of Colorado. The hasty and urgent efforts to restore various Southern states to their old places in the Union, as recited in the last chapter of this work, were influenced by the same considerations. Stevens on May 7 reported the bill to admit the Africanized state of Arkansas to representation in Congress.[4] It was hurried through the House the next day,[5] reached the Senate on the 12th of May and two senators were at hand ready to take the oath.[6] Reverdy Johnson assumed that no member contemplated for one

---

[1] Cong. Globe, 40th Cong. 2nd sess., pp. 2544, 2548-55, 2597-99, 2622.
[2] Ibid., 3rd sess., p. 1865.   [3] Ibid., 2nd sess., p. 2379.
[4] Ibid., p. 2375. [5] Ibid., p. 2399. [6] Ibid., p. 2417.

moment the possibility of allowing these men to constitute a
part of the court of impeachment. No one, said he, "controlled by a sense of justice, controlled by any, the least,
sense of propriety," could believe that they were to be brought
in to participate in the issue of that proceeding.[1] But this
was the object of Stevens's haste in reference to Arkansas, as
it was his object a few days later in presenting the bill to
bring senators and representatives into Congress from North
Carolina, South Carolina, Louisiana, Georgia and Alabama.[2]
If they could not be made available "to operate on that
question," [3] which by good fortune they were not, it at least
could be brought to everyone's understanding that new Radicals soon would be added to the membership of the Senate,
numerous enough to dispose of the President at some later
date.

The session was not allowed to end without renewed threats
of impeachment. Stevens on July 7 offered three additional
articles for presentation to the court, which he was
pleased to say had adjourned "without completing its judgment," with sundry characteristic remarks expounding them.[4]
Thomas Williams on the same day offered fourteen articles.[5] On July 25 a new Congressman from Florida, named
Hamilton, who had now taken his seat, read a tirade on the
same subject to have it referred to the Committee on the
Judiciáry.[6]

Stanton, when he found that he was not to have the vindication from the court of impeachment which he had sought
and the opportunity of continuing to be Secretary of War in
the new Cabinet of "glorious Ben" Wade, gradually removed
the barricades with which he had surrounded himself. He
sent a letter to the President on May 26 when the result
of the vote on the second and third articles reached him, saying that he now "relinquished charge of the War Department."
Still not recognizing Lorenzo Thomas he stated that he had

---

[1] Cong. Globe, 40th Cong. 2nd sess., p. 2437. Sumner said that, "of
course," they could be added as members of the court.—Ibid., p. 2516.
[2] Ibid., p. 2445.   [3] Ibid., p. 2465.   [4] Ibid., p. 3786.
[5] Ibid., pp. 3792-3.   [6] Ibid., pp. 4473-4.

SCHOFIELD, SECRETARY OF WAR   149

turned over the books, archives and other property in his custody as Secretary of War to General Townsend.[1]

For some time it was known that General Schofield had been requested and had consented to act as Secretary of War. The disposition of the office in this manner was the subject of a kind of treaty secretly negotiated by Mr. Evarts, while the trial was in progress,[2] which has given rise to the thought that one side used little more care than the other to regard the case as one to be determined by the quiet rules of a court of justice, apart from its relation to politics. For the friends of the President to approach Schofield and offer him the place and, for him to consent to accept it was a piece of manipulation meant to propitiate public opinion and to influence the mind of the court.[3] At any rate the name of Thomas Ewing, Sr., on which the Senate had never acted, was withdrawn and on April 23 Schofield's was substituted for it. Now, on May 30, after the President had been acquitted and Stanton had gone, the nomination was confirmed, though not without further senatorial flings at the President and much wrangling in executive session as to the exact language to be used on the occasion,[4] and on June 1 Schofield took charge, soon to appear at meetings of the Cabinet.[5]

The Radicals offered a resolution tendering Stanton the "thanks of Congress" for his "great ability, purity and fidelity to the cause of the country" as Secretary of War, "amid the open dangers of a great rebellion," and afterward, "when assailed by the opposition, inspired by hostility to the measures of justice and pacification of Congress." [6] There was objection in debate and an effort to change the wording of the resolution, so that reference might be made only to Stanton's services during the war, but without success, and it was adopted

[1] Gorham, Life and Public Services of E. M. Stanton, vol. ii, p. 456; Dewitt, p. 592.
[2] J. M. Schofield, Forty-Six Years in the Army, pp. 413-9; Century Magazine for August, 1897.
[3] Gorham, vol. ii, pp. 449-55; cf. Dewitt, pp. 547-8.
[4] Executive Journal, vol. xvi, pp. 236, 238-9.
[5] Welles, vol. iii, p. 375.
[6] Cong. Globe, 40th Cong. 2nd sess., p. 2727.

in the Senate on June 1 by 37 yeas and 11 nays, three of the recusant seven—Fowler, Henderson and Ross—voting with the Democrats.[1]   The House concurred on June 19.[2]

The President desired to reinstate Mr. Stanbery in the Attorney General's office, but the Senate vindictively refused its assent.   Only 11 members voted for the confirmation of his name; 29 opposed it.[3]   Mr. Johnson then proffered the office to Mr. Curtis, who declined it,[4] whereupon it was tendered, through Seward, to Mr. Evarts who, after taking the subject under advisement for a short time, expressed a willingness to serve, though he alleged that it would be at "some sacrifice of personal convenience and interest." [5]   The Senate agreed to this arrangement [6] and he entered the Cabinet to act for the few remaining months of Mr. Johnson's term.

[1] Cong. Globe, 40th Cong. 2nd sess., pp. 2727-36.
[2] Ibid., p. 3311.
[3] Sherman was the only member voting to convict Johnson who supported Stanbery.—Executive Journal, vol. xvi, p. 249.
[4] Under date of June 8 in Johnson Papers.
[5] Letters from Seward to Johnson of June 11 and from Evarts of June 20 in Johnson Papers.
[6] Seven Radicals voted against the confirmation of Evarts—Harlan, Howard, Stewart, Sumner, Tipton, Wade and Welch, a carpetbagger from Florida.—Executive Journal, vol. xvi, p. 313.

CHAPTER XI

THE CAMPAIGN OF 1868

THE position of Grant, while the impeachment trial progressed, was in complete harmony with his character as it had been disclosed in the preceding months. He was playing the "dumb inarticulate man of genius." [1] His quiet reticence in regard to Johnson and the imbroglio with Stanton over the possession of the War Department was consistently maintained, although his epistolary exchanges with the President had put him before the country as clearly on the Radical side. His was the one name on the lips of the party leaders as their candidate for the Presidency in the campaign of 1868. He would be nominated at the convention which was to be held in Chicago in May. As a result of a canvass resounding with the rancor of the past two years he would be swept into the office on a triumphal wave, expressive of national loyalty and patriotism.

While Grant's silence was as inscrutable as it was tactful and shrewd, it is quite plain that he now was ready to see Johnson convicted and Wade installed in the place. To his friends, as to General Schofield, he revealed a feeling of complete distrust of the President's designs and purposes. If Johnson were acquitted he must be held under the watchful eye of Congress all summer lest he trample the laws under foot. Escape from punishment would serve to increase his audacity; he would bring upon the country evils greater than any which yet had come to it from this baneful source.[2] Grant's warmest friends in Congress made no secret of his opinion that the President ought to be removed. Washburne, Logan, Roscoe

---

[1] J. L. Motley, Letters, vol. ii, p. 283.
[2] J. M. Schofield, Forty-Six Years in the Army, p. 416; cf. N. Y. Nation, April 9, 1868.

Conkling, undeviating in their support of Grant as the Republican candidate, let it be known at every opportunity that he was an inveterate advocate of the conviction of the culprit whom the Radicals had laid their hands on and were bent on sending back in disgrace to a village in Tennessee.[1]

His taciturnity about this great matter concerning which every one spoke was extended to cover the entire field of politics. He smoked on in silence,[2] doing offense to neither Democrat nor Republican.[3] He talked about horses to men who came to him full of other thoughts. To a delegation from Kentucky he spoke of the soil, climate and crops of their state.[4] In March and April General Sherman was still entirely in the dark as to his friend's intentions. He did not know what Grant meant by such silence "in the midst of the very great indication of his receiving the nomination." [5] Wade at one time was in so much uncertainty that he journeyed down from his home in Ohio to see Grant's father and mother at Covington, Ky., where old Mr. Grant was postmaster. They were away from home, but he met Dr. Cramer, the brother-in-law who was afterward made United States minister to Denmark, and who gave so favorable an account of Grant's radicalism to the visitor that he threw his hat into the air and broke a globe of the chandelier.[6] The "hero" of the war was quietly awaiting the stroke of the hour when he should leave soldierly associations, and, at the wish of advisers whose fair words concealed a deal of selfish interest and design, he, for better or worse, should enter the field of politics.

No other name except that of Chief Justice Chase presented itself to the minds of those who canvassed the political situation. That it was his wish to be the nominee could admit of no doubt. He had failed in 1856, 1860 and 1864 to realize

[1] Dewitt, Trial and Impeachment, p. 532.
[2] Phila. Ledger, July 29, 1867.   [3] Ibid., July 30, 1867.
[4] Ibid., Nov. 21, 1867.   [5] The Sherman Letters, pp. 314, 316.
[6] M. J. Cramer, U. S. Grant, Conversations and Unpublished Letters, pp. 68-9.

the ambition which all knew that he entertained. It was
more than a suspicion that Lincoln had placed him upon the
bench to relieve the party of his design to subject it to his
personal leadership. But by interview, letter and speech he
still kept himself prominently before the country as one who
had opinions upon current questions of politics and who would
be glad if the day should come when he might be President.
He had been among the first to advocate the enfranchisement
of the negro. Why not nominate him so that the Republican
party might get the electoral votes of the reconstructed states
at the South?[1] The country needed a statesman and a jurist
for President, not a military man. The arguments which Clay
knew so well how to use against Jackson and William Henry
Harrison and Zachary Taylor would apply as well now to
Grant. The "man on horseback" who stalked through the
history of France was a vision rising to appall not a few
Americans.[2] The New York Tribune on many occasions had
held the name of Chase before its readers as that one to which
Republicans could well and properly rally in the campaign of
1868.[3] The New York Independent gave its influence to
Chase.[4]

But if there were those who believed that a soldier should
not be President there were many more to say that a Chief
Justice should not trail his toga in partisan politics. For the
judiciary there must be respect and a feeling of complete confidence. In the Supreme Court there was "enough to satisfy
the noblest and purest ambition." It must not be used "as a
resting place on the way to something more attractive
in the political field."[5] That so good a judge could think

[1] N. Y. Nation, Jan. 9, 1868.   [2] Ibid., Jan. 16, 1868.
[3] As recently as on Jan. 3, 1868.—"We want a statesman; we desire
Mr. Chief Justice Chase. The party contains no purer, no worthier,
no more gifted man." As for Grant he would talk only about horses
and tobacco. The Tribune printed the following from Washington:
"Inquiring Republican (to General Grant).—'Well, General, what do
you think will be the effect of negro suffrage, fairly carried out?' General Grant.—'Have you seen Marshal Brown's pups? They are the
finest in the District.' "—N. Y. Tribune, Jan. 6, 1868.
[4] N. Y. Nation, April 30, 1868.   [5] Ibid., Jan. 16, 1868.

of being anything else than a judge was "little short of a scandal."[1]

The impeachment trial as it proceeded involved Chase more and more deeply in political discussion. His honest opinions offered as the presiding officer of the court were ascribed to base motives. The very Radicals who a few weeks before were commending him for his robust Republicanism were now ready to read him out of the party, and call him a Democrat.[2] The stock of Grant rose until no one had a thought of any other being the nominee of the convention. The New York Nation found him to be "a man really great and genuinely American." He was "a son of the soil, if ever there was one," who, "conscious of merit," knew how "to wait in silence and at his post for his reward."[3]

The vote taken on the eleventh article in the impeachment court on May 16, the scene shifted with suddenness to Chicago where the Republican national convention was to meet on the 20th. So absorbed had the nation been for weeks past in the issue of the trial that discussion of candidates and platforms had practically ceased. Grant's nomination was "conceded by acclamation."[4] But who should be the party's candidate for Vice President, and what should be done with the Chief Justice and the "recreant seven" with a view to securing the conviction of Johnson on the other articles when the court should reconvene? Seventeen coaches bore the Congressmen and their friends to Chicago. Bingham, Logan and other leading figures in the trial of Johnson were on the ground which shook with the echoes of the days just past at Washington. Immediately prior to the meeting of the nominating convention a large number of soldiers and sailors as-

---

[1] N. Y. Nation, April 30, 1868. He lobbied for the black man in the halls of Congress, said the Nation, harangued the people, gave to reporters of newspapers his opinions on political questions, ostentatiously returned to his home in Ohio to vote at a state election, proclaiming the fact in speeches from his window in Cincinnati to crowds in the street.— Ibid., Jan. 16, 1868.

[2] Ibid., March 19, 1868.   [3] Ibid., Jan. 16, 1868.

[4] Chicago corr. Phila. Press, May 18, 1868.

sembled in the German Turners' Hall to impart some of the
fervor of the victorious war to the proceedings, and to link
the causes for which the Republican party stood with loyal
service on the field of battle. The veterans marched through
the streets with "Old Abe," an eagle which had been the mas-
cot of a Wisconsin regiment during the war, sang "Old Grimes
is Dead," gave three groans in front of the office of the Chicago Tribune which had apologized for Senator Trumbull and
the other recreants, and cheered themselves hoarse for Grant
and the Union.

General Fairchild, the young Governor of Wisconsin, presided. Grant's father was conducted to a seat on the platform
while the band played "Hail Columbia" and he was compelled to make a brief speech. General Stokes declared that
it was the immediate duty of Congress to swear in fourteen
new senators from seven Southern states and vote Andy Johnson out of the White House. The recreant seven would go
down to posterity covered with more shame than Benedict
Arnold. He hoped the country would "spew them out," and
consign them to oblivion. Resolutions were adopted in favor
of the nomination of Grant and declaring that any senator
voting for acquittal in the impeachment trial was "unworthy
of the confidence of a brave and loyal people." The delegates
rose and gave three groans for Andrew Johnson and "all traitorous Republicans" while the band played the "Rogues'
March." [1]

The nominating convention met in Crosby's Opera House,
a spacious hall which lent itself well to such a use. Delegations were present from the Southern states, a dozen or more
negroes appearing to arouse comment. A not more curious
sight than the black men was a "reconstructed rebel" of "one
of the rebellious states," ex-Governor Joseph E. Brown of
Georgia, who when he spoke explaining how he had come
within the fold of the Republican party was greeted with "tremendous applause." [2] Grant's father found a place on the
stage here as in the Soldiers' and Sailors' Convention. Carl

[1] Chicago corr. Phila Press, May 20, 1868.   [2] Ibid., May 21, 1868.

Schurz took the temporary chairmanship and delivered a ringing party speech, soon turning over the gavel to General Hawley of Connecticut.

A brief platform of twelve "planks" was brought in by the Committee on Resolutions and adopted. It declared for "equal suffrage" at the South. Repudiation of the public debt was denounced as a "national crime." Payment must be made "in the utmost good faith to all creditors." But the rate of interest should be reduced wherever possible and the period for redemption of the principal should be "fair." The government should be administered with the "strictest economy" and the "corruptions" which had been "so shamefully nursed and fostered by Andrew Johnson" called "loudly for radical reform." A fling was taken at Great Britain for the pleasure of the Irish voters in America and it was made the duty of the government to interfere in behalf of "naturalized citizens," arrested and imprisoned by foreign powers. Sympathy was expressed for all oppressed peoples who were "struggling for their rights." Bounties and pensions were promised Union soldiers and their widows and orphans. Liberal encouragement should be extended to foreign immigration. The most strenuous efforts were put forth to secure the incorporation in the platform of a resolution ex-communicating the recreant seven, but better counsels prevailed. Unrestrained condemnation of Andrew Johnson was indulged in for his omissions and commissions, his treacheries and usurpations, but the convention contented itself on the subject of the trial by saying that he had been "justly impeached for high crimes and misdemeanors and properly pronounced guilty by the votes of 35 senators."

Logan nominated Grant in the name of the loyal people and soldiers of the republic. The whole convention rose to its feet while the band played "Hail to the Chief." There was not one dissenting vote out of 650. A portrait of the candidate, supported by a figure of liberty, with the motto "Match Him," was disclosed at the back of the stage amid loud cheering. In a few minutes the convention proceeded to ballot for candidates for Vice President. Massachusetts nominated Henry Wilson; Indiana, Colfax, whose name awakened great enthusiasm; Ohio, Wade who was "wildly" cheered; Pennsylvania, its "war governor," Curtin; New York, its governor since 1865, Reuben E. Fenton; Kentucky, ex-Attorney-General Speed; Maryland, J. A. J. Creswell; Iowa, James Harlan; Maine, Hannibal Hamlin: Kansas, Senator Pomeroy; a delegate from Alabama, Congressman William D. Kelley. The first ballot resulted in 170 votes for Wade, 149 for Colfax, 140 for Fenton and 113 for Wilson. Wade gained up to the fourth ballot when he had 204 votes to 186 for Colfax. On the fifth ballot there was a stampede to Colfax who received 522 votes, 326 being necessary to a choice. The amiable [1] but entirely partisan Speaker of the House was, therefore, declared to be the choice of the Republican party as its nominee for Vice President. One hundred guns were booming outside the convention hall before the friends of the various candidates for the second place on the ticket had yet finished their complimentary speeches. The celebration was general from Portland, Me., to San Francisco. At military headquarters in Washington the telegraph informed Grant of his nomination. Stanton and other friends came to offer him their congratulations and he nonchalantly smoked a cigar with them "as if nothing had happened." In the evening he held an impromptu reception at his home. Colfax was in his room at the Capitol while the balloting proceeded. His popularity caused many to crowd around him to felicitate him when the news of his nomination was received, and his house was filled with callers at night.

The next evening a procession was formed in the street. Headed by the Marine Band it marched to Grant's home. He appeared at the door. Boutwell standing at his side speaking for the assemblage expressed its gratification. His fellow citizens would support his administration knowing that it would

[1] "Was there ever such a good-tempered, chirping, warbling, real canary bird of a Speaker?"—Washington corr. N. Y. Tribune, Jan. 6, 1868.

be "characterized by firmness, by integrity, by patriotism, by good sense—all the manly qualities" which had marked his "past career." "I have now the pleasure of presenting to you the next President of the United States," said Mr. Boutwell as he reached the end of his remarks, "General Grant, the commander of your armies!" There was loud applause and for the first time, so far as his friends knew, Grant was prevailed upon to make a speech. It was brief but they were delighted that he had broken his silence at last. "Being entirely unaccustomed to public speaking and without any desire to cultivate that power," he began, "it is impossible for me to find appropriate language to thank you for this demonstration. All that I can say is that to whatever position I may be called by your will, I shall endeavor to discharge its duties with fidelity and honesty of purpose." Amid cheering, hundreds of persons entered the house to grasp the general's hand. In a little while the crowd moved on to Speaker Colfax's home and called him out. He was introduced as "the next Vice President of the United States," and in reply, with easy oratorical grace he put Grant beside Washington as "first in war, first in peace and first in the hearts of his countrymen." [1]

The action of the convention was received with great favor. "The choice of this distinguished patriot and soldier," said the Philadelphia Inquirer, "makes the nomination not partisan but national." [2] "His administration," said the Philadelphia Press, would "recall the simplicity and virtues of the early hours of the republic." The Republican party tendered to the nation "as a nominee the nation's favorite son—whom no state can own, no section claim—General Grant of Appomattox." [3] The convention "could not have chosen a better ticket," said the New York Herald.[4] Grant was "stronger than his party." The "enthusiasm and confidence in his popular strength" had never been "surpassed in any party convention over any other name." [5] It was not necessary to

[1] Washington corr. Phila. Inquirer, May 23, 1868.
[2] May 22, 1868.   [3] Phila. Press, May 22, 1868.
[4] N. Y. Herald, May 23, 1868.   [5] Ibid., May 22, 1868.

hold a convention, said the New York Tribune, to designate the party candidate. The people had decided that question. "We tried for a while," observed Greeley, recalling his advocacy of Chase, "to persuade them that they could do better but they would not hear us." It had become clear that there was "no other American in whom all interests and all sections cherished so profound a trust."[1]

On May 29 Grant wrote a letter to General Hawley formally accepting the nomination. He endorsed the party platform. If elected to the office of President it would be his "endeavor" to "administer all the laws in good faith, with economy and with the view of giving peace, quiet and protection everywhere." He concluded his little statement of principles with the words "Let us have peace!" Colfax accepted his nomination with more fluency and at more length, and the ticket went to the country, for the campaign; Grant and Colfax were the standard bearers of the "National Union Republican party."

What now would be done by the Democrats whose national convention would meet in New York city on July 4? Whom would they name for a canvass which on its face from the start seemed to be nearly hopeless? The convention at Chicago had spoken of "repudiation" as a "national crime." These words concealed a contention of political forces which had developed with rapidity, especially in the West. The war had left behind it much economic and financial disorder. Prices which had been high and which it was expected would fall with the coming of peace were still burdensome. For many life was stern. Gold was still being sold at a substantial premium. A greenback dollar was worth $1.39\frac{3}{4}$ on June 1 and $1.40\frac{3}{8}$ on July 1, 1868, in New York. Intelligent men were concerning themselves in Congress, in the press, in private discussion about a return to specie payments. The use of a paper currency had been designed to be but temporary—for the duration of the war only. Now the time had come for a readjustment of values and prices based upon the standards from

[1] N. Y. Tribune, May 22, 1868.

which the country had departed six years before. Herein agitators, seeking to gain the favor and applause of ignorant elements in the population, found their opportunity. Congress on
April 12, 1866, had passed a law authorizing the Secretary of
the Treasury to purchase $4,000,000 worth of greenbacks a
month and burn them up.[1] The process promised to be slow,
but, if it had been pursued for a period of years, it would have
led to the complete retirement of the "legal tenders." Men
of little property, urged forward by those who, for unworthy
ends, wished to convince this class that it was suffering from
unmerited poverty, at once raised a hue and cry about "contraction." The currency was being reduced in volume, said
they, the government was laying an oppressive hand upon the
farmer, trader and mechanic. Secretary of the Treasury
McCulloch was not led astray by the agitation, but the President, true to his type as a "people's man," placed himself
by speech and interview on the side of the anti-contractionists.
Congress, sensitive to such criticism, in February, 1868, repealed the law which it had passed less than two years before
and on the money question the country stood on the ground
it had occupied at the end of the war.

One plan led to another. This man proposed to tax the government war loans, that man to fund them in a manner which,
in greater or less degree, would mulct the owners. The scheme
which reached the widest measure of effrontery called for a
statement by Congress that such bonds as were not made payable in gold in distinct terms upon their face should be redeemed as they matured in "lawful money," i.e., in greenbacks.
When the "five twenties" were sold by Secretaries Chase and
Fessenden and the Treasury Agent, Jay Cooke, it was understood and plainly declared in Congress, in the newspapers, by
the sellers in the presence of the subscribers that these were
gold bonds. The principal as well as the interest was to be
paid in gold. It was with this explanation and on this promise
that the issues were distributed to the people and the money

[1] Not more than $10,000,000 in the first six months following the
enactment of the law and thereafter "not more than $4,000,000 in any
one month."

was brought into the Treasury to meet the large daily costs of the war.[1] Now orators in political conventions, and on the hustings, newspaper editors, oracles in village inns and at corner stores were ready to declare that, as nothing had been printed upon the five twenty bond about its redemption in coin, and as the government had received only greenbacks for it no more valuable money should be returned to the holder when the obligation matured. "The dead should bury their dead; the greenbacks should settle the score of the greenbacks," said the New Orleans Times. "As the national debt was contracted by inflation by inflation it should be paid," said George Francis Train.[2]

Men like Thaddeus Stevens and Benjamin F. Butler in the Republican party espoused the cause of the "repudiators" and "inflationists." Once, not long since, the people had been importuned to take the loans of the government as a patriotic duty. The bondholders, when they had made over their savings to the government, had been figures to be honored on every side. Now Butler declared that nine-tenths of them resided east of a meridian drawn through Lake Ontario. It was the rich East against the poor West. Stevens, though in 1862 he had said in Congress as chairman of the Committee on Ways and Means, in common with others who spoke at that time on the same subject, that the loan was "at six per cent, redeemable in gold in twenty years, the best and most valuable permanent investment that could be desired," [3] now, in 1868, declared that he would vote "for no such swindle upon the taxpayers." "If I knew," said he, "that any party in the country would go for paying in coin that which is payable in money, thus enhancing it one-half—if I knew there was such a platform and such a determination this day on the part of my party I would vote for the other side." [4] Senator John

[1] Oberholtzer, Jay Cooke, vol. i, pp. 239, 249, 257; F. Fessenden, Life of W. P. Fessenden, vol. ii, p. 303.
[2] New Orleans Times, Aug. 28, 1868.
[3] Cong. Globe, 37th Cong. 2nd sess., p. 686, Feb. 6, 1862; cf. N. Y. Tribune, July 23, 1868.
[4] Dewey, Financial History of the U. S., p. 348; cf. N. Y. Nation, July 23, 1868.

Sherman of Ohio, Senator Morton of Indiana, General Logan and other Republican leaders, while not of a mind to go so far to gain the acclamation of the inflationists, made pretense of favoring their schemes. Sherman had wavered and temporized in the court of impeachment; he was ready to do so again, and, though he was chairman of the Committee on Finance in the Senate, embraced a part of the heresies of the "rag money" men. He would pay or fund the bonds on a green-back basis, but he would not increase the volume of paper currency.[1]

The Republican party of Indiana had declared that "the public debt should be honestly paid, and all bonds issued there-for should be paid in legal tenders, commonly called green-backs, except where by their express terms they provide other-wise." [2] Similar resolutions were adopted by Republican conventions in other Western states. The party committees in local communities were controlled by this element, even when the state organizations were kept out of their hands. Campaigners, such as Carl Schurz, were told, when they came to speak for Grant, that they must say nothing to offend the greenback men.[3]

Yet, in the main, even in the West, the Republican party gave little encouragement to the inflationists, and the clear declarations of the Chicago platform served to discourage the agitation which was nearly forgotten as the campaign proceeded, and its issues were made plain questions of loyalty to the country and of gratitude to General Grant for bringing the war to an end.

Not so, however, with the Democratic party; nearly every-where it fell an easy prey to the doctrines so insinuatingly expounded by the greenback men. In Ohio in particular "anti-

[1] To his ignorance or dishonesty on this occasion Sherman has made too slight a reference in his Recollections, vol. i, p. 439; cf. N. Y. Nation, Dec. 28, 1871.

[2] N. Y. Nation, Feb. 27, 1868.

[3] Schurz characteristically disregarded the injunction and converted at least one hostile community to his views.—Reminiscences, vol. iii, pp. 289-91.

contraction" became a very popular cry, and it was soon generally known as the "Ohio idea." The Democrats in convention in that state said that the payment of the principal of the bonds in gold would "virtually add more than a thousand millions to the burden of the debt." They were opposed "to the whole insane financial policy" of which this scheme was a part. The five twenties should be paid "in the same currency received by the government for their issue." The country must be saved "from the reproach of paying a favored class in gold, while discharging its debts to all others, including pensions to widows and soldiers, in an inferior currency." Democratic conventions in Indiana, West Virginia, Nebraska and other states made similar declarations.

The more the "idea" was fought in the East the more it seemed to thrive in the West. Never in its long period of notable service did the New York Tribune keep so faithfully to the path of honorable duty. The value of its daily explanations of the fundamental principles of finance, and its protests against the "tomfooleries" that were thought and uttered on such questions was peculiarly important, because it was heard with so much respect in the "infected districts." [1] The "greenback dodge," said the Tribune, was nothing but "sneaking repudiation." It was an "unequivocal and dastardly cheat." [2] It was but a plan for the government "to fix and alter the value of its debt of two and a half billions of dollars at its own good pleasure." [3] The country was to be flooded with irredeemable paper money. The people who wanted such a thing were in debt and wished to stay there, or to get out cheaply; they would not pay what they fairly owed at specie par. [4]

The Tribune, and the Nation, as well as some other well edited journals, constantly kept before their readers a history of the issue and sale of the war loans. Who were the lenders? Not the great banking houses of New York, Boston and Philadelphia; not the great capitalists of foreign countries. Every day the boast had been uttered in the gazettes that the gov-

[1] N. Y. Nation, Jan. 16, 1868.
[2] N. Y. Tribune, Feb. 10, 1868.
[3] Ibid., Jan. 14, 1868.
[4] Ibid., Jan. 4, 1868.

ernment loans represented the savings of multitudes of poor men and women over all the Northern part of America. When the government first offered the five twenties to the people there was but little difference between paper and gold values. Until the public credit declined and the premium on gold increased it was not a great matter in any one's mind whether the principal should be paid in coin or greenbacks. Whenever the question was raised, it was stated plainly and categorically that the contract called for gold. Those who now advocated the redemption of the debt in a depreciated currency had stood by silently until the money had been received and spent. They were repudiators.[1] The greenback scheme as a swindle "far surpassed the old mediæval plan of adulterating and clipping the coinage," said the New York Nation.[2] The man who would do in private life what the Western politicians proposed to do in public life would be "a scoundrel."[3] To follow such leadership would be to destroy the last vestige of the nation's credit. Without credit nationality was impossible. "The nation as a nation would cease to exist." Its life gone, "it would simply hold together till somebody chose to upset it, and the rising generation of Southerners would probably live to see what their fathers died in vain to bring about." Were we to pay our debt with our rags it would be "one of the greatest blows" ever directed at "public morality."[4]

For months it had been quite clear that the Democratic national convention would be largely under the control of, if it should not be captured completely by the inflationists. As the representative of the "Ohio idea" that state offered for the presidency George H. Pendleton. He had been the Democratic nominee for Vice President on the McClellan ticket on the Baltimore platform of 1864 in which the war was declared to be a failure. Of Southern ancestry, and with sympathies for the Confederacy, which had been ill concealed, he with some

[1] Cf. N. Y. Tribune, Jan. 13, 1868; N. Y. Nation, Feb. 6 and July 23, 1868.
[2] N. Y. Nation, Jan. 16, 1868.   [3] Ibid., March 5, 1868.
[4] Ibid., Feb. 6, 1868.

right was called a Copperhead. But his personality was engaging. Fastidious in his dress and polite and chivalrous in
his bearing he was generally known as "Gentleman George."
When he had been a member of Congress in 1862, at the time
the greenbacks were issued by the Republican party as a
measure to forward the war, he had denounced them.[1] Now
he espoused the paper money cause and advocated the entire
inflationist program with all the arts and wiles of a demagogue which his political career abundantly proved him to
be. His leadership was accepted in other states, as well
as in his own, and he was trumpeted throughout the West as
the candidate whom the party must accept, if it were to
receive the support of the people settled beyond the Alleghany
Mountains.

President Johnson was not without a thought that he might
be the Democratic nominee. Many wrote him filling him with
the idea.[2] But he must reconstruct his Cabinet, so his advisers said, and give definite recognition to the party of which
he would be the candidate. Particularly necessary would this
be with reference to the Treasury, the Post Office and the
Interior departments. In any event McCulloch must be displaced. The treatment which was accorded Democrats in the
matter of appointments to subordinate positions by the Secretary of the Treasury had done the leaders of the party serious affront.[3] The removal of this man who was so "treacher-
ous" would be the price of Mr. Johnson's nomination at New
York. To such a suggestion the President paid no heed. To

[1] E.g., on Jan. 29, 1862—"I firmly believe that it [the government]
cannot maintain itself against the shock of the accumulated and manifold dangers which follow, inevitably, closely in the wake of an illegal,
unsound and depreciated government paper currency. . . . Borrow to
the full extent that may be necessary and let us adhere rigidly, firmly,
consistently, persistently and to the end to the principle of refusing
to surrender that currency which the Constitution has given us."—
Cong. Globe, 37th Cong. 2nd sess., pp. 549, 551.
[2] Johnson Papers.
[3] One of McCulloch's leading enemies, R. W. Latham, called him a
"corrupt, debauched incubus." Not for another day should the President
in his "suit of white flannel" continue "to wrestle with this chimney
sweep."—Letter to Johnson dated June 15, 1868, in Johnson Papers.

friends who addressed him on June 24, asking if he would permit his name to come before the convention he replied at length on the 2nd of July. After explaining his courses and policies in familiar language he concluded that he now, as always before, was "in the hands of the people and at their disposal." [1]

General Frank P. Blair of Missouri, a member of a family which had come to think itself almost indispensable to the nation, if it were to have wise guidance, was also asked if he would stand. On June 30 in a letter to Colonel James O. Brodhead he explained his views to the country. There was, he averred, only one way "to restore the government and the Constitution," and this was by the election of a President who would declare the Radical reconstruction acts "null and void," compel the army "to undo its usurpations at the South," and "disperse the carpet bag state governments," which must be superseded by new white governments. Whatever the Senate might do, if the next House were Democratic it would receive the representatives sent to Washington by those white governments. Other men spoke of gold and greenbacks, of the public faith and the public credit. As for him he would restore the Constitution of the country before he would restore its finances.[2] Blair, like Johnson, revealed himself, therefore, as a constitutional Democrat impelled by principles which were the fair inheritance of the party. During the war both had been Republicans of the most outspoken type; now they had gone over completely and unreservedly to the other side.

General Hancock's course in New Orleans, in conciliating the Southern people and undoing some of the mischiefs which were ascribed to Sheridan, made him a favorite with those who believed that the convention should present a military name to offset Grant's claim upon the country as the Republican nominee. Others advocated the nomination of Senator Hendricks of Indiana, an able leader for many years of the Democratic party in the upper branch of Congress.

[1] The draft of this paper, carefully edited, is to be found in the Johnson Papers.
[2] American Annual Cyclopedia for 1868, p. 746; McPherson's Handbook of Politics for 1868, pp. 380-1.

The most astounding suggestion in connection with the convention involved the name of Chief Justice Chase. The movement in his behalf proceeded cautiously. That he would consent to become the candidate of the party was incomprehensible to most of his old friends. Even to suggest such a change of his political allegiance, said the New York Tribune, was to insult a man whose integrity was without a blot.[1] The New York Nation which had criticized him "for seeking the Republican nomination" condemned him "still more strongly" for "coquetting with the Democrats." It was "the greatest scandal of the day,"[2] and proof of his "moral downfall."[3] But if it were not revolting to Mr. Chase on his side to contemplate such associations it was concluded that the party would find it impossible to accept the leadership of a man holding such views on public questions as he was known to entertain. He was "one of the originators of Radicalism," said Welles, "and the promoter of its vagaries, heresies and wrongs."[4] "On any platform," said the New York Tribune, he would be "a pretty candidate for the men whose chief political creed is that the negro is the descendant of the gorilla."[5] It was inconceivable that he would abate any of his faith in universal suffrage of which he had been an advocate from the beginning; impossible also that he, the Secretary of the Treasury under whom the five twenties had begun to be sold, would hold out the right hand of fellowship to repudiators.

But in defiance of all reasonable prediction and expectation the movement to make him the Democratic candidate proceeded and gained in strength. From a party standpoint several considerations recommended his nomination. The New York Herald became his warm advocate. The party which would defeat Grant must adopt heroic measures. Were the Democrats to name Chase as their candidate, said the Herald, they would be taking advantage of the "Republican split" brought about by the impeachment and trial of Johnson. The

[1] March 27, 1868.   [3] N. Y. Nation, June 25, 1868.
[2] Ibid., July 16, 1868.   [4] Welles, vol. iii, p. 379.
                    [5] N. Y. Tribune, March 27, 1868.

Chief Justice practically had been read out of the party by the Radicals. He was in the same position as the seven proscribed Republican senators who had voted for the acquittal of the President. Indeed, he was regarded by many as "the particular marplot who by his rulings and his example" had saved that evil man from the consequences of his multiplied offenses. His course made him "the champion around whom the conservative Republicans ought to rally." [1] With that support, plus the force of the Democratic party, his election might be achieved. He was, said the Herald, "the greatest civilian with a popular name." He would stand as "the great type and representative of the supremacy of constitutional government." [2] Indeed, he was "the only man" suggested for the nomination under whose leadership victory could be expected, the only man who could stand even for a moment against the hero of Appomattox. Grant had given "blood and courage" to the fight; Chase had given "bread and cash." There would be "success" with him; "defeat and death without him." [3]

A considerable body of opportunists within the party, especially in the East, were moved by these and similar arguments to give Chase's candidacy their more or less sincere support. He, on his side, at first to the unconcealed astonishment of his old Republican associates, reaching later to dismay and even to disgust, gave encouragement to the undertaking. Could it be that he would consent to lead the party which had been wrong about slavery, wrong about the war? Could it be that he would surrender his principles so abjectly and bring himself and his great office into the open disrepute in which they together would be held if he were to accept a nomination at the hands of the New York convention? A certain pique because of Radical attacks upon his course during the impeachment trial, which had been entirely correct and which was deserving of praise rather than criticism, was without a doubt influential in determining his action. But over

[1] N. Y. Herald, May 30, 1868.   [2] Ibid., June 1, 1868.
[3] Ibid., June 24, 1868.

and beyond this was the unsatisfied ambition which everyone knew he entertained of reaching by one avenue or another the Presidential office. If he could not attain the desired honor from one party, men said he would accept it from the other.

It was not quite so plain a case for condemnation, for the slightest acquaintance with Mr. Chase would furnish any with assurance that whatever he might do would be done in order and with dignity. There was that in his character which would effectually prevent him from truckling to man or party, from yielding his opinions or his principles. But the fact remains that this episode in his career brought as much personal humiliation to a national figure of great talent and indubitable integrity as his ill-starred intrigue to take the Presidency from Mr. Lincoln in 1864.

He was made to believe that the wish for him to be the New York convention's candidate in 1868 was in the nature of an uprising of the people. It was almost a demand not confined to party lines. Considering "its origin, its growth, its unselfishness," said his friend John D. Van Buren, a son of President Van Buren, and a Democratic leader in New York, "nothing like it" had ever been seen "in politics in any country." He could "well be proud" of such a manifestation of the confidence of men hitherto opposed to him. "No artificial efforts, no organized machinery" could have brought it about.[1] Committees and clubs were formed to promote his interests. In Philadelphia in June one hundred prominent citizens were appointed to visit New York and to present his name to the convention.[2] This man and that wrote him "confidential" and "strictly confidential" letters to which he guardedly replied. He sought no political office, said he. He was "neither candidate nor aspirant." [3] He wanted "no more political distinction or position." [4] But it would gratify him deeply to see the Democracy "turn away from past issues and

[1] Van Buren to Chase, June 9 and September 5, 1868, in Chase Papers, Historical Society of Pa.
[2] Warden, Life of Chase, p. 703.
[3] March 23, 1868, in ibid., p. 683.   [4] Ibid., p. 684.

take for its mottoes: suffrage for all; amnesty for all; good money for all; security for all citizens at home against military despotism and abroad against governmental invasion." [1]

Though he would "greatly prefer to remain disconnected from all political responsibilities," on such a platform already on April 19 he told a correspondent that he "should not be at liberty to refuse the use" of his name.[2] Other statements followed in a similar tone; the press of the country generally discussed the question of his nomination. But if any expected him to abandon his principles they were completely deceived. "What should it profit a man to gain the whole world and lose his own soul?" he wrote to Hiram Barney. He could "refuse the throne of the world" at the price of surrendering the cause of "equal rights."[3] As men continued to write him and visit him to assure him of their willingness to take him without respect to his views he was filled with "surprise." It was "pretty obvious," he believed, that "a large number of the Northern Democrats" had "wearied of the formulas under which for the last ten years they had been led to defeat."[4]

The impeachment trial was not yet done when the Democratic National Committee addressed a letter to the Chief Justice inquiring about his political views with the purpose of finding out if he would be available as a nominee. On May 30 he replied, telling how he had been a Democrat before the war, how he had left the party because of the slavery question, how he had become a Republican, in what respects he had lately agreed with Johnson, in what others he had disagreed with the President. In the main he seemed to be a Democrat on the large constitutional question of state rights. But he adhered to his program for giving the vote to the negroes and for a reconstruction of the South with their active aid. In

---

[1] Warden, p. 684.
[2] To Alexander Long, ibid., p. 686; cf. letter to Theodore Tilton, ibid., pp. 687-9, and letter to Colonel William Brown, ibid., p. 690.
[3] May 29, 1868, in Schuckers, Life of Chase, p. 583.
[4] Schuckers, p. 588, Chase to W. C. Bryant, June 19, 1868.

conclusion he with propriety averred that he did not desire the office of President, or a nomination for it. "Nor do I know," he continued, "that with my views and convictions I am a suitable candidate for any party. Of that my countrymen must judge."[1] Of the plan to repudiate the debt, which he as Secretary of the Treasury had helped to create, he said nothing. On this subject, too, he had the most definite views and everyone knew that they would be held inflexibly. Yet negro suffragist as he was, opposed definitely to the "Ohio idea" as he must be, his candidacy continued to gain friends.

The delegates came from all parts of the country. They were to meet in the garishly decorated new Tammany Hall.[2] It would seat 4,000 people. The heat was intense as the "unterrified" and the "great unwashed"[3] reached the city. Many prominent "rebels" and Copperheads were drawn to the meeting. The long hair, the slouch hats, the Confederate gray clothing of some of the Southern delegates were the subject of Republican comment, meant to reawaken all the angry feelings of the war. Among the number who had come were General N. B. Forrest, the "hero of Fort Pillow"; Wade Hampton, ex-Senator James Chesnut, R. B. Rhett and General Bonham of South Carolina; B. H. Hill and General John B. Gordon of Georgia; General Garland of Arkansas and General Price of Missouri; and that chief of Copperheads, Vallandigham of Ohio whose face had been so unwelcome in the Philadelphia Convention of 1866. What more could be needed in proof of the party's fellowship with disloyalty? The attempt to allay the unfavorable impression created by such scenes through a Soldiers' and Sailors' Convention, called

[1] Schuckers, Life of Chase, pp. 584-6.
[2] A "magnificent temple," said August Belmont, chairman of the National Committee, in welcoming the delegates, "erected to the Goddess of Liberty by her staunchest defenders and most fervent worshippers," the "time-honored Society of Tammany." Cf. Myers, Hist. of Tammany Hall, 2d ed., p. 216.
[3] Again with acknowledgments to the New York Tribune and other Republican gazettes.

to meet in the city at the same time in the hall of the Cooper
Institute, went but a little way in that direction. Such a
"side-show" had invigorated the Republican convention in
Chicago. Here now were Democratic veterans of the war
who upon return to their homes were bidden to persuade their
"late comrades in arms" to yield such candidates as might be
named by the convention in New York "an earnest support."

Henry D. Palmer of Wisconsin was elected temporary chairman and Horatio Seymour of New York permanent chairman
of the nominating convention. The two-thirds rule prevailed;
at least two-thirds, or 212 votes, must be cast for a candidate
before he should be considered the choice of the convention.
The names of as many as eleven men were formally presented,
—Andrew Johnson by his friend Judge Nelson of Tennessee
who had so flamboyantly defended him in the impeachment
trial; Pendleton by General McCook; Sanford E. Church,
whom the New York delegation had determined to support in
the early balloting, by Samuel J. Tilden; General Hancock by
Anderson of Maine.

The suspicions of the Pendleton men had been aroused when
it was announced that the convention would be held in New
York. It was "too near Wall Street." [1] They must be on
their guard lest the meeting fall into the hands of Belmont
and a clique of capitalists. The Ohio delegates came to the
city with counterfeit five dollar bills pinned to their coat
lapels. The West would support Pendleton to the last because he was "right" on the money question, the South because he had been a Copperhead.

The friends of Mr. Chase on the other hand were men who
had correct views in regard to the national finances and "War
Democrats." Headquarters were hired on Fifth Avenue, funds
were assembled and spent. While Chase himself remained in
Washington, playing croquet, as he awaited the letters and telegrams informing him of the progress of events, his accomplished daughter Kate, the wife for some years of the wealthy
young calico manufacturer, the governor of and now United
States senator from Rhode Island, William Sprague, was on

[1] N. Y. corr. Phila. Ledger, July 4, 1868.

the ground representing his interests with devotion. In private
conferences, by letter, through every avenue of acquaintance
and friendship she was constantly in communication with the
leaders in the city upon whom she hoped to exert by her acknowledged graces an influence great enough to bring about
her father's choice. Few women, indeed, have been so eager
or so able to play a prominent part in our politics. It was her
spirited ambition for him and, through him, for herself which
in some degree had brought Mr. Chase to this strange cross-
way in his career.[1]

The text of a platform, which Mr. Chase and Mr. Van Buren
together had written,[2] and upon which the candidate felt that
he could stand, was circulated. It was passed from hand to
hand as a statement of principles "acceptable to some New
York Democrats." Chase himself read it to "several gentlemen of various opinions" in Washington and on July 2 said
that as yet he had "met with no one not ready to accept it."
He "verily" believed that if it should be adopted by the convention it would mark the beginning of "a new era of Democratic ascendency analogous to that inaugurated by Jefferson."[3] But resolutions as different from those which he had

[1] Many letters which passed between her and her father at this time
are to be found in the collection of Chase Papers in the Library of the
Hist. Soc. of Pa. They begin "dearest father" and "dearest Katie"
and evidence the warmest affection. "Oh, if the convention would
only have the courage to do right," she wrote on July 7 from New York.
She wished to see "this bright jewel" added to his "crown of earthly
distinction," she said again. But she continued—"we can love and be
very happy and just as proud of you without it." Another time she
signed herself "affectionately and ambitiously for country, the Democracy and its noblest Patriot and Statesman." Men had written to
Chase from New York with great admiration of her abilities. "I am
afraid, my darling," he said in a letter to her on July 7, "that you are
acting too much the politician. Have a care! Don't do or say anything which may not be proclaimed from the house tops. I am so
anxious about you that I cannot help wishing you were in Narragansett
or here, where I take all things very quietly and play croquet nearly
every evening and sleep as soundly as the heat will let me every
night."
[2] Chase in writing to Van Buren called it "your platform."—Letter
dated July 2 in Chase Papers in Library of Hist. Soc. of Pa.
[3] Chase to Van Buren, July 2, 1868, in Chase Papers in Hist. Soc. of
Pa. This platform is to be found in American Annual Cyclopedia for
1868, pp. 750-51, and Schuckers, Life of Chase, pp. 567-70.

approved as language could make them were reported out of
the committee on Tuesday, the third day of the convention.
The obligations of the government, except when it was stated
positively that they should be discharged in coin, "ought in
right and in justice to be paid in the lawful money of the
United States," i.e., in greenbacks. The whole Republican
policy of reconstruction, including the enfranchisement of the
negroes which had led to black supremacy in ten states, was
condemned as "unconstitutional, revolutionary and void." The
utterances on the money question were received with "thunders
of applause." [1] After the fifth resolution was read and cheered
—"One currency for the government and the people, the la-
borer and the officeholder, the pensioner and the soldier, the
producer and the bondholder" there were shouts of "Read it
again." It was again read and again cheered. Not a phrase
or sentence which Mr. Chase had suggested went into the platform. Having satisfied the West on the money question, and
the South and the Copperhead element in the North on the
subject of reconstruction the convention began to ballot for
candidates.

On the first ballot Pendleton led all others with 105 votes,
while Andrew Johnson had the next highest number, 65. Pendleton gained up to the eighth ballot when he was the choice
of 156 delegates. Then Hendricks came forward under the
leadership of New York, which through Mr. Tilden announced
the withdrawal of "Governor" Church, until on the 21st ballot
the senator from Indiana had polled 132 votes. Meanwhile
Hancock also developed strength; on the 18th ballot he commanded the support of 144 delegates.[2]

Johnson's agents on the ground were industrious and fully
expected that at the crucial hour they could attach a large
body of delegates to his name. They gave him telegraphic
accounts of the "general good feeling" which was entertained

[1] General press report of the proceedings of the convention in Phila.
Ledger, July 8, 1868.
[2] "Leading the men he fought at Gettysburg," a Republican allusion
to the large number of "rebels" and "Copperheads" in the convention.
—Phila. Press, July 8, 1868.

for him. Friends drank toasts to him.[1] His vetoes were "magnificent" and his conduct during the impeachment trial had been "sublime."[2] But he was still importuned to remove McCulloch. There must be a Democrat in the Cabinet so that the country might know that the President was a party man. Groesbeck and others were in mind. But Johnson still stood his ground. He had performed the important feat of carrying away from the Radical Republican party seven Cabinet officers, the Chief Justice and seven of "their most respected, talented and influential senators." It was no time to change front now. He had provided the Democrats with the "only live issue" with which they could go before the people and he was their logical candidate.[3]

Chase had not been named by any delegate until Wednesday, on the 12th ballot, when a Californian gave him a "half vote." This was the signal for "great and long continued applause in the galleries," which delegates on the floor hissed.[4] The hall, said the anti-Chase men, had been packed by the people of New York. Motions were made to clear it. Scenes of "delirious excitement" ensued; the cheering inside the building was taken up in the streets and for ten minutes business was suspended.[5]

The sphinx in the convention, as one day followed another, was the presiding officer. Horatio Seymour had studied law. Inheriting a considerable estate he had retired from practise and was known as a large and prosperous dairy farmer at Utica. Several times before the war he had been the Democratic candidate for Governor; once he had been elected. Again he had been his party's nominee in 1862 and served for

---

[1] As at the Parker House in Boston—

"Once more the bright stars and broad stripes will be floating
   O'er a country united, great, happy and free,
And the hero who conquered the Radical dragon
   Will our country's St. George in our history be."

                                             —Johnson Papers.

[2] R. J. Walker in Johnson Papers.   [3] Johnson Papers.
[4] General press report of the proceedings; see, e.g., Phila. Ledger, July 9, 1868.   [5] Schuckers, p. 585.

two years during the period marked by the memorable draft riots. He then made a record which called down upon his head criticisms from the Republicans affecting his loyalty to the Union and lately, though the West held him to be bound to "Wall Street," had made some equivocal statements on the money question. In the New York state Democratic convention, suiting himself to his hearers, he had said that the bondholder was receiving coin while honest labor was paid in "a debased paper money." Once there were free and slave states; now, the bonds being held in the main "in one corner of the country," there were "debtor states and creditor states." [1]

Such utterances were accounted the more reprehensible because of Mr. Seymour's better knowledge. He was playing the demagogue. His friends admired his easy address and winning manners, while to the other party he was merely a cool, wily and ingenious politician.[2] There had been a wish on several sides, before the convention met, to bring him forward as a candidate. In emphatic terms he had declined at that time and afterward; while the fourth ballot was being taken, when nine votes were cast for him, he said that he "must not be nominated," as he could not accept. His inclinations had led him earlier to refuse; "honor" now impelled him to like action. His name would not be mentioned in the convention against his protest. Thereafter the two very antagonistic elements in the convention, representing West and East, led by Ohio and New York, continued to talk and trade and vote without taking into account a possible change in his mind.

New York would not support Pendleton nor would the delegates, barring a few, from any of the other Eastern states. Ohio spoke of bolting the convention if Chase were nominated.

[1] N. Y. Nation, March 19, 1868.
[2] "Subtle, artful and not always sincere," said Welles. (Vol. iii, p. 383.) His "partyism" predominated over his patriotism. (Ibid., p. 398.) He was a past master in the "slippery use of words," said the Philadelphia Press; "a Democrat disguised as a gentleman."—Phila. Press, Sep. 17, 1868.

From the first the Chief Justice had had friends in the New York delegation which was now voting for Hendricks, and it was given out and believed that at the propitious moment the state would present his name, which in the opinion of good judges of the situation would start a stampede. The Ohio men with their antipathies and feuds would be overwhelmed by the general enthusiasm. The activity of the Chase managers to bring about an understanding between the candidate and the party continued. In order that they might the better secure the votes of delegates who were ready to say that he was not a Democrat they wished to bind him in writing beforehand to an approval of whatever candidates should be nominated, of whatever platform should be adopted. He refused to make such a pledge.[1] His "self respect" was worth more to him "than fifty presidencies." [2] But after resolutions so distasteful to him were adopted by the convention, with a shrewdness which it must have been difficult to assume, he did forbear denouncing them. Only a part of the platform, he said, "a telegraphic abstract," had come before his eyes; he could not approve or condemn until he had seen the whole.[3]

Tilden was openly opposed to the nomination of Chase. But Seymour was supposed to be sincerely in favor of it, and, while in New York, he was a guest in the home of John

---

[1] Alexander Long of Cincinnati had asked for an "unconditional pledge," which Chase would not give. Never in his life had he bound himself to the support of "unknown candidates upon an unknown platform," nor had he ever "asked such promises from anybody." But he did write Long on July 1: "It will afford me great satisfaction to give my vote to all of the distinguished citizens whose names have been prominently mentioned in connexion with the office and who may be selected by the convention, unless, contrary to my expectations, a platform shall be adopted to which I cannot yield my assent without disregard of my settled convictions of duty and of the whole trend of my public life." Fearing that, perhaps, he had gone "too far" he wrote almost immediately afterward to John Van Buren. He hoped that the convention would nominate "upright, honorable and capable men on a right platform," but he could not "assume this in advance" and the more he thought of the subject "the more unwilling" he felt "to make any pledge whatever." Van Buren was asked to visit Long and to "allow no mistake to be made."—Letters in Chase Papers in Hist. Soc. of Pa.

[2] To Long in Schuckers, p. 589.   [3] Warden, pp. 706, 707.

Van Buren so that his movements were under observation.[1]
It was due to his personal influence, according to Mr. Van
Buren, that the sentiment of the New York delegation, which,
when he came to town, contained only 10 Chase men, was
changed until 37 out of 61 expressed a willingness to vote
for the Chief Justice.[2] Thus was a majority gained, and thus
was the state committed to action in the convention. All but
one of the New York city delegates, John Morrissey, pugilist
and gambler, who had been elected to Congress from a Tammany district, all but one from Brooklyn were for Chase.[3]
A majority of the New Englanders favored his nomination and
he had friends in every delegation.[4]

At the last moment Seymour, according to Van Buren, went
so far as to send a carriage for General McCook, the Pendleton leader, in an effort to bring the Ohio men over to the Chase
side.[5] But meanwhile other things came to pass. Mrs.
Sprague and her father's friends, who were buttonholing delegates and making a hundred plans, were told that the Pendleton men, who were "very fractious," must not be offended.
To prevent this there must be no demonstrations prematurely.
The "popular voice" was "all one way."[6] Nothing would be
done to-day; the Chase men must wait until to-morrow. Wisconsin would second the nomination. Massachusetts, Michigan, Tennessee and Rhode Island stood ready to present the
Chief Justice's name, but they were restrained out of consideration for the wishes of New York which desired the honor
for itself.[7]

For days the New York Herald had been predicting treachery on the part of the "old Albany Regency." The scheme
was revealed. Chase was being used merely to bring about the
defeat of Pendleton. There might be honesty among thieves

[1] Kate Chase Sprague to her father, July 2, 1868, in Chase Papers in
Hist. Soc. of Pa.
[2] Van Buren to Chase, Sep. 5, 1868, in Chase Papers, loc. cit.
[3] Van Buren to Chase, July 2, 1868, in Chase Papers.
[4] Schuckers, p. 564.
[5] Van Buren to Chase, Oct. 24, 1868, in Chase Papers.
[6] Mrs. Sprague to her father, July 2, 1868, in Chase Papers.
[7] Alexander Long to Schuckers, July 15, 1868, in Chase Papers.

SEYMOUR AND BLAIR 179

but there was none "among New York politicians."[1] What
was foreseen happened. It was made clear to the Western
delegates that they could not have both the man and the platform. Their repudiation and greenback planks had received
the approval of the convention; they could not fairly expect
to name the candidate.[2] Chase, they were told, was certain to
be nominated on the next ballot and nothing was left to Mc-
Cook and Washington McLean but to make a treaty with New
York. The voting on the 22nd ballot, on Thursday, the fifth
day of the convention, was proceeding without excitement.
Minnesota, Missouri, New York, North Carolina voted for
Hendricks. Then came the thunderbolt. Ohio was called and
McCook rose, at the "unanimous request and demand" of his
delegation, with the assent of Mr. Pendleton, to cast the state's
21 votes for "a man whom the Presidency has sought and who
has not sought the Presidency." He had declined but he must
yield to the desires of the convention. It would be the solution of the problem which had taxed the mind of the party
and the nation and drive from power "the vandals" who now
possessed the capital of the country. Ohio put in nomination
Horatio Seymour of New York.

Men leaped upon their seats, waved their handkerchiefs and
hats, and shouted. The galleries cheered and wild commotion
prevailed, until Seymour came forward upon the platform,
waved his hand for order and in a speech, expressive of his
grateful feelings, again declared that he could not lead the
party. "May God bless you for your kindness," he said, "but
your candidate I cannot be." No account was taken of his
protests. One man after another spoke. One delegation after
another, though it had already voted, added its voice to Ohio's.
Cannon boomed and a band played "The Battle Cry of Freedom" in the street outside, while inside the hall, there was
veritable pandemonium. Every vote, 317 in all, was cast for
Seymour. He was declared to be the convention's unanimous
choice for President. Frank P. Blair of Missouri was quickly

[1] Issue of July 7, 1868.
[2] N. Y. corr. Phila. Ledger, July 8, 1868.

nominated for Vice President and the convention was ready to adjourn.

Seymour's friends had persuaded him to relinquish the chair and he was taken out of the convention. Both he and Blair were found at the Manhattan Club where they were notified of their nomination. On the evening of the next day they attended a ratification meeting in Tammany Hall which was presided over by Samuel J. Tilden. By way of apology for the change which had come over his mind Seymour said that he had been caught by "the overwhelming tide," the pressure of which he had found himself "unable to resist." He promised a more formal acceptance and a full statement of his principles at a later time.

While Blair promptly entered the canvass with the militant vigor which he had displayed in the Brodhead letter Seymour on his side maintained a studied silence. That he personally had played fast and loose with Chase to further his personal ambitions does not seem to accord with the facts. His disinclination to enter the contest was sincere, and he can be fairly charged only with weakness which impelled him at the end to yield to Tilden and the leaders who had prepared the scheme to put him forward as the candidate. This appearance of an infirmity of purpose had caused him disquietude while the convention was in session, and a feeling that he had not explained it away followed him afterward into the campaign.[1]

Men in the convention predicted that he would carry New York by 100,000 [2] and sweep the Union. There is no evidence that he attributed to himself any such power over the American people and little was said now, outside the most narrowly partisan circles, which could serve to increase his courage for

[1] He was called "the Great Decliner." A wag wrote in the New York Tribune (July 17, 1868):

> "There's a queer sort of chap they call Seymour,
> A strange composition called Seymour,
>   Who stoutly declines,
>   Then happiness finds
> In accepting, does Horatio Seymour."

[2] Report of proceedings of convention in Phila. Ledger and N. Y. corr. of same newspaper, July 10, 1868.

the canvass. He knew as well as any that his statements in New York city on July 4, 1863, while he had been governor of the state, in criticism of the military management of the national administration, which was followed so soon by the draft riots,[1] could be used effectively in such a campaign as this was certain to be. The New York Tribune and every other Republican newspaper immediately referred to his record during the war. He had been "the deadliest, most implacable enemy throughout of the ideas which triumphed in the abolition of slavery." If such a man could be elected President over U. S. Grant then "the patriot blood poured out like water at Gettysburg, Vicksburg, Mission Ridge and in the advance to Richmond was shed in vain."[2] To the Philadelphia Press the nomination was "an affront to every Union soldier, an insult to the friends and memory of every dead hero and an offense to every loyal man."[3] The New York Herald which had been advocating the choice of Chase spoke of "the blockheads of the Democratic party." Led by Seymour, who was "the embodiment of Copperheadism," it was a "clear field for General Grant."[4]

The poignancy of Mr. Chase's disappointment, however great it may have been, was concealed by a proud and discreet silence. He had written one of his lieutenants, while the convention was still in session, that he could not "forget the difference between outside speculation and inside decision."[5] But he had been led by his advisers to expect the nomination. So many men had spoken of the result with assurance that a shock must have attended the receipt of the telegram bearing the news. To Mrs. Sprague it brought bitter grief which she also knew how to control.[6]

[1] He had said that "the bloody and treasonable and revolutionary doctrine of public necessity" could be "proclaimed by a mob as well as by a government."
[2] N. Y. Tribune, July 10, 1868.
[3] Phila. Press, July 10. He was "the mob law candidate on a repudiation platform."—Ibid., July 13, 1868.
[4] N. Y. Herald, July 10 and 11, 1868.
[5] To Fred'k A. Aiken on July 4, 1868, in Chase Papers in Hist. Soc. of Pa.   [6] Warden, pp. 705-6.

The manner in which Chase's defeat was accomplished could but increase the painfulness of the wound. It was not difficult to understand how insincere were the pledges and professions of some of the men who were accounted to be his friends. The platform in the first place was but a series of indignities in view of his known opinions upon public questions, if ever there had been serious thought of asking him to stand upon it as the party candidate. As the calm and impartial presiding officer of the impeachment court of but six weeks ago it was ungrateful to him to find among the resolutions adopted by the convention a declaration that Andrew Johnson, "in exercising the powers of his high office, in resisting the aggressions of Congress upon the constitutional rights of the states," was "entitled to the gratitude of the whole American people." Still less to his mind were the propitiatory words, a sop as it appeared to one who could not be given more, about "the learned Chief Justice" who had been "subjected to the most atrocious calumnies, merely because he would not prostitute his high office to the support of the false and partisan charges preferred against the President." [1]

No one of all the candidates, not even Pendleton, held views so irreconcilable with Chase's as Frank Blair, a member of a family which had antagonized him in Lincoln's cabinet and the advocate of policies directly at variance with his own.[2] Yet this enemy was nominated unanimously for Vice President. The leaders of his own state of Ohio by their uncompromising opposition had accomplished his defeat with the assistance of Mr. Tilden, who did not try to conceal his hostility, the vacillating Mr. Seymour and other men in New York who had seemed to be acting as friends.[3]

The press by its course, as is its wont, made the disappoint-

---

[1] Specifically mentioned by Chase as being distasteful to him in later correspondence with Van Buren in Chase Papers in Hist. Soc. of Pa.

[2] Cf. Letters of the Blairs to Tilden, Letters and Memorials of S. J. Tilden, vol. i, pp. 232-3, 240, 246.

[3] Seymour's nomination, Welles said, was intended from the first. It was effected by "duplicity deceit, cunning management and sharp scheming."—Vol. iii, pp. 379, 381, 382, 383, 396, 398.

ment no easier to bear.[1] But no regret or recrimination escaped the Chief Justice. Not now, nor at any later day did he indulge in criticism of those who had had a hand in bringing to his door this great humiliation.

The managers of his campaign were not disposed to follow the good rule which he had laid down for the guidance of his own conduct. They believed, with some justice, that they had been thimblerigged and they were in no pleasant humor. They would yet compel Seymour to withdraw. They wished the Chief Justice to become the candidate of a third party. This suggestion was made to him after he had failed to receive the Republican nomination in May,[2] without winning his favor. Now again on several sides he was requested to become a "people's candidate."[3] In these movements Chase himself had no hand. When he did speak to one of his intimates it was to say that his nomination had been desired only for the sake of "bringing the Democratic party into a just and generous assertion of democratic ideas which would enable it to command success." "Except as the representative of such ideas" his name was of "no value to the party," and "unless taken as the representative of such ideas," the nomination

---

[1] "Concerning Chase it turns out now that it was rather a deep game that the Democratic leaders had been playing. The game was to toy with him long enough to detach him from his party and then drop him."—N. Y. corr. Phila. Ledger, July 10, 1868. The Sandusky Register published the following advertisement—"Wanted—A knot-hole of unusually small size. Address S. P. Chase, Washington, D. C."

[2] Warden, p. 698.

[3] There are a number of letters asking him to lead a third party movement in the Chase Papers in the Hist. Soc. of Pa. (Cf. Warden, p. 703.) The "disgust" because of "the treachery of Tammany Hall" was widespread. (Chas. S. Halpine to Chase, July 11, 1868, in Chase Papers, loc. cit.) Money had passed between New York and Ohio. The corrupt instrument in this dirty deal was Washington McLean. (Long to Schuckers July 15, 1868, in Chase Papers.) Long, who had gone back to his home in Ohio, was busily pressing Chase's friends to write and telegraph to Seymour. All knew that he did not desire the nomination; it was received coldly by the country and doomed the party to defeat. (Long to Seymour from Cincinnati, July 14, 1868, in Chase Papers.) Seymour was weak and timid, said Long. The thing to do was "to thunder away at him" and compel him to withdraw. (Long to Schuckers, July 15, 1868, in Chase Papers.)

would have had "less than no value" to him. He wanted this understood, and he wanted it understood also that his position removed him "from active participation in party strife."[1] He had no thought of "going into a third party movement." Nothing now, in his judgment, made this course advisable. He would leave such labors to younger men.[2]

To Andrew Johnson and those who moved in his circle the nomination was equally unwelcome.[3] They completely distrusted Seymour and, with reason, for he had told them that he would decline the nomination in the President's interest, just as he had made similar promises to the Chase men with reference to their candidate.[4] Johnson had been "swindled in the very moment of victory."[5] McCulloch and Browning said that Seymour next to Pendleton was the "worst selection that could have been made."[6] Doolittle had been in New York; his resentment approached disgust.[7] He, like Chase, was urged to let his name be used as the candidate of an independent third party.[8] The New York Democrats by their trickery, said Welles, had "put in jeopardy an election which they might have made certain."[9]

Meanwhile the Republican nominee was travelling through the West. Sage students of the subject of the conduct of nominees for popular office now directed Grant's movements, and his own impulses led him to flee the political scene, leaving the conduct of the campaign to other men.[10] For a time he should re-establish his home at Galena, where he, at the outbreak of the war, had been employed in his father's store, buying hides and selling leather; he should again become a

[1] Chase to Schuckers, July 20, 1868, in Schuckers, Life of Chase, p. 590.
[2] To John Colyer in Schuckers, p. 591.
[3] Welles, vol. iii, pp. 398, 402, 403.
[4] Philo Durfee to Johnson, July 8, 1868, in Johnson Papers.
[5] Johnson Papers.   [6] Welles, vol. iii, p. 401.
[7] Ibid., pp. 402, 405.   [8] Ibid., p. 405.   [9] Ibid., p. 399.
[10] A crowd surrounded Grant at Jersey City while he was hurrying to a train. "What do you think of the present political prospect?" said one. "I don't think of it at all at this time," Grant replied. "My principal object just now is to catch the train."—Phila. Ledger, June 22, 1868.

resident of Illinois. He left Washington in a special car on the last day of June to visit his parents in Covington, Ky. The Fourth of July found him at his birthplace, Point Pleasant, a little town in Ohio near Cincinnati. He spent several days in this neighborhood, visiting the places in southern Ohio and northern Kentucky at which he had attended school, meeting friends and relations, and renewing the associations of his youth. Committees received him, guns were fired in his honor, bands played. He was the victorious general, now a candidate for the Presidency, coming near to the people, quietly asking them for their votes.

Soon he was at Sherman's headquarters in St. Louis, and two favorite military names could be linked in the minds of the people. While here he visited his farm, located a few miles out of the city on the Gravois Pike. Grant and Sherman started west together to meet Sheridan at Fort Leavenworth, sent there by Johnson in unmerited exile, as the Northern Radicals believed, for his policy in New Orleans. Now the three commanders of the Northern armies stood side by side, appealing to the political imaginations of the people, as they had appealed earlier to the nation's sense of loyalty and patriotism. All together proceeded over the line of the new Kansas Pacific Railroad to Denver, and returned by the Union Pacific to Omaha and Council Bluffs. Early in August Grant was in Chicago and in a little while in his old home in Galena, to which he returned after an absence of three years to occupy the house which his townsmen had presented to him at the end of the war. The locomotives of the trains which bore him from place to place were decorated with flags and wreaths. Everywhere committees met him, crowds acclaimed him, guns boomed and music filled the air.[1]

It was alleged by the Democrats that he was a "drunkard," but so much also was said by the Republicans for Blair; that he was a "butcher" in the light of his campaign in the Wilderness; that his military reputation was an accident and with-

[1] N. Y. Tribune, July 23, 24, 28 and Aug. 3 and 4.

out foundation in knowledge or skill; that he had been involved in corrupt contracts during the war.[1] He knew nothing of statesmanship. He could not make a speech. The party might have "a deaf and dumb candidate"; the country could not afford to elect "a deaf and dumb president." [2] But the favorite argument of his opponents in the campaign was to call him "a man on horseback." He was a military hero who would become a dictator. Once in the White House he would remain there, serving as a kind of uncrowned emperor who would lead the republic to its fall.

Whatever might be said about Grant, truly or falsely, it was certain that he was not a "show candidate." He was of little use to his campaign managers for "spectacular purposes." [3] He shook hands with thousands, but without enthusiasm. Appeals to him for addresses were invariably declined, or were responded to so briefly and awkwardly as to awaken the sympathy rather than the admiration of his auditors.[4] But there was refreshment in the sight of such a candidate. He was taken for a plain, rugged, unassuming man who had had no affiliation with politicians, who was now gaining no acquaintance with their arts, who would in future keep himself free from their influences. Colfax was the orator on the ticket. He stumped the West as far out as Denver with the affable fluency for which he had been valued when the leaders in the convention were looking around them for a candidate for Vice President.

The campaign increased in warmth as the time drew near for a test of strength in the September and October states. The Republican National Committee was organized with Wil-

[1] Amusing summaries of the various campaign libels upon the candidates are to be found in the N. Y. Nation, July 16, 23, 30, Aug. 6, 20, 27.

[2] N. Y. World, June 29, 1868.   [3] N. Y. Nation, Sep. 24, 1868.

[4] A speech which he was importuned to make at St. Joseph, Mo., is reported as follows: "I thank you for this very cordial reception, but I cannot make you a speech. I have been travelling all the time for the past two weeks in the western country and it is the first time I have ever been in the west. I am tired and worn out and dusty. I would like to make you a speech but I cannot do so."—N. Y. Tribune, August 3, 1868, quoting St. Joseph Union.

liam Claflin of Boston as chairman, and William E. Chandler
as secretary. They appealed to the country for funds to conduct the campaign, exacting large sums from the promoters
of land grant railroads and the leaders in those branches of
finance and industry who had been enriched by the war and
were hopeful of receiving future benefits from the government.
At no time before in the history of presidential elections had
demands been so insolent; never, as later appeared, though
it was without Grant's present knowledge, was a candidate put
under so great a burden of obligation to rich men, which he
would be asked to repay.[1]

No place was too small for a mass meeting. Stump speakers
appeared in every hamlet. Not a township that did not have a
pole raising and a flag. Grant had been a tanner. "Tanneries"
were built. Men formed campaign clubs, called themselves
"Tanners" and marched about carrying lighted flambeaus, and
transparencies lettered in praise of the Republican candidates
and policies and in derogation of the Democracy and its alliances with rebellion. The soldiers returned from the war were
organized as "Boys in Blue," and in bright new uniforms under
banners, amid red fire and bursting bombs, swarmed in torchlight processions through the streets of towns and cities.

It was certain that Grant would be elected, so thought, so
said nearly every one, but nowhere was effort to be relaxed
until the sure expectation became an accomplished fact. Every
impulse of loyalty to the Union, every patriotic consideration,
all the grateful instincts of the nation awakened by his prominent part in bringing the war to a successful end were called
upon as the canvass proceeded. Day after day the New York
Tribune headed its political news with Miles O'Reilly's—

> "So, boys! a final bumper
>   While we all in chorus chant,
> For next President we nominate
>   Our own Ulysses Grant;
> And if asked what state he hails from,
>   This, our sole reply shall be,
> From near Appomattox Court House,
>   With its famous apple tree."

[1] See e.g., an account of the demands made on Jay Cooke by William
E. Chandler in Oberholtzer, Jay Cooke, vol. ii, p. 69-71.

More effective than any other device of the campaign, than speech by Colfax, or Henry Wilson, or Sumner, or Stanton, or any parade of "Tanners" or "Boys in Blue" was the activity of the late leaders of the rebellion in the South in espousing the cause of Seymour. "Scratch a Democrat and you'll find a rebel under his skin," said the New York Tribune.[1] Robert Toombs, Benjamin H. Hill, General Forrest, "Pirate" Semmes, Howell Cobb, Wade Hampton, Zebulon Vance and many others, some of them delegates to the New York convention, all known as leaders in the war on the Southern side, were speaking for Seymour. Nothing that they said was allowed to escape the readers of Republican newspapers.

Meantime in the South itself disorder was rampant. Both parties strove to carry the reorganized states for their candidates. The bitterest feeling prevailed everywhere. Some of the affrays between white and black men reached the proportions of riots. Assassinations and massacres were daily occurrences. These crimes of the Democrats upon the Republicans, as they were represented to be in the North, were set forth day by day to inflame the popular mind. The war was refought from Sumter to Appomattox.

The campaign on the Democratic side for this reason and on other accounts made no very favorable progress. General Blair actively stumped the West, giving voice to his violent opinions as they had been presented to the country in his "bloody letter" to Brodhead. Seymour made public a letter of acceptance on August 4, when he again relapsed into silence, except for some short addresses in response to serenaders at Utica, and a speech or two at county fairs. Three of Chase's lieutenants, William Brown, Henry Reed and Alexander Long, came forward early in September and told some of the secrets of the charnel house, to create a flutter of amusement throughout the country. They distinctly charged Seymour with double dealing. He had been shown the Chase platform, which in the plainest terms advocated negro suffrage and the honest payment of the public debt, and had approved it. The im-

[1] Aug. 4, 1868.

plication was plain, therefore, that as a candidate on a Blair-Pendleton platform the head of the Democratic ticket was an insincere man. Moreover, so it was said, he had in his pocket at the very moment of his treachery a speech which he was to deliver to the convention when Chase should be nominated, congratulating the delegates upon the wisdom of their choice. After his breach of faith in accepting the honor for himself he had wept in a private room "for hours like a newly weaned baby." As a "weeper" he was the equal of Job Trotter.[1]

Such revelations were extremely unwelcome to the Democrats, as it was known by those who made them that they would be. Van Buren and others had cherished the hope that for the assistance of the Democratic party in the campaign the Chief Justice might be induced to make a declaration in favor of Seymour. Now it would not be easy to bring so much about. Van Buren reviewed the whole subject from his standpoint in correspondence with Chase. Seymour had shrunk from the nomination "with absolute dread,"[2] and he had "never ceased a single day since the convention to reproach himself for yielding."[3] The nomination had "plunged him into a sea of troubles."[4] Doolittle had announced his intention of supporting the ticket and Chase was asked to follow the example. The Chief Justice was reminded that 4,999 out of every 5,000 in New York and Brooklyn had been ready in July to take the man and ask no questions about his views. Would he "throw away this mass of new made but earnest personal friends?" His political future lay in this direction. The party yet would be brought to accept his leadership.[5]

Before the convention had met Chase, in writing to Van Buren, had said that, of course, whether he should be nominated or not, his "judicial position" would forbid his taking "any active part in the election." He could only cast his

---

[1] N. Y. Nation, Sep. 10, 1868; N. Y. Tribune, Sep. 4 and 5, 1868.
[2] To Chase, Sep. 5, 1868, in Chase Papers in Hist. Soc. of Pa.
[3] To Chase, Oct. 24, 1868, in Chase Papers.
[4] Seymour to a friend, N. Y. Nation, Sep. 10, 1868.
[5] Cf. Van Buren to Chase, July 27, 1868, in Chase Papers.

vote.[1] He easily resisted the attempts made on the Democratic as well as the Republican side to involve him personally in the canvass. He deplored the outburst of his lieutenants in September, which was meant to embarrass Mr. Seymour, but avoided making a public statement on the subject.[2] If he had soiled his gown, as his enemies alleged, in expressing his willingness to be a candidate for the Presidency, his course now during the campaign cannot have given the most cavilling of his judges ground for fair criticism.

The election in Vermont for state officers and Congressmen on the first day of September would furnish an index of the state of popular feeling in the country at large. That day came. The majority for the Republican candidate for governor was about 27,000, nearly 7,000 greater than in the previous year, indeed, it was almost as large as Lincoln's in 1864. There was great rejoicing among the Republicans and they now looked forward confidently to the result in another "September state." "As goes Maine so goes the Union" was an old adage in American politics. The election on September 14 gave the Republicans a majority of about 22,000. The receipt of this news was the signal for mass meetings and torchlight processions in all parts of the Union, and particularly in those states which would vote in October. The entire strength of the party organization was brought to bear upon the wavering in Pennsylvania, Ohio and Indiana. Ex-Secretary Stanton, General Sickles, John Sherman and Hannibal Hamlin were the speakers announced for a meeting in Philadelphia on the 15th. Thousands of marching men formed "a line of fire" in the streets. Grant's words "Let us have peace!" stood upon transparencies everywhere. One club bore aloft a banner with the inscription "William Penn was a carpetbagger." Another presented a rude picture of Seymour being overturned by smoke from Grant's cigar blown towards him by a blast from Maine. Still another depicted Grant in an apron. He had tanned the hides of Lee and the Southern

[1] Chase to Van Buren, July 1, 1868, in Chase Papers.
[2] Chase's letter to Brown in Schuckers, pp. 592-93.

generals; he offered now to do as much for Seymour and Blair.[1] On the same night in Cincinnati, Cleveland and other cities there were similar scenes and as the days passed the excitement increased.

On October 1 and 2 the campaign reached its climax in Pennsylvania, where so much energy was being expended in behalf of the Republican ticket on account of the state's action in returning a Democratic majority in 1867. To invigorate the voters the Grant managers organized a "national mass convention" of soldiers and sailors and a meeting of "loyal governors and ex-governors." The delegates met in the open air in Independence Square, which was decorated lavishly for the occasion. General Burnside presided. Scores of major and brigadier generals were named as vice presidents and secretaries. A characteristic letter was received from Sherman, affirming his love for Grant but an unalterable determination "to keep out of political assemblages, conventions and controversies altogether"; another similarly characteristic of its author, from Sheridan, saying that it was "as essential" to elect Grant in 1868 as "to have an Appomattox in 1865." The streets of the city both day and night again were filled with processions of marching men. Resolutions emphasizing the Democratic party's alliances with the South and its efforts to foment "a new rebellion" were adopted, and "every citizen who wore the Union blue, whether on land or sea," was implored to cast his vote for Grant and Colfax. Thousands of persons were drawn to Philadelphia for this crowning effort to carry Pennsylvania for the Republicans.

Tuesday, October 13, was the eventful day. The allegations that large numbers of thugs were brought into Philadelphia from New York and Baltimore and were allowed to vote the Democratic ticket, that men from Kentucky were "colonized" in Ohio and Indiana for the same purpose, that foreigners were naturalized and enfranchised illegally to affect the result were made and could not be denied.[2] Fisticuffs, shootings

---

[1] Phila. Press, Sep. 16, 1866.
[2] See, e.g., N. Y. Nation, Oct. 15, 1868.

and small riots marked the day in Philadelphia as well as in other places.[1] Satisfactory majorities were obtained for the Republican candidates in all of the "October states" to the great delight of the Radicals. Ohio was carried for Grant by about 17,000, Pennsylvania, by 10,000, Nebraska, by 2,000, Indiana, by 1,000. The party came out of the election, said the New York Nation, "with a perfect certainty of success in the Presidential contest." The Democracy had nothing whatever to hope for except within the limits of New York City.[2]

The New York World, which was aggressively leading the Democratic press, embraced the opportunity to suggest that Seymour and Blair should retire and that other candidates should be designated. The hour had struck. If "mistakes" had been made they "should be corrected now."[3] "A bold manœuvre after a repulse in the field of battle" had often saved the day.[4] The blame was laid at the door of Blair, Seymour's "misplaced associate."[5] It was he, in particular, who was antagonizing the country and solidifying the opposition to the ticket. He was not a Democrat and the convention had gravely erred when it nominated him.[6]

The National Intelligencer in Washington suggested that the party take refuge behind the name and achievements of Andrew Johnson. Many wrote to the President to express the wish that he might be selected even at this late day and he was ready, if the opportunity had presented itself, to lead the campaign.[7] Friends did not cease to remind him of the party's "ingratitude." He had done "more than any living man" to give it "vitality." "All is due to your noble course," wrote Senator Dixon. "But for your courage and patriotism what would the Democracy now be?" He would receive the

---

[1] Phila. Press, Oct. 14, 1868.   [2] N. Y. Nation, Oct. 15 and 22, 1868.
[3] N. Y. World, Oct. 15, 1868.   [4] Ibid., Oct. 16, 1868.
[5] Ibid., Nov. 5, 1868.
[6] This notwithstanding the fact that the World, speaking the day after the nomination had been made, approved it on the ground that he was "a Westerner" and a Republican who was "disgusted with the revolutionary measures of his party."—N. Y. World, July 10, 1868.
[7] Welles, vol. iii, pp. 454, 455, 458, 459.

"thanks of posterity"; the future historian would point to his messages as "the best defense and illustration of the constitutional principles of our government." [1]

Others turned to Chase and advocated his nomination. To all who conversed with him upon the subject he was quite non-committal. But his sentiments were not incorrectly interpreted by Van Buren, who was at Utica at the time, and who took it upon himself to decline the honor for the Chief Justice. Those who had placed Seymour on the ticket should hold him there. The candidate himself felt it a duty "to stick"; it would be "mean," he told Van Buren, "to shift his misfortunes upon some other's shoulders," which in his heart, however, he was still willing enough to do. [2]

The World's suggestion was widely discussed. Members of the Democratic National Committee said that the proposal was "absurd"; the masses of the party had received it "with astonishment, derision and indignation." [3] Tilden and August Belmont made a statement over their joint signatures in which they alleged that "to change front" now would be "totally impracticable and equivalent to disbanding" their forces. [4]

"It is the business of leaders to lead," said the New York World. The crisis was "supreme." The Democratic masses awaited "the inspiring voice and the authentic word." [5] At last Seymour was goaded into activity. Johnson in a telegram urged him to stump the country against "the despotic power now ready to enter the very gates of the citadel." It was hoped that he would speak with an "inspired tongue." [6] Seymour was at Buffalo when the President's appeal reached him. From that place he proceeded west to Cleveland, Chi-

---

[1] Johnson Papers.
[2] Van Buren to Chase, Oct. 24, in Chase Papers in Hist. Soc. of Pa.
[3] Letters and Memorials of S. J. Tilden, vol. i, p. 250.
[4] Washington despatch in Phila. Press, Oct. 17, 1868. Cf. their statements of Oct. 20 to the Democracy of the country as chairmen of the national and New York state committees respectively in Phila. Press (Oct. 22, 1868), which called them "farewell addresses" and "death rattles."   [5] Oct. 17, 1868.
[6] Despatch from Buffalo to Phila. Press, Oct. 24, 1868; cf. N. Y. Nation, Oct. 29, 1868.

cago (where he was on October 24) and Detroit, and came back by way of Indianapolis, Columbus, Pittsburgh and Philadelphia, addressing Democratic crowds in these cities and in many smaller places. Fatigue led him to decline invitations to speak in New Jersey and New York. He returned to his home in Utica through Wilkesbarre and other towns in northern Pennsylvania.

The Republican candidate quietly pursued his way in the West. He was again with Sherman at St. Louis in October, but remained for the greater part of the time in semi-seclusion at his home in Galena. The impression created by his unobtrusive conduct was excellent. The poet, George H. Boker, voiced the nation's determination to

> "Crown his shy worth with gratitude and lay
> The nation's rod at his scarce willing feet
> That so his mission may be made complete."[1]

The Democratic effort to turn the strong tide of enthusiasm for Grant was unavailing. The elections on the 3rd of November gave him decisive majorities. Those states which had chosen governors in September and October now increased their Republican majorities. It was a pleasant triumph for the Radicals. Their newspapers proclaimed the victory in such lines as "The Second Rebellion Closed"—"Peace! Peace! Peace!"—"The Union Men of the South Rescued"—"Repudiation Repudiated"—"Blair Declared Unconstitutional, Null and Void"—"The Union Ballot Like the Union Bullet Invincible"—"The Men Who Saved Shall Rule the Republic."[2] The majority in Massachusetts was 77,000; in Illinois, 51,000; in Iowa, 46,000; in Ohio, 41,000; in Pennsylvania, 28,000; in Missouri, 25,000. The Democrats carried only eight states—Delaware, Georgia, Kentucky, Louisiana, Maryland, Oregon, New York and New Jersey—New York by a majority of about 10,000, by reason of the peculiar exertions of "Tammany" in New York City, and New Jersey by a majority of less than 3,000. Frauds of the grossest kinds were undoubt-

[1] N. Y. Tribune, Oct. 13, 1868.
[2] Phila. Press, Phila. North American, N. Y. Tribune, Nov. 4, 1868.

edly perpetrated by the Democratic managers in the interest
of their ticket in both states.[1] In New York at the instigation
of the Union League Club the irregularities became the subject of a Congressional investigation.[2]

Georgia and Louisiana had been captured for Seymour by
"intimidation" of the negroes who were made to believe that
if they tried to vote it would be at the peril of their lives.
Three Southern states, still in course of reorganization, Mississippi, Virginia and Texas, were not ready for the election
and did not participate in it.

On election day Grant quietly visited the polls in Galena
and in the evening received the reports as they came in over
the telegraph wires at the home of his friend, Congressman
E. B. Washburne. He soon made ready to return to Washington. A great demonstration awaited him there, but he
eluded those who had arranged to welcome him. He arrived
at the railway station at an unexpected hour and was driven
to his home in a public hack. Few knew that he was in the
city until he was espied walking about the streets on the following day on his way to headquarters which, during his
absence of four months had been in charge of General Rawlins.
Committees urged that he consent to a formal reception to
be prepared in his honor, but he so much discouraged them
that they were constrained to abandon their plans.

The prospect was viewed with complete satisfaction by the
friends of good government. Grant's election, it was believed,
would bring tranquillity to the turbulent South. It gave assurance of an honest payment of the public debt, a feeling
now voiced in the exchanges dealing in government securities,
both at home and abroad. The new President would be free
of all alliances with politicians and might improve upon the
methods of Lincoln in the distribution of the offices,—these
could be held for worthy and efficient men. He had been bred
in a school in which the meaning of the words "honor" and

[1] N. Y. Nation, Nov. 5 and 12, 1868; Myers, Hist. of Tammany Hall,
2d ed., pp. 218-9.
[2] House Reports, 40th Cong. 3rd sess., no. 31 and no. 41.

"merit" were understood. Through his administration of the
army he had come to know good men when he saw them, and
would "clasp" them to him "with hooks of steel." Both by
"education and temperament" he was "the foe of jobbers, in-
triguers and blatterers" and soon he would make several important branches of the public service what the army and the
navy were—"a credit to the country instead of a shame and
scandal." [1]

The four months left to President Johnson, after the election
of Grant, droned on for him and the members of his unhappy
administration. He lost no enemy and gained no friend.
Congress counted the days until he should be remanded to
private life in the obscure town in Tennessee where he had
operated the tailor's goose, had been alderman and the rest
of it which by much repetition he had made so familiar to
the people of the land. No whit of his political creed did he
surrender. Whatever else history shall say of him there must
be agreement in the view that unto the end he kept to his
course consistently. While the Democrats were assembling
for their nominating convention in New York he had seized
upon the sentiment attached to the Fourth of July as an
excuse for issuing a proclamation extending, since the late
"lamentable civil war" had "long since altogether ceased," full
pardon and amnesty to all who had been engaged in the rebellion, except such as might be at the time under presentment
or indictment in any court of the United States upon the
charge of treason.[2] The Christmas season induced him, on
December 25, to return to this subject. In another proclamation all, without condition, were restored to their rights,
privileges and immunities under the Constitution.[3] These
state papers were couched in language fully expressive of the
President's dissent from the new view of the nature of the
Federal government, which the Radicals in Congress were
finding it to their convenience and advantage to expound.

[1] N. Y. Nation, Oct. 29, 1868.
[2] McPherson, Hist. of Recon., p. 344.
[3] Ibid., p. 419.

But they fell heavily upon the public ear. None would waste a word upon the author of them.

The Fourteenth Amendment had gone out to the states. It had been ratified by 23 in the North and by Tennessee and West Virginia. Several Southern states which had just been readmitted to the Union followed. But two, Ohio and New Jersey, having elected Democratic legislatures, now attempted by resolution to withdraw their approval. The right to do this was clearly doubtful [1] and on July 20 Secretary Seward issued a statement certifying to the ratification of the amendment. He counted all the states, including those which had not yet been reconstructed. He found that there were 37 and, by some explanation and evasion, reached the conclusion that three-fourths had now regularly acted with favor upon the measure. The next day Congress, reciting that 29 states had ratified it, directed Seward to promulgate it as a part of the Constitution of the United States,[2] an act which he performed under date of July 28.[3]

Congress had adjourned on July 27 until the third Monday in September, faithful to its policy of keeping watch upon the President. A considerable number of senators and representatives assembled in their respective halls in the Capitol on that day. It was merely to adjourn until October 16, when, after prayers, four senators and a handful of representatives formally met and adjourned until November 10, at which time five senators and a few members of the other house, after hearing from the chaplains, adjourned until the first Monday in December, the regular meeting day.

The "short session," which would come to an end with President Johnson's term, was largely occupied with efforts to insult him. One after another of his nominations to office were rejected by the Senate. Two whom he had named for the Russian mission, three named to be minister to Ecuador,

---

[1] A state, said Charles Sumner, could no more withdraw its assent to a constitutional amendment than it could withdraw from the Union. —American Annual Cyclopedia for 1868, p. 196.
[2] McPherson, Hist. of Recon., pp. 379-80.   [3] Ibid., pp. 417-19.

five for the commissionership of internal revenue failed of confirmation and the places remained vacant. S. S. Cox and H. A. Smythe were rejected in turn when they were nominated to be minister to Austria. Any one known to be a friend or a partisan of the President met the opposition of the Senate. Practically all the names sent in in connection with Federal offices in his own state of Tennessee were rejected. Not one man nominated to officer the new territory of Wyoming was allowed to qualify.[1]

Johnson's annual message in December, 1868, his fourth and last, was a re-statement of his views in advocacy of a strict construction of the Constitution and of his part in the attempt to make these views prevail against the opposition of Congress. It was "an axiom in the government of states," said he, "that the greatest wrongs inflicted upon a people are caused by unjust and arbitrary legislation." With this in mind he entered upon a denunciation of the enactments of Congress concerning reconstruction during the past three years. The policies of that body had been tried and they had failed. Evil had accrued not only to the South but to the entire Union.

Finishing with this topic he addressed himself to the national finances. Contrary to the advice of members of his Cabinet and to their regret [2] he made it plain that he was on the side of the fiat money men, who, through the efforts of Stevens, Butler and others, had been undermining the sound foundations of the Republican party on this subject, and had captured the whole Democratic party organization, following the lead of the Pendleton men. The President's allusions to "favoring a few at the expense of the many," to a "moneyed aristocracy," and the "rights of the people" were the words of a demagogue. He spoke with favorable expectation of a return to specie payments, but he clearly indicated his sympathy for the elements in the West and the South which were preaching mischievous doctrines about the national debt.

---

[1] Senate Executive Journal, vol. xvi.
[2] Welles, vol. iii, pp. 478-9.

There was gold in interest and principal, said he, for the owner of a five twenty bond, but only "depreciated paper" in pension money for the wounded soldier of the war; in salaries for men engaged in government service, whether civil or military; in "just and hard earned dues" for the farmer and the artisan. He advocated some arrangement with the bond-holders by which all payments of interest should be counted as payments of principal. A man who received six dollars a year for sixteen years and a fraction was to be brought to feel that he had received the principal of one hundred dollars in full.

Johnson's scheme was "more impudent," said the New York Nation, than any which yet had been devised.[1] Hitherto it had been a question whether the debt should be paid in green-backs or in coin, said Senator Cattell; now the President proposed that it should not be paid at all.[2] The "unvarnished proposition" was, said Senator Frelinghuysen, that this "young Christian republic" should pay the interest on its debt for 16 or 17 years, and then that the debt itself should be repudiated.[3]

The other outstanding feature of the message was a re-statement of Mr. Johnson's plans for the amendment of the Constitution which he had presented to Congress in July, providing (1) That the President and Vice President should be elected by a direct vote of the people; (2) That some one should be designated to act as President in the event of vacancies in the offices of both President and Vice President; (3) That United States senators should be elected by popular vote; (4) That Federal judges should serve only for limited terms of years. This series of proposals, like the President's utterances on the financial question, were held to be inexpedient by members of the Cabinet noted for their good sense; that Mr. Johnson had insisted upon making them a part of his message was a subject of regret.[4]

[1] Issue of Dec. 17, 1868.
[2] Cong. Globe, 40th Cong. 3rd sess., p. 66.
[3] Ibid., p. 44.   [4] Cf. Welles, vol. iii, pp. 406-8, 478.

The message was well written and was the work, like those which had preceded it, of another hand. The President's secretary, Colonel Moore, presented it at the bar of the Senate and the reading began. It was not quarter done; Congress was being denounced for the cost of executing laws in the South "both unnecessary and unconstitutional," when Conness of California rose with a motion to print. Further reading should be dispensed with. It was a "tirade against Congress"; it was "an offensive document." Time could be better employed than in hearing it. Howe supported Conness, as did Cameron, and upon a motion to adjourn, offered by Edmunds, the Senate did so by a vote of 26 to 22.[1] The next day Edmunds called up the subject and asked that the reading be resumed "for the benefit of the country," that the people could see "what sort of an official" they had "at the head of the government." So the secretary proceeded to the end, when the Senate agreed to a motion that the message be laid upon the table and be formally printed.[2]

In the House the reading proceeded without interruption. But it was no sooner finished than many rose to denounce the paper. Some did not wish to have it printed. Others thought that Johnson was so "dead," killed by his own hand, that to make so much ado about what he said and did not say was honor which he should not enjoy. Here, too, the message was laid on the table with an order to print.[3]

The Radical press also found no merit in the document. The New York Nation described it as "a disquisition on public affairs" which was "marked by stupidity and dishonesty in about equal measure." To discuss the President's theories would be a "waste of time and paper." [4] It was, said the New York Tribune, "his worst and fortunately his last insult to the American people." Congress had never more truly expressed "the spirit of the nation than when it trampled contemptuously upon this miserable message and left it to be

[1] Cong. Globe, 40th Cong. 3rd sess., pp. 28-9.   [2] Ibid., p. 44.
[3] Ibid., pp. 34-5; cf. Welles, vol. iii, pp. 479-80, 482.
[4] Issue of Dec. 17, 1868.

swept up with the dust and dirt and waste paper of the floor."[1]
It was "an ebullition of bile" from a "disappointed, disre-
spected and universally despised official," said the Philadelphia Press. After reading the message the contempt of the
American people for its author would reach "its profoundest
depths."[2]

In the excitement a resolution had been offered in the House
condemning the President's plan of repudiation; it was "odious
to the American people."[3] Cattell and Willey presented similar resolutions in the Senate; they would "repudiate the
repudiator."[4]

The counting of the electoral vote on February 10 in accordance with the terms of the Constitution, led to unusual scenes.
Congress in July, 1868, had resolved to exclude from the
electoral college the votes of states which had not been reorganized. It was clear that Virginia, Mississippi and Texas
could not participate in the election. But Georgia had done
so and the state had been carried by the Democrats. Since
that time, under circumstances to be related elsewhere, she
had been returned to military control. While the election of
Grant and Colfax in no way depended upon the action of
Georgia it was not easy to decide how to manage the question
when it should come before the Senate and the House.

It was thought that Congress had shrewdly disposed of the
subject, when, a few days before the date set for the meeting,
it had resolved to make a conditional statement—if the votes
of Georgia were counted the result would be this; if they were
not counted it would be that—in either case Grant and Colfax
were elected President and Vice President of the United
States.[5] But account was not taken of Ben Butler, who
nearly succeeded in precipitating a riot.

[1] Issue of Dec. 10, 1868. [2] Idem.
[3] Cong. Globe, 40th Cong. 3rd sess., p. 34. The resolution was passed
on December 14.—Ibid., pp. 71-2.
[4] Ibid., pp. 65-8. The subject was referred to the Committee on
Finance and a resolution was adopted by the Senate on December 17
by a vote of 43 to 6.—Ibid., p. 128.
[5] McPherson, Hist. of Recon., pp. 393-4.

The Senate at the appointed hour, headed by Wade, its president *pro tem.* and its sergeant-at-arms, proceeded to the hall of the House of Representatives and was seated. Wade took the chair to preside over the joint convention. The tellers were given the votes of the several states. When Louisiana was reached a member of the House, named Mullins, from Tennessee, objected. He said that the election in that state had not been valid. Thereupon the two houses separated to discuss the matter and both determined in favor of counting Louisiana's votes.[1] Georgia was called and Butler rose. He offered his objections in writing and they were read. He was reminded by Wade that the resolution of Congress of a few days before covered the case. Butler would re-open the question. Upon the retirement of the Senate the House by a vote of 150 to 41 determined to reject the votes of Georgia, thereby supporting Butler, while the Senate, on its side, after a lively discussion, decided that his objections were out of order.

Upon the return of the senators, when the announcement was made that they had overruled Butler, notwithstanding the action of the House, that obstreperous man rolled up his sleeves and shouted and stormed, like the ruffian he had proven himself to be during the impeachment trial and on other occasions.[2] Wade would not brook interruption and directed the tellers to proceed. Butler appealed from the decision of the chair. A score of men were on their feet calling for order. No debate was admissible. Butler spoke for the "representatives of the people." By no such "arbitrary proceedings" could the privileges of the House be overridden, he continued amid great uproar. Senators might not determine points of order for the joint convention and Butler moved that they "have leave to retire," so that the representatives might have the hall to themselves. On this motion he demanded a vote so that the room might be cleared of "inter-

---

[1] Seven Radical senators voted against this proposition,—Chandler, Howard, Nye, Robertson, Sumner, Thayer and Wilson.
[2] Cf. N. Y. Nation, Feb. 18, 1869.

lopers." But Wade was resolute and the tellers were ordered
to declare the result. It was announced that 214 votes had
been cast for Grant and Colfax and 80 for Seymour and
Blair, if the votes of Georgia were included; 214 for Grant
and Colfax and 71 for Seymour and Blair, if Georgia's were
excluded. "Wherefore," said Wade, "whether the votes of the
state of Georgia be included or excluded, I do declare that
Ulysses S. Grant of the state of Illinois, having received a
majority of the whole number of electoral votes, is duly elected
President of the United States for four years commencing on
the 4th day of March, 1869." [1]

After the Senate had retired Butler continued his scene,
speaking to a resolution which denounced Wade's order as "a
gross act of oppression and an invasion of the rights and privileges of the House," [2] while in the Senate Garrett Davis
brought forward a resolution condemning the "noisy, disorderly and tumultuous conduct of Benjamin F. Butler, a representative of the state of Massachusetts." [3]

Morton of Indiana, on the part of the Senate, and James F.
Wilson of Iowa and Pruyn of New York, representing the
House, formed a committee to wait upon Grant and Colfax
to notify them of their election. This duty was duly performed. The delegation met Grant at the office of the general of the army in Washington in the presence of some twenty
members of his staff. "The friends of liberty throughout the
world," said Senator Morton, rejoiced at his election. They
believed that he would bring to the Presidency "unalloyed
patriotism, inflexible integrity, great powers of intellect and
all the high qualities" which had enabled him "to achieve such
distinguished success in another sphere of duty."

In reply, he said, that it would be his endeavor to call
around him as assistants "such men only" as in his opinion
would carry out the principles which the country desired to
be "successful." Much had been said about his Cabinet
appointments. Many names had been suggested to him. He

---

[1] Cong. Globe, 40th Cong. 3rd sess., pp. 1062-3.
[2] Ibid., pp. 1064-1148 passim.   [3] Ibid., p. 1069.

had reached no determinations. He would make no announcements even to those whom he had it in mind to choose until two or three days before the time of sending their names to the Senate, if indeed, he should speak to them at all beforehand. Speculation upon this subject, therefore, might cease. Nothing would develop until the 4th day of March.[1] This declaration like earlier statements of the President-elect concerning his selections for office met with warm public approval.

By way of making it still clearer to Mr. Johnson that the Tenure of Office act as to removals, which had been passed in 1867, was aimed at him only, and was not meant to be a settled policy of government Congress now proposed to repeal the measure. The bill passed the House on January 11, but the Senate did not act upon it before adjournment. No definite action was taken until after the inauguration of Grant.[2]

The national platform of the Republican party adopted by the convention in Chicago while pronouncing for "equal suffrage to all loyal men in the South," under Congressional guaranty, declared that "the question of suffrage in all the loyal states properly belongs to the people of the states."[3] As an issue in the campaign the Republican leaders approached the subject timidly and evaded its discussion, but now, after Grant's election, they pretended to believe that they had received a mandate from the people in favor of the general enfranchisement of the African race.[4]

[1] American Annual Cyclopedia for 1869, p. 695. Already in November it was stated that 72 persons were "sure" of having places in Grant's cabinet. Some one computed perhaps correctly, that there were no less than 100,000 applicants for places of all kinds. The President-elect told his secretaries to make cigar-lighters of all applications for office. (Phila. Ledger, Nov. 11 and 12, 1868.) "Good evening," said an office-seeker one night to Grant. "I have not been to see you since the election." "Plenty have," the general answered. "I've not been lonesome." (Ibid., Feb. 1, 1869.)

[2] Cong. Globe, 40th Cong. 3rd sess., p. 282; McPherson, Hist. of Recon., pp. 397-8; Welles, vol. iii, p. 503.

[3] McPherson, Hist. of Recon., p. 364.

[4] The plan in the platform of forcing negro suffrage upon the South, while leaving it optional with the Northern states was "too brazen" to last long.—Horace White, Life of Trumbull, p. 338.

The first day of the session was not done before proposals for a constitutional amendment which would guarantee suffrage to the negro appeared in Congress. The profound discovery was made, after 80 years of nationality, that unless he were to vote we should not have a "republican form of government" within the meaning of the Constitution of the United States.[1] In the elections of 1868 in the South it had been made plain to the Radicals that action by the states would not suffice. Moreover provisions on this subject inserted in state constitutions might be repealed. A score of proposals in the Senate, as many in the House, led at the end of February, 1869, to conferences and the adoption of a simple declaration that—

"The right of citizens of the United States to vote shall not be denied or abridged in the United States, or by any state on account of race, color or previous condition of servitude." [2]

This was essentially the language which had been employed by Senator Stewart of Nevada in reporting the measure out of the Judiciary Committee in the first instance.[3] It had been submitted to the President-elect who in conversation endorsed the measure.[4] But to secure its final adoption, so that it could be forwarded to the states, called for several prolonged evening sessions, and at least one sitting which ran continuously through the night and into the next day.[5] Democrats offered many arguments against it from the standpoint of policy and denounced it on constitutional grounds, because it took from the states the power to regulate the suffrage and gave it to the national government. It was "another invasion of the jurisdiction and rights of the states by the Federal authorities." Party ends were to be gained, even if

[1] Without negro suffrage, said Sumner and Boutwell, any government was "unrepublican."—Cf. Cong. Globe, 40th Cong. 3rd sess., pp. 5, 558.
[2] McPherson, Hist. of Recon., for a convenient summary of the various votes taken upon the amendment, pp. 399-406; also American Annual Cyclopedia for 1869, pp. 120-71.
[3] On Jan. 15, 1869. Cf. Cong. Globe, 40th Cong. 3rd sess., p. 379.
[4] W. M. Stewart, Reminiscences, pp. 233-4.
[5] Cf. Welles, vol. iii, p. 524.

thereby this party were to "revolutionize the government, overthrow the constitution and destroy the republic." [1] One usurpation developed another, encroachment followed encroachment until soon "all the original landmarks of liberty" would be lost.[2] Instead of being a movement toward republicanism this plan to take away from the states the power to determine and establish, each for itself, the qualifications of its own voters was an attack upon the very foundations of republican government.[3]

Sumner on his side, a law unto himself, though at all times an eager Radical upon the subject of the negro, obstructed the progress of the measure. Congress already had power to enfranchise the blacks in all parts of the Union, so he averred, and it could and should act without amendment of the Constitution. Already the states were possessed of the power to "regulate" the manner of elections. It was "an insult to God and to humanity" to say that regulation could be disfranchisement of a race. In the exercise of this constitutional power you could not "degrade the country," you could not "disgrace the age." [4]

A few senators and representatives advocated, though only feebly and without response, the giving of the ballot to women.[5] Others spoke for educational tests as "an encouragement to popular intelligence," and as a means of preserving "the jewel of liberty," against "incoming floods of ignorance and barbarism." [6] And what of the Chinese? Trumbull said that in seeking "to carry out the great principles of human rights" it would be "paradoxical" to exclude from the ballot the citizens of the oldest empire on earth, renowned in the art of learning from antiquity, while declaring that "the Hottentots and cannibals from Africa shall have the right to vote and hold office." [7]

---

[1] Cong. Globe, 40th Cong. 3rd sess., p. 642.
[2] Ibid., p. 692.	[3] Ibid., p. 708.
[4] Ibid., pp. 986, 1041; cf. E. L. Pierce, Memoir and Letters of Sumner, vol. iv, pp. 365-6.
[5] Cf. Cong. Globe, 40th Cong. 3rd sess., pp. 543, 557.
[6] Ibid., p. 1037.	[7] Ibid., p. 1036.

But it was not the Chinaman's day. The eye of the Radical philanthropist, as well as the Radical politician, was fixed upon the negro only. Thus at the end of February was the Fifteenth Amendment passed and made ready for the action of the states.

CHAPTER XII

THE departure of Andrew Johnson and the members of his Cabinet from their places was attended with embarrassment. In their own minds they had convicted Grant of equivocation and falsehood at the time of his surrendering the War Office to Stanton during the unfolding of the impeachment plot.[1] It was observed that he did not appear at Johnson's reception on New Year's day; he had gone to Philadelphia to avoid it. He absented himself from another reception given by the President three weeks later. He had not permitted his children to attend a juvenile party in the White House. Seward, whose talent for riding two horses at the same time had stood him in excellent stead throughout the administration, entertained Grant at dinner, thus increasing the suspicion and distrust in which the Secretary of State was held by his associates in the Cabinet.[2] The President-elect's dislikes, once they were awakened, were bitter, and since the acquittal in the impeachment trial, which in some way he took to be a rebuke to himself, his antipathy to Johnson was angry and obstinate.[3]

It was clear that it would be the part of wisdom for John-

[1] Johnson said that he knew Grant to be "a liar, guilty of duplicity, false to his duty and his trust." (Welles, vol. iii, p. 500.) Grant, Johnson said another time, was "not a fair representative of the nation, mentally, morally or physically. The people should have seen his attitude and looks as he withdrew from the Cabinet meeting the day his duplicity was exposed. The goddess of history should have been present to inscribe the scene upon her tablets. It would have shown General Grant in his true colors. Lee will go down in history as a greater man than Grant. Grant was a mere figurehead who by fortuitous circumstances won a reputation far above his real deserts "—Moore's Notes in Am. Hist. Review, Oct., 1913, p. 129.

[2] Welles, vol. iii, pp. 508, 511.

[3] McCulloch, Men and Measures, p. 403.

son to leave the White House as quietly as possible at the
hour of noon on March 4, at the expiration of his term
of office. Some of the members of the Cabinet were of
opinion that they should remain to welcome their successors,[1]
but this plan met with little favor. If Grant were to
return "proffered civility with churlish discourtesy," as
Welles suspected that he might, none need remain to receive it.[2]

While they could write in their diaries that he had been
"a porter in a leather store," who but for the war still would
have been in that place,[3] he on this occasion had the advantage of his adversaries. He was able to inform the committee on ceremonies that he would not ride in the same carriage with Johnson, nor speak to him on inauguration day,
and the gentlemen in charge devised an elaborate scheme for
the outgoing and the incoming presidents to occupy separate
vehicles, leading separate processions, moving side by side
through Pennsylvania Avenue. It was practically agreed by
Seward and Evarts in Cabinet meeting that matters should
take this course.[4] But at the last moment the President
wisely followed his own inclinations. He would remain in
the White House surrounded by his Cabinet officers to transact public business. Here he stayed and when the clock
struck twelve he shook the hand of each in token of farewell, descended to the portico, entered his carriage and drove
to Secretary Welles's house, to which place his daughter,
Mrs. Patterson, and her children had gone a few hours before.[5] The mansion was left in charge of General Schofield,
the Secretary of War, whom Grant, in friendliness and military comradeship, had asked to continue in office for a few
days.[6]

A long valedictory by President Johnson which he addressed
to the people had been sent to the press. In this paper he
again presented the account of his contest with the Radical

[1] Welles, vol. iii, pp. 529-30, 532. [2] Ibid., p. 533.
[3] Ibid., pp. 497-8. [4] Ibid., pp. 536-8.
[5] Ibid., pp. 541-2. [6] N. Y. Tribune, Feb. 24, 1869.

Congress to prevent that body from overriding the Constitution. He indicted its members for their "usurpations" and their "crimes," and defended himself from their censures, which had reached a climax in their impeachment of him and their attempt to convict him in the high court. "It is a matter of pride and gratification in retiring from the most exalted position in the gift of a free people," he said at the conclusion of his address, "to feel and know that in a long, arduous and eventful public life my action has never been influenced by the desire for gain, and that I can in all sincerity inquire 'Whom have I defrauded, whom have I oppressed, or off whose hand have I received any bribe to blind my eyes therewith?' . . . My thoughts have been those of peace and my effort has ever been to allay contentions among my countrymen. Forgetting the past let us return to the first principles of the government and, unfurling the banner of our country, inscribe upon it in ineffaceable characters 'the Constitution and the Union, one and inseparable.' "[1]

Thus departed the official scene a President whose honesty none can fairly impugn, and whose devotion to the Constitution, as he understood its letter and its purpose, no magistrate has ever surpassed. He remained in Washington for a fortnight as a guest of friends. Mayors of cities and innkeepers on routes which he might take on his way home wrote to proffer him their hospitalities.[2] But he declined them and made the journey to Greenville quietly to receive the kindly greetings of the friends and neighbors from whom he had long been separated.[3]

It was expected that he would go abroad during the summer and all the steamship companies, English, French and German, tendered him and his family free passage over their lines.[4] But he was soon taken ill which led to a false report of his death—his son did die—and upon his recovery, in a little while he was again in the midst of political strife. He

[1] American Annual Cyclop. for 1869, pp. 589-92.
[2] Johnson Papers.
[3] Greenville corr. N. Y. Tribune, March 24, 1869.
[4] Johnson Papers.

had been welcomed home as an "instrument" for "redeeming Tennessee," and almost at once he was making speeches which his admirers believed would lead him to the governor's chair or a seat in the United States Senate.

Out of Washington with Johnson went most of his friends in Congress who had clung to Lincoln's reconstruction policy and had refused to go down the new way prepared for them by the Radicals. Four senators, Doolittle of Wisconsin, Dixon of Connecticut, Norton of Minnesota and Edgar Cowan of Pennsylvania—all elected as Republicans, had taken part in the "Arm-in-Arm Convention" in Philadelphia in 1866 and ever since had stood like martyrs in the fiery furnace. Cowan's term had expired in 1867; Dixon and Doolittle, long since branded as Democrats, retired with Johnson; Norton, who yet had a few months to serve, died in July, 1870, before the completion of his term.

The seven "traitors," who joined these four as party outcasts after the impeachment trial, followed a similar course. Grimes, stricken with paralysis before the proceedings had yet ended, resigned and took himself from the scene of strife. Henderson was defeated for re-election in Missouri, indeed he made no pretense of being a candidate to succeed himself, though long years afterward he was reinstated in the good opinion of his party.[1] Fessenden, whose term would have ended in 1871, died in September, 1869, and was spared the struggle which impended had he offered himself for re-election in the state of Maine.[2] Van Winkle's successor appeared at Washington with the beginning of the administration of President Grant. Ross of Kansas yet had two years to serve; when these passed he was destined to forty years of life in poverty and obscurity.[3] So soon as the legislature of Tennessee could reach Mr. Fowler his activities as a statesman were brought to an end. Only Trumbull, who had five years more assured to him, a fact which galled the Radicals

[1] Cf. Horace White, Life of Trumbull, p. 326.
[2] F. Fessenden, Wm. Pitt Fessenden, vol. ii, pp. 327-9.
[3] A little eased by a term as governor of the territory of New Mexico by appointment of President Cleveland.

immeasurably, remained a factor in the Senate, but when the period for which he had been elected expired in March, 1873, he was returned to the shades of private life.

Meantime brighter scenes were being enacted in another part of Washington. On the 3rd of March Grant had transferred the command of the army to General Sherman. The city was filled with people. Early on the morning of the 4th the troops, the visiting campaign clubs, the fire companies and other bodies of citizens with their bands of music were massed in eight "grand divisions," and, with the President-elect seated in an open carriage at their head, followed by the Vice President-elect, Schuyler Colfax, escorted by details of cavalry, infantry and artillery from the regular army, the procession passed along Pennsylvania Avenue. The windows and porticoes were crowded with onlookers waving handkerchiefs and flags. The pavements were thronged. Cheers rent the air on every side. Arriving at the Capitol Grant proceeded to the east portico where he was surrounded by the justices of the Supreme Court, senators, representatives, members of the diplomatic corps, visiting governors of states and territories, army officers and other invited guests. Near him sat his wife and children. Boys hung from the boughs of trees. Dense masses of people extended into space a quarter of a mile away. Chief Justice Chase administered the oath. Cannon boomed, the crowds shouted and General Grant was President of the United States. He read his inaugural address, which was audible to but a few persons who were placed quite near him, and reached the White House about two o'clock, where he was greeted by General Schofield, ready to begin the work appertaining to his high position.

The place had come to him "unsought," he said in his address; he assumed its duties "untrammelled." He would fill the office to the best of his ability "to the satisfaction of the people." On all subjects he would have "a policy to recommend," but none, he continued, with only a half-veiled allusion to his predecessor, "to enforce against the will of the people." If his opening statements were platitudes his references to the payment of the debt, principal and interest, in gold and the return of the country to a specie basis were bolder, and in the confusion of the hour on this subject worthy of hearty commendation. "Let it be understood," said he, "that no repudiator of one farthing of our public debt will be trusted in public place," and at this moment by this act alone the national credit will be strengthened throughout the world. He advocated the ratification of the Fifteenth Amendment by the states. As for the rest of the speech—about the value of the gold mines of the West as a national asset, executing the laws in good faith, collecting the revenues, making disbursements with economy, respecting the rights of other nations and requiring them to respect ours, the "proper treatment" of the Indians and the wish that men would have "patient forbearance" one for another, the address was no guide for the future and spoke but ill of the author's intellectual powers.[1]

The country, however, received the new President's words indulgently and was determined to believe, except in quarters influenced by partisan feeling, that an era of good government with happier social and political relationships had begun. Everywhere there was a sense of relief. The brawl between the executive and legislative branches of the government, which had been continuous for three years, had now come to an end.[2]

No one had ever entered the White House with so little experience concerning matters of state, indeed with so little education of whatever variety fitting him for high public office,[3] except Zachary Taylor, who in a similar manner owed his political elevation to military service. But the gratitude of the country for what as a soldier Grant had been the

[1] A "mess of trite, flat, newspaper partyism," said Welles, "in a day and time when noble utterances ought to be expected."—Vol. iii, p. 544.
[2] Schurz, Reminiscences, vol. iii, p. 303. The inaugural address was received with "the greatest satisfaction," said the New York Nation, "by the press of all parties."—Issue of March 11, 1869.
[3] "As ignorant of civil government as of the characters on the Moabitish stone."—Richard Taylor, Destruction and Reconstruction, p. 256; cf. Hugh McCulloch, Men and Measures, pp. 357, 361.

instrument to achieve was great, and his very detachment from politics had filled right thinking citizens with hope that his administration would be distinguished by honesty and common sense. The choice of his Cabinet officers, which he promised would be announced only in his own time, was a secret he had kept to himself. Many had guessed what it might be and then, like John Lothrop Motley, gave up the attempt.[1] Now on the 5th of March, the day after his inauguration, he forwarded the names to the Senate. When they were posted on the bulletin boards in New York the crowds were incredulous. Men said it was a hoax; the telegraph had been "sold."[2] Words could not express their surprise and disappointment,—some who had friends in view for the places because these were not chosen, others with high ideals for the public service because several of the appointees were mere "sycophants" and "money givers," named to please the President's personal tastes,[3] and possessed so few qualifications and so little experience.[4] Nor were those who had been selected the less astonished since several of the number were without previous notice of the President's intentions regarding them.[5]

The office of Secretary of State which had had so many distinguished occupants, with but rare exceptions the first

[1] The general said to Mrs. Grant, who had made an inquiry of him in February: "Jule, if you say anything more about it I'll get leave of absence, go off West, and not come back till the 4th of March." (Corr. of J. L. Motley, vol. ii, p. 302.) He gave no indication of his intentions even to his close friend, Rawlins. J. H. Wilson, Life of Rawlins, pp. 350-2.

[2] N. Y. corr. Phila. Ledger, March 6, 1869. The prophets in Washington were astounded. (J. H. Wilson, Life of C. A. Dana, p. 140.) The Cabinet was "a conglomerate which stupefied the politicians." (Horace White, Life of Trumbull, p. 333.) How far afield the guesses were is proven by the fact that Sumner was supposed by many to be Grant's choice for Secretary of State.—F. Fessenden, Life of W. P. Fessenden, vol. ii, p. 322.

[3] Sumner's Works, vol. xv, p. 126; Welles, vol. iii, pp. 545-6.

[4] The Radicals were "astounded, thunderstruck, mad, but after taking breath" tried to be thankful that things were no worse, that Grant had not "besides kicking them to one side selected Democrats."—Welles, vol. iii, p. 544.

[5] Adam Badeau, Grant in Peace, pp. 156-7, 163, 166.

statesmen in the land, which for eight years had been directed by the able hand of Seward, was bestowed upon the President's friend and advocate of many years, Elihu B. Washburne. Washburne had been a member of the House of Representatives from the Galena district for several terms. As he did not possess the least special knowledge about foreign affairs, as he had never concerned himself with the precedents and principles underlying international law, and had some personal qualities, including an impulsive and a combative nature, unfitting him in a marked way for the duties of such a place,[1] the President's acumen in judging of the character of men with reference to their aptitude for public office at once became a subject of distrust.

A. T. Stewart of New York, the first of America's great department storekeepers, was named to be Secretary of the Treasury. Some years before he had come to this country from the north of Ireland. At first a school teacher, he soon turned his talents to merchandising, and by his diligence and integrity built up a large business as well as a great fortune. Only Astor and Vanderbilt now had a higher place on the list of America's rich men.[2] Stewart was an excellent advertiser and attached a good deal of merit to himself for his rapid rise to financial power. The new President owed the wealthy merchant much for his services, hospitalities and gifts. Through a meeting in Cooper Institute he had early brought the millionaires of New York into the movement to nominate Grant on a simple platform of admiration for his "past record" and confidence in his "judgment in the future."[3] Only a day or two since he had handed Grant a check for $65,000, representing a purse made up by himself and other opulent men, purporting to be pur-

---

[1] Horace White, Life of Trumbull, p. 333. Cf. Welles, who calls Washburne "coarse, comparatively illiterate, a demagogue without statesmanship or enlarged views, with none of the accomplishments or attributes that should belong to a Secretary of State."—Vol. iii, p. 543.
[2] Stewart returned an income of over $3,000,000 in 1868.—N. Y. Tribune, July 19, 1869.
[3] Phila. Ledger, Dec. 31, 1867.

chase money for Grant's home in Washington.[1] No one knew
whether Stewart was a Republican or a Democrat, but the
nomination was well received by the press.[2] Here was a
business man who, without previous entanglements with political subjects, might bring good sense to the public service.

Adolph E. Borie of Philadelphia, not at all known away
from his home, and there principally for his wealth and his
recent connection with a scheme to present Grant with a
house[3] in that city, was appointed Secretary of the Navy.
Even Admiral Farragut, it was said, had never heard of the
man[4] and he himself seems to have been entirely averse to
the assumption of his strange new duties.[5] Neither the state
of his health nor his interests in life fitted him for useful
service.[6]

The appointment of Governor Jacob D. Cox of Ohio as
Secretary of the Interior was rather warmly commended,
though he was charged with too much earlier friendship for
President Johnson.[7] J. A. J. Creswell of Maryland, the new
Postmaster General, for some time a most outspoken Radical,
had been a secessionist in the first days of the war, indeed,
he had raised troops for service in the Confederate army.[8]
E. Rockwood Hoar, the Attorney General, taken from the
supreme bench in Massachusetts, was the one man among
them all for whose selection there was general praise. If
the country had been "searched through," said the New York
Nation, "a fitter man for the place could not have been
found."[9]

[1] Some time before this house had been bought by public subscription for Grant for $30,000. What was originally a gift to him was now
"purchased" from him for more than twice as much as it was worth,
to be presented in turn to General Sherman.—N. Y. World, March 4
and 10, 1869; N. Y. Nation, March 18, 1869; Welles, vol. iii, p. 545;
Badeau, Grant in Peace, p. 168.

[2] Horace White, Life of Trumbull, pp. 335-6.

[3] Phila. Ledger, May 1, 1865; N. Y. Sun, April 1, 1869.

[4] Sumner's Works, vol. xv, p. 126.

[5] Adam Badeau, Grant in Peace, p. 166.

[6] Sumner's Works, vol. xv, pp. 138-9; J. H. Wilson, Life of C. A. Dana,
p. 411.

[7] Cf. N. Y. Nation, March 11, 1869.

[8] Welles, vol. iii, p. 543.

[9] N. Y. Nation, March 18, 1869.

In a few days it was made clear that Washburne had been appointed to the State Department merely to compliment a patron and a friend. It had been intended that James F. Wilson of Iowa should have the place and he had accepted it. A leading member of the House of Representatives and chairman of its Judiciary Committee, in which place he had long and courageously combatted the project to impeach President Johnson, he had declined re-election to Congress in 1868, and was on the point of retiring from public life. But Grant, who had been consulting him about matters connected with the quarrel with Johnson over the *ad interim* tenure of the War Office, urged him to enter the Cabinet as the successor of Mr. Seward. He had even agreed to the plan for Washburne to occupy the place for a time, when it became clear that it was Grant's desire to honor the congressman from Galena in this manner, on the condition that no steps should be taken by the temporary incumbent to make appointments or define policies in the department. The agreement was violated. Wilson reported this fact to Grant, who urged Washburne to haste in leaving the place. But it was then too late, for Wilson had gone to New York on his way to his home in Iowa, and, though a messenger was sent after him to explain the situation, he refused to return.[1] Washburne had now gained what he desired—the prestige of having held a great office before proceeding abroad as our minister to France, to which post he was now assigned and for which his unfitness seemed to be as notable as for the higher place.[2]

Wilson being out of the way, Grant turned to Hamilton Fish of New York, a man of influence and social position who once had been governor of his state, once a representative in Congress and for six years a United States senator,—

[1] Horace White, Life of Trumbull, p. 34; cf. J. R. Young, Around the World with General Grant, vol. ii, p. 276; Adam Badeau, Grant in Peace, p. 162; Washington corr. N. Y. World, March 17, 1869.
[2] Cf. N. Y. Nation, March 18, 1869. Washburne had wished to be minister at London, so it was said, and he might have been this, "but his want of knowledge of the English language was insurmountable," on which account he was sent to France.—Moran's Diary, Oct. 22, 1869.

all prior to the war.[1] He had been a colorless figure in politics and had made no impression upon his times. But to his handsome homes in New York city and on the Hudson River Grant came as a guest.[2] His name was sent to the Senate without his knowledge, indeed he had declined by telegraph in response to a letter proffering him the place, and "with a heavy heart" and "unnumbered misgivings" he determined to go to Washington "at the sacrifice of personal ease and comfort" to undertake duties for which he felt he had "little taste and less fitness."[3] The appointment was so good in contrast with Washburne's that it was received in discriminating quarters with gratefulness and content.

An impression still worse than that which was created by the series of events touching the disposition of the first place in the Cabinet came from the nomination of Mr. Stewart to be Secretary of the Treasury. The Senate had hastily confirmed this with the other appointments. Now the discovery was made that by an act of September 2, 1789, no one might hold the place if he were "concerned in carrying on the business of trade or commerce." So Grant sent the Senate a message asking that Stewart be exempted by a joint resolution of the two houses from the disabling provisions of the old law.[4] There was objection and three days later Grant withdrew his message.[5] Mr. Stewart, eager to qualify, had proposed that he place his business in the hands of trustees, the profits going to public charities,[6] but in the midst of the argument the Radical politicians, aroused to a high pitch of resentment because of the little recognition they had

[1] He was "politically superannuated," said Hugh McCulloch. (Men and Measures, p. 351.) "Out of politics so long that the people seem to have forgotten him," said the New York Tribune, March 12, 1869. Cf. J. H. Wilson, Life of C. A. Dana, p. 410.

[2] Cf. N. Y. Tribune, Feb. 8, 1869.

[3] So he wrote Sumner. (E. L. Pierce, Memoir and Letters of Sumner, vol. iv, pp. 374-9.) In marked contrast with the words of Grant in his inaugural which had been commented upon so unfavorably on many sides. Grant had said: "The responsibilities of the position I feel but accept them without fear."

[4] Richardson, Messages and Papers, vol. vii, p. 9.

[5] Ibid.   [6] N. Y. Tribune, March 10, 1869.

received, pressed the claims of Representative Boutwell of
Massachusetts, who seems at first to have been offered the
Secretaryship of the Interior,[1] and Grant surrendered to their
demands.[2] This man had been a country storekeeper. Later
he had studied law. Very indifferently educated and, with
experiences entirely parochial, he had come to be governor
of his state for a term before the war, at which time he was
a Democrat. For a few months after it was first established
he had been at the head of the bureau for collecting the new
internal revenue taxes and then entered Congress. Everywhere he was a pre-eminent partisan.[3] He had been a foremost and vindictive advocate of the plan to impeach President
Johnson and his reward now was the great office so intimately
responsible for the financial and economic future of the country, safely directed during and since the war by Chase, Fessenden and McCulloch.

General Schofield in a few days made way for John A.
Rawlins, Grant's confidential staff officer during the war and
like Washburne a fellow townsman in Galena, Ill. He had
had a dour youth. Studying law he had gained some prominence in a small neighborhood as an attorney and at the outbreak of civil hostilities entered the volunteer army to stand
at Grant's side from Belmont through to Appomattox. Since
the war he had served as Grant's chief of staff in Washington.[4] Outspoken and impassioned in utterance and, when
aroused, often rough in manner, he had a loyal heart. He
had been Grant's good genius in many emergencies, offering
him advice, commanding him, indeed, to many a course when
he wavered and would have taken the wrong road, and guarding him from the ruinous dram which often threatened his
fall and destruction.[5] Of all human beings it was he, so it

---

[1] Boutwell, Sixty Years in Public Affairs, vol. ii, p. 204; cf. J. D. Cox,
Atlantic Monthly, August, 1895. Cf. Welles, vol. iii, p. 550.

[2] Cf. Welles, vol. iii, p. 550.

[3] Cf. N. Y. Nation, March 18, 1869, and Sep. 7, 1871.

[4] J. H. Wilson, Life of Rawlins, p. 18.

[5] At City Point on July 28, 1864, Rawlins wrote to his wife—"I find
the general in my absence digressed from his true path. The God of

seemed, who best understood the character of the new President.[1] But Grant was being "changed by prosperity." Amid his great and rich friends he was in danger of forgetting the rungs of the ladder by which he had risen to his amazing eminence. By his exposures during the war Rawlins's health had been broken. He was growing feebler from a pulmonary disease, and was under the constant care of a physician.[2] His needs were great, and, out of Grant's confidences for the time being and in suspense, he asked some friends to see the President in his behalf. They were told that Rawlins was to have a command in Arizona in the hope that life there would restore him to health. They answered that he wished to be Secretary of War and thus it was that he came into the Cabinet.[3]

In June, having been three months in the office, Mr. Borie, under newspaper attack, resigned his position as Secretary of the Navy and, after offering the succession to two other Philadelphians whose fitness for such service was not manifest,[4] George M. Robeson, a respected but inconspicuous lawyer of Camden, N. J.—at the time attorney general of his state— was appointed on Borie's recommendation to the place. Two members of the Cabinet came from the same state, Massachusetts, indeed from the same county in Massachusetts, but this seemed to be of little moment except to writers of gossip in the press.[5] Grant's group of official advisers was now complete. His private secretaries were four members of

Heaven only knows how long I am to serve my country as the guardian of the habits of him whom it has honored."—J. H. Wilson, Life of Rawlins, p. 249; cf. ibid., p. 242.

[1] Cf. ibid., pp. 61-3; J. H. Wilson, Life of C. A. Dana, p. 418; Horace White, Life of Trumbull, p. 37; Welles, vol. iii, pp. 551; J. D. Cox, Atlantic Monthly, August, 1895.

[2] J. H. Wilson, Life of Rawlins, p. 362.

[3] Ibid., pp. 351-2, and Wilson, Life of C. A. Dana, pp. 405-6.

[4] George H. Stuart and Lindley Smyth. (J. R. Young, Around the World with General Grant, vol. ii, p. 277.) Stuart had been chairman of the committee which had presented Grant with a house in Philadelphia. (Phila. Ledger, May 1, 1865.)

[5] Cf. J. D. Cox, Atlantic Monthly, August, 1895; Boutwell, Sixty Years in Public Affairs, vol. ii, p. 210.

his staff who still held commissions in the army—Generals
O. E. Babcock, Adam Badeau, Horace Porter and F. T. Dent,
the latter a brother-in-law, one of the large number of relations and married connections whom he invited into the public
service.   In the President's entourage military forms were
substituted for those of civil life.[1]

What candid men saw was not very reassuring to them.
Grant told Farragut that he had given the office of Secretary of State to Washburne as a "compliment." [2] "Who before ever heard of a member of the Cabinet being appointed
as a compliment?" exclaimed Fessenden.[3] To their surprise
senators heard that the President was about to remove a
Federal judge, a most capable man in one of the territories.
No reason was given or sought for.   It was said, simply, that
the governor of the territory could not "get along with that
judge at all" and was "very anxious to be rid of him."   The
President, being an army man in his whole outlook, thought
that a governor should have "control of his staff." [4]

Such views, too, did he entertain about the members of his
Cabinet. They were subordinates whose functions he might
any day assume if he liked.[5] He himself directly addressed
senators concerning the confirmation of his nominees for office.
He urged Schurz to support J. R. Jones, a politician in Illinois, who had been chosen to represent the United States in
Brussels. In a few days the name appeared before the Committee on Foreign Relations.[6] William A. Pile, an ignorant

[1] Sumner's Works, vol. xv, pp. 131-2.
[2] Welles, vol. iii, p. 546.
[3] Pierce, Memoir and Letters of Sumner, vol. iv, p. 374.
[4] Schurz, Reminiscences, vol. ii, p. 306.
[5] Cf. Recollections of John Sherman, vol. ii, p. 449.
[6] Knowledge about the man was asked for and Senator Morton,
staunch Radical as he was, replied, "Well, Mr. Jones is about the most
elegant gentleman that ever presided over a livery stable." The members laughed. Jones, having some connection with the street car lines
of Chicago, had much to do with horses, which, so it seemed, had
created a bond of sympathy between him and the President. Yet more
potent was the fact that he had lived in Galena and was a friend of
Grant's friends, Washburne and Rawlins. (Schurz, vol. iii, pp. 309-10;
Welles, vol. iii, p. 577; Sumner's Works, vol. xiv, p. 260.)

frontier evangelist, was nominated for the Brazilian mission.
His name was rejected by the Senate, though he afterward
was allowed to serve as governor of the territory of New
Mexico.[1] A scamp named Wadsworth, of so evil a record
that the nomination must be withdrawn, was chosen to be
United States marshal in New York.[2] The "original im-
peacher," the corrupt Ashley, of Ohio, was made governor of
the territory of Montana.[3] But the most unfit appointment
to a conspicuous place in the public service was that of General Sickles to be minister to Spain. It is true that he had
come back from the war with a record for gallantry and had
been one of the Radical martyrs in Andrew Johnson's contest
with Congress upon the subject of reconstruction. But his
earlier life had been morally abominable. He had entered
the army, said the New York Nation, simply as "a refuge
from disgrace." To choose one of his private reputation to
represent us at a foreign court was a shock to the sensibilities of many men.[4] Unsuitable persons by the score were
brought forward for diplomatic and consular posts [5] as well
as for the offices at home which were in the gift of the Presi-

[1] Welles, vol. vii, p. 577.   [2] N. Y. Nation, April 15, 1869.
[3] Ibid., April 15, 22 and 29, 1869. [4] Ibid., July 1 and 8, 1869.
[5] "We make diplomatists as we do town constables," Moran complained as he watched them file through London on their way to their
posts. "Unpolished," "ill-mannered," "vulgar," "ignorant" were some
of the words which he used in designating them as they called from
day to day at the American legation. Again Moran writes: "Curtin
[Minister to Russia], Jones [Minister to Belgium], Washburne [Min-
ister to France] are all at Homburg talking American politics and
drinking mineral waters. These men are a set of loafers and act like a
set of bar room politicians at home. In fact, they have just transferred
their talk from one side of the Atlantic to the other." Shellabarger,
the new minister to Portugal, when taken to meet the Minister of
Foreign Affairs at Lisbon, suddenly, in the midst of the audience, asked
his predecessor, who stood by as an interpreter, whether he had spoken
French before coming out. When told that the use of the tongue
had been acquired Shellabarger said: "Tell him [a Portuguese marquis]
that I have a private secretary who speaks the [sic] French." An
assistant secretary just arrived in the legation in London, after dining
officially in a distinguished company of guests, asked how he had liked
the experience, said it "surpassed any circus performance he had ever
dreamed of."—Moran's MS. Diary in the Library of Congress.

dent and the new heads of the departments.[1] Grant thought
that "office seeking" had become "one of the industries of
the age." It gave him "no peace."[2]

The advocates of a responsible civil service[3] founded upon
education, fitness and experience, whose claims for a hearing
in some quarters were reaching a demand, had been filled
with high hopes as they saw Grant assume the presidential
office. A few days, a few weeks had not passed before they
were shaking their heads with apprehension.

In the army, too, disappointment soon ensued. Sherman
was elevated to Grant's vacated place as general, which was
as it should have been, and he came to Washington, soon to
be made very uncomfortable, because of nearly everything
being taken out of his hands by law or regulation, for which
conditions he was unable to get redress from the President,
to whom he frequently complained.[4]

But the saddest blow was that aimed at General Meade,
the senior major general, if Halleck's claims were not respected, which seemed to be foreordained, when he was not
raised to the lieutenant generalship in succession to Sherman.
As the head of the Army of the Potomac his performances
in the last months of the war were of the greatest importance.
Indeed, he was indispensable to Grant, whose dispatches to

[1] Welles, vol. iii, pp. 577-8.
[2] Under date of March 31, 1869.—M. J. Cramer, U. S. Grant, Conversations and Unpublished Letters, p. 108.
[3] If there were to be a system of civil service examinations, said the
New York World, the first question to be asked of a candidate for
office under the administration should be, "Were you a contributor to
either of Grant's three houses in Philadelphia, Washington or Galena,
or have you made gifts to him or to any member of his family?"
The second question should be, "Are you a member of the Dent family
or otherwise connected by blood or marriage with President Grant?"—
N. Y. World, March 17, 1869.
[4] Cf. General Orders, no. 11, of March 5, and order of March 26, 1869,
rescinding the earlier order in Richardson, Messages and Papers, vol.
vii, pp. 20, 22; The Sherman Letters, pp. 331-2; J. H. Wilson, Life of
Rawlins, pp. 356, 361-7. Grant in contact with politics soon totally
changed his views about the position which should be held by the
general of the army with reference to the War Department.—Schofield,
Forty-Six Years in the Army, p. 421.

Washington were in large degree the work of Meade, by whom, however, he was always reluctant to deal fairly. He had spoken of advancing 'Meade with Sherman but had not done so. Then Sheridan was to be put forward at the expense of the commander of the Army of the Potomac, who protested with so much vigor that he succeeded in obtaining his major generalship.[1] Now with Grant in the presidency Sheridan's position was to be improved at once. The spectacular cavalryman, who during the war had stirred the popular imagination and afterward had endeared himself to the Radicals by a tactless and really vindictive administration of his office as commander in Louisiana and Texas, would be raised over the head of a soldier who was to have nothing more than the chance to go to his home in Philadelphia at the head of the Military Division of the Atlantic.[2]

After a few days in command in Louisiana, as. a vindication for his removal by President Johnson, Sheridan was assigned to the new Military Division of Missouri, with headquarters in Chicago, while Howard of the Freedmen's Bureau took command at New Orleans.

That favorite of the Southern conservatives, Gillem, in the Fourth District, was summarily disposed of. Though a brevet major general, his rank was colonel and he was ordered to turn over the command to the next senior officer and go back to his regiment. The Department of the South,

[1] From accounts of that excellent military historian, Isaac R. Pennypacker. Cf. Carswell McClellan, Personal Memoirs of Grant vs. the Record, and Notes on the Personal Memoirs of P. H. Sheridan. Grant had said that Meade was "one of the fittest officers for a large command he had come in contact with." Again he "defied any man to name a commander who could do more than he had done with the same chance."—Life and Letters of General Meade, vol. ii, p. 297. For Rawlins's estimate, not less full of praise, see J. H. Wilson, Life of Rawlins, p. 229.

[2] Meade regarded this as "the cruellest and meanest act of injustice." It was "low conduct" which he could resent only in that "calm, dignified" way which it merited. He hoped if there was "any sense of wrong or justice in the country" that "the man who had perpetrated it" would some day be appropriately rebuked.—Life and Letters of General Meade, vol. ii, p. 300. See Grant's excuses in J. R. Young, Around the World with General Grant, vol. ii, pp. 298-300.

the old Second and Third Districts, where Meade had been, was given to General Terry. Canby, who had been in Louisiana, was sent to Virginia to replace Stoneman. Reynolds was returned to command in Texas. Hancock was sent to Dakota.[1] Shortly, when the new Military Division of the South was established, Halleck, who had been on the Pacific coast, was brought on to take general command.[2] Grant's course with reference to the supersession of the conservative commanders in the South was entirely partisan, but their assignment to service there by Johnson had been so in the first place, and the North found satisfaction in their transfer to other scenes.

Grant's early failures to meet all the expectations which had been formed for him, respecting his appointments to office, were soon supplemented by a strange effort to impose upon the Senate a treaty of annexation with the black republic of San Domingo. Following his secret negotiation with Russia as to Alaska, which encountered so much opposition, Seward, giving his imagination full rein, turned to the tropics. In conversation he told Sumner, so it appears, that in thirty years the City of Mexico would be the capital of the United States.[3] He sought to annex the Sandwich Islands,[4] and brought President Johnson to the advocacy of this course.[5] He used to say that he would have the Union extend "up to the pole and down to the tropics."[6] He actually had entered into a negotiation for the transfer to the United States of the Danish West Indian islands, of which there were three of any size—St. Thomas, St. John and Santa Cruz—in consideration of the payment of $7,500,000 to the Danish government, $300,000 more than Russia received for Alaska. The treaty called for the cession of the islands of

[1] General Orders of March 5, 1869, McPherson, Hist. of Recon., pp. 424-5.
[2] General Orders of March 16, 1869, ibid., pp. 424-5.
[3] Pierce, Memoir and Letters of Sumner, vol. iv, p. 328.
[4] Seward at Washington, vol. iii, pp. 372-3, 383.
[5] Richardson, Messages and Papers, vol. vi, p. 689.
[6] Seward at Washington, vol. iii, p. 372.

St. Thomas and St. John, and it was signed at Copenhagen in October, 1867.

Seward's interest in the West Indies went back to the year 1866, when he had made a voyage for his health, covering a month, on a government steamer in these waters.[1] It is likely that the scheme in any event would have been viewed with disfavor, both on account of the stealth with which it had been arranged and the disinclination on the part of Congress to lend support to any measure emanating from the Johnson administration. But it was completely discredited after a hurricane which at this inopportune moment burst upon St. Thomas, to be followed by several shocks of earthquake.[2] The discussion proceeded for many months. General Raaslaff, at one time Denmark's consul general in New York and later her minister in Washington, visited this country to press the ratification of the treaty. He distributed pamphletary matter, urged the enterprise in the press and approached political leaders through the pleasant channels of society at the national capital. He was granted the unusual distinction of appearing before the Senate Committee on Foreign Relations though not one member seemed to share Seward's enthusiasm for the project.[3] At Seward's instigation President Johnson inserted some ringing passages in favor of annexation in his message of December, 1867. A "comprehensive national policy," he said, seemed "to sanction the acquisition and incorporation into our Federal Union of the several adjacent continental and insular communities as speedily" as this end could be attained "peacefully" and "lawfully." He dwelt upon the need of a naval base in the West Indies which would save us apprehension of danger in the future "from any transatlantic enemy," recalling the words

[1] Seward at Washington, vol. iii, pp. 302-9.

[2] "We had not fairly swallowed our icebergs," said the New York Tribune, alluding to the annexation of Alaska, "when we were summoned to rinse them down with a few earthquakes."—Issue of March 23, 1869.

[3] E. L. Pierce, Memoir and Letters of Sumner, vol. iv, pp. 328-9; Seward at Washington, vol. iii, pp. 370-1.

of "our early statesmen" on this subject.[1] The time set for
the final ratifications was extended and President Johnson in
his last message referred to the fact that the treaty was still
in the Senate's hands.[2]

When Grant came into office he dismissed the subject as
one to which it was not worth while to give serious consideration. On March 30, 1869, the Committee on Foreign Relations laid the treaty on the table and a year later, in order to
be finally rid of it, rejected it. Thus ended this unfortunate
adventure in foreign diplomacy.

While Seward had been in the West Indies gathering enthusiasm for the purchase of St. Thomas he paid a visit to Hayti
and San Domingo, two negro republics which not too happily
for many years had shared jurisdiction over the ancient Caribbean island of San Domingo. Hayti, of French traditions,
with the harbor of Port-au-Prince, occupied the western portion of the island while the Dominican Republic in the east,
inhabited principally by Spanish negroes and mulattoes, had
for its capital the old city of San Domingo, placed on a site
first seen by white men when Columbus came hither on his
historic voyage in 1492. From 1822 to 1844 the people had
lived under one government. A civil war lasting for years
ensued and ended with independence for San Domingo which
comprehended two-thirds of the superficial area of the island,
though it had but one-fifth of the population. Internal revolution followed internal revolution in Dominica, and at most
times the two republics were not far from war with each other.

Two leaders, named Cabral and Baez, for some years al-
ternately held power in Dominica. By Thaddeus Stevens's
favor, which Seward had secured, a sum of money was appropriated for Admiral Porter and F. W. Seward, the son of the
Secretary of State and his assistant in the State Department,
to proceed secretly to San Domingo to arrange, if possible,
for purchasing the gulf and peninsula of Samana, a harbor
coveted for some time by the prophetic eyes of travellers, as

---

[1] Richardson, Messages and Papers, vol. vi, p. 580.
[2] Ibid., p. 688.

a naval outpost.[1] They were authorized to offer the Dominican government $2,000,000.[2] Obstacles arose to prevent the
consummation of this plan. But the trip of Admiral Porter
and young Seward directed attention to the subject and in a
few months a sable representative of the Dominican government arrived in Washington, ready to sign a treaty along the
lines which had been suggested by our State Department.[3]
As Seward's tenure of office drew to an end there were assurances from Baez, who had returned to power in 1868, that
the whole of Dominica might be ceded to the United
States.[4]

President Johnson in his last message in 1868, expressed himself as favorable to the acquisition of both Hayti and Dominica.[5] The scheme had its friends in Congress. In January
and February, 1869, General Banks of Massachusetts and
Mr. Orth of Indiana introduced resolutions in the House on
the subject of annexation, though they did not gain more than
the feeblest support for their measures.[6]

Grant had had Quixotic ideas about our duties in Mexico
with reference to Maximilian, which very certainly would have
led us into war with that country as well as with France,[7] and
he was in the President's office for but a short time when he
was revolving in his mind plans for the future of Cuba. He
would have added that island to the national domain, if he

[1] Seward at Washington, vol. iii, pp. 310-16.
[2] Senate Ex. Doc., 41st Cong. 3rd sess., no. 17, p. 6.
[3] Seward in Washington, vol. iii, pp. 344-5, 372.
[4] Ibid., pp. 392-3; Senate Ex. Doc., 41st Cong. 3rd sess., no. 17, pp.
4-8.
[5] Richardson, Messages and Papers, vol. vi, p. 689.
[6] The first plan called for a protectorate to cover Hayti and San
Domingo in the interest of peaceful social conditions and orderly government upon the island. This scheme was rejected by a vote of 226
to 36. (Cong. Globe, 40th Cong. 3rd sess., pp. 317-9, 333-40.) The
second plan provided for the annexation of the Dominican portion of
the island and its incorporation in the American Union as a territory.
It was laid upon the table by a vote of 110 to 63. (Ibid., pp. 769,
972-3.)
[7] See vol. i of this work, p. 510. "When our war ended," Grant said
to J. R. Young, "I urged upon President Johnson an immediate invasion of Mexico." (J. R. Young, Around the World with General Grant,
vol. ii, pp. 163-4; cf. Adam Badeau, Grant in Peace, p. 180.)

could have brought so much about. But for Secretary Fish's services, as we shall soon see, the country, through Grant's brashness, would have been involved in a war with Spain.[1] Thwarted here the President's zeal for tropical annexions was concentrated upon San Domingo. He listened to the industrious leaders who came themselves or despatched their representatives to Washington to labor in behalf of the sale of their distracted country, and espoused their cause. Instead of confiding the subject to the State Department Grant, after failing to enlist the services of another person, called in one of his private secretaries, General Orville E. Babcock. The subsequent career of this man afforded complete proof of his unfitness to enjoy any public or private trust,[2] but in May, 1869, ten weeks after the new administration was begun, the Secretary of the Navy was asked to put a war ship at his disposal. He started away in July to inquire into the resources of the island, the social condition of the people and their temper, touching a possible change of their political allegiance.[3] Robeson, who by this time had come to the Navy Department, soon ordered a second war ship to the scene, thus giving an appearance of force to the mission, and on September 4 Babcock, as "aide-de-camp to his excellency Ulysses S. Grant, President of the United States of America," signed a protocol which he had entered into with the authorized agents of the Dominican republic, stipulating that in consideration of the payment of $1,500,000 to extinguish the debt of the country, they would transfer it to the United States. It was specified, furthermore, that "his excellency, General Grant, President of the United States," would promise "privately to use all his influence in order that the idea of annexing the Dominican republic to the United States may acquire such a degree of popularity among members of Congress as will be necessary for its accomplishment."

Babcock returned to Washington. From time to time there

---

[1] Cf. Pierce, Memoir and Letters of Sumner, vol. iv, 428.
[2] Cf. ibid., p. 429, and authorities there carefully cited.
[3] Cf. Cong. Globe, 41st Cong. 3rd sess., p. 233.

had been casual references by the President in Cabinet meetings to his plan to send an agent to Dominica, and there had been—perforce—a quiet acquiescence in the mission. The impression was given out that it was a mere tour of observation and inquiry. But now one day upon their coming together the heads of the departments found the table in the President's room filled with specimens of the mineral and vegetable products of the island, the great value of which Babcock was ready to explain. As he was rather frigidly received he left the apartment, and Grant immediately proceeded to state the case. "Babcock is here and has brought with him a treaty of annexation," said the President. "I suppose it is not formal, as he had no diplomatic powers, but we can easily cure that." All were dumbfounded.[1] Favor for what had been done was expressed on no side, the President passed to other subjects and never again referred to San Domingo in meetings of the Cabinet.[2]

Having been kept in ignorance of the negotiations the Secretary of State felt that he had no recourse but to resign. Twice he did so, once in writing, but later reconsidered his action at Grant's desire and gave his support, however reluctantly, to the enterprise.[3]

[1] "To say that never before in the whole history of government had any President made such a naïve exhibition is quite within safe bounds. Ignorance of law and usage and an utter absence of the sense of propriety were about equally pronounced." (C. F. Adams, Lee at Appomattox, p. 131.) "One of the strangest, not to say most astounding things that ever occurred in the history of the country."—H. McCulloch, Men and Measures, p. 353.

[2] Cox asked the question—"But, Mr. President, has it been settled, then, that we want to annex San Domingo?" This inquiry embarrassed Grant who colored and "smoked hard at his cigar." He looked at Fish at his right who was impassively gazing at the portfolio before him, and at Boutwell on the left, where also there was no response. (J. D. Cox, Atlantic Monthly, August, 1895.) In reviewing his administration, Grant, while he was travelling around the world after stepping down from the presidency, said "I never allowed the Cabinet to interfere when my mind was made up."—J. R. Young, Around the World, vol. ii, p. 154.

[3] Mr. Fish was wont to say in later years in recalling this incident that upon presenting his resignation the President had remonstrated with a "Please do not do this. We cannot spare you. Mrs. Grant

After his conference with the President Babcock in November returned to San Domingo and, on December 3, concluded two treaties with the Dominican government, one for the annexation of the republic, the other for the lease of the bay of Samana. President Grant, meanwhile, until all the arrangements should be completed, would guarantee Dominica against Haytian or other foreign intervention. Babcock sent officers of the navy ashore at Samana to raise the American flag. During 1870 no less than twelve different American war ships were employed in these waters. In plain terms they were serving the revolutionist, Baez, against the rival revolutionist, Cabral. They were used even to convey Baez himself, members of his staff and the troops enlisted in his interest from port to port, so that for a time the navy of the United States was the navy of this Spanish negro. Admiral Poor steamed into Port-au-Prince and threatened the Haytian government, if it should adopt any policy calculated to shake the precarious hold of Baez upon the reins of power.[1] Nothing that was done in this connection was disavowed by the President. He afterward said publicly that Babcock had acted in accordance with his instructions.[2]

The "aide-de-camp" having completed his work early in December, 1869, returned to Washington with the treaties. So much had been done on Grant's personal authority and the matter must now go to the Senate. With a view to bringing the subject before that body the President adopted an extraordinary course. One night early in January he appeared at Sumner's house. The senator from Massachusetts was at dinner and had for his guests two Republican journalists, John W. Forney and Ben. Perley Poore. The President was brought

and I need you in the administration as our social guide." (Based on the conversations of several men with Mr. Fish. Cf. J. F. Rhodes, vol. vi, p. 348; Pierce, Memoir and Letters of Sumner, vol. iv, p. 443; Sumner's Works, vol. xiv, p. 259; J. D. Cox, Atlantic Monthly, August, 1895; C. F. Adams, Lee at Appomattox, pp. 222, 247.)

[1] The correspondence with and the orders issued to the commander on duty in these waters may be found in Senate Ex. Doc., 41st Cong. 3rd sess., nos. 34 and 45.

[2] E. L. Pierce, vol. iv, pp. 430-3.

in; a little later all adjourned to the library where he began to speak of the business which was the occasion of his visit to the chairman of the Committee on Foreign Relations, whom he addressed, however, as the "chairman of the Judiciary Committee." From this most informal proceeding on Grant's part much came very soon. Although the precise nature of the treaties was not communicated to Sumner, if, indeed, President Grant himself had full acquaintance with the details, he said—"Mr. President, I am an administration man and whatever you do will always find in me the most careful and candid consideration." [1] The next day Babcock called upon the senator to show him, and to explain to him the treaties, which on January 10, 1870, were sent to the Senate [2] to be referred to the Committee on Foreign Relations.

In the same way Grant aimed to bring the subject to the favorable attention of other senators. He advanced across the room at an evening reception in Washington to speak to Schurz, who was asked to the White House for a conversation. Coming there the President without introduction attacked the topic in hand. Would Schurz vote for annexation? The new senator from Missouri, with the frankness which characterized him, said that he could not do so, for such an extension of the national domain in his belief would be contrary to the best interests of the republic. Moreover, since he felt certain that the proposal could not receive a two-thirds vote in the Senate, he expressed regret that the administration should expose itself to defeat by committing itself irrevocably to the enterprise.[3] But the President seemed quite unconvinced of the value of the advice which Schurz had offered him, relapsed into silence as was his wont when he was opposed, and, with that tenacity which had marked his career on the military field, prepared himself for battle.

Little public approval was shown for the scheme anywhere and not one member of the Committee on Foreign Relations,

---

[1] Cf. B. P. Poore, Reminiscences, vol. ii, p. 280.
[2] Richardson, Messages and Papers, vol. vii, pp. 45-6.
[3] Reminiscences of Carl Schurz, vol. iii, pp. 307-8.

except Morton, expressed favor for it.[1] Sumner acted without haste or appearance of partiality; he aimed to influence no one's mind for or against the undertaking. But many things were being brought to his attention. He was informed that the navy was being used to support one revolutionist against another; that San Domingo's independence and, likely, as well Hayti's was menaced. But yet more potential was the fact that these countries were republics, and that their inhabitants were black people. He would raise no hand to extinguish them and bring to naught their efforts for self government.

As opposition grew and the prospect of the treaty being reported favorably out of the committee diminished, Grant, full of the idea that he was commander in chief, looked about him for the underlings in camp who were thwarting his will. He soon found Sumner. No men at ground could have been more uncongenial than these two. By training, by tradition, by temperament, in person and in mind—one almost without education, the other overweighted with it; one simple and informal, the other proud and austere; one set upon the realization of a material object, the other roaming the sphere of thought to serve some human cause—they were antitheses.[2]

Industrious meddlers put forth efforts to widen the breach between them. Sumner had not enthusiastically favored Grant's nomination for the Presidency. Already in November, 1867, at a private meeting in Washington, attended by Babcock (later no doubt the informant) Sumner had said that for the party to choose a military leader was a confession of weakness, and a reflection upon its interest in and capacity for civil administration.[3] He had rather conspicuously objected to the plan for excepting A. T. Stewart from the provisions of law when Grant wished to make the New York merchant Secretary of the Treasury. It was clear to Grant, too, that

---

[1] Pierce, Memoir and Letters of Sumner, vol. iv, p. 436.
[2] Cf. G. F. Hoar, Autobiography, vol. i, pp. 211-2; Boutwell, Sixty Years in Public Affairs, vol. ii, pp. 214-5; C. F. Adams, Lee at Appomattox, pp. 109-10.
[3] D. C. Forney in Cincinnati Commercial, cited in Pierce, vol. iv, p. 358.

some of his appointments, though as a rule they were obligingly confirmed, were distasteful to the senator from Massachusetts.[1]

The President chose to say that he had called upon Sumner to ask him to support the treaty with San Domingo. Sumner had promised to do so; now he opposed it. This misunderstanding on Grant's side was the excuse for the unrelenting war which he waged upon the Titan of the Senate. Less than a year after the new Radical administration had begun, therefore, the elements were at loggerheads. Grant was trying to impose upon a co-ordinate branch of the government a policy to which it was hostile, with a madness not very different from Andrew Johnson's. For smaller offenses not long since the House had impeached and the Senate had tried that man.[2]

The prospect of defeat but goaded Grant, who was possessed of what Badeau called the "soldier's instinct" for victory, to new endeavors. He read the riot act to the members of his Cabinet, as if they were a headquarters staff, saying that he would have their unquestioned support.[3] He called senators to the White House and to his room at the Capitol to urge them to ratify the treaty. Babcock appeared before the Committee on Foreign Relations. Four months were allowed for action. On March 14, 1870, Grant notified the Senate that the specified limit would expire on the 29th day of that month, expressing an "earnest wish" that action should ensue before the time named, and a "sincere hope" that this action would be favorable.[4] But without avail for the next day the committee made an adverse report over the names of Sumner,

[1] Pierce, vol. iv, p. 380.

[2] Sumner a little later said as much. "The whole case," he declared, was "more reprehensible and also plainly more unconstitutional and more illegal than anything alleged against Andrew Johnson on his impeachment." (Speech in Senate, May 31, 1872, Works, vol. xv, p. 89.) He had exclaimed at a dinner in Washington when an Englishman had intimated that Grant would be elected for a second term: "No, he'll be impeached for high crimes and misdemeanors. I tell you he will be impeached." (Reminiscences of Wm. M. Stewart, p. 247.)

[3] C. F. Adams, Lee at Appomattox, pp. 142, 218, 232.

[4] Richardson, Messages and Papers, vol. vii, pp. 52-3.

Patterson, Schurz, Cameron and Casserly. Harlan supported
Morton in favor of the treaty.[1]

The debate which began on the 24th, and was continued behind closed doors, was opened by Sumner in a speech four
hours in length, only parts of which, because of the enforced
secrecy of the proceedings, came to public knowledge. His
condemnation of the proposal to acquire San Domingo took
rank, however, in the estimation of men who were present,
with his exhaustive and brilliant defence three years earlier
of Seward's plan for the purchase of Alaska.[2] The points
made were numerous, but those which met the warmest approval related to the impolicy of embarking upon schemes having to do with the annexion of tropical lands which contained
populations not easy to assimilate; the conditions of incessant
revolution which gave promise, should the country come to
the United States, of new wars; and the injustice of interfering
with the course of the colored race in the West Indies. "To
the African," said Sumner, "belongs the equatorial belt and he
should enjoy it undisturbed." [3]

The discussion upon both sides continued for several weeks.
On May 31 the President again addressed the Senate, submitting an additional article, extending the time which, contrary to his wish, had been allowed to expire, and stating at
some length the merits of the annexation. The people "yearned
for the protection of our free institutions and laws, our progress and civilization." They must look for "outside support."
If they were not to come to us they would with certainty seek
a refuge with some European power. The island's value as
a naval outpost was dwelt upon; its riches were described;
its importance to us commercially was referred to and magni-
fied. In short the President believed, so he averred, that the
ratification of the treaty, for which he had "unusual anxiety,"
would "redound greatly to the glory of the two countries interested, to civilization and to the extirpation of the institu-

[1] Pierce, vol. iv, p. 440.
[2] Cf. N. Y. Tribune, March 25, 1870.
[3] Pierce, vol. iv, p. 441.

tion of slavery." It would be "a rapid stride," said he, "toward that greatness which the intelligence, industry and enterprise of the citizens of the United States entitle this country to assume among nations." [1]

But few of the leaders of the Senate could see the subject through his eyes. The press, also, except for a journal here and there, bent upon courting the favor of the President, openly antagonized or else ridiculed the scheme. Popular approval for the project, said the New York Evening Post, did not appear on any side.[2] The sense of the country, said the New York Nation, was "firmly opposed to the annexation of the Dominicans." [3] Senator Wilson, Sumner's colleague, though he finally was brought to vote for the treaty, said that nine-tenths of the people of Massachusetts were opposed to it. A meeting in Cooper Institute in New York, which it was expected would reflect the great interest felt in that city for the plan to annex the little negro state, came to nothing. Resolved upon achieving success at any cost Babcock, cooperating with two speculators who were keeping Baez in power, as against his old rival, Cabral, caused a citizen of Connecticut, named Hatch, to be imprisoned in San Domingo, lest he come to the United States to make his influence felt against ratification. Such a person as Babcock, said Senator Ferry of Connecticut, ought no longer to be an officer of the United States army. Sumner said he should be "cashiered at once." [4]

Fish, with a loyalty which was noteworthy in view of his earlier friendship for Sumner and his personal convictions on this subject, visited the senator to persuade him to forego his opposition, even hinting at his appointment as minister to England in Motley's room as a reward for a change of his attitude.[5] At any rate Sumner understood that the sugges-

[1] Richardson, vol. vii, pp. 61-3.
[2] Issue of July 1, 1870.   [3] Issue of Dec. 29, 1870.
[4] Cong. Globe, 41st Cong. 2nd sess., p. 4195; Pierce, vol. iv, pp. 442-3.
[5] Sumner's Works, vol. xiv, p. 260; Pierce, vol. iv, pp. 443-4; cf. Adam Badeau, Grant in Peace, p. 216, for another view of the meaning of this interview.

tion might be a tender of the office, and, whether Fish was
an authorized agent or not, it is known that the clique around
Grant had such a scheme in mind. By sending Sumner to England they would be rid of him in the Senate. The President
favored the plan, but he would make the appointment, so he
declared, only with the understanding that the senator should
be removed from his new office as soon as his name should be
confirmed.[1]

Sumner had no intention of being so served and publicly,
with vigor, repelled the suggestion at the time it was made,
and afterward. Debate upon the treaty was resumed by the
Senate in executive session on June 29, when Morrill of Vermont made a speech of some length against it. The next day
a vote was taken. There were 28 senators for and 28 against
it, and, as less than two-thirds had expressed themselves in
favor of ratification, it was rejected. Among the number in
favor of the treaty were eight of the new senators from the
Southern states, and Northern Radicals like Cameron, Cattell,
Conkling, Drake, Harlan, Thayer and Wilson. In the opposition with Sumner were Edmunds, Ferry, Fowler, Morrill of
Maine, Morrill of Vermont, Patterson of New Hampshire,
Ross, Schurz, Scott of Pennsylvania, Sprague, Willey and all
the Democrats. Sherman refrained from voting.[2]

For some time the President had been using his appointing
power to forward the cause of San Domingo,[3] and now he
was ready to take a step which, to many persons, revealed
him in a more unfavorable light than any under which he
had been seen since coming to his great office. When the
Senate had refused to confirm General McClellan as minister
to England to succeed Charles Francis Adams, in 1868, President Johnson had forwarded to that body the name of one
of its own members, Reverdy Johnson of Maryland. This
distinguished jurist had been a senator of the United States
as long ago as in 1845, and during the war had returned to the

[1] C. F. Adams, Lee at Appomattox, p. 137.
[2] Pierce, vol. iv, p. 445; Executive Journal, vol. xvii, pp. 502-3.
[3] C. F. Adams, Lee at Appomattox, p. 218.

upper house of Congress. He was confirmed without opposition [1] and proceeded to London. That he would not remain
very long was clearly understood, and in view of some of
Grant's appointments to diplomatic posts it was accounted a
fortunate thing, when, on April 12, 1869, he announced that
he had chosen John Lothrop Motley for the court of St. James.

Throughout the war the noted historian of the Netherlands
had been our minister to Austria. But he had been taken to
task for his political opinions by President Johnson in a manner which he considered to be insulting and in 1866 he resigned. To his surprise his resignation was accepted.[2] The
incident rather widely advertised him and he took his place
in the Radical Martyr Book. He had returned from Europe
in the summer of 1868 and had made an address during the
campaign very flattering to the claims of General Grant.
Companion and friend of George Bancroft, still at Berlin, and
of Bismarck (all had been students at the University of Goet-
tingen) well known and much liked by Fish and Sumner, he
was a prominent figure in Washington, whither he had come
to spend a few weeks prior to the inauguration. He met the
President-elect over the cigars, an hour which Grant used for
getting acquainted with other men, and the nomination followed as a matter of course.[3] Many believed that the appointment had been made at Sumner's urgent personal desire.
In some degree this was the truth. Grant now chose to have
it appear that this was the case,[4] and Sumner, on his side,
seems to have felt a sense of proprietorship in the minister.[5]
To punish the senator from Massachusetts, for opposing the

[1] Pierce, vol. iv, p. 383.
[2] O. W. Holmes, Life of Motley, pp. 120-39; Seward at Washington,
vol. iii, pp. 355-6.
[3] Following Pierce and his cited authorities, vol. iv, pp. 380-1; Sumner's Works, vol. xiv, p. 270. C. F. Adams told Moran that Motley
had made "a dead set at President Grant" through Sumner and Hooper.
(Moran's Diary, Nov. 30, 1871.) At one time, according to Badeau,
Motley's name was under discussion for secretary of state. (Grant in
Peace, pp. 152-3.)
[4] Cf. Boutwell, Sixty Years in Public Affairs, vol. ii, p. 214; Adam
Badeau, Grant in Peace, pp. 152-3, 197-8.
[5] C. F. Adams, Lee at Appomattox, p. 246.

annexation scheme, and Motley, for having adopted some of Sumner's views on the *Alabama* question, the minister's resignation was demanded on the day following the rejection of the San Domingo treaty. Fish, as the President's agent, expressed his regret that it must be his hand to serve a friend so cavalierly. The news sent many to the President to protest against a measure which bore the appearance of being marked by plain vindictiveness,[1] but Grant was immovable and on July 15, 1870, the last day of the session, he nominated Senator Frelinghuysen of New Jersey as Motley's successor.

In his message in December, 1870, Grant returned to his obsession and reiterated the extravagant statements about the value of San Domingo to the United States which had marked his communication to the Senate in May. A part of an island in the Caribbean Sea, though now inhabited by only 120,000 negroes living in "cave huts" on bananas and cocoanuts,[2] would, so he asserted, support "in luxury" a population of 10,000,000. The acquisition of Dominica would reduce our importations by $100,000,000, turn the balance of foreign trade in favor of the United States, lead to the employment of multitudes of laborers, reduce the cost of living and contribute in a large way to the extinguishment of the national debt.[3] The moment the project was abandoned, he said, some European nation would step in to seize the prize which in our folly we had rejected. He would have a commission visit San Domingo to make arrangements for its acquisition by the

[1] George Jones, publisher of the New York Times, told Moran in London that Motley's removal was solely due to Sumner's "haughty demeanor and hostility to the President." Grant told Jones that he had appointed Motley to please Sumner, since he himself had known nothing of him and never saw him until after his own election. Now he would remove the man to please himself because of "the San Domingo business." (Moran's Diary, Aug. 22, 1870.)

[2] Capt. George B. McClellan's Report in 1854 in House Ex. Doc., 41st Cong. 3rd sess., no. 43, p. 8.

[3] Richardson, Messages and Papers, vol. vii, pp. 99-100. Such assertions, however strongly they might attest to their author's tenacity of purpose, betrayed him as one of the most truly ignorant persons on the subject of political economy whom the American people have ever elevated to the President's office. Cf. N. Y. Nation, June 16, 1870.

United States. He proposed, too, since it seemed certain that a two-thirds vote could in no manner be secured for a treaty, that the end should be brought about by a joint resolution. On nine different days in the last session Ben Butler, who was further to round out his career as a violent "San Domingo man," endeavored without success to get a hearing for himself on this subject.[1] Now the President advocated this policy.

The first step was to obtain authority for the commission which again brought Sumner into the debate. San Domingo was now no longer a subject for speech behind closed doors. On December 21, 1870, Sumner took the floor and in a finished address, in which a friend has said that "all the fire of youth came back again," he reviewed the whole "long drawn machination" to take this island from the negroes who were entitled to it "by right of possession, by their sweat and blood mingling with the soil, by tropical position, by its burning sun and by unalterable laws of climate," and to impose it upon the United States, which wished for no such territory and would not be benefited by its annexation to our domain. Baez and his agents, who kept up the agitation for the cession, were described as "political jockeys." Babcock's part in the conspiracy and the despatch of war ships to these waters for a "dance of blood" were scathingly denounced. The President, said Sumner, had not only interfered in the internal affairs of San Domingo but he had also menaced the independent existence of Hayti.[2] Likening Grant's course now to the repeal of the Missouri Compromise by the passage of the Kansas-Nebraska bill and the attempt to make a slave state out of Kansas under the Lecompton constitution, he passionately called upon Colfax, who sat in the chair, to go to the President and "to address him frankly with the voice of a friend to whom he must hearken," urging him to shun "the example of Franklin Pierce, James Buchanan and Andrew Johnson."[3]

[1] April, May and June, 1870; cf. Pierce, vol. iv, p. 453.
[2] What had been done Sumner later described as "a prolonged war dance" about the island. Sumner's Works, vol. xiv, p. 318.
[3] Cong. Globe, 41st Cong. 3rd sess., pp. 226-31; Sumner's Works, vol.

The debate which ensued was marked by great asperity. Finally, near dawn, after an all night session, the resolution, which took the form of an authorization of the President to appoint a commission to investigate the subject, was passed by the Senate [1] and it was sent to the House where it was approved on January 10, 1871, but only with an amendment distinctly stating that such action should not be understood to be expressive of a desire on the part of Congress to annex the island.[2] The Senate concurred in the amendment,[3] though not before Sumner had had the opportunity to apply to the situation a famous phrase, which was suggested by the "painful news," contained in the daily press, of the spread of civil war in the island. The whole scheme, said he, was "nothing less than buying a bloody law suit." [4]

The House amendment put the mark of death upon the measure which only awaited the formality of later interment. The President appointed Benjamin F. Wade, Andrew D. White and Samuel G. Howe to be members of the commission, who, accompanied by the negro leader, Frederick Douglass, as a secretary, and several other men, including a considerable number of scientific experts and journalists, set sail for the island on January 18, where their observations were continued for about five weeks.

Motley in London had been asked to resign. He refused to do so. Sumner called the removal "brutal"; it was "heartless and cruel." [5] The bitterness of the senator's relations with Grant increased. He often was under terrific excitement.

xiv, pp. 89 et seq. This speech he afterward printed under the title "Naboth's Vineyard."

[1] Cong. Globe, 41st Cong. 3rd sess., p. 271. The vote was 32 to 9, 30 senators being absent from the chamber.

[2] Ibid., p. 416. The papers bearing on the subject sent into Congress at this time are in Senate Ex. Doc., 41st Cong. 3rd sess., no. 17, and House Ex. Doc., 41st Cong., 3rd sess., nos. 42 and 43.

[3] Cong. Globe, 41st Cong. 3rd sess., p. 431.

[4] Ibid., p. 404. Sumner had said on December 21 that "no prudent man" would buy a lawsuit. In taking Dominica "we should buy a bloody lawsuit."

[5] Pierce, vol. iv, p. 448.

Following a guest to the door of his home he would roar, said Fish, "like a bull of Bashan" in his rhetorical denunciations of the President, who in the White House, across Lafayette Square, many thought, must hear the loud words.[1] The President on his side was inflamed by the young staff officers with whom he had surrounded himself and other friends who dealt in much tale-bearing to Sumner's disadvantage. Grant had declared, one said, that if he were not President he would hold the senator personally responsible for his insults, and there was talk of a challenge to mortal combat. According to another story Babcock, who took up Grant's cause, was ready to thwack Sumner over the head.[2] On indubitable testimony Grant was in so angry a state of mind one night that, while walking with George F. Hoar near Sumner's house in Washington, the President shook his closed fist at the windows. "The man who lives up there," he said, "has abused me in a way which I have never suffered from any other man living."[3]

In his correspondence in the Motley matter Fish had used words at which Sumner took new offense. It was now clearly understood that the senator, who, so long and with so much real distinction, had served as the chairman of the Committee on Foreign Relations would be expelled from that place in further punishment for his attitude toward the President. His vanity was increasing with his years. More than ever was he arrogant and overbearing. Fish, so long on the most pleasant and trustful intimacy with him, now held him to be a "monomaniac"; he was "partially crazy," and he was forfeiting many of even his oldest friendships.[4]

The threat to depose him from his chairmanship had been heard for many months, and when the Forty-second Congress should meet on March 4, 1871, it was predicted that his name would not be found upon the list prepared by the Republican caucus. So it was. Three of the five members of the commit-

[1] C. F. Adams, Lee at Appomattox, pp. 246-7.
[2] Cong. Globe, 41st Cong. 3rd sess., pp. 217-18.
[3] George F. Hoar, Autobiography, vol. i, p. 211.
[4] C. F. Adams, Lee at Appomattox, pp. 249, 252.

tee designated for the preparation of the "slate" gave the place
to Simon Cameron, who was the ranking member, though he
had the least possible talent for its duties, either on intellectual
or moral grounds. In the caucus the vote against Sumner was
26 to 21, and he was removed with the excuse that he had
ceased to represent the views of a majority of his Republican
colleagues in the Senate, and that he was no longer on terms
with the President and the Secretary of State which would
allow him to converse or associate with them for the conduct
of public business. He was to be consoled by the chairmanship of a new Committee on Privileges and Elections which
he promptly declined.[1]

If the unhappy San Domingo scheme were not already dead
such action was well designed to finish it.[2] At the end of
March Sumner again secured the floor and delivered his second
speech against San Domingo. For hours previous to the
time set for him to begin crowds besieged the Capitol, seeking·
admission to the Senate galleries. The House adjourned and
the members thronged in upon the floor. Ministers came
from the legations. Justices of the supreme court, members
of the Cabinet, high officers in the army—in all 2,000 people,
many of them of great distinction, were gathered within reach
of Sumner's voice, which for three and a half hours, in solemn
and earnest measure, discussed the question of policy involved
in the annexation of Dominica.[3]

It was accounted by the "San Domingo men" a most inopportune occasion for a further assault upon the scheme, for
the commissioners that very day were to arrive home from

[1] Pierce, vol. iv, p. 470; Horace White, Life of Trumbull, pp. 343-7;
John Sherman, Recollections, vol. i, pp. 470-3; Sumner's Works, vol.
xiv, pp. 254-76; C. F. Adams, Lee at Appomattox, pp. 225-44.
[2] The removal, said Harper's Weekly, was "a grave political blunder."
(March 25, 1871.) The "general impression" was that it was "a fatal
blunder," a "fatal blow to the San Domingo scheme," said the New
York Nation. (March 16, 1871.) "That it was a mistake," said the
New York Tribune, "we cannot doubt."—March 13, 1871.
[3] Sumner spoke to resolutions which he himself had introduced and
which are printed in Cong. Globe, 42nd Cong. 1st sess., pp. 294-304,
Senate Mis. Doc., 42nd Cong. 1st sess., no. 35; Sumner's Works, vol.
xiv, p. 168.

the tour of inspection upon which Grant had sent them. On April 5 the President communicated to Congress their report which, as everyone had anticipated, was favorable to annexation. Indeed, he observed, still making the cause his own, what the commissioners now stated "in regard to the productiveness and healthfulness" of the country, "of the unanimity of the people for annexation to the United States, and of their peaceable character" more than sustained all that he had heretofore said on this subject.[1] A few days more of argument and the enterprise was heard of in Congress for the last time.[2] It was impossible to obtain the approval of two-thirds of the senators for a treaty, equally impossible to get a majority vote in the House for a joint resolution, and San Domingo did not become a part of the United States.[3]

Not a whit more enlightened or creditable to Grant personally was his course with reference to Cuba. Since September, 1868, insurrection had been again in progress on that island. Plantations were laid waste, men were murdered and assassinated, savage battles were fought. Scores of prisoners were slaughtered in cold blood by the Spanish military authorities, while, on the other hand, General Quesada, the insurgent chieftain, boasted that in one day he had deliberately slain 650 captives.[4] The contest was being waged on both sides in violation of the principles of humanity and the established rules of war—"with a degree of ferocity and a disre-

[1] Richardson, Messages and Papers, vol. vii, pp. 128-31. The commission's report is in Senate Ex. Doc., 42nd Cong. 1st sess., no. 9. Cf. A. D. White, Autobiography, vol. i, pp. 483-507, for his recollections of the journey.
[2] Sumner's resolutions were laid on the table on March 29, 1871, by a vote of 39 to 16.—Cong. Globe, 42nd Cong. 1st sess., p. 329.
[3] Grant, however, surrendered none of his faith in the undertaking which he had so determinedly espoused. In his last message in 1876 he repeated his account of the great and various advantages which would have accrued to the country as a result of the annexation of the little black republic.—Richardson, Messages and Papers, vol. vii, pp. 411-3; see also U. S. Grant, Personal Memoirs, vol. ii, p. 550, and A. D. White, Autobiography, vol. i, p. 179.
[4] Grant's message, Richardson, vol. vii, p. 64.

gard of human life," it was said, "unknown in modern warfare." [1] The government plainly was unable to suppress the
revolt.

Such methods rightly aroused the indignation of the American people and horrified the world. Agitators came to the
United States, as they had done on like occasions before, to
awaken sympathy for the cause of "Cuban independence."
A nest of Cuban refugees in New York exhibited great zeal
in publishing a newspaper,[2] organizing and advertising meetings, making speeches and giving concerts, the proceeds of
which were to be used to aid the revolution. Soft-hearted
ministers were persuaded to deliver sermons and to say prayers
in their churches in behalf of the cause. Indeed the "junta"
formed in New York what they called the "independent
government of Cuba," and designated one of their number as
an agent to go to Washington, where they audaciously supposed he might be received as their diplomatic representative.[3]
They supported a lobby to work upon the feelings of Congress,
offered for sale the bonds of their imaginary future Cuban
republic and purchased and shipped away arms and munitions
to the insurgents. From time to time filibustering parties left
our shores, and, when they were not intercepted and prevented
from going on their way by our authorities, were landed on
the island.[4] Such activity was certain to lead to diplomatic
representations by Spain [5] and to a retaliatory course on the
part of that government's agents in Cuba. The rights of
American citizens were brought into question and the State
Department was busily employed with the cases, some of
which threatened grave outcome. The American brig, *Mary
Lowell*, laden with war material for the revolutionists, was
seized by a Spanish frigate in March, 1869. Early in 1870
the *Colonel Lloyd Aspinwall*, flying the American flag, was

[1] American Annual Cyclopedia for 1870, p. 687.
[2] Called La Revolucion.
[3] Cf. Senate Ex. Doc., 41st Cong. 2nd sess., no. 7, pp. 14, 69.
[4] Geneva Arbitration, vol. ii, pp. 260-1.
[5] Papers Relating to Cuba presented in the House of Representatives,
Feb. 21, 1870, pp. 133-8.

captured and towed into Havana. The *Champion*, an American sloop, aleak, made port at Santiago and was hauled under the guns of a Spanish man-of-war. Two Americans, named Speakman and Wyeth, charged with having participated in a filibustering expedition, were shot as pirates at Santiago. Other men, held to be under the protection of our flag, were executed without proper trial. Thirty-six of our citizens were unlawfully imprisoned; the property of 20 was confiscated.[1]

Fish inherited from Seward some of the duties imposed upon the State Department by the Cuban situation. But more soon came to him. His first important act was to address the Spanish minister at Washington as to the recent order of the captain-general, declaring that all persons found on board vessels which were carrying arms, munitions and men in aid of the revolution, when seized in Spanish waters or on the high seas near the island, would be shot.[2] Spain on her side asked Fish to cause the President to issue a proclamation, as Fillmore had done in 1851, generally warning the people to desist from acting in behalf of the insurgents in violation of the law of nations, and reciting the penalties for engaging in such enterprises.[3]

So much the Secretary of State declined to do. The conditions in 1851 and 1869 he found not to be analogous. He did not "perceive the necessity or the propriety at this time" of such action. The government would interpose its power against every improper or unlawful exercise of sympathies likely to lead to infractions of neutrality. But more it would not do.[4] He had frequently remonstrated with the Spanish authorities "in the interest of humanity" against the atrocities which marked the progress of the war,[5] and Sickles, when he went to his post late in June, 1869, bore with him instructions to inquire of the gov-

---

[1] Senate Ex. Doc., 41st Cong. 2nd sess., no. 108.   [2] Ibid., no. 7, p. 12.
[3] Ibid., p. 16; cf. Geneva Arbitration, vol. i, pp. 711-2.
[4] Senate Ex. Doc., 41st Cong. 2nd sess., no. 7, pp. 16-8.   [5] Ibid., p. 74.

ernment at Madrid, in the name of the President, if they would not accept the good offices of the United States to terminate the conflict. He was to ask whether there might not be a relinquishment of Spain's rights in Cuba, in return for the payment by the people of the island of a sum which might be mutually agreed upon. Slavery was to be abolished and pending the result of the negotiations an armistice should be declared.

The inquiry, it was added, might also cover Porto Rico. To secure a compliance with the suggestion Sickles was authorized to intimate that the granting of belligerent rights to the insurgents by the United States was imminent. Such action probably could be not much longer withheld.[1] When asked to name a sum Sickles spoke of $125,000,000.[2] The exchange of conversations and notes continued for some time, Spain returning with a plan for a plebiscite to ascertain the sense of the Cuban people, which Fish declared to be impracticable, since no vote that could be taken in the disorganized condition of the country would indicate the popular will.[3]

While these events quietly proceeded the country was profoundly incensed by the news which daily continued to come from the island, and a formidable demand arose for a recognition by Congress of its independence from Spain, or, at the very least, of the insurgents as a people entitled to belligerent rights. The Secretary of War, General Rawlins, had been won over by the advocates of Cuban freedom and pressed the cause upon Grant.[4] On June 9, 1869, only two months after he had come into office, the President was suggesting a recognition of belligerency to Sumner, who opposed the idea.[5] It would be doing for Spain, argued Grant, only that which she had so promptly done for us at the outbreak

---

[1] House Ex. Doc., 41st Cong. 2nd sess., no. 160, pp. 15-7.
[2] Ibid., p. 18.
[3] Ibid, pp. 25, 31, 41; cf. Moran's Diary.
[4] J. H. Wilson, Life of Rawlins, p. 359.
[5] Pierce, vol. iv, p. 409.

of the Southern rebellion.   He persisted against advice in his
characteristically dogged manner, directed that a proclamation be written recognizing the insurgents, signed it on August
19, 1869, in the cabin of a Fall River steamboat on his way
to Boston, and forwarded it to Washington by Assistant Secretary of State Bancroft Davis with instructions to Mr. Fish to
attach the official seal to the paper and issue it. But Fish,
fortunately, was able to be of more service to the administration and to the country in this emergency than he yet had
been, or would be, on the subject of San Domingo.   He chose
to stand or fall on the Cuban question.   He saw that the
insurgents had no army, no courts, no seaport, no capital city.
Indeed, they did not occupy a single town or hamlet.[1]   Their
warfare consisted of ambushes and massacres, the burning of
estates, the attacking of convoys and other guerrilla operations.   Great Britain or France, he wrote privately afterward,
might as well have recognized the belligerency of the Indians
in our "Black Hawk War."   So, while he signed the proclamation, he, instead of publishing it, put it in a safe in the State
Department, where it was permitted to remain.[2]

Fortunately for the course of affairs with reference to Cuba,
Rawlins died in a few days of his pulmonary disease and
Grant's attention was diverted by other events.   Thus the
President was prevented from embarking upon an active anti-
Spanish policy by Fish's "steadiness and wisdom."[3]   In his
message in December, 1869, he, under the guidance of his
Secretary of State, said that, while sympathizing with "all
people struggling for liberty and self government," it was
"due to our honor" to abstain from "enforcing our views upon
unwilling nations and from taking an interested part without
invitation" in other men's quarrels.   There was in Cuba no
war "in the sense of international law," and no "political

[1] Cf. words of Spanish minister at Washington in letter to Fish.—
House Ex. Doc., 41st Cong. 2nd sess., no. 160, p. 77.
[2] C. F. Adams, Lee at Appomattox, pp. 118-19; cf. Pierce, vol. iv, pp.
402-3.
[3] C. F. Adams, op. cit., p. 119.

organization of the insurgents sufficient to justify a recognition of belligerency." [1]

But the insurrection continued and the agitation for the intervention of our government went on actively. It was pointed out that Mexico, Chile, Colombia and Peru had declared the revolutionists to be belligerents. Several ex-Confederate officers had made their way to the island to espouse the insurgent cause. One of these, a General Jordan, who might not have been able to get amnesty for himself at Washington, came there, and, by much going about on the floor of Congress and in the lobbies, secured the promises of 100 members, it was said, for Cuban recognition. [2] A few millions of dollars worth of Cuban bonds, their payment made conditional upon our granting the revolutionists belligerent rights, mere "bets" on the action of the United States, [3] were flourished about. Whether any found their way into the hands of Congressmen or not, the very suggestion that they were available to influence votes led to corrupt charges and a committee of investigation. [4] Bills and resolutions on the subject of recognition appeared in the Senate and the House from the hands of impulsive and perfervid members. State legislatures passed resolutions urging Congress forward. Private organizations of many kinds in all parts of the country called for action in the interest of liberty and civilization. Petitions, bearing no less than 72,384 names, were presented in the House to be referred to the Committee on Foreign Affairs, whose chairman was that indefatigable "people's man," General N. P. Banks.

It was very well known on June 13, 1870, what that committee proposed to do on the next following day. Banks was a redoubtable advocate of Cuban independence and he

[1] Richardson, Messages and Papers, vol. vii, p. 31.
[2] He was rebuffed by only one, Representative George F. Hoar.— Cong. Globe, 41st Cong. 2nd sess., app., p. 540.
[3] Cong. Globe, 41st Cong. 2nd sess., p. 4487.
[4] Ibid., pp. 4318-22, 4486; N. Y. Evening Post, June 8, 1870; Washington Evening Star, June 9, 1870.

had prepared a report in favor of recognizing the insurgents. Four members, headed by Representative Orth of Indiana, would sign a minority report opposing the policy, but Banks's sonorous voice would ring with eloquence, as he denounced Spain's atrocious course in Cuba against an heroic people, who were suffering to be free.[1] Fish had striven for months to set the country right on this question. He had been laboring with Sherman and other senators and representatives, and he wrote a message on the subject for Grant. The President had refused to let it go out, and now another was prepared by the secretary's hand.[2] At the time Grant was fishing in Pennsylvania. Upon his return the paper was presented to him and, with the aid of Hoar, Cox and Robeson, he was induced "with great hesitation and with much reluctance to sign it."[3]

The President now was made to reiterate what he had said in December and more. Escaping their own island and "congregating in this country at a safe distance from the scene of danger" a large number of Cubans were endeavoring to embroil us in a fight which they themselves had come here to avoid. He unfolded their plot. They were selling bonds the value of which rested only on the expected declaration by us of the insurgents' belligerent rights. They were speculating upon their ability to involve us in the contest. The course of other presidents, from Washington onward, under like conditions was described. "The strict adherence" to a traditional rule of neutrality in such contests had been "one of the highest honors of American statesmanship." Fighting, "though fierce and protracted," did not "alone constitute war." There was still no "*de facto* political organization" which we could recognize. Action of the kind which was recommended, "if not justified by necessity," would be "a gratuitous demonstration of moral support to the rebellion."

[1] The majority and minority reports are in Cong. Globe, 41st Cong. 2nd sess., app., p. 454, and House Reports for the same Congress, no. 80.
[2] C. F. Adams, Lee at Appomattox, pp. 217, 228.
[3] Ibid., pp. 219-20.

The new risks and responsibilities which we should assume by such a movement were pointed out. Our commercial marine would become liable to search. Our coastwise as well as our foreign trade would suffer and the consequences were commended to the serious consideration of Congress.[1]

The surprise and anger of the "Free Cuba" men, when the message was received in Congress was boundless. The President had practically read them out of the party. Nothing was left for Banks but to bring in his report and for two or three days the orators raged. It was a step on Grant's part, said Representative Swann of Maryland, a member of the committee, "without precedent in our past legislative history." His anticipating the action of the House was a "deliberate attempt" to influence the course of that body. It was a "budget of assumed facts, illogical inferences and undigested absurdities"—an insult to Congress and to the country. The President had betrayed "the patriot cause of Cuba," and, "taking his position at the clerk's desk," had declared himself "an advocate of Spain."[2] He had "disrobed himself of the executive mantle," declared Fitch of Nevada.[3] The message had been prepared by "counsel," said Swann. Logan would support Grant "when he was cool, when he deliberated for himself, when he had not men around him to bother him and annoy him with their peculiar and interested notions." But the message was not from the President's hand. It did not express his views. It had been written when he was fishing up in Pennsylvania, whither it was not worth while to go "for more fish." They had all they needed in Washington.[4] Banks, beside himself with rage, said that upon hearing the paper read it sounded to him as if the person who had prepared it was in the pay of Spain and of the United States at the same time. He might be wrong on this point and he "hoped to God" that he was, but this was his belief. A

---

[1] Richardson, Messages and Papers, vol. vii, pp. 64-9.
[2] Cong. Globe, 41st Cong. 2nd sess., p. 4438.
[3] Ibid., p. 4443.   [4] Ibid., app., p. 500.

lawyer, who, for anything but money, should send to the representatives of the people such doctrines to act upon "ought to be forever reproved and forbidden the presence of civilized men." [1]

Fish was "grossly maligned and assailed." [2] The ugliest charge was to the effect that in December, 1869, he had released a fleet of thirty gunboats which had been designed by Ericsson and built by an American citizen, Cornelius Delamater, fifteen in shipyards in and around New York and fifteen on the Mystic River in Connecticut, for the account of the Spanish government. While still in port, it was said, they were armed for service against Cuba and Peru and in August they were seized by the United States authorities, on complaint of the Peruvian minister,[3] long to lay in custody at the foot of 13th Street in North River, the subject of much rumor and argument. Finally they were allowed to leave our shores [4] with Fish's favor, so it was alleged, based upon a retainer paid to his son-in-law. He had "sold himself to Spain." [5] But the contest was brief and decisive and Fish's victory was complete. Action on Banks's resolution was taken on June 16 and the hotheads were defeated by a vote of 101 to 88.[6] Hoar and Cox in congratulating the Secretary of State on the result said that it was "the greatest triumph" the administration had yet achieved, and Robeson added— "Yes, and the first triumph." [7]

Even after the message was forwarded to Congress Grant

[1] Report of speech in Phila. Ledger, June 15, 1870. Banks's speech was to have appeared in the Appendix of the Globe, but it seems to have been suppressed as it is not to be found there. His allusions are held to have been to Caleb Cushing, engaged in confidential service for the State Department. Cf. N. Y. Tribune, June 15, 1870.
[2] From his diary in C. F. Adams, Lee at Appomattox, p. 220.
[3] N. Y. Tribune, Aug. 4, 1869.
[4] Ibid., Dec. 9, 11, 20, 1869.
[5] Cong. Globe, 41st Cong. 2nd sess., pp. 4443, 4445; ibid., app., p. 541.
[6] Cong. Globe, 41st Cong. 2nd sess., p. 4507. Diplomatic correspondence relating to Cuban affairs for this period is brought together in Geneva Arbitration, vol. i, pp. 714 et seq. Cf. ibid., vol. ii, pp. 260-61. For the case of the gunboats in particular, ibid., vol. i, pp. 732-55.
[7] C. F. Adams, Lee at Appomattox, p. 219.

feared that he had "made a mistake," an opinion which he
continued to hold until he found that the House was ready
to sustain the policy. Then he expressed satisfaction with
what had been done.[1] And still later he gratefully acknowledged his indebtedness to Fish, both for the message of 1870
and for the secretary's bolder action on another "important
occasion," in August, 1869, when, in complete disregard of
his instructions, he had withheld the proclamation signed on
the Fall River steamboat.[2]

An attempt to repeal the Tenure of Office act, which had
been aimed at Andrew Johnson and formed the principal
basis for the impeachment proceedings, was put forth while
that President was still in his place, so that the way would
be clear for Grant. But the movement was frustrated in the
Senate which, having gained this new power, was reluctant
to part with it. The members had developed a fondness for
authority which, whether founded on right and reason or not,
they were determined to retain. The Republican leaders in
the House resumed the effort to unfetter Grant soon after
his inauguration. He himself had every expectation that the
restrictions set upon a predecessor for a temporary partisan
purpose would be removed for his own advantage. But, when
the proposal appeared, Sumner, fit spokesman for the Senate
in its hours of arrogance, asked for delay,[3] a fact which did
not escape Grant's notice.[4] Trumbull, Edmunds,[5] Conkling
and others opposed the unconditional repeal of the law. Those
who desired to place the subject where it had been before
1867, finding themselves in a minority, called a caucus in
the hope of using the party machinery to bring the unwilling
into line. But this scheme failed. Senators visited Grant,
who had been acting rather boldly, at least in conversations
with applicants for office. He for a time sent no nomina-

---

[1] C. F. Adams, Lee at Appomattox, pp. 219-20, 233.   [2] Ibid., p. 119.
[3] On March 9, Cong. Globe, 41st Cong. 1st sess., p. 32.
[4] Pierce, vol. iv, p. 374; Sumner's Works, vol. xv, pp. 141-2.
[5] "Is the race of bad presidents extinct?" asked Edmunds.—W. D.
Foulke, Life of O. P. Morton, vol. ii, p. 129.

tions to the Senate, saying that he was under no obligation to make removals until Congress had repealed the measure which curbed his power. But he was now made to believe that it would be well to agree to a compromise. In this plan the House refused to concur and insisted upon doing away with the law entirely. At the end of March, 1869, the subject went to a committee of conference, the Senate gained its point and the bill, continuing that body's power over removals, was rushed through both houses to be signed by the President.[1]

Haste was made by many states to ratify the Fifteenth Amendment, conferring suffrage upon and guaranteeing it to the negro in all parts of the Union. Congress had passed the joint resolution proposing the measure in the last days of February, 1869, and it was sent out for ratification by telegraph at once. The first state to respond was Kansas on February 27, the very day it was approved in Washington.' There was a unanimous vote in the senate; only seven members said nay in the house. Louisiana, Missouri, Nevada and West Virginia followed ere Grant had taken the oath of office. Before March was done Massachusetts, Maine, Pennsylvania, North Carolina, South Carolina, Wisconsin and Arkansas had ratified. Kentucky, Ohio, Delaware and Georgia rejected the amendment. Votes in favor of and against it continued to be received throughout 1869 and the first months of 1870. In the Maryland legislature not a single member voted for it; New York which had ratified the amendment in April, 1869, the next year attempted to rescind its action, while Ohio which had rejected it in 1869, approved it by a majority of one vote in the senate and two in the house in the following January. New Jersey rejected it.

Its adoption by a number of states sufficient to make it

[1] Grant was "defeated and overreached" by the lawyers of the Senate, said Welles. He had "neither the sagacity nor obstinacy" for which some had given him credit.—Welles, vol. iii, pp. 555, 556, 557, 558, 560, 564, 567-9, 571; McPherson, Hist. of Recon., pp. 413-5; Sumner's Works, vol. xv, pp. 141-2; Cong. Globe, 41st Cong. 1st sess., p. 395.

effective was bound up with the course of reconstruction in the South. On that rock Johnson had wrecked his ship, and the Radicals, with both Congress and the Executive at their beck and call, might now develop their policies without more hindrance. Virginia, Mississippi and Texas were still out of their places in the Union when Grant came to the Presidency. They had not participated in the elections of 1868. Georgia had been "reconstructed" and had voted for Seymour, as we have seen, but her return to self government had proven to be premature, and soon she was again out of the Union, so that it was an initial task of the new administration to apply the machinery of restoration to four of the units of the disrupted Confederacy.

On April 7, 1869, President Grant issued a proclamation covering the cases of Virginia, Texas and Mississippi. He recommended that they hold elections upon their pending constitutions, permitting separate votes as to sections, whereupon it might be expedient to have separate opinions. In a few days Congress sent the President a bill embodying his suggestions, adding the requirement that the legislatures should ratify the Fifteenth as well as the Fourteenth Amendment, which had been a condition to be fulfilled by states returning to the Union under the terms of the general reconstruction acts.

The measure was approved on April 10, and the President fixed July 6, 1869, as the date for the election in Virginia. Two clauses in the constitution of the state, relating to test oaths and disabilities, were made the subject of separate votes.[1] An active canvass in the radical interest was begun; many speakers were imported from the North for service on the hustings. The conservatives were successful by substantial majorities after an exciting campaign and the constitution was adopted without the clauses which were so obnoxious to the old elements in the population.[2]

[1] Senate Ex. Doc., 41st Cong. 2nd sess., no. 13.
[2] For the constitution, 210,577; against the constitution, 9,136.—Senate Ex. Doc., 41st Cong. 2nd sess., no. 3, pp. 102-3, 137-8.

The result was most displeasing to the Radicals in the North as well as in Virginia and they sought to influence Congress, if possible, to set aside the election. It was a "Confederate triumph" which had been achieved by "artifice, intimidation and fraud." A mistake had been made in submitting the clauses aimed at the "rebels" to a separate vote. Quiet acquiescence now would "extinguish the last hope of republican liberty in Virginia." Congress must remember the "heroic sufferings and dauntless bravery" of those who "on quarter deck and battle field had given of their heart's blood to redden the crest of the billow and the bayonet of their foemen," unseat conservatives by test oaths and order a new election which should be supported by Federal military force.[1]

Forty-five members of the legislature protested against the state's return to the Union,[2] although Wells, the defeated Republican candidate for governor, as well as General Canby were distinctly favorable to abiding by the result.[3] The Fourteenth and Fifteenth Amendments were ratified, United States senators were elected and it was with little grace that the re-admission of the state could be further delayed. Nevertheless to Congress the subject passed. Many pages of statement and argument on the topic were put into print. While the debates proceeded the galleries were filled with partisans, and politicians from Virginia freely moved about on the floor of the two houses, buttonholing and importuning the members.

The election, Sumner said, had been "one huge colossal fraud." The state was "still smoking with rebellion."[4] Its constitution was "dabbled in blood."[5] He called the new conservative Governor Walker, a "traitor." The Congress of the United States would become "partakers in the crime"

---

[1] Language used in an address to Congress by a Radical Republican convention which met in Richmond in November, 1869.—American Annual Cyclopedia for 1869, p. 714; House Mis. Doc., 41st Cong. 2nd sess., no. 8, p. 3.
[2] Cong. Globe, 41st Cong. 2nd sess., p. 545.
[3] House Mis. Doc., 41st Cong. 2nd sess., pp. 4, 13-4.
[4] Cong. Globe, 41st Cong. 2nd sess., p. 565.   [5] Ibid., p. 569.

should they commit "this great trust to such a man."[1] If
Virginia were at this time to come back into the Union at
all certain "fundamental conditions" should be imposed upon
her. Test oaths must be required of her officers and there
must be guarantees as to her future conduct. It was but a
"surly welcome" to the state which had been called the mother
of states, the mother of presidents, said Representative Cox.
Should this great commonwealth come back "handcuffed like
a criminal," or "unshackled like an upright man"? [2]

The debate in the Senate called forth a notable series of
exchanges between Sumner and Trumbull, who, for himself
and as chairman of the Judiciary Committee,[3] contended for
the generous treatment of the state. The war was over, said
he.[4] He argued with conclusive force and great talent to
prove the unconstitutionality as well as the impolicy of the
proposed course of the Radicals. Other Republican senators
came to his support. It was not the design of the Republican
party, said Stewart of Nevada, "to keep up perpetual warfare." [5] Congress in an utterly unworthy way was "higgling
upon technicalities," said Senator Ferry of Connecticut. The
vote to admit the state without conditions was very close, 28
to 31 in one case and 29 to 30 in another. Conkling, Carpenter
(Doolittle's Republican successor from Wisconsin), Corbett,
Ferry, Fowler, Morrill of Maine, Nye, Ross, Scott, Stewart,
Tipton, Trumbull, Willey, Williams and others had the
courage to ally themselves with the Democrats on this question. But the effort failed, the Radicals had their way and on
January 26, 1870, the President approved the bill, with the
hampering conditions which they had attached to it, for the
restoration of Virginia to its old place in the Union of
States.[6]

---

[1] Cong. Globe, 41st Cong. 2nd sess., p. 545.   [2] Ibid., p. 497.
[3] The members of the Committee on the Judiciary were Trumbull,
Edmunds, Conkling, Carpenter, Stewart and Rice, Republicans, and
Thurman, Democrat.
[4] Cong. Globe, 41st Cong. 2nd sess., p. 565.   [5] Ibid., p. 567.
[6] McPherson, Hist. of Recon., pp. 572-6.

The Radicals in Mississippi were not long content with their situation. On the face of the returns the constitution of 1868 was defeated by some 7,000 votes. But in view of what Congress had done in admitting Arkansas in spite of the narrowest of majorities, resting on gross frauds, and Alabama, though the provisions of the reconstruction acts in that state had been in no manner complied with, there was hope that a way might be found to put the government of Mississippi in the hands of the carpetbag-scalawag-negro party.

So much might have been effected, but for the fact that the Democrats had elected their candidates for governor and other state offices and had gained control of the legislature. The proof of intimidation and fraud here was as convincing as in Arkansas and Alabama. The negroes had been threatened with dismissal from employment if they voted for the constitution. They were set upon and were physically prevented from acting in answer to their own inclinations. When they did vote they were "spotted" for later proscription and punishment. It was an effective argument to Radical ears to say that General Gillem, in command in the district, came from Tennessee, and was on the Southern side of the reconstruction question. He had interfered to bring about the unwelcome result. But he had been temporarily superseded just before the election by General McDowell who removed the civil governor, Humphreys, and the attorney general of the state for their political activities, and he had returned to command only after the election was at an end.

General Adelbert Ames whom McDowell installed in Humphreys's place was a young West Point graduate, a native of Maine. He used the troops to gain possession of the office in the state house and, after being refused admittance to the executive mansion, had rather roughly expelled Humphreys and his family from their home by military power.[1] In the Democratic victory the ejected governor found his vindica-

[1] Garner, Recon. in Miss., pp. 213-6; Pub. of Miss. Hist. Soc., vol. i, pp. 385-9; American Ann. Cyclop. for 1868, article on Miss. Humphreys yielded only to what he called "stern, unrelenting military tyranny."

tion. He had been a candidate to succeed himself and to everyone's amazement was re-elected over General Eggleston, a carpetbagger [1] whom the Radicals had nominated for the place.

Ames's position now was in no wise pleasant but he held his ground as best he could. A "Committee of Five," appointed by the constitutional convention, came forward and presumed to represent the Radical interests in the state at large and at Washington. General Gillem had been asked to institute an investigation of the charge of irregularities at the polling places. He reported that the returns were a correct expression of the views of the people. The constitution had been defeated because of clauses in it disfranchising the whites. The convention had exceeded the demands of Congress and had prescribed conditions for voting and office-holding which were not contemplated by the reconstruction acts.[2] He would not change his report to please the "Committee of Five" which proceeded to issue statements on its own account. In seven counties the elections, it said, had been "mere farces" [3] and they should be regarded as illegal and void.

On the strength of these declarations the House of Representatives at Washington passed a bill on July 24, 1868, providing that the convention should be re-assembled and that a new constitution should be framed and submitted to the people. But the Senate rejected the plan and the subject continued to be discussed with acrimony. The Republican state convention, when it met, declared that the Democrats had carried the state only by "bribery, threats, misrepresentation, fraud, violence and murder." It sent a "Committee of Sixteen" to Washington to badger Congress.[4] But they made no progress until after the inauguration of President Grant. Then Gillem, who had been charged with so much friendliness for the conservative element in Mississippi, was

[1] In Mississippi usually called "Buzzard" Eggleston.
[2] House Mis. Doc., 40th Cong. 3rd sess., no. 53, p. 63.   [3] Ibid., p. 2.
[4] Ibid.; Pub. Miss. Hist. Soc., vol. i, pp. 391-8; Garner, Recon. in Miss., pp. 216-36.

summarily removed and Provisional Governor Ames took command of the troops. He at once turned out practically all the incumbents of civil offices in the state down to the lowest in the local districts by insisting, in response to the resolution of Congress of February 6, 1869, that they take the test oath of 1862, and installed negroes, carpetbaggers and scalawags in their places.[1]

So the case stood when Grant issued his proclamation of April 7 in relation to Mississippi, Virginia and Texas. The arrangements of the Mississippi Radicals for gaining control of the state went forward and in July the President designated November 30, 1869, as the date for a re-submission of the constitution. The three obnoxious and proscriptive clauses as to voting and office-holding, which it was believed had resulted in defeat· in 1868, were treated separately as in Virginia and were rejected by great majorities, as in that state, while· the constitution itself was ratified by a nearly unanimous vote.[2] The conservatives had nominated Judge Louis Dent, a brother-in-law of President Grant, for Governor, though he had but a tenuous hold upon citizenship in Mississippi, in a hope, which proved to be illusive, of winning official favor in Washington for their ticket.[3] The Radicals named James L. Alcorn, a "rebel brigadier," who had been converted to negro suffrage.[4] Alcorn was elected by an overwhelming majority, the legislature adopted the Fourteenth and Fifteenth Amendments and its claims for reinstatement in the Union were ready to present to Congress. Butler, who had fallen heir to Thaddeus Stevens's place as chairman of the dictatorial Reconstruction Committee, reported a bill to the House which was "word for word" like the bill under which Virginia was re-admitted to representation in Congress. It was adopted without debate to encounter Trumbull and

---

[1] Cf. Garner, Recon. in Miss., pp. 231-2; American Ann. Cyclop. for 1869, p. 455.

[2] 105,223 for and 954 against the constitution.

[3] Garner, Recon. in Miss., pp. 239-40.   [4] Ibid., p. 180.

his Judiciary Committee in the Senate, who opposed its conditions on the grounds which had actuated them a few weeks earlier in dealing with the Virginia bill. Trumbull wished it to be a "Union of co-equal states." He would have no "inferior and subordinate states." [1] He was supported by a considerable number of his Republican colleagues as before, but by not enough to suffice. The bill as it came from the House was adopted. The President signed it on February 23, 1870, and Mississippi was ready to resume her old position in the Union.[2]

The convention in Texas, it will be remembered, had broken up in disorder. General Canby had brought together its proposals for the consideration of the people. The two factions which had been fighting over the work from the first day, under E. J. Davis and A. J. Hamilton, took their dispute to Washington, where the whole subject rested, not without exchanges which reflected the enmities of the rival parties, until Grant issued his proclamation. On July 15, 1869, he ordered the submission of the constitution to the voters of the state on the following 30th day of November. The two leaders, Davis and Hamilton, were the candidates of their respective factions for governor. Davis was befriended by President Grant and, aided by Federal patronage and Federal troops,[3] he was elected with a few hundred votes to spare amid general accusations of fraud. The constitution was adopted by a large majority,[4] and by act of Congress, approved on March 30, 1870,[5] Texas was "reconstructed."

Georgia was face to face with the tedious processes of "re-reconstruction." [6] The legislature had contained a large number of Democrats who, supported by some "North Georgia Republicans," representing a part of the state in which there

[1] Cong. Globe, 41st Cong. 2nd sess., p. 1174.
[2] McPherson, Hist. of Recon., pp. 576-7.
[3] Ramsdell, Recon. in Texas, pp. 276-82.
[4] 72,366 votes for and 4,928 votes against.—Senate Mis. Doc., 41st Cong. 2nd sess., no. 77, p. 35.
[5] McPherson, Hist. of Recon., pp. 577-9.
[6] Ku Klux Report, Georgia Testimony, p. 315.

were few negroes and a strong race prejudice existed,[1] reached
the opinion that under the new constitution only white men
could occupy seats in the body. One of the blacks sent to
Atlanta to make laws for the commonwealth was the same
infamous Aaron Alpeoria Bradley who had been turned out
of the convention. All the negroes now were expelled from
both houses of the legislature. "A greater outrage," said the
New York Tribune, had not been "perpetrated under a free
government."[2] "In the name of justice and of liberty" there
would be appeal from "a company of unwhipped and stiff
necked rebels" to the great American people.[3]

For his own purposes Governor Bullock at once regarded
himself as a "provisional governor" only, and he took the
case to Congress. He said that at least 40 members of the
house and 15 or 18 members of the senate could not take the
test oath. If these men were unseated the negroes could be
reinstated; then Georgia might fulfill the fundamental conditions of the reconstruction acts.[4] For his action Bullock was
violently denounced by the conservatives. He was branded
by the mayor of Savannah as "a traitor to his state, to civilization and to humanity."[5] "Perfectly reckless," said Robert
Toombs, he was making himself dictator.[6] He would remand
the people to military rule. Nelson Tift, a Democratic con-
gressman-elect, actively led the opposition to Bullock at Washington.

The governor adduced a mass of testimony to prove that
there was disorder on every hand and that the state was unfit
for self control. The negroes held a convention in Macon,
some of them walking 50 or 100 miles that they might be
present to protest against the treatment they had received in
the legislature. Accounts of the hard and cruel usage which
was their lot throughout the state were forwarded to Wash-

[1] House Mis. Doc., 40th Cong. 3rd sess., no. 52, p. 6; cf. Thompson,
Recon. in Ga., pp. 211-4; Wooley, Recon. in Ga., pp. 56-7.
[2] Issue of Sep. 9, 1868.   [3] Ibid.
[4] House Mis. Doc., 40th Cong. 3rd sess., no. 52, p. 2.   [5] Ibid., p. 176.
[6] Annual Report of American Hist. Assoc. for 1911, vol. ii, pp. 707-8.

ington.[1] Tift wrote to all the judges, ordinaries, mayors and
other men of light and leading in Georgia, and soon was able
to present an imposing collection of opinions on the other
side of the question, which, as might have been foreseen, went
for nothing in the sight of the Radicals in Congress.[2] The
state's senators never had been received; its representatives
ceased to occupy their seats in the House at the end of the
term of life of the Fortieth Congress, on March 3rd, 1869.

Bullock and Tift continued their arguments and the Reconstruction Committee in April, 1869, brought forward a bill
to restore "republican government" to the state of Georgia,
but definite action was postponed until the meeting of the
long session in December.

Meantime the question of law involved in unseating the
negroes reached the supreme court of Georgia, and a majority of the judges found that a "person of color" was eligible
to office in the state.[3] The accounts of outrages upon the
negroes continued to be received in the North and Senator
Henry Wilson was induced to write President Grant calling
Georgia the "worst of all the states." Martial law should
be proclaimed that the criminals might be caught and punished. The letter was referred to General Sherman, who in
turn consulted Terry, who by this time had taken Meade's
place in command of the troops. Terry found that the situation called for "the interposition of the national government"
in the interest of the "rights and liberties" of the freedmen.[4]
Grant alluded to the state's condition in his first message to
Congress. He thought that it would be wise "without delay,"
as Bullock had proposed, to authorize the governor to con-
vene the legislature which had been elected in 1868, and
to purge it of those who could not take the required oath.
This was done at once and the bill was in the President's

[1] House Mis. Doc., 40th Cong. 3rd sess., no. 52, p. 11.
[2] Ibid., pp. 140-236.
[3] McPherson, Hist. of Recon., pp. 466-74; C. M. Thompson, Recon. in
Ga., pp. 215-6.
[4] American Annual Cyclopedia for 1869, p. 308.

hands for signature before the Christmas holidays.[1] **The**
state was returned to military rule. The "District of Georgia"
was created and Terry, in addition to his general duties as
commander of the Department of the South, took it under his
separate special care.[2]

Bullock reconvened the legislature and amid much excitement, induced by the arbitrary action of a great carpetbagger, over 300 pounds in weight, named Harris who had
been appointed to organize the house in the governor's interest,[3] the colored members were seated. Whites who were
disqualified from taking the oath, with the assistance of
General Terry, were sent back to their homes to make way
for those who had received the next highest number of votes
at the election in 1868, which, of course, brought in more
negroes and white Republicans attached to the governor's
cause. A Democratic legislature was converted into a Republican legislature which proceeded to adopt the Fourteenth
Amendment, which it had approved before, when it was, as it
was now held to have been, only a "provisional body," and the
new Fifteenth Amendment, which it earlier had voted to reject.

A violent contest ensued in Congress. Butler, chairman of
the Committee on Reconstruction, proposed that Georgia
should return to the Union under the conditions which were
being imposed upon Virginia, Mississippi and Texas. He

[1] Cong. Globe, 41st Cong. 2nd sess., pp. 232, 292; McPherson, Hist. of
Recon., pp. 609-10.
[2] General Orders no. 83, American Annual Cyclopedia for 1869, p.
310, and General Orders no. 1, ibid., for 1870, p. 331.
[3] "A great 'tun of a man' from the state of Ohio . . . who enthroned
like another Falstaff acting the part of King Henry IV before his
profligate son overawed and thundered into silence the representatives
of the people." There was amazement "when a stranger, a man
wholly a stranger to the legislature and almost to the whole people
of the state appeared there and occupied the chair of the speaker,
thundering out his edicts to the representatives of the people," etc.
(Senator Hill in Cong. Globe, 42nd Cong. 1st sess., p. 541.) The real
power behind Harris as well as Bullock was a corrupt "boss" named
Foster Blodgett, who later tried to force his way into the United States
Senate. Cf. Article on Georgia in Why the Solid South, pp. 131-2;
Thompson, Recon. in Ga., pp. 221-2; Senate Reports, 41st Cong. 2nd
sess., no. 58.

would also incorporate in the bill a provision that the next election should not take place until 1872, thus granting two more years of life to Bullock and his friends, to which end they visited Washington. The governor and other scalawags and carpetbaggers from Georgia moved about among the members in the interest of this scheme to prolong their power. Negroes were summoned and arrived upon the scene with a view to further stirring party fires. But, though all of them together labored diligently, while Butler bellowed and charged, he had not Stevens's control over the party. In the course of the contest he encountered his parliamentary enemy, Bingham, who succeeded in inducing the House by a vote of 115 to 71 to reject the measure.

The members of the Committee on the Judiciary in the Senate, meanwhile, with an honest public devotion and a respect for constitutional learning entitling them to national gratitude, found recent proceedings in Georgia to have been without warrant in justice or law. The "Lecompton swindle" in Kansas, said Trumbull, was "not more iniquitous" than the proposal to continue Bullock's government in power without a new election, set up as it had been by a minority and held in place against the popular will.[1] Edmunds now supported the chairman of the committee, as he had not done during the debates on the Virginia and the Mississippi bills. Sumner, on the other hand, found that the "republican government," guaranteed to all the states under the terms of the Constitution of the United States, about which he had prated so long, called for the continuing intervention of Congress. Georgia was "in peril." Were they now to desert the Unionists of the state in an hour of need? Would they "descend to this vileness"?[2] "Law or no law," said Senator Wilson, with complete frankness, "we want to keep this state government in power."[3]

So active and offensive did Bullock and the lobby become

---

[1] Cong. Globe, 41st Cong. 2nd sess., p. 1928.   [2] Ibid., p. 2422.
[3] An opinion paraphrased in Schurz's speech, ibid., p. 2064.

that the Senate in April directed the Judiciary Committee to institute an investigation as to their operations. Hints there were that sums of money and other considerations of a valuable kind were influential in deciding votes of members of Congress in favor of giving the present Georgia government an extension of authority. Nothing conclusive was adduced, except the fact that nearly $15,000 had been paid out by Bullock, or his representatives, for the travelling expenses of negroes summoned to Washington, for favorable articles in the Radical press and for the printing and distribution of pamphlets.[1]

By 25 to 24, 31 to 30 and other close votes on divisions the Radicals were defeated for the first time in the history of the Congressional treatment of the reconstruction question. A plain statement of fact that the state had complied with the terms of the reconstruction acts and had ratified the Fourteenth and Fifteenth Amendments in good faith and was, therefore, entitled to representation in Congress was made to suffice. On July 15, 1870, the bill received the approval of President Grant,[2] and, after another election in December, senators and representatives of the state, early in 1871, six years after the war had ended, were allowed to take their seats in the Capitol at Washington.[3]

Before Georgia had ceased to trouble Congress the Fifteenth Amendment had come to be a part of the Constitution. On March 30, 1870, three-fourths of the states, or 29—North Carolina, West Virginia, Massachusetts, Wisconsin, Maine, Louisiana, Michigan, South Carolina, Pennsylvania, Arkansas, Connecticut, Florida, Illinois, Indiana, New York, New Hampshire, Nevada, Vermont, Virginia, Alabama, Missouri, Mississippi, Ohio, Iowa, Kansas, Minnesota, Rhode Island, Nebraska, and Texas—having signified in official documents on file in the State Department that their legislatures had ratified the measure, Secretary Fish, evad-

---

[1] Cf. Senate Reports, 41st Cong. 2nd sess., no. 175.

[2] Cong. Globe, 41st Cong. 2nd sess., pp. 1771, 5619, 5621; ibid., app., p. 738; McPherson, Hist. of Recon., pp. 609-13.

[3] Thompson, Recon. in Ga., pp. 269-70.

ing the question of the legality or illegality of New
York's action in rescinding its vote, as Seward had done
in reference to the Fourteenth Amendment in the cases
of New Jersey and Ohio, and offsetting this defection with
Georgia's change in the other direction, declared it to be a
valid part of the Constitution. President Grant at the same
time forwarded a special message to Congress, penned by his
own hand,[1] directing attention to the amendment which was,
he said, "of grander importance than any other one act of the
kind from the foundation of free government to the present
day." He urged the "newly enfranchised race" to fit themselves for their new duties, the white race "to withhold no
legal privilege of advancement to the new citizen," and Congress "to take all means within their constitutional powers to
promote and encourage popular education throughout the
country."[2]

The hour of jubilee had come. "From this day forth," said
the New York Tribune, the republic would move responsive to
"the sublime faith which her founders proclaimed nearly a
century ago—all men were free and equal."[3] Grant and Sumner were serenaded and called out for speeches in Washington. For a month the accounts of the celebrations of the
colored people filled the newspapers. In Philadelphia the
city council gave the negroes the use of Independence Square.[4]
They organized a great procession in which they carried the
Liberty Bell.[5] In New York the whole colored population
swarmed the streets to watch thousands of other blacks parade
through the city.[6] Everywhere they were marching to music
from their own trumpets and drums under evergreen arches.
Houses were decorated with the national colors. Mottoes indicative of the day and the cause were flung out for all to read.
Pictures of Lincoln, Grant, Sumner, Colfax and Thaddeus

[1] G. F. Hoar, Autobiography, vol. i, p. 204.
[2] McPherson, Hist. of Recon., pp. 545-6.
[3] Issue of March 31, 1870.
[4] Phila. Ledger, April 1, 1870.   [5] Ibid., April 27.
[6] N. Y. Tribune, April 9, 1870.

Stevens were hung upon both sides of the way through which the negroes passed, while thousands of onlookers acclaimed the new free race. At religious services, in mass meetings and at balls their rejoicing continued in the presence of the old Abolitionist leaders and many of the Republican politicians who hoped to profit on election day by such proof of zeal. The Anti-Slavery Society celebrated the occasion by disbanding, after an existence of 37 years.[1] "Encased in three boxes—the jury box, the cartridge box and the ballot box," said Fred Douglass, the negro was at last a man.[2]

Against the policies which were productive of continued bitter feeling between the sections there was a growing revulsion of sentiment. It had been revealed in the discussions called out by the bills relating to the reconstruction of Mississippi, Virginia, Texas and Georgia. A time had come, enlightened Republican leaders believed, for dealing, if not magnanimously, at least justly with the South. The movement gained special force in Missouri. During the war the Unionist and Secessionist elements, dwelling there side by side, had wrought themselves into a peculiarly proscriptive state of mind, and a distinct demand arose for measures in the interest of peace. Universal suffrage and universal amnesty had been a cry on many tongues almost ever since the war had ended. Suffrage now there was for everyone, but the forgiveness of political offenses was still an unrealized ideal.

A constitutional convention which had met in Missouri in 1865 had prescribed such tests for voters and office-holders that a considerable part of the citizens of the state were barred from participating in the elections. Efforts to have these features of the constitution declared invalid in the courts were unsuccessful and every political campaign was "little less than a civil war in itself."[3] A meeting was held in St. Louis as early as in 1866, and a movement inside the Republican party was instituted by B. Gratz Brown, a lawyer from Kentucky who

[1] N. Y. Nation, April 14, 1870.
[2] Phila. Ledger, April 27, 1870.
[3] American Annual Cyclopedia for 1870, p. 517.

had represented Missouri in the United States Senate for a few years during the war, to secure citizen's rights for the disfranchised. Finally, in 1870, amendments changing and liberalizing the constitution were submitted to the people. Carl Schurz who had lately come to the state to edit a newspaper in St. Louis and who spoke with power to and for a large body of Germans, gaining a seat in the United States Senate in 1869, where he had already distinguished himself, joined Gratz Brown and they and their "liberal" delegates seceded from the Republican state convention, leaving the old radical element in control. The Brown-Schurz party organized a separate meeting, nominated Brown for governor and declared itself "unequivocally" in favor of the constitutional amendments. "The extension of equal political rights and privileges to all classes of citizens without distinction" was demanded "by every consideration of good faith, patriotism and sound policy." It was "essential to the integrity of republican institutions, to the prosperity of the state and to the honor and preservation of the Republican party." After a vigorous campaign in which the Democrats joined the "Liberals" the amendments were adopted and Brown was elected by a majority of more than 40,000.[1]

By the provisions of the Fourteenth Amendment the disability to hold office in the case of men who had violated their oaths to engage in rebellion against the United States could be removed by a two-thirds vote of each house of Congress. This amendment made President Johnson's amnesty proclamations inoperative except in the remission of penalties. Congress now took complete control of the work of deciding when "rebels" should be restored to the right of holding office.[2] In the Fortieth Congress 1,431 persons were amnestied; in the Forty-first Congress, ending on March 4, 1871, 3,185.[3]

The echoes of the struggle in Missouri were heard over the whole nation. The need of some action to satisfy the rising

[1] American Annual Cyclopedia for 1870, article on Missouri.
[2] Blaine, Twenty Years in Congress, vol. ii, pp. 211, 281-2.
[3] Rhodes, vol. vi, p. 324.

opinion on the subject was reflected in Congress and Grant in
his message in December, 1871, recommended the passage of
a bill granting general amnesty to all but some of the "great
criminals" of the war.[1] A measure of this kind was presented
at once and would have been enacted promptly by the necessary two-thirds vote if Sumner had not interposed in behalf
of a supplemental civil rights bill for which he had been diligently laboring for the last three sessions.[2] This was to be
fastened on the amnesty bill as an amendment. It would
guarantee to negroes equal rights in railway stations and
trains, and on steamboats. They were to sit with whites in
theatres and churches, eat with them in hotels, lie in death
beside them in cemeteries. Their children were to attend the
same schools. There should be no discrimination for color
in jury service in any court in the land. In a word all that
the South had been asked to do by the most fanatical of the
old Northern Abolitionists to make the negro an equal, which
the South most defiantly declared that it would not do, and
which the North itself never had done, was to be enforced by
stringent Federal law. Congress must be just to the colored
race, said Sumner, before it should "play the generous to
rebels."[3] He returned to his doctrine that the Declaration
of Independence and the Constitution were of equal authority.
"Every word in the Constitution," he said, must be "interpreted so that liberty and equality shall not fail."[4]

Trumbull and other senators used their influences upon
Sumner to induce him not to press his favorite measure at this
time, so that harmony and good feeling among the people in
all sections of the land might be restored. But such obduracy
as his was not to be overcome. The result was failure for
both the original bill and the amendment. When the vote
was taken on February 9, 1872, there were 33 yeas and 19

[1] Richardson, Messages and Papers, vol. vii, p. 153.
[2] Sumner's Works, vol. xv, pp. 357-8.
[3] Ibid., vol. xiv, pp. 415, 470; Cong. Globe, 42nd Cong. 2nd sess., p.
3736.
[4] Sumner's Works, vol. xiv, pp. 425-6; cf. ibid., pp. 457-65.

nays, not two-thirds of the membership of the Senate.[1] Sumner's amendment to the amnesty bill was adopted only by the casting vote of Vice President Colfax, the Senate being equally divided, 28 to 28, Morrill of Maine, Trumbull, Ferry of Connecticut and Schurz being numbered among the Republicans in opposition to the measure.[2]

Another general amnesty bill which had passed the House [3] was taken from the calendar and reached consideration in the Senate on May 8 to have Sumner's civil rights bill attached to it, as in the case of the measure which had been defeated in February.[4] It, therefore, likewise failed.[5] Another House bill on the same subject was at hand, and by design it was brought up for consideration by Sumner's enemies at the end of an all night session on May 21. Indeed, it was early in the morning of May 22 when a messenger hurried to Sumner's house to apprise him of the trick. Though in ill health he appeared on the floor, as soon as he could, and made his familiar plea for the rights of the negro. But his amendment this time in a "thin Senate," when so many of the members were in their beds, was rejected,[6] and the amnesty bill itself, rid of this encumbrance, was passed by a vote of 38 to 2.[7]

Political disabilities were now removed from all participants in the rebellion, except senators and representatives of the Thirty-sixth and Thirty-seventh Congresses which covered the period of the secession of the Southern states, cabinet officers of the United States, officers of the judiciary, of the army and navy, and in the diplomatic service of the United States, who had violated their oaths and allied themselves with

---

[1] Cong. Globe, 42nd Cong. 2nd sess., pp. 928-9.
[2] Ibid., p. 919.   [3] Ibid., p. 399.
[4] By a like vote of 28 to 28, the Vice President again deciding its fate.—Ibid., p. 3268.
[5] Ibid., p. 3270. The vote was 32 to 22.
[6] By a vote of 13 to 29.—Ibid., p. 3738.
[7] Sumner and Nye in opposition. (Ibid., p. 3738.) For summaries of the proceedings on this subject see McPherson's Handbook for 1872, pp. 72-85.

the Confederacy. From 150,000 to 160,000, so it was supposed, had been excluded from office; now the number who were denied political rights was reduced to 500, or possibly 600.[1]

All the Southern states had been returned to the Union, but some of the men whom they had sent to Congress to act as their senators and representatives were ineligible for office. On April 23, 1872, every seat in the Senate and on May 22, 1872, every seat in the House was occupied for the first time since 1861.[2]

The election of Grant on a fairly satisfactory platform on the money question and the defeat of Seymour, whose party had committed him to the indefinite circulation of the greenback and the repudiation of the national debt, did not dispose in any final way of the nonsense which was uttered on these subjects. Loose thinking and dishonest counsel, concerning the currency, and the payment of the principal and the interest of the great war loans, marked the speeches of Congressmen, the conversation of large classes of the people, and the outgivings of the newspapers.

Representative Coburn of Indiana said in Congress that

[1] Washington corr. N. Y. Tribune, May 23, 1872; Washington corr. Phila. Ledger, May 23, 1872; Merriam, Life of Samuel Bowles, vol. ii, p. 123. Men like Generals Joseph E. Johnston, P. G. T. Beauregard, Jubal Early, W. J. Hardee, Fitzhugh Lee and Braxton Bragg, who left the United States Army to serve the South; D. L. Yulee and S. R. Mallory of Florida, C. C. Clay of Alabama, J. C. Breckinridge of Kentucky, A. G. Brown of Mississippi, James Chesnut, Jr., of South Carolina, L. T. Wigfall of Texas and Thomas Bragg of North Carolina, who had left the United States Senate to engage in secession; James L. Pugh, Roger A. Pryor, Zebulon B. Vance, L. Q. C. Lamar and J. L. M. Curry, who had sat in the lower branch of Congress; William A. Graham, who at one time had been secretary of the navy, and John A. Campbell, who left the Supreme Court bench at the outbreak of the war still labored under their disabilities. Congress by special action at its leisure amnestied those who still remained under the ban with exceptions for those whose offending seemed to be too gross to be forgiven, as in the cases of Jefferson Davis and a few others. Full amnesty was granted by an act of June 6, 1898, thirty-three years after the war had ended, when Davis was dead. Rhodes discusses this subject well in vol. vi of his work, pp. 329-30.

[2] Cong. Globe, 42nd Cong. 2nd sess., pp. 2716, 2783.

none could complain of suffering loss, if his bonds were paid off in currency; he would receive all except what he had hoped to gain by speculation. To leave the subject in doubt would increase the desire of holders to exchange old bonds for new ones bearing a lower rate of interest.[1] The demand that 5-20s should be redeemed in gold rather than the "money of the people," said Representative Beatty of Ohio, proceeded from capitalists who wished the value of their bonds enhanced fifty per cent.[2] It was a scheme, said Cary, another representative from Ohio, to make the "laboring classes," who were "the producers of all wealth," into "mere vassals of a privileged class." He believed in the sacredness of an obligation, but there were duties in this world more imperative than redeeming national bonds. When government left the citizen only rags and an empty cupboard, taking everything else to fill the coffers of "an untaxed moneyed aristocracy," it ceased to be a government and became a "robber."[3]

But the most rampageous of all the inflationists was "Ben" Butler. To him gold and silver were "monarchical standards of value"; they were the "instruments of tyrants," he alleged. Having divested the government of "every trait of the despotisms, every attribute of the monarchies and every vestige of the slaveries of the old world," except one, the coinage of money, now it, too, must be abolished. This strange blatterer stood for "inconvertible paper money," which he alleged had fought our battles and saved our country, which had been held by us as a just equivalent for the blood of our soldiers, the lives of our sons, the widowhood of our daughters and the orphanage of their children. To the greenback four millions of people owed their emancipation from slavery, to the greenback labor was indebted for its elevation from that thrall of degradation in which it so long had been enveloped.[4] Representative Ela, developing Butler's theories, said that he

[1] Appendix to Cong. Globe, 40th Cong. 3rd sess., p. 231.
[2] Ibid., p. 229.   [3] Ibid.
[4] Cong. Globe, 40th Cong. 3rd sess., pp. 303 et seq.

"would as soon abuse the soldier who stood by the country and fought the issue through to victory as the greenback legal tender, which came to our aid and his relief when specie left for Canada, following or preceding other deserters from the army and the draft."[1]

In a word, said Representative Phelps of Maryland, Butler proposed "to shingle the country with shinplasters, fundable into unpayable bonds, these again being dissolvable into irredeemable shinplasters." Thus would the debt furnish the currency and the currency pay the debt.[2] Once not long since the people had been importuned to take the loans of the government as a patriotic duty; now such as had done so were "bloated bondholders" to be mulcted in the most convenient way at the first opportunity.[3]

The fact that Andrew Johnson had taken an extraordinary position in his last annual message regarding the payment of the debt had its influence, without a doubt, upon many Republicans. They would adopt an opposite course, and now, on this account, were the more easily led away from the "greenback swindle" to correct views on the money question. Sherman, Morton and Logan, who had shown signs of unsettlement, put themselves into conformity with the declarations of their political party.[4] The Committee on Finance of the Senate, of which Sherman was chairman, had reported in December, 1868, in the closing session of the 40th Congress, an "act to strengthen the public credit," which declared that the 5-20 bonds should be redeemed in coin and looked to the resumption of specie payments.[5] It was passed in the last moments of the session to die in the hands of the President.[6]

[1] Cong. Globe, 40th Cong. 3rd sess., p. 886.
[2] Ibid., app., p. 299.
[3] The "rascally bondholder," said the New York Nation with fine irony, "the detested fellow who in 1863-4 brought army after army into the field, covered the South with hostile troops and horses and munitions, when millions of Southern ears were listening for the news of Northern bankruptcy."—Issue of July 23, 1868.
[4] N. Y. Nation, March 4, 1869.
[5] John Sherman, Recollections, vol. i, p. 440; American Annual Cyclopedia for 1869, pp. 183-90.
[6] McPherson, Hist. of Recon., p. 397.

This measure formed the basis for another of similar meaning which made its appearance in Congress soon after the inauguration of Grant. It was approved by the House on the 12th, by the Senate on the 15th, by the President on the 19th of March, 1869. Hereby, "in order to remove any doubt as to the purpose of the government to discharge all just obligations to the public creditors," the "faith of the United States" was "solemnly pledged" to the payment of them in coin, unless there was express provision to the contrary, and to the redemption of the greenbacks in specie "at the earliest practicable period." [1] This was excellent. At the moment nothing more could have been desired. A confident feeling took possession of bankers and financiers; the orderly progress of business seemed to be assured.

Further legislation to give effect to the promises of Congress was now expected. The plan of Secretary McCulloch for the retirement of what he called "a dishonored and disreputable currency" [2] had been discarded because of the cry that arose about contraction. Since no step forward could be taken along this line plans were evolved for "resumption without contraction." The debt would be paid off as rapidly as possible out of the surplus revenues. It would be funded into issues bearing lower rates of interest. Thus, it was argued, the credit of the government might be improved and the subject of bringing gold and paper to parity could be approached from another direction. [3] A bill to some extent expressive of this policy made its way through Congress in the summer of 1866 as a campaign measure. It was a mere partisan manœuvre and was the subject of a "pocket veto" by the President. [4] Secretary Boutwell in his first report for December, 1869, presented his ideas about funding. He proposed that the reissue should consist of three classes of bonds of $400,000,000 each, running from 15 to 25 years and bearing interest at the

[1] Sherman, Recollections, vol. i, p. 448; American Annual Cyclopedia for 1869, pp. 196-7.
[2] Report of December, 1868.
[3] Sherman, Recollections, vol. i, p. 440.
[4] Ibid.; McPherson, Hist. of Recon., p. 382.

rate of 4½ per cent.[1] General Schenck, chairman of the Committee on Ways and Means in the House, and Sherman, chairman of the Committee on Finance in the Senate, both from Ohio, the state which seemed to exhibit the greatest confusion of mind on the financial question, in conference with Boutwell, brought forward bills in Congress.

In February Sherman was ready with a project of a law which had the approval of his committee. Following Boutwell three new series of bonds of $400,000,000 each were proposed, but at this point there was divergence from his plan. One running for ten years was to bear five per cent, another for fifteen years, four and a half per cent and the third for twenty years, four per cent interest. The bill passed the Senate with only ten dissenting votes and went to the House where, at length, a substitute appeared, providing for one issue of thirty year four per cent bonds to the amount of $1,000,000,000. The advocates of the House bill observed that the bonds would be more readily taken, if they did not so soon mature. The extension of the loan over a greater period at a lower rate of interest would be economical; it would result in gain for the government. Soon the House passed its measure and the subject in July was in the hands of the conferees for a compromise. It was finally agreed to authorize $200,000,000 ten year five per cent bonds, $300,000,000 fifteen year four and a half per cent bonds and $1,000,000,000 thirty year four per cent bonds. It was now confidently expected that the national debt which on March 1, 1870, had been brought down to $2,500,000,000, could be reduced still further, so that before the refunding operations were completed the $1,500,000,-000 named in the act would cover all existing liabilities of the United States, except the "legal tenders" about the redemption of which nothing yet was said.[2]

The work of conversion could proceed only slowly. It was

[1] Report of Sec. of Treasury in House Ex. Doc., 41st Cong. 2nd sess., no. 2, p. xvii; cf. Boutwell, Sixty Years in Public Affairs, vol. ii, p. 140.
[2] Sherman, Recollections, vol. i, pp. 451-7.

midsummer before the bill was finally approved. The opinion had been held that a large part of the debt could be distributed in Europe. There was a prevailing belief, so uninformed was the public mind regarding financial questions, that the most of what the United States needed to do in order to sell its loans abroad was to issue long time bonds bearing a lower interest rate. If they were made to resemble those of England and France in these particulars they would be taken by investors in all parts of the world.[1] On the other hand many were ready to say that it was humiliating and in some measure degrading to go abroad to borrow money, and a debt in the hands of foreigners would be a menace to national independence.[2]

The arrangements to "entrap capitalists" were too transparent to bring them to the support of the Treasury.[3] The guarantee that the bonds were to be redeemed in "coin," given both in the "act to strengthen the public credit" and in the new funding act, was reassuring in high degree. It was specified in the funding act, however, that the secretary could not call in the sixes until their price was equal to par in gold; he must sell the new bonds at par. The market, if left to itself, would not work itself into a position making possible such an operation, for as soon as the price of the 5-20s approached par in gold it would recede, because of each buyer's knowledge that in passing this point they were in danger of being converted into bonds bearing a lower interest rate. Practically, therefore, the secretary was deadlocked.[4]

Of this, however, he at first was not assured, and he early conferred with bankers in Washington on the subject of the issue. He would offer bonds of all three of the authorized classes to a total amount of $700,000,000, sending one-half of them to Europe.[5] From the beginning he had had the pur-

[1] N. Y. Nation, July 7, 1870.
[2] Cf. Boutwell, Sixty Years in Public Affairs, vol. ii, p. 141.
[3] N. Y. Nation, July 27, 1870.
[4] Ibid., Aug. 24, 1871; Oberholtzer, Life of Jay Cooke, vol. ii, pp. 268-9.   [5] Oberholtzer, Jay Cooke, vol. ii, pp. 266-7.

pose of making the conversion without agents, although the
law provided one-half of one per cent for the operation.[1] He
had come to the office with experience which some had believed would qualify him for its duties, but so impracticable
were his schemes that many soon spoke of him in the most dis-
paraging terms. So little skill did he evidence, indeed, that
there were rumors of his supersession.[2] His opportunities for
action were few, for the Franco-Prussian war ensued and all
Europe was disturbed by the overthrow of the empire of Louis
Napoleon, the establishment of a new government in
Paris amid the ruins of the old and the creation of the German Empire under the hegemony of Prussia. The derange-
ment of regular monetary relations in France was complete
and the influence of such a collapse was wide.[3]

As conditions improved Boutwell, realizing that the fours
and four and a halfs were at the time unsalable, in February,
1871, determined to offer the $200,000,000 of five per cent
bonds authorized in the funding act. Levi P. Morton, the
New York banker and his partner in London, Sir John Rose,
pledged their aid in the promotion of the negotiation. Jay
Cooke, the Philadelphia banker, who had so successfully sold
the war loans, had lately opened an office in London. Hugh
McCulloch upon leaving the Treasury Department went
abroad to become the head of Cooke's business in that city.
The experience of McCulloch and all the facilities of the
Cooke banks in London, New York, Philadelphia and Washington were put at the disposal of Boutwell, who, however,
was fixed in a determination to grant no special privileges.
Indeed, nearly all who asked him for a share in the business
were bidden to proceed with the sale at a commission of one-
fourth of one per cent. The department would advertise the
bonds and await the result.

Everybody's became nobody's business and there was prac-

---

[1] Report of Sec. of Treas. for 1869, House Ex. Doc., 41st Cong. 2nd
sess., no. 2, p. xvii.
[2] Oberholtzer, Jay Cooke, vol. ii, pp. 267-8, 274, 287.
[3] N. Y. Nation, Aug. 18, 1870.

tically no response except from the national banks to which
a warm appeal was made by Jay Cooke, who during the war
had been so influential in their organization.[1] It was a question always of raising the price of the 5-20s to par in gold.
When Boutwell began his operation the difference was about
one per cent, and it increased, as time passed, to nearly or
quite two per cent. Bankers, like the Cookes, knew that only
the manipulation of the market by a bold and powerful hand,
supported by all the agencies of the Treasury Department,
could make the negotiation a success. Though Boutwell had
advertised the issue continuously for several months he was
able to distribute only $66,000,000 worth, and of this amount
$64,000,000 represented exchanges by the national banks, so
that only $2,000,000 had been taken by the public. In the
summer of 1871 some $134,000,000 of the $200,000,000 remained unsold and the Secretary of the Treasury began to
look about him for the means of bringing his operation to an
end.[2] Several times he spoke of forming parties to take the
rest of the issue. The name of this or that well known European banking house was mentioned in connection with the deal.
Agents were sent abroad and repeatedly it was given out that
English and German financiers, acting alone or in combination, were about to purchase large blocks of the bonds.

Meantime the Cookes continued to remind Boutwell of their
ability and willingness to complete the operation. In midsummer, without any other resource, he was induced to make a
contract with them and they proceeded to form a group which
they called a syndicate.[3] Indeed they organized two syndicates of bankers, one in Europe which made itself responsible
for $15,000,000 in gold, another in America which obligated
itself to gold payments amounting to $10,000,000. Cooke's
London house soon brought into a group twenty or more rich
and prominent firms located in that city, and in Frankfort,

[1] Oberholtzer, Jay Cooke, vol. ii, pp. 272, 273-4.
[2] N. Y. Nation, Aug. 24, 1871; Boutwell, Sixty Years in Public Affairs,
vol. ii, p. 186.
[3] Not before had the French word *syndicat* been given an Anglicized

Hamburg, Amsterdam, Berlin, Paris, Brussels and other money centres on the Continent, while in this country his alliances were with the firms and national banks which had been identified with his large operations for the government during the war.[1] Simultaneously the managers began to manipulate prices to insure the success of the undertaking. $80,000,000 were assigned to the European syndicate. The books were opened on August 22 and at the end of the first day the sum was oversubscribed. The American syndicate's share was $50,000,000; in a few days the books were closed in this country. The operation was a conspicuous success. The credit for it was eagerly taken by President Grant and Secretary Boutwell who now called the five twenty bonds of 1862, and gave notice that interest payments would cease on December 1. Holders demanding gold for their bonds would be paid from the fund which had been assembled by the syndicates, or they would be given the new five per cent bonds, a course which they preferred when they saw that the price was being held above par.[2]

The exchange proceeded in Cooke's London banking office where the government was represented by Assistant Secretary of the Treasury William A. Richardson. The new bonds had been sent abroad in various passenger steamers in locked safes in charge of Treasury Department clerks[3] and in a few

form for general use in America. Instantly it rolled off every tongue. In Congress, in the newspapers it was the subject of quip and pun. Some one addressed the New York Tribune:

> "Pray what is a syndicate
> Intended to indicate?
> Is queried abroad and at home.
> Say, is it a corner
> Where Jay Cook-y Horner
> Can pull out a very big plum?"
> —Oberholtzer, Jay Cooke, vol. ii, p. 275.

Cf. Cong. Globe, 42nd Cong. 2nd sess., p. 741, where "syndicate" is spoken of as a word "very unfamiliar to American ears" and again as "a new word so far as this country is concerned in reference to fiscal negotiations." Also Cong. Globe, 42nd Cong. 2nd sess., pp. 749-50.

[1] Oberholtzer, Jay Cooke, vol. ii, pp. 277-9.

[2] Ibid., pp. 279-80.

[3] Boutwell, Sixty Years in Public Affairs, vol. ii, p. 188.

months, though the process was slow, since some of the holders were peasants on the Continent who could not be communicated with immediately, the business was brought to an end.

By act of January 20, 1871, Congress had authorized an increase in the amount of bonds in the five per cent class from $200,000,000 to $500,000,000, wherefore $300,000,000 more might be offered immediately on similar terms.[1] As the way had now been found it was supposed that Boutwell would continue his funding business. The Rothschilds, who stood forth at this time as the principal Crœsuses of the world, had been impressed so favorably with the success of the syndicate that they agreed to assist in further operations. The Cookes and the Rothschilds together made a proposal, covering the sale of four and a halfs, indeed, as well as fives.[2]

But at the opening of the session on December 4, 1871, "Sunset" Cox introduced a resolution in the House charging Boutwell with having increased the debt and with having expended more than the one-half of one per cent allowed him for the negotiation.[3] The syndicate was charged with having made a profit of more than $3,000,000. Boutwell and Cooke were hauled before the Committee on Ways and Means to which the subject had been referred for an investigation. Through its chairman, Mr. Dawes, it in January made a report,[4] exonerating Boutwell, and on February 1, 1872, the opinion was made to express the sense of the House by a vote of 110 to 86.[5] But Grant's anxiety concerning his re-election now governed every movement of the government. The timidity of the party managers dictated the course of the Secretary of the Treasury. When he was ready to act it was too late and plans for continuing the work must await the transition of the country into better times. No bonds bear-

---

[1] Cong. Globe, 41st Cong. 3rd sess., app., p. 330; Sherman, Recollections, vol. i, p. 457.
[2] Oberholtzer, Life of Jay Cooke, vol. ii, pp. 288, 359-60, 361.
[3] Cong. Globe, 42nd Cong. 2nd sess., p. 12.   [4] Ibid., p. 501.
[5] Ibid., p. 777; House Reports, 42nd Cong. 2nd sess., no. 7; Oberholtzer, Life of Jay Cooke, vol. ii, pp. 288, 359-60.

ing interest at a rate lower than five per cent were sold until 1877.[1]

Boutwell's course back to specie payments was "a long road." [2] Day after day the New York Tribune declared that "the way to resume is to resume." Charles Sumner said as much in other language. But it was advice not more sage or practical, the New York Nation remarked, than saying that the way to fly is to fly.[3] When McCulloch's operation of calling in the greenbacks and destroying them had been stopped the amount of notes still outstanding was $356,000,-000. There were in circulation besides some $38,000,000 of small notes of different denominations, beginning at ten and running up to fifty cents. The national bank notes had the same purchasing power as the greenbacks. For all purposes, except in the payment of import duties and interest on the public debt, and everywhere except on the Pacific coast, where gold continued to be the medium of exchange, paper money was in general use. The measure of its depreciation was found in the quotations which came to the people day by day from the "Gold Room" in New York City. As gold had been driven out of circulation so, too, had silver coin. Neither one nor the other was to be had east of the Rocky Mountains except by purchase like any other commodity.[4]

If specie payments were to be resumed the value of the greenbacks must be advanced to par in gold, and this was a feat not to be accomplished by writing editorials in Greeley's newspaper office. A preeminent difficulty was found in the fact that large numbers of men wished the country to remain on a paper money basis, while others were without any concern whatever for the subject. What very many were unwilling to perceive was that the greenbacks were promissory notes, promises to pay in gold the sums stamped upon their face;

---

[1] Dewey, Financial History of the United States, p. 356.

[2] N. Y. Nation, Nov. 26, 1869.

[3] Ibid., Nov. 25, 1869. Chase had said in a letter to a friend on June 5, 1866—"The only way to resume is resumption."—Chase Papers in Hist. Soc. of Pa.

[4] "A five-cent piece, the largest coin we have."—Letter of J. R. Lowell in 1869 in Rollo Ogden, Life of E. L. Godkin, vol. ii, p. 72.

they had been given out by the government of the United States
in return for merchandise or services purchased from the people. They represented a part of the whole sum of money borrowed for the conduct of the war. For one portion of the
amount thus borrowed bonds were given in acknowledgment
of the debt, and it was stated at what time the principal would
be paid and what the rate of interest should be meanwhile.
For another portion of the borrowed sum greenbacks were
given. Upon them no statement appeared as to when or how
they would be redeemed. They bore no interest and had value
only because of their capacity to pay debts, in other words
to circulate as a legal tender currency.[1]

A decision of the Supreme Court in Hepburn v. Griswold
on February 7, 1870, was calculated to exert a wholesome influence upon the public mind with reference to the question.
A certain Mrs. Hepburn in 1860 had given a promissory note
for $11,250. Before it was paid the legal tender act of Febru-
ary 25, 1862, was passed. She tried to extinguish the debt with
greenbacks. They were refused and the case reached the Kentucky court of errors which declared the law unconstitutional,
this being the only state among some fifteen, which had passed
upon the subject, to reach this conclusion. Appeal was taken
to the Supreme Court of the United States to which the case
came during the term of 1867-8. What the decision would
be was anxiously anticipated. In three cases in 1868 the
court had decided that greenbacks were not legal tender for
state taxes;[2] that being "obligations" and evidence of national
debt they were exempt from taxation;[3] and, yet more important, that when a contract was made specifically promising
payment in specie it meant specie—legal tender paper money
would not suffice.[4] It was still to be determined what was
the position of debt in which the manner of payment was not
named in the contract.[5]

The Chief Justice delivering the opinion on this subject in

[1] N. Y. Nation, Dec. 10, 1868.
[2] Lane Co. v. Oregon, 7 Wall., p. 71.
[3] The Bank v. Supervisors, 7 Wall., p. 26.
[4] Bronson v. Rodes, 7 Wall., p. 228.
[5] Hart, Life of Chase, pp. 392-3.

the Hepburn case, argued that the acts authorizing the legal
tenders had impaired the obligation of contracts and, therefore, that these acts contravened the provisions of the Constitution. In compelling creditors to accept dollars worth less
than the dollars they had lent these creditors were deprived
of property without due process of law.[1] Four justices were
in agreement with Chase—Nelson, Clifford, Field and Grier—
though Grier, brought to incapacity by age, resigned before
the opinion was read.[2] Two—Swayne and Davis—agreed
with Miller, a Republican swayed by partisan feelings, who
delivered a dissenting opinion and who held that, though the
Constitution forbade the states to pass laws impairing the
obligation of contracts, Congress was not so inhibited. The
legal tender acts had been acquiesced in universally. Many
debts contracted in gold prior to February 25, the date of the
passage of the first of the series of laws authorizing the greenbacks, had already been paid in paper. A still larger amount
of debt, contracted since that time, would be discharged in
notes. A great weight of opinion, represented by the action of
Congress, by the approval of the President, as indicated by his
appending his signature to the bills and by the decisions of
the state courts, whose duty it was "as much as it is ours to
pass upon it in the light of the Constitution," lay on the side
of the validity of the policy. With many patriotic allusions
to the greenback's part in winning the war Justice Miller declared that he would not reverse the action of so many potential individuals and bodies.[3]

To most persons of understanding the opinion of the court
was very welcome. It closed the loophole which debtors found
in the greenback to evade their just pecuniary obligations and
to repay in paper what had been borrowed in gold. The legal
tender was set before the country in its real character; it was
seen for what it was—a makeshift only, a constant source

[1] 8 Wall., p. 603.
[2] As to his resignation which was enforced by his colleagues see J. P.
Bradley, Miscellaneous Writings, p. 73.
[3] 8 Wall., p. 638.

of irritation and disturbance to be got rid of at the earliest
day. Indeed the decision was quite clearly an attempt to
make up for the failure of Congress to bring the country back
to a specie basis.[1] To gain the desired result by "contraction"
through the Treasury Department was rendered impossible
by the Republican leaders whom popular opposition had intimidated.[2]

But instantly a great pother ensued. The inflationists were
up in arms at once. The same influences which had seized the
Democratic party and had nearly captured the Republican
organization in 1868—the debtor class and the demagogues
who sought the favor of the poor on election day, made themselves heard over all the land. Again it was the "blood
stained" greenback; it had won the war and preserved the
Union, and, though many who said this a few years since had
been Copperheads and had cared little enough about the
Union, they were listened to now with sympathy. So proscriptive was public opinion that the court, which had not felt
itself at liberty to express its will with reference to the en-
croachments of Congress upon the executive power, a judgment for which Johnson had waited so hopefully, though in
vain, was also not to be allowed its freedom on a money question,[3] when it ran counter to Radical political sentiment.

To many it seemed strange enough that Chase who, as Secretary of the Treasury had issued these notes, now as Chief
Justice could deliver an opinion declaring that action to have

[1] Hart. Life of Chase, p. 398. Cf. N. Y. Nation, Feb. 25, 1869.
[2] Chase wrote to a friend on June 5, 1866, that "a fearless and sagacious secretary [the slur was aimed at McCulloch] would have resumed
a year ago and let contraction take care of itself. Contraction as a
policy preliminary to resumption was a mistake." (Chase Papers in
Hist. Soc. of Pa.) Here was another way to the same end. Indeed Chase
himself would have gone farther than in the Hepburn case, if he could
have done so, for the sake of the great national object which he had
in view and there was fear that he might do so much should the matter
come within his reach again. He would have declared the legal tender
acts unconstitutional for all contracts,—for those made after Feb. 25
1862, as well as prior to that time.—Hart, Life of Chase, p. 396; McPherson, Hist. of Recon., p. 523, note.
[3] Cf. N. Y. Nation, March 24, 1870.

been invalid. But he had been governed in the first instance
by the necessities of war. He had levied a forced loan; justification for it he found in the grant of the money making
power to Congress by the Constitution. At this later day the
event could be considered with judicial calm; "examination
and reflection under more propitious circumstances" had satisfied him that his earlier judgment was erroneous, and it was
quite within his authority, indeed it was his duty, if his opinion inclined him to it, to declare that what he himself had
earlier done under the stress of the hour was unconstitutional.[1]

Nevertheless he came in for nearly as much calumny and
abuse as had been heaped upon his head for the part he had
played as the presiding officer in the impeachment court.
His prominence as a Democratic candidate in the convention
which had nominated Seymour for the presidency in 1868, and
the expectation that his name would again come before the
country as a possible nominee of the Democrats in 1872,[2]
further embittered the judgment of the country. The opinion
Radical Congressmen declared to be as infamous as the Dred
Scott decision.[3] Several railways and other corporations,
having outstanding bond issues dating back to a period
anterior to 1862, exerted their influences through political
channels to discredit the Chief Justice.[4]

The Radical politicians were still manipulating the Supreme
Court as they manipulated Congress and the President. During Johnson's administration it had been determined that the
number of justices should be reduced from nine to seven, as
soon as the lower number should be reached by retirement
or death, a movement to curb the distrusted President's power,
and to prevent him from putting conservatives upon the
bench.[5] When Grant came into office the number was almost

---

[1] Cf. Chase's own explanations of and excuses for his course in 8
Wall., p. 625, and 12 Wall., p. 576; Hart, Chase, pp. 389-90, 407-11;
G. F. Hoar, Autobiography, vol. i, p. 286.
[2] Cf. G. F. Hoar, Autobiography, vol. i, p. 282.
[3] N. Y. Nation, March 24, 1870.
[4] Cf. A. B. Hart, Life of Chase, pp. 397-8; Schuckers, Life of Chase,
pp. 260-1. [5] Act of July 23, 1866.

instantly restored to nine.[1]   The law was to take effect in
December, 1869.   Wayne had died and Grier resigned.   To
the vacant places Grant nominated ex-Secretary of War Edwin
M. Stanton, who died four days after his confirmation by the
Senate without being able to take his seat, and Attorney General Hoar who was rejected by the Senate for reasons which
are to be given in another place.[2]   Thus there were two seats
to be filled when the legal tender decision was handed down
and the President at once nominated William Strong of Pennsylvania and Joseph P. Bradley of New Jersey to occupy
them.

The reorganized court proceeded to its task.   The new justices immediately displayed their sympathies.   Both allied
themselves with the minority justices and made a dramatic
effort to bring up two legal tender cases previously passed
over, so that the opinion of Chase might be reversed at the
same term of court in which it had been rendered.   The effect
of such an exhibition of zeal was instant.   The good which
had been done by the opinion of the Chief Justice and his associates was at once undone.   The financial and business world
took note of what had come to pass, the premium on gold was
not reduced, as there had been signs that it soon might be,
and the country was as far as ever away from specie payments.

But meantime the cases which Strong and Bradley were so
eager to reach were withdrawn,[3] and two other cases, Knox v.
Lee from Texas and Parker v. Davis from Massachusetts,
were brought forward.   On these a decision was announced
in May, 1871,[4] although the opinion was not read until January 15, 1872.[5]   Now five justices, Strong, Bradley and the
three who had dissented in the Hepburn case, gave the majority opinion, overruling Chase and his three associates, and
declaring that the acts of Congress creating the legal tenders

[1] Act of April 10, 1869.
[2] By a vote of 24 to 33.—Senate Executive Journal, vol. xvii. p. 357.
[3] 9 Wall., p. 145; cf. Hart, Life of Chase, pp. 402-3; Schuckers, Life
of Chase, pp. 262-4.   [4] 11 Wall., p. 682.   [5] 12 Wall., p. 457.

were constitutional as applied to contracts made either before or after their passage.

Bitterness marked the transactions of the justices in reaching this result.[1] They shared the turbulence which characterized the relations of the factions in Congress and throughout the country. On both sides, from the first appearance of the subject in the court, the guiding influences were less legal than political. The arguments of Strong and his associates reflected the emotional feeling which came to the defence of the greenbacks. They had done the country a service during the war and they were held to have acquired some of the sanctity of a tattered regimental banner or a soldier's grave, on which account it seemed to be impermissible to doubt their legal validity.[2] Chase occupied a sounder position because he had in view a good and an important object, the country's return to principles from which he felt a responsibility for having induced it for a time, under necessity, to depart.

It was easy to conclude and to assert that the court had been "packed." Chase himself believed it.[3] The fact that the new appointments came so soon after the decision had been rendered and the spectacle of the new justices hurrying to the task of reversing and discrediting the Chief Justice naturally gave rise to such a charge. The accusation was true only in the sense that Strong and Bradley were railroad attorneys, as, indeed, most prominent lawyers were likely to be, and very recently had been directly concerned for the interests of their clients on this subject;[4] and that they were Republicans with the aggressive and arrogant bias with which most of the adherents of that party came out of the war. They held and uttered, as soon as they could, the partisan *post bellum* opin-

[1] Hart, Life of Chase, p. 403; Schuckers, Life of Chase, p. 403.

[2] "Something revived the drooping faith of the people; something brought immediately to the government's aid the resources of the nation, and something enabled the successful prosecution of the war and the preservation of the national life. What was it if not the legal tender enactments?"—Justice Strong in the majority opinion in the Legal Tender Cases, 12 Wall., p. 541.

[3] Boutwell, Sixty Years in Public Affairs, vol. ii, p. 210.

[4] "The most serious objection to the action of Justices Strong and Bradley," said the New York Tribune, "is that they overturned and

ion of the dominant political organization. The court, therefore, was "packed" for the Radical Republican party and the
Grant administration, as might have been anticipated, but
in no other sense.[1]

The taxes which were levied to defray the costs of the war,
now that it was ended, were bearing upon the nation with a
fearful weight. It is true that they were being used to pay
the public debt at a rate which found "no precedent in the
history of any other nation."[2] But the people could not well
stand under such burdens indefinitely. A "mountain of taxation" rose before your eyes wherever you turned, said the
Chicago Tribune.[3] Many branches of business were "taxed
into stagnation," said the New York Nation; others had been
"actually taxed out of existence." There was "intolerable
pressure" upon the people who were bleeding "at every pore."[4]
It had been said with truth, Morgan of Ohio declared in the
House—

> "We are taxed for our clothing, our meat and our bread,
> On our carpets and dishes, our table and bed,
> On our tea and our coffee, our fuel and lights,
> And we're taxed so severely we can't sleep o' nights.

brought into contempt a recent very careful decision of their own
court by ruling, with little argument and in unusual haste, on the
side on which they had but a short time before been paid advocates."
—Issue of May 1, 1871.

[1] This subject is discussed in many places as in Hart, Life of Chase,
pp. 399–402; Hoar, Autobiography, vol. i, pp. 286-8; Boutwell, Sixty
Years in Public Affairs, vol. ii, pp. 208-10; J. P. Bradley, Miscellaneous
Writings, pp. 45 et seq. This is a bootless controversy. It is said for
Miller, Strong and Bradley that they were jurists of unquestioned
ability. Their careers give us proof of this. But when they could
write in judicial opinions prepared for the highest court in the land
that a piece of paper money was a legal issue because it had helped
the country to win a war, and offer us this in the room of a constitutional argument one can be permitted to doubt their capacity for forming unpartisan judgments at this period of their lives. That at a later
day Strong, Bradley, Judge Hoar, who after the rejection of his nomination to the Supreme Court still served as Attorney General, and his
brother, Senator Hoar, should have come to the defence of the court
for its course at this time may be taken to be evidence of nothing so
much as unquiet consciences.

[2] David A. Wells, in second annual report, House Ex. Doc., 40th Cong.
2nd sess., no. 81, p. 6; cf. Wells in N. Y. Nation, April 18, 1872.

[3] Quoted in Cong. Globe, 39th Cong. 1st sess., app., p. 286.

[4] N. Y. Nation, June 18 and Nov. 21, 1867.

"We are stamped on our mortgages, checks, notes and bills.
On our deeds, on our contracts and on our last wills,
And the star-spangled banner in mourning doth wave
O'er the wealth of the nation turned into the grave.

"We are taxed on our offices, our stores and our shops,
On our stoves, on our barrels, on our brooms and our mops,
On our horses and cattle, and, if we should die,
We are taxed on our coffins in which we must lie.

"We are taxed on all goods by kind Providence given,
We are taxed for the Bible that points us to Heaven,
And when we ascend to the Heavenly goal
You would, if you could, stick a stamp on our soul."[1]

Congress in 1865 before the war had ended[2] had authorized the Secretary of the Treasury to appoint a commission to study the subject of the excise and customs revenues. It was composed of David A. Wells of New York, Stephen Colwell of Pennsylvania and S. S. Hayes of Illinois. The object had been the discovery of new sources of income to support the war, but as Lee surrendered before its activities began the three officers found it to be their duty instead to suggest methods of readjusting the taxes with a view to reducing their burden.[3] It was a "novelty in American experience." The commission, after six months in taking testimony and assembling information, in January, 1866, submitted its findings to Mr. McCulloch who said that the work had been "admirably performed." He forwarded the report to Congress with his hearty approval in the hope that its recommendations would be made the basis of revisory legislation.

When the commission's term had expired Mr. Wells, in accordance with the provisions of the revenue act of 1866, was designated by Secretary McCulloch to continue the work as a "special commissioner of revenue."[4] The commission and its successor, the "special commissioner," found that often, in the eager and unscientific search of Congress for the means

[1] Cong. Globe, 40th Cong. 2nd sess., p. 2724.
[2] Act of March 3, 1865.
[3] See Report in House Ex. Doc., 39th Cong. 1st sess., nos. 34, 51, 62 and 68.
[4] Stanwood, American Tariff Controversies, vol. ii, pp. 158-9.

of carrying on the war, the same article was taxed many times. It was computed that from 8 to 20 per cent of the value of every finished manufactured product found its way into the United States treasury. Before a book could reach its readers from 12 to 15 different taxes were paid upon it, or the materials going to complete it. Distilled liquors which had borne a tax of only 20 cents a gallon in 1863 now were made to pay $2 a gallon, so exorbitant a charge that it gave encouragement to frauds which attained scandalous proportions. It was estimated that the Federal taxes at the end of the war amounted to nearly 5 per cent of the gross annual earnings of the entire population, an average of $14 in a year upon every man, woman and child in both the Northern and the Southern states.[1]

Plainly some of these taxes were unjust and contrary to the public welfare. It was proposed by the experts that those which impeded the industrial development of the country should be abolished, and that, in so far as this might be possible, trade should be freed of the restrictions which had been temporarily imposed upon it. An act of July 13, 1866, repealed the taxes on coal and pig iron and made other changes in the internal revenue system, all together effecting a reduction in the Federal income of $45,000,000 annually. The next year [2] the taxes on many kinds of manufactured products were reduced or were done away with entirely. Incomes up to $1,000 were exempted. The tax on cotton which had been lowered in 1867 was abolished in 1868.[3] In that year many other kinds of goods were finally freed from taxation, with exceptions for gas, kerosene, tobacco, liquors and a large variety of articles which brought the government a revenue through adhesive stamps.[4] The tax upon spirituous liquors was reduced from $2 to fifty cents a gallon.[5] Finally, on July 14, 1870, the internal revenue system was put into the position which it held until 1883.

[1] Ibid., vol. ii, pp. 144-5.   [2] Act of March 2, 1867.
[3] February 3, 1868.   [4] March 31, 1868.   [5] July 30, 1868.

Banks and bankers, a few manufactures, spirits, malt liquors, tobacco and some articles bearing stamps were alone left to recall to the popular mind the system of war finance. What remained were regarded as taxes upon luxuries. Nearly all the license taxes except those upon distilleries, breweries and shops for selling liquor and tobacco were repealed. The income tax was reduced to 2½ per cent for incomes in excess of $2,000. It was to be abolished entirely in 1872.[1]

But it was a very different matter when the commissioner turned to the imposts. The system of duties was based upon the provisions of the "Morrill Tariff Act" which had become effective on April 1, 1861, at the beginning, therefore, of Lincoln's administration. Many rates were advanced with a view to increasing the revenues on August 5, 1861. Two more acts with the same ends in view followed on December 24, 1861, and July 14, 1862. Again on March 3, 1863, June 30, 1864, March 3, 1865, May 16 and July 28, 1866, the rates were advanced. Duties were compounded; *ad valorem* were added to specific duties. On some kinds of woolens the charge was 24 cents a pound plus a 40 per cent tax on their imported value. Raw wool of certain grades paid as much as 10 cents a pound. The cheapest calicoes were subject to a tax of 6½ cents a square yard and 10 per cent *ad valorem*. The rate upon railroad iron was $22.40 a long ton. Duties on many articles were so high that the import trade in these articles ceased.

Tax was added to tax without meeting more than casual and formal opposition. The manufacturers paid a license to carry on business, taxes on their raw materials and on their finished products, and, in the end, an income tax upon their profits. No one particularly begrudged them protection. They were supporting the government; the government might well aid them by giving them a secure control of the home market for the sale of their goods.[2]

[1] Dewey, Financial History of the United States, pp. 391-4; Cong. Globe, 41st Cong. 2nd sess., app., pp. 701-3.
[2] Edward Stanwood, American Tariff Controversies, vol. ii, p. 130.

During the war it had been stated repeatedly that we must have protection, as John Sherman had expressed it, "against our own laws," i.e., against the paper currency and the internal taxes, by which influences the cost of manufactured goods was increased. The tariff must be raised to hold the domestic market against foreigners who were free of such burdens. When the excise, which in great part had justified the higher customs charges, should be reduced or abolished it was understood that the duties on imports would be lowered also.[1]

But instead of a willingness to return to pre-war conditions what was seen? Loud and insistent demands were heard on every hand. The manufacturers descended upon Washington and, when they themselves were not present, the halls of Congress were filled with their lobbyists.[2] They not only declined to keep to the terms of the bargain to return to lower duties, but they asked for still higher tariffs. The Démocratic leader, Representative Brooks, called it "impudence," and it seemed like this to many other men.[3]

The protectionist influences radiated from two principal centres. A group of manufacturers in Pennsylvania, and the politicians whom they sent to Congress and kept in other places of power, found it convenient to adopt the theories of Henry C. Carey of Philadelphia, a social economist who advocated the protective system with peculiar pertinacity and with some appearance of scientific learning. William D. Kelley, known his life through as "Pig Iron" Kelley for his earnestness in defence of Carey's doctrines, was the principal expositor of these views in Congress. The members of this group were unyielding Brahmins and the effects of their tireless activity were profoundly felt for a generation.

Yet more potential was Horace Greeley who spoke in the

---

[1] Cong. Globe, 39th Cong. 2nd sess., app., p. 712; ibid., 40th Cong. 3rd sess., app., p. 63; ibid., 41st Cong. 2nd sess, app., p. 193.

[2] Congressman Marshall spoke of the "hordes of monopolists and manufacturers who have infested the capital during the entire session." Ibid., 39th Cong. 1st sess., app., p. 283.

[3] Ibid., 40th Cong. 3rd sess., app., p. 63.

columns of the New York Tribune. The most of what he knew about the tariff was acquired by a reading of the speeches of Henry Clay.[1] While he was addressing the farmers of the Mississippi Valley as to the wrongs of slavery, gaining their confidence as he proceeded, he sought to open their minds to the necessity of protection. He essayed to write a treatise on political economy which appeared in parts in the Tribune[2] to be brought together afterward in a book. He had the simplest notions about the subject. The do all and be all of political economy for him was a tariff which was designed and justified as a means of holding the home market —of keeping the American market for Americans. Insuperable barriers, ironically called a "Chinese wall," should be erected on the national boundaries to exclude the products of other countries. A people must consume what they themselves raised and manufactured, making themselves independent of the rest of the world. He would not enrich other nations by trading with them. In this manner would a country's industries be fostered, strengthened and diversified. Here was the true road to national wealth.

Greeley, to make his theories more acceptable to the people, belittled "abroad" and sought to raise a prejudice against foreigners. He was helped forward on this line by the distrust and hatred so generally felt in the United States for England because of the sympathy which had been expressed there for the Confederacy, fomented and exaggerated all the while by the large numbers of Irish settled in this country who were so eager to involve us in some kind of a quarrel with Great Britain, which they conceived might be in the interest of Irish independence. The workingmen of Europe were pictured as "paupers";[3] cheapness was a thing to be despised. The presentation of opposing doctrines was dismissed as a "free trade howl." The scorn with which a

[1] Cf. Tarbell, The Tariff in Our Times, p. 17.

[2] Beginning on May 29, 1869.

[3] Grant in his second message of December, 1870, spoke of the "pauper labor of the old world."—Richardson, vol. vii, p. 108.

Carey-Greeley protectionist could cast out of the temple a "free trader," usually made still more odious by being branded a "British free trader," was not exceeded by the contempt which the same man expressed for a "rebel" or a "Copperhead." Now and again he was heard to say that if the Maker of the universe had been a good political economist, with the welfare of the United States close to His heart, He would have separated us from Europe with a sea of fire.[1]

When Greeley began his preaching protectionist sentiment among the farmers of the West was nascent, if, indeed, it can be said to have existed at all. Signs were many at the end of the war that their views had undergone a change. It was particularly notable with reference to wool upon which manufacturers had come to rely in large degree as a fibre for their weaving mills because of the cutting off of the cotton supply. Clothing and blankets for the army kept the looms in action incessantly, and the high prices had attracted an increasing number of farmers to sheep raising. In 1868 it was said that the American flock was 70 per cent larger than at the outbreak of the war seven years before.[2] It was thought that there were 36,000,000 sheep in the United States, half of them grazing upon the pastures of Ohio, and that the clip amounted to 100,000,000 pounds annually.

The wool manufacturers had formed a national association in 1864 and were making their demands heard in Republican newspapers, like the New York Tribune, and in Washington. They wished to continue to sell their cloth, however inferior it might be, at high prices, safe from the competition of the very efficient manufacturers of Great Britain.

---

[1] "If I had my way, if I were king of the country," said Greeley to Garfield, "I would put a duty of $100 a ton on pig iron and a proportionate duty on everything else that can be produced in America. The result would be that our people would be obliged to supply their own wants. Manufactures would spring up, competition would finally reduce prices and we would live wholly within ourselves." (Dewey, Financial History of the United States, p. 397.)

[2] N. Y. Nation, June 25, 1868.

For the wool grower they had no concern, if they themselves could be protected by tariff laws. Indeed, they were in favor of free wool; with cheap materials they could obtain larger profits on their finished products.

But the sheep farmers of Ohio had come to believe that what was good for the manufacturer would be equally good for them. They were active politicians and they said that if there were to be tariffs on woollens so should there be on wool itself. They saw wool coming into the country from South America and the Cape of Good Hope where land was cheap and the flocks were tended by "pauper labor," and they wished to put a stop to the trade. They also viewed with great disfavor the large importations of shoddy to be worked up into cloth in the manufacture of which wool should have been employed. "A greater legislative wrong" there had never been, said Columbus Delano, than this which had been "practised on the wool growers of the land." God helping them, they would bear such ills no longer. For years without end the West had supported the tariff bills made for the profit and advantage of the East and now, Delano continued, "if you will not help us, then when we get strong enough, as we soon shall be, we will help ourselves and you may help yourselves." "As you have so long had protection and had it at our expense," he cried, "come now to the work."[1] He and others were ready to predict that if flockmasters should receive the encouragement which was their due, sheep would soon cover the prairies of the West as they now covered the downs and hummocks of Ohio. It was shepherds on the plains of Judea who first saw the star resting over the babe in Bethlehem and no class of men were "better entitled to the care and protection of a beneficent government."[2]

In the same way the West wanted a duty on flaxseed, while the New York linseed oil makers wished to buy it cheap and to import it at will from other countries free of duty.

[1] Cong. Globe, 39th Cong. 1st sess., app., pp. 260, 261.
[2] Ibid., p. 204.

Thus was the issue made for the Republican party; it was confronted with a problem which it continued to face for a generation. It must reconcile the East and the West—the interests of the farmer and the interests of the manufacturer. The basis was laid for that system of log-rolling in protective tariff politics, which consisted of giving a duty to the farmer for some agricultural product in return for his support of a duty upon a manufactured product.[1]

Representative Morrill of Vermont whose name was attached to the tariff act of 1861 presented a bill in the summer of 1866 which was largely the compilation of Stephen Colwell, though in other respects it followed suggestions and recommendations of Mr. Wells. If there were some reductions there were many increases in duties to satisfy the Careyites of Pennsylvania, the "wool lobby" of Ohio and other interests active at Washington.

To the Democrats the rising duties were a "system of robbery." That all the rates were not instead to be reduced was "a disgrace to the civilization of the age." The manufacturers who wished these benefits were "plunderers" whose "unholy demands" were "ever increasing." They were "lordly" men, "building palatial residences, sporting princely equipages" and regularly declaring dividends of from 20 to 200 per cent annually upon their businesses. The day the bill should pass it would add $200,000,000, the New York Herald said $500,000,000, to the wealth of the manufacturers, importers, warehousemen and other holders of goods affected by its provisions.[2] The New York Mercantile Journal said that it would change the rates on 4,000 separate articles of commerce, raising the duties from 20 to 150 per cent. It would add 30 per cent to the cost of living. To the Chicago Tribune it was a "pure scheme of plunder without the slightest excuse or palliation."[3]

The wool growers and the woollen manufacturers had held

[1] Stanwood, American Tariff Controversies, vol. ii, p. 158.
[2] Cong. Globe, 39th Cong. 1st sess., app., pp. 283-4, 286.
[3] Ibid., p. 286.

a joint meeting in Syracuse, N. Y., to reconcile and pool their interests and had reached a compromise. The sheep men must have higher duties on raw wool—this was foreordained. The manufacturers would give their adhesion to this policy if they could have proportionately higher duties on woollen cloth. It was a strange bargain. Interests in no official relationship with the government had struck hands and carried their scheme to Washington to have it accepted by the Republican leaders in the Thirty-ninth Congress, as though it had been the product of their own committee rooms.[1] The general tariff bill, including the provisions relating to wool and woollens, failed of passage in the first and went over to the second session. It was seen that it could not be approved and at the last moment, on the eve of adjournment, the sheep men, whose requirements were so urgent, pressed through both houses a bill of their own, embodying the terms of their bargain with the manufacturers, and by their importunities induced President Johnson on March 2, 1867, to sign it.[2] Such was the history of the measure which is usually known as the "Wool and Woollens Act of 1867."

Special Commissioner of the Revenue David A. Wells was a Republican. At first he had been a protectionist, but as he proceeded with his inquiries, coming in contact with the selfish interests dictating tariff legislation at Washington and meeting the corrupt men, who often moved under a thin disguise of pretended knowledge of political economy, he reacted strongly to the other side.[3] Though his annual reports were written in a controversial style and were marked by much partisanship they contained cogent and unanswerable

[1] Cf. Cong. Globe, 39th Cong. 2nd sess., p. 3466, and app., p. 74; Stanwood, American Tariff Controversies, vol. ii, pp. 147-9; D. A. Wells's Report, Senate Ex. Doc., 39th Cong. 2nd sess., no. 2, pp. 50-1; House Reports, 41st Cong. 2nd sess., no. 72, pp. 8-9; F. A. Taussig, Tariff Hist. of the U. S., 4th ed., pp. 198 et seq.

[2] Cong. Globe, 39th Cong. 2nd sess., pp. 1924, 1949, 1952; Stanwood, American Tariff Controversies, vol. ii, pp. 154-8.

[3] N. Y. Nation, Dec. 1, 1870. He was "educated," as he said, "by his own investigations."—House Reports, 41st Cong. 2nd sess., no. 72, p. 120.

arguments in favor of lower duties.[1] Wells advocated free
raw materials in the interest of lower manufacturing costs.
Product should be exchanged for product—that one on which
labor had been expended by the processes of manufacture
for some rough one—a fibre, a root, a hide or a gum. As it
was now prices were made abnormally high by import duties,
so that little or nothing could be exported to other countries
and accounts had to be settled expensively by bills of exchange on England. The tariff, he said, was a tax upon the
consumer. He would have it reduced for the relief of the
poor. If not in these words, he spoke in plain enough terms
of the rights of the masses to existence without the payment
of tribute to a class of men who were enriching themselves
behind a wall erected for their advantage by politicians with
whom they stood in league.

Wells was soon quoted approvingly by Democrats and condemned by Republicans. It was clear to the protectionists
that he had come under the influence of Great Britain. Like
the editor of the New York Nation and others who made
themselves prominent as the advocates of tariff reform, which
was held to be only another name for free trade, he had been
bought by "British gold" out of the famous coffers of the
"Cobden Club." Radicals spoke of "kicking him out of the
party." In the face of reports which indicated the most
laborious research, "Pig Iron" Kelley called him a "dreamy
and indolent theorist";[2] Greeley a "Munchausen" and a
"humbug." [3] They would abolish his office and deny government publication to his reports, so that his "pestiferous
utterances" should not go out to corrupt the American mind.
Boutwell and the Radicals made certain that Wells should
not receive a re-appointment and at the end of his term

[1] Report of the commission, House Ex. Doc., 39th Cong. 1st sess.,
no. 34; Wells's first report, Senate Ex. Doc., 39th Cong. 2nd sess., no.
2; second report, House Ex. Doc., 40th Cong. 2nd sess., no. 81; third
report, House Ex. Doc., 40th Cong. 3rd sess., no. 16; fourth report,
House Ex. Doc., 41st Cong. 2nd sess., no. 27.
[2] Cong. Globe, 40th Cong. 3rd sess., app., p. 120.
[3] Quoted in N. Y. Nation, March 3, 1870.

on June 30, 1870, he was excused from further public service.

The "special commissioner" received a parting shot in a report of the Committee on Manufactures of the House to which had been referred innumerable petitions from members of outraged wool growers, window glass, iron puddling and stocking weavers' associations, all of whom repelled with indignation his imputations upon them as true and patriotic Americans. The committee informed him that he had erred in "supposing that the promulgation of any system of political economy was within the limits of his duty or his authority." Congress was competent to draw its own conclusions when put in possession of the facts. He had in his heart no pride which an American ought to feel with reference to his country's efforts to gain its "industrial independence." His reports were made in the interest of the "cotton lords of Manchester." Although seemingly at peace we were "really engaged in unrelenting warfare" with the "trained legions of England" which was incessantly launching missiles from its workshops and mines "to subjugate and impoverish" America. A minority of the committee gave Wells an opportunity in their report to reply to his detractors, of which he availed himself.[1]

A bill proposing a general revision of the tariff similar to that which was defeated in the Thirty-ninth was brought forward in 1868 for the approval of the Fortieth Congress. Its sponsor was Representative Moorhead of Pennsylvania. It was "gloved and furred and velvet-pawed to suit certain Pennsylvania interests," said James Brooks, and it was generally known as the "Pennsylvania bill." [2] It was a declaration of war upon light, as represented by window glass, and upon salt and iron, "three great elements of life." There were to be "fresh levies" upon the people "to satiate the insatiate maws" of the "Pennsylvania cormorants." [3] When

---

[1] House Reports, 41st Cong. 2nd sess., no. 72.
[2] Cong. Globe, 40th Cong. 3rd sess., app., p. 64.
[3] Ibid., p. 66.

tariff laws were to be passed, Brooks continued, let interests be heard other than "those tremendous monopolies now thronging the halls of this Capitol and overwhelming us with their cries for protection, protection, everlasting and eternal protection, more and more, louder and louder, the more we give." [1]

The net result in this Congress was a bill increasing the duties on copper and copper ores, which was vetoed by President Johnson on the ground that it imposed "an additional tax upon an already overburdened people" who should not be further impoverished "that monopolies" might be "fostered and corporations enriched," [2] but the measure was passed over his veto on February 24, 1869, and became a law in his despite. [3]

Pelion was piled on Ossa. From 1861 to 1869 there had been thirteen different tariff acts in each one of which the rates of duties had been increased. While striking the manacles from 4,000,000 blacks we had been riveting chains on 36,000,000 white men. [4] From the 5 and 10 per cent protection of Alexander Hamilton, an old Whig said, we had advanced to the 20 and 30 per cent of Henry Clay and Daniel Webster. Now it was from 30 to 500 per cent and still more was demanded. [5] The average rate, said Wells, was nearly 50 per cent. [6] James Brooks declared the United States to be "the most tariffed, the most taxed" nation on earth. [7]

The opposition to the taxes on tea, coffee and sugar, the so-called "taxes on the breakfast table," grew until it could no longer go unheeded. Likewise the duties on coal, salt and many other articles essential to the comfort of the people were adjudged oppressive, and Congress was asked to do away

[1] Cong. Globe, 40th Cong. 3rd sess., p. 69.
[2] Richardson, vol. vi, pp. 705-7.
[3] Cong. Globe, 40th Cong. 3rd sess., app., p. 304.
[4] Ibid., 41st Cong. 2nd sess., app., p. 159.
[5] Ibid., 40th Cong. 3rd sess., app., p. 63.
[6] Senate Ex. Doc., 39th Cong. 2nd sess., no. 2, pp. 40-1; House Ex. Doc., 41st Cong. 2nd sess., no. 27.
[7] Cong. Globe, 41st Cong. 2nd sess., app., p. 159.

with them. The outspoken course of some Western representatives, notably William B. Allison of Iowa (later to serve
with distinction for so many years in the United States
Senate) in the Committee on Ways and Means of which he
was a member, and on the floor of the House was proof of
the earnestness of the people inhabiting that part of the
Union on the side of a more moderate tariff policy.[1] Garfield declared that at least 50 of the 57 Republican and Democratic representatives from the region lying west of the state
of Ohio, north of Arkansas and east of the Rocky Mountains, were in favor of lower duties. "If I do not misun-
derstand the signs of the times," said he, unless we ourselves
revise the tariff "prudently and wisely, we shall before long
be compelled to submit to a violent reduction, made rudely
and without discrimination, which will shock, if not shat-
ter, all our protected industries." He was in favor of protection, but of protection leading to "ultimate free trade."[2]

The bill was brought forward by General Schenck, chairman of the Committee on Ways and Means, and it was usually known, therefore, as the "Schenck bill." Washington
was again filled with manufacturers and their legislative
agents. It was a "free for all scramble," said the New York
Nation, for "such trades and callings as have the strongest
lungs and longest arms." Now as before, and as in so many
cases since, our "vast wealth of ingenuity" was diverted from
"the ennobling work of mechanical invention and contriv-
ance to the barren and debasing work of lobbying."[3] "Something is surely wrong in a modern state," the Nation continued, "when manufacturers who stand in the very foremost rank, such as our edge tool makers for instance, on finding foreign rivals underselling them, instead of sitting down
to study their processes and overhaul their books, have to
leave their factories to take care of themselves to go to Washington to have long palavers with men who hardly know a
hawk from a handsaw."

[1] Cong. Globe, 41st Cong. 2nd sess., app., pp. 190 et seq.
[2] Ibid., pp. 271, 272. [3] N. Y. Nation, May 5, 1870.

The changes which were proposed in the schedules by the
"Schenck bill" were in the direction of lower duties, but the
number of articles affected was few and the reductions were
small. The debates were productive of much speech, colloquy and rejoinder. The bill went to ,the conferees early
in July and was signed by the President on the 14th day of
that month to take effect on the 1st of January following.
In answer to popular demands the duty on tea was cut from
25 to 15 cents, on coffee from 5 to 3 cents. The rates on
sugar and spices were reduced. The duty on pig iron which
had been $9 henceforth would be $7 a ton. For the satisfaction of the manufacturers who were pressing for free raw
materials some 130 articles were added to the free list, including india rubber, fur skins, hair, horns, round timber,
oak and hemlock bark, phosphates, rags and wood for paper
making, and many kinds of drugs.[1]

It was thought that what had been done might suffice.
But this was a mere tub to the whale. The tone of the press
and of political feeling generally in the West was such as
to indicate that yet more concessions must be made to the
"revenue reformers." A number of leaders of the movement
who had been acting within the Republican party, including
ex-Secretary of the Treasury Hugh McCulloch, Mr. Wells,
General Hawley of Connecticut, Horace White and Amasa
Walker met in Washington in April to discuss the situation,
and they reached the conclusion with Adam Smith that "taxes
should be so contrived as both to take out and keep out of
the pockets of the people as little as possible over and above
what they bring into the public treasury of the state."[2]

Republican journals, like the Tribune in Chicago and the
Missouri Democrat in St. Louis, insistently demanded lower
duties. The Republican revolution in Missouri in 1870 concerned itself with tariff reform as well as disfranchisement.
The "Liberals" were "unequivocally hostile to any tariff"
which fostered "one industry or interest at the expense of

[1] Cong. Globe, 41st Cong. 2nd sess., app., pp. 703-7.
[2] N. Y. Nation, April 28 and May 5, 1870.

another." [1] The Republican platforms in other states, as Illinois, Indiana, Connecticut and Maine, indicated a similar tendency in public feeling.[2] Not only did Gratz Brown sweep Missouri but the results of the autumn elections throughout the country gave emphatic proof of a rising sentiment hostile to the Grant administration. In the new House of Representatives the majority of the Republicans would be reduced from 97 to 35. For the first time since their contest with Johnson began they had lost their useful two-thirds majority, and the opposition could at last put effective obstacles in their way. The Democrats also gained several seats in the Senate.[3]

The free traders made the most of the situation. In November, 1870, a call was sent out by the secretary of the New York Free Trade League for a conference of "revenue reformers" in New York city with a view to some activity which would influence Congress to lower the tariff.[4] Not knowing how much this issue had had to do with the result in 1870, nor the force of the movement with reference to the campaign of 1872, the Republican leaders manifested many signs of alarm. In March, 1871, the House voted to put tea, coffee, salt and coal on the free list.[5] But the matter rested there until the next session when the subject was attacked in earnest.√ The speaker, James G. Blaine of Maine, who had followed Colfax in that office,[6] though a

[1] American Annual Cyclopedia for 1870, p. 520.
[2] Ibid., in articles concerning those states; N. Y. Nation, Sep. 8 and 15 and Oct. 13, 1870.
[3] Cf. N. Y. Tribune Almanac for 1871, p. 45, and 1872, p. 52. "It is safe to say," the New York Nation declared, "that the Republican party has just passed a crisis from which only extraordinary luck or extraordinary behavior will enable it to recover."—Issue of Nov. 17, 1870.
[4] Horace White, Life of Trumbull, p. 353; N. Y. Nation, Dec. 1, 1870; Rollo Ogden, Life of E. L. Godkin, vol. ii, p. 100.
[5] Cong. Globe, 42nd Cong. 1st sess., pp. 81-2; N. Y. Nation, March 16, 1871.
[6] Blaine had been elected in March, 1869, over Dawes after an animated contest, his election having been achieved largely by Butler's services in bringing a number of "carpetbaggers" and other Southern Congressmen to Blaine's support."—Cf. Hoar, Autobiography, vol. i, p. 201.

protectionist, realizing the need of strategy for party success, after visiting Chicago for a conference with the Western "revenue reformers," appointed Representative Finkelnburg, a Schurz Republican from Missouri, and Representative Burchard of Illinois, both "tariff reformers," as members of the Committee on Ways and Means.[1] This action meant that Dawes, who was chairman, had been deposed to all practical purposes, and it paved the way for two laws, of May 1 and June 6, 1872, which entirely repealed the duties on tea and coffee, reduced the rates on coal, salt, leather, tin, soda ash and several other articles, and added to the free list hides, jute, paper stock, saltpetre, books twenty years of age and material for ships in the foreign trade. The call for some reductions in the tariff on manufactured goods, which had never been heeded was now met by the slight horizontal cut of 10 per cent on cotton, wool, metal, paper, india rubber, glass and leather products. John Sherman but voiced the view of other shrewd party leaders when he told the manufacturers that the reduction was in their interest which was "so connected with the general interest," i.e., "with the maintenance of the protective system" that it would be "a misfortune to them if this concession to the consumers of the country should now be refused." It were better for them to submit to "this slight modification of duties" rather than "invite a contest" which would "endanger the whole system." It was time, said he, "to abate somewhat, not the principle of our protective duties, but the maximum amounts that were imposed during the war."[2]

Grant had begun badly in the exercise of the appointing power and his selections for public office rapidly grew worse. Rawlins died in September, an irreparable loss to the administration because of his peculiar power over the President. He was friend as well as adjutant. The two men had been "as but one soul." Though Grant, after his election to the Presidency, had begun to feel that he must be possessed of

[1] White, Life of Trumbull, p. 354; cf. N. Y. Nation, April 18, 1872.
[2] Cong. Globe, 42nd Cong. 2nd sess., pp. 2017-8.

some superior quality of which even he himself had hitherto been ignorant,[1] Rawlins's influence was still great. In the Cabinet it was he, and he only, who had seen Grant develop from a simple clerk in the Galena leather store to a victorious chieftain commanding a million men; he, and he only, who knew the President's real capacities and limitations and "stood not in the slightest awe of him." As Secretary of War, says General Wilson, Rawlins "wielded the same potent and controlling influence over the President, when he chose to exert it, that the chief of staff had wielded over the commanding general."[2] Now another must be found to head the War Department. The choice fell upon General W. W. Belknap of Iowa, commended for the place through an act of kindness to a member of Grant's family, a man of whom at the time almost nothing was known,[3] and who, in the end, contributed one of the darkest chapters to the history of an administration which throughout was singularly wanting in worthy figures or creditable deeds.

At first "Greeks bearing gifts" and patrons, those who had the power of accumulating money, a talent which was so alien to Grant that when he found it in others he seemed to give it an exaggerated value, were in many cases preferred for office. He was moved by flattery and not a few conspiring persons reached his heart through this avenue.[4] Places continued to be found for a large number of brothers-in-law and other relations and family connections. Some statisticians alleged that 42 persons allied to the President by blood or marriage were on the pay rolls of the government; it was positively ascertained that there were 13 of these "billeted on the country."[5] These 13 became centres of influence for procuring appointments for others in their circles, thus extending the presidential family indefinitely. The charge of

---

[1] J. H. Wilson, Life of Rawlins, p. 376.

[2] Ibid., pp. 359, 369, 376.

[3] J. H. Wilson, Life of C. A. Dana, p. 419.

[4] Cf. McCulloch, Men and Measures, p. 355.

[5] Cf. N. Y. Nation, Dec. 14, 1871, quoting N. Y. Times and Brooklyn Eagle; Sumner's Works, vol. xv, p. 102.

nepotism was heard on every hand. With a kind of egotism difficult to reconcile with the simplicity which had seemed earlier to characterize him he looked upon the presidency as a reward bestowed upon him for his personal services, to be used in turn to reward his kindred and friends and to punish his enemies.[1] When the President ceased obeying his own impulses the appointees were chosen creatures of the Radical party managers who pressed around him. With unctuous tongues and outstretched hands they took possession of the government. Never before had the hacks and flunkies of "practical politics" made their way in such numbers into the civil service. It was the beginning of that compact organization of spoilsmen who were to cast an evil spell over our public life for the next quarter of a century. The expectation of those who had set much store by Grant's administration on the strength of his training in the army where supposedly competent men were assigned to tasks, promoted for valuable service and faithfulness to duty, and dismissed when they were proven to be incompetent, was immense. But the hope for civil service reform through his agency did not survive his first year of office. Already in September, 1869, the New York Nation felt itself justified in saying that he had "not only made bad appointments but probably some of the worst ever made by a civilized Christian government."[2]

It was noted with grave regret that the President was repairing to his room in the Capitol for long conversations with senators and representatives as to the bestowal of offices.[3] Moses H. Grinnell, a respectable New York merchant,[4] who was presiding over the affairs of the New York custom house, was dismissed because he would not lend himself to Conkling's schemes for distributing the patronage in that city.[5] Thomas Murphy, an illiterate hatter, an army contractor and a speculator in real estate, an ally of Tweed and other leaders of

[1] Merriam, Life and Times of Samuel Bowles, vol. ii, p. 112.
[2] N. Y. Nation, Sep. 16, 1869.   [3] Ibid., March 24, 1870.
[4] Welles, vol. iii, pp. 560-1.   [5] N. Y. Nation, June 2, 1870.

Tammany Hall in many a disreputable transaction,[1] was appointed in Grinnell's stead, soon to become one of the President's most intimate friends. They smoked together in New York and Washington and told each other stories about horses at Long Branch, which became the nation's summer capital. "Tom" Murphy's appointment to collect the customs revenues of the United States at their principal source, the New York Times said, "set rational explanation at defiance." It was proof that "the parasites of the party" were its "masters."[2] His activities consisted in taking great fees which he held to be the perquisites of the place and in filling the custom house with his own and Conkling's tools who were to strive to keep Grant in the White House for a second term.[3]

Ill paid though they were levies were made upon these poor men for campaign funds which they helplessly paid under threat of dismissal from office, an abuse which had been developing for a long time, but which now was so openly practised that it gave general offense.[4] Office holders were assessed, as scoundrels were allowed to rob the South, under the cover of loyalty and "to help save the country from traitors," i.e., from anti-Grant Republicans and Democrats. General Barlow, the United States marshal in New York, was asked to pay the usual two per cent not only upon his salary but also upon the supposed filchings of his office. In his view this was too much to be borne. As he was administering his place honestly he published the correspondence.[5]

Federal appointments in Louisiana were made at the dictation of Grant's brother-in-law, Casey, who was collector of the port in New Orleans to strengthen the so-called "Custom House party" which was acting in opposition to Warmoth.[6] Offices had been distributed with a view to winning

[1] N. Y. Nation, Sep. 14, 1871.   [3] Cited in ibid., Oct. 26, 1871.
[2] Ibid., Sep. 14 and Oct. 26, 1871.   [4] Ibid., Nov. 17, 1870.
[5] Ibid.   [6] Ibid., Jan. 25, 1872.

support of senators for Grant's San Domingo scheme. Sumner was driven from the chairmanship of the Senate Committee on Foreign Relations, his friend Motley was asked to resign the English mission and other friends of the senator from Massachusetts were removed from or kept out of office vindictively without "a shred of a reason" that would "bear examination." [1] When Schurz led the revolt against the old party organization in Missouri Federal officers who sided with him in that state were punished by dismissal. As for Schurz himself, when he came to Washington in December, 1870, and called upon the President at the White House he was refused admittance.[2]

Boutwell, who had so many places to bestow, withheld nothing from the "gang" which pressed around him; the Treasury Department was a "hotbed of low jobbery." [3] Attorney General Hoar and Secretary of the Interior Cox refused to lend their departments to such a use and immediately incurred the unconcealed displeasure of the men who stood at Grant's elbow and guided his political course. These were the only members of the Cabinet of distinct personal force. Rather than dismiss Hoar or permit him to resign the President in December, 1869, had coupled his name with that of ex-Secretary of War, Edwin M. Stanton, and nominated him for the Supreme bench. Stanton, as we have seen, was immediately confirmed by a large majority, though he did not live to occupy the place, while Hoar, who had done affront to some of the politicians, when he had guided Grant's hand aright in choosing judges for the new circuit court, was opposed. These politicians would have their revenge, and, although on every account, his was one of the worthiest names which Grant had sent them they dallied with the subject discourteously for several weeks and finally rejected the nomination. The same Senate which had said that a man like General Sickles would be a good minister to Spain unblushingly refused to permit Judge Hoar to enter the Su-

[1] N. Y. Nation, Aug. 25, 1870. [2] Ibid., Dec. 15, 1870.
[3] Ibid., Oct. 13, 1870.

preme Court.[1] Its manners as well as its morals had been
ruined in its angry contest with Andrew Johnson, and, still
intent upon pursuing an arbitrary course, it exhibited little
more fitness than the President for exercising the appointing
power with which they together were vested by the Constitution.

In June, 1870, Attorney General Hoar was actually dismissed. Some senators in the clique which had come to
control Grant's judgments informed him that they would
not again visit the Department of Justice while Hoar stood
at its head.[2] A group of Southern leaders required a place
in the Cabinet in return for their support of the San Domingo scheme and their demands were to be satisfied.[3] Furthermore, as Hoar, like Cox and Boutwell, clearly had no
enthusiasm for the treaty with the black republic of the
Antilles, and had also opposed Grant's plans with reference
to Cuba,[4] Grant in military manner seems to have been glad
to dismiss some one of his official family in order to discipline
those who remained.[5] To make his action the more impressive his department heads were not told beforehand of
his design; knowledge of it came to them through the newspapers.

To Judge Hoar himself it was a bolt out of a clear sky.
A messenger entered his office with a letter from the President containing a "naked statement" that it had been found
necessary to ask for his resignation. No explanation was
vouchsafed; no reason of any kind was assigned for the act.
Hoar, putting aside his first impulse to go to Grant to inquire
why such a course had been taken, promptly wrote out his

[1] N. Y. Nation, Dec. 23, 1869, and Feb. 10, 1870. Butler took the
credit for bringing about the rejection of Hoar's name.—Butler's Book,
p. 925.
[2] Boutwell, Sixty Years in Public Affairs, vol. ii, p. 211.
[3] J. D. Cox, Atlantic Monthly for August, 1895.
[4] Pierce, vol. iv, p. 403.
[5] C. F. Adams, Lee at Appomattox, p. 142. But see Grant's reason
in J. R. Young, Around the World with General Grant, vol. ii, p. 278.
"Of course it would not do," said Grant to Young, while he was lotus
eating somewhere in the Indian Ocean in 1879, "to have two Cabinet
officers from Massachusetts and Mr. Hoar retired."

resignation and sent it in, to have it as promptly accepted. Secretary Fish was asked to place the great seal of the State Department upon the paper nominating Amos T. Akerman, a Southern Republican, to the vacancy. Thus was Fish informed of the departure of a friend and colleague. Nor was there at any time in Cabinet meeting afterward a reference to the occurrence, Grant making a studied effort to avoid occasion for inquiry or explanation.[1] Akerman was a native of New Hampshire who had practised law for several years in Georgia, had taken a small part in the war on the rebel side, and had been prominent in the constitutional convention of the state. Still more recently he had been United States district attorney for Georgia.[2] His term was short, for in January, 1872, he resigned and the President appointed George H. Williams, recently United States senator from Oregon, to the place.

A still more determined effort was made to gain possession of the Interior Department. Secretary Cox had organized it on the merit system in accordance with the provisions of an old law of 1853.[3] He surrounded himself with capable and well educated men. The Indian service, the Patent Office and the Census Bureau, which would employ so many persons in connection with the work of compiling the census of 1870, he put into capable hands in spite of the

---

[1] J. D. Cox, Atlantic Monthly, loc. cit.; Fish's Diary for June 17, 1870, in C. F. Adams, Lee at Appomattox, p. 219. Grant, Cox said, "lacked the faculty of conversational discussion which is the very essence of the successful conduct of business where co-operation is necessary." (Article in Atlantic Monthly, loc. cit.) "He unconsciously treated his Cabinet rather as staff officers than as his constitutional advisers," says General J. H. Wilson, "rather as clerks than as counsellors." They in turn "stood in awe of the victorious and taciturn soldier."—Life of Rawlins, p. 358.

[2] Described as a "third rate rebel and a fourth rate lawyer." (N. Y. Nation, June 23, 1870.) It was remarked with some irony that when he became a member of the Cabinet he might have influence enough to get his state into the Union. Everyone asked "who is Akerman?" He was "even more obscure, if possible," said the New York Tribune, "than Borie, Robeson or Belknap."—Washington corr. of Tribune, June 17, 1870.

[3] N. Y. Nation, Nov. 17 and Dec. 1, 1870.

clamor of the office jobbers. But they were levying assessments upon his employees. They were going over his head and he was no longer master in his own house. For good reasons he had resisted an evil scheme called the McGarrahan claim which involved property in some mining lands, again doing affront to that group of corruptionists who pressed around the President.[1] Cox appealed to Grant, who accorded him no support,[2] and in October, 1870, he resigned,[3] the President soon giving the place to Columbus Delano, a Congressman from Ohio, advocate of the sheep growers of that state for a high tariff on wool and since the beginning of Grant's administration Commissioner of Internal Revenue. Hoar's departure from the cabinet had led to general expressions of regret and Cox's resignation, when it came, was declared by men of all parties and by newspapers of all shades of opinion to be a very real and large loss to the government.[4] It was believed that Secretary Fish would go also. Though he honestly wished for relief,[5] he patriotically continued at his post to contribute what wisdom and honor he could to the administration. He was the "bulwark," said Judge Hoar, "standing between the country and its destruction." [6]

It was plain to everyone now, if it had not been before, that the politicians had got hold of Grant. He had taken office "with a splendid fame and with an amount of confidence which had fallen to the lot of no president since Washington," said the New York Nation,[7] but he was now sunk deeper in the mire of abuse than any of his predecessors except Andrew Johnson. The "wreck" of his reputation was a "national misfortune." [8]

[1] Merriam, Life of Samuel Bowles, vol. ii, p. 129; N. Y. Nation, Feb. 9, 1871.
[2] N. Y. Nation, Nov. 3, 1870.
[3] Without much regret to Grant, again on account of San Domingo. —C. F. Adams, Lee at Appomattox, p. 222.
[4] N. Y. Nation, Nov. 3 and 10, 1870.
[5] From his diary in C. F. Adams, Lee at Appomattox, pp. 219-23.
[6] Ibid., p. 221.
[7] Issue of Nov. 17, 1870.
[8] N. Y. Nation, Nov. 8, 10 and 17, 1870.

It was pointed out that there was no proper or adequate law governing the civil service. But Grant could have set a worthy example to the heads of the departments by choosing capable and respected citizens for the higher offices. He could have seen to it that Boutwell and other men did not make a "farce" of the provisions of the law of 1853. He could have accorded his support to Secretary Cox who had respected the provisions of that law. He could have refrained from putting his name to a letter asking Judge Hoar to resign, and saved him to the government. He did none of these things and, after three years in office, it could be said with truth that "not the smallest step" had been taken by him to bring about a civil service based upon merit in any one of the departments.[1]

Grant's charitable judges attributed his failures to his "simple and confiding" nature. The politicians studied him "as the shoemaker measures the foot of his customer," said Senator Hoar.[2] He was "totally unfamiliar with their arts and totally unable to detect even the worst of their snares."[3] His habitual reticence made him the victim of sophistries which there were none to expose and which his tenacity of purpose caused him to cling to even after he himself must have known how fearfully he had erred.[4]

The office holders were banded together in legions by states under some Radical leader, such as Senator Cameron in Pennsylvania and Senator Conkling in New York. "Ben" Butler, that low spoilsman and constant advocate of rascality, whatever its variety, now audaciously essayed to seize the Republican party organization in Massachusetts. He was narrowly defeated in the state conventions in 1871 and 1872 as a candidate for governor. Though he had been denounced by the general who had become President for his incompetency as a commander, though he would not speak to Grant at the end of the war,[5] though he had opposed as well as

[1] N. Y. Nation, June 8, 1871.
[2] Autobiography, vol. i, p. 197.
[3] N. Y. Nation, Oct. 20, 1870.
[4] J. D. Cox, Atlantic Monthly for August, 1895.
[5] B. P. Poore, Reminiscences, vol. ii, p. 220.

he could the movement which carried Grant into the White House,[1] he stood forth now as a principal ally and friend of the administration.

This, that and the other chieftain of similar kind came forward with insolent demands and the President took them into his private circle. Ambitious, intriguing, sordid and corrupt men with the lowest standards for the public service became the impelling forces in the government. Appointments in a vast majority of cases were dictated and controlled by "an influence unknown to the Constitution or the laws."[2] Every custom house, assessor's office and post office became a radiating centre for activity in answer to the will of the leader in the Congressional district or the state who, with this horde at his heels, could overwhelm his opponents on election day. In return for soft words, promising Grant a second term in the White House, they were permitted to build up a great and reprehensible organization founded on offices for their henchmen. The country was at the mercy of "a mercenary political class, an oligarchy of stipendiaries."[3] Now committed to the fortunes of Grant, in a little while they would turn to some other man whom they would hope to bring forward and use in the same way.

It was very clear to a small but determined body of men that the civil service must be put on other foundations before the "tide of corruption" should rise higher.[4] The value of Mr. Godkin's services to this unpopular reform, not only at first, but constantly for years afterward cannot be overstated. "To the victor belong the spoils of the enemy" had been the motto of every administration since Jackson's day, but we were come now to a worse pass than at any time before. The "evil complained of," said Garfield, addressing the members of the House, was "so deep, so wide, so high

[1] Private and Official Correspondence of B. F. Butler, vol. v, p. 720.

[2] Report of Civil Service Commission, Senate Ex. Doc., 43rd Cong. 1st sess., no. 53.

[3] G. W. Curtis in Introduction to D. B. Eaton's Civil Service in Great Britain, p. 5.

[4] N. Y. Nation, Nov. 17, 1870; cf. Rollo Ogden, Life of E. L. Godkin, vol. ii, pp. 40-2.

that some brave Congress must meet it, must grapple with it, must overcome it, if we propose to continue a worthy and noble nation." The "old mad whirl of office brokerage, of coining the entire patronage of the United States into mere political lucre" should be brought to an end.[1]

For many years Representative Jenckes of Rhode Island, "the father and pioneer of civil service reform," [2] had presented bills in Congress providing for the examination of applicants for office. Those proven fit should be put into classes, to be drawn upon in filling vacancies. His attention was forcibly directed to the evil by the great increase in the number of government offices and by the "new and extraordinary doctrines and practices in regard to their distribution." [3] In speech and report [4] he described the development of the "spoils system" in this country, explained the better methods of Europe and fearlessly demanded reform. Schurz signalized his appearance in the Senate with a measure extending the classes of office holders which should be affected by the examinations.[5]

None of the "practical politicians" gathered around Grant wanted a competitive system based upon intelligence or merit. Their power rested on the practice of bartering salaried places for party service. So they sneered at and ridiculed such a reform, when they did not openly denounce it as undemocratic. It was a step toward the bureaucracy which belonged to the despotic states of Europe. It would breed the "insolence of office" which came with tenure for life; 10,000 men, thus ensconced in place, could revolutionize the government.[6] The system would operate against the interests of crippled Union soldiers; the clerkships would go to ex-rebels or shirkers who had stayed at home during the war studying in schools and

[1] Cong. Globe, 42nd Cong. 2nd sess., p. 235.

[2] Harper's Weekly, March 25, 1871.

[3] G. W. Curtis in Introduction to D. B. Eaton, Civil Service in Great Britain, p. v; cf. article on Curtis in Atlantic Monthly, January, 1893.

[4] See, e.g., House Reports, 39th Cong. 2nd sess., no. 8; House Reports, 40th Cong. 2nd sess., no. 47.

[5] N. Y. Nation, Jan. 13, 1870; Schurz, Reminiscences, vol. iii, p. 317.

[6] W. D. Foulke, Life of O. P. Morton, vol. ii, p. 215.

colleges, and who might, therefore, succeed in passing the examinations [1] with higher rank. It was unconstitutional in that the appointing power was vested in the President who could not be relieved of his full responsibility by a transfer of the trust to a "board of schoolmasters." [2]

Many made a pretense of favoring the measure in the abstract, but recoiled when they were brought to the point of taking steps toward its realization. The Liberal Republican party platform in Missouri in 1870 contained ringing declarations in favor of "thorough reform" of the service, based upon "ability and moral worth." Grant himself rather earnestly and, perhaps, sincerely [3] asked for legislation on this subject in his message to Congress in December, 1870. He would have the law "govern not the tenure but the manner of making all appointments." He complained of the embarrassing duty of selecting government employees. No more "arduous and thankless labor" was imposed on senators and representatives. "The present system," he said truthfully, "does not secure the best men and often not even fit men" for public places. He would do away with it. "The elevation and purification of the civil service of the government" would be "hailed with approval by the whole people of the United States." [4]

Finally on March 3, 1871, to quiet the agitation, if possible, as in the case of the tariff bill which was offered to the "revenue reformers," a clause was tacked on the sundry civil bill authorizing the President "to prescribe rules and regulations for the admission of persons into the civil service of the United States as will best promote the efficiency thereof." With this object in view he might appoint a commission to

[1] This from "Ben" Butler, who further declared the scheme "visionary, futile, theoretical and useless"; it had been "devised by newspaper editors."—Cong. Globe, 42nd Cong. 2nd sess., p. 2351.

[2] Cf. Senate Mis. Doc., 42nd Cong. 2nd sess., no. 30; Article on G. W. Curtis in Atlantic Monthly for January, 1893.

[3] How much sincerity certain Congressmen attributed to him may be inferred from their speeches in Cong. Globe, 42nd Cong. 2nd sess., pp. 2370-72.

[4] Richardson, Messages and Papers, vol. vii, p. 109.

conduct the necessary inquiries.[1]   But he delayed action until
summer when he named George William Curtis of New York,
who had so frequently spoken for and written on the subject,[2] and would do so with so much grace, skill and devotion
again,[3] ex-Senator Cattell of New Jersey, Joseph Medill of
the Chicago Tribune, Dawson A. Walker of Pennsylvania and
three officers representing respectively the Treasury, Interior
and Post Office Departments.

The commission made unexpected haste in the performance
of its duties.   It found that "the whole machinery of the
government" was "pulled to pieces every four years."   The
business of the nation, the legislation of Congress, the duties
of the departments were "all subordinated to the distribution"
of what was well called "the spoils."   The "great officers of
the government" were "constrained to become mere office
brokers."   Thus "the moral tone of the country" was "debased," the "national character" deteriorated.   No country or
government could "safely tolerate such surely increasing demoralization."   The report was an eloquent and unanswerable statement of the case.   "The improvement of the civil
service," said the commissioners in conclusion, "is emphati-
cally the people's cause, the people's reform, and the administration which vigorously begins it will acquire a glory only
less than that of the salvation of a free Union."[4]   In his
annual message the President said that the "experiment"
should have a "fair trial,"[5] and on December 19, 1871, he
transmitted to Congress the rules which the commissioners
had adopted, declaring that they would go into effect on
New Year's day.[6]   In April, 1872, he called upon officers in
all branches of the public service for "the utmost fidelity and
diligence."   Political assessments were forbidden and "hon-

[1] Cong. Globe, 41st Cong. 3rd sess., app., pp. 370-71.
[2] Nowhere better than in his address to the American Social Science
Association in New York in October, 1869.—G. W. Curtis, Orations and
Addresses, vol. ii, pp. 3-28; cf. N. Y. Nation, June 8, 1871.
[3] Atlantic Monthly, Jan., 1893.
[4] G. W. Curtis, Orations and Addresses, vol. ii, pp. 3-80.
[5] Message of Dec., 1871, in Richardson, vol. vii, p. 155.
[6] Ibid., pp. 156-9.

esty and efficiency, not political activity" were hereafter to "determine the tenure of office." [1]

Men laughed at such zeal. It was eleventh hour virtue for the presidential campaign. Soon Congress would not give the board enough money to meet its necessary expenses,[2] and in a little while altogether refused it pecuniary support. In some departments which had adopted the system it was almost immediately suspended.[3] The rules, said George William Curtis, were never effectively carried into practice "at any point in the service." [4]

What Grant really thought of civil service reform may be inferred, perhaps, from his remarks to John Russell Young in 1879 when he attributed "cant" to those who interested themselves in the movement and threw doubt upon their "sincerity." No country in the world, said he, had a more efficient civil service. The way to virtue was through the Republican party. Every day that it continued in power amended and improved the service. That party had given the United States "an educated, tried and trusty body of public servants" who could not be displaced "without injury." The only danger to the civil service so far as Grant could see lay in the possible triumph, at some time in the future, of the Democrats.[5] The spoilsman's philosophy had taken complete possession of his mind.

[1] Richardson, vol. vii., p. 180; cf. Grant's statements in his message of 1872. (Ibid., p. 205), and Report of Commission for 1874, which gives much historical matter.—Senate Ex. Doc., 43rd Cong. 1st sess., no. 53.

[2] Cong. Globe, 42nd Cong. 2nd sess., pp. 2350, 2370, 2373.

[3] Cf. G. W. Curtis, Orations and Addresses, vol. ii, pp. 198-9.

[4] G. W. Curtis in Introduction to D. B. Eaton's Civil Service in Great Britain, p. vii.

[5] J. R. Young, Around the World with General Grant, vol. ii, pp. 264-9.

CHAPTER XIII

THE KU KLUX KLAN

The reconstruction of the late rebel states by the Radical Congress brought into office a type of man hitherto unknown to the politics of the South. Those who had been organizing the Republican party there, and had established themselves and their friends in the conventions were now ready to seize the governorships, the judgeships and the seats in the Senate and the House of Representatives at Washington. They would procure themselves places in the legislatures, use the taxing power, lend the public credit and expend the public funds. Counties, cities, all jurisdictions from the greatest to the least, fell into the hands of the elements which enjoyed the favor and support of the Radical leaders in Congress, and these were the carpetbaggers, the scalawags and their dupes and tools, the enfranchised ex-slaves.

Powell Clayton, a native of Pennsylvania, who had been in Kansas when the war broke out, and had only lately settled in Arkansas as a planter, became the governor of that state. W. W. Holden, the publisher of a small newspaper, who, after various tergiversations in politics, had become Johnson's governor of North Carolina, now suffered further change of his opinions and came forward as the Radical candidate for governor of the state under the "black and tan" constitution. Henry C. Warmoth, a native of Illinois, later a lawyer in Missouri, a soldier in the war with a dubious career, a judge in the Department of the Gulf under General Banks and a member of the "Torch and Turpentine" party of Southern Loyalists which invaded the North in 1866, still only 26 years old, soon to make for himself an infamous reputation, became governor of Louisiana.[1]

[1] For his record, cf. House Reports, 42nd Cong. 2nd sess., no. 92, pp. 28, 349-50.

General R. K. Scott, born in Pennsylvania, who had recently been serving as an officer of the Freedmen's Bureau, was elected governor of South Carolina. Harrison Reed, a Massachusetts man, who had been a newspaper editor in Wisconsin, and, after the war, a mail agent in Florida, became governor of that state. Rufus B. Bullock, who had gained wide advertisement as the governor of Georgia, was a native of New York, had gone South before the war to organize an express business and had remained there. W. H. Smith, governor of Alabama, was of Southern birth and ancestry, though after his defeat for a seat in the Confederate Congress he had become a Unionist and had crossed the Federal lines, as had members of his family.[1] The lieutenant governor, Powers, was a most illiterate and dishonest Union soldier who had remained in the state. General Edmund J. Davis of Texas, like Smith, had left his state at the outbreak of the war to seek service on the Union side. Alcorn in Mississippi was a native of Illinois, but he had lived in the South long enough to become identified with its interests and enjoyed a good reputation as a lawyer, a planter and a Whig politician. Though he was a "rebel brigadier" he had been a Falstaffian soldier. But a luke warm defender of the Southern cause, his military performances in behalf of the Confederacy had consisted of but a few weeks' service, in the Mississippi militia.[2] He resigned his governorship in a short time to take a seat in the United States Senate, to be succeeded by the lieutenant-governor, a carpetbagger.

Some of the members of the legislatures never had seen the districts which they had been elected to represent. A number of those who may have visited their constituencies during the campaign to ask for the votes of the people did not return. A friend of Governor Warmoth was elected in a private room in a New Orleans hotel at midnight to represent a parish 300 miles away.[3] In Alabama twenty members of the legis-

[1] To the Alabama people a "Tory." See Fleming, Recon. in Ala., pp. 534, 735-6.
[2] Garner, Recon. in Miss., p. 291.
[3] House Reports, 42nd Cong. 2nd sess., no. 92, p. 21.

lature were then or had been at an earlier time under indictment for crime.[1] Seven sworn charges of burglary had
been made against a Republican leader of the house of representatives in Louisiana.[2] A negro preacher who had raped
a child sat in the general assembly in Texas.[3]

All the legislatures contained considerable bodies of negroes. In South Carolina only 46 of the 124 members of
the lower chamber were white men; only 10 of the 31 senators. One, Dunn, a colored house painter, had been chosen
lieutenant-governor of Louisiana. Cardozo, who had been
prominent in the convention in South Carolina became secretary of state in that state; Lynch, an eloquent mulatto
preacher, held the same office in Mississippi. Many of the
blacks, thus suddenly introduced to public life, could barely
read. Negroes who saw white members of the legislature absorbed in newspapers, also took up journals which, legs on
desks, they held before their eyes upside down, so unused
were they to the printed page.[4] If they could make their
letters at all it was merely in a signature, slowly and me-
chanically affixed, after painful rehearsal that none might say
they could not write their names.[5] Some of the wealthiest

[1] Fleming, Recon. in Ala., p. 739.
[2] House Reports, 42nd Cong. 2nd sess., no. 92, p. 27.
[3] Ramsdell, Recon. in Texas.
[4] M. L. Avary, Dixie After the War, p. 254.
[5] Reynolds, Recon. in S. C., p. 121; cf. Lonn, Recon. in La., p. 9;
Garner, Recon. in Miss., p. 269; N. Y. Nation, June 9, 1870. And yet
the representative, presumably, was a more intelligent man than the
voter who had sent him to the state capital. In Louisiana the members of a Congressional committee examined a negro who had voted
at the Presidential election in that state in 1868 with the following
result:
Question.—"You say that you would like to have voted for Grant.
What office was he running for?"
Answer.—"We heard he was running for equal rights of both parties.
If we are free people we want to be free."
Q.—"Is that the office he was running for?"
A.—"That is what we understood."
Q.—"Who was Colfax?"
A.—"Mr. Colfax and Mr. Blair from what we understood, one was a
black man, the other is a white man. I have seen their pictures."
Q.—"Which was the white man and which the black man?"

counties in Mississippi were represented solely by men who a few years before had been negro slaves.[1]

The debates were more ignorant as to matter and more dis-

A.—"Mr. Colfax is a black man and Mr. Blair is a white man from the pictures. I cannot read."

Q.—"What is Seymour running for?"

A.—"I suppose he was running for the same thing that Blair was."

Q.—"What was Blair running for?"

A.—"God Almighty knows; it is a judgment which never has come out yet. We voted for him; but what he ran for we have never found out."

Q.—"Have you found out what Mr. Colfax ran for?"

A.— Mr. Colfax! Colfax! Colfax and Seymour and Blair and Grant! Well, I cannot tell you much about Mr. Colfax, nor about Mr. Grant," etc., etc.—House Mis. Doc., 41st Cong. 2nd sess., no. 154, pt. 2, pp. 165-6.

Another Louisiana negro, who had been a sergeant in the Union Army, a preacher of the gospel and a campaign speaker for the Democrats in 1868, underwent the following examination:

Question.—"You are a pure black, are you not?"

Answer.—"Not a pure black. I am a kind of a snuff colored fellow."

Q.—"Have you any white blood in you that you know of?"

A.—"It is the same as the blood of any other man. No one ever saw any white blood yet."

Q.—"Your wife is a colored woman, is she not?"

A.—"Yes, I never have stared no woman in the face but a colored woman. I am not obscriptious."

Q.—"Did you not think that Grant would make a better president than Seymour?"

A.—"I will tell you what my thinking is. General Grant is a prompt man. General Blair is a prompt man. They are two generals who lead the field. I do not know that they lead the field into any tangle."

Q.—"Do you not mean General Seymour?"

A.—"Yes, I mean General Seymour. . . . General Grant was Lieutenant General Grant. Did he see how soldiers fared in Texas when we were all dying of the scurvy? No, sir. So I thought I would rather try the man who I do not know."

Q.—"You did not know anything about Seymour?"

A.—"No sir. There is another point that General Grant should have done and he didn't do it. At the time my colonel took my corporal's wife away he put him under a beef skin and General Grant didn't know anything about that, although he was Lieutenant General, and then they turn and put him in the Capitol. I said to myself I will have to say to Grant, whom I know, I will try Seymour, whom I do not know."

Q.—"Was that the way you talked to the boys?"

A.—"I did not tell them so, but that is the way I talked to myself. I had a certain platform for them and when I got up I stated that case to them. I just said to them, 'Come my b'loved,' or 'Away, you cursed; there is the fork; there is the road to dignition and there is the road to glory. Take your choice.' "—Ibid., pp. 381-2.

[1] Garner, Recon. in Miss., p. 270.

graceful as to form than any ever heard in parliamentary
bodies in our Anglo-Saxon world. Personal abuse, coarse allusion, profane oaths marked the speech of the members.
Horse play and buffoonery characterized the sessions and personal encounters, both inside and outside the meeting halls,
were of frequent occurrence.[1] The legislature of Louisiana
was "a shameful and disgraceful burlesque upon republican
institutions," said General Rousseau.[2] When a member of the
British Parliament came with a letter of introduction to J. B.
Eustis of New Orleans, later a United States senator of
Louisiana and for some years our ambassador to France, the
visitor asked if there were any great curiosity in the city.
Mr. Eustis replied that they had such a curiosity as was
not to be seen in any other civilized country, and he took
the man to look at the legislature.[3] Robert Somers, an English traveller, visited the South Carolina legislature. It was
a "proletariat parliament," he said; its "like could not be produced under the widest suffrage" in any other part of the
world.[4]

Judges, sheriffs, assessors, treasurers, clerks, supervisors,
commissioners and other officials in counties and towns,
whether white or black, were ignorant and incompetent.[5]
School officers were so illiterate that to keep their records
in order Democrats must be employed to act as clerks. In
many cases not one member of a board of supervisors, charged
with the most important duties, could perform the smallest
operation in arithmetic.[6] Many justices of the peace could
not make out a warrant for an arrest. Some in South Carolina could not correctly spell three words in succession.[7] Prisoners must be relied upon to prepare the papers committing
them to jail. In a county in Mississippi there was not a sin-

[1] Cf. Hamilton, Recon. in N. C., pp. 386-7; Fleming, Recon. in Ala.,
p. 740; Lonn, Recon. in La., pp. 21-5.
[2] To President Johnson, Sep. 26, 1868, in Johnson Papers.
[3] House Reports, 42nd Cong. 2nd sess., no. 92, p. 27.
[4] Robert Somers, Southern States After the War, p. 41.
[5] Cf. Fleming, Recon. in Ala., pp. 742-3.
[6] Garner, Recon. in Miss., p. 308.
[7] Ku Klux Report, South Carolina Testimony, p. 94.

gle justice who could write his name.[1] Negro, carpetbagger
or scalawag sheriffs often received $15,000 or $20,000 a year
in fees. When they were incapable of performing their duties
they "farmed out" their offices to more intelligent persons
who served as deputies, and with whom the emoluments were
shared.[2]

White as well as black office-holders under the constitutions, like the members of the conventions, were without property. Not only were they not identified with the history, traditions and social life of the communities in which they lived,
but they also were without a stake in the material prosperity
of those communities. There were eight Republican nominees
for elective office in South Carolina in 1868. One, Boozer
by name, the candidate for lieutenant-governor, had some
property, paying the state $1,599. Another paid a poll tax of
one dollar. But the other six, headed by the candidate for
governor, General Scott, paid no taxes.[3] The total sum of
money coming into the treasury in taxes from the 124 members of the house and 31 senators in the South Carolina legislature was $635.23; the names of 91 did not appear upon the
tax books at all.[4] In Alabama five of the eight candidates
for state office were non-resident attachés of the Freedmen's
Bureau.[5] All of the members of the legislature in that state,

[1] Garner, Recon. in Miss., p. 308. For Alabama cf. H. A. Herbert's
article on Alabama in Why the Solid South, p. 64. A public document
in Richland county, S. C., written by a negro school commissioner,
who was a licensed preacher of the African Methodist Episcopal Church,
read: "The foller-ring person are Rickermended to the Board [list of
names follows] for the Hower [Howard] Schoole Haveing Given fool
sat es fact Shon in thi tow Last years." (Reynolds, Recon. in S. C.,
pp. 121-2.) The following is in the handwriting of a North Carolina
constable: "Notis wil be sole next tusdy was a week at John Engh's sicks
mills on Rolly rode won hoss 4 yerr ole. won cow and cafe. Won silver
spune. Won sow with pigs by me G. Imbles, Constable."—For this and
similar reprints see Hamilton, Recon. in N. C., pp. 344, 417, 418; Lonn,
Recon. in La., pp. 9-81.
[2] Garner, Recon. in Miss., pp. 305-6.
[3] Reynolds, Recon. in S. C., p. 87; Ku Klux Report, South Carolina
Testimony, on the authority of Wade Hampton, pp. 1220, 1238-40.
[4] Reynolds, Recon. in S. C., p. 108; cf. Ku Klux Report, South Carolina Testimony, pp. 1244-8.
[5] Herbert in Why the Solid South, p. 47.

it was said, paid less than $100 in taxes.[1]   Only ten of the Republican members of the Louisiana legislature were taxpayers.[2]

In the judiciary, said the Raleigh, N. C., Sentinel, summing up the subject from the Southern standpoint, were "mountebanks, ignoramuses, and men who bedraggled the ermine in the mud and mire of politics"; in executive offices "mercenary squatters and incompetents"; in legislative halls "where once giants sat, adventurers, manikins and gibbering Africans."[3]   Nor was the Federal service in the South in better hands.   Illiterates, incompetents, defaulters, embezzlers and other felons occupied profitable posts as rewards for partisan service.   They were "pestiferous ulcers feeding upon the body politic."[4]

Six states were reorganized in time to seat senators and representatives in the 40th Congress in 1868 and 1869.   Ten of the twelve senators were carpetbaggers.   Three were natives of New York; the others came from New Jersey, Ohio, Pennsylvania, Connecticut, Massachusetts, New Hampshire and Vermont.   One-half of the 32 members returned to the House of Representatives were carpetbaggers.   The rest were in large part scalawags.[5]

The first negro to appear in Congress was J. Willis Menard of New Orleans, elected to fill a vacancy in the House of Representatives in 1869.   Though he held a certificate from Governor Warmoth his title to the place was contested.   After hearing him in a speech in his own behalf[6] the House rejected his claims.[7]   No negro was seated until Mississippi was reconstructed, when that state sent to the United States Sen-

---

[1] Fleming, Recon. in Ala., p. 739.
[2] Article on La. in Why the Solid South, p. 401.
[3] Raleigh Sentinel, Dec. 10, 1868, quoted in Hamilton, Recon. in N. C., p. 378.
[4] Hamilton, Recon. in N. C., pp. 418, 491.
[5] The "whole set of representatives in Congress" from Alabama, except one man, said Governor Smith, were "unprincipled scoundrels."—Fleming, Recon. in Ala., p. 738.
[6] Feb. 27, 1869, Cong. Globe, 40th Cong. 3rd sess., p. 1684.
[7] Ibid., p. 1696; cf. A. K. McClure, Recollections, p. 252.

ate a colored preacher, named Revels,[1] and its late military governor, General Adelbert Ames of Maine.[2]

It was announced with vast satisfaction by the Northern Radicals that Revels would occupy the seat of Jefferson Davis, and when he reached the capital it was to be welcomed in an ostentatious manner by the negrophiles. For three days, before galleries which were densely packed with colored people, Democrats, like Davis of Kentucky and Saulsbury of Delaware, strove to prevent the seating of the dusky senator. It was an innovation unheard of in the history of the government. The Dred Scott decision was appealed to to show that the negro was not a citizen. But no protest could avail. It was the slave power "dying in the last ditch," said Senator Wilson of Massachusetts. The seating of this black man in the halls of the Federal government would close the great struggle of forty years. Now "caste and privilege" would be "disowned forever." To Sumner it was "an historic event, marking the triumph of a great cause." The Declaration of Independence was made a reality. For a long time a word only it now became a deed. What was being done was for mankind, for God himself.[3] Forty eight senators voted for, only eight against seating the negro senator and Wilson escorted him to the bar to take the oath.[4]

What was begun in the conventions was continued in the

[1] How he was chosen is described by a negro ex-Congressman from Mississippi, John R. Lynch, in The Facts of Reconstruction, pp. 40-47.

[2] Ames did not pay a dollar of taxes in Mississippi and could not claim even a technical residence there. He had seized the senatorial toga before taking off his military coat. (Garner, Recon. in Miss., p. 291; cf. Pub. Miss. Hist. Soc., vol. ii, pp. 387-8.) Not only was he not a citizen of the state, said the Jackson Clarion, but he did not have "the slightest idea of ever again being within her borders after crossing the Tennessee line on his journey to Washington."—Issue of Jan. 20, 1870.

[3] Cong. Globe, 41st Cong. 2nd sess., pp. 1503-68 passim. The vote was taken on Feb. 25, 1870. For the man himself cf. Pub. Miss. Hist. Soc., vol. ii, pp. 386-7; A. K. McClure, Recollections, p. 252.

[4] For the parts played by negroes and carpetbaggers in the United States Senate during this period see C. M. Thompson, Studies in Southern Hist. and Politics, pp. 161-76; cf. A. K. McClure, Recollections, pp. 254-8. The first negro to take a seat in the House was Joseph H. Rainey of South Carolina, who was sworn in on Dec. 12, 1870.—Cong. Globe, 41st Cong. 3rd sess., p. 64.

legislatures. Bills appeared to make blacks and whites
"equal." Their children were to attend school in the same
houses. The races were to ride side by side on railway trains,
on steamboats and in street cars. They were to sit at the
same tables in restaurants and hotels, occupy adjoining seats
in theatres. Hereafter no one should be called a "nigger,"
nor so much, indeed, as a "negro." New offices of various
kinds were created that there might be the largest possible
number of salaried posts for the Radical leaders and their
henchmen. State constabulary systems were established ostensibly to preserve the peace, really to make more jobs. "Financial agents" were appointed to negotiate loans for which
service they were paid large bonuses and commissions. Old
public institutions were ruined, new ones which served no
purpose were created. The common schools which were organized, often to be directed by negroes, were not adapted to
the needs of the people. Superintendents and teachers frequently were "without respectable antecedents and of a low
character." [1] There were large and incessant demands for
money in behalf of these inefficient educational systems.
Boards and commissions to perform useless tasks were authorized and large sums were appropriated for their support.

Beginning with small peculation corruption soon assumed
gross forms. Local and state treasuries were pillaged in a
thousand ways. Subsidies, exemptions, grants and endorse-
ments of different kinds to the advantage of railroads, canals,
levees and other private enterprises, robbery here and fraud
there, often forwarded by bribery, filled the air in every Southern state. Men were paid for land which they never delivered,
for erecting school houses and other edifices which they never
built. [2] Companies which asked for charters distributed their

---

[1] Publications Miss. Hist. Soc., vol. ix, p. 151.
[2] In Washington County, Miss., a negro photographer of Cincinnati
was president of the school board; his son was its clerk. Both at the
same time held other salaried offices. One bought a building lot for
$200 and transferred it to the other for $2700 cash in school money.
No house was ever built upon it and the lot in due time was sold for
taxes.—Publications of Miss. Hist. Soc., vol. ix, pp. 150-51; ibid., vol.
ii, p. 402.

stock at the state capitals in return for their incorporation
papers; they paid large sums outright for subventions of land
and the public endorsement of their bonds. Rings made up
of members, clerks and their friends were formed to control
every valuable contract. That the scoundrels might have
fuller assurance of success in the promotion of their villanies
they installed public bars in the state houses. In North Carolina a refreshment room was located in the west wing of the
capitol, on which account it was called the "third house." [1]
The bar in South Carolina which was kept open daily for six
years was crowded with men smoking and drinking, often until
two and even four o'clock in the morning, while they discussed
the various schemes under consideration in the legislature.
Liquors and cigars, purchased with public money, were sent
to the members in their homes and boarding houses. [2]

Acts of legislature were printed and reprinted. The debates
were published in the newspapers at the cost of the state.
Contracts were given to favorite Radical presses on the most
expensive terms. The public printing cost Louisiana about
$1,500,000 in three years and of this sum a newspaper in
New Orleans, controlled by Governor Warmoth, received about
$700,000 in two years. [3] The expense to the state on this ac-
count in previous years had been only $37,000 per annum. [4]
In one year in South Carolina the amount appropriated on
account of printing was $450,000. To secure the passage
through the legislature of a bill for $250,000 lobbyists and
corrupt members of the house and senate took nearly one half,
or $112,550, as their share of the spoil. [5]

The stationery bills were padded by purchases of miscellaneous articles intended for private use. In Alabama material which could have been bought in Montgomery for

[1] Hamilton, Recon. in N. C., p. 353; Vance, Article on North Carolina
in Why the Solid South, p. 80.
[2] Reports on Public Frauds in S. C., quoted in Fleming, Doc. Hist. of
Recon., vol. ii, pp. 59-65; Article on S. C. in Why the Solid South,
p. 89.
[3] House Reports, 42nd Cong. 2nd sess., no. 92, p. 21.
[4] Article on La. in Why the Solid South, p. 408.
[5] Article on South Carolina in Why the Solid South, p. 100.

$4,000 was ordered in New York at a cost of $7,000.[1] Shameful overcharges were found in a bill for furniture for the state house of South Carolina. A mirror for $750, clocks at $480, chandeliers at $650, 200 porcelain spittoons at $8 apiece made up a total of more than $50,000. Large as it was the sum was increased to $95,000 to cover the claims for services of men who had been engaged in lobbying the measure through the legislature.[2] Nearly every procurable room in Columbia was a "committee room" where, with "state house furniture" around them, the members lodged and ate their meals.[3] Material after being received was sold and the money was pocketed by any rogue who could lay his hands upon it. The legislature voted $1,000 to the speaker of the house of representatives to reimburse him for what he had lost by betting on a horse race.[4]

"Hell Hole Swamp," a tract of land near Charleston, was purchased by a group of men for seventy-five cents an acre, a total sum of $26,100, to be sold in a little while to the state for $120,000.[5] Six thousand acres of land in North Carolina which the owner was about to give to the negroes to escape the taxes were bought for sixty cents an acre. Two thousand acres more, acquired at a very low price, were added to the purchase and the tract was transferred to the state as a penitentiary site for $100,000.[6]

Governor Bullock had for his guide and mentor a man named Hannibal I. Kimball who had come to Georgia from the West. Wherever you saw the footprints of one, said a committee of the Georgia legislature in 1872, you might look for the track of the other.[7] They had an actual, if not a legal partnership, and openly drew money from the same bank

[1] Fleming, Recon. in Ala., p. 577.
[2] J. S. Pike, The Prostrate State, pp. 201-3; Reynolds, Recon. in S. C., p. 161; Article on S. C. in Why the Solid South, p. 89.
[3] Ku Klux Report, South Carolina Testimony, p. 121.
[4] J. S. Pike, The Prostrate State, pp. 197, 199-200.
[5] Ku Klux Report, S. C. Testimony, p. 95; Article on S. C. in Why the Solid South, p. 91.
[6] Hamilton, Recon. in N. C., pp. 379-80.
[7] C. M. Thompson, Recon. in Ga., p. 218.

account. Kimball bought an uncompleted opera house in Atlanta for $30,000, finished it and sold it to the state for a capitol for $400,000. He built a large hotel in that city with public funds and in a little while was president of three or four railroads, which were in receipt of subventions from the legislature.[1]

The bonds of 37 railroads in Georgia were endorsed for a total sum of $30,000,000, 32 of them at one time during a single session of the legislature. The affairs of these roads were so inefficiently and dishonestly conducted that all but one soon went into the hands of receivers.[2]

A man named Littlefield from Maine, a native scalawag named Swepson and a few others induced the legislature of North Carolina to authorize the issue of bonds of a face value of $25,000,000 on the faith of the state for the construction of a system of railways. They never put down a mile of iron in the commonwealth.[3] Moving from North Carolina to Florida they gained control of three railroads in that state, free of all old encumbrances, for about $2,000 a mile, paid in money which Swepson had embezzled in North Carolina. By bribing the negroes, the carpetbaggers and the native scamps who held seats in the legislature at Tallahassee they obtained a charter and state endorsement, which enabled them to sell millions of dollars worth of their stocks and bonds.[4]

Governor Scott, John J. Patterson, who later bribed his

---

[1] On the authority of General Gordon in Ku Klux Report, Georgia Testimony, p. 314; cf. Somers, Southern States After the War, p. 97; Article on Georgia in Why the Solid South, pp. 135-6. Among the Republicans at the capitol he was "the epitome of munificent and open-handed wealth." The negroes had a popular song with a refrain which ran—

> "H. I. Kimball's on de floor,
> Taint gwine ter rain no more."
> —C. M. Thompson, Recon. in Ga., p. 218.

[2] C. M. Thompson, Recon. in Ga., pp. 236-8; Article on Georgia in Why the Solid South, p. 134.

[3] Vance in Article on N. C. in Why the Solid South, pp. 80-82.

[4] Davis, Recon. in Fla., pp. 657-61. The Supreme Court of the United States described some of their operations as "the most shameful frauds."
—Senator Pasco in Article on Florida in Why the Solid South, p. 148.

way into the United States Senate, and a financial agent in New York named Kimpton manipulated two railroads in South Carolina—the Blue Ridge and the Greenville and Columbia—in such a way that they were soon in possession of the lines without the expenditure of a dollar of their own money. They bought in the properties at a secret sale for $59,699.50 abstracted from the public funds and saddled the state with a debt of $6,000,000 in guarantees.[1]

High per diem rates of compensation for members and mileage charges (the allowance was eighty cents a mile in 1870 in Mississippi),[2] vast forces of attachés,[3] extra sessions to increase their rewards, double payments to cover services rendered in committee work, travelling expenses incurred on needless journeys, inquiries into extravagance and fraud, often more costly than the enterprises to be investigated, called for large appropriations. It was said, indeed, that members would instigate outrages and start riots so that they might appoint themselves on committees to visit the scene, examine witnesses and issue reports at public expense.[4]

The first session of the legislature of North Carolina, though it lasted for but 47 days, cost the taxpayers $80,000 for per diem and mileage charges alone.[5] The expenses incident to the next session which continued for 115 days reached a total of $195,000, while with printing bills and other contingent outlays the amount was not less than $250,000.[6] The first session of the South Carolina legislature of 72 working days took from the treasury of that state $130,000.[7] A later session of 106 days in 1870-71 entailed an expense to the taxpayers of $679,000,[8] while the session of 1871-72 cost them

---

[1] Article on South Carolina in Why the Solid South, pp. 96-7.

[2] Garner, Recon. in Miss., p. 325.

[3] The South Carolina legislature for the session of 1871-72 had 475 clerks, 212 messengers, 74 pages, 23 porters, 16 doorkeepers, 14 chaplains, 27 solicitors and 7 sergeants at arms.—Reynolds, Recon. in S. C., p. 174.

[4] Ku Klux Report, South Carolina Testimony, p. 1010.

[5] Hamilton, Recon. in N. C., p. 360.   [6] Ibid., p. 377.

[7] Reynolds, Recon. in S. C., p. 117.   [8] Ibid., p. 161.

$1,174,177.[1] The annual ordinary expenses of Georgia in 1860 were $325,000, but in 1870 they had been increased to $924,000.[2]

In 1869 the members of the legislature of Louisiana voted themselves $250,000, and in 1870, $500,000.[3] The session of 1871 cost the state nearly a million dollars, an average of $113.50 a day for each member of the body, the sum being distributed to senators and representatives and their clerks, and to sergeants-at-arms, doorkeepers and pages for compensation and for travelling and other expenses; to printers, many of them controlling presses in obscure parish towns; and to contractors to supply "stationery," which Governor Warmoth declared was made to include articles so foreign to the writing table as ham and champagne.[4] Men said and believed that more had been stolen in Louisiana and South Carolina since the war "than in all the Southern states put together from the Revolution to 1860."[5] The corruption in Louisiana was "utterly astounding."[6] All society was contaminated by the rascality which reigned in high places. Gambling became an openly licensed business in New Orleans, which took on the appearance of some wild town on the Western frontier. Lotteries and other evil contrivances received the endorsement of the state. The greatest of these, the so-called Louisiana Lottery, was given a charter for 25 years which enabled it to extend its baneful influence into a period otherwise cleared of the moral wreckage of this unfortunate age.[7]

No Radical in Louisiana seemed to escape the charge of being involved in the corruption of the time. Office holders

---

[1] Reynolds, Recon. in S. C., p. 174.

[2] Ku Klux Report, Georgia Testimony, pp. 153-4; cf. Article on Ga. in Why the Solid South, p. 134.

[3] Lonn, Recon. in La., p. 30.

[4] Ibid., p. 86; cf. House Report, 42nd Cong. 2nd sess., no. 92, p. 21.

[5] Ku Klux Report, Georgia Testimony, p. 828, quoting Cincinnati Commercial.

[6] House Report, 42nd Cong. 2nd sess., no. 92, p. 24.

[7] Article on Louisiana in Why the Solid South, p. 428; cf. A. K. McClure, Recollections, p. 173.

grew rich while the people struggled daily for food to eat.[1]
One declared that he knew no official in the state who did not
deserve to be impeached.[2] Governor Warmoth came to be
called the "Boss Tweed of Louisiana."[3] So poor in 1865 that
the negroes who sent him to Congress must contribute to a
fund to pay the expense of his journey to Washington,[4] it
was alleged in 1872 that he was worth a million dollars.[5] He
said openly that he did not pretend to be honest. Corruption
was the fashion and he was not better than other men.[6]
Government in South Carolina, said a visitor to the state, did
not deserve the name of government; it was nothing but "a
huge system of brigandage."[7] The state treasurer had been
a barkeeper in Massachusetts; at the end of the war he had
settled in South Carolina where he had failed in business,
paying only twenty-five cents on the dollar to his creditors.
Though two years since he could scarce buy himself a pair
of boots, in 1871 he was "dashing through Columbia in one
of the finest vehicles in the state" behind a pair of $1,000
horses with gold mounted harness upon them. He boasted of
his diamonds and the stocks which he owned.[8] The handsome
residences in Columbia of the white thieves who had stolen
their half million or more apiece were pointed out to every visitor.[9] When men were asked how they had got their money
they replied that they had stolen it. If any one should suggest the possibility of punishment for such offending he was
defied to prove his charge.[10] Governor Scott who had had no
property to tax, when he was elected to office, two years

[1] J. B. Eustis in testimony before a Congressional committee, House
Mis. Doc., 42nd Cong. 2nd sess., no. 211, p. 533.

[2] Lonn, Recon. in La., p. 88.

[3] S. S. Cox, Three Decades of Federal Legislation, p. 560.

[4] Lonn, Recon. in La., pp. 3-4.

[5] Ibid., pp. 90-91; House Reports, 42nd Cong. 2nd sess., no. 92, p. 25;
Somers, Southern States After the War, p. 228.

[6] Article on La. in Why the Solid South, p. 429.

[7] J. S. Pike, The Prostrate State, p. 58.

[8] Weekly Union Times of Union, S. C., Feb. 24, 1871, quoted in Ku
Klux Report, S. C. Testimony, pp. 1009-10; cf. N. Y. Nation, June 9,
1870.

[9] J. S. Pike, The Prostrate State, p. 29.   [10] Ibid., p. 28.

later, in 1870, paid $500 in Columbia alone, and he owned houses and lands in other parts of the state.[1]

The riot of wrong continued until nothing remained for the corrupt to exploit or for the thief to steal. The states were without credit in the money markets of the world. Loans falling due were converted into new ones on extravagant terms; interest was paid by new bond issues. More than one commonwealth was brought to the verge of bankruptcy.[2] Public securities were for sale for a song and schemes of repudiation were freely discussed.

The indebtedness of South Carolina in less than three years had been increased from $5,500,000 to $18,500,000. At the end of the year 1870 all but two of the counties of the state were in debt.[3] In Georgia in 1870 Bullock and his "plundering dynasty"[4] had increased the public debt more than $20,-000,000 and the governor had approved bills which would raise the total to $30,000,000. The "toiling farmers," taking up what little they could collect, said the treasurer of the state, would be "forced to flee their homes for safety from the tax gatherers."[5] In 1872 bonds, scrip and other obligations issued by the state and the counties and towns of Alabama had reached a total sum of more than $52,000,000.[6] In Arkansas the state debt in a short time was increased four or five fold; many counties were bankrupt.[7] In Florida where the debt in 1866 was about $600,000 it had been increased in January, 1872, to more than $5,000,000.[8] The debt of Louisiana as a result of the activities of two legislatures was multiplied by five. In 1872 it was $48,000,000; if parish and municipal debts were added the total became $76,000,000.[9]

---

[1] On the word of Wade Hampton in Ku Klux Report, S. C. Testimony, p. 1225.

[2] For North Carolina cf. Hamilton, Recon. in N. C., p. 386; for Alabama, Fleming, Recon. in Ala., p. 583.

[3] Reynolds, Recon. in S. C., p. 134.

[4] Called so by Representative Farnsworth (Republican).—Cong. Globe, 41st Cong. 2nd sess., p. 4781.

[5] Ku Klux Report, Georgia Testimony, pp. 153-4.

[6] Fleming, Recon. in Ala., p. 582.

[7] Nordhoff, The Cotton States, pp. 29-31.

[8] Davis, Recon. in Fla., p. 679.

[9] Article on La. in Why the Solid South, p. 405.

The taxes were enormously increased. Mr. Eustis said that
in New Orleans, including both city and state, they were 4⅝
per cent.[1] In one of the country parishes the rate was 7₁⁹₀
per cent.[2] The Louisiana state tax in 1872 was 21½ mills;[3]
it cost 12 per cent to collect the taxes.[4] The expense attached
to the collection of the poll tax (the negroes as a rule were
subject to no other), the auditor of the state complained, exceeded by 140 per cent the net amount which came into the
treasury from this source.[5] In Mississippi in 1872 the taxes
were eight and a half times what they had been in 1869
and the end was not yet in sight.[6] The people of North
Carolina were paying taxes five times as great as formerly.[7]

In the North criticism of misrule usually was dismissed as
the voice of rebellion. Opposition even to obvious oppression
and proven theft by the poltroons who held the fate of the
country in their hands was the subject of summary legislation
or executive rescript at Washington. They were trying "to
live off Northern patriotism and humanity," said the New
York Nation. Any one who directed attention to their performances was represented as "an enemy of the colored man
and the Unionist." The greater the scoundrel the more intense was his loyalty and the higher did he seem to stand in
the favor of the Northern Radicals. But many were beginning
to be repelled by the spectacle. It was high time, the Nation
continued, "to bring this little comedy to an end." No longer
should "the plea of faithful service in the war" be accepted
"as a defence of roguery."[8] It should be understood "once
for all," said the Chicago Tribune, that "long and weary years
given to the Republican party" may not be "pleaded in bar
of punishment for any sort of rascality whatever."[9] It came

[1] House Mis. Doc., 42nd Cong. 2nd sess., no. 211, p. 535.
[2] Article on La. in Why the Solid South, p. 406.   [3] Ibid.
[4] Lonn, Recon. in La., pp. 83-5; Article on La. in Why the Solid
South, p. 403.
[5] Somers, Southern States After the War, pp. 227-8.
[6] Senate Reports, 44th Cong. 1st sess., no. 527; Miss. Election of
1875, vol. i, p. 457.
[7] Ku Klux Report, North Carolina Testimony, p. 313.
[8] N Y. Nation, June 16, 1870.   [9] Quoted in ibid.

to be said with cynical truth that loyalty meant stealing by statute.[1]

The Southern bandits as they proceeded on their shameless courses involved themselves in family quarrels. One accused another. They divided into groups and factions and with the echoes of the trial of President Johnson at Washington ringing in their ears impeachment became the resort of every man in reference to a political enemy.

The disturbances which had attended the work of framing a constitution in Florida were continued after it was adopted by the people. Each faction sought recognition at Washington that it might direct the distribution of Federal patronage in the state. Judge Jenkins who had presided over one wing of the convention, now a member of the legislature, in November, 1868, preferred articles which were accusatory of Governor Reed, some of them of so grave a character that proof of their truth would have sent the governor to the penitentiary. The house impeached him of "high crimes and misdemeanors" by a vote of 25 to 7 and there ensued an unseemly wrangle with the lieutenant-governor, who was ineligible to any office because he was not a citizen of the state, for the possession of the place, pending the trial, which, however, never was held.[2]

Reed's immunity was but temporary. Later attempts were made to displace him in the same manner. In January, 1872, the house again adopted articles for presentation to the senate. This time the case came to trial, but in the midst of the proceedings the legislature adjourned. There were appeals to the courts; when the legislature reassembled the case was dismissed, the governor was discharged and he was allowed to complete his term.

The Radicals in Arkansas were divided into factions known as "Brindle Tails" and "Minstrels." An effort to impeach the lieutenant governor failed by one vote. Then the House turned its attention to Governor Clayton and impeached him

---

[1] Hamilton, Recon. in N. C., p. 400; cf. Fleming, Recon. in Ala., p. 582.   [2] Davis, Recon. in Fla., chap. xxi.

of corrupt conduct in office. A large body of senators absconded for eight days to prevent the presentation of the articles by which means the proceedings were quashed.[1]

In Louisiana Warmoth involved himself in a quarrel with the auditor of the state, who was arrested and indicted by a grand jury. Injunctions and counter injunctions led to a prolonged and discreditable quarrel between the two men and their friends. Finally, in 1870, the auditor was impeached and removed from office.[2] Warmoth himself, after for some time escaping the threats of his enemies, was impeached in 1872 by a vote of 57 to 6, but his term came to an end before the senate had made any progress with the case.[3]

Governor Scott in South Carolina narrowly missed a similar experience as did the treasurer of the state. Only by expending nearly $50,000 of public money, through warrants drawn in favor of three fictitious persons to bribe the members of the house of representatives at rates varying from $200 to $5,000 each, did they succeed in bringing about the rejection of the resolutions calling for their impeachment.[4]

As the legislatures came into the control of the Democrats impeachment proceedings were begun under their auspices. Governor Bullock resigned in 1871 on the eve of the meeting of a legislature in Georgia which would have impeached and convicted him of high crimes and misdemeanors. Only by fleeing the state did he escape the fate which was prepared for him.[5]

Jonathan Worth in North Carolina, elected governor under the Johnson constitution of 1865, would not recognize Holden and surrendered his office to that turncoat only "under military duress."[6] As soon as the conservatives gained control of the legislature Holden was impeached. He had been a

[1] Senate Reports, 42nd Cong. 2nd sess., no. 15, pp. 36-8; Powell Clayton, Aftermath of the Civil War in Ark., pp. 261-2, 319-28.
[2] Lonn, Recon. in La., pp. 47-51.
[3] Ibid., pp. 105, 208, 225.
[4] Reynolds, Recon. in S. C., pp. 172-3; Article on South Carolina in Why the Solid South, pp. 95-6.
[5] American Annual Cyclopedia for 1871, p. 351.
[6] Ibid., for 1868, p. 555.

"blatant secessionist during the war" and now was persecuting "with rabid vindictiveness" his "secession neighbors."[1] He was the most notorious scalawag who had appeared in the South since "Parson" Brownlow. His case reached trial on eight counts. Found guilty of six of the charges he was in 1871 remanded to private life.[2]

But amid the traditions which belonged to the Southern people constitutional processes under such provocation were too uncertain and slow. In their semi-feudal society extra governmental methods of regulating civilization were looked upon as natural and necessary. If conditions before the war had justified such a course these conditions now were infinitely worse. Upon the surrender of the Confederate armies the country abounded in regulators, jayhawkers and "black cavalry."[3] Wild young soldiers from both armies, and desperadoes drawn to the country for adventure and plunder, rode hither and thither, committing lawless acts without restraint. It was in accounts of these disorders that Congress had found an excuse to set aside the Johnson system of reconstruction and had returned the South to military rule.

Now the negroes were banded together in a huge federated society, the sinister Loyal League, with branches in every county in every state.[4] By systematic effort, as we have seen, infamous leaders were filling them with sentiments of distrust and hatred with reference to the white people. Promises of land and mules to work it were repeated on every hand. Swindlers were still selling ignorant darkies four pegs for four dollars, and the purchaser was told that he could stick them down at the four corners of a piece of land which, when he had made his choice, would be deeded to him by the government at Washington.[5] Many a negro thus was led to lay claim to his old master's finest acres.

[1] Hamilton, Recon. in N. C., p. 521.
[2] Ibid., pp. 545-58.
[3] Senate Ex. Doc., 39th Cong. 2nd sess., no. 6, p. 55; Fleming, Recon. in Ala., p. 660.
[4] For its Ritual, Constitution and By-Laws see Ku Klux Report, South Carolina Testimony, pp. 949-60; Fleming, Recon. in Ala., pp. 553-68, and Doc. Hist. of Recon., vol. ii, pp. 3-29.
[5] Ku Klux Report, Ala. Testimony, pp. 238, 314.

He was deliberately encouraged, so it seemed, to prey upon the country. Cattle, horses and mules were run off at night. A planter near Baton Rouge complained that the negroes had killed and carried away the meat of all but 6 of his 33 hogs. Another was enabled to save 60 out of 110 by killing them himself. Sheep and goats disappeared in the same manner.[1] In South Carolina and Alabama the negroes had shot and stolen so many pigs that planters no longer tried to raise them.[2] Animals were slaughtered in the woods, a part of the flesh being taken while the rest was left to putrefy on the ground. Smoke houses were broken open and emptied of their bacon.[3] Cotton fields were pillaged under cover of darkness. Corn fields were robbed of their roasting ears. A great pile of cobs in a field in the morning told of the depredations of the night. Chickens, fruit, vegetables, farm and garden tools, household utensils and movable property of all kinds were gathered up by the blacks preparatory to locating themselves on their new lands.[4] Indeed robberies were so numerous and frequent that editors could not find space to record them in their newspapers. Many of the thieves betook themselves with "seed" cotton (unginned cotton) and other produce, full of the evidence of theft, to "deadfalls," small shops or stores set in nooks and corners of the South, where they received money and whiskey in return for their ill gotten spoil.[5]

Drunkenness increased. White women and girls were assaulted in the woods and ravished, some of the outrages assuming the most odious forms.[6] Unattended they feared in many parts of the country to venture out of doors even in broad daylight. Those who must go to town with produce would not travel singly as before, but were gathered together

[1] Baton Rouge Advocate, Dec. 6, 1867; New Orleans Picayune, Dec. 12, 1867. For Florida see Davis, Recon. in Fla., p. 594.
[2] Ku Klux Report, South Carolina Testimony, p. 121; ibid., Alabama Testimony, pp. 230-31, 1132, 1688, 1714, 1717; cf. Transactions of Ala. Hist. Soc., quoted in W. L. Fleming, Doc. Hist. of Recon., vol. ii, p. 310.
[3] Ku Klux Report, South Carolina Testimony, p. 1014.
[4] New Orleans Picayune, Dec. 8, 1867; Fleming, Recon. in Ala., pp. 561-2; Ku Klux Report, Georgia Testimony, p. 172.
[5] Fleming, Doc. Hist. of Recon., vol. ii, pp. 318-20; Ku Klux Report, South Carolina Testimony, pp. 124-5.
[6] Cf. New Orleans Picayune, May 3, 1867, quoting Mobile Times.

into large companies for safety. Barns, dwellings and gin houses were burned.[1] Incited to idleness, arrogance, and violence by the most dastardly of white leaders, the negroes had forfeited right to the sympathy of those who had been their real friends, and invited the retaliation which was to descend upon their heads in horrible measure for so many years to come.

The people, said Senator James Chesnut of South Carolina, were "at the mercy of ignorance and of corruption, foreign and domestic."[2] They were committed to the hands of "camp followers, horse holders, cooks, bottle washers and thieves," said General Clanton of Alabama.[3] No longer under the care of the Northern troops but subject to the jurisdiction of the "reconstructed" civil governments, with such a magistracy that the enforcement of order by regular agencies was out of the question, it seemed a hopeless, to many a completely desperate situation.

As if by magic hundreds of protective and revolutionary clubs of white men appeared in all parts of the South. There were the Pale Faces in Tennessee; the Constitutional Guards and the White Brotherhood in North Carolina; the "K.W.C.'s," or the Knights of the White Camelia in Louisiana and Arkansas;[4] the Council of Safety in South Carolina; the Men of Justice in Alabama; the Society of the White Rose, the '76 Association and the Robertson Family in Mississippi; the Knights of the Rising Sun and the Sons of Washington in

[1] Fleming, Recon. in Ala., pp. 561-2; Publications Miss. Hist. Soc., vol. iv, p. 131.

[2] Ku Klux Report, South Carolina Testimony, p. 449.

[3] Ibid., Ala. Testimony, p. 244.

[4] This order seems to have numbered 17,000 men in New Orleans alone and was intended to have a general organization like the Ku Klux Klan covering the whole South. (House Mis. Doc., 41st Cong. 2nd sess., no. 154, pt. 1, p. 19.) It was, as one member said, "a white man's association to keep white men in their present state and to prevent the negro being elevated above him" (Ibid., p. 275), or as another declared "to prevent the supremacy of an inferior race and to oppose miscegenation." (Ibid., p. 290.) It had been organized by an officer of the Confederate Army, a Creole, Colonel Alcibiade Le Blanc. (Ibid., p. 556. For Ritual, etc., see ibid., pp. 276-7, and Fleming, Recon. in Ala., pp. 669-73.)

Texas, while many were entirely local and without name or reputation except in their own small neighborhoods.[1]

Soon one of these societies spread and grew until it gained a prominence surpassing that of any rival. It came, indeed, to comprehend the entire South. It began as little more than an idle jest in Pulaski, Tenn., a county town of 2,500 persons, late in the summer of 1866, by a group of young men returned from service in the Confederate army. They had formed a "circle" which they found to be "kuklos" in Greek.[2] This was converted into Ku Klux, and for the sake of alliteration the word Klan was added, the foundation for the mysterious symbols "K.K.K." which in a short while met the eyes of the affrighted negroes and excited the curious interest of the readers of newspapers in all parts of the country.[3]

But the growth of the little club in Pulaski into nation wide prominence was gradual. The members of the "circle" passed to other towns and carried the idea of the Klan with them. Thus new clubs were formed. The possibility of using what at first seems to have been without any very definite purposes for the social and political advantage of the South in its existing plight was soon understood. The Klan would take its place beside the other secret societies and, through a great secret confederation of men, sworn to loyalty to one another and the common cause, it would crystallize and give expression to the sentiment of the Southern people as to their common danger at a dire hour.

A convention was called to meet in Nashville in April, 1867, when delegates from the Ku Klux clubs adopted a prescript to govern the body. A year later the Klan held another meeting at which time this prescript was revised and improved in form.[4]

---

[1] Fleming, Doc. Hist. of Recon., vol. ii, pp. 349-54; W. G. Brown, Lower South in American History, pp. 209-10.
[2] Cf. Ku Klux Report, Ala. Testimony, p. 661.
[3] Cf. N. Y. Tribune, April 14, 1868.
[4] The original prescript is in possession of W. L. Fleming. The revised and amended paper is in the Library of Columbia University. See the Reprint of the Louisiana State University's Department of History; Fleming, Doc. Hist. of Recon., vol. ii, pp. 346-49; Lester and Wilson, The Ku Klux Klan, appendices; Ku Klux Report, vol. xiii,

In this paper we find a full statement of the principles and the system of organization of the order. The society was established as "an institution of chivalry, humanity, mercy and patriotism."[1] Its members would defend the Constitution of the United States and assist in the execution of "all constitutional laws." They would "protect the weak, the innocent and the defenceless from the indignities, wrongs and outrages of the lawless, the violent and the brutal, relieve the injured and oppressed, succor the suffering and unfortunate," with special regard for the widows and orphans of Confederate soldiers.

Candidates for membership in the order were to be asked whether they belonged to the "Radical Republican party," the Loyal League, or the Grand Army of the Republic. Were they opposed to the principles and policies of these organizations? Had they served in the Federal army during the war to fight against the South? What were their views on the subject of "negro equality"? Were they in favor of "a white man's government," of "constitutional liberty," of "maintaining the constitutional rights of the South," of the re-enfranchisement and emancipation of the Southern people? If the various questions were answered to the satisfaction of those who propounded them the candidate was sworn to "the most profound and rigid secrecy" amid skulls, vials of blood and other symbols which were a part of the hocus pocus of the society and he became a "ghoul." To no one should he ever reveal the fact that he belonged, or that he had the acquaintance of any who belonged to the body. Grave penalties would be imposed upon that man who should violate his oath in this regard.

The whole South, including Maryland, Virginia, the Carolinas, Georgia, Florida, Alabama, Mississippi, Louisiana, Texas, Arkansas, Missouri, Kentucky and Tennessee, was

pp. 35-41; Powell Clayton, Aftermath of the Civil War in Ark., pp. 58-61; House Mis. Doc., 41st Cong. 2nd sess., no. 144, pp. 32-8; Cong. Globe, 41st Cong. 3rd sess., app., pp. 214-5.

[1] It was "a military organization," says a young Southern historian, "in which was mingled the glamour of chivalry and the awe and reverence inspiring mysticism of a ritualistic religious order."—Pub. of Miss. Hist. Soc., vol. xi, p. 246.

called the "Empire," often the "Invisible Empire," which was presided over by a "Grand Wizard" and his ten "Genii." Each state was a "Realm" under a "Grand Dragon" and eight "Hydras." A group of counties, constituting a Congressional district, formed a "Dominion" under a "Grand Titan" and six "Furies." Each county was a "Province" under a "Grand Giant" and four "Goblins"; while the local unit was a "Den" ruled over by a "Grand Cyclops" and his two "Night Hawks."

Some Radicals professed to believe that the "Grand Wizard" was Andrew Johnson, the general malefactor of the age; others connected the name of Frank Blair with the Klan. But it was recognized in the South that that intrepid soldier, General N. B. Forrest, stood at the head of the society. In 1868 it was "spreading like wild fire." [1] Forrest is reported to have said at that time that there were as many as 40,000 clansmen in Tennessee—no less than 550,000 in the whole South.[2]

It is clear that at first the principal, if not the sole purpose of the order, was to discipline the negroes. It was a secret society to operate against their secret oath-bound leagues.[3] There had been "slave patrols" before the war. At night planters, planters' sons and overseers mounted horses, and rode along the roads and over the fields to frighten vagrants and hurry them back to their cabins.[4] Such methods were in

---

[1] Augusta, Ga., corr. N. Y. World, April 7, 1868.

[2] Interview with correspondent of Cincinnati Commercial which Forrest afterward partially denied, though the value of this denial is not high in view of statements he made in his examination by the Ku Klux Committee that it was not complete. Still more of what he was reported to have said was now declared to be untrue. (Ku Klux Report, vol. xiii, pp. 4-6, 32-5.) For numbers in Texas, cf. Testimony in contested Congressional election case of Grafton v. Connor, House Misc. Doc., 41st Cong. 2nd sess., no. 114, p. 25. Also Powell Clayton, Aftermath of the Civil War in Ark., pp. 58-60. Manifestly the numbers are mere guesses. No proof is at hand that the confederation of the local camps was close enough to admit of anything like an accurate statement of the membership.

[3] Richmond Examiner, quoted in N. Y. Tribune, April 6, 1868.

[4] Garner, Recon. in Miss., p. 338; Fleming, Recon. in Ala., p. 657; W. G. Brown, Lower South in American History, pp. 193-4; Ku Klux Report, Georgia Testimony, p. 242, and Ala. Testimony, p. 873.

the interest of good order. Recourse would again be had to this system of policing the country.

Much of the force of such sporadic volunteer regulation was founded upon the well known superstitions of the blacks. The gruesome names of the officers of the order—Dragons, Goblins, Giants, Night Hawks—were fear inspiring as were all their movements. The very words, Ku Klux Klan, were full of ominous sound. The rendezvous was a swamp, a wood or a graveyard, and the time of meeting was at night. Grotesque costumes, in many cases contrived by the needles of the wives and sisters of the South [1] from their old dresses, or bed sheeting, or "domestic"—home made cloth, spun often on hand looms from the cotton of their own plantations—were donned for a disguise, which, while it would increase the terror of the negroes, might serve at the same time to make detection more difficult.

The traditional and, perhaps, the most usual type of costume was a white gown with wide sleeves. The face was covered with a mask, either of cloth, with orifices for the eyes, the nostrils and the mouth, or a "doughface," a crude plastic false face used in masquerades, and kept for sale in the stores. The head was likely to be surmounted by a high conical hat built around card board, designed to increase the height of the wearer. Sometimes a tassel was fastened to the apex of the structure. Very often it was trimmed with scarlet in imitation of blood. A false nose of great length and a long tongue of red flannel with large jagged teeth made of quills might be added, if it should please the taste of the clansman or the ladies concerned in his adornment. False beards made from a mule's or a cow's tail might depend from the headpiece, which, for convenience, could be turned around to hang down the back, while the "Ku Klux" was riding and needed room for fuller breath and clearer sight. Horns, to suggest

---

[1] Women were often elected to membership in the camps so that they would be under oath while performing this service.—Pub. of Miss. Hist. Soc., vol. xi, pp. 252, 311; North Carolina Booklet, vol. ii, no. 1, p. 13.

to the negroes that their visitors were animals or devils, were in many cases attached to the masks. These came from rams or cattle, or were pointed pouches of cloth stiffened by whale-bones taken from women's corsets and stuffed with cotton, which sometimes were allowed to stand upright and some-times to depend like mules' ears. Various devices, sugges-tive of the impish employment of those who wore the cos-tumes, such as skulls, cross bones and daggers, might be painted or sewed upon the white gown. At times the flow-ing garment was starched so that it would rustle and glisten in the moonlight. A white bed sheet would be thrown over the back and haunches of the horse or mule which bore the rider and sometimes it covered even the neck and head of the animal.

But there was no certain pattern or style for the attire of the members of the order. Some wore black robes; others were in spotted calico. Some again did not wear the robe at all but appeared in black trousers which were striped with red or white. Still others were seen in red clowns' suits. The masks and head dress were similarly various. And many of these knights who went forth from Southern homes in behalf of "chivalry, humanity, mercy and patriotism" were content to bind a handkerchief over their faces like Western train robbers, perhaps merely smutting their faces with lamp black, and turning their hats and their coats wrong side out. It was as ill-assorted a company of masqueraders as ever possessed the streets of a Pennsylvania town on an Allhallowe'en, or New Orleans on the night of Shrove Tuesday.[1]

The white robe was designed to create the illusion that the Ku Klux were ghosts. They were the shrouded Confederate dead come back to earth to right the wrongs of the South. As such it was understood that they were incapable of being wounded in combat. They could not be stopped by doors or windows because they "flew." When the negroes met a rider

[1] Pictorial reproductions of Ku Klux costumes may be found in Ku Klux Report, Miss. Testimony, p. 1158; Harper's Weekly, vol xvi, p. 73; Fleming, Doc. Hist. of Recon., vol. ii, p. 364; Lester and Wilson, The Ku Klux Klan.

they were likely to be told that he had just come from the moon, or from some place "betwixt the moon and the seven stars," or again, and more often, from hell. "Here we come!" a squadron of the white-robed horsemen would shout as they galloped through a black settlement on one of their forays. "We are the Ku Klux, right from hell."

Nearly always they had been killed at Shiloh, or Chickamauga, or Manassas Gap, or Gettysburg, at which places they had just issued from their graves, magically traversing great distances, perhaps, 60 or 100 miles in a night. There were blacks to believe that one, a more agile imp of Inferno than the rest, had travelled 1,000 miles in a few brief hours—all the way from the battle field of Shiloh. Over one who had died to be buried at Manassas they had built a pike, and he had been able only with great difficulty, so he averred, to scratch his way up through the gravel. Now and again the negro women were warned not to let their children cry; it disturbed the slumbers of these dead who were come to life for a night. One wanted a negro's horse for a "charger to ride to hell" with which place the Ku Klux were in communication by courier nine times a day.[1] Sometimes the phantom figure would ask for a drink of water to quench the thirst he had gained while dwelling amid the eternal fires. If but a tin cup full should be offered him he would require the entire pail. Tipping it he would pour it through his fantastic visor into a cowhide or rubber bag concealed beneath his robe, and then call for another to be disposed of in the same way, to the amazement and confusion of every sable beholder.[2] Then, his thirst slaked, a negro might be asked to carry this disembodied spirit of the Confederacy back to the graveyard.

From Tennessee came the story of a "Ku Klux" who had

[1] Ku Klux Report, Alabama Testimony, p. 814.

[2] "Why you drink a great sight of water," said a black woman after a Ku Klux in ghostly uniform had taken his second pail full. "Yes, old lady," he answered, "and if you were dead and in hell as long as I was you would drink a sight of water, too."—House Mis. Doc., 41st Cong 2nd sess., no. 154, pt. 2, p. 163; cf. ibid., p. 397, and Fleming, Doc. Hist of Recon., vol. ii, p. 365; Pub. Hist. Soc. of Miss., vol. xi, p. 311; Reminiscences of Basil W. Duke, pp. 409-10.

ridden up to an unfinished building and swallowed a hand saw. Another stole a side of beef from a butcher shop and left a note saying that he had eaten it all and had gone away hungry. In Louisiana several masqueraders entered a market. Though, when they came, they had looked like "ordinary humans," they suddenly shot up to a height of fifteen feet, drank gallon upon gallon of hot coffee and ate all the raw meat.[1] Now and again the midnight prestidigitator would offer a hand which when it came to the negro to be shaken was found to be but a clattering skeleton of bone or wood extended from the gown sleeve. Or the rider might have a false head set upon an artificial framework affixed to his shoulders, a skull made, likely, from a gourd, which he could take off at will, asking a negro bystander to hold it for him until he could "fix his backbone," or tighten the cork leg he had been obliged to wear ever since he had been killed at Shiloh,[2] thus leading to the rather widespread impression among the blacks that the Ku Klux could "take themselves all to pieces whenever they wanted to."

They would rattle chains and shake cow bones in a sack to scare the darkies. From an ear of corn the pith in the cob would be removed. The hole, then, might be filled with powder and when lighted it would be thrown into a crowd to explode, the grains flying out in all directions.[3] A negro had heard a "Ku Klux" tell of a horrible monster, which lived in the swamps, possessed of an insatiable appetite for "fried nigger meat." One time a "ghost" rapped at the door of a Loyal League lodge room. "Hold on a minute," the "Ku Klux" cried, "till I turn this screw and let a little more power into my steam arm," wherewith the darkies tumbled out of the windows and dashed for the woods.[4]

Usually the clansmen would designate one of their number to speak for them so that their voices might not be recog-

---

[1] House Mis. Doc., 41st Cong. 2nd sess., no. 154, pt. 2, p. 120.
[2] Ibid., pt. 1, pp. 153, 526, 543.
[3] Publications of Miss. Hist. Soc., vol. xii, p. 237.
[4] House Mis. Doc., 41st Cong. 2nd sess., no. 154, pt. 1, p. 543.

nized. This "ghost" would use deep sepulchral tones or perhaps a high treble, which further wrought upon the fears and superstitions of the blacks. Sometimes the conversation was in Irish or German dialect, and the words were frequently so mysterious that they could not be understood by the affrighted darkies. This was "talking Ku Klux"; in Mississippi and Tennessee it was known as "mummicking." [1] With the same object in view, to obviate the use of names when it was necessary for one to communicate with another, the members of a party of riders would be numbered and, if grave work were to be done, "brothers" were brought from distant places further to mystify the community. A "den" in another county, or, perhaps, in another state would be called upon to visit the culpable and punish them for their sins.

Often the Ku Klux would ride by silently—mere apparitions in the night for negroes and children to shudder at as they looked out of their windows. On recorded occasions, as in Pulaski, Tenn., and Huntsville, Ala., the ghostly cavalry entered a town for parade, marching and countermarching to create the impression of great numbers. In such a case the men sat their horses like statues, after a while disappearing as mysteriously as they came. Again their antics took other forms. They used whistles as signals of communication. These they would blow shrilly as they galloped into a group of negro cabins in order to start the dogs to barking. Perhaps, as they passed, they would fire four or five shots through a door, thus terrifying the whole settlement. Again they would halloo and whoop and yell. If they should dismount they might make an uncanny noise by beating their clubs against a fence; or they would bellow like bulls, bark like dogs, grunt like pigs, howl like wolves, hoot like owls, or call like whippoorwills. If they wished to enter a cabin to compel a negro to give up his gun, and there was a latch upon the door a half dozen would rush against it and break it down, then pouncing upon the fellow before he could get out of bed. At signs of

[1] Garner, Recon. in Miss., p. 340; Cong. Globe, 42nd Cong. 1st sess., p. 452.

sunrise the "ghosts" would "squander," as they said in Mississippi, i.e., put the habiliments of the grave in their saddlebags or in some cave in the wood, and disperse to their homes.

Frequently placards would be posted on houses and walls and trees—awkwardly contrived notices in threatening and mysterious language, written perhaps in red ink, with rude drawings of coffins, owls, crescent moons, hounds, coiled snakes, bugles and daggers, signed with the cryptic "K.K.K." Letters of similar authorship were despatched hither and thither through the mails to white and black leaders of the Radical party. These pronunciamentoes of destruction and death purported to come from "Crow Hall," or the "Old Graveyard," or "Wolf Hole," or the "Hell-a-Bulloo Hole," or the "Den of Skulls." The time was "Midnight," or "The Last Hour of the Sinking Moon," or the "Dark Moon," or the "Bloody Moon," or the "Silent Moon," or the "First Year of Revenge." Then followed terse phrases and sentences which any could understand—"Daggers Glimmer"—"Blood to be Drawn"—"Some Live Today, Tomorrow Die"—"The Dark and Dismal Hour Draws Nigh"—"Unholy Blacks, Cursed of God, Take Warning"—"Twice Hath the Sacred Serpent Hissed"—"To be Executed by the Grand White Death and the Rattling Skeleton"—"When the Black Cat is Gliding Under the Shadows of Darkness and the Death Watch Ticks at the Lone Hour of Midnight, then we Pale Riders are Abroad"—"To Your Dens, Hyenas! Come Forth, Ghosts of the Shiloh Dead! Prepare and Note the Signals! The Owls Shall Repeat Them!"—"Perish the Guilty! When the Finger of the White Skeleton Points to the New Made Grave, Brothers Strike! Spare None!" [1]

Digging graves along all the roads of approach would keep the blacks from coming into a town. Setting a coffin at a man's door or smearing red paint here and there to suggest a flow of blood created wild excitement. A single rider posted in a lonely road would send a negro flying at top speed. A

[1] Cf. House Mis. Doc., 41st Cong. 2nd sess., no. 154, pt. 2, pp. 384-5; Fleming, Recon. in Ala., pp. 678-81.

few ghostly figures seated on a tombstone in a graveyard furnished a prolific subject of conversation for months to come. It soon came about that the mere cry of "Ku Klux" would strike panic into an entire countryside. The sound of more than two horsemen passing down a road was enough to make the negroes leave their beds and spend the night in the woods.[1] They would tremble with fear if in the night they saw anything white. The very children of white families, denied some whimsy they had wished to gratify, had but to say, to gain their ends, that if this or that were not done to their minds old "uncle" or "mammy" would be "kukluxed."

There were blacks ready to swear, not only that the Ku Klux were fifteen feet high, but that they rode mules ten feet high which had ears six feet long.[2] They left holes in the ground like seventeen year locusts which they had made in coming up through the earth. When the negroes saw ten Ku Klux they averred that they had seen five hundred or a thousand. At times they thought the air was full of white riders on white horses flying at all speed to join the resurrected rebel cavalry at some mysterious rendezvous, whence they would issue to compel all "niggers" to obey "old Marster" again.[3]

It is said by friendly historians of the Ku Klux that to affright the negroes during the disturbed period of reconstruction was the office of the Klan. Its founders at no time intended that it should become a scourging and murder society. It is impossible for any who will steep himself in the subject,

[1] Hamilton, Recon. in N. C., p. 479.
[2] Ku Klux Report, Georgia Testimony, p. 244.
[3] Cf. House Mis. Doc., 41st Cong. 2nd sess., no. 154, pt. 1, p. 542.— For general accounts of the Ku Klux see Lester and Wilson, The Ku Klux Klan, Its Origin, Growth and Disbandment; Fleming, Doc. Hist. of Recon., vol. ii, p. 369; Powell Clayton, Aftermath of the Civil War in Ark., pp. 56 et seq.; Ficklen, Hist. of Recon. in La., p. 222; Wilson, The Ku Klux Klan, Century Magazine, vol. vi, pp. 398-410; W. G. Brown, The Lower South in American History, pp. 191-225; Hamilton, Recon. in N. C., pp. 452-81; Garner, Recon. in Miss., pp. 338-53; C. M. Thompson, Recon. in Ga., chap. xiv; Fleming, Recon. in Ala., pp. 660-93; Speech of Horace Maynard in Cong. Globe, 41st Cong. 3rd sess., app., pp. 214 et seq.

as it is presented in the written and printed records of the
time, to gain a confident feeling that merely to discipline the
negroes by scaring them was its sole original purpose. It
was plainly designed to be a body of Vigilantes or Regulators,
a "Raw Head and Bloody Bones" society, to "straighten" the
blacks, and to admonish, and, if necessary, punish the carpetbaggers, scalawags and white Radicals generally, who were
an affront to the sentiments of the Southern people. It was
evident, said the Richmond Examiner, already in April, 1868,
that this was not a "meaningless Merry Andrew organization,"
but that "under its cap and bells" it had a purpose, "resolute,
noble and heroic." It was being formed for action, "wherever
the insolent negro, the malignant white traitor to his race,
and the infamous squatter" were plotting to make the South
"utterly unfit for the residence of the decent white man." [1]

> "Strike for your altars and your fires,
> Strike for the green graves of your sires,
> God and your native land!"

repeated the Montgomery, Ala., Mail. "From the valleys
should go up the defying shouts of an outraged people. From
the hill tops should blaze forth the fiery cross of vengeance
and the soil of Alabama should thrill once more beneath the
feet of freemen." [2] From "every quarter of the South," said
the Tuscaloosa Monitor came accounts of the "singularly
beneficial" effect of the operations of the armed Ku Klux
bands.

It is to the credit of the better leaders of the Southern
people that they withdrew from the Klan when they discovered, in 1868, that they could not control the turbulent men
who had found their way into the "dens." It may be accepted as true that the "Grand Wizard," General Forrest, officially disbanded the organization late in that year or early
in 1869. But his authority over the camps was loose. [3] No
power could put an end to the order by a mere gesture of the

[1] Quoted in N. Y. Tribune, April 6, 1868.
[2] Quoted in Cong. Globe, 40th Cong. 2nd sess., p. 3304.
[3] Cf. Lester and Wilson, The Ku Klux Klan, pp. 128-31

hand or a stroke of a pen. If some members resigned, others came in to take their places. The cover had been prepared for a reign of outrage and crime which, all taken together, forms a record of wrong among the most hideous in the history of any modern state.

In 1869 the Klan had absorbed "all the horse thieves, cutthroats, bushwhackers and outlaws of every description" who unhindered continued to use its "signs, passwords, robes, and masks for their own purposes."[1] It had "degenerated into a mob of rioters and marauders who plundered and abused friend and foe alike, sparing neither party nor sex," said a leading lawyer in North Carolina. It became "a dangerous and fearful conspiracy against society."[2] The negroes were visited in their cabins and they were seized to be scourged, at which time it came to be very well understood that the Ku Klux were not ghosts but "folks." Hundreds running into thousands were laid out upon the ground, while brutes stood upon their heads and feet, or were tied face downward upon logs or barrels, or were fastened in a standing position to trees with their backs to a mob of rowdies, to be beaten with fence palings, hickory withes, ram rods, clubs, hoe handles, cart whips, harness straps, pine tops and fishing poles. Women were stripped of their clothing to be "bucked" and paddled, and often indeed to be thrashed like the men. Even cripples were not spared from these brutalities. Many a victim was left naked, bleeding and freezing in wood or swamp. Released, after the ruffians had made good their threat to cut his back "as fine as dog's hair," he was told to run home while shots were fired at his fleeing form. Others were freed only to be ridden down by horses or were pursued by "nigger hounds." Many died of their frightful wounds.

Before they were scourged both men and women at times were subjected to strangely abasing and disgusting experiences amid profane and filthy language, in some cases so vile that it could not be printed in the records of the hearings before

[1] Report of War Department for 1868-69, vol. i, p. 185.
[2] Ku Klux Report, North Carolina Testimony, p. 385.

investigating committees or in the proceedings of courts. Men were castrated and women were mutilated for the amusement of beasts. Whites as well as blacks were shot, stabbed, hanged. Stones were tied to them and they were thrown into rivers and ponds. Helplessly wounded they were put upon heaps of brush to be burned to death. Bodies of the slain were eviscerated so that they would sink in the water and trace of crime would disappear. Men were bound to railway irons for trains of cars to pass over. Sheriffs were overtaken, jails were opened, prisoners were seized and lynched. School houses and churches were burned. Teachers were assaulted and driven out of the country, so that the people might be rid of the tax levied upon them to meet the cost of educating black children. Reverdy Johnson who had been retained to defend the accused in some Ku Klux trials in the United States courts in South Carolina said that he had listened to the testimony with "unmixed horror." The outrages which were proven, he continued, were "shocking to humanity"; they admitted of "neither excuse nor justification"; they demonstrated that the "parties engaged were brutes insensible to the obligations of humanity and religion." [1]

From the very beginning some of the wiser of the Southern leaders had frowned upon the organization. For example the New Orleans Picayune said that it was "all folly," and did "an infinitude of harm." Young men who went about the country frightening simple negroes should be at home planting corn and working it. The worst of it was that such performances strengthened the Radical party at the North. The smallest incident of this kind was trumpeted far and wide. "Wild young men among us," the editor continued, should be "put behind the plow." Each idle young white man was "a greater curse to the country than two vagrant negroes." [2] After the order fell into the hands of desperadoes and it became a mere murder society criticism increased. The Macon (Miss.)

---

[1] Ku Klux Report, South Carolina Testimony, p. 1821.
[2] New Orleans Picayune, April 14, 1868; cf. Ficklen, Hist. of Recon. in La., p. 223.

Beacon denounced the "midnight banditti." It should be "made disreputable to countenance such outrages" which were "foul ulcers" upon the name and reputation of the South.[1] A Freedmen's Bureau agent in Tennessee said that in his travels he had not encountered "a single citizen of any standing" who did not deplore these manifestations of lawlessness.[2]

In Georgia the better classes of the people deprecated the outrages.[3] "The Ku Klux business," said B. H. Hill, "is the worst that ever afflicted the South. Every day that we let it continue we cut our own throats. . . . It is a curse upon our land, a blight following slavery and war and the greatest blunder our people ever committed."[4] The time was at hand, said the Augusta Constitutionalist, for the people to rise up and speak out. Georgia must display a capacity for protecting the lives of its own citizens. "Secret organizations and midnight mobs" must be condemned in the "strongest language," and the people exhorted to vindicate the "peace, good order and dignity of the state."[5] Nine-tenths of them, said Judge Wright were opposed to the Ku Klux.[6] There was not a reputable man in Alabama, said Governor Lindsay in 1871, who did not rejoice when one of these disguised outlaws was shot.[7] The men who perpetrate such outrages, said General Clanton, are "the worst enemies of our people on God's earth," and "every decent man" in the South was ready to say so.[8]

The "thing" had "gone far enough" in South Carolina.[9] Many in that state it was said did not hesitate to express their "abhorrence" of it "in unmeasured terms."[10] In North Carolina ex-Congressman Davidson declared that "all the reliable men who have at heart the good of the state and the peace and

[1] Issue of May 14, 1870, quoted in Garner, Recon. in Miss., p. 345.
[2] Report of Sec. of War for 1868-69, vol. i, p. 185.
[3] House Mis. Doc., 40th Cong. 3rd sess., no. 52, pp. 29-44; Ku Klux Report, Georgia Testimony, p. 373.
[4] Ku Klux Report, Georgia Testimony, p. 773.   [5] Ibid, p. 1217.
[6] Ibid, p. 966.   [7] Ibid., Alabama Testimony, p. 213.
[8] Ibid., p. 241.   [9] Ibid., South Carolina Testimony, p. 1115.
[10] Letter in Charleston News, quoted in ibid., p. 1009.

order of society" gave the Ku Klux organization not "any encouragement whatever." [1]

So much could be said in sincerity, though it was intended in some measure for the ears of the Northern people with the purpose of breaking the force of their condemnation. As a matter of fact those who held such sentiments, unless they were men of independent position and marked consequence, found it discreet to keep their judgments to themselves. There was a vast amount of quiet as well as open indulgence of and apology for the Ku Klux Klan. In particular it was observed that the Southern women who had exhibited so much feeling during the war were now (possibly because of the prevalence of house burning and rape) applauders of the deeds of the masked riders.[2] It would be said that no such order as the Ku Klux was in existence; lawlessness at the South was greatly exaggerated; cases were sporadic; much of what passed for outrages were mere "cock and bull stories" of the negroes.[3] Some, indeed, so it was seriously alleged, were contrived and staged by ex-Federal soldiers and negroes for the express purpose of shocking the North and of re-directing attention to the "inherent bad nature" of the Southern people.[4] Many a political scoundrel of the Radical party who wished to steal from a county or a state would "get up an outrage" and make off with his booty in the midst of the excitement which attended this new evidence of unquelled rebellion.[5]

Anyhow the Ku Klux were just a few "boys on a frolic," "a parcel of dare devil young men," or, perhaps some "drunken vagabonds" who went out to punish a negro who had burnt a gin house or committed a rape.[6] They were simply regulators of people who were not "toteing fair." [7] Thus fared horse thieves, white men who consorted with negresses and

---

[1] Senate Reports, 42nd Cong. 1st sess., no. 1, p. 132.
[2] Ku Klux Report, South Carolina Testimony, p. 1038.
[3] Ibid., Georgia Testimony, p. 243.
[4] Ibid., p. 787; Alabama Testimony, p. 380.
[5] South Carolina Testimony, p. 97.
[6] Ibid., pp. 97, 627.
[7] Alabama Testimony, p. 1143.

negroes who dwelt with white women.[1] There was lawlessness in the West, even in Philadelphia and Massachusetts;
not more of it existed in the South than in other parts of the
country.[2] It was a species of "wild justice," a "terrible thing"
indeed, but made necessary by incompetent local government
in the interest of social order.

Arrests for crime were not to be expected. If the negroes
and objectionable Radicals were prosecuted and convicted the
carpetbag governors would soon intercede and release the prisoners. Long lists of pardons granted for partisan considerations were prepared in justification of the rule of "Judge
Lynch."[3] It was defended as the "only manner of punishing
criminals" in the South.[4] After the remedy had been applied
the community felt "safer" and "more at ease."[5] Through
lawlessness would lawlessness be cured. It was the "shortest
and most humane road to becoming civilized." Otherwise the
South must have been the scene of "a general conflict of
races."[6]

It is true enough that the provocation had been great.
The Southern people had been told in effect, said General
Gordon—"You are unworthy to vote; you cannot hold office;
we are unwilling to trust you; you are not honest men; your
former slaves are better fitted to administer the laws than
you are." The burning of Atlanta and Sherman's devastations on the march to the sea had "never created a tithe of the
animosity" which now resulted from the North's proscription
of the Southern people. Scarcely any other population, he

---

[1] Ku Klux Report, Georgia Testimony, p. 832.

[2] Cf., e.g., ibid., p. 965, quoting Atlanta Constitution, Oct. 25, 1871.

[3] Governor Bullock in Georgia, so it was said, since August, 1868,
had had 420 applications for pardon before him. He had granted 321
of these, many of them of men held for murder, and in a number of
instances before trial.—Georgia Testimony, pp. 153, 156, 767, 825.

[4] South Carolina Testimony, p. 995.

[5] Ibid., p. 1115.

[6] Ibid., p. 1116. The organization had been formed, said General Forrest, "to prevent a general slaughter of women and children." On all
sides men feared an uprising which might become as bloody as the
revolution in San Domingo.—Ku Klux Report, vol. xiii, pp. 7, 24, 29.

said, would have behaved so well "in the same situation."[1] There would have been no Ku Klux Klan, said General Gordon, but for a class of men, come into the South since the war without property interests there, or reputation for character at home, whose object it seemed to be to excite animosity and strife. The order had included "some of the very best citizens of the state"; it was "a brotherhood of the property holders," of the "peaceable, law-abiding citizens" for their own protection.[2]

The country was as free of lawlessness, said Judge Wright of Georgia, as any other circumstanced as the South had been.[3] It was not, said Wade Hampton, an evidence of "settled hostility to the general government," but "solely the sporadic effort of a people to throw off the incubus" of their local government.[4] The resentment of the South was the greater since the harpies were flourishing on money which was taken from the people when they were "desperately poor."[5] Under such circumstances "evil disposed persons" might "Indian-like take revenge haphazard."[6] There were times when it became "almost a virtue to meet despotism and connivance with crime with swift retribution."[7] What was seen in the South would "make the most pure Christian in the world commit bloody deeds."[8] The only way to break up the Ku Klux Klan was to disperse the thieves who were plundering the Southern states and to install honest men in their places.[9]

It was alleged, with appearance of truth, that the perpetrators of these outrages were not men who had owned negroes before the war, but those who hated and despised them.[10] In very many cases it was proven that the outlaws were renegades recruited from the "poor whites" who had the idea that

[1] Ku Klux Report, Georgia Testimony, pp. 316, 317.
[2] Ibid., p. 308.   [3] Ibid., p. 966.   [4] South Carolina Testimony, p. 1221.
[5] Ibid., p. 1001.   [6] Georgia Testimony, p. 171.
[7] Augusta Constitutionalist, Nov. 9, 1871, quoted in Georgia Testimony, p. 1217.
[8] Ku Klux Report, South Carolina Testimony, p. 1010.   [9] Ibid.
[10] Ibid., Mississippi Testimony, pp. 507-8.

if they could drive the negroes out of the country they would be able to command a higher price for their labor.[1] Midnight crime was more prevalent in the hills than in the bottoms— where the negroes were few in comparison with the white population rather than where they predominated, as in the so called "black belts."[2] It was plainly contrary to the interests of the old planter element that the negroes should live in a state of fear and panic. For weeks at a time in some neighborhoods they could not be induced to sleep in their cabins; they sought safety in the woods. No labor could be got out of them while they were in this disturbed condition, on which account it was understood in many places that there would be no "kukluxing of niggers" while the crop was being put in the ground, or when it was time to lay it by. Offenses at these seasons would be overlooked; scores would be settled at a more suitable day.[3]

Without a doubt in some cases in the "poor white" mountain districts "kukluxing" was bound up with the business of illicit distilling. Blacks were whipped and otherwise maltreated because they had informed or were suspected of the intention of informing upon those who were violating the internal revenue laws.

In some places negroes were migrating and were seeking homes in other states, and a new impetus was given to the scheme to return them to Africa. The American Colonization Society was ready to celebrate its fiftieth anniversary in 1867. It had been sending out a little vessel in the spring and another in the fall laden with emigrants and freight for Liberia. Glowing accounts were put into circulation of this "free and thriving republic with its nigh 600 miles of once barbarous coast dotted with 60 towns and settlements, schools, a college and churches shedding their elevating and hallowing light . . .

[1] Ku Klux Report, Alabama Testimony, p. 1139, and South Carolina Testimony, p. 448.

[2] Cf. Fleming in Introduction to Lester and Wilson's Ku Klux Klan, pp. 23-4.

[3] Ku Klux Report, Alabama Testimony, pp. 924, 935.

with commerce extending, and literature, industry, and African nationality established." Colonists wrote back to say that coffee grew in the woods, that the cotton plant attained the size of a tree, that farmers could raise potatoes all the year round. They had "no more use for America." They wished every colored man in the South to come over to Africa. Inquiries for passage thither increased when the Ku Klux began to ravage the South. The society purchased a new ship called the *Golconda* which late in 1866 sailed away with 600 blacks, principally drawn from the neighborhood of Macon, Ga. In 1867 parties made up in the Marion district in South Carolina and at Columbus, Ga., were taken out to their ancestral homes under the Equator. No less than 2,000 negroes made application for passage in 1868. Parties organized in the Edgefield district in South Carolina, at Eufaula and Decatur in Alabama, at Elizabeth City in North Carolina, in Louisiana, Florida and Georgia wrote to the offices of the society in Washington.

But the courage of most of the intending emigrants failed them as the day of departure approached. They made their excuses. Some still expected the government to give them land and mules, and would not go on this account. Others were promised higher wages at home. Very unfavorable reports of Liberia were printed in the newspapers, by design said the agents of the society, who even suggested that the "head men" of companies of colonists were paid by Southern employers or by the Radical politicians to dissuade the negroes from emigration. The exportation of labor met with increasing disfavor which led the society to say in its own defence in its report in 1873 that the number of persons sent away under its auspices was "too insignificant for serious consideration." In truth it was so, for while in 1867 it had forwarded 633 colonists to Liberia the number in 1869 was only 160, in 1870, 196, in 1871, 247 and in 1872, 150. From the close of the war up to 1872 the total was only 2,833.[1]

[1] Annual Reports of American Colonization Society, 1868-73; Ku Klux Report, South Carolina Testimony, pp. 1410, 1412.

Such a secret organization, whatever its original or later purpose—whether it was meant merely to terrify unruly negroes; or was designed as an agency to administer punishment in the absence of trustworthy constables, sheriffs and courts; or was, as it soon clearly came to be, a mere name to cover the hideous depredations of roving bands of desperadoes, was very certain to be put to political use. That this was not the intention of the founders of the order may, indeed, be true. From the first, however, such a purpose was not far in the background. The Loyal League was an organization to assist the Republican party to win elections in the South. The Ku Klux would have an opposite use and no denials, of which there were many throughout these years, on the part of the conservative leaders, were sufficient to make any other view prevail.

Republicanism in Georgia, said General Gordon, meant "nothing in the world but creating disturbance, riot and animosity, and filching and plundering." [1] So much was believed and said in other Southern states and such political rule was to be resisted by any means which opportunity and circumstance could suggest. A dozen or a hundred sheeted ghosts on phantom chargers would enter a county town and silently parade the streets on the eve of an election. "A wink was as good as a nod for a blind horse," said one negro when he was asked if he knew what was expected of him by the old master class. If the Ku Klux should ride into town casting a voodoo spell upon a circle about which their horses paced, black voters would be certainly kept from crossing it on the following day. The records of the period attest to the great number of whippings and assassinations which were inspired by partisan hatreds and political rivalries. Many were flogged for voting the Republican ticket; others in anticipation that they would do so. Scalawags and carpetbaggers were visited by masked men and were persuaded not to accept, or to vacate local offices. Some were warned to leave the country under penalty of death.

[1] Ku Klux Report, Georgia Testimony, p. 309.

The first outrage which directed attention in a prominent way to the Ku Klux Klan was the murder of G. W. Ashburn, a scalawag who lived in Columbus, Ga. He had been a cruel overseer of slaves before the war. Now, for his own selfish purposes, he was a Republican. He caused himself to be elected by the negroes to the constitutional convention of Georgia, and, like Hunnicutt in Virginia, played the part of an incendiary and a demagogue to gain their good will and win their votes. He aspired to the governorship of the state. One night in 1868 he was visited by a party of masked men who killed him. No trace of the murderers could be found. Although many held that he had abundantly merited his fate, since he had been living in adultery with a negress, thus doing affront to the decent sensibilities of the community in which he dwelt,[1] the North demanded reparation for such a wrong. General Meade was instructed to proceed to the place. He removed the mayor and aldermen and other civil authorities, and proclaimed martial law. Scores of persons, some drawn from the best families in the town and the surrounding country, were arrested and confined in cells in an improvised prison of planks in an open field under the hot sun. Nothing was proved against them by the military commission convened to try the cases and all finally were released, the whole incident serving to awaken the further resentment of the conservatives.[2]

So it went from month to month and year after year in inexorable reiteration toward one inexorable result. Senator Chesnut had found "the true secret of all this thing." The law breaking associations of the South were similar to the associations formed in other countries at other times where the people were living under a "despotism." Nowhere, said he, were they "countenanced by thinking or good men," but when power was exercised in an arbitrary way "parties ardent

[1] Cf. Columbus, Ga., Sun, which after his death called him "one of the most obnoxious pests that ever afflicted a civilized community."— Quoted with like opinions in Cong. Globe, 40th Cong. 2nd sess., p. 3304.
[2] Ku Klux Report, Georgia Testimony, pp. 184, 317, 782; Article on South Carolina in Why the Solid South, pp. 127-30; C. M. Thompson, Recon. in Ga., pp. 385-6.

and seeking redress for real or fancied wrongs" which they thought could not be "avenged through the government" would spring into life.[1] They were not different, except in period and name, from the Moss Troopers who flourished in England under the iron rule of the Normans and who reappeared in Scotland prior to the Union; the Illuminati who strove to overturn tyranny in Bavaria and in other parts of Europe; the Tugendbund which rose in northern Germany during the period of the Napoleonic occupation; the Carbonari, active at the same time in the kingdom of Naples; and the Nihilists of Russia.[2]

Scourgings and assassinations developed into riots. The total toll of life and the sum of mutilation, injury and maltreatment reached appalling proportions. Allowance could be made for partisan exaggeration. On one side there was possibility of overstatement of the case with reference to the number of brutish outrages committed by the negroes; on the other side there was beyond a doubt much systematic falsification by the Radicals as to the amount of crime and violence which was to be laid at the door of the whites with regard to the so called Loyalists.[3] The truth in all reason, if it could have been arrived at, was bad enough.

Conditions in Texas were awful. Here in a state nearly as large as North Carolina, South Carolina, Georgia, Alabama, Mississippi and Tennessee, all combined, was seen

> "Old Chaos ere the breath of God
> Moved it to harmony."

In thirty counties there was no civil government; in many others, still in 1869, the organization was very imperfect. Some were so remote that it required from 25 to 40 days for the commander in charge of the district to address inquiries

[1] Ku Klux Report, South Carolina Testimony, p. 449.

[2] Garner, Recon. in Miss., p. 353; Lester and Wilson, The Ku Klux Klan, p. 25; Minority Report of Ku Klux Committee, vol. i, p. 515; Cong. Globe, 42nd Cong. 1st sess., p. 453.

[3] The New York Tribune each day during the campaign of 1868 headed a department of the paper devoted to accounts of Southern outrages, "The New Rebellion."—Cf. Issues of Oct. 21, 22 and 23, 1868.

to them and receive replies.[1] While Sheridan was in command of the state there were nine murders in a month, not including assaults with intent to kill, rapes and other crimes. If he owned both hell and Texas, he said upon one occasion, he would rent out Texas and live, by preference, in the other place, a picturesque statement which was repeated up and down the country for a generation.[2]

This was quite enough, but under Hancock, Sheridan's successor in command, it was asserted that there were 54 murders in a month in the state. The population was only 700,000; it was as if 700 men, women and children in New York City should be assassinated annually.[3] Governor Pease in January, 1868, presented a list of 100 homicides for the preceding year, and he complained that no attempt was made to apprehend the guilty or to bring them to punishment. Not one-tenth of the perpetrators of these murders, he said, had been arrested and less than one-twentieth had been tried. Even when United States officers and soldiers were killed their slayers continued to go about with impunity. Negroes could be convicted, but white men went free.[4]

The committee on "lawlessness and violence" of the constitutional convention of 1868 stated on partial returns from the counties that 1,035 men had been murdered in Texas since the close of the war. The real number in the opinion of a Federal attorney for the district might have been 2,000. The secretary of state reported to the Texas senate 905 homicides for the two years ending May, 1870, and he believed that if all the facts were known the total would be 1,500.[5] In 1870,

[1] House Ex. Doc., 40th Cong. 3rd sess., no. 97.

[2] Another speech of the same character reflecting upon the condition of Texas at this period is attributed to Benjamin F. Wade. "All that Texas needs to make it a paradise is water and good society," said a native of that state. "Yes," Wade replied, "that's all they need in hell." —A. D. White, Autobiography, vol. i, p. 489.

[3] N. Y. Nation, July 16, 1868.

[4] House Mis. Doc., 41st Cong. 2nd sess., no. 144, p. 31.

[5] House Ex. Doc., 42nd Cong. 2nd sess., no. 268, p. 47; Ramsdell, Recon. in Texas, pp. 219-20. Cf. N. Y. Nation, Nov. 12, 1868, for figures given by General Reynolds and Report of Sec. of War for 1868-9, vol. i, pp. 262-71, for statistics prepared by the Freedmen's Bureau.

after the new state government was organized, it was officially reported from 108 of the 127 counties that 2,970 persons charged with crime in those counties were evading arrest. In some cases two and even seven murders were attributed to a single individual.[1] There was no security for life, it was said, beyond what each man's character might afford him in the community in which he dwelt.

General Thomas reported "murders, robberies and outrages of all kinds" in the country districts of Tennessee without any attempt on the part of the civil authorities to arrest the offenders. Union men and negroes were "in constant danger of their lives." Memphis was the "Sodom of the South." The absence of a daily account from that place of a riot, a murder or some other outrage was conclusive evidence, said a Northern newspaper, that the telegraph wires were down.[2] The Freedmen's Bureau of Tennessee collected the names of 162 persons who had been murdered in that state during the year ending July 1, 1868,[3] and not very dissimilar conditions prevailed in Kentucky.[4]

Lynchings and assassinations were daily occurrences in Arkansas. The "dark catalogue of crimes," Governor Clayton said, would probably never be "entirely disclosed." The state was in the midst of a "reign of terror" which "threatened to obliterate all the old landmarks of justice and freedom."[5] The sheriff of Fulton county arrested seven men for murdering a registrar. Ninety outlaws under a leader named Monks came into the state from Missouri and seized four of the prisoners. Answering a writ of habeas corpus the men were given up to a deputy sheriff, but he, while riding away with them, encountered a party of fifty desperadoes. They demanded one of the prisoners, who, under threat, was surrendered to them to be taken into the woods and shot. In

[1] House Ex. Doc., 42nd Cong. 2nd sess., no. 268, p. 47; American Annual Cyclop. for 1870, p. 718.
[2] Phila. Ledger, Feb. 10, 1868.
[3] Report of Sec. of War for 1868-9, vol. i, pp. 717-24.
[4] Ibid. for 1867-8, vol. i, pp. 182-3.
[5] Clayton, Aftermath of the Civil War in Ark., pp. 68-9, 71.

a few hours 600 men congregated to deal with Monks whom they drove out of the state.[1]

In a period of eighteen months, ending on June 30, 1867, General Canby reported 197 murders and 548 cases of aggravated assault in North and South Carolina.[2] In August, 1868, Governor Warmoth said, though others came forward to deny the statement, that in six weeks 150 men had been murdered in Louisiana.[3] As the summer and autumn of 1868 wore on, and the excitement attending the Presidential election rose high, crime and disorder increased. "I can compare the population here to nothing so apt as a volcano ready for an explosion at any moment," General Rousseau wrote to President Johnson from New Orleans.[4] The gun stores were thronged with buyers and the price of Colt's revolvers advanced from $10 to $20 and even $25. For ten days prior to the election of November the streets were filled with men carrying shot guns, rifles, pistols and knives. A band of "Sicilian cutthroats" [5] called the "Innocents," made up largely of fruit dealers, fishermen, oystermen and other elements drawn from the markets, roamed the city, hunting negroes. Soon none could be found in the streets. Then the ruffians entered the houses to drive out the blacks, shooting them like rabbits as they ran. A colored man feared to sleep two nights in the same place.[6] This bloody club had 2,000 members. There were more than 70 other clubs in New Orleans bearing such names as the "Seymour Knights," the "Seymour Legion," the "Seymour Southrons," the "Seymour Infantas," the "Seymour Tigers," the "Blair Knights," the "Swamp Fox Rangers," the "Hancock Club" and the "Rousseau Guards."

---

[1] Report of Sec. of War for 1868-9, vol. i, pp. 318-9; Harrell, Brooks and Baxter War, pp. 75-83, quoted in Fleming, Doc. Hist. of Recon., vol. ii, pp. 73-6.

[2] Report of Sec. of War for 1868-9, vol. i, p. 350.

[3] N. Y. Nation, Aug. 13, 1868; Ficklen, Hist. of Recon. in La., p. 206.

[4] Under date of Sep. 26, 1868, in Johnson Papers.

[5] New Orleans Times, quoted in House Mis. Doc., 41st Cong. 2nd sess., no. 154, pt. 1, p. 109.

[6] Louisiana Contested Election, House Mis. Doc., 41st Cong. 2nd sess., no. 154, pt. 1, p. 22.

Their appearance in parades led to riots in which many were killed and injured.

Disorder extended to other parts of Louisiana. In one month, said General Hatch, of the Freedmen's Bureau, 297 persons were slain in the parishes adjacent to New Orleans.[1] The sheriff of St. Mary's parish was shot and killed in his hotel. A patrol passing through the streets the same night found the dead body of the parish judge.[2] In St. Landry parish the editor of a Radical newspaper was seized by three men and flogged. A race riot followed and several whites and blacks were killed and wounded. In the parish of St. Bernard a negro was killed; a black mob killed a white man. Three steamboats filled with armed ruffians left New Orleans for the scene of the riot. Before the trouble could be composed a dozen or fifteen men were slain.[3]

Frightful conditions prevailed up the Red River around Shreveport, in Caddo and Bossier parishes, a trading centre for Texas, Arkansas and the Indian Nations. A United States army officer on duty in this place saw two or three men shot down in the street in front of a store in which he sat. He picked up the bodies of eight men who had been killed in one night. Never had he heard of any one being punished for murder in that country.[4] One hundred and twenty corpses were found in the woods or were taken out of Red River after a "negro hunt" in Bossier parish.[5] Over 2,000 persons, so it was said, were assassinated or murdered, or were maltreated without fatal result in Louisiana during a few weeks in 1868.[6] Not less than 900, according to other estimates, had been killed.[7] Although conditions during the

[1] House Mis. Doc., 41st Cong. 2nd sess., no. 154, pt. 1, pp. 32-3.
[2] Report of Sec. of War for 1868-9, vol. i, pp. 303-4; N. Y. Nation, Oct. 22, 1868.
[3] Report of Sec. of War for 1868-9, vol. i, pp. 308-9; cf. Ficklen, pp. 225-9.
[4] House Mis. Doc., 41st Cong. 2nd sess., no. 154, pt. 1, p. 109.
[5] Ibid., p. 131.
[6] Ku Klux Report, vol. i, pp. 21-2.
[7] House Mis. Doc., 41st Cong. 2nd sess., no. 154, pt. 1, pp. 39, 161-2; Senator Ames of Miss. in Cong. Globe, 42nd Cong. 1st sess., p. 197.

next two years showed improvement, General Mower, in command in New Orleans, said, in 1869, that the country around Winnsboro in Franklin parish was "infested by a gang of desperadoes and thieves" who totally defied the civil authorities.[1]

In many parts of Georgia, said General Terry in August, 1869, there was "practically no government." The abuse of the negroes was "too common to excite notice." Murders were frequent. The "worst of crimes" were committed and no attempts were made to punish the guilty. Local magistrates who were not in sympathy with the insurrectionary organizations were "overawed" by them.[2] In Camilla in the southwestern part of the state in September, 1868, a white man who was running for Congress on the Republican ticket appeared at the head of a procession of negroes. They were armed and provisioned for a long electioneering campaign. As they were marching under flying flags to music in a country road near the town the sheriff approached and bade them lay aside their muskets. They refused, whereupon he returned to the village and formed a posse of citizens to preserve the peace. A drunken man discharged a gun and a riot in which several persons were killed ensued.[3]

Civil officers, said General Ames, were "unequal to the task" of bringing criminals to justice in Mississippi. Disorderly persons were shielded by their neighbors and could not be arrested. Under such circumstances the commander declared that "the protection of persons in their lives and property" was "impossible."[4] Governor Alcorn said that 124 murders had been committed in the state from April, 1869, to March, 1871. In April, 1871, he found that there had been more than 60 murders in the preceding three months.[5]

The negro secretary of state, Jonathan Gibbs, in Florida,

[1] Report of Sec. of War for 1869-70, vol. i, p. 98.
[2] Ibid., pp. 89-90.
[3] American Annual Cyclopedia for 1868, p. 315; N. Y. Nation, Sep. 24, 1868; Senate Doc., 57th Cong. 2nd sess., no. 209, p. 126.
[4] Report of Sec. of War for 1869-70, vol. i, p. 100.
[5] Garner, Recon. in Miss., p. 288.

when called before a committee of Congress in 1871 reported
153 murders in Jackson county in that state.[1]

The Radical governors and legislatures did not stand by
idly. One reconstructed government followed another in
enacting laws designed to suppress the Ku Klux Klan. Brownlow sounded the charge in Tennessee. He was powerless, he
declared, in face of the widespread disorders in the middle
and western portions of the state. Therefore, in the summer
of 1868, he convened the legislature in extraordinary session.
The "rebellious elements," he said, as he waved his flaming
sword to the Republican part of the nation, both North and
South, had "secretly" armed themselves and perfected a "military organization known as the Ku Klux Klan, composed of
ex-rebel soldiers and those who were in sympathy with them—
thus violating their paroles at the time of their surrender
and violating the laws of the state, and plotting and planning
mischief in every respect." Throughout the year past they
had been at work with an eye to overthrowing the state government and of carrying Tennessee for the Democratic party
in the Presidential election of 1868.[2] The organization rami-
fied "almost every part of the eleven states that once constituted the Southern Confederacy." The members of it should
be "declared outlaws" and be "punished with death wherever
found."[3]

The legislature soon gave effect to Brownlow's recommendations in an "act to preserve the public peace," usually
called the "Ku Klux Law." Any person uniting with, asso-
ciating with or encouraging secret organizations engaged in
night prowling to the disturbance of the peace, or sheltering
and shielding the members of such an organization was to
be punished by a fine of not less than $500 and imprisonment
in the penitentiary for a term of not less than five years,
and he should be "rendered infamous." Informers were to

[1] Ku Klux Report, vol. xiii, pp. 231-2; Davis, Recon. in Fla., p. 582.
[2] Acts of Tenn., Extra Sess. of 1868, p. 5.
[3] Ibid., p. 9. For report of the legislative committee on outrages see
N. Y. Tribune, Sep. 7, 1868.

receive one-half of the fines if they were citizens; three-fourths if they were public officers, bonuses intended to serve as a fillip in the business of breaking up the outlaw bands. Any person might arrest a "Ku Klux" on sight "without process." The making of masks, robes and other disguises for the prowlers was forbidden. Any officer, before being inducted into his place, should swear that he did not belong to the Klan and had not directly or indirectly supported or countenanced the organization.

Pecuniary damages were to be assessed upon communities chargeable with neglect, or indifference, or connivance on the subject of Ku Klux outbreaks. Thus it was believed that the common purse would be reached and that the substantial tax-paying part of the population, as an economic measure, would unite to bring the evil to an end. A county which permitted a culprit wanted on a Ku Klux charge to live within its borders without arrest and punishment would be subject to an assessment of not less than $500, or more than $5,000. The sum must be paid into the state treasury for the benefit of the school fund. Furthermore the costs of prosecution might be laid upon the perpetrators of such outrages, if they were men of property. The amount of injury sustained under Ku Klux attacks should be fixed by the jury at the trial of the offender and, if it were not paid, it would be entered as a lien against his property. The price of entering a house against the owner's will was fixed at $10,000; of killing any peaceable person in the night at $20,000.[1] A committee of the Tennessee legislature appeared in Washington and presented an address to the President reciting the outrages of the Klan.[2]

Following Tennessee the Alabama legislature soon enacted a law aimed at the Ku Klux in that state. "Ample and undoubted evidence" of the existence of the organization was

---

[1] Acts of Tenn., Extra Sess. of 1868, pp. 18-23. The act was approved by the governor on Sep. 10, 1868. It was repealed in 1869.—Acts of Tenn. for 1869-70, p. 131. Cf. Lester and Wilson, The Ku Klux Klan, pp. 105, 113-23.

[2] N. Y. Tribune, Sep. 12, 1868.

at hand.[1] Fines and prison sentences were prescribed for men found in masks, or otherwise disguised, outside of their homes by day or by night. The commission of or threat to commit offenses would be punished by from five to twenty years in the penitentiary. The fact of a man's hiding his face and wearing a costume was *prima facie* evidence of guilt.[2]

A Ku Klux law was passed in Arkansas in March, 1869,[3] in North Carolina in April, 1869,[4] in Mississippi in July, 1870,[5] in South Carolina in March, 1871.[6] In at least three states—Tennessee, Alabama and Arkansas—hunting for Ku Klux with deadly weapons was made a legalized pursuit. The entire year was an "open season" for killing disguised men. They were to be shot like raccoons and foxes. Taking such lives was immune from prosecution and under the protection of the state.[7] As a further measure the governors in several states appointed special constables, employed detectives and

[1] "Whereas," the act ran, "there is in the possession of this General Assembly ample and undoubted evidence of the secret organization in many parts of this state of men who under the cover of masks and other grotesque disguises, armed with knives, revolvers and other deadly weapons, do issue from the places of their rendezvous in bands of greater or less number on foot or mounted on horse, in like manner disguised, generally in the late hours of the night to commit violence and outrages upon peaceable and law-abiding citizens, robbing and murdering them upon the highway and entering their houses, tearing them from their homes and the embrace of their families, and with violent threats and insults inflicting on them the most cruel and inhuman treatment," etc.—Acts of Ala. for 1868, pp. 444-6.
[2] Ibid. Act passed Dec. 26, 1868.
[3] Approved March 13, 1869. Its provisions were similar to those found in the law of Tennessee. It was aimed at "the secret organization known among the members thereof as the Knights of the White Camelia, but more generally known as the Ku Klux."—Acts of Ark. for 1868-9, pp. 63-9.
[4] Approved April 12, 1869. Directed against the person who should "disguise himself by painting his face, wearing any mask or any other device for the concealment of the face or person, with intent to terrify or frighten any citizen or the community or part thereof."—Acts of N. C. of 1868-9, p. 613; cf. Hamilton, Recon. in N. C., p. 483.
[5] Acts of Miss. for 1870, pp. 89-92.
[6] Statutes at Large of S. C. for 1871, pp. 559-62.
[7] This provision was kept out of the North Carolina law. To have included it would have made it "an act to legalize murder."—Hamilton, Recon. in N. C., p. 383.

offered large rewards for the apprehension and delivery to
the public authorities of persons guilty of this midnight out-
lawry. All of it was of no avail. There were few arrests
and no successful prosecution of any man for a Ku Klux outrage in any state court, and this was pronounced by Federal
officers on the ground to be "utterly impossible."[1] He could
not be brought to justice "no matter how plain the evidence."[2]

There must be recourse to military power. The Southern
commanders, either in answer to the appeals of the governors
in states which had been reconstructed, or in other cases on
their own motion, asked for troops from Washington. Their
small contingents were inadequate to meet all the demands
of the hour. Brownlow urgently called upon Thomas of the
Department of the Cumberland, who on October 1, 1868,
reported "the strange operations of a mysterious organization"
called the Ku Klux Klan which "within a few weeks had
spread over a great part of the state." He said that "organized companies of men, mounted and armed, horses and riders
being disguised, patrolled the country," carrying "terror and
dismay" everywhere. President Johnson who shared the view
of the conservative element, that conditions were much better
than they seemed, at first used his influences to prevent the
despatch of greater numbers of soldiers to the South.[3] But
such a position he could not long maintain. "Lawless and
diabolical" acts continued to be reported to Thomas and
other commanders. With the beginning of Grant's administration as President the conservative generals whom Johnson
had sought out for service in the South were, as we have seen,
replaced in favor of men Radical in their sympathies and the
arm of the Federal government was extended more freely and
with a view to fuller control.

[1] Words of the U. S. District Attorney for S. C., House Ex. Doc., 42nd
Cong. 2nd sess., no. 268, p. 19; cf. Lester and Wilson, The Ku Klux
Klan, pp. 106, 125.
[2] Words of Major Merrill in command at Yorkville, S. C., Report of
Sec. of War for 1872-3, p. 90.
[3] Report of Sec. of War for 1868-9, vol. i, pp. 144-7; Acts of Tenn.,
Extra Sess. of 1868, p. 6.

The state legislatures quite generally enacted militia laws
and bodies of local troops were organized by the Radical
governors. The special session of the general assembly which
had passed the "Ku Klux Law" in Tennessee also adopted
an "act to enforce the laws of the state," providing for the
enlistment of militia companies to be known as the "Tennessee State Guards." [1] On September 16, 1868, Brownlow
appealed for volunteers and in January, 1869, he was ready
for a vigorous military campaign against "those masked vil-
lains called Ku Klux," which he said were taking prisoners
from jails and hanging them without trial, abducting passengers from railway trains and driving men of Northern
birth from the state. He was not to be "cajoled or trifled
with." Offenders were to be tried by military commission and
punished summarily. On February 20, 1869, he proclaimed
martial law in nine counties and imposed the expense of his
policy upon the people of those portions of the state which
were in insurrection against his authority.[2]

Governor Powell Clayton was not far behind Brownlow in
an effort to enforce the law in Arkansas. Indeed his drastic
measures preceded Brownlow's. The law was openly defied
in many parts of the state. In three counties the judges were
driven from their seats. Armed men rode through the country
expelling peaceable people from their homes and burning their
houses, farm buildings and crops. Hundreds of persons, many
of them occupying prominent places in the community, were
killed. The Ku Klux organization. said the governor, was
striving to create vacancies in office "by assassination and
intimidation." Its objects were "treasonable and murderous
and subversive of all government." A militia law was passed
by the legislature and the governor called for volunteers.
They came down from the mountains, many of them mounted
for cavalry service, and on November 4, 1868, he proclaimed
martial law in ten counties. He ordered the Ku Klux to dis-

[1] Acts of Tenn., Special Sess. of 1868, pp. 23-5.
[2] Senate Doc., 57th Cong. 2nd sess., no. 209; Federal Aid in Domestic
Disturbances, pp. 118-9.

band at once; otherwise they would be "treated as outlaws." [1]
Later three more counties were declared to be in a state of
insurrection. Several skirmishes, which in some places took
on the character of pitched battles, occurred between the
militiamen and the desperadoes. A number of notorious outlaws were publicly executed and the situatior in the opinion
of the governor was so much better before the end of March
that he felt justified in restoring civil authority in all the
thirteen counties.[2]

South Carolina in an "act to suppress insurrection and rebellion" gave the governor the power to suspend the privilege
of the writ of habeas corpus. He might call out the militia
to deal with "unlawful obstructions, combinations or assemblages of persons, or rebellion against the authority of the
government of the state." [3]

So, too, in North Carolina the governor might form and
use local military associations. Any county in which the civil
authorities were unable to protect the citizens he could declare, at his discretion, in a state of insurrection.[4] Holden
issued a number of proclamations commanding the people to
forego violence. In the summer of 1870 he had reached the
conclusion that it was "all in vain." Magistrates were intimidated and rendered afraid to perform their duties; "assassination and outrage" went unpunished. To the inhabitants of
many parts of the state the approach of night was "like the
entrance into the valley of the shadow of death." Men dared
not sleep beneath their own roofs and fled to the woods for
safety.[5] In March, 1870, he declared Alamance county in
a state of insurrection and in July he proclaimed martial law

[1] Powell Clayton, Aftermath of the Civil War in Arkansas, pp. 62-5,
68-105.
[2] Ibid., pp. 164-5; cf. Senate Doc., 57th Cong. 2nd sess., no. 209, pp.
125-6.
[3] Statutes at Large of S. C. for 1868, p. 85.
[4] Acts of N. C. for 1869-70, pp. 64-6; Hamilton, Recon. in N. C., p.
485.
[5] American Annual Cyclopedia for 1870, p. 551; Hamilton, Recon. in
N. C., pp. 508-9.

in Caswell county.[1] He was confronted, said he, in reporting his action to President Grant, by "a secret, oath-bound, armed organization," hostile to the state government and the government of the United States. He could not rely upon the militia. Only a suspension of the privilege of the writ of habeas corpus and military trials would avail. The remedy would be "sharp and bloody," but it was "as indispensable as was the suppression of the rebellion."[2] Holden's course was taken amid violent opposition; it was charged that he was being influenced entirely by considerations affecting himself and the future of the Radical party in North Carolina.[3]

But the governors were in grave difficulty as soon as they adopted such measures as a means of restoring good order. If white citizens were enlisted as militiamen they would be, with few exceptions, members of or sympathizers with the Ku Klux organization. If negroes should be employed for this service few could foretell, in the excited state of society, what dire result might follow. In enrolling and officering the militia more salaried places were created for the carpetbaggers.[4] Tennessee, North Carolina,[5] Arkansas and Louisiana[6] formed companies of both black and white troops. Governor Scott in South Carolina was brought to rely entirely, perhaps perforce, if he were to have a military organization of any kind, upon the black population. Some companies of white volunteers he refused to receive; others which he enrolled must be abandoned upon the demand of the negroes. The force at one time on paper amounted, it appears, to 96,000 men and at least 20,000 were put under arms.[7]

---

[1] Senate Ex. Doc., 41st Cong. 3rd sess., no. 16, pt. 1; Hamilton, Recon. in N. C., pp. 512-5. [2] Ibid., pt. 2, p. 41.

[3] Hamilton, Recon. in N. C., pp. 482-533.

[4] The simple enrollment of the militia in South Carolina cost the state $200,000.—Article on S. C. in Why the Solid South, p. 93.

[5] The North Carolina State Militia—the "N.C.S.M.."—was now interpreted to mean the "Negro, Carpetbag, Scalawag Militia."—Hamilton, Recon. in N. C., p. 347.

[6] Warmoth had about 2,500 white and 2,500 black militiamen in service in 1872.—House Mis. Doc., 42nd Cong. 2nd sess., no. 211, p. 295.

[7] Reynolds, Recon. in S. C., pp. 137, 145, 182-3; W. L. Fleming, Sequel

The conduct of the negroes who thus were turned against the white people of the state was far from exemplary. They would march "company front" through the streets, jostling white men and insulting ladies as they passed.[1] Life on such terms, from the standpoint of the old, intelligent, respectable and propertied classes of the state, was in a fair way to become "unendurable."[2] "No more diabolical wrong" could have been committed, said ex-Governor Perry in a letter to Governor Scott, than putting powder and ball into the hands of the blacks when these were denied to the white people.[3]

Inevitably the subject would lead to action by Congress. The strange word, Ku Klux, was on every tongue. Every Radical editor and politician engaged in new denunciations of the "rebels," and, if so much were possible, exaggerated the South's lawless condition. This Ku Klux was a "hell-born cabal," said John W. Forney, which had its lodges in every Southern state.[4] It was "another secession snake," said the New York Tribune, whose fangs must be drawn by loyal power.[5] Again the rebel flag was being flaunted in the South, said Senator John Sherman. This "rebel organization" had brought about a condition which was "revolting to every instinct of humanity." In looking over the record of crime in all ages no one could name a band of men "who combined in their acts and in their purposes" more that was "diabolical."[6] The "bloody orgies" of the "fiendish organization" met the denunciations of Charles Sumner.[7] It would be "eulogy" to call such miscreants "brigands," said Representative Perry of Ohio.[8] Congressman Merriam of New York

---

of Appomattox, p. 236; Report on Public Frauds in S. C., quoted in Fleming, Doc. Hist. of Recon., vol. ii, pp. 19-80; Article on S. C. in Why the Solid South, p. 93.

[1] Reynolds, Recon. in S. C., pp. 183-5.   [2] Ibid., p. 156.

[3] Porcher, Last Chapter in the Hist. of Recon. in S. C. in Southern Hist. Soc. Papers, vol. xii, p. 176.

[4] Quoted in New Orleans Picayune, April 16, 1868.   [5] April 6, 1868.

[6] Cong. Globe, 42nd Cong. 1st sess., pp. 153, 154, 157.

[7] Ibid., 41st Cong., 2nd sess., p. 640.

[8] Ibid., 42nd Cong., 1st sess., app., p. 78.

spoke of it as a "blood dance." It was a war on defenceless
people "outvying the remorseless savagery of the tomahawk
and scalping knife." [1] The members of the Klan were "fiendish monsters and enemies of the Union," said D. H. Starbuck,
the district attorney of the United States for North Carolina.[2]
Congress began to adopt acts to "enforce" the Fourteenth
and Fifteenth Amendments. On May 31, 1870, a bill was
approved guaranteeing the voting privilege to the negroes
in the Southern states. Any one who should hinder, or obstruct, or control qualified electors in the exercise of the
franchise would be fined and imprisoned. Threat, intimidation, bribery, cheating in the registration offices and at the
polls would be stopped by Federal authority. Ku Klux and
other men in disguise, acting to prevent any one from enjoying the rights and privileges secured to him by the Constitution or the laws of the United States, were to be adjudged
guilty of felonies. On conviction the offender would be·fined
in a sum not exceeding $5,000, imprisoned for a period not
exceeding ten years, and be disabled in future from holding
public office. The whole subject was committed to the control
of the Federal district and circuit courts. United States
marshals and other officers entrusted with the making of
arrests might form posses of bystanders to aid them in the
performance of their duties, and, at need, the President might
employ the land and naval forces of the country.[3]
Summer and autumn passed without any amendment of
the conditions. A mass of material—reports of military officers stationed in the South, appeals of governors and other
civil officers of the Southern states, petitions of bodies of men
and of individuals, the sworn accounts of the sufferings of
victims of violence and abuse—had come to the President,
and on December 16, 1870, the Senate by resolution asked
for these documents. Grant forwarded them on January 13,

[1] Cong. Globe, 42nd Cong., 1st sess., p. 282.

[2] House Ex. Doc., 42nd Cong. 2nd sess., no. 268, p. 29.

[3] Cong. Globe, 41st Cong. 2nd sess., pp. 3809, 3884; ibid., app., pp.
661-2; McPherson, Hist. of Recon., pp. 546-57.

1871.[1] Four days later the Senate received from the President
another collection of papers bearing particularly upon the
acute situation in North Carolina.[2] Action ensued at once.
On January 19, the Senate agreed to appoint a committee
of five members to conduct an inquiry into conditions in the
South. The Vice President promptly designated John Scott of
Pennsylvania, Henry Wilson of Massachusetts, Zachariah
Chandler of Michigan, Benjamin F. Rice of Arkansas—all
Republicans, and Thomas F. Bayard of Delaware, a Democrat, to serve on this committee. Before long two more names
were added—James W. Nye of Nevada, Republican, and the
notorious General Frank P. Blair, after his defeat in 1868
elected a senator by the Democrats who had gained control
of the legislature of Missouri. The life of the Forty-first
Congress was nearing its end but the committee went to work
with a will, subpoenaing and examining state and Federal
officers, district attorneys, political editors, preachers, private
citizens, Ku Klux leaders, local magistrates and constables,
blacks and other men who had been "kukluxed"—all from
North Carolina. Time was not at hand for the investigation
of conditions in other states. The five Republican senators
reached the unanimous conclusion that, "as against the violence of the Ku Klux organization, the authorities of the state
cannot secure to its citizens life, liberty and the pursuit of
happiness," as enjoined by the Constitution of the United
States. The matter, as it affected North Carolina, rested
with Congress. What should be done with appeals made to
the committee from other states, which seemed to be in a like
situation, was referred to the Senate.[3]

Bayard and Blair, on their side, presented a minority report in which they said that the suggestion of the existence
of anarchy in North Carolina was "absurdly untrue." Holden
and his satrapy had been rejected by the taxpayers of the

[1] Senate Ex. Doc., 41st Cong. 3rd sess., no. 16, pt. 1.
[2] Ibid., pt. 2.
[3] This Report of Select Committee of the Senate to Investigate
Alleged Outrages in the Southern States is printed as Senate Report,
42nd Cong. 1st sess., no. 1.

state, and now Congress was asked to intervene to "force North Carolina down again under the feet of her Radical masters." [1]

The response of Congress to this inquiry, and the agitation which attended it, was an act approved by the President on February 28, 1871, amending the "Enforcement Act" of the preceding May. The provisions of that law were made more stringent in several respects. New safeguards were thrown about the registration of voters and the conduct of elections of representatives in Congress; supervisors of elections were to be appointed by the Federal courts; interference with them in the performance of their duties was made the subject of fine and imprisonment; and process was brought within the range of jurisdiction of the judiciary of the United States.[2]

The new Congress met immediately after the adjournment of the old, and in a few days the Senate and the House passed a resolution authorizing the appointment of a "Joint Committee" whose duty it should be "to inquire into the condition of the late insurrectionary states." It should consist of seven senators and fourteen representatives. The Vice President named five Republican senators—Scott, Chandler and Rice of the old committee, together with John Pool of North Carolina and Daniel D. Pratt of Indiana, and the two Democrats who had served during the North Carolina inquiry—Bayard and Blair. The Speaker of the House appointed eight Republicans—Luke P. Poland of Vermont, Horace Maynard of Tennessee, Glenni W. Scofield of Pennsylvania, John F. Farnsworth of Illinois, John Coburn of Indiana, Job E. Stevenson of Ohio, Benjamin F. Butler of Massachusetts and William E. Lansing of New York, together with six Democrats—S. S. Cox of New York, James B. Beck of Kentucky, Philadelph Van Trump of Ohio, A. M. Waddell of North Carolina, J. C. Robinson of Illinois and J. M. Hanks of Arkansas.

Meantime outrageous conditions had come to prevail in South Carolina. Many clashes between the races had oc-

[1] Senate Report, 42nd Cong. 1st sess., no. 1, pt. 2.
[2] McPherson's Handbook for 1872, pp. 3-8.

curred, due in great part to the swaggering and insolent conduct of Governor Scott's negro militia. The weeks preceding the election in October, 1870, were marked by much disorder, especially in Laurens county. A scalawag named Joseph Crews had made himself a leader of the blacks after the manner which had been adopted by Hunnicutt in Virginia and Ashburn in Georgia. Before the war this despicable white man had been a slave trader. He had evaded military service, though he had professed to be a secessionist, and now, during Reconstruction, was beguiling the negroes in order to gain their votes that he might serve his own ends under the protection of the Republican party. The militia companies were composed of the most turbulent young blacks in their respective neighborhoods and they were supported by a white constabulary, made up of men who had been hired for the service in, and were imported from the North. Crews was their leader in Laurens county and used them to promote his candidacy for office. Scott sent him large quantities of arms for distribution to the blacks and he had stored the material in a wooden building which he owned at Laurens Court House and in his barn. The militiamen, as a kind of body guard, escorted him to public meetings which he addressed. As they swung along the roads they shot at dogs and insulted the whites, both men and women. Crews himself in his speeches to the blacks, it was charged, used the most inflammatory language. He urged them to vote as often and wherever they liked. If the Republican ticket were defeated the freed people would be sent back into slavery. They should meet force with force. Matches were cheap. Even women and children could apply the torch.

Mobs were active at Newberry, then at Clinton and, on October 20, at Laurens around the building which Crews used as an armory. Firing between two men led to a general altercation. At a sign two or three thousand armed whites swarmed into the town from the surrounding country and many were killed and wounded before quiet could be restored.[1]

[1] Ku Klux Report, South Carolina Testimony, pp. 1303-30; Senate Doc., 57th Cong. 2nd sess., no. 209, pp. 119-20.

On the last day of the year, 1870, some negro militiamen in Union county met a white man, an ex-Confederate soldier, driving a wagon in a road. They used abusive language which he resented, whereupon they attacked and killed him. This unprovoked murder led to an uprising of the white people. Several blacks were arrested and lodged in jail. The building was surrounded and the prisoners were seized. Two were shot. Several escaped, again to be captured, again to be imprisoned, and again to be taken out by an armed mob which hanged them. In other counties similar conditions prevailed. Multitudes of negroes slept in the woods throughout the winter of 1870-71 in fear of their lives. The governor asked for United States troops. These were sent to Yorkville, but before they reached that place the night riders had robbed the county treasury and torn up a railway to obstruct the passage of the soldiers.[1]

The facts were laid before President Grant. On March 23, 1871, he addressed Congress in a message. "A condition of affairs" now existed in some of the states, said he, "rendering life and property insecure and the carrying of the mails and the collection of the revenue dangerous." The power of the state authorities "to correct these evils" had been exhausted; it was "not clear" that the President's authority was "sufficient for present emergencies." He, therefore, recommended legislation which would enable him to secure the enforcement of law.[2] The next day, March 24, he issued a public proclamation. He had been informed that "combinations of armed men, unauthorized by law," were "disturbing the peace and safety of the citizens of the state of South Carolina and committing acts of violence" which rendered the power of the state itself "unequal to the task of protecting life and property and securing public order." He commanded the insurgents "to disperse and retire peaceably" to their homes within twenty days.[3]

[1] Senate Reports, 42nd Cong. 2nd sess., no. 209, p. 120.
[2] Richardson, Messages and Papers of the Presidents, vol. vii, pp. 127-8.
[3] Ibid., pp. 132-3,

Shellabarger of Ohio introduced the bill in the House and it quickly made its way through both chambers. One wag, amid laughter, suggested that the Republican members should once more be sworn; they had forgotten their oaths to support the Constitution.[1] Pass the bill, said Waddell, one of the conservative representatives from North Carolina, and you would tear down the last column on which rests the still fair but disfigured temple of American liberty. What was proposed was "violent, unconstitutional and revolutionary"; it would lead to "absolute despotism."[2] As the surf "tramples down the seaweed" upon the shore, the South was to be "Yankeeized" until her people should talk through their noses, smell of codfish and acquire all the vices of the Puritans.[3] It had been "reconstructed" and "re-reconstructed" and "re-re-reconstructed" and now it was to be "re-re-re-reconstructed."[4]

But whatever might be said was dismissed as coming from "rebels" and "Copperheads." To a man the Democrats were still drinking to the old toast—

> "Damn the goose
> Which grew the quill
> That wrote the Proclamation
> Of Emancipation."[5]

More significant was the attitude of Republicans like Garfield in the House, and Schurz and Trumbull in the Senate. Garfield pronounced the bill an "extreme and unprecedented measure" which would "alarm the country." If the sword were to be sent to the South at all it should be accompanied by the olive branch.[6] There are, said Schurz, "many social disorders very difficult to cure by laws," just as there are many diseases which it is impossible to cure by medicines. Such a measure would be "an encroachment of the national authority upon the legitimate sphere of local self government." It was giving the President a power which Schurz said that

[1] Cong. Globe, 42nd Cong. 1st sess., p. 398.   [3] Ibid., p. 378.
[2] Ibid., p. 424.   [4] Ibid., p. 399.   [5] Ibid., p. 392.
          [6] Ibid., appendix, p. 155.

he "would confide to no living man," however great his confidence might be in that man's ability or fidelity.[1] What would be the need of the state governments, asked Trumbull, if the Federal government should take to itself "the entire protection of the individual in his rights of person and property." He believed that "the rights of the people, the liberties of the people, the rights of the individual" were "safest among the people themselves and not in a central government extending over a vast region of country."[2]

But voices from their own party were not more heeded by the Radicals than if it were counsel offered by the Democrats. The bill soon passed both houses by large majorities.[3] The President approved it and it became a law on April 20, 1871.[4] This was the third "Enforcement Act," which at once came to be known as the "Ku Klux Law." The activity of "unlawful combinations," so it ran, might be deemed a "rebellion against the government of the United States," and while these conditions existed in any state, or portion of a state, the President might suspend the privilege of the writ of habeas corpus therein, and proclaim martial law. Those having knowledge of "wrongs conspired to be done," if they made no motion to prevent them, were rendered liable in a pecuniary way to the person injured, or his legal representatives.

A fortnight later the President issued another proclamation directing public attention to the act which Congress had passed and he had approved. It was, said he, "a law of extraordinary importance." He would act only reluctantly, but if the occasion arose he would "not hesitate to exhaust the powers" vested in him, "whenever and wherever it shall become necessary to do so."[5]

The South's reception of the plan to investigate its social and political state by a Congressional committee and to enforce order through the "Ku Klux Law" was far from hos-

[1] Cong. Globe, 42nd Cong. 1st sess., pp. 687, 690.
[2] Ibid., p. 579; Horace White, Life of Trumbull, pp. 356-8.
[3] Cong. Globe, 42nd Cong. 1st sess., pp. 522, 808, 831.
[4] Ibid., app., pp. 335-6.
[5] Richardson, vol. vii, pp. 134-5.

pitable. The committee was generally called the "Outrage Committee." Its members were "corpse-hunting, graveyard-ransackers." The Radicals had defeated Seymour and Blair in 1868 by eloquent accounts of outrages in the South; if they could they meant again in 1872 to elect their candidates on this issue.[1] Moreover, it was unconstitutional to appoint committees of Congress to "investigate matters over which the states have sole control." [2] President Grant's proclamation of May, 1871, announcing his intention of declaring martial law in the South was "barefaced" and "incredible." The republic had become an "empire"; states were being ridden over; rights "once as sacred as liberty itself" were being destroyed; "military despotism" would hurl the people into a "yawning gulf." [3]

The Joint Committee was organized for work in Washington on April 20, the very day the President signed the "Ku Klux Law." Sub-committees were appointed to proceed to the South to take testimony in state capitals and in towns located in or near districts where riots and other race disturbances had occurred. The examination of witnesses occupied several months. Men like Wade Hampton, Senator Chesnut, ex-Governor Orr and Attorney General Chamberlain were called in South Carolina; Linton Stephens, General John B. Gordon, ex-Governor Joseph E. Brown and Benjamin H. Hill, in Georgia; Judge Busteed, ex-Governor Parsons, General Clanton, General Pettus and Governor Lindsay, in Alabama; and General N. B. Forrest, now building railroads in Mississippi, reputed to be the head and front of the secret order—together with numbers of Southern leaders of less distinction, planters, lawyers, teachers, clergymen, editors, "poor whites," "carpet-baggers," "scalawags," negroes, both male and female, who had been scourged, the ruffians who were charged with whip-

[1] Southerner and Commercial of Rome, Ga., Feb. 17, 1871, quoted in Ku Klux Report, Georgia Testimony, p. 886.
[2] Atlanta Constitution, quoted in Ku Klux Report, Georgia Testimony, p. 965.
[3] Ibid., quoted in Ku Klux Report, Georgia Testimony, pp. 995-6.

ping them—in all several hundreds of persons drawn from every social class. They were questioned and cross questioned by Republican and Democratic committeemen in turn.

The yield in proof of guilt was amazingly small. It had been said that the Ku Klux was a society whose members were bound by oath to protect one another. They would not inform upon a "brother." As legal officers they would not prosecute him. They would not take the witness stand against him in a court room. They would not vote to convict him if they were members of a jury to judge his case. Therefore, so it was said, hope of breaking up the order by regular process, through the established agencies of local government, could not be entertained.

All of this was abundantly confirmed by the dense ignorance concerning the whole subject of every Southern man who was brought before the committee and the sub-committees. The existence of such an order was denied. Men who were part and parcel of it perjured themselves for hours at a time as they parried the thrusts of the examiners. The secret society to which they belonged, if an admission of membership was extracted from any of them, bore another name and had good purposes. They never were able to remember who had asked them to join or had initiated them into the order. If a name or two should be given it was of men who were dead or had emigrated to Brazil.

Why were the facts not reported to the prosecuting officers? Why were arrests not ordered and made? Why were culprits not tried and convicted? Why were murderers not hanged? Their identity could not be established. How, indeed, could it be that the most hideous of outrages were committed in an intelligent community without one inhabitant coming forward with the name of the perpetrators of the deed? Were there not men who sold the stuff and women who fashioned it to disguise the outlaws? The raids were made on horse back. Whence came the animals? Were there not jaded steeds with the lather and sweat upon their flanks in many a stable the next day? Not a gleam of light was thrown upon any phase of the subject by the volume upon volume of testimony. The two or three turncoats who had "puked," [1] i.e., who had dared to tell what they had seen in meetings of the Ku Klux camps were inconspicuous persons in possession of so little knowledge that their revelations were of small account. If those who were whipped and shot were fornicators and adulterers who had done affront to society—in many cases, so the Republican members of the committee believed, an excuse invented after the fact—whence came the South's fastidious morality? Did not the griffes, mulattoes, quadroons and other men of all degrees of mixed blood to be met with everywhere attest in an indubitable way to the carelessness of the people as to the relations between the races? Marriage between the blacks and whites, indeed the mere association now was abominated, yet every light-colored negro over the length and breadth of the South was proof of its previous immoral living covering a long period of time. It was strange enough to see a sudden new development of feeling about the cohabitation of the races, so quick and sensitive that it called for the organization of parties of armed men who must scourge and slay to uphold the fine standards of Southern society.

The testimony went around in a circle and at length it was incorporated, together with the reports in thirteen volumes.[2] The investigation had covered inquiries in six of the "insurrectionary states"—North and South Carolina, Georgia, Mississippi, Alabama and Florida, and resulted, as could have been foreseen, in two vigorous statements in which diametrically opposite and wholly partisan conclusions were reached. By the majority [3] protective measures in the form of Federal law supported by the Federal power were recommended. These should be continued until there remained "no further

---

[1] Reynolds, Recon. in S. C., p. 198.
[2] Senate Reports, 42nd Cong. 2nd sess., no. 41, pts. 1-13; House Reports of same Congress, no. 22, pts. 1-13.   [3] Ibid., pt. 1, pp. 1-100.

doubt of the actual suppression and disarming of this widespread and dangerous conspiracy." The committee urged the
people of the North to exercise patience and forbearance in
their judgments. The existence side by side of the planter
class, which had been accustomed to govern the state and to
hold absolute sway over their black and white dependents,
the poor white element which felt itself to be degraded by
the elevation of the blacks to political equality with them, and
the negroes now ruling this former master class—begot preju-
dices and resulted in "disorders" to which Northern communities were "strangers." The strong feeling which had led
to the rebellion and which had been so long and gradual in
its growth could not be expected to subside "at once nor in
years." More than "reluctant obedience," the North was
reminded, might not be hoped for, but "less than obedience"
the government would not accept.

The minority report was a Democratic stump speech.[1] The
investigation had not touched Virginia, Tennessee, Arkansas,
Texas and Louisiana which presumably, therefore, so it was
concluded, were "free from the suspicion of lawlessness."
Whatever violence there may have been in the past few years
in the South was ascribed to the unparallelled corruptions
of the Republican party which were dwelt upon in detail and
at great length. In the states infested by bands of disguised
marauders these had not been seen in more than 40 of the
420 counties, on which account Federal intervention under
the Enforcement Acts was the "grossest outrage, the foulest
calumny ever perpetrated or circulated upon or against a
helpless people by their rulers."[2] The national election of
1872 impended and the minority placed the responsibility
upon the shoulders of the "imperious, not to say imperial
President."[3] He was submitting himself to "the dictates
of party vengeance." He was betraying complete indifference
to the "terrible results" likely to follow "the maladministra-
tion of affairs in the Southern states."[4]

[1] Senate Reports, 42nd Cong. 2nd sess., no. 41, pt. 1, pp. 290-588.
[2] Ibid., p. 292.   [3] Ibid., p. 292.   [4] Ibid., p. 588.

Meanwhile the President, after his proclamation of May 3, 1871, patiently awaited the course of events. He continued to receive alarming accounts of the condition of affairs in various parts of South Carolina. To satisfy himself as to the truthfulness of the reports he requested Attorney General Akerman to visit the disturbed communities. In nine counties, this officer said, there were hostile combinations embracing at least two-thirds of the "active white men" resident there. A majority of the remaining one-third were in sympathy with these combinations which were a part, he alleged, of "a grand system of criminal associations pervading most of the Southern states." Their oaths as members of an order were higher obligations than lawful oaths taken before civil magistrates; wherefore witnesses were terrified, juries controlled and courts intimidated.[1]

Grant hesitated no longer. "Unlawful combinations and conspiracies" having long existed in nine counties of South Carolina—Spartanburg, York, Marion, Chester, Laurens, Newberry, Fairfield, Lancaster and Chesterfield—he, on October 12, 1871, commanded all persons concerned to disperse within five days and deliver their arms to the United States marshal or his deputies, or to the officers of the United States army on garrison duty within the affected district.[2] As his directions were not obeyed he, on October 17th, suspended the privilege of the writ of habeas corpus in the nine counties which he had earlier named and prepared the way for summary military arrests.[3] A few weeks later he freed Marion county from martial law and extended it to Union County instead.[4]

The first important trials under the "Ku Klux Law" were held at Oxford, Miss., in June, 1871. The town was filled with strangers—prisoners, witnesses, soldiers—and a riot was narrowly averted.[5] Indictments were found against twenty

---

[1] Richardson, Messages and Papers, vol. vii, pp. 163-4.
[2] Ibid., pp. 135-6.   [3] Ibid., pp. 136-8.   [4] Ibid., pp. 138-41.
[5] Edward Mayes, Life of L. Q. C. Lamar, pp. 131-4.

or thirty night riders.[1] So much brought fear into the hearts of evil-doers.

Now that martial law had been proclaimed in South Carolina something akin to a panic prevailed among the "conspirators" in that state. Federal troops usually accompanied the deputies while they were making arrests to obviate the possibility of resistance and subsequent rescue of the culprits by their friends.[2] Seeing that there was no escape from the net which had been spread for them many absconded, some of them to Mexico and the West Indian islands, while others came in and voluntarily surrendered to the authorities.[3] The trials were begun in the United States district court at Greenville and were continued in the circuit court in Columbia.[4] Many of the offenders were found guilty and were sentenced to pay heavy fines or to serve long terms in prison.[5] Hundreds were arrested in North Carolina to be tried before the United States courts in Raleigh in an effort to improve the situation in that state.[6]

Again charges of partisanship and corrupt management ran through the South. Witnesses whom it was desired to favor, so it was said, were summoned from long distances under subpœnas that they might receive the per diem and mileage fees. Those who were put under arrest were often very poor men. They were accompanied in their distress by their wives and children, who were compelled to live away from their homes for tedious periods at their own expense. Vacant lots in the court house towns frequently were covered with tents to shelter the unfortunate people.[7] "Never since the reign of

---

[1] Ku Klux Report, Miss. Testimony, pp. 936 et seq.

[2] Report of Sec. of War for 1872-3, vol. i, p. 89.

[3] House Ex. Doc., 42nd Cong. 2nd sess., no. 55, p. 5.

[4] Ku Klux Report, South Carolina Testimony, pp. 1615 et seq.

[5] Fleming, Doc. Hist. of Recon., vol. ii, p. 128. For detailed accounts of the numbers arrested and tried see Reports of Attorney General for 1871 and 1872, House Ex. Doc., 42nd Cong. 2nd sess., no. 55, and Senate Ex. Doc., 42nd Cong. 3rd sess., no. 33.

[6] Ku Klux Report, North Carolina Testimony, pp. 417 et seq.; Hamilton, Recon. in N. C., pp. 576-81.

[7] Edward Mayes, Life of L. Q. C. Lamar, p. 165.

judicial tyranny in the days of Jeffreys," said the Jackson, Miss., Clarion 'were such outrages practised in the name of justice." [1]

Some of the hardships imposed upon the prisoners and their families and friends were unavoidable. The facilities for the disposition of cases, the United States district attorney for South Carolina complained, were "utterly inadequate." The courts were choked with them. The judges could not hear a fifth of all that awaited their attention.[2] Congress must increase the number of Federal judges in the South or "permit most of the prosecutions to fail." [3] The Ku Klux Committee also recommended such a measure in order to "leave no hope of impunity to criminals by the law's delay." [4]

Bodies of Federal troops continued to be moved from place to place in the interest of good order. In December, 1871, three white men killed a negro in Chicot county in Arkansas. The murderers were taken out of jail and lynched by a mob of black men who were assisted by some of Governor Clayton's "irresponsible militia companies," and the Secretary of War was asked for soldiers to preserve the peace at Chicot Landing.[5] In January, 1872, the United States district attorney for the northern district of Mississippi said that five witnesses before the United States grand jury had been killed there within a few weeks. "Men of the highest standing" were refugees from their homes. The prosecution of offenders and the enforcement of law were interfered with. A "perfect reign of terror" prevailed in portions of Lee and Union counties. Attorney General Williams asked for the assistance of the Secretary of War and cavalrymen were drawn from Missouri for service in the disaffected region.[6]

In August, 1871, the Federal troops had intervened to dis-

[1] Edward Mayes, Life of L. Q. C. Lamar, p. 166, for quotation.
[2] Report of Sec. of War for 1872-3, vol. i, p. 90; House Ex. Doc., 42nd Cong. 2nd sess., no. 55, p. 5.
[3] House Ex. Doc., 42nd Cong. 2nd sess., no. 268, pp. 19, 42.
[4] Ku Klux Report, vol. i, p. 100.
[5] House Ex. Doc., 42nd Cong. 2nd sess., no. 209, pp. 23-4.
[6] Ibid., pp. 26-34.

perse a mob of 4,000 or 5,000 persons who had gathered around
the custom house in New Orleans. When the legislature met
in January, 1872, demonstrations which promised to bring on
bloody riots were resumed. Governor Warmoth had gained
the enmity of a faction, led by a number of Federal office
holders, called the "custom house party," who pretended to
be "reformers." A group of members of the lower house of
the legislature friendly to Warmoth were in session at the
capitol which was guarded by 600 men armed with muskets
and artillery under General Longstreet. A rival body directed
by a man named Carter met in another hall.[1] To break a
quorum and prevent the senate from organizing, Collector of
the Port Casey, a brother-in-law of President Grant, put a
revenue cutter at the disposal of several members in sympathy
with the "custom house party" leaders, and for a week, at
public expense, they cruised about in the Mississippi River.[2]
For a month or more the city was on the verge of civil war.

The vigorous supervision exercised by the Federal government in all parts of the South was instantly effective. The
example made of culprits in the United States courts had a
"most salutary effect."[3] The rapid movements of the troops
into disturbed neighborhoods intimidated outlaws, and soon
it could be said with truth that the power of the Ku Klux Klan
was broken.[4] Political disorders and race riots continued, but
they were not planned and executed by bands of men held
together by secret oaths in revolutionary clubs.

[1] Senate Doc., 57th Cong. 2nd sess., no. 209, pp. 146-7.
[2] House Reports, 42nd Cong. 2nd sess., no. 92, pp. 16 et seq.
[3] Attorney General Williams in Annual Report dated January, 1873,
in Senate Ex. Doc., 42nd Cong. 3rd sess., no. 33, p. 11.
[4] House Ex. Doc., 42nd Cong. 2nd sess., no. 268, pp. 29-30.

CHAPTER XIV

THE ALABAMA CLAIMS

THE war had left behind it in all parts of the North a vast legacy of bad feeling for England. No time was lost by the State Department, when hostilities were seen to be imminent, in communicating with our legation in London. Action of the British government favorable to the South would be forestalled, if this were possible.[1] Three representatives of the new Confederacy, W. L. Yancey, Judge Rost and Dudley Mann, were soon on the ground.[2] Their arrival preceded that of our new minister, Charles Francis Adams, and, while Seward was writing despatches to say that he would not receive communications from a government which should hold the Southern rebels to be lawful belligerents, and that privateers would be treated as pirates and their commanders and crews hanged as such,[3] the British ministry was conferring with France on the subject of a proclamation of neutrality. This came at once. On May 13, 1861, only a few days after the news of the attack on Fort Sumter had reached England, the Queen announced that she had accorded belligerent rights to the Southern insurgents.[4] France soon followed with her declaration and other governments made like concessions to the rebels.

Action was taken on "mere rumor." Jefferson Davis had said that he would issue letters of marque. President Lincoln had declared a blockade of the Southern coasts, but official notification of this event had not yet come to hand. No in-

[1] Correspondence concerning Claims against Great Britain, vol. i, pp. 7-9. Hereafter referred to as "Corr."
[2] Cf. Diary of Benj. Moran, Proceedings of Mass. Hist. Soc., vol. 48, p. 441. [3] Corr., vol. i, pp. 51-2, 62-71.
[4] British Case in Geneva Arbitration, vol. i, pp. 215-8.

quiries were instituted, no information was asked for.[1] Minister Adams would arrive in London in a few hours, but the proceedings were to be hurried through before he should come upon the scene.[2] Beyond any kind of doubt there was a show of eagerness in the matter which was unfriendly. Particularly did England's action wound and rankle, since it had come at a time when the North still believed that they would deal quickly with secession and in a few weeks stamp it out.

When the portentous shots were fired upon the flag of the country in Charleston harbor Captain J. D. Bulloch of the United States Navy was in command of a mail steamer at New Orleans. A Georgian, ready to "go with his state," he was asked by the new government at Montgomery to proceed to Europe where he was to contract for the purchase or construction of cruisers, to be used in breaking the blockade and in harrying Northern commerce. He ran his boat back to New York, returned home and, perfecting his plans for the service to which he had been assigned, proceeded at once by way of Louisville and Detroit to Canada, where he found passage out of Montreal. Early in June he was in Liverpool where credits were established and complete war, naval and fiduciary agencies of the rebel government were organized.[3]

A statute dating from 1819, called the Foreign Enlistment Act, governed England's attitude as a neutral power.[4] Bulloch sought advice as to its meaning. It was asserted that the loose terms of this old law would permit a belligerent to build a ship in a British yard, if this ship were not at the same time supplied with guns and other equipment appertaining

[1] This conclusion is not affected by a request for information at the American legation in London at a time when it was as yet without advices on the point. (Moran's Diary, Proceedings of Mass. Hist. Soc., vol. 48, pp. 238-9 note.)

[2] Mr. Adams left Boston on May 1 and reached Liverpool on the morning of the 13th, arriving in London on the afternoon of that day. The morning papers on the 14th printed the Queen's proclamation. (Corr., vol. iii, pp. 660-61 note; Case of the U. S. in Geneva Arbitration, vol. i, pp. 25-9, 30-31.)

[3] Bulloch, Secret Service of the Confederate States, vol. i, pp. 52-4; Geneva Arbitration, vol. i, p. 91; Corr., vol. vi, pp. 181 et seq.

[4] For text of the act see Corr., vol. iv, p. 86, and vol. vii, pp. 1-9.

to a war vessel. The mere act of construction did not contravene the statute. Nor did the separate and complementary act of manufacturing and furnishing batteries and munitions for the vessel, taken by itself, constitute a violation of the law.[1] All then was simple enough—the finished ship could be built, and launched, and sent to sea; the war material could be forwarded in another vessel simultaneously and, coming together at some point one marine league distant from the British shore, the guns could be put in place and the cruiser could be transferred to the belligerent's flag ready for its destructive career. Here was a situation which all could comprehend. Though it bore "a close family resemblance to piracy"[2] it was a course of conduct which was defended by England's cabinet officers, her law officers, her newspaper press, and the way for the Confederate agent was clear.[3]

Bulloch made haste to order of a firm of shipbuilders named Miller in Liverpool, through Fawcett, Preston and Co., a wooden screw steamer designed for the Confederate naval service. The contract was written in his name. The keel was laid at once and the ship was known in the dockyard as the *Oreto*. She was completed in March, 1862, the agent paid for her and received her, and, under the British flag with a British captain and crew, who gave it out that she was bound for Palermo, she put to sea. The "fact of her true destination was notorious all over Liverpool."[4] Instead of making the trip to the Mediterranean she proceeded to Nassau in the Bahamas, "consigned" as the *Manassas*,[5] where she was to meet her commander, Captain J. N. Maffitt, a young

[1] Bulloch's adviser is said to have been an excellent English lawyer named Mellish, afterward Lord Justice.—Sir Roundell Palmer, Family and Personal Memorials, vol. ii, p. 417.

[2] C. F. Adams, Lee at Appomattox, p. 40.

[3] If Bulloch were doing only what was lawful, as he was assured by high authority that he was, the subterfuge and trickery to which he was obliged to resort should have been unnecessary. If these were a belligerent's rights in England he was excusable in thinking that at times he was treated with small consideration by the British government. See his Secret Service of the Confederate States in Europe.

[4] Corr., vol. i, p. 241.   [5] Ibid., vol. vi, p. 83.

United States naval officer, like Bulloch gone over to the Confederacy, who promised the Confederate Secretary of War that his "whole soul" would be "devoted to giving éclat to our cause and annoyance to the enemy." [1]

At the same time a consort, containing her equipment, was despatched from England to the same place. After thirty-seven days the ship reached port where, however, the United States consul had been active. He complained to the colonial government and, after much difficulty, caused her to be detained. Her purposes were "notorious to every one." [2] But she was shortly released by a decree of the vice-admiralty court, after proceedings which our consul declared to be "a burlesque on justice and neutrality," [3] to be cleared out as a vessel in ballast destined for St. John, N. B., and Maffitt, the armament and the cruiser were brought together off Green Cay, a small desert island on the edge of the Bahama Bank, about 60 miles from Nassau. There the guns were transferred to the vessel, Maffitt took command, the Southern flag was hoisted at her peak and she was renamed the *Florida* to start away upon her spectacular career.

But under the circumstances connected with her leaving Nassau Maffitt had not succeeded in assembling a sufficient number of men, and in the transshipment some essential parts of the equipment were lost or mislaid. Fever broke out on board. The captain himself was stricken, and, unable to make the ship effective, he ran her through the blockade into Mobile Bay. [4] She was much injured by gun fire, as she passed the patrols, and could not be made ready for a re-

---

[1] Corr., vol. vi, p. 236.   [2] Ibid., p. 260.

[3] Ibid., p. 250. See ibid., pp. 262 et seq., for proceedings. "Usually," says Sir Spencer Walpole, "the finding of a court should be respected until it has been reversed," but this one, he thinks, could not be "defended on this ground," since it was condemned at Geneva by Sir Alexander Cockburn, an authority whose judgment was "certainly not tainted with any unfriendly disposition" toward England.—Hist. of Twenty-Five Years, vol. ii, p. 47.

[4] U. S. Commander Preble's account of the affair in Corr., vol. vi, p. 332.

sumption of service until January, 1863, when she successfully dashed out under cover of a norther. Sailing back and forth across the shipping lanes she captured no less than 55 prizes which she sank, burned or bonded,[1] until compelled to seek refuge in Brest for rest and repairs.

Her performances created a veritable panic in maritime circles in New York and New England. The insurance premium was advanced. American merchants sought British registry to save their property. After refitting the ship Maffitt retired on account of broken health, and, under a new commander, she proceeded on her course, until, anchored in the port of Bahia, under the protection of the Brazilian government, she one night was deliberately rammed by the U. S. corvette *Wachusett*. It was "assassination," said Bulloch.[2] Seward admitted in his correspondence with Brazil that such action was "unauthorized, unlawful and indefensible."[3] But the nation rejoiced, the ship, having been towed up to Hampton Roads, was allowed to founder there, and reparation ended in apology.

Meantime a vessel which was to lead a still more famous career had been put under contract at the Laird yards in Birkenhead, on the other bank of the Mersey at Liverpool. She, too, was to be delivered to Bulloch. Her cost would be about a quarter of a million dollars. Her dockyard number was 290 (the 290th ship which Lairds had built) and under this name she was the subject of manifold comment and speculation. When she was launched she was christened the *Enrica* and was ready for her trial trip in July, 1862. The work of construction had proceeded without concealment of her ownership. Bulloch himself often boarded her, though the ship was closed to others. He selected her cabin fitings.[4] All seemed to go well with his enterprise. In reviewing his operations afterward he was pleased to boast that "no mystery or disguise was attempted,"[5] but he had for-

[1] Bulloch, vol. i, p. 178. [2] Ibid., p. 185.
[3] Ibid., p. 217. [4] Corr., vol. iii, pp. 3, 10.
[5] Bulloch, vol. i, p. 229.

gotten his experiences with the watchful and energetic American consul at Liverpool, Thomas H. Dudley of New Jersey, who had come to England soon after Minister Adams to take the place vacated by Beverly Tucker of Virginia, a partisan of the Confederacy. Dudley, secured legal advice, employed detectives and assembled statements and affidavits for use in proof of the character of the vessel.

Bulloch, who seems to have had timely notice of the proceedings,[1] made haste to get his ship out of reach of the authorities. On July 29, 1862, he decked her in colors, invited a number of guests, both men and women, to come on board and, amid "music and frolic," [2] under pretense of another trial of her sailing qualities, departed. At the end of the day they were informed that the ship would remain out all night for further tests and they were sent ashore in a tug, whereupon she was headed for a bay on the Welsh coast to take on seamen and supplies. Early on the morning of the 31st she started up the Irish Sea, Bulloch himself debarking at the Giant's Causeway, while she rounded the north of Ireland on her way to her rendezvous, a quiet little bay on the east side of Terceira, one of the Azore Islands. There she would meet a barque, the *Agrippina*, laden with her guns and other war equipment, which at about the same time slipped out of the Thames.

Bulloch himself was to have commanded the *290*, but plans were changed. Captain Raphael Semmes had been harrying the United States merchant fleet in the *Sumter*, a passenger boat which had been running between New Orleans and Havana. This vessel, converted into a cruiser, had escaped from the mouth of the Mississippi through the blockade early in the war, making some eighteen captures before she had been compelled to put into Gibraltar for repairs, where, it being impracticable to continue her in the service,[3] she was sold. Semmes was at Nassau on his way home when he was

[1] Bulloch, vol. i, pp. 238, 251, 261; Diary of B. Moran in Proceedings of Mass. Hist. Soc., vol. 48, pp. 481-2, 483.

[2] Sumner's Works, vol. xiii, p. 66.

[3] Cf. Semmes, Cruise of the Alabama and the Sumter, p. 94.

intercepted with orders to report to Bulloch in Liverpool to take command of the *290*, and upon his arrival the two men together proceeded to the Azores. The plans were executed without mishap and on August 24, at the appointed place, the *290*, later the *Enrica*, became the *Alabama*.[1] The white ensign with the blue cross was unfurled in her rigging. Semmes set foot upon a deck which he was to tread for nearly two years, during which time, without the help of the telegraph to locate her, the cruiser defied all her pursuers, in voyages north and south of the Equator on the American coast, in mid-Atlantic, off the shores of Europe and Africa, in the Indian Ocean and as far eastwardly as an island off the coast of French Indo-China in the China Sea.

It was in June, 1864, that she limped [2] into Cherbourg, of no further use without going into dry dock for a general refit. The *Kearsarge*, a United States ship under command of Captain Winslow, was at Flushing, not far distant, and came down the channel. Unprepared though he was, Semmes brought his boat out of the roadstead, and, after an historic engagement, the *Alabama* was overpowered and sunk. From September 6, 1862, when she captured and made a bonfire of the *Ocmulgee*, the first of a number of whalers which she found near the Azores, until April 27, 1864, when the *Tycoon*, intercepted on the way from New York to San Francisco, was burned off the coast of Africa, she had taken 65 or 70 American ships.

For some time the Confederate naval authorities had been contemplating the despatch of a cruiser to the North Pacific to scatter the New England whalers which repaired to those waters. But the Confederacy was now sorely pressed for

[1] A proceeding which Minister Adams described to Seward as "the change of the chrysalis 290 into the butterfly Alabama."—Corr., vol. iii, p. 43.

[2] Semmes, half poet and half warrior, living amid natural beauties during the day and studying the starry sky at night, likened his ship at this period of her career to "the weary foxhound limping back after a long chase, footsore and longing for quiet and repose."—Bulloch, vol. i, p. 278.

money and the enterprise must await more favorable days. Bulloch had under observation in the fall of 1863 a full-rigged ship, with auxiliary steam power, which was being built in a yard on the Clyde. She was called the *Sea King*, but he was without means of buying her and she proceeded on her maiden voyage for a British owner to India. Upon her return the *Alabama's* skeleton lay at the bottom of the English Channel and he was pressed by the government at Richmond to find a ship to take up the work which she could not continue. He accordingly entrusted to an agent, whose identity none could suspect, the duty of purchasing the *Sea King*, and she was cleared out for Bombay. The familiar device of sending away a tender, or supply vessel, at the same time was again successful. The equipment was transferred near an uninhabited island hard by Madeira. Confederate Lieutenant Waddell took command. The *Sea King* became the *Shenandoah* and, before any one knew what Bulloch was about, she was off for Australia on her way to the whaling grounds, capturing and lighting the skies with American merchantmen as she went. For weeks after the war had ended her cruise was continued, since she was out of communication with the world, and it was November, 1865, before she was back in Liverpool, where Waddell, "without a government," surrendered her into the hands of the British officers of customs, who in due time made her over to the United States.[1]

Commander M. F. Maury, who was a scientist rather than the practical and efficient naval man Bulloch proved himself to be, also was commissioned by Secretary Mallory to procure ships in Europe to prey upon the commerce of the United States. In March, 1863, he purchased on the Clyde a new iron screw steamer, the *Japan*. She cleared from Greenock for the East Indies in ballast. Her guns met her off the

[1] The ship came to New York, where she was knocked down at auction to the Sultan of Zanzibar for his use as a private yacht. But he was unable to support such a luxury and she went into the tropical trade. In 1879 she struck a coral reef in the Indian Ocean, where she was left to crumble to her death.—Bulloch, Secret Service, vol. ii, p. 187; Corr., vol. vi, p. 706.

French island of Ushant. She became the *Virginia*, and then the *Georgia*, making some captures, but her type ill fitted her for the service, and, after a few months, she returned to Liverpool where she passed through the formality of a sale. Under British registry she was soon converted into a blockade runner.

The rebel cruisers had burned or, when destruction was not practicable or politic, had bonded their prizes; in some cases they had fitted out captured vessels as tenders which set forth independently as harriers of American shipping. All told it is estimated that the Confederate privateers accounted for more than 250 ships, nearly all of them having fallen victims of three—the *Alabama*, the *Florida* [1] and the *Shenandoah*.

The British government throughout our Civil War was in the hands of the Liberal party, with Lord Palmerston serving as Prime Minister and Lord John Russell [2] as Secretary of State for Foreign Affairs. No inquiry into the speech and writing of the period can furnish us with ground to believe that anywhere in England in the first years of the war, except in a few uninfluential circles, there was aught but open and unreserved friendliness for the South. The public men of the country generally were pro-Southern.[3] While Palmerston avoided distinct public expressions of opinion,[4] at least two members of his cabinet, Lord Russell and W. E. Gladstone, Minister of the Exchequer, exercised much less care. Russell said at Newcastle in October, 1861, and again in Parliament in 1864 that the war was a struggle between empire and independence; it was the war of 1776 over again.[5]

---

[1] Six millions of dollars, Maffitt wrote to Bulloch from the Florida while she was still at sea in April, 1863, would "not make good the devastation this steamer has committed." (Corr., vol. ii, p. 629.)

[2] For whom an earldom was created in 1861.

[3] There were so few exceptions as to make notable the cases of John Bright, Richard Cobden, John Stuart Mill and W. E. Forster.

[4] Cf., however, declarations by him cited in Geneva Arbitration, vol. i, pp. 42-3; Bulloch, Secret Service, vol. i, p. 307; Diary of B. Moran, Proceedings of Mass. Hist. Soc., vol. 48, pp. 442-3.

[5] Corr., vol. i, p. 220; Geneva Arbitration, vol. i, p. 43.

400 GLADSTONE'S SYMPATHIES

In 1862 he declared in debate in the House of Lords that the area of the American republic was great enough to support two independent nations, and he hoped the people would agree to a peaceful separation.[1] He wrote as late as in 1863 that the success of the North would be a "great calamity."[2]

Gladstone in a speech at Newcastle on October 7, 1862, satisfying himself that the South had made an army, that they were making a navy[3] and what was "more than either," that they had "made a nation,"[4] added in the House of Commons on June 30, 1863, that the reunion of the two sections was unattainable, in which opinion he knew that he was supported by the "unanimous" feeling of Great Britain. There was no "real or serious ground for doubt as to the issue of the contest."[5] Lord Derby, leader of the Conservative party, spoke in the same sense. The "restoration of the Union," he declared, was "absolutely impossible."[6] It seemed to Cobden early in 1863 that nineteen-twentieths of the people of the upper classes in London were on the side of the South.[7] Bulloch found the proportion to be five out of seven in the middle and upper classes throughout the country.[8] Nine-tenths of the Tories and almost as many Liberals were pro-Southern, said the London Saturday Review.[9] Bulloch had

[1] Corr., vol. i, p. 235.
[2] Cf. C. F. Adams, Lee at Appomattox, pp. 64-5; Hackett, Reminiscences, p. 40; Geneva Arbitration, vol. i, p. 41.
[3] If instead of saying that the South were making a navy Gladstone had said that England was making one for her it would have been "nearer the truth," Consul Dudley wrote to Seward on Oct. 14, 1862.—Dudley Papers.
[4] Geneva Arbitration, vol. i, p. 41. "There spoke the spirit of the Liverpool slave trader and the Confederate bondholder," said a writer in Fraser's Magazine, "rather than of the English statesman and Chancellor of the Exchequer."—Issue for June, 1872.
[5] Geneva Arbitration, vol. i, p. 43; cf. C. F. Adams, op. cit., pp. 64-5. Gladstone's attitude toward the North during the war is explained as favorably as it may be in Morley's Life of Gladstone, vol. ii, pp. 68-86.
[6] Walpole, History of 25 Years, vol. ii, p. 58.
[7] Speeches, vol. ii, p. 103; cf. newspaper quotations in Adams, op. cit., pp. 75-8.
[8] Secret Service, vol. i, p. 294; cf. Sir R. Palmer, Family and Personal Memorials, vol. ii, p. 438. [9] Issue of Jan. 18, 1863.

never met an army or navy man in England who did not
sympathize with the South.[1] G. W. P. Bentinck, a member
of Parliament, declared that in his travels over the kingdom,
which had been very extensive, he had seen not one Englishman who did not say—"My wishes are with the Southerners."[2]

Liverpool in particular was a hotbed of anti-Northern sentiment.[3] There sympathy for the South was "almost universal."[4] "I think sometimes," Dudley wrote to Seward, "that
the whole community is banded together to assist them [the
Southern people] and to baffle us";[5] the merchants of
the city as late as in 1864 were still petitioning the government to recognize the independence of the Confederacy.[6]
Manchester and Lancashire generally, tied to the South by
bonds of trade, now deprived of the cotton for their spindles
and looms, made no attempt to conceal their sympathies.
With many, in truth, it was a profoundly grave matter.
The Liverpool Daily Post said that thousands of persons
in and about that city were "dying a lingering death for want
of food."[7] In December, 1862, half a million persons were
living upon the relief they could procure from the local rates
and private charity.[8] Flour for bread was forwarded by generous men in our Northern states to save the poor from starvation, yet the sentiments of the people underwent little altera-
tion.

Consul Dudley, for his protection, often disguised himself
when he went upon the streets. Skulls and cross bones were
chalked upon the walls of his house. Once a window of his

[1] Secret Service, vol. ii, p. 303.
[2] London Morning Post, Nov. 4, 1862, quoted in Adams, op. cit.,
pp. 63-4; cf. Diary of B. Moran, Proceedings of Mass. Hist. Soc., vol.
48, p. 439.   [3] Cf. Adams, op. cit., p. 76.
[4] Dudley Papers date of April 26, 1862.
[5] August 15, 1863, in Dudley Papers.   [6] Corr., vol. vi, p. 152.
[7] Corr., vol. ii, p. 370; cf. Wemyss Reid, Life of W. E. Forster, vol. i,
p. 354.
[8] M. Bernard, Neutrality of Great Britain during the American Civil
War, p. 469; cf. Dudley Papers, letter from the consulate, under date
of Aug. 29, 1862.

home was stoned in order that a mob might reach an American flag hanging inside.[1]

The tone of public feeling was not better in the British colonies, especially in the Bermudas and Bahamas where the storage and transshipment of war supplies for the rebels was a lucrative pursuit for all classes of the people. American naval officers were insolently treated in the streets.[2] Consul Whiting and his wife in Nassau were "almost isolated." He was jeered as "Abe Lincoln's spy" in driving through the town.[3] He told Secretary Seward that he was afraid to go out at night.[4]

When the Confederate government offered a loan of £3,000,-000 in England it was quickly taken five times over and the bonds actually rose to a premium on their sale price. For several months they were quoted higher than United States bonds.[5] "Every Southern victory," said the Index, a Confederate paper published in London,[6] "was welcomed as if it had been won by the British army; every Southern defeat was spoken of as if it had been a national reverse."[7] There was not one of her Majesty's ministers, said an English observer of the period, "who was not ready to jump out of his skin for joy when he heard of the escape of the *Alabama*."[8]

The *Alabama* was received with expressions of friendship and found coal and rest in British colonial ports.[9] One of the Lairds, the builders of the ship, was a member of Parlia-

---

[1] From E. L. Dudley, a grandson.
[2] Corr., vol. vi, p. 47.   [3] Ibid., p. 97.   [4] Ibid., p. 114.
[5] Bulloch, vol. i, p. 109, and vol. ii, p. 35; Life of C. F. Adams, pp. 329, 345-6.
[6] Cf. Diary of B. Moran, Proceedings of Mass. Hist. Soc., vol. 48, p. 482.   [7] Quoted in Corr., vol. vi, p. 181.
[8] Thomas Mozley, Reminiscences, vol. ii, p. 141; Walpole, Hist. of 25 Years, vol. ii, p. 51, and Life of Russell, vol. ii, p. 367 note. This was an obvious exaggeration in view of the fact that one or two of the number betrayed some friendliness for the North. Cf. Sir R. Palmer, Family and Personal Memorials, vol. ii, p. 430.
[9] "Everywhere" she was "hailed with joy and treated with hospitality as a legitimate cruiser."—Bulloch, vol. i, p. 309.

ment. He was cheered when he rose to speak,[1] while men like Bright and Forster, friends of the Union, were listened to only with "cold indifference." [2] Supplies were constantly forwarded to the ship at designated points as she pursued her course at sea. The families of members of her crew were paid monthly in Liverpool.[3] It seemed to many, as it did to Consul Dudley, that there was "nothing about her but what was English" with the exception of Captain Semmes.[4] These things were done "openly and notoriously." The persons and places of business of the rebel agents were well known in the communities in which they lived.[5]

The British ensign was hoisted on the government flag staff in Trinidad when the *Sumter* visited that port.[6] The *Florida* upon entering St. George's in the Bermudas in the summer of 1863 was saluted by the forts, the first attention of this kind, the rebels boasted, "which the flag of the Confederate states had ever received in a foreign port." [7] Maffitt was entertained at mess by the officers of a British regiment stationed on the island.[8] Waddell and his men when they visited Melbourne in the *Shenandoah* were "little lions." He was made an honorary member of clubs and was dined in "select society." [9] The English press, led by the London Times, the Standard, the Morning Post and the Saturday Review, generally applauded the deeds of derry of the *Alabama* and her consorts as their work of pillage proceeded throughout the four long years of the war. Nine out of ten persons in Liverpool deplored the loss of the *Alabama* when she was

[1] As on March 27, 1863; cf. London Times, March 28, 1863; Geneva Arbitration, vol. i, p. 41; Semmes, The Cruise of the Alabama, app., iii; Sumner's Works, vol. xiii, p. 70.
[2] Corr., vol. vi, p. 181.
[3] Ibid., vol. ii, p. 210. "Always keeping the umbilical connection with England out of whose womb she sprung."—Sumner in Cooper Institute speech in 1863, Works, vol. vii, p. 354.
[4] Dudley to Adams, Sep. 29, 1862, in Dudley Papers.
[5] Geneva Arbitration, vol. i, p. 91.
[6] Corr., vol. vi, pp. 191 et seq.
[7] Ibid., vol. vii, p. 57. The act, however, was disavowed by the British government.—Geneva Arbitration, vol. ii, p. 355.
[8] Corr., vol. vi, p. 348.   [9] Ibid., p. 688.

sunk by the *Kearsarge*,[1] and popular ovations awaited Semmes there and at Southampton.[2] Hearty abuse of the "Federals" was publicly indulged in by the most influential leaders of English society wherever they were gathered together. Lord Russell's replies to Mr. Adams's notes were "discourteous in their indifference" and often "insolent in their disregard of truth."[3] On all sides in his "forlorn outpost of London," as Lowell called it,[4] our minister met with cold glances. Only "the wonderful self command of a very strong man" enabled him to treat with "mute disdain" the social incivilities which he received.[5] In regard to Lincoln and Seward "English society seemed demented." The belief in Lincoln's "brutality" and Seward's "ferocity" became a dogma of popular faith.[6] Wolfe was scarcely more sincerely mourned than Stonewall Jackson.[7] Monuments in his honor were projected. The North, therefore, felt it not wrong to conclude that the course of the ministry was part of a general plan to disrupt the Union. Incidentally American shipping would be swept from the seas and our carrying trade would be transferred to British bottoms, which was early seen to be the practical effect of the policy.[8]

Quite within the bounds of law as their action was declared to be Secretary Seward from first to last unremittingly pur-

[1] Dudley to Seward, June 21, 1864, in Dudley Papers; Corr., vol. iii, p. 257.
[2] Corr., vol. iii, pp. 257, 270.
[3] Education of Henry Adams, p. 128. Henry Adams was his father's private secretary in the American legation.
[4] Life of C. F. Adams, p. 345.
[5] Lord Coleridge in Macmillan's Magazine, Jan., 1888, quoted in A. Lang, Sir Stafford Northcote, vol. i, p. 184; Education of Henry Adams, p. 123.
[6] Education of Henry Adams, p. 131.
[7] Corr., vol. vi, p. 181.
[8] "The main object the nation has in view," Adams said in July, 1862, "is the final disruption of the Union." (Corr., vol. i, p. 416.) "It is not too much to say that as a body the government looked and was known to look with confidence and without displeasure to a disruption of the American Union." (Fraser's Magazine for June, 1872.) "Every act of Russell from April, 1861, to November, 1862, showed the clearest determination to break up the Union." (Education of Henry Adams, p. 163; cf. N. Y. Nation, March 25 and April 1, 1869.)

sued the English government with inquiry, admonition and
protest. But his course was beset with difficulties. Dudley
said that those who served him as witnesses were marked
as "spies" and were subjected to the insults of their neighbors and friends. They would be dismissed from employment if they gave testimony for use against the rebel government; they were blacklisted and barred from work elsewhere.[1] The Confederate agents in the prosecution of their
plans had the "secret sympathy of her Majesty's officers in
the port of Liverpool," said Minister Adams. He declared
them to be the "most gullible, or else the most corrupt body
of civil servants in any civilized land," and their "wilful
blindness and credulous partiality," he believed, went far to
determine England's policy toward the United States.[2] Their
"connivance and stupidity" were remarked and condemned by
Reverdy Johnson.[3]

The *Oreto*, or *Florida* had got away from Liverpool without
Bulloch's encountering much opposition, although her destination was fully reported by Consul Dudley to Lord John
Russell through Minister Adams. The neglect of the government to act with a view to preventing her escape was denounced with all the force our State Department could command.[4]

The *290* was on the ways in the Mersey. At any cost, if
there were weight in the depositions of witnesses and diplomatic argument, she must be detained. Late in July, under
pressure from our legation, Russell referred the papers bearing on the case to the law officers of the crown.[5] One of
these fell ill,[6] occasioning a delay of a few days. An order

[1] Corr., vol. ii, p. 323. "Every man who takes the side of the North,"
Dudley declared, "is marked, if not persecuted."—Ibid., p. 358.
[2] Ibid., vol. ii, p. 598.
[3] See his Reply to Sir Roundell Palmer, pp. 32-3, 36.
[4] Cf. Geneva Arbitration, vol. i, pp. 99, 135; Corr., vol. ii, pp. 595,
604, and vol. vi, pp. 214 et seq.
[5] The attorney-general, the solicitor-general and the Queen's advocate.
[6] Corr., vol. ii, p. 35; Walpole, History of 25 Years, vol. ii, p. 48; Sir
R. Palmer, Family and Personal Memorials, vol. ii, pp. 422-30; J. B.
Moore, International Arbitrations, vol. i, pp. 679-82.

came, indeed, for the detention of the ship, but she, meanwhile, through Bulloch's devices, had left port, and, though she was still near the Welsh coast, where she remained from 7.30 P. M., July 29, until 3 A. M., July 31, upward of 31 hours, collecting her crew and making ready for her long journey, no attempt was put forth by the authorities of the port to reach her.[1]

Consul Dudley was enabled to collect an impressive number of papers bearing upon the character of a small wooden screw steamer called the *Alexandra* which was being built in Miller's yard in Liverpool. He satisfied himself that she was intended for use as a gunboat rather than a merchantman,[2] and, after much exertion, caused the vessel to be seized.[3] The case was tried in the Court of Exchequer in London. The Lord Chief Baron who presided at the trial in instructing the jury said that a belligerent might buy muskets, cannon, gunpowder or ammunition, "in short whatever can be used in war for the destruction of human beings." Why then, he asked, "should ships be an exception?" Concerning the interpretation to be put upon the terms of the Foreign Enlistment Act he said that its purpose was simply to prevent hostile naval engagements in British waters. Therefore, it had been required that equipment should not be put on board before the ships of belligerents left port.[4] The jury under such advice found for the owner of the ship, a verdict which was received with applause by the crowd assembled in the court room.[5]

[1] Geneva Arbitration, vol. i, p. 150. "This lamentable proceeding," John Morley called it, "for which the want of alacrity and common sense at the Foreign Office and the bias or blundering of the customs agents at Liverpool may divide the grave discredit."—Life of Gladstone, vol. ii, p. 394.

[2] Bulloch avers that the boat was not designed for the Confederate naval force, but he draws distinctions which are without a difference.—Bulloch, Secret Service, vol. i, p. 352. Cf. Geneva Arbitration, vol. i, p. 105, note.

[3] Corr., vol. ii, pp. 258 et seq.; Bulloch, vol. i, pp. 330 et seq.

[4] Geneva Arbitration, vol. i, pp. 105-6; cf. Diary of B. Moran, Proceedings of Mass. Hist. Soc., vol. 48, p. 464.

[5] Cf. Adams, Lee at Appomattox, pp. 60-1. Appeals to higher courts ended in "a mere contest about forms" and in the end Minister Adams concluded that "there never was such a comedy performed on a grave

It was clear now, said the government organ, the London
Morning Post, that the Confederates might "with ease obtain
as many vessels in this country as they pleased without in
any manner violating our laws." This might be "a great
hardship to the Federals," but, "like many other hardships
entailed on belligerents," they must submit to it with what
grace they could.[1]

The Confederate agents had made their arrangements to
go farther. Encouraged by the escape of the *Alabama* Bulloch had been instructed to order a fleet of turretted iron-
clads from Lairds for use in opening and protecting the blockaded Southern ports, particularly with a view to regaining
possession of the Mississippi River, or possibly of ascending
the Potomac for a sensational attack upon Washington, with
raids upon some. Northern cities, such as Portsmouth, N. H.,
and Philadelphia.[2] A question arose in Bulloch's mind. Was
armor plating equipment within the meaning of the act of
1819? Counsel said no and two of the rams, the *294* and the
295, were in process of construction in 1862 and 1863 in Birkenhead. All possible haste was being made to complete
them. Night gangs hammered upon the hulls.[3] Consul Dudley and his "Yankee spies" relaxed no energy. "Scarcely a
man, woman or child in the place but what knows these rams
are intended for the Confederates," he wrote. They were
a leading topic of conversation day by day on 'Change in
Liverpool.[4]

subject in the whole history of law."—Corr., vol. ii, pp. 304-5. For
account of proceedings see Parliamentary and Judicial Appendix, Corr.,
no. xv.

[1] Cf. Adams, op. cit., pp. 65-6.

[2] "I designed these ships for something more than harbor or even
coast defense," wrote Bulloch to the Confederate Navy Department
on Dec. 18, 1862, "and I confidently believe, if ready for sea now, they
could sweep away the entire blockading fleet of the enemy." They
could "sweep the blockading fleet from the sea front of every harbor
from the Capes of Virginia to Sabine Pass, and, cruising up and down
the coast, prevent anything like permanent, systematic interruption of
our foreign trade for the future."—Bulloch, vol. i, pp. 394, 411-2.

[3] Cf. Corr., vol. ii, pp. 314 et seq. [4] Ibid., p. 358.

If these "British built, armed and manned vessels" were sent out to raid our coasts it would stir the whole nation, Seward wrote to Adams, and make "a retaliatory war inevitable." [1] The building of these formidable ships, Adams told Lord Russell on July 11, 1863, must be regarded by the government and the people of the United States as "virtually tantamount to a participation in the war by the people of Great Britain to a degree which, if not seasonably prevented, cannot fail to endanger the peace and welfare of both countries." [2] But Russell responded that the depositions which Mr. Dudley had presented were "mere hearsay, surmise, conversation and conjecture." He, therefore, could not "interfere in any way." [3] Mr. Adams responded on September 5 with a dispatch which contained plain prophecy of an early rupture of friendly relations between the two countries. After again reciting the facts he declared that no nation "retaining a proper degree of self respect" could "tamely submit" to such indignities. "It would be superfluous in me to point out," said he, "that this is war." [4]

Public opinion in the United States was at white heat. In the midst of the excitement Charles Sumner made a speech in Cooper Institute in New York. His utterances, solemn and impressive as always, held the attention of a great audience. Never before had England been set forth so plainly as a partner of slavery. [5]

"Come unto us, rebel slavemongers, whippers of women and sellers of children," England cried (said Sumner), "for you are the people of our choice whom we welcome promptly with ocean rights, with Armstrong guns and naval expeditions, equipped in our ports, and on whom we lavish sympathy always and the prophecy of success; while for you who uphold the republic and oppose slavery we have hard words, criticism, rebuke and the menace of war." [6]

[1] Corr., vol. ii, p. 362.   [2] Ibid., p. 327.   [3] Ibid., pp. 360-61.
[4] Ibid., p. 365; Life of C. F. Adams, pp. 342-3; Bulloch, vol. ii, p. 62.
[5] Sumner's Works, vol. vii, pp. 329-492.   [6] Ibid., p. 367.

The speech was published in full in many of the newspapers and made its way in the mail steamers across the sea to excite wide comment. The Emancipation Proclamation of September, 1862, had met response in the British conscience, and it could not fail to cause large numbers of men in the middle classes in England to perceive the underlying meaning of the conflict, a reaction reflected plainly enough in public meetings, expressive of sympathy for the North, which were organized in many towns.[1] Sumner spoke to high as well as middle class, to whom his name as an emancipator was as well known as Wilberforce's or John Bright's, and his words sank into the head as well as the heart of the British nation.

But much else, more potent than phrase of Seward, or Adams, or Sumner had lately come to pass. The news of Lee's repulse at Gettysburg and the fall of Vicksburg, which had electrified the North in time for its Fourth of July celebration in 1863, was carried to England in a fortnight. It caused "great depression" in Liverpool.[2] Upon many minds it had begun to dawn that the eventual outcome of the war might not be what the nation had so generally hoped for and expected.

However the unthinking might applaud the feats of the *Alabama*, Lord Russell himself recoiled as he contemplated the logical consequences of his course in permitting this vessel to proceed to sea. Much might befall the great British merchant shipping interests at some future day, if any state, without a port or a mile of seaboard, at war with England, should be at liberty to construct cruisers in the shipyards of neutral countries. What if "innumerable *Alabamas*," said the London Morning Post, with some frank purpose, should some day issue from American ports to prey upon the com-

---

[1] Cf. Dudley to Seward, Jan. 6 and Feb. 20, 1863, in Dudley Papers; Walpole, Hist. of 25 Years, vol. ii, p. 86.

[2] Dudley to Seward, July 22, 1863, in Dudley Papers. It was a paralyzing blow to the Confederate agents in Europe, as will appear from their despatches in Southern letter books preserved among the Dudley Papers.

merce of Great Britain?[1] Lord Russell with the support
of the Duke of Argyll, another member of the government,
had drawn up a despatch directing colonial authorities to
detain the ship, if she came within their reach. When the
subject was brought before the Cabinet "there was a perfect
insurrection," and the measure must be abandoned.[2] Nevertheless many had come to understand that it was time to
pause before going farther down this dangerous way. At
this very moment there was ominous movement on the Continent. Prussian advances northward into Schleswig bore
hard upon England whose crown through family ties was
concerned for the welfare of Denmark.[3]

Meanwhile Bulloch had taken fright and the "Laird rams"
were sold to a French banking house professing to represent
the Pasha of Egypt, though the Confederacy relinquished only
the title in them, and still had the hope of applying them
to its uses. Russell had said that he could and would do
nothing in the case. But at the last moment he changed
his mind and ordered them detained.[4] Gunboats were lashed
alongside, guards were mounted on deck where they lay in
the Birkenhead yards, and, after several months, arrangements were completed whereby they should pass into the British navy. The Admiralty purchased the boats on motion
of Lord Russell at a price indicating a considerable profit to
the builders, in order to clear himself of an incident which
threatened his ministry with serious embarrassment.[5]

Another ironclad, the *Pampero*, in course of construction

---

[1] May 14 and 18, 1864, quoted in C. F. Adams, Lee at Appomattox,
p. 74. That there was a change of sentiment is corroborated by Bulloch, vol. i, pp. 353-4.

[2] Walpole, Life of Russell, vol. ii, p. 355; Walpole, Hist. of 25 Years,
vol. ii, p. 51; Sir R. Palmer, Family and Personal Memorials, vol. ii,
p. 431.

[3] Sir R. Palmer, Family and Personal Memorials, vol. ii, pp. 452-4;
C. F. Adams, op. cit., pp. 69-72.

[4] Corr., vol. i, p. 365; cf. C. C. Beaman, National and Private Alabama Claims, p. 165; Education of Henry Adams, pp. 172-3, 176-8.

[5] Sir R. Palmer, Family and Personal Memorials, vol. ii, pp. 450-51;
Education of Henry Adams, p. 178; Bulloch, vol. i, p. 442; Life of
C. F. Adams, p. 67.

for the Confederates at Glasgow, was under surveillance during the summer of 1863. The frigate was seized in January, 1864. The Scottish regulations were much less favorable to such operations. The case came before judges who gave the ship short shrift; she was condemned and sold to Denmark.[1] The turning point in British policy on this subject had been reached at last.

In our international relations, as in the conduct of the war at home, we were acting upon the principle that "the integrity of the republic" remained unbroken. The government at Washington continued to be supreme over all the states.[2] The South was in insurrection and the insurrection was to be quelled. The blockade had been established to hasten this end. It was "effective" and other nations must respect it. Here as a neutral Great Britain had failed also, so it was thought and alleged, for blockade runners were constantly permitted to leave English ports bound for the South with material which was calculated to prolong the war. Consul Dudley wrote to Seward on November 7, 1862, that nine vessels flying the British flag were then loading at Liverpool for the South; four more were in port ready to take on cargo. On November 28, 1862, he reported twenty-one steamers which had recently been built or purchased for blockade running; on December 2 he gave the names of seven more destined for the same use. On April 8, 1864, forty new steamers were being built for this trade. Blockade running was as clearly a part of "the business of the country," he declared, as its commerce with China, or Italy, or France. One sea captain boasted that he had made thirty successful trips through the cordon of American ships guarding the Southern coast.[3]

Bermuda, Havana in Cuba and the Bahamas became bases of supplies for the Confederacy. In particular did the island of New Providence, since it lay so near the blockaded South-

[1] Bulloch, vol. ii, pp. 271, 272-3; C. C. Beaman, National and Private Alabama Claims, pp. 153-61.
[2] Corr., vol. i, p. 214.   [3] Dudley Papers.

ern coast, prove of great service to the rebels.[1] Nassau was
openly used as a relay station by their secret agents in Europe. Here large ships broke bulk. Warehouses and even
private dwellings were bulging with war material; cotton on
its way back to England stood on the wharves; boxes of rifles,
sabres and ammunition plainly marked with the letters,
"C. S. A.," were drawn through the streets [2] to be reloaded
into small steamers expressly designed for the service, of
light draught and great speed, painted usually a bluish white
to resemble the sky at dawn, the hour chosen for dashing
across the bars into bayous along the coast.[3] The rebel and
British agents, who were engaged in receiving and forwarding
freights for the Confederacy, distributing pilots and supply-
ing the boats with coal, filled the hotels in Nassau and St.
George's.[4]

Come what might out of the controversy about the blockade
runners the Foreign Enlistment Act of 1819 was denounced
as a municipal law which was being interpreted and enforced in such a way that it was made to supersede the general law of nations. It was a plain mockery of the statute,
said Mr. Adams, if a ship ready for arms was to be built
and sent away from one dock while at another dock the arms
for her awaited despatch to her side. Such vessels did not
issue from a home port; from first to last they never entered
a Confederate harbor. They could not take their captures before prize courts, except such farcical tribunals as Semmes
organized on deck. They were "chartered libertines." [5] They
were "corsairs," "pirates," "ocean incendiaries," "gypsies of
the sea," said Sumner, "disturbers of the common highway,

[1] Geneva Arbitration, vol. ii, pp. 277-80.
[2] Corr., vol. vi, p. 260.
[3] Geneva Arbitration, vol. i, pp. 92-8. "Swarms of swift steamers,"
said Sumner, " 'a pitchy cloud warping on the eastern wind' always under British flag with contributions to rebel slavery."—In Cooper Institute speech in 1863, Works, vol. vii, p. 352.
[4] Corr., vol. vi, p. 238; Bulloch, vol. ii, pp. 232-3; letter books of
Southern agents in Dudley Papers; American Case in Geneva Arb.,
vol. i, pp. 126-7.
[5] Reverdy Johnson, Reply to Speech of Sir Roundell Palmer, p. 8.

outlaws and enemies of the human race," "a rib taken out of the side of England and prostituted to rebel slavery."[1] Neither the *Alabama* nor any other rebel cruiser fitted out in England could be regarded by the United States as "a ship of war of a lawful belligerent power."[2] It was "a fraud on neutrality," yet Great Britain had "virtually assumed" that the construction and equipment of a rebel war vessel, if it were "successfully completed," was "at once entitled to recognition as a legitimate transaction."[3] It was immaterial whether or not a nation should have municipal law to enforce its general obligations in the family of nations. This was its own affair. A local understanding of the meaning of a Foreign Enlistment Act, or whatever its name, was of no importance to us when our shipping was being destroyed in violation of the principles of a higher body of law. Puerile, indeed, did it seem to refer such a question to a petty criminal court, as had been done in the case of the *Alexandra*. Plainly stated, here was the case of a nation, or a ministry representing that nation, which was ready to alter international law by municipal law and which, when driven into a corner, appealed to trial by jury.

"Our commerce on the high seas," said Seward, "is perishing under the devastation of ships of war that are sent out for that purpose from British coasts."[4] It was "rapidly vanishing from the face of the ocean," while the shipping trade of Great Britain was "multiplying in nearly the same ratio." It was "substantially the destruction of the whole mercantile navigation belonging to the people of the United States," Adams told Russell in April, 1865.[5] The pirates, said Sumner, more rhetorically, "raging from sea to sea," turned the ocean "into a furnace and melting pot of American commerce."[6]

The whole train of troubles had begun with the "unneces-

---

[1] Sumner's Works, vol. vii, pp. 459, 461.
[2] Corr., vol. iii, p. 295.   [3] Ibid., vol. ii, p. 702.
[4] Ibid., vol. i, p. 264.   [5] Ibid., vol. iii, p. 346.
[6] Sumner's Works, vol. vii, p. 353.

sary and premature concession of belligerent rights." [1] This
was "the first grave error" [2] from which "all the grievances"
alienating the American people from Great Britain were "de-
ducible." [3] The conclusion that the proclamation was issued
in a kind of hostile glee was unavoidable. Called a declaration of neutrality it had not been this, for "it had depressed
the spirits of the friends of the government" and it had
"raised the courage of the insurgents." [4] In lifting "the disaffected states up to the level of a belligerent power," [5] said
Mr. Adams, in declaring the war *justum bellum,* before there
was yet any kind of warfare except within one of the insurgents' own harbors, and a "marine power" before they yet
had a single privateer upon the ocean, British action had been
too rapid. It inferred "the existence of an intention, more or
less marked, to extend the struggle." [6] The insurgents were
not a "navigating people." They of themselves had fitted out
nothing but a few old steamboats. [7] They had become a
"belligerent on the ocean solely by reason of the facilities
furnished them in her Majesty's ports." [8] It "can never be
regarded by my government in any other light than as precipitate," Mr. Adams said again, to acknowledge persons "as
a belligerent power on the ocean before they had a single
vessel of their own to show floating upon it." [9] "In all the
history of the United States or of Great Britain," or, indeed,
in that of any civilized country in the world there was "not
an example" of "so precipitate a recognition of belligerent
rights to insurgents." [10] If this action were revoked, and revo-
cation was asked for by the State Department, the "revolution," Secretary Seward alleged, would "become extinct at
once"; [11] the war, he said confidently, would "end to-
morrow." [12]

[1] Corr., vol. i, p. 226.
[2] Ibid., p. 235.
[3] Ibid., p. 242; cf. ibid., p. 270.
[4] Ibid., p. 199; cf. ibid., p. 240.
[5] Ibid., p. 39.
[6] Ibid., p. 184.
[7] Ibid., p. 199.
[8] Ibid., p. 306.
[9] Ibid., p. 292; cf. ibid., p. 304.
[10] Ibid., pp. 240-1.
[11] Ibid., p. 226.
[12] March 6, 1862. Ibid., p. 227; cf. ibid., pp. 230, 233.

For such offending long continued, compounded and re-compounded by the *Alabama* and the other corsairs, "the off-spring of the violated law of this land," there must be repara-tion.[1] Requests became demands. "The nation that recog-nized a power as a belligerent 'before it had built a vessel and became itself the sole source of all the belligerent character it has ever possessed on the ocean," Adams wrote to Russell at the war's end, "must be regarded as responsible for all the damage that has ensued from that cause to the commerce of a power with which it was under the most sacred of obliga-tions to preserve amity and peace." [2]

That there had been conferences with France over the mat-ter before action was taken was disliked and denounced; it was confirmatory of unfriendly intent.[3] The partiality with which the *Alabama* and the other cruisers were received in British colonial ports was noted and made the subject of pro-tests. Rules as to the period of stay and the receipt of coal and other supplies, which were rigidly enforced against the United States, were not only relaxed, but were oftentimes entirely disregarded in reference to rebel cruisers.[4] Allowed to stand outside of ports within or just beyond the three mile limit to catch American vessels, bound in or out, they virtually blockaded these ports for days at a time. The *Shenandoah* remained for more than three weeks in Melbourne to fit her-self out for her cruise to the whaling grounds, and in that port actually essayed the recruitment of seamen for her voyage.[5] The kingdom of Great Britain, Mr. Adams declared in April, 1865, must be regarded as having "not only given birth to this naval belligerent, but also as having nursed and main-tained it to the present hour." [6]

And yet it might be accounted good fortune that England had not delayed her declaration until after the rout of the

[1] Adams to Russell, Corr., vol. iii, p. 379.
[2] May 20, 1865. Corr., vol. i, p. 316.
[3] Ibid., p. 180.   [4] Geneva Arbitration, vol. i, p. 141.
[5] Corr., vol. vi, pp. 588-95; Geneva Arbitration, vol. i, pp. 171-5.
[6] Corr., vol. i, p. 292.

Northern army at Bull Run, or the withdrawal of McClellan from his positions before Richmond, else she might not have been satisfied with a limited concession.[1] The emissaries of the Confederacy in Europe were received by Lord Russell at his home where they presented their plea for a full recognition of independence,[2] which they did not cease to advocate. The subject was repeatedly before Parliament. At one time such action was not far away, for in September, 1862, Palmerston had proposed so much to Russell, and a Cabinet meeting was called to discuss the matter. But by the time it had convened General Lee had been stopped at Antietam. The ministry on this account was constrained to think better of the North and feared to pursue the plan.[3]

Our minister in London in summing up the case in correspondence with Seward, in 1862, said: "That Great Britain did in the most terrible moment of our domestic trial, in struggling with a monstrous social evil she had earnestly. professed to abhor, coldly and at once assume our inability to master it, and then became the only foreign nation to verify its prejudgment, will probably be the verdict made up against her by posterity on a calm comparison of the evidence." The governing classes had "inscribed for the whole nation a moral and political record which no subsequent action" would "ever avail to obliterate."[4]

Russell on his side peremptorily refused to intervene on the subject of blockade running. Vessels could go to sea bound for Southern ports as they liked. If the blockade were "effective" the North could enforce the penalty, namely the capture and condemnation of maritime property the owners of which would subject it to such a risk.[5] But he intimated that it was not "effective"; therefore were ventures of this kind stimulated and hence the North's complaints. While once he

[1] Life of C. F. Adams, p. 174.
[2] Corr., vol. i, pp. 37-8; cf. ibid., pp. 417, 419-20, 425.
[3] Walpole, Life of Lord John Russell, vol. ii, pp. 349-52; Morley, Life of Gladstone, vol. ii, pp. 77, 80; Diary of B. Moran, Proceedings Mass. Hist. Soc., vol. 48, p. 462; Walpole, Hist. of 25 Years, vol. ii, pp. 53-9; Fitzmaurice, Life of Walpole, vol. ii, pp. 442-4.
[4] Corr., vol. i, p. 529. [5] Cf. ibid., p. 533.

did remark in conversation with Mr. Adams that the escape
of the *Oreto* and the *290* was "a scandal and in some degree a
reproach to our laws,"[1] later telling Mason, Slidell and Mann
that the fitting out of the vessels "by such shifts and strata-
gems" was "a proceeding totally unjustifiable and manifestly offensive to the British crown,"[2] he nevertheless repeatedly and with the greatest vigor contended on other occasions, that the neutrality of the country had been perfectly
preserved at this as well as at every other point.

England was sending munitions to both belligerents—to the
Federals as well as to the Confederates. Of the latter's share
the North had captured a great part and he could not sympathize with the Northern people in their contention that there
had been a want of neutrality in his course on this subject.[3]
He had a *tu quoque*. Many subjects of Great Britain had
enlisted in the Federal armies and they had been paid bounties to "induce" them to do so. This was a violation of neutrality on the side of the United States.[4] American agents
had visited Ireland to obtain soldiers to fight against the
South.

When pressed concerning the construction of a war ship
in one dock and the despatch of the guns from another dock,
to be put in place in the Bahamas or the Azores, Lord Russell would say that they were "unable to go beyond the law,
municipal and international." Again and again he returned
to this position and when it was proposed that the "municipal law" be changed, that the old act of 1819 be amended
in Parliament, he retorted that such action would be conditional upon the adoption of a similar course on the part of
the United States with reference to our enlistment act. But
when assurances were given that such amendment would be
made by Congress the offer was withdrawn.[5]

[1] Cf. Corr., vol. i, p. 585; C. C. Beaman, National and Private Alabama Claims, p. 210; Sumner's Works, vol. xiii, p. 66, and cited authorities in that place.
[2] Feb. 13, 1865. Corr., vol. i, p. 631.
[3] Cf. Russell, Speeches and Despatches, vol. ii, p. 249.
[4] Corr., vol. iii, p. 90.   [5] Ibid., pp. 91-2, 98-100, 544.

It had been a necessity on England's side to acknowledge
the blockade, he would say in answer to the charge concerning
the Queen's proclamation of 1861. To have insisted that
British subjects should continue to trade freely with Southern
ports was impracticable.[1] Had the United States stopped
British ships and exercised the right of search without a declaration of belligerency the most serious consequences would
have ensued immediately. England had chosen the course
which was "at once the most just and most friendly to the
United States,"—one that had been recommended by those
who wished us well.[2] The North itself did not treat the
Southern combatants as pirates, and when they were captured neither the opinion of the civilized world nor the ex-
igencies of war could have justified hanging them.[3]

Confronted by the depredations of the *Alabama* the government disclaimed "all responsibility" for any of her acts
or the acts "of any other Confederate cruiser," and Lord
Russell said, on September 14, 1862, as if to bring the discussion to an end—"I have only in conclusion to express
my hope that you may not be instructed again to put forward claims which her Majesty's government cannot admit
to be founded on any grounds of law or justice." [4]

He was so indiscreet at one point in the controversy as
to confuse the subject of law with the material interests of
the country. A great object which the government had in
view, he said, was to preserve for the nation "the legitimate
and lucrative trade of shipbuilding." [5] They must "decline

---

[1] Corr., vol. iii, p. 351.

[2] Wemyss Reid, Life of W. E. Forster, vol. ii, pp. 12, 21. "On what
other footing they could have established a blockade of the Southern
ports, visited and searched British merchant ships at sea and seized
British vessels for carriage of contraband or breach of blockade was
not explained."—Sir R. Palmer, Family and Personal Memorials. vol. ii,
p. 384.

[3] Corr., vol. i, p. 199; ibid., vol. ii, p. 351. For a review of the entire
history of England's policy from Russell's standpoint see his letter to
Adams, Corr., vol. ii, pp. 548 et seq. Cf. C. F. Adams in Proceedings
Mass. Hist. Soc., vol. 48, pp. 239-41; Walpole, Hist. of 25 Years, vol. ii,
pp. 40-2.

[4] Corr., vol. iii, p. 164.   [5] C. F. Adams, Lee at Appomattox, p. 54.

to be responsible for the acts of parties who fit out a seeming merchant ship, send her to a port or to waters far from the jurisdiction of British courts, and then commission, equip and man her as a vessel of war," for, if this were done, "the trade of shipbuilding in which our people excel and which is to great numbers of them a source of honest livelihood would be seriously embarrassed and impeded." [1] "It is difficult to find a reason," he wrote Adams on September 11, 1863, "why a ship that is to be used for warlike purposes is more an instrument or implement of war than cannon, muskets, swords, bayonets, gunpowder and projectiles to be fired from cannon and muskets." A ship, like a musket, might be sold to a belligerent; it would cease to be neutral only when it was "employed in war." [2] Russell marvelled that the United States with its powerful and expanding navy should be unable to catch two or three boats about whose performances the nation expressed to him its unending concern.

"I have to point out to you," Russell said again to Adams in 1865, "that her Majesty's government, having used all the means in their power to prevent the fitting and arming of vessels in their ports to cruise against the vessels of the United States . . . cannot consider themselves bound to answer for the acts of every individual who may evade the operation of the laws, by fitting out and arming vessels bought in this country in some distant port or on the seas beyond her Majesty's jurisdiction." [3] The war ending in a complete victory for the North, the statesmen and the pro-Southern newspapers of Great Britain were in a difficult position. Their hopes defeated and their prophecies falsified they displayed no dexterity in extricating themselves from it. [4]

A time was at hand when, by a little management, a settle-

---

[1] Oct. 23, 1863. Corr., vol. iii, p. 201.

[2] Corr., vol. ii, p. 374; cf. Bulloch, vol. i, p. 450; Russell, Speeches and Despatches, vol. ii, pp. 251-3.

[3] Feb. 8, 1865. Corr., vol. i, p. 630.

[4] For the change of tone in the debates in Parliament when Northern success was near see Diary of B. Moran, Proceedings of Mass. Hist. Soc., vol. 48, p. 473.

ment of the controversy, as grave as it was, could have been effected. For the North it was an hour of self congratulation and complacency. In "our oblivious good nature," Sumner said, we would have "accepted anything."[1] The conviction that England had done this nation infamous wrongs was deep, but Seward, press, and public sentiment generally, in answer to a graceful acknowledgment of her mistake, would have welcomed a basis of understanding.[2] Giving the United States the satisfaction of achieving a diplomatic victory to supplement its great military triumphs might have hurt the English minister's personal pride, but to have said frankly that he had been led into a false attitude and regretted it could have done his government no injury. It would have the better prepared the way for the nation to take that position which, at length, interest as well as right would compel it to assume.

On October 23, 1863, Adams, writing to Russell, had said that there was "no fair and equitable form of conventional arbitrament or reference to which they [the United States] will not be willing to submit."[3] On August, 30, 1865, Russell chose to revert to this suggestion and remarked to our minister that such questions could not be put "to a foreign government with any regard to the dignity and character of the British crown and the British nation. Her Majesty's government," he continued, are "the sole guardians of their own honor," and they must decline "either to make reparation and compensation for the captures made by the *Alabama*, or to refer the question to any foreign state." They would,

[1] Pierce, vol. iv, p. 393; Salter, Life of Grimes, p. 370.
[2] C. F. Adams, Lee at Appomattox, pp. 82-5. Likewise the pendulum in Great Britain seems to have swung to the other side. "Wonderful," said Sir Roundell Palmer, "was the good will towards the victorious party which some of those whose sympathies had been with the South began to display."—Personal and Political Memorials, vol. i, p. 206.
[3] Corr., vol. iii, p. 182. For early suggestions as to the arbitration of the dispute cf. Thomas Balch, International Courts of Arbitration; T. W. Balch, The Alabama Arbitration, pp. 40 et seq.; Sir Roundell Palmer, Personal and Political Memorials, vol. i, p. 205; Reverdy Johnson, Reply to Sir Roundell Palmer, pp. 13-8.

however, consent to the appointment of a commission to which should be referred "all claims arising during the late civil war which the two powers shall agree to refer to the commissioners." [1] As this proposal was understood by Mr. Seward to exclude cases arising from the "captures and spoliations made by the *Alabama* and other vessels of her class," and he was confirmed in the understanding by Lord Russell, it was repelled.[2] To show Great Britain plainly to what a point her course was leading her the House of Representatives at Washington in the summer of 1866, without one dissenting vote, passed a bill to repeal such provisions in our neutrality laws as forbade the fitting out of ships of war for the use of belligerents, which led England to look at her old Foreign Enlistment Act, though she did not change its terms until 1870.[3]

Palmerston died in the autumn of 1865 and Russell became Prime Minister. Lord Clarendon was installed in the Foreign Office. But Russell and Clarendon continued to speak as Palmerston and Russell had spoken. Diplomatic exchanges proceeded without bringing the question nearer to a settlement, Clarendon "closing the correspondence" with the observation "that no armed vessel departed during the war from a British port to cruise against the commerce of the United States," and that throughout these years the British government had "steadily and honestly discharged all the duties incumbent on them as a neutral power," and had "never deviated from the obligations imposed on them by international law." [4]

The Liberal government went out of office in the summer of 1866 and a Conservative ministry, headed by Lord Derby and Benjamin Disraeli, with Lord Stanley as Secretary of State for Foreign Affairs, came in. The outlook now was better. From a government which had not made the blunder

[1] Corr., vol. ii, p. 562.
[2] Ibid., pp. 576, 579, 581-8; cf. Walpole, Life of Lord John Russell, vol. ii, p. 359, for Russell's views as to the arbitration of the dispute.
[3] Adams, Lee at Appomattox, p. 79.   [4] Corr., vol. iii, p. 625.

some rectification of it might be expected. Lord Derby intimated [1] that a plan for the adjustment of the claims would be entertained. The subject was reopened. The inspired London Times asked if it would be inconsistent with the national dignity "to reconsider dispassionately" the questions arising out of the *Alabama* case. This course it advocated and no better time than the present, it said in October, 1866, "could be selected for this attempt." If a commission, after inquiry, should find that reparation was due the United States "no false pride" should prevent Great Britain from making it "with a good grace." [2] It must be accounted impolitic, whatever the precedent, to make neutrals "the sole judges of their own obligations." [3] A foreign enlistment act in the United States, or France, or Prussia, or any other state, interpreted by a petty jury in a criminal court, as in the case of the *Alexandra*, could not be allowed to be of greater weight than the general law of nations. [4] Here was gain and correspondence was resumed.

Secretary Seward and Minister Adams went back and pointed to the trouble at its source, the "precipitate and unprecedented" proclamation of belligerency, on May 13, 1861, and led up to the responsibility of the government for the destruction of American commerce by the cruisers which subsequently had issued from British ports. [5] Lord Stanley categorically declined to consider the question as to whether there had been warrant for the recognition of the Confederates as belligerents, but he was ready to arbitrate other classes of claims. [6] From the beginning, we had insisted upon an adjustment of damages computed somehow with reference to the Queen's proclamation and the country now was "not at all likely," said Mr. Seward, "to yield the attitude" it had "hitherto maintained." [7] The negotiation, therefore, again came to a standstill. [8]

[1] At a Guildhall dinner. Corr., vol. iii, p. 641.
[2] Issue of Oct. 4, 1866.
[3] Issue of Nov. 17, 1866.   [4] Adams, op. cit., p. 91.
[5] Corr., vol. iii, pp. 645-6.   [6] Ibid., pp. 652, 669.
[7] To Adams, Nov. 16, 1867.—Ibid., p. 683.   [8] Ibid., pp. 673-4, 686, 688.

More was not done until Reverdy Johnson reached London
in the summer of 1868. He bore instructions to address himself at once to the naturalization question—the assumption of
Great Britain that she could hold naturalized citizens of the
United States, if born in that country, amenable for offenses
under laws and before tribunals not applied to native born
citizens of the United States, of immediate importance because
of the plight of certain Fenians held in dungeons and otherwise mistreated, as it appeared to their Irish sympathizers
in America.[1] He should likewise seek a determination of the
San Juan boundary question which had been in train of settlement before the war began. Did this island, the ownership
of which was in dispute under the terms of the treaty of
1846, belong to Great Britain or to the United States? Having disposed of these matters a joint commission for the
settlement of the *Alabama* claims was suggested, to be
constituted on the lines of the commission of February 8,
1853.[2]

A lavish welcome was accorded Minister Johnson in England. He was a Democrat, he came from Maryland, he was
the choice of Andrew Johnson for the mission and he was
soon sitting beside and conversing with men who had been
outspoken enemies of the North during the war. Disraeli,
Lord Cairns, Lord Derby, Lord Devon, the Duke of Argyll
and many more invited him to their homes.[3] He attended
feasts which discretion should have enabled him to avoid.
The name of Roebuck, who had labored so long in and out of
Parliament for the recognition of the Confederates, was as
much disliked in the North as that of Jefferson Davis, Robert
Toombs or Clement Vallandigham; yet Mr. Johnson consorted
with this man and addressed him as a "friend." He shook
hands with Laird, who had built the *Alabama,* and was soon
in exceedingly hot water. His associations and utterances
were violently condemned by the English haters and the
entire breed, seed and generation of jingoes who write and

[1] J. B. Moore, International Arbitrations, vol. i, p. 501.
[2] Letter of Instructions from Seward—Corr., vol. iii, pp. 692-3.
[3] Reverdy Johnson Papers in Library of Congress.

speak in an American presidential campaign, as they were
sincerely regretted by more thoughtful men.[1]

In answer to his critics, Johnson said, in a despatch to
Seward, that he had determined "to lose no time in culti-
vating the growing friendly feeling for the United States"
which was "so strongly exhibited" upon his arrival in England, "whilst never forgetting scrupulously to regard the rights
and honor of our country." This had been his "sole motive";
he deemed "the existence of such a feeling . . . essential to
the interest of both countries." [2]

Seward had a keen desire to effect a settlement of the national differences while he was still in office and the President
shared his Secretary of State's eagerness to make progress
with the old subject. So, too, did the Tory ministry in
England wish to enjoy the honor of concluding the negotiation before, by a turn of the wheel, they should be discharged from power. It would be a good cry on the hustings
if they could point to their skill in repairing Liberal mistakes.

So rapidly, under the influence of social intercourse, or on
other accounts, did the *rapprochement* proceed that in October, 1868, Johnson was asking for final instructions on the
subject. The cable had been laid and the course of diplomacy was quickened by cipher communications under the sea.
The minister inquired if the *Alabama* question might be left
to the arbitration of the King of Prussia.[3] Seward replied
that the Senate and public opinion would not approve of the
appointment of any umpire in advance of the meeting of the

[1] C. F. Adams to W. E. Forster in Wemyss Reid, Life of Forster, vol.
ii, p. 13; Lowell's Letters, vol. ii, p. 26; N. Y. Nation, Oct. 1, 1868,
and Jan. 28, 1869; Harper's Weekly, Sep. 26, 1868. Sumner described
Johnson's career in England as "maudlin."—Wemyss Reid, Life of
Forster, vol. ii, p. 17.

[2] Corr., vol. iii, pp. 751-2. For Seward's view of Johnson's course at
this time, which he commended, see MS. letter in State Department
quoted in J. B. Moore, International Arbitrations, vol. i, pp. 506-7.
But see Moran's Diary for references to the "garrulity" of the "old
man," a view which seems to have been held by Clarendon.—Entry in
MS. Diary in Library of Congress for May 22, 1869.

[3] Oct. 20, 1868. Corr., vol. iii, pp. 695-6.

commission to which the questions in difference were to be referred. He urged Johnson to haste.[1] Such progress was made that on November 10 a convention "for the settlement of all outstanding claims" of citizens of the United States against the government of Great Britain and of subjects of Great Britain against the government of the United States, which had arisen since 1853, the date of the last convention, was signed. Four commissioners, two chosen by the Queen and two by the President of the United States, were to meet in London, when before proceeding farther they should appoint an arbitrator or umpire to dispose of questions upon which they might be unable to come to a decision. In the event of failure to agree upon a man for this position he should be chosen by lot from two persons, one of whom should be named by the commissioners on either side. Each government was to designate an agent to represent it before the commission in all matters connected with the investigation. A majority should determine any question except a claim arising out of the depredations of the *Alabama* and ships of her class. In this case, unless the decision were unanimous, reference would be made to "some sovereign or head of a friendly state as an arbitrator." The correspondence and evidence already in possession of the two governments were alone to be considered, without the submission of further argument or testimony, unless there were a unanimous request for new material.[2]

Seward immediately telegraphed that the commission ought to sit in Washington instead of London in view of the "highly disturbed national sensibilities." This was "absolutely essential." With this change "all will be well," said the Secretary of State [3] and on November 23 Stanley and Johnson appended their signatures to a supplementary article making this amendment in the scheme.[4]

The completed text reached Seward on November 24. It

[1] Corr., vol. iii, pp. 695, 697.
[2] For text of the Stanley-Johnson Convention, see ibid., vol. iii, pp. 70 et seq.   [3] Ibid., p. 706.   [4] Ibid., p. 708.

surprised and disappointed him. Instead of an adjustment the "whole thing was wrong—contrary to instructions," he said in Cabinet meeting in Washington.[1] Members wished to know what claims England would make on her side. Evarts said that our *Alabama* claims would amount to only about eight millions while the English would probably demand a hundred millions from us.[2] Welles suspected that they might ask payment for their cotton and other property destroyed during the war, as well as for prizes condemned in our courts.[3] Unless the convention were amended, Seward informed Minister Johnson, it would be "useless."[4] The *Alabama* claims were now "prejudicially discriminated against." They must be put on the same basis as other questions. Further evidence and argument must be admissible. These and other changes which were necessary were indicated by cable. "Time is important," Seward repeated. Explanations followed by post.[5] The treaty was sent back for "better terms."

Astonishment was expressed by Lord Stanley that what had been done by Minister Johnson was not with full authority,[6] and the matter was in this position when the Tory government resigned and the Liberal party came back to power early in December, with Gladstone as Prime Minister and Lord Clarendon again in place as Secretary of State for Foreign Affairs. This was the end of the Stanley-Johnson Convention. But it was only a little while until the negotiations were resumed. Clarendon and Johnson in London, and Seward and Sir Edward Thornton, the British minister at Washington, hastened to introduce the amendments which it

---

[1] Welles, vol. iii, p. 468. "On exchanging salutations" with Welles, Seward said, "he was sick, quite sick." Welles "asked his malady," and he replied that "he had got the damnedest strange thing from Reverdy Johnson for a protocol." For Johnson's defence of his course, see Corr., vol. iii, pp. 721-2.
[2] Welles, vol. iii, p. 470.   [3] Ibid., p. 474.
[4] Corr., vol. iii, p. 709.   [5] Ibid., pp. 709 et seq.   [6] Ibid., pp. 727-30.

was thought would make the scheme acceptable in America. Again the cable was used freely and on January 14, 1869, the new convention, generally known as the Johnson-Clarendon Convention, was signed at the British Foreign Office. The features of the earlier draft to which particular objection had been made at Washington were changed, namely as to the exceptional treatment to be accorded the *Alabama* claims and the introduction of new evidence. Now, if on the question of any claim of whatever kind the commissioners, or any two of them, desired the arbitration of "a sovereign or head of a friendly state," such person could be called in only after referring the subject back to their respective governments. They were bound to consider not only the official correspondence which had already taken place as to any claim, but also "all other written documents or statements" which might be presented to them.[1]

Andrew Johnson's and Seward's days now were numbered. The verbal text of the convention was received in Washington by cable the day it was signed in London. It still met with little favor in the Cabinet, Welles and McCulloch being outspoken in their opposition, but the President gave his support to Seward,[2] and submitted it to the Senate at once, on January 15, without waiting for the mails.[3]

At the same time Reverdy Johnson signed a convention referring to the arbitration of the President of the Swiss Confederation the disputed line of water boundary in the Northwest under the treaty of 1846, involving the possession of San Juan island. He had earlier sent to Seward a protocol on the naturalization question. The plans for the settlement of these minor matters were forwarded to the Senate with the claims convention,[4] and Minister Johnson was assured by Seward of the "President's high satisfaction" with the manner in which he had conducted "these important negotiations." [5]

[1] Text in Corr., vol. iii, pp. 752-5.
[2] Welles, vol. iii, pp. 506-7, 579.
[3] Richardson, vol. vi, p. 696.
[4] Ibid.   Corr., vol. iii, p. 757

From the first day there was not a chance for the ratification of the convention concerning the depredations of the
Alabama. Seward wrote Reverdy Johnson that "the confused
light of an incoming administration" was spreading itself
over the country. Indeed it was so, and no kind of desire
was felt to see the treaty in a favorable aspect, or to give
Andrew Johnson the honor of a settlement of this great international controversy.

Any arrangement which did not "by its terms concede the
liability of the English government for acts of her protegées,
the *Alabama* and her consorts," said a resolution in the legislature of Massachusetts would be "spurned with contempt by
the American people." [1]

The whole North rose to proclaim this or sentiments more
violently in disagreement with the convention.[2] By a unanimous vote Sumner's Committee on Foreign Relations opposed
its ratification.[3] President-elect Grant expressed himself in
conversation in the same sense. It was freely asserted in the
press that the claims of English holders of Confederate bonds
were to be arbitrated, and on the strength of the negotiation
of the treaty their quotations in England rose from the price
of old paper to ten.[4]

Seward left office with Andrew Johnson and Fish came in
with Grant before the Senate was ready to act, and Minister
Thornton was not wrong in the prophecy made to Lord
Clarendon that it would fail to receive the necessary two-
thirds vote.[5]

---

[1] Corr., vol. iii, p. 772.

[2] The friendly London Spectator characterized the state of mind of the
Northern people, "They were insulted, so they were, and they won't
take the bracelet, so they won't, and they never were in the wrong,
and Edwin shall say so before they'll kiss and be friends, and if not
they'll wait, they will, and pay him off some day. They will not be
content with damages, even though submission to the award is under
the circumstances an.open acknowledgment of error, but will have the
British government say in the teeth of all the facts that they had no
right to acknowledge the South, that it was an 'unfriendly act,' " etc.

[3] Corr., vol. iii, p. 772; Pierce, vol. iv, p. 384.

[4] Sumner's Works, vol. xiii, p. 58.   [5] Corr., vol. iii, p. 775.

On April 13 in executive session Sumner rose to speak
to the question. He submitted the adverse report of his
committee and urged the rejection of the treaty in an address of an hour in length. It exhibited "a haste" in its
preparation, he said, which had found "few precedents in
diplomacy." It could not have been completed at all to
be set before the Senate before the dismissal of the administration, but for the agency of the Atlantic cable. To this
he would not object, except that the treaty concealed "the
main cause of offence." It purported to do no more than
settle individual claims on both sides—of American citizens
who alleged injuries at the hand of England, of British subjects, at the hand of the United States, "putting the two
batches on an equality." Further and later negotiations as
to wrongs suffered at any date prior to the exchange of the
ratifications were barred. This commission was to make "a
full and final settlement of every claim upon either government."

The great matter was untouched. It was proposed, indeed,
to adjudicate the losses sustained by those whose ships and
cargoes had been seized or destroyed by the Confederate
cruisers, but in the treaty there was no recognition of "the
vaster damage to commerce driven from the ocean and that
other damage, immense and infinite, caused by the prolongation of the war," all of which Sumner said might be called
"national in contradistinction to individual." Concerning the
expense of the blockade, the prolongation of the war, the
destruction in a general sense of our commerce the treaty
was silent, yet the losses from these sources stood "mountain high with a base broad as the nation and a mass stupendous as the rebellion itself." The damage which the United
States had sustained was "vast beyond precedent." It was
"a massive grievance." There was "a deep seated sense of
enormous wrong as yet unatoned and even unacknowledged."
The attempt to close the negotiation "without a complete
settlement." was "little short of puerile." The treaty was
a "surrender," a "capitulation."

No account had been taken of the proclamation granting
the rebels belligerent rights. Thus had England, "little more
than a month after the bombardment of Fort Sumter,. when
the rebellion was still undeveloped, . . . flung a sword into
the scales with slavery." It was "unfriendly in the precipi-
tancy with which it was launched" and "more unfriendly in
substance." But for this "tremendous concession" not a
ship could have been built in Great Britain for the use of
the Confederacy. Every movement in this direction would
have been piracy. The departure of the blockade runners,
"kindred to the pirates," would have been barred. If a concession of belligerency were to have been granted at all it
could by no right have been made to extend to the ocean as
well as to operations on land, for the rebels were without
ships, without prize courts, indeed "without any of those
conditions which are the essential prerequisites of such a concession." Belligerency was a "fact" and not a "principle"
and there was, in 1861, or afterward, no ground for regarding
it as a "fact" in the South with reference to the sea.[1]

The *Alabama* case began with the "fatal concession" of
belligerency which enabled the rebels to build ships in England, extended to their construction, armament and escape,
"with so much negligence on the part of the British government as to constitute sufferance if not connivance," and re-
appeared in the "welcome and hospitality" accorded these
ships in British ports "when their evasion from British jurisdiction was well known." Their depredations which had
"made the ocean blaze all proceeded from England, which by
three different acts lighted the torch."

The commission to which the claims were to be submitted
was "an anomalous tribunal." In the case that an arbitrator
could not be agreed upon he was to be chosen "by lot" from
two persons, one named by each side. If such a proceeding
were "a proper device in the umpirage of private claims,"

[1] Sumner used the words "ocean belligerents" and "land belligerents."
Works, vol. xiii, p. 59. For a fuller discussion of this subject from his
point of view see his Cooper Institute speech of 1863.—Ibid., vol. vii,
pp. 329-492.

said Sumner, it was "strangely inconsistent with the solemnity which belongs to the present question." [1]

Sumner's speech met with the warm approval of his fellow senators. Even those whose relations with him were unfriendly came forward to congratulate him. They commended his conciliatory spirit and his moderate tone. Though Chandler and others suggested the surrender of Canada and, indeed, England's complete retirement from this continent by way of an indemnity,[2] Sumner at this time refrained from advocating any specific form of settlement. Men had spoken of war; here was no breath of anything but peaceful reparation. He had tried, he wrote Lieber, "to make England see what she had done to us." He would expose the national wrongs suffered at her hands "as plainly, but as gently as possible."[3] Our grievance, according to Senator Schurz, was presented in "the strongest light" to prepare the way for a removal of all questions of difference and restore and confirm a friendship between the nations "which ought never to have been interrupted."[4]

The Senate immediately rejected the treaty by a vote of 54 to 1[5] and removed the injunction of secrecy from the speech, that it might go out to the journals in all parts of the country and to England in the interest of a fuller understanding of the case.[6] By this act it became "practically the authorized statement of the Senate."[7] The President thanked and congratulated Sumner. Fish said that he was in hearty accord with the senator's sentiments. Leading men, both inside and outside of Congress, called upon him and wrote to him to express their approval. Welles spoke of the "manly vigor and true statesmanship" which the speech displayed.[8] Indeed, as Sumner himself averred, it

[1] Sumner's Works, vol. xiii, pp. 53-93.
[2] Corr., vol. iii, p. 784.
[3] Pierce, Sumner, vol. iv, p. 388.
[4] Ibid., p. 387.
[5] McCreery of Kentucky.
[6] Senate Executive Journal, vol. xvii, p. 163.
[7] C. C. Beaman, National and Private Alabama Claims, p. 300.
[8] Diary, vol. iii, p. 579.

represented the views of all "from the President down to the doorkeeper." [1] The newspapers joined in the praise. [2] It was, said Harper's Weekly, "the most popular speech" in the history of this remarkable orator. [3]

Even the highly intelligent and carefully critical applauded. The New York Nation found it "happily superior" to many of Sumner's recent utterances. It received "the approval of a great majority of the people of the Northern states" and could be taken to voice "the general sentiment of the country." [4] It "expressed the feeling of the country very truly," said James Russell Lowell. [5]

Its reception in England was naturally of a different character. Sir Roundell Palmer called it a "most violent" deliverance. [6] Judging from the tone of the press, said Reverdy Johnson, there seemed "not the remotest chance" that the demands of the nation, as they were voiced by Sumner, would ever be recognized. To do so much would be taken to be "an abandonment of the rights and a disregard of the honor" of the British government. [7] Sumner's acquaintance with English history and English life, and his intimate and affectionate friendships with many English men and women made his utterances the more surprising and disappointing. But for this reason, perhaps, was he listened to with the greater attention, and the fact soon sank into the consciences of the British nation that the United States had a conviction of the gravest wrong, for which nothing but humiliation of spirit, if not very large material sacrifice, would atone. [8]

It was said afterward by Sumner's unfriendly judges that,

[1] Wemyss Reid, Life of W. E. Forster, vol. ii, p. 18.
[2] Cf. Corr., vol. iii, p. 786.
[3] Issue of March 16, 1872.
[4] N. Y. Nation, April 22, 1869.
[5] But Lowell added—was Sumner not trying "rather to chime in with that feeling than to give it a juster and manlier direction?"—To E. L. Godkin under date of May 2, 1869, in Rollo Ogden, Life and Letters of E. L. Godkin, vol. ii, p. 81.
[6] Personal and Political Memorials, vol. i, p. 210.
[7] To Fish, May 10, 1869.—Corr., vol. iii, p. 789.
[8] Cf. Moorfield Storey, Charles Sumner, pp. 367, 368; T. W. Balch, The Alabama Arbitration, pp. 109-10.

by his irreconcilable words and extravagant demands, he had undone all that had been brought to fruit by months of diplomacy. The terms of the settlement which he proposed were, by strong inference if not by plain statement, extreme and unreasonable. An adjustment there could not be because of his insistence upon large indirect or consequential damages, as they everywhere came to be called, though he had used the word "national." In this, however, he but voiced the general popular sense. It was clear that nothing less would have been acceptable to our State Department in 1868 and 1869 except upon the theory that one administration was nearly done and another was about to begin.

Even Reverdy Johnson had taken into account the subject of the Queen's proclamation. "Upon this ground," he wrote Seward on February 17, 1869, after denouncing "so speedy a recognition" of the South's revolutionary effort, "the obligation of Great Britain to meet the losses" seemed to him to be "most apparent." He believed that by the terms of his convention this matter would be brought before the commission and the umpire, and the decision he could not doubt would be in favor of the United States.[1] He, however, was opposed to the view that anything could be asked for by the government for the government—an indemnity in money to go into the national treasury.[2] If such demands were to be made by us Great Britain on her side might "bring forward claims to compensation for damages done to British subjects by American blockades, which, if the Confederates were not belligerents, were illegally enforced against them."[3] In some quarters in England it was far from clear that the commission, created by the Johnson-Clarendon convention, might not have the right to hear the case of the United States on the subject of consequential damages.[4]

That a partisan like Sumner should give his favor to a treaty sent to the Senate by Andrew Johnson would have

---

[1] Corr., vol. iii, p. 764.   [2] Ibid., pp. 766-7.   [3] Ibid., p. 774.
[4] Fitzmaurice, Life of Granville, vol. ii, p. 83.

been too much to expect.[1] That the Republican party, strengthened by the majorities recorded in November for Grant, would have obligingly approved a settlement arranged by those against whom political feeling had run so high was outside the range of probability. In view of the popular antipathy, akin to hatred, for England which had been aroused during the war, the demonstrations of the Fenians which did not abate and the American sympathy which their performances aroused, the statements of our government in the correspondence induced by the controversy what else, indeed, could Sumner have done, especially when he was able to offer the most weighty reasons, as his most intelligent critics will not dispute, for the rejection of the treaty?[2] He was a party leader. He was the principal spokesman of the Senate and, through it, of the nation in making a bargain. He was stating the case in its worst form and later, in the official conduct of the negotiation on the American side, there was no material departure from his line of statement and argument. He was speaking in a parliamentary hall and his discourse was rhetorical. He was seeking to create an effect in England as well as at home, and his utterances seem to have met the demands of the occasion. It can be granted that he gave expression to some of what the New York Nation called the "sentiment" in the case[3] and mixed this with the law, as it was so generally intertwined in the American mind.[4]

[1] Cf. Reverdy Johnson, Reply to Sir Roundell Palmer, pp. 10-11.
[2] "The fault of the treaty was that it offered absolutely nothing and might have left matters in a worse condition than they now are." —Fish to Fessenden in Adams, Lee at Appomattox, p. 209.
[3] N. Y. Nation, March 18, 1869.
[4] Whatever Sumner's failings, and they were obvious, much injustice has been done him for his course on this subject. See for instance C. F. Adams in "The Treaty of Washington" in Lee at Appomattox and other papers; J. C. Bancroft Davis, Mr. Fish and the Alabama Claims; F. W. Hackett, Reminiscences of the Geneva Tribunal, pp. 50 et seq. On the other side see D. H. Chamberlain, Charles Sumner and the Treaty of Washington; Pierce, Sumner, vol. iv, chap. 56, and app. ii. The interest of the Adamses on the anti-Sumner side of this controversy may be referable in part to Sumner's opposition to C. F. Adams's appointment as minister to England. (Cf. Education of Henry Adams, p. 110.) The other writers were plainly partisans of Grant.

Fish, meanwhile, observed the course of events. He had said that he liked the speech and reiterated his admiration of it. Many of the senators who had listened and had praised it, he said, "dissented from the argument while agreeing in the conclusion."[1] Like Fessenden, he took it for what it was—"a statement of our grievances, not of our claims."[2] To his credit as a publicist he made no account of the distinction which Sumner had tried to draw between belligerency on land and "ocean belligerency."[3] The North had been on the point of exercising the right of search with reference to neutral vessels bound to Southern ports. We would stop them, and seize and condemn contraband, and in this exercise, but for a proclamation of belligerency, we soon would have been at war with Great Britain as well as with the seceded states. The South had seaboard in plenty. It was at least twice as far from the Virginia capes to the Rio Grande as from those capes to Passamaquoddy Bay. Jefferson Davis proposed to issue commissions or letters of marque to private vessels and several of these ships were armed and went to sea to catch prizes.[4] President Lincoln had proclaimed a blockade of the coastline of the Southern states, with which Great Britain was carrying on a large trade. Clearly Palmerston was right in concluding that the rebels were belligerents on the ocean.[5]

[1] Adams, Lee at Appomattox, p. 208.   [2] Ibid., p. 209.
[3] In this, too, Sumner had the support of Seward and Adams, and expressed the view long current in writing and speech touching the controversy.
[4] British Case in Geneva Arbitration, vol. i, pp. 214-5.
[5] Though Sumner had said, "As well invest the rajahs of India who never tasted salt water with this ocean prerogative, so that they too may rob and burn; as well constitute land-locked Poland, now in arms for independence, an ocean belligerent, or enroll mountain Switzerland in the same class, or join with Shakespeare in giving to inland Bohemia an outlook upon the ocean," an allusion to words in "The Winter's Tale,"

> "Our ship hath touched upon
> The deserts of Bohemia."

—Cooper Institute Speech, Works, vol. vii, p. 458; cf. Adams, Lee at Appomattox, p. 199.

The act was precipitate—Mr. Fish agreed with others on this point. England had promised to await Minister Adams's arrival but had anticipated it.[1] "Under the circumstances," Senator Fessenden wrote, "it was a grievous wrong and coupled with subsequent avowals and conduct would have justified a declaration of war."[2] But the proclamation as a basis for damages, said Fish, could be complained of "only as leading to, as characterized by, and authorizing in its execution and enforcement" the fitting out of the *Alabama* and other cruisers, the acts of hospitality accorded them in colonial ports, etc., and "as leading to the moral support given in England to the rebel cause."[3]

Reverdy Johnson came home and Motley who went out to take his place was empowered in his letter of instructions to make a treaty on the subject of naturalization on the lines laid down in the Johnson protocol. England was to be informed that the San Juan treaty awaited the ratification of the Senate, which might be delayed for a few months. In the matter of the *Alabama* convention the government abandoned neither its own claims nor those of its citizens. It had been "disapproved by the people with an approach to unanimity." Now Secretary Fish recommended "for a short time" a "suspension of the discussion" until the emotions of the people should subside.[4]

In September it was believed that a sufficient period had elapsed and the correspondence was resumed. The subject was reviewed in a brilliant way in one of the finest despatches which, in the entire course of the controversy, had yet left the State Department. There was still no want of allusion to the Queen's proclamation and its "unseasonable precipi-

[1] Cf. Corr., vol. i, pp. 34, 179, 193, 199; Geneva Arbitration, Case of the U. S., vol. i, p. 23.

[2] Adams, op. cit., p. 209.

[3] Fish to S. B. Ruggles, May 18, 1869, in Adams, op. cit., pp. 206-8. The New York Nation also was clear on this point. Issue of April 22, 1869.

[4] May 15, 1869, in Corr., vol. vi, pp. 2-4. "A fair chance" would be allowed England for "quiet consideration."—Schurz to Secretary Fish in Adams, Lee at Appomattox, p. 209.

tancy." After they had been converted into belligerents aid given in England to the Confederates, which otherwise would have been piratical, was lawful. Thus "Great Britain became and to the end continued to be the arsenal, the navy yard and the treasury of the insurgents." The losses sustained directly and consequentially were recited, though Mr. Fish said that he was not prepared to speak of the reparation due from the British government for "the vast national injuries" inflicted upon the United States. He with much force declared that, if England's municipal law were defective, it was "a domestic inconvenience of concern only to the local government." No sovereign power could "rightfully plead the defects of its own domestic penal statutes as justification or extenuation of an international wrong to another sovereign power." [1]

What Grant himself may have thought about the subject is of little moment except as the state of his mind may have contributed to the working out of the negotiation through Secretary Fish. He had regarded England as an "enemy" during the war; he had spoken of an invasion of Canada as well as of Mexico. [2] What he said in his first message to Congress in December, 1869, on this subject was what Secretary Fish bade him say. The provisions of the Johnson-Clarendon convention were "wholly inadequate for the settlement of the grave wrongs that had been sustained by this government as well as by its citizens." Grant, too, spoke of "national" damages, which were never out of any one's mind, to atone for injuries expressed "in the increased rates of insurance, in the diminution of exports and imports and other obstructions to domestic industry and production, in the effect upon the foreign commerce of the country, in the decrease and transfer to Great Britain of our commercial marine, in the prolongation of the war and the increased cost

[1] Fish to Motley, Corr., vol. vi, pp. 4-14.
[2] Adams, Lee at Appomattox, pp. 104-5, 153, 157-60; J. R. Young, Around the World with General Grant, vol. ii, pp. 167-70; J. H. Wilson, Under the Old Flag, vol. ii, pp. 378-9, and Life of J. A. Rawlins, p. 328.

(both in treasure and in lives) of its suppression." All these matters were treated in the convention simply as "ordinary commercial claims" without a word calculated "to remove the sense of the unfriendliness of the course of Great Britain in our struggle for existence which had so deeply and universally impressed itself upon the people of this country." [1]

The President's eyes now, as we have seen, were cast in the direction of San Domingo and Cuba. To Fish as to Seward, to any one, indeed, with a sense of proportion our relations with Great Britain presented not only the greater opportunity for skill in statesmanship but also for national service. Without sympathy for Grant with reference to the plan to add a few thousand Spanish negroes to the population of the United States Fish, nevertheless, was willing to support this adventure, if thereby he could gain a free hand on the larger subject of a treaty with Great Britain. Indeed, he might have extended his favor to Rawlins's scheme for an espousal of the cause of the Cuban insurgents which Grant had embraced. But here the policy which the State Department was asked, if not commanded, to assume directly conflicted with the English negotiation. It was in August, 1869, that Fish put into a safe, from which it never emerged, a proclamation conceding belligerent rights to the Cubans and in June of the next year that he wrote Grant a message which caused the defeat in the House of a resolution bearing on the same subject. Mr. Fish saw plainly enough, however much his policy at ground may have diverged from Mr. Sumner's, that the American case against Great Britain, as it had been developed, could not stand for a moment, if we were to be led away in this direction. What would become of our contention that England had been without justification in making belligerents of the Southern rebels, who had 3,000 miles of shore line, for a war between great armies in a multitude of battles covering a period of four years, if we ourselves were now to extend the same rights to a parcel of outlaws in Cuba and some paper warriors in New York who were without a

[1] Richardson, vol. vii, pp. 33-4.

coast, without a seaport, without a *de facto* government or,
for the matter of that, a *de facto* war? The United States
would have been brought into a preposterous place in reference to her great dispute with England. By our own act we
should have thrown our case out of court, returning to the
basis of the "commercial claims" of the Johnson-Clarendon
convention, if, indeed, we should have been in so good a position to secure an adjustment of the controversy.[1]

It is very clear that Sumner from his station as chairman
of the Senate Committee on Foreign Relations, with his friend
Fish at the head of the State Department, and Motley, another friend, in London, expected to direct, if he did not dictate the policy of the administration with reference to the
Alabama dispute. Sumner and Motley were writing to each
other on the subject, while the time passed in which England
was expected to recover from the shock she had received in
the rejection of the Johnson-Clarendon convention and to
bring herself to an understanding of the American point of
view. Fish at Washington, while he was still on the most
cordial relations with Sumner, availed himself of the advice
of other men, notably of Caleb Cushing, a competent coun-
sellor of large experience in practical diplomacy, as well as
with the subject of international law. Soon Sumner felt that
he was being shown less attention in the conduct of the negotiation than he had expected to receive, and he was visibly
irritated. He communicated his feelings to J. C. Bancroft
Davis, Mr. Fish's assistant, and the instructions to govern
Motley's course at London were in some degree altered to
meet Sumner's views.[2] All might have been well but for the
imbroglio over the annexation of San Domingo. Grant got
himself into such a position on this subject that to disapprove
of the scheme became a test of loyalty to the administration.
The stubbornness with which the President pursued this idea

[1] For the analogy cf. correspondence of Secretary Fish, Attorney General Hoar and the Spanish minister at Washington on the subject of
the Spanish gunboats.—Geneva Arbitration, vol. i, pp. 732-55.
[2] Davis, Mr. Fish and the Alabama Claims, pp. 31-6, 114-6; Adams, op.
cit., p. 115; Pierce, vol. iv, p. 405.

brought Fish to the parting of the ways. He felt himself
bound to go with Grant if he should continue in office at all.
He sincerely wished to be of service to the country in the settlement of the controversy with England,[1] and, little by little,
he inevitably, with unconcealed regret, drew away from Sumner.

Motley was placed at a disadvantageous distance from the
scene; indeed, his temperament did not entirely fit him for
diplomacy,[2] and in a short time he became hopelessly involved on the Sumner side. In his first interview with Lord
Clarendon he again pointed to the Queen's proclamation, the
old Pandora's box from which all the evil of whatever kind
had come. Here was "disobedience" which was "flagrant,"
Davis told Sumner. When he was sent out he was instructed
to make one statement; when he arrived he did the reverse.[3]
He himself knew that he had "overstated the case," but he
was ready to defend his course,[4] when he was censured for
it by Fish,[5] and he was told that hereafter the negotiation
would be conducted at Washington instead of at London, a
rebuke which some men would not have borne without resigning.[6] He was in conference with his own and Sumner's enlightened friend George Bemis of Boston, who was in London
at the time and who had definite and very well known views
upon the subject, and was carrying on a private correspondence
with Sumner to whom, indeed, Moran avers, he sent his de-

[1] To be an agent in this he should esteem "the greatest glory and the
greatest happiness of my life," he wrote a friend in 1869.—Adams, op.
cit., p. 125.
[2] Motley was unquestionably out of sympathy with the rank and file
of his countrymen. He, Mrs. Motley and their daughters in an obvious
way were interested in their own social advancement. They "hugely
loved the company of lords." They were "not republicans but aristo-
crats," said Moran. In their household the servants were instructed to
call Motley "His Excellency" and Mrs. Motley "Her Excellency." He
was charged with snobbishness, fussiness, a suspicious nature, indecision
and vanity. Cf. Daily entries in Moran's MS. Diary covering the
period during which Motley was minister.
[3] Davis's Diary in Library of Congress, entry for July 26, 1870.
[4] Moran's Diary, July 15, 1869.
[5] Letter No. 23.   [6] Moran's Diary, July 10, 1869.

spatches to the State Department in duplicate, an "unpardonable" violation of usage and law.[1]

It is safe to conclude that Grant knew almost nothing about the Queen's proclamation in its relation to international law in general or to this particular dispute. But he did know that he desired to make a similar concession of neutral rights to the insurgents of Cuba, and, bent upon this policy, he would have Motley find other ground for the English negotiation, though this feature of the American case had played so large a part in the correspondence thus far, and Fish, as we have seen, set so high a value upon it that he had disobeyed the President's orders on the subject.

The fact remained that Motley had made an unfavorable impression upon Grant which was heightened by the tattling of an impudent sot, General Adam Badeau, who had attached himself to the President, and went out as assistant secretary of legation at London. This man pretended in England that he "owned" Grant. He did not scruple to declare that he had obtained Motley the appointment as minister—he himself should have had the place. Not receiving the social attention which he thought his due, while Motley's position in this respect was very high, he spread the report that the minister was to be recalled, and otherwise sought to degrade him in the sight of the English people and in America.[2] Letters from Badeau reached the President and, as Sumner's opposition to the San Domingo project became more outspoken, a resolution to humiliate and punish the senator through Motley took firm possession of Grant's mind.

Desire to support the minister and to cooperate with him did not exist. Instead there was apparently a design to badger him out of the office. That Motley was to be caught for a

[1] Moran's Diary, July 29, 1869.
[2] Cf. Moran's Diary for this period. Grant said to Bancroft Davis that Motley was a "dangerous man, bad-tempered and violent in language and an intellectual dandy." (Davis's Diary, Aug. 18, 1870.) The President's antipathy, it is said, dated from the day he discovered that Motley "parted his hair in the middle."—Henry Adams, The Education of Henry Adams, p. 276; N. Y. Nation, Jan. 19 and Feb. 23, 1871. This story is repeated in Badeau's Grant in Peace.

drum-head court martial was clear when on October 11, 1869, he was instructed to approach the British Foreign Office in the spirit which he had been censured for manifesting in July. Indeed Motley asked Fish by cable if he might not soften the language of the note. Permission to do this was denied, though he was told to avoid giving Clarendon a copy in writing, unless it should be particularly requested.[1]

One thing led to another until in July, 1870, Motley was asked to resign. Sumner himself was removed from the chairmanship of the Committee on Foreign Relations in March, 1871. The whole train of events was animated by vindictive personal feeling. Whatever may have been thought of the worth of Sumner's advice and leadership in the great matter having to do with our relations with England, it was infinitely more valuable than Grant's ever could be, because it was founded upon knowledge of the history of the controversy and by experience in statesmanship. Grant grew angry, Sumner followed or preceded him. Had the senator been dealt with considerately his unreasonableness would have been less manifest. Had he had the responsibility of leadership his management of the affair would have been marked by a conciliatory spirit which was not wanting in him when he faced a great question of this kind. As it was, after suffering such indignity and abuse, when early in 1871 he was asked by Secretary Fish for a statement of his views as to a basis of settlement, he spoke of England's surrender of Canada,[2] a suggestion frequently heard in Congress and the press, led by the New York Tribune.[3] Annexation was in many men's minds. It was an eventuality seriously and favorably contemplated by President Grant and Secretary Fish who in turn earnestly discussed the matter with the British minister in Washington, Sir Edward Thornton, who seems to have been not averse to

[1] Fish's No. 70 quite similar to Motley's No. 43 in July. The "insult" was found in the words "speculated improvidently and to their own discomfiture in the expected dismemberment and downfall of the great American republic."—Moran's Diary, Oct. 11, 1869.

[2] Davis, Mr. Fish and the Alabama Claims, pp. 65-6.

[3] Cf. Adams, op. cit., pp. 152-3; N. Y. Nation, Feb. 23, 1871.

listening to the suggestion.[1] Sumner, therefore, said nothing
which could have occasioned any one great surprise when he
declared that "the withdrawal of the British flag from this
hemisphere, including the provinces and islands," could not
be abandoned "as a condition or preliminary" of a treaty.[2]

Such a statement on Sumner's side was taken to be the
measure of his capacity to deal with the *Alabama* question.
Rather was it an angry retort meant, not for England, but
for those men in his own country who were plotting his downfall and who were on the point of bringing it about.

What Motley had not succeeded in doing in London, what,
indeed, he had been barred from doing, was being adroitly
achieved by unofficial agents in Washington. Sir John
Rose, or Mr. Rose as he still was in 1869, was a Scotchman
who had been prominent for a number of years in business
and politics in Canada. In Washington on official matters he
was thrown into friendly relations with Caleb Cushing.[3] They
together, shortly after the rejection of the convention in 1869,
discussed the question of reopening negotiations. In a little
while Mr. Rose visited England where other public men,
John Bright and William E. Forster among them, were laboring to the same end.[4] Indeed Rose, while in London, was
secretly commissioned by Lord Granville, by direction of
Gladstone and the Queen, to go about the task of beginning a
negotiation which would effect a "reconciliation with the
states." [5] It was intimated now, in full understanding with
Fish, that "a kindly word or an expression of regret" in a
new convention would be of more value "than the most irre-
fragable reasoning on principles of international law." The

[1] Adams, op. cit., pp. 156-9, 161.
[2] J. B. Moore, International Arbitrations, vol. i, pp. 525-6; Adams,
op. cit., p. 147. In my opinion C. F. Adams has done injustice to
Sumner on this point, although I perceive what is clear enough, that
Sumner made the suggestion with the object, in some degree at least,
of preventing a settlement by those who had, with not a little spite-
fulness, desired to conclude it without him.—Adams, op. cit., pp. 148,
149, 165; cf. Pierce, Sumner, vol. iv, pp. 480, 481, 635-8.
[3] Cf. F. W. Hackett, Reminiscences of the Geneva Tribunal, p. 57.
[4] Cf. Education of Henry Adams, p. 125.
[5] Fitzmaurice, Life of Granville, vol. ii, pp. 29, 86.

advantage of conducting the negotiations at Washington rather than London, as a means of propitiating public opinion in the United States, was pointed out and the cause was being steadily advanced.[1]

Urging England forward were considerations having to do with the rapid development of events on the Continent of Europe. There Count Bismarck was beginning to cast a long shadow. Ill omen in that direction had hastened the Johnson-Clarendon negotiation. Now more had come to pass. The outbreak of the war between Prussia and France, which was so quickly concluded, to prepare the way for a united and powerful Germany, caused the public men of England to look about them seriously. Confession of wrong at once, without more ado, were wiser than to face the *Alabama* precedents. With such a danger at the door the sooner such views of international law were disavowed the better,[2] and in some degree this end was achieved in the sight of the world in 1870 by the appointment of a commission to revise the British neutrality laws. As a result of its recommendations the Tory administration passed an act to take the place of the old Foreign Enlistment Act of 1819, which had been the subject of so much controversy, thus putting the country on solid ground at last.[3]

Motley when he was asked to resign had refused in vigorous language. A cablegram demanding a reply was received the same day, perhaps before the letter came. The minister, who suspected with good reason that Badeau was behind the movement for his displacement, since that man had lately returned to London as consul general, again to spread reports of the minister's recall, bade Fish tell the President that he was "compelled to decline the offer which he makes in giving me an opportunity of resigning my post." [4] Instantly Motley got into an unbecoming rage, swearing at Grant and berating

---

[1] Adams, op. cit., pp. 126-8; Davis, Mr. Fish and the Alabama Claims, p. 48.   [2] Adams, op. cit., pp. 130, 133, 135.
[3] Sir Roundell Palmer, Family and Personal Memorials, vol. i, p. 416.
[4] Moran's Diary, July 14.

his country and its people.[1]   He could not compose himself
until he learned that Frelinghuysen, who had been nominated
to his place, had declined to take up the succession.[2]   Motley,
therefore, remained in possession of the mission.

In August the President tendered the post to Trumbull,[3]
who could not be induced to accept the office.   Grant's im-
patience increased.   Some one must be found soon, he said.
The names of George William Curtis [4] and Horace Greeley,[5]
were suggested.   Fish himself was in mind, if he should insist
upon the execution of his plan to leave the State Department,
though none, barring Motley, who seemed to think that the
Secretary wished the place for himself, entertained the opinion
that he would accept.[6]   In September Samuel G. Howe was
offered the post but declined.   Pierrepont and Andrew D.
White were under discussion.[7]   Senator Morton of Indiana
was nominated; he declined.[8]

In the legation the weeks and months wore on, Motley
"damning" Grant each morning before he began his day's
work.[9]   Finally, in November, while he was visiting the·Mar-

[1] He "damned his countrymen as vulgar and brutal and wished the
damned government might be destroyed," says Moran.   He would
"never go among the vulgar brutes again, but would lay his bones in a
foreign land."   Moran agreed that Motley had been badly treated but
found in this no reason why he should not "act the gentleman."
—Moran's Diary, July 15 and 17, 1870.
[2] N. Y. Nation, Aug. 25, 1870.
[3] Horace White, Life of Trumbull, pp. 347-8.
[4] Edward Cary, Life of G. W. Curtis, p. 215.
[5] Hollister, Life of Schuyler Colfax, p. 359.
[6] Moran's Diary.
[7] Bancroft, Davis's Diary, Sep. 8, 1870.   Both Howe and White soon
afterward were put upon the San Domingo commission.
[8] N. Y. Nation, Sep. 29 and Oct. 27, 1870; C. F. Adams, Lee at Appomattox, pp. 161-2.   Morton declined, said Grant, because "a bitter
Copperhead" would take his place in the Senate should he go.—Adam
Badeau, Grant in Peace, p. 472.
[9] He was "like a bear with a sore head," said Moran.   He continued
to abuse his fellow Americans and opposed the plan for the government
to buy a house for the minister lest they be quartered upon him when
they came to London.   However, he was not alone in a feeling that
such as travelled abroad and visited our legations were a nuisance.
Motley's successor, General Schenck, also complained of being "run
down with these damned Americans."—Moran's Diary, Sep. 26, 1871.

quis of Salisbury at Hatfield he received his "letter of recall."
He was to have gone thence to stay with Disraeli at Hugh-
enden Manor and with Gladstone at Hawarden. Socially he
had made himself a distinguished success, but he was now
peremptorily dismissed, and after he had had his "audience
of leave" with the Queen the legation was put in charge of
Moran. In a little while the President named Robert C.
Schenck of Ohio, a respected Whig in the days of Webster
and Clay, now for some years one of the leaders of the House,
where he was a vigorous debater, who accepted the post.[1]
The new minister did not reach London until June, 1871, but
the country was relieved to think that the contention as to
the possession of the office had come to an end.

Motley out of the way, Sumner was yet to be eliminated
and his statement regarding the withdrawal of the British flag
from the American hemisphere, which earlier had been quite
as much an idea of Grant as of Sumner, was to be used to
mask personal excuses for driving him from the Committee
on Foreign Relations. It was made to appear that a settlement with England could not be effected unless he were set
aside and, as we have seen, this end was accomplished without delay.

In his message of December, 1870, Grant spoke of Great
Britain's unwillingness to concede that she had been "guilty
of any negligence, or had permitted any act during the war
by which the United States has just cause of complaint."
Saying that "our firm and unalterable convictions" were "directly the reverse," he recommended Congress to authorize
the appointment of a commission "to take proof of the amount
and the ownership" of the private claims, and urged that they
be settled by the United States, thus giving the government
responsible control of all the demands against Great Britain.[2]

The London newspapers remarked the "menacing" tone of
the President's message; its meaning was well understood and,

---

[1] "A gentleman whose eminent fitness for this high position is generally acknowledged, even by his political opponents."—Harper's
Weekly, Jan. 21, 1871.   [2] Richardson, vol. vii, p. 102.

in a little while, on January 9, 1871, Mr. Rose was again in Washington on a confidential mission, ready for a conversation with Secretary Fish. On the 11th he called at the State Department and submitted a memorandum which formed the basis of the agreement.[1] The conversations behind the curtain proceeded. The cables were busy again. The "expression of regret" was demanded; "less than this" would not satisfy the United States. Assurances on this subject were secured,[2] and, on January 26, Sir Edward Thornton, under instructions from the Gladstone ministry, through Lord Granville, now, since Clarendon's death in 1870 Secretary of State for Foreign Affairs, wrote to Mr. Fish proposing a Joint High Commission, composed of members "to be named by each government" to meet in Washington to discuss questions in difference between the two nations with regard to the Canadian fisheries.[3]

This was the wedge and the way opened. Fish replied that the fishery subject might be discussed, if at the same time attention should be given to "the acts committed by the several vessels" during the rebellion which had "given rise to the claims generically known as the *Alabama* claims." On February 1 Thornton was ready to say that he had been authorized by Granville to submit these matters "to the consideration of the same high commission," if the United States would include the claims of British subjects which had arisen out of the war.[4] The papers were sent to Congress and on February 9 the President forwarded to the Senate the names of five persons who should represent us in the negotiation. He had chosen the Secretary of State, Hamilton Fish; Justice Samuel Nelson of the Supreme Court; ex-Attorney General Hoar; the new minister to Great Britain, General Schenck;

[1] J. C. B. Davis MS. journal, quoted in J. B. Moore, International Arbitrations, vol. i, pp. 523-5; cf. Davis, Mr. Fish and the Alabama Claims, pp. 59-64, 145. For Rose's authority to act for the British ministry, see Fitzmaurice, Life of Granville, vol. ii, p. 29.

[2] Geneva Arbitration, vol. ii, pp. 586-7.

[3] How grave these had become can be gleaned from President Grant's message of December, 1870.—Richardson, vol. vii, pp. 102-4.

[4] Corr., vol. vi, pp. 15-18.

and George H. Williams of Oregon who had just ceased to
be a senator from Oregon. Assistant Secretary of State J. C.
Bancroft Davis was made secretary of the commission on the
part of the United States. Great Britain named Earl de Grey
and Ripon, a member of the Gladstone cabinet; Sir Stafford
Northcote, later Lord Iddlesleigh, a Tory leader; Sir Edward
Thornton, British minister to the United States; Sir John A.
Macdonald, Premier of Canada; and Professor Mountague
Bernard of Oxford University.[1] Lord Tenterden, Under Secretary of State for Foreign Affairs, was appointed secretary
of the commission on the part of Great Britain.[2]

The High Commissioners met in Washington on February
27, and continued their sessions for nearly six weeks. On May
8 the treaty was signed with pleasant ceremonies,[3] and on
the 10th the President submitted it to the Senate, which referred it to the Committee on Foreign Relations of which
Sumner was no longer a member. That he still would be
a factor, not to be disallowed in executive session and in directing public opinion in the country at large, both the British
and the American commissioners very well knew.[4] He played
a manly part and forbore opposition to the ratification of the
treaty which another might have offered under similar irritation.

The expression of contrition which Rose had urged as a
point of beginning was found in the first article. Here it was
distinctly set down that "her Britannic Majesty" authorized
her "high commissioners and plenipotentiaries to express in
a friendly spirit the regret felt by her Majesty's government

[1] Professor Bernard had but lately completed his Historical Account
of the Neutrality of Great Britain during the American Civil War, a
careful examination of the subject from the English standpoint.

[2] Granville's instructions to the commissioners, under date of Feb. 9,
1871, are in British Case and Papers, vol. iii, pp. 945-9.

[3] A. Lang, Life of Sir Stafford Northcote, vol. ii, n. 17.

[4] That they systematically flattered him and gave him social attentions to propitiate him is an allegation of C. F. Adams in his unfriendly
essay, "The Treaty of Washington," in his Lee at Appomattox and
Other Papers, pp. 183-6; cf. Lang, Life of Sir Stafford Northcote, vol.
ii, p. 23; Pierce, Sumner, vol. iv, pp. 488-9.

for the escape, under whatever circumstances, of the *Alabama* and other vessels from British ports, and for the depredations committed by these vessels." It was provided that the claims should be referred to a "tribunal of arbitration," composed of five men to be named, one each, by the President of the United States, the Queen of England, the King of Italy, the President of Switzerland and the Emperor of Brazil. The arbitrators were to meet at Geneva "at the earliest convenient day." Each of "the high contracting parties" should name one person to attend the tribunal as its agent. The "case" of each party, accompanied by the documentary and other evidence upon which it relied, was to be put into the hands of the arbitrators in duplicate within a period of six months after the ratification of the treaty, and within four months, subsequently, the parties might present a "counter case" by way of rejoinder with additional evidence. The respective agents were to furnish their written or printed arguments within two ensuing months and might have counsel.

In Article VI three rules were laid down binding neutrals to use diligence in time of war to prevent the fitting out and departure from their ports of such vessels as the *Alabama*, and naval operations generally of one belligerent directed against another. While the British government did not admit these rules to have been in force during the Civil War, that government, "in order to evince its desire of strengthening the friendly relations between the two countries and of making satisfactory provision for the future," agreed that, "in deciding the questions between the two countries" arising out of the *Alabama* class of claims, the arbitrators should "assume that her Majesty's government had undertaken to act upon the principles set forth in these rules."[1]

The decision of the tribunal should, "if possible," be made within three months after the closing of the argument. In case the arbitrators found that there had been any failures on

---

[1] Called by Lord Russell "an ex post facto law." By this law and by its "arbitrary interpretation" the conduct of the British government was to be tried "many years after the event."—Recollections and Suggestions, p. 325.

Great Britain's part it was suggested that there be an award of "a sum in gross," to be paid in coin to the United States within twelve months. The first eleven of the forty-three articles comprising the treaty had to do with the *Alabama* question.[1] The rest related to other classes of claims against either government by citizens of the other, growing out of the war, which were to be referred to a mixed commission of three members to be convened at Washington "at the earliest convenient period"; to differences as to the use of the fisheries on the British North American coast for the adjustment of which there was to be another mixed commission of three members to meet in Halifax; to the San Juan boundary question which was referred for arbitration and award to the new Emperor of Germany;[2] the navigation of the St. Lawrence and the connected canals and of Lake Michigan; the transit of goods in bond through Canada and the United States, and the exemption from duty of lumber cut on the banks of the St. John River.[3]

On May 24, 1871, the treaty was ratified by the Senate by a vote of 50 to 12.[4] Ratifications were exchanged by the two governments on June 17, and it was proclaimed on the 4th of July. The arbitrators now could be named. Great Britain appointed the Lord Chief Justice, Sir Alexander J. E. Cockburn; the United States, most properly,[5] its minister to

---

[1] Corr., vol. vi, pp. 19-27.

[2] The convention arranged by Reverdy Johnson in 1869 which provided for a reference of the question to the President of the Swiss Confederation was not ratified by the United States Senate; the period in which it might have done so expired without action.—Caleb Cushing, Treaty of Washington, pp. 204-5; J. B. Moore, International Arbitrations, vol. i, p. 224; British Case and Papers, vol. iii, p. 948.

[3] J. H. Haswell, Treaties and Conventions, pp. 478-93; J. B. Moore, International Arbitrations, vol. i, p. 553. Cf. Granville's instructions to the commissioners to attend the conferences at Washington in 1871 in British Case and Papers, vol. iii, pp. 945-9.

[4] Senate Executive Journal, vol. xviii, p. 108.

[5] Objected to, however, on some sides in England because he had had so prominent a part in the development of the dispute, wherefore to appoint him for this service was "undoubtedly contrary to the traditional rules of judicial etiquette."—Sir Roundell Palmer, Personal and Political Memorials, vol. i, p. 232.

England during the war, Charles Francis Adams; the King of Italy, Count Frederic Sclopis of Turin, a senator and a distinguished jurist; the President of Switzerland, Jacques Staempfli, himself three times president of the Confederation,[1] and the Emperor Dom Pedro, Viscount d'Itajubá, at the time the Brazilian minister in Paris. J. C. Bancroft Davis was designated to act as agent for the United States, Lord Tenterden for Great Britain. To serve as counsel for the United States William M. Meredith of Philadelphia, an eminent lawyer, once secretary of the treasury, and Caleb Cushing, a veteran international jurist and a general master of diplomacy, were chosen. But Mr. Meredith was unable to proceed to Europe and his services could not be made available, whereupon Benjamin R. Curtis and William M. Evarts, who had acted together so brilliantly in the Johnson impeachment trial, were asked to join Mr. Cushing. Curtis declined and his place was tendered to Morrison R. Waite, a lawyer of Toledo, Ohio, who accepted.[2] Sir Roundell Palmer, later Lord Selborne, in turn Solicitor General and Attorney General of the crown, while our war was in progress, now enjoying a large if not the largest practice at the English bar,[3] was chosen to act as counsel for Great Britain.

Instantly there was great activity in the State Department. Under Secretary Fish's general direction Bancroft Davis, who was to take charge of the interests of the United States at Geneva, prepared the "case."[4] Clerks wrought until midnight through the fervor of a Washington summer.[5] The documentary evidence was put in order and printed. The cantonal

[1] An appointment very unwelcome to Great Britain.—Bancroft Davis Papers.

[2] F. W. Hackett, Reminiscences, pp. 73-83, 388-92.

[3] London Times, Jan. 26, 1872. For descriptive accounts of the arbitrators, agents, etc., see Hackett, pp. 213-25; Davis, Mr. Fish and the Alabama Claims, pp. 85-6; J. R. Young, Men and Memories, pp. 359-61; Cushing, The Treaty of Washington, pp. 26-7, 78-99; Sir R. Palmer, Personal and Political Memorials, vol. ii, pp. 246-53.

[4] Geneva Arbitration, vol. ii, p. 415; ibid., vol. iv, pp. 3-4; Davis, Mr. Fish and the Alabama Claims, p. 86; Hackett, p. 88.

[5] Geneva Arbitration, vol. ii, p. 413.

government tendered the tribunal the use of the Hotel de Ville at Geneva and the arbitrators, agents, counsel and a retinue of secretaries repaired to that place to attend the opening session which was set for December 15, 1871. As neither Lord Chief Justice Cockburn nor Charles Francis Adams, the ranking members, could preside, because of their relationship to the controversy, the choice fell upon Count Sclopis, the Italian arbitrator, further commended for the place since he was the only one of the three neutral members who had knowledge of the English tongue—the other two could not as much as read the language.[1]

Beyond the organization of the body and the presentation of the "case" on each side nothing could be done, and on the following day, December 16, adjournment was taken [2] for a period covering the six months allowed each side to prepare its "counter case" and the evidence which it should choose to offer in rebuttal, and to make ready its "argument." The winter could be spent in Paris or London in study of the subject. Mr. Adams, who had contemplated a trip up the Nile, returned for personal reasons to America.

In this conjuncture Fish, who had so reluctantly assumed the duties of the State Department, again resigned. At Davis's departure he had announced that such a step was in prospect. Throughout the summer Grant was confronted with the problem of finding a new Secretary of State. He offered the place to Colfax,[3] and had Andrew D. White and other men under discussion for the succession. When Congress opened in December, 1871, the President had still made no progress with his work. He had promised Fish not to urge him to remain and now did not do so; Grant said simply that the situation "distressed him," that he "regretted it extremely," that he was "at a loss to fill the place." He went to Fish's rooms and repeated these words. His expressions were enforced by a letter signed by Vice President Colfax and 44 senators, "earnestly

[1] Bancroft Davis Papers.
[2] Geneva Arbitration, vol. iv, p. 17.
[3] On August 4, 1871. See Hollister, Life of Colfax, pp. 356-7.

pressing" the secretary to remain, and by "personal importunities" from other sides, so that he was prevailed upon to
stay yet a while in the place.[1]

Bancroft Davis's "case" was a volume of nearly 500 pages
divided into six parts.[2] It reviewed the course pursued by
Great Britain toward the United States, beginning with the
Queen's proclamation conceding the insurgents belligerent
rights, which the author alleged had been actuated "by a conscious unfriendly purpose." His statement of grievances in
proof of the "insincere neutrality of the British cabinet of that
day" outdid in its eloquence the utterances of any jingo who
yet had spoken on the question. Passing to a discussion of
"the duties which Great Britain as a .neutral should have observed toward the United States," which involved a consideration of the law bearing on the case, and Lord Russell's failure
in the performance of these duties, there followed specifications of these failures with reference to particular ships—the
Sumter, the *Nashville,* the *Florida* and her three tenders; the
Alabama and her tender, the *Tuscaloosa;* the *Retribution,* the
Georgia, the *Tallahassee,* the *Chickamauga* and the *Shenandoah.* He, in conclusion, asked for an award of "a sum in
gross."

Careful computations were made by the Navy Department
indicating that the United States had expended not less than
$7,000,000 in attempting to capture the cruisers which England
had allowed to depart from her shores, and had not arrested
afterward in her colonial ports or on the high seas, though
it was clear that they had violated the law of neutrality. The
direct losses inflicted upon shipping by the *Alabama* were
thought to reach $6,547,000, by the *Shenandoah* $6,488,000, by
the *Florida* $3,698,000. The increased war premium item was
$1,120,795 more. Here was a total of $19,000,000.[3] To be
added were two other items, (1), the loss in the transfer of

---

[1] Fish to Davis in Bancroft Davis Papers.
[2] The Case of the United States to be Laid Before the Tribunal of
Arbitration. Reprinted in Geneva Arbitration, vol. i, pp. 9-190.
[3] Corr., vol. vii, pp. i-ccxlvii.

the American commercial fleet to the British flag, and, (2),
"the prolongation of the war and the addition of a large sum
to the cost of the war." [1] As for the compensation which
might be appropriate on the first account Mr. Davis quoted
a speech in the House of Commons by Mr. Cobden, who had
declared that at the outbreak of the war two-thirds of the
commerce at New York was carried in American bottoms,
while three years later three-fourths of it was brought in and
taken out of the port in foreign bottoms. The "vast" mercantile property of the United States had been "virtually
made valueless." [2] The tribunal was asked to estimate the
amount which ought to be paid us on this account. The sum
which we should receive by reason of the prolongation of the
war likewise was indeterminable. Great Britain had been
"the real author" of our "woes." The measure of her responsibility it would be "impossible" to state, but it was "vast
injury" for which we should be compensated.[3] Moreover
there should be interest upon the claims from July 1, 1863,
to the date of payment. Finally he uttered a threatful prophecy: if the tribunal should find that the operations of Bulloch and the other Confederate agents in London were "legitimate" the "foundation" would be laid, he declared, "for endless
dissensions and wars." [4]

Davis was much complimented for the form and tone of
the "case." His uncle George Bancroft wrote—"Your argument is masterly, the *culpa* of England is stated more clearly
than ever before and Lord John Russell's character as Secretary for Foreign Affairs damaged beyond reparation." [5] Bancroft sent copies of the "case" to Bluntschli, Gneist, Holtzen-
dorff, Heffter and other German publicists. Their favorable
opinions were sought and received. To Caleb Cushing it was
a "most able, thorough, complete, learned and effective exposition of the claims of the United States against Great Britain
. . . worthy in all respects of the subject, and honorable

[1] Geneva Arbitration, vol. i, p. 185.
[2] Ibid., pp. 187-8.   [3] Ibid., pp. 188-9.   [4] Ibid., p. 82.
[5] From Berlin, Dec. 12, 1871, in Bancroft Davis Papers.

alike to its immediate author, to the Department and to the government." Evarts joined Cushing in praise of the document, when it was said in America that the counsel were not in accord with the agent as to the presentation of the matter in controversy.[1]

The "case" was translated into several languages. Ministers and consuls of the United States in Europe were asked to bring it to the attention of the leading statesmen and the editors of influential newspapers and reviews in those countries in which they were stationed. With an enterprise characteristic of America, if little in accord with the idea of weighing evidence and securing justice in an international court, press agents were employed under Davis's direction to shape public sentiment favorable to our side of the controversy.[2]

However much admiration may have been expended upon his work the plain truth is that he presented the subject in an "intemperate way."[3] The "case" was characterized by much of what Europe has been wont to regard as "Yankee swagger." The assumption of a wrong purpose, the confidence in a deliberate hostility which had made England virtually a partner of the South, the suggestion that new dissensions would follow a decision unfavorable to the United States gave the paper an unpleasant tone. To Sir Roundell Palmer its spirit seemed "acrimonious"; the manner of stating the subject was "totally wanting in international courtesy."[4]

The British "case," on the other hand, the work of Mountague Bernard and Lord Tenterden, acting under the direction of Sir Roundell Palmer,[5] was a simple and respectful presenta-

---

[1] The N. Y. Evening Post had printed what Bancroft Davis called "unfounded slanders" on this point. Cushing and Evarts replied on Dec. 7, 1871. See Bancroft Davis Papers.
[2] Bancroft Davis Papers.   [3] Moran's Diary, Feb. 10, 1872.
[4] Sir Roundell Palmer, Personal and Political Memorials, vol. i, pp. 229, 230; cf. ibid., vol. ii, p. 277. The "case" had an "attorney-like smartness," says the younger C. F. Adams, "more appropriate to the wranglings of a quarter sessions court than to pleadings before a grave international tribunal."—Adams, Lee at Appomattox, p. 190.
[5] Palmer, Personal and Political Memorials, vol. i, pp. 227, 228-9; Hackett, Reminiscences, p. 149.

tion of the fact and the law touching the controversy from the opposite standpoint.[1] The proclamation of neutrality was defended. It rested upon a perfectly sound basis. There had been absence of "precipitation" in issuing it. No other course could have been adopted. Great Britain had but little preceded other governments in conceding the South belligerent rights.

The steps which had been taken to detain the *Alabama*, the seizure of the *Pampero* and the "Laird rams," and the care given to hearing and examining the. facts as to other vessels at home and in the colonies, concerning which Minister Adams had made representations to the British government on the ground of violations of neutrality, were recited with reference to the documents. Only four vessels, so it was said, had been made the subject of claims. The *Georgia* and the *Shenandoah* were never "in any manner or degree" fitted out for war in her Majesty's dominions, or were they "specially adapted to war-like use." No information of any kind respecting them had been furnished to Great Britain until they were out of reach.[2] The controversy, therefore, was reduced in the worst case to the *Florida* and the *Alabama;* and of these the *Florida* had been seized in a colonial court and released because of a want of evidence to hold her, and the *Alabama* got to sea before the order to take her into custody was given, though "the utmost expedition" had been used by Russell in referring the complaints as to her character "to the proper departments of the government for inquiry."[3]

The cruisers were at large because, as it appeared, "no serious endeavors" were put forth by the United States "to intercept or capture" them. The losses which they inflicted upon the United States's mercantile fleet would have been averted or materially diminished "had reasonable activity and diligence been exerted" by our government and its officers for that purpose. The "general course of her Britannic Majesty's

[1] Cf. Adams, op. cit., pp. 190-91.
[2] Geneva Arbitration, vol. i, p. 407.
[3] Ibid., p. 408.

government throughout the war was governed by a strict regard for the obligations of neutrality."[1]

Upon a reading of the "cases" as they were presented to the arbitrators the distance separating the two governments never seemed to be greater. One asked for damages for losses sustained from the depredations of thirteen vessels, plus vast sums to cover both direct and consequential injuries on account of the pursuit of these ships, increased insurance rates, the destruction of the American mercantile marine and the prolongation of the war, with interest to date. The other denied any responsibility whatever except in relation to two vessels, the *Florida* and the *Alabama*, and asserted that it had exhausted its powers in trying to prevent the escape of these ships.

Bancroft Davis was not done receiving congratulations from America and the Continent for the skill he had shown in the preparation of the "case" when a great pother arose in England. The people, animated anyhow by a really "bitter dislike" of the United States, had "consented but unwillingly" to the plan for an international tribunal,[2] and the whole negotiation, even after it had reached the arbitrators, was in danger of falling to the ground.

At first English public opinion seemed to be dazed.[3] Soon

[1] Geneva Arbitration, vol. i, p. 409. Of the British case the London Times said: "Not only is it far more colorless and temperate in its tone, but it is far more limited in its scope, proceeding, as it does, on the assumption that international law alone is the standard by which the conduct of Great Britain must be judged."—Issue of Jan. 30, 1872.

[2] Fitzmaurice, Life of Granville, vol. ii, p. 107; Walpole, Life of Lord John Russell, vol. ii, p. 305. The settlement in general was gall and wormwood to Lord Russell and the political characters who had been responsible for the British policy which now was to be reviewed and in all probability discredited. (Sir Roundell Palmer, Personal and Political Memorials, vol. i, pp. 216-20.) "No swindler or pickpocket ever had worse terms applied to him than those which were applied to us by the American government," said Lord Russell after reading Davis's "case."—Cf. Bancroft Davis Papers.

[3] The "case" lay in Granville's hands for seven weeks without action. At a dinner which Schenck tendered Evarts in London on Jan. 18, though both Palmer and Tenterden were present, nothing was said to indicate the coming of the storm.—Moran's Diary.

there was such an outburst of feeling as had not been seen since the rejection of the Johnson-Clarendon convention; it was even more violent. Press and people were in a state of panic. We had acted in bad faith. To present such demands the London Telegraph declared to be "effrontery"; the Spectator called it "sharp practice."[1] The indirect claims were "preposterous," said the Standard. We seemed to be acting "under the advice of a sharp and unscrupulous attorney." The "case" was a "malignant composition," said the Saturday Review; the narrative was "perverted and spiteful." To the Times it was "a most distorted version of events and circumstances." It was impossible, said the Saturday Review again, to discuss questions with a power which had "an ethical code of its own." The claims, in the view of the Daily News, were intended merely as "an electioneering card" in the Presidential campaign.[2]

It had been understood by the British members of the Joint High Commission, when they were in Washington, so it was said now, that all the claims for "national" damages were *ultra vires*. The treaty had been signed and ratified under an impression that this part of the subject had been eliminated from the arbitration.[3] This was denied by Secretary Fish and all the other commissioners who had acted in behalf of the United States.[4]

True some in England uttered other views, as, e.g., the Earl of Derby and Lord Cairns speaking in the House of Lords on June 4, 1872.[5] The "national" claims, said Fraser's Magazine, were "the sole and only point in dispute. The course of

[1] This, too, was it called by W. E. Forster.—Wemyss Reid, Life of Forster, vol. ii, p. 23.

[2] Geneva Arbitration, vol. v, pp. 4-5; Bancroft Davis Papers; Hackett, Reminiscences, pp. 165-6; Cushing, Treaty of Washington, pp. 41-2.

[3] Sir Stafford Northcote stated in a speech at Exeter in May, 1872, that he and his colleagues at Washington had understood the American commissioners to make a distinct promise that the claims for indirect damages were not to be pressed (Geneva Arbitration, vol. ii, pp. 593-5, 603-4; cf. Davis, Mr. Fish and the Alabama Claims, pp. 90-5; A. Lang, Life of Sir Stafford Northcote, vol. ii, pp. 1-12). Sir Edward Thornton in New York and Lord Ripon in the House of Lords spoke definitely in the same sense.—Bancroft Davis Papers.

[4] Geneva Arbitration, vol. ii, pp. 596-601.   [5] Ibid., vol. iv, pp. 551-3.

action upon everything else was already decided." In view of
this fact the writer wished to know what title the British
commissioners might have "to be considered men of ordinary
intelligence and judgment." [1]

But, with few exceptions, Tory and Liberal alike said that
they had been deceived. In the House of Commons Disraeli
called the indirect claims "wild and preposterous"; they were
likened to tribute exacted from "a conquered people." [2] Gladstone declared that they were demands which "no nation with
a spark of honor or spirit left could submit to, even at the
point of death." [3]

The dispute waxed warmer and warmer. To Moran's displeasure Schenck made no note of the utterances of the English press until February 2, when he telegraphed Fish that
the London journals "all" demanded a withdrawal of the
claims for "indirect damages" as not within the "intention"
of the treaty. [4] Mr. Fish replied that there would be "no withdrawal of any part of the claim." For Great Britain to take
this position amounted to a "repudiation of the treaty." [5]

[1] Fraser's Magazine for June, 1872.
[2] Monypenny and Buckle, Life of Disraeli, vol. v, p. 178.
[3] Morley, Life of Gladstone, vol. ii, p. 406. Walpole suggests that
"the differences of opinion [as to the meaning of what had been done
at Washington] were not from any lack of straightforwardness on either
side, but from the constraining desire to arrive at an agreement which
made each side anxious to devise some words which the other could
accept."—Hist. of 25 Years, vol. iii, p. 100.
[4] Moran's Diary for the period; Geneva Arbitration, vol. ii, p. 425.
[5] Geneva Arbitration, vol. ii, p. 425. "The withdrawal of any part
of the claim or 'case' as presented," Fish wrote personally and unofficially to Davis, "is as impossible as it was impossible to have omitted
the claim for indirect damages." (Under date of Feb. 12, 1872, in Bancroft Davis Papers.) Davis felt himself on firm ground and he was
strengthened in this position by the opinion which he and George
Bancroft had shaped and called out on the Continent, especially in
Germany which stood, so Bancroft said, as "solid as a rock." Bismarck
greatly enjoyed the discomfiture of the British ministry. They had
nothing to do, said he, but to go forward under the treaty and abide
the result of the arbitration. Of the British policy he spoke in this
wise to Bancroft—"When we were at Versailles much was said to me
both by the French and the English on the conduct of England during
your civil war. I always answered that I could not comprehend the
conduct of Great Britain. If she wished to make an end of you and
was willing to act for that end she should have set in motion all her

Granville meanwhile had written to Schenck that it was "not within the province" of the tribunal "to decide upon the claims for indirect losses and injuries." [1] The Queen was made to express the prevalent English view of the matter in her address to Parliament.

The cable was used more freely than ever before. Hurried meetings of cabinet officers were held in London and Washington. Ministers were got out of bed in the middle of the night to decipher despatches. These indirect losses and claims, Fish continued, were "not now put forward for the first time." For years they had been "prominently and historically" a part of the dispute. All were to go to arbitration that the two governments might be forever rid of their differences of every kind growing out of the war.

Granville replied at length. The correspondence was enriched by another treatise descriptive of the whole course of the controversy, in proof of the view that the understanding arrived at in Washington had been violated. [2] The sum which Mr. Davis intimated should be paid by Great Britain by way of reimbursement of the United States for its expenditures on account of the prolongation of the war beyond July, 1863, the date named in the "case," would apparently amount to $3,000,000,000. It was "an incredible demand." They were "enormous estimates." [3] Elsewhere it was computed that the sum might be 1,600 millions sterling or $8,000,000,000. [4] The different heads of loss, when put together, amounted to more than the total of the British national debt. [5] With the immense punitive sum, five billions of francs, which had

army and all her navy, and made earnest work of her co-operation with your enemies. If she did not mean that she should have acted as we did. I told them that I did not understand this business of going out against a lion and incensing him and then not killing the lion."— Bancroft's letters to Davis in Bancroft Davis Papers.

[1] Under date of Feb. 3, 1872.—Geneva Arbitration, vol. ii, pp. 425-6.

[2] Geneva Arbitration, vol. ii, pp. 436-59.

[3] On the basis of a total cost for the war of $9,000,000,000 from which $2,700,000,000 could be deducted to cover the operations of the Confederates.—Geneva Arbitration, vol. ii, p. 458.

[4] Wemyss Reid, Life of W. E. Forster, vol. ii, p. 24.

[5] Sir Roundell Palmer, Personal and Political Memorials, vol. i, p. 230.

been levied upon the French by Bismarck at the end of the war with Prussia, fresh in the popular mind, the possibilities of a like award against England by the tribunal occasioned great alarm.[1]

The time was at hand when the "counter cases" must be exchanged by the agents at Geneva, and it was highly problematical whether the British representatives would not put an end to the arbitration. Their agent desired to know if their "counter case" could be filed "without prejudice to their position in regard to consequential damages." Fish replied that they were bound to file it. The rights of both parties afterward would be the same as before.[2]

Great Britain's rejoinder consisted, in the first place, of an allusion to Bancroft Davis's charges as to the insincerity of the nation's course. A discussion of this subject would not be entered into because it would be "inconsistent with the self respect which every government is bound to feel," because it involved the "irrelevant" question of motives, and because it was calculated to "inflame the controversy." All references to the subject of indirect losses were omitted. The "counter case" would be confined to the claims for damages arising from the acts of cruisers which, as the Americans alleged, had left England in violation of her neutrality laws.

Surprise was expressed that the demands should have been made to cover the depredations of more than four cruisers. Claims for money expended in endeavoring to capture these boats would not be admissible, nor did claims for the payment of interest rest on tenable ground. The losses to be taken into account by the arbitrators "at the utmost" would be "only" those arising from the destruction by the cruisers of ships and property owned by the United States or its citizens, and the extent of Great Britain's liability could not exceed "that

[1] Walpole, Hist. of 25 Years, vol. iii, p. 105. It is likely that the personnel of the body may have accounted in some degree for the changed attitude in England toward the arbitration. At least two of the arbitrators it was felt were hostile to the British position in the case.—Monypenny and Buckle, Life of Disraeli, vol. v, p. 178.

[2] Geneva Arbitration, vol. ii, p. 460; cf. ibid., p. 203.

proportion of them" which could be deemed "justly attributable to some specific failure or failures of duty" on the part of the government.[1]   The tribunal, of course, would arrive at its conclusions by a consideration, not of what the government of the United States might "allege," but of what they might "be able to prove."

The "counter case" of the United States, in view of the excitement which had ensued upon the publication of the "case," consisted of but a brief statement, indicating certain "errors of sense," and various points of difference in the two lines of argument.   Further discussion of the subject on the American side would be left to the counsel when the tribunal should re-assemble.   A mass of additional documentary matter, largely historical, on the subject of neutrality laws and their execution, as illustrated by the practise of the United States as well as of other governments, was appended to the paper.[2]

In both countries the discussion as to the meaning of what had been said and done in the conferences at Washington continued.   Schenck, in touch with English opinion, made himself a force in the interest of a more moderate course on our side.   "I shrewdly suspect," he wrote to Fish, "that there are some in power who have come to wish they had not taken up such an extreme position."[3]   England had acted "under fear of the newspapers."   The "panic" they had produced was "quite beyond their power of retraction."   To Schenck it seemed "very like a collision between the two trains head on"; neither could "back off," so "the next question comes to this—what side track is there by which we may switch around."[4]

Sir John Rose whose heart, it was needless for him to say, had been "in this business from the first" still wanted no "miscarriage," and he actively busied himself in behalf of a pacific result.   Portions of the press in America began to discredit the indirect claims—to say that they ought never to

[1] Geneva Arbitration, vol. ii, p. 392.
[2] Ibid., vol. i, pp. 429-856, and vol. ii, pp. 1-196.
[3] Under date of Feb. 14, 1872, in Bancroft Davis Papers.
[4] Schenck to Davis in Bancroft Davis Papers.

have been included in the "case" and to urge that they be
withdrawn.

Davis himself was entirely unconvinced that he had gone
too far. His "case," he wrote Fish, as it was passing, through
Bancroft, to a publisher in Leipsic for a German edition, was
"the most notable political book of the day in Europe." [1]
Again he told Fish with truth that his "definition of our
claims," was "in strict accordance with all previous negotiations between the two governments, with the action of the
Senate of the United States and with the official expressions
of the President to Congress." [2]

Davis could prove by the protocol that the British commissioners in Washington had had a full understanding of
what the arbitration was to comprehend. We would have
concluded a treaty "in more limited form," he wrote to John
Jay, the American minister to Austria, "but they were unwilling to do so." Great Britain was trying "to repeat the San
Juan dodge, make a treaty and then construe it so as to un-
make it." [3] He had not supposed that any organ of opinion
in the United States could be induced to make the assertion
that we "ought to have omitted the essence and life of our
case," though some journals were doing so. When "the lapse
of years" should permit an "impartial judgment," he felt confident men would say that nothing was claimed by the United
States which "the provisions of the treaty" had not "justified." [4]

[1] Bancroft Davis Papers.

[2] Geneva Arbitration, vol. iv, pp. 1-2. Sumner, who has been put
forward as the radical on this subject, though he spoke in and to a
legislative assembly rather than to an international court, at no time
had taken a more advanced position. Here again it is impossible not
to note the conspicuous injustice of the treatment accorded him by a
group of commentators who have dealt with this episode in our history.
More preposterous than any other one *arriére pensée* on this subject
is Grant's reference in later years, intended to discredit Sumner, to the
"indirect damage humbug." His own demands for reparation for consequential losses were as clear and as extreme as any man's.—Cf. Adams,
Lee at Appomattox, pp. 188-9.

[3] Under date of Jan. 20, 1872, in Bancroft Davis Papers. Cf. Davis's
letter to Fish in Geneva Arbitration, vol. iv, pp. 1-2.

[4] From a "confidential" publication of Bancroft Davis, dated Wash-

Fish wrote to Davis on March 1, 1872—"Bull has made an ass of himself," thereby jeopardizing "the whole treaty."[1] But the secretary was changing his ground. Suddenly, on April 23, 1872, he addressed General Schenck in another tone. "Not doubting the correctness of the position which the government has occupied," said he, and "fully convinced that the indirect claims," were not "eliminated from the general complaint of the United States," he alluded to his desire "to preserve the example" which the treaty afforded of "a peaceful mode" of settling international differences of the gravest character. "Neither the government of the United States, nor, so far as I can judge, any considerable number of the American people," Mr. Fish continued, "have ever attached much importance to the so-called indirect claims, or have ever expected, or desired any award of damages on their account." No "pecuniary award" was sought; a "judgment" only was asked for that they might be finally disposed of. As they had been set forth in the protocol, where they were "unchallenged," they could not be omitted from the "case," etc.[2] Upon this basis the exchanges continued in the hope that some satisfactory adjustment could be arrived at. Proposals and amended proposals passed back and forth. The dispute took such a turn that the arrangement at length was incorporated in a supplementary article for submission to the Senate,[3] which altered the wording in some particulars, and ratified it. In this new form it was returned to England,[4] where it was rejected by the Cabinet.[5]

Agreement was as far away as ever. The furore was so great at times as to threaten the life of the ministry.[6] In-

ington, May, 1873, entitled "A Few Remarks upon Some Criticism on the Case of the United States," etc., in Bancroft Davis Papers. His many protestations, said Moran, prove "that his conscience troubled him for having raised this needless storm."—Moran's Diary.

[1] Bancroft Davis Papers.
[2] Geneva Arbitration, vol. ii, pp. 475-6, 477-8.
[3] Ibid., p. 500.   [4] Ibid., pp. 525-6.   [5] Ibid., p. 529.
[6] Wemyss Reid, Life of Forster, vol. ii, p. 27; Fitzmaurice, Life of Granville, vol. ii, pp. 96-7. Russell, out of office and a deeply interested

discreet men in both countries spoke of war. As the day for
the arbitrators to meet to receive the arguments, June 15,
drew near the tension increased. Fish instructed Davis and
the counsel to proceed to Geneva in order to be present at
the appointed time, regardless of any action which Great
Britain might be supposed to be likely to take on this occasion.[1]

The tribunal reconvened and Great Britain through her
agent, Lord Tenterden, immediately moved an adjournment
because of the difference existing between the two governments as to the competency of the body to pass upon the
indirect claims.[2] The arbitrators, to the great relief of everyone, now took the matter into their own hands. The result
was brought about by General Schenck, Sir John Rose and
Mr. Evarts, who were acting secretly in London,[3] and, in
large degree, by Mr. Adams, who on his way home had stopped
in England where he had met W. E. Forster. This man, who
had been a staunch friend of the Union during the war, was
advising moderation in the Cabinet.[4] In America Adams had
put himself in communication with Secretary Fish and on his
return was again in London conferring with Forster, Schenck,

spectator, was goading the government from his seat in the House of
Lords as Sumner was annoying Mr. Fish in Washington. (Wemyss
Reid, Life of Forster, vol. ii, p. 29; Lord Russell, Recollections and
Suggestions, pp. 325-34.) He would blow into the air "both the treaty
and the government with it." (Fitzmaurice, Life of Granville, vol. ii,
p. 191.) He thought that the Gladstone ministry had "not sufficiently
defended his own action as Secretary of State or resented with adequate
warmth the charges brought against him in official documents." Now,
"for the first and only time in his life," he found himself drawn into
confidential communications with the leaders of the Conservative party.
(Granville, Life of Russell, vol. ii, p. 366.) In his later years, however,
the old statesman took the blame to himself for the escape of the
Alabama, rather frankly owning up to his mistake. (See, e.g., his Recollections and Suggestions, pp. 235, 334.) "There was something touching
in his confession that the four days' indecision as to the Alabama was
all his own fault; it cost the country a million a day." (Lord Houghton
to Granville in 1875, in Fitzmaurice, Life of Granville, vol. ii, p. 81.)

[1] Geneva Arbitration, vol. ii, p. 567.
[2] Ibid., vol. iv, pp. 17-8; cf. Hackett, p. 237.
[3] Bancroft Davis Papers. [4] Wemyss Reid, Life of Forster, vol. ii, p. 25.

Rose and others.[1] Difficult, indeed, was it to bring about any basis of understanding because of the assaults in England upon Gladstone with a view to overturning his ministry, if he should not exclude the indirect claims—because of the angry criticism which would be aimed at Grant in America, if these claims were not insisted upon by our representatives. Such truckling to Great Britain by Fish would most certainly alienate the formidable Irish vote in the Presidential campaign of 1872.

Adams continued his conciliatory service at Geneva.[2] He and Cockburn spoke French with ease, and the conversations which ensued in the presence of the three neutral arbitrators were carried on in that language. In a little while they all were brought to the point where they were ready to say in an "extra judicial opinion"[3] that they had read what the United States had to offer on the subject, and that they "individually and collectively" had reached the conclusion that these claims did not constitute, "upon the principles of international law applicable to such cases, good foundation for an award of compensation, or computation of damages between nations, and should upon those principles be wholly excluded from the consideration of the tribunal in making its award, even if there were no disagreement between the two governments as to the competency of the tribunal to decide thereon."[4]

Thereupon the counsel of the United States recommended that their government receive this as a final judgment on the point. Davis transmitted their opinion by telegraph to Fish, who laid it before the President, who accepted the declaration as the tribunal's "judgment upon a question of public law" which it had been felt that "the interests of both governments required should be decided." It was "the attainment of an end" which the United States had had in view from the first.[5]

[1] Adams, Lee at Appomattox, pp. 191-2; Reid, Life of Forster, vol. ii, p. 28; Fitzmaurice, Life of Granville, vol. ii, pp. 98-100.
[2] Extracts from Bancroft Davis's account of the proceedings behind the scenes are contained in Hackett, Reminiscences, pp. 240-53.
[3] Life of C. F. Adams, pp. 394-6; Bancroft Davis, Mr. Fish and the Alabama Claims, pp. 98-103.
[4] Geneva Arbitration, vol. ii, pp. 577-8, and vol. iv, pp. 19-20.
[5] Ibid., vol. ii, pp. 578-9. Grant's want of rudimentary knowledge on

The claims were to be not further insisted upon and could be excluded from all consideration in any award that might be made.[1] The work of the tribunal could now proceed in order to its end.

The "arguments" in behalf of the two governments were presentations of the subject from the opposite standpoints. That of the United States, signed by Caleb Cushing, William M. Evarts and M. R. Waite, and prepared by them jointly, surpassed in length the "case" of Bancroft Davis.[2] The British "argument" was much briefer and included a report of a committee of the Board of Trade formed to pass upon the justice of individual demands for reparation, which it examined and scaled down. The claims on the subject of increased insurance were disallowed, and, since they were "indirect," [3] were deducted, leaving, according to the United States's revised statement, a total of about $19,000,000 in losses which were ascribed to the various cruisers. This sum was reduced by the British calculation to $8,600,000.[4] The expenditures on account of the pursuit of the cruisers were brought down to $910,000.[5]

Throughout the course of the proceedings supplementary arguments on particular points were introduced by the counsel on both sides, either orally or in writing, notable among the number being a long address at the conferences on August 5 and 6 delivered by Mr. Evarts.[6]

The tribunal at the end of August was ready to vote upon

such a subject is further illustrated by his demand upon Fish to instruct Adams to remain at Geneva if Great Britain withdrew by reason of our insistence upon damages for indirect losses. Our representative in the tribunal could sign the decision alone and make the award if the others left the scene. Fish directed the President's attention to the fact that the Treaty of Washington required action by a majority.—Adams, Lee at Appomattox, p. 189; Around the World with General Grant, vol. ii, p. 279; N. Y. Herald, Sep. 25, 1877, containing interview with Grant in Edinburgh; cf. Wemyss Reid, Life of Forster, vol. ii, pp. 28-9.

[1] Geneva Arbitration, vol. ii, p. 580.
[2] Ibid., vol. iii, pp. 1-225; cf. Hackett, Reminiscences, pp. 124-30.
[3] Geneva Arbitration, vol. iii, p. 315.   [4] Ibid., p. 338.   [5] Ibid., p. 370.
[6] Ibid., pp. 442-85; Hackett, Reminiscences, pp. 303-4.

the question of the responsibility of Great Britain for the acts of the various vessels. The arbitrators unanimously answered "no" when they were asked if damages should be awarded the United States for the depredations of the *Sumter, Georgia, Nashville, Tallahassee* and *Chickamauga.* Mr. Adams said "yes" as to the *Retribution,* while Mr. Staempfli held Great Britain liable for one loss occasioned by this vessel. Guilt was fixed upon Great Britain for losses sustained through the activity of three vessels only—the *Alabama* and her tender, upon which the judgment was unanimous; the *Shenandoah* for her acts after her departure from Melbourne by a majority of three to two voices, Viscount d'Itajubá and Lord Chief Justice Cockburn dissenting; and the *Florida* and her three tenders, the Lord Chief Justice in this case alone dissenting.[1]

The cost of pursuing the cruisers was held to be indistinguishable from the United States's general expenses in the conduct of the war, but it was determined to allow interest at a reasonable rate. The deliberations as to suitable damages to be paid by Great Britain were held behind closed doors. As a result of computation and mutual arrangement it was agreed on September 2 that a lump sum of $15,500,000 in gold should be awarded the United States, the British arbitrator dissenting.[2] Having concluded its labors the tribunal on September 14, 1872, was dissolved amid salvoes of artillery.

Sclopis, Staempfli, d'Itajubá and Adams filed brief separate explanatory opinions. Chief Justice Cockburn at the last moment, after he had declined to sign the decision, presented a voluminous statement, three times as long as the opinions of all the other arbitrators together, and twice the length of

---

[1] Geneva Arbitration, vol. iv, pp. 37-8.

[2] For the decision and award see Geneva Arbitration, vol. iv, pp 49-54; J. B. Moore, International Arbitrations, vol. i, pp. 653-9. Some intimate history of how the agreement was reached is to be found in Sir Roundell Palmer, Personal and Political Memorials, vol. ii, pp. 256-7. Staempfli wished us to receive reparation for all the acts of the Shenandoah, both before arriving at and after leaving Melbourne, and for the Sumter. He was accused of "a strong animus" in favor of the United States.

the American "case," which not unnaturally, when it came to be read, aroused much comment. It was written in a partisan spirit, even more unbecoming than the narrative of Mr. Davis, who had been an advocate, while the Lord Chief Justice was a member of the court and the representative of the government, which had just been adjudged guilty of great wrong. He pounded his desk and stormed about in strange anger.[1] He might well have remained wholly silent but he proceeded to say that the "case" of the United States was filled with "abuse" and the "pent up venom of national and personal hate." He complained of the "hostile and insulting tone, thus offensively and unnecessarily adopted toward Great Britain, her statesmen and her institutions." Our counsel were accused of "strange misrepresentations" and "assertions without the shadow of a foundation." At one point in their argument Sir Alexander found "an extraordinary series of propositions." Mr. Cushing, Mr. Evarts and Mr. Waite had been guilty of "the most singular confusion of ideas, misrepresentation of facts and ignorance, both of law and history, which were, perhaps, ever crowded into the same space."[2]

The Cockburn statement was "an extraordinary document," said Secretary Fish, when it was brought to his notice; it was "a very remarkable paper," laying down principles as to neutral rights by a representative of the British government which were worthy of remembrance in future wars.[3] The Lord Chief Justice's course did not escape criticism even in Great Britain.[4] Naturally the decision and the award were ungrateful to Englishmen and expressions in this sense made their appearance in the press. The authoritative London Times, however, accepted the result in a good spirit. "We simply wanted the

[1] Cf. Davis to Fish, MS. letter cited in Hackett, pp. 289, 292; J. R. Young, Men and Memories, pp. 360-61.

[2] Davis to Fish, Geneva Arbitration, vol. iv, pp. 12-13. For the opinion see ibid., pp. 230-544. Cf. Hackett, Reminiscences, pp. 342, 356-7; Cushing, Treaty of Washington, pp. 128-49; J. B. Moore, International Arbitrations, vol. i, pp. 659-61.

[3] Geneva Arbitration, vol. iv, pp. 546-9.

[4] Sir Roundell Palmer, Personal and Political Memorials, vol. i, p. 250.

judgment of five men of sense and honor," that journal said. "We have obtained it and we cheerfully abide by it." [1]

The part which Charles Francis Adams had officially and unofficially taken in the settlement, especially in the accommodation of the difficulty over the indirect claims, met with generous and grateful acknowledgment in England. Many public men complimented and thanked him. [2] The Queen desired Lord Granville to convey her appreciation of the "distinguished statesman's" labors and the "ability and indefatigable industry" he had displayed during the "long protracted inquiries and discussions" attending the arbitration. Through the British embassy at Washington the President was asked to make known her Majesty's sentiments to Mr. Adams, to whom this acknowledgment was highly pleasing, as it was to his countrymen, in view of his experiences in London during the war while a drama which had so disagreeably excited the national sensibilities was being enacted before his eyes day by day. [3]

The sum was promptly paid and was converted into United States bonds in connection with the Treasury redemption operations which were in progress under the funding act in London. [4] The proceeds were now to be distributed to those who were entitled to indemnity for their sufferings at the hands of the Confederate cruisers. In 1874 Congress authorized the President to appoint a court of five commissioners to consider the cases of the various claimants. It continued its labors until the end of 1876, and there were paid out on its judgments more than $9,000,000. Some $10,000,000, as a result

[1] Cited in Hackett, p. 347; cf. J. B. Moore, International Arbitrations, vol. i, pp. 664-5.

[2] Cf. Sir R. Palmer, Personal and Political Memorials, vol. i, p. 247.

[3] Geneva Arbitration, vol. ii, pp. 584-5; J. B. Moore, International Arbitrations, vol. i, pp. 663-4. The task of conveying such a message to Mr. Adams may have led to some change of feeling in General Grant. He had written to Adam Badeau on October 23, 1870—"The Adamses do not possess one noble trait of character that I ever heard of from old John Adams down to the last of all of them, H. B. [Henry Adams]."—A. Badeau, Grant in Peace, p. 472.

[4] J. B. Moore, International Arbitrations, vol. i. pp. 664-7.

of accumulation, remained and the government must go out to find others who alleged that they had sustained damages and who hitherto, by the terms of the law creating the court, had been barred from appearing before it. They waged an active contest in Congress for recognition. As a result, the act of June 5, 1882, was passed and another court was established. Its work proceeded for more than three years, until the end of 1885, and thus the rest of the sum was distributed.[1]

The other arbitrations provided for by the Treaty of Washington attracted less public attention. The mixed commission which was to adjust the Civil War claims depending between Great Britain and the United States, other than those which had arisen out of the depredations of the *Alabama* and her consort ships, was made up of a former justice of the supreme court of Indiana, James S. Frazer, representing the United States, and Russell Gurney, a member of Parliament, representing Great Britain, while the third commissioner, named jointly by the President and the Queen, was the Italian minister to this country, Count Louis Corti. It convened in Washington in September, 1871, adjourned to Newport for the summer, and made its first award in September, 1873. As many as 478 British claims were presented to the commission, nearly all for property which it was said had been taken or destroyed by the military or naval authorities of the United States, or for the unlawful arrest of British subjects. There were 19 claims for injuries which it was alleged had been sustained by American citizens. These were disallowed. But 181 British cases were favorably acted on and the awards amounted in all to $1,929,819. This sum was paid out of the Treasury of the United States to Great Britain.[2]

The Emperor of Germany was to determine the water line separating the Territory of Washington from Vancouver's Island. Should it run through the Haro Channel or the Rosario Straits? A decision of this question would determine

[1] J. B Moore, International Arbitrations, vol v, chap. k.
[2] Ibid., vol. i, chap. xv; Cushing, Treaty of Washington, pp. 188-9.

the ownership, not only of the island of San Juan but also of an archipelago of smaller islands and islets. For the conduct of our case before the arbitrator the United States chose as its agent George Bancroft, minister to Germany, whose fitness was preeminent, because of his distinguished position as an historian, and also because he had been concerned with the controversy while he had been our minister at the court of St. James during the administration of President Polk. Great Britain appointed Admiral Prevost, almost as well qualified by practical experience with the subject. The claims of each government were ably presented and the Kaiser referred the subject to three experts, drawn from that class of scholarly men for whom Germany has enjoyed so much merited distinction. After considering the question they made a report to the Emperor who on October 21, 1872, rendered his decision and award in favor of the claim of the United States. The line should pass through the Canal de Haro. The British government at once withdrew a detachment of Royal Marines stationed on San Juan and the dispute which had been in progress for 26 years was brought to an end.[1]

The fisheries commission was not immediately organized for its tasks. Sir Alexander T. Galt was named as British commissioner, Ensign H. Kellogg, as commissioner on the part of the United States, while the third arbitrator was the Belgian minister at Washington, Maurice Delfosse. The first meeting was held in Halifax on June 15, 1877. The decision was announced on November 23 following, and the United States was condemned to pay $5,500,000 in gold to the British government. For a long time expressions of dissatisfaction were heard on many sides concerning the composition of the commission and the manner of making the award, but in 1878 the sum was reluctantly paid.[2]

Thus as a result of the Treaty of Washington the United

[1] J. B. Moore, International Arbitrations, vol. i, chap. vii; Cushing, Treaty of Washington. pp 203-25.

[2] J. B. Moore, op. cit., vol. i, chap. xvi; Documents and Proceedings of Halifax Commission. House Ex. Doc., 45th Cong. 2nd sess., no. 89 (3 vols.); Senate Ex. Doc., 45th Cong. 2nd sess., nos. 44 and 100.

States won two and lost two decisions. We had gained an award of **$15,500,000**, covering the *Alabama* claims and secured San Juan and the neighboring islands at the northern end of Puget Sound, and were made to pay sums aggregating nearly **$7,000,000** by the Civil War Claims and the Halifax Commissions.

CHAPTER XV

PROGRESS upon the Central Pacific and the Union Pacific Railway line from Omaha to Sacramento was unexpectedly rapid. In November, 1867, the railhead from the east had reached Cheyenne, 510 miles west of the Missouri and in January, 1868, when a temporary bridge had been thrown across the river, it could be said with truth that there was unbroken railway communication from New York to the base of the Rocky Mountains, a distance of 2,000 miles.[1] It was only 54 hours from Chicago to Colorado, while a year before many days were needed for the journey.

It had been the hope of the Union Pacific contractors to bring the road to the summit before the winter should set in. But this hope was not to be realized. The passes were bound with snow until late in the spring and it was mid-April, 1868, before the track layers advanced the railhead to the top of the range which they scaled at a height of more than 8,000 feet, where a station called Sherman in honor of General Sherman, was established, a greater altitude than the locomotive had reached up to this time anywhere in the world. This point, which was the highest to be attained on the entire line to the coast, was about 20 miles west of Cheyenne.[2] The rails throughout the summer and fall of 1868 were laid with speed over the elevated plateau in Wyoming. In late July the end-of-track had reached Benton, nearly 700 miles west of Omaha. The continental divide was crossed at Creston, 40 miles farther on, at a height of 7,000 feet, and when 200 miles more of track had been completed, late in the year, it rested upon the topmost ridge of the Wahsatch Mountains at Aspen, 7,400 feet

[1] Phila. Ledger, Jan. 6, 1868.
[2] N. Y. Tribune, April 15, and Phila. Ledger, April 28, 1868.

above sea level, ready to descend into the Great Salt Lake basin.

In January, 1869, the railhead passed the 1,000th mile post, a lone evergreen tree, in Weber Cañon,[1] and it was but a short way to Ogden, a little city built and occupied by the Mormons. This peculiar people, comfortable in their isolation, had at first looked with disfavor upon the construction of the railroad. Then, seeing that their opposition would be unavailing, they had demanded that it pass through Salt Lake City. But the engineers, bent upon finding the best route to the coast, had taken no more note of this considerable place than of Denver, and Brigham Young, with characteristic thrift, now offered to build a portion of the line. He enlisted the services of several thousand men and laid down sections of the track, thus hastening the Union Pacific Company's advance into the west.[2]

At the other end of the line the Central Pacific engineers had blasted their way with nitroglycerine through the Sierras, and trains in June, 1868, were running to Reno, only 20 miles from that important objective, Virginia City.[3] The problem of protecting the line from the heavy winter snows, which disturbed so many minds, was being solved by the construction of sheds, which quite roofed over the tracks for a distance of many miles. Twenty-eight saw mills, employing 2,000 or 3,000 men, were at work in the mountains preparing the 4,000,-000 running feet of lumber which were required for this purpose.[4]

The two companies in the summer of 1868 had as many as 25,000 or 30,000 men in their employ, mostly Irishmen on the Union Pacific, principally Chinamen on the Central Pacific.[5]

[1] Phila. Ledger, Jan. 15, 1869.
[2] Ibid., July 31 and Aug. 18, 1868.
[3] Ibid., May 15, June 23 and July 31, 1868; N. Y. Tribune, July 6, 1868, quoting Alta California.
[4] N. Y. Tribune, Aug. 13, 1868, quoting San Francisco Bulletin; Phila. Ledger, March 23, 1869; J. E. Lester, The Atlantic to the Pacific, pp. 57, 60.
[5] Cf. Phila. Ledger, Aug. 13, 1868.

A rivalry which was almost ludicrous sprang up between the contractors and their respective forces. They worked with feverish activity, each to outdo the other in the number of miles laid in a day, and in reaching the point at which the rails could be joined to complete the iron trail over the continent.

The act of Congress allowed the companies until July 1, 1876, to span the country, but the line would be ready for use seven years before that date. Now it was predicted that the work could be finished in time for a national celebration of the event on July 4, 1869. But as the weeks wore on it was clear that the ends could be brought together early in May. So much came to pass. In some favorable seasons the gangs of laborers had laid three, four, even five miles of track in a day. Taunted to greater exertion by a record which had been established by the Chinamen, the Irish on the Union Pacific had responded by putting down seven and a half miles. Crocker, the Central Pacific contractor, resolved to build ten miles. It was at sunrise, on April 29, when the end was very near, that he set his Chinese gangs at the task. There was a wager upon the result, and before the sun had set his men were several hundred yards beyond the point which he had fixed for them and he won. Only a few more rail lengths remained to be set in place and fastened down, and these would be reserved for the day when the junction of the tracks could be fittingly celebrated.

The Chinese and the "Paddies" faced each other on a summit in the desert north of the Great Salt Lake. A few tents and shanties, the inevitable gambling resorts and liquor shops stood here at a place called Promontory Point. Trains from the east and west, bearing officers of the two companies and their guests, must be given time to arrive upon the scene. Saturday, May 8, was designated as the day of jubilee.

Vice President Durant [1] was stopped on his way by some

---

[1] An appreciation of this man is to be found in N. Y. Tribune, May 29, 1869.

workmen who alleged that he had not paid them their wages. He ran into a rain storm which led to further delays, so that the event must be postponed until Monday, the 10th. Meanwhile California, having made all of its arrangements, went forward with its celebration in honor of the achievement. Booming cannon hailed the dawn in San Francisco. The Federal forts in the harbor fired salutes, bells were rung, military and civic societies paraded the streets. All business was suspended. Flags were flung to the breeze. Buildings were gaily decorated. At night the city was illuminated. In Sacramento like scenes were enacted. The railways carried passengers free of charge and all the inhabitants of the surrounding country came to town. Thirty locomotives, decked in red, white and blue, were ranged in front of the city. Their whistles, blown in unison, awoke the echoes in the Sierras.[1]

Monday found Durant on the ground and all in readiness at Promontory Point. President Stanford and his friends from Sacramento came up in a special train drawn by the locomotive "Jupiter," while Durant's luxurious "palace" cars, behind the Union Pacific engine "119," stopped on the eastern side of the gap. A crowd gathered around the track ends as the hour set for the ceremonies approached. Ingenious plans were laid for apprising the country of the "wedding of the rails." Spikes of gold and silver were contributed by California, Nevada, Idaho, Montana and Arizona and were presented with appropriate sentiments. A sleeper of polished California laurel, bearing an inscribed silver plate, was inserted under the rails. The spikes were set in place to be driven into it. A silver sledge was provided and wires were connected with it so that each stroke could be instantaneously recorded on the instruments in all the principal telegraph stations in the land. A prayer was said, Governor Stanford made a brief address on behalf of the Central Pacific, while General Grenville M. Dodge, chief engineer of the Union Pacific, spoke for his company. Stanford standing on one rail and Durant

[1] N. Y. Tribune, May 10, 1869.

on the other in turn used the hammer. The blows upon the "last spike," as the silver struck the gold, were taken up and flashed away to the groups of people who were assembled in various cities awaiting the news of the culmination of the hopes and ambitions of so many years. The two men shook hands while the crowd cheered. The locomotives were drawn up to "touch noses" and champagne bottles were broken over their pilots. The bands blared, the people shouted again, telegrams were sent to President Grant and Vice President Colfax, the officers of the roads ate, drank and made merry on their private cars, while joy was unconfined in the dance halls and bar-rooms of the "shanty town." [1]

The entire country responded with enthusiasm. Congratulatory messages passed between the Atlantic and Pacific coasts. Separated hitherto by thirty days of travel they were now but seven or eight days apart. New York in holiday dress fired a hundred guns and held thanksgiving services in Trinity Church; Philadelphia rang the bell on Independence Hall; Chicago formed an impromptu procession seven miles in length which wound its way through the principal streets. The new little city of Omaha was beside itself. "Omaha and San Francisco," so ran the words upon a banner, "What God hath joined together let no man put asunder." The celebration was renewed on the Pacific coast. From Maine to California powder crackled, cannon sounded, bonfires were lighted, men and women sang "The Star Spangled Banner" and "Hail Columbia."

On January 1, 1866, only 40 miles of track had been laid at the Omaha end and 60 miles in California—a mere 100 of the nearly 1,800 miles to be traversed, so that practically all of the work had been done in three years and four months "in a country which abounded in the most forbidding difficulties and obstacles to such an undertaking." [2]

[1] A florid account of the ceremony is found in E. L. Sabin, Building the Pacific Railway; see also J. P. Davis, The Union Pacific Railway, pp. 152-6; Crofutt, New Overland Tourist, pp. 117-21, and Williams, Pacific Tourist, pp. 164-6.

[2] Phila. Ledger, April 29, 1869.

General Sherman, who at first had not been confident of success, telegraphed his congratulations to the "thousands of brave fellows who fought out this glorious national problem in spite of deserts, storms, Indians and the doubts of the incredulous." [1] It was "one of the greatest, if not the greatest work of modern times," said the Public Ledger of Philadelphia.[2] The rapidity with which it had been completed "must challenge the admiration of the whole civilized world." [3] It was an "epoch not below in its national significance the Declaration of Independence, the emancipation of the slaves or the acquisition of California," said the New York Tribune It was a "definite bond and material guarantee for the perpetuity of an oceanbound Union.[4] The London Times found it to be "a feat of railway enterprise unparallelled, and, indeed, hardly admitting of parallel in any other country." The completion of a line over which one could take "the longest railway journey in the world" had been accomplished with "astonishing expedition." It was impossible, the Times continued, to "withhold" admiration from such "enterprise, energy and power." [5]

The regular transportation of passengers, merchandise and mails across the continent was begun at once. On May 1 as many as 15,000 persons in California, it was said, had bespoken passage east over the road.[6] Communication between Sacramento and San Francisco must proceed entirely, or in part, by boat on the Sacramento River until the completion of the Western Pacific line, which would bring the trains to Oakland on the opposite side of the bay. The first through passengers, 500 in number, reached Omaha in a train of two sections on May 16.[7] A Pullman car arrived in New York in six and a half days from Sacramento on July 26, the thirty passengers on board being welcomed at the Hudson River

[1] Phila. Press, May 15, 1869.   [2] Phila. Ledger, May 12, 1869.
[3] Ibid., April 29, 1869.   [4] N. Y. Tribune, May 10, 1869.
[5] London Times, Nov. 30, 1868.   [6] Phila. Press, May 28, 1869.
[7] Phila. Ledger, May 18, 1869.

Railroad station by a crowd eager to know if they had seen any Indians or buffalo on their novel trip from ocean to ocean.[1]

San Francisco which had had a population of but 56,000 in 1860 had come to be a city of 150,000, nearly one-fourth of all who dwelt upon the Pacific slope. Its harbor was "a forest of masts." Spread over its hills were fine hotels, substantial business houses, handsome residences. From tall chimneys issued the smoke of industry. The streets were crowded with horse cars, omnibuses, coaches, drays and human beings speaking many tongues. The place had the commercial activity and the social atmosphere of a great capital. In spite of a damaging earthquake in 1866 its physical progress was remarked by every visitor.

California's geographical position, its climate, its various and curious resources, its scenic beauty stirred the imagination of the people of the East. This marvel state extended over nine degrees of latitude, a distance, which if it were laid off on the Atlantic seaboard, would reach from Plymouth Rock to Charleston. Its trees and plants, its fruits and grains in the north belonged to the temperate zone; in the south they were semi-tropical in their luxuriance. It was the "Italy of America."

Within the boundaries of California were three times as much arable land as in Great Britain and Ireland, nearly as much as in all France. In 1867 it was said that 6,000,000 bushels of wheat had been exported, while 7,000,000 had been held for use at home. The flocks had yielded 9,000,000 pounds of wool; 2,000,000 bushels of potatoes had been taken from the fields.[2] There were 25,000,000 vines in the vineyards from which the vintners in 1868 had expressed several million gallons of wine and brandy,[3] which already were coming east over the Pacific Railroad. Cars ventilated by air pumps conveyed the luscious fruits to new markets. Pears two weeks

[1] Phila. Ledger, July 27, 1869.
[2] Ibid., Oct. 23, 1868.   [3] Ibid., June 19, 1869.

in transit were soon for sale in New York at fifty cents each.[1]

A German in 1870 carried to Washington a flag 36 feet long and 20 feet wide made of silk grown and woven in California, and presented it to the Senate of the United States.[2] A factory to make sugar from beets was in operation near Sacramento; another was at work in the neighborhood of San Francisco, and the crop was declared to be equal to any grown in Germany.[3] A future of nearly unlimited grandeur lay before the state and there were many whose dearest wish it was to view its wonders, while not a few would emigrate from the Eastern states and establish their permanent homes in this bountiful land.

During the summer of 1869 the entire Ways and Means Committee of the House of Representatives made a trip to the coast.[4] A large party of merchants and politicians from Chicago, including Senator Trumbull, Governor Oglesby and Congressman Judd, visited California in the interest of closer trade relations.[5] Vice President Colfax boarded a train at Omaha to contrast the experiences on the new railway with those he had enjoyed four years before on a transcontinental stage coach. Seward, released from the duties of the State Department, ready for a sight of the distant places in his own country and abroad to which, while in office, his broad enthusiasms had drawn him, was soon in San Francisco. Ben Holladay of the "Overland," now a steamship owner on the Pacific coast, offered him the use of a vessel for a trip to Alaska to inspect the great new territory, which he had added to the national domain.

The hospitality of the people was exhibited abundantly as travellers from the East came to Denver, Ogden, Salt Lake City, Virginia City, Sacramento and San Francisco. Seward and Colfax were particularly marked out for cordial recep-

[1] Phila. Ledger, July 8 and Aug. 17, 1869.
[2] Ibid., July 26, 1870; cf. N. Y. Tribune, July 28, 1869.
[3] Phila. Ledger, Dec. 27, 1869, and June 16 and Dec. 20, 1870.
[4] Ibid., July 29, 1869.   [5] Ibid., July 17, 1869.

tions. Their friendly expressions for the West and their political services in behalf of the Pacific coast had endeared them to the population. They were greeted with dinners, levees, mass meetings and other attentions which they were called upon to acknowledge with many a hand clasp and a speech. Seward's welcome in Sitka, in the "Walrussia" which had been the butt of so much ridicule, reached the proportions of an ovation. The days which he spent there were numbered among the happiest in his life.[1]

Temporary bridges, connecting Omaha and Council Bluffs, were swept away by the ice. In 1868 a contract was let for a fine iron structure of eleven spans, set fifty feet above high water. It would be supported by iron caissons, sunk until they reached the solid sandstone, then to be filled with boulders and concrete, and it was finished on Washington's Birthday in 1872.[2]

The tariffs were "inexcusably high." [3] The Central Pacific company was charging ten cents a mile in gold for transporting passengers over the western end of the line. It was "an outrage and an extortion to which the American people would not submit," said the Chicago Tribune.[4] The freight rates also were exorbitant. No less than eleven cents a ton a mile was paid by a shipper of hides from Ogden to Omaha. For the conveyance of the same goods from Omaha to Chicago the charge was only four and a quarter cents.[5] Tea came from China to New York by sea for two cents a pound, but from San Francisco to New York by rail the rate was thirteen cents. To ship a ton of flour from coast to coast cost $136, while from Chicago to the Atlantic seaboard, a third of the distance, the charge was only $10.[6]

[1] Seward in Washington, vol. iii, chap. lxiv.
[2] Williams, Pacific Tourist, p. 18; Crofutt, New Overland Tourist, pp. 21-2; J. E. Lester, The Atlantic and the Pacific, pp. 274-81.
[3] N. Y. Tribune, July 12, 1869.
[4] Quoted in Phila. Press, May 28, 1869.
[5] Phila. Ledger, June 30, 1869.
[6] Ibid., July 21, 1869; cf. J. P. Davis, The Union Pacific Railway, p. 207.

The two companies, which at first found it difficult to cooperate, gradually adjusted their differences and, under general criticism of the high rates, rendered more angry in view of the bounty which they had received from the government, changes to the public advantage ensued. In a few weeks the passenger rates to Omaha were reduced to $133 in currency, to Chicago or St. Louis, $153 and to New York, $173. The extra cost for meals and sleeping car berths amounted to $5 or $6 a day.[1] In August the fares were further reduced to $150 for a first class ticket from coast to coast, with a second class rate of $70, and promise of a $50 rate for emigrants.[2] In October the Pennsylvania, with a line shorter than the Erie or the New York Central, led in a general reduction of the travelling time between New York and Chicago to 30 hours. This express train made connections for Omaha where travellers once a week met a "hotel train" of Pullman "palace" cars, to one or more of which kitchens were attached, so that meals could be served on the way. Leaving New York on a Tuesday a passenger might thus reach San Francisco on the following Sunday. But a considerable delay was necessary at Ogden for transfer from the Union Pacific "Pullmans" into the Central Pacific "silver palace cars" and the service was soon discontinued.

The restaurant on the train, whether in the separate "diner," or by way of a buffet attachment to the "sleeper," was now a fact. While facilities for cooking and serving meals had been installed in Durant's and a few other private cars, manufactured in the Pullman shops, the "hotel car" for general public use was yet regarded as a great curiosity.[3] Three times a day stops had been made at "meal stations" which were established at intervals along the line. With the stage coach, as it labored across the plains and up and down the mountain trails, still fresh in mind, it was sufficiently remarkable to be

---

[1] Phila. Ledger, June 28, 1869.

[2] N. Y. Tribune, Aug. 17, 1869.

[3] Samuel Bowles, The Pacific Railroad—Open; J. E. Lester, The Atlantic to the Pacific.

able to occupy a soft seat by day, to lie upon a clean bed at
night, to exercise the legs by a walk up and down the aisles,
to play cards and chess, to converse, sew, knit, look at the
scenery from an observation platform and to gather around a
cottage organ for a song, while moving forward smoothly and
rapidly to journey's end. But to eat at a table from a bill
of fare worthy of a good hotel, while the train ran on, was a
new delight.

The "palace" cars were heavy with silver plate and glittered
with crystal, symptomatic of the vulgar taste of the day. So
new to wealth and luxury were many of our people that the
opportunities, while travelling, to recline in "velvet cushions"
and be "pictured in a score of mirrors" were cited in the railway company advertisements as reasons for men to leave
their homes in the East for a transcontinental tour.[1] These
cars served their day until simpler beauty could be enjoyed.[2]

Work proceeded also upon the branch which was to serve
St. Louis and pass west through Kansas, now known as the
Kansas Pacific. It was 639 miles from Wyandotte at the
mouth of the Kansas River to Denver and 500 miles of the
road was finished before June 30, 1870. But Denver, isolated
as she was while the trains ran on from Omaha to the Pacific,
100 miles to the north, had awaited the coming of the locomotive from St. Louis impatiently. The Denver Pacific which
took over the franchises of the Kansas Pacific to build the
connecting link to Cheyenne in Wyoming, in accordance with
the act of Congress of March 3, 1869, was laying rails and
sleepers. About two and a quarter millions were expended
on this line and the last spike was driven on June 22, 1870.
The first train rang its bells in Denver that night.[3] Less than
two months later, on August 15, the completion of the road
through Kansas, built at a cost of about 17 millions, was

[1] Weston's Guide to the Kansas Pacific Railway, p. 150. This "palace"
car gave birth to the contemptuous sentence which architects have long
been wont to pass upon a coarse production when they say that it is a
mixture of "early Pullman and late North German Lloyd."
[2] Americanization of Edward Bok, pp. 251-3.
[3] N. Y. Tribune, June 23 and July 23, 1870.

celebrated.[1] A passenger could leave Kansas City in the morning and reach his destination in Colorado the next afternoon, making the round trip for $50.

The first bridge over the Missouri was opened for traffic at Kansas City on July 4, 1869, so that from the first day trains could be run through to St. Louis. It was a structure of six spans with a draw of 360 feet which for the convenience of shipping could be swung about by four men in two minutes and ten seconds. In two years, so it was said, there would be five "magnificent iron bridges" across the "Big Muddy." [2] Upon the completion of the great bridge over the Mississippi at St. Louis there would be direct communication without change of cars with New York. Colorado, therefore, after September, 1870, had two lines to the East—one over the Union Pacific tracks through Cheyenne and Omaha whence three lines led to Chicago—the other through Kansas City and St. Louis.

The Atchison, Topeka and Santa Fé followed the Kansas Pacific across Kansas on a more southern route. In large degree this road was the product of the enthusiasm of Cyrus K. Holliday, a free state pioneer, drawn from Pennsylvania while the slavery contest was at its height. Chartered in 1859 as the Atchison and Topeka it received important land grants from Congress in 1863, but actual construction was not begun until November, 1868. Then rails were laid upon the prairie for a few miles out of Topeka. They had reached Emporia, a distance of 62 miles, by the summer of 1871. The next year they were advanced 75 miles farther to Newton, 285 miles from the state line, headed south and west over the route of the old Santa Fé trail.

Holliday courageously pursued the project. If the country would support the buffalo, as it did abundantly, he argued that it would support man. A large part of the government grant would be lost unless the rails should reach the Colorado boundary before the end of 1872. This feat was accomplished,

[1] N. Y. Tribune, Aug. 15, 1870.
[2] Phila. Ledger, Aug. 20, 1869.

and in the first report of March, 1873, it could be announced
that the company had 497 miles of road in operation. Here
it stood when the great national panic, so near at hand, came
on to bring every form of financial and commercial activity
to a pause, pending the long and slow readjustment of the
business world which was the penalty of the high, eager and
misguided living of these restless years.[1]

As the locomotives sped over the prairies antelope raced
beside them until the little animals were winded with the exercise, passengers shot big game from the windows and platforms of the cars,—the prairies held a mixture of wilderness
and civilization such as man had never seen before. The most
interesting, the most picturesque wild creature of the plains
was the buffalo. On the Union Pacific he was seldom found
near the tracks, for the American pack by this time had
been definitely divided, one part having gone north toward
Montana and British America, while the other ranged from
Kansas down to and west of the great Staked Plain in Texas.
The feeding grounds of the southern herd were penetrated by
the Kansas Pacific and the Santa Fé. In 1868 an English
traveller in western Kansas passed through "millions" of the
animals. The plain was "completely covered with them as far
as the eye could reach."[2] The locomotives ran into the lum-
bering beasts as they crossed the rails, or in blind madness
charged the trains. In one week on the Santa Fé cars were
twice derailed, and the engineers were taught by experience
to stop when they met a group of the animals.[3]

A multitude of "gentlemen" hunters from the East and from
England, as well as many who adopted the chase as a commercial pursuit, were seen on every hand. In Fort Hays on
the Kansas Pacific, Dodge City on the Santa Fé, or at
other places in central Kansas, the parties were outfitted for
incursions upon the constantly dwindling herds. Some of the

---

[1] G. D. Bradley, The Story of the Santa Fé, pp. 63-4, 75, 85, 86;
Brown's Industrial Gazetteer of the A. T. and S. F., pp. 7-8.
[2] W. A. Bell, New Tracks in North America, vol. ii, pp. 233-4.
[3] R. I. Dodge, Plains of the Great West, p. 122.

meat, which men on the plains said was as good as the beef
of Texas cattle selling at $20 a head—and particularly
the tongues, accounted a great delicacy—was smoked and
corned for shipment to Eastern markets; but the hunt went
on primarily, when not in wanton sport, for the skins.[1] Though
these were selling in Kansas in 1872 at one dollar each, many
found the pursuit profitable.   Even at this low price it was a
simple matter around Dodge City for a hunter to take enough
in a day to yield him $100.[2]

Such "imbecility" was the buffalo's that when an experienced man "got a stand," which consisted in attracting animals to a dying fellow, he could shoot a score without moving
from a given spot.   One observer saw 112 carcasses inside of
a semi-circle of a radius of 200 yards, all of which had been
brought down by a single hunter in less than three quarters
of an hour.[3]   Another told of a man who had shot 99 in a short
time.   Not a pound of the meat was taken away; all was left
to fatten the wolves or to rot on the ground.[4]

The waste was awful.   For one "robe" sent to market it
was estimated in 1872 that three, four or even five animals
were slain.   To all appearances, said Harper's Weekly, an
effort was being made to exterminate the species in "the shortest convenient time."[5]   The killing was not sport; it was mere
butchery, and it awakened the resentful protest of our army
officers and Indian agents on the plains.   The brutes were
"harmless and defenceless," said Colonel Brackett; they could
be killed as easily as cows, said General Hazen.   The aid of
the Society for the Prevention of Cruelty to Animals was invoked to stop the slaughter.[6]   Bills appeared in Congress
making it a misdemeanor for any one to kill buffalo on the

[1] R. I. Dodge, op. cit., p. 131; Cong. Globe, 42nd Cong. 2nd sess., app.,
p. 179.
[2] Bradley, The Story of the Santa Fé, p. 94.
[3] Dodge, op. cit., p. 136.
[4] Cong. Globe, 42nd Cong. 2nd sess., app., p. 179.
[5] Harper's Weekly, Feb. 24, 1872.
[6] See speech of Delegate McCormick of Arizona in House of Representatives April 6, 1872.—Cong. Globe, 42nd Cong. 2nd sess., app., p. 179.

public lands except for the purpose of "using the meat for food or preserving the skin." Violation of the law would be punishable by a fine of $100 for each animal taken. Wanting better means of enforcement it was proposed that one-half of the sum should be paid to the informer.[1]

But the slaughter continued. Many buffalo not reached by the hunters were starved or frozen to death during the severe winter of 1871-2.[2] Soon where throngs of the beasts had been were myriads of decaying carcasses. In a year or two they were seldom seen in numbers in Kansas, though they served for some time as a subject for railway advertisements to allure tourists to the West. No sooner did a herd appear upon the Kansas line, coming out of Indian Territory, whither a hunter feared to go lest he be arrested, than it was destroyed.[3] Colonel Dodge has computed that the three principal "buffalo roads"—the Santa Fé, the Kansas Pacific and the Union Pacific, carried to market in 1872 nearly 500,000 and in 1873 750,000 hides. About 5,000,000 pounds of meat, it is said, were shipped east in 1873. In 1874 the railroads in Kansas and Nebraska conveyed to the fertilizer mills 21,000,000 pounds of bones which men were beginning to collect upon the plains.[4]

With the skin trade as a basis. for the reckoning Colonel Dodge has reached the. conclusion that in three years the number of buffalo killed for shipment east over these lines was not less than 3,000,000 head. Making additions for shipments south and west, and for what may have been taken by the Indians and parties from British America, he has fixed the total mortality from gunpowder in 1872, 1873 and 1874, with no account taken of death by snow and cold, at 5,500,000 head, which brought the species appreciably near the point of extinction.[5]

[1] See speech of Delegate McCormick of Arizona, loc. cit.; Cong. Globe, 42nd Cong. 2nd sess., p. 1063.
[2] J. H. Beadle, The Undeveloped West, p. 436.
[3] Dodge, op. cit., pp. 132-3.
[4] Ibid., p. 140.   [5] Ibid., pp. 142, 143-4.

The town which had so rapidly risen at the railhead folded its shanties and sped into the west, leaving behind it scarcely a trace.[1] Julesburg in the northeastern corner of Colorado which had had 5,000 inhabitants in 1867 was the home, a year later, of barely 50. Meadow Lake which had had a municipal government, two theatres, 13 hotels, 75 barrooms, a daily paper and a stock exchange was left with a population of 35. A building which had cost $6,000 was sold for $75.[2] So, too, was it at Benton[3] and Bryan on the Union Pacific, Hays City and Kit Carson on the Kansas Pacific and nearly all the rest of the "roaring towns," where men played three card monte, "chuck-a-luck," rondo coolo, faro and in a hundred other ways gambled the day and night away, where vice of all kinds flourished unashamed and "six shooter" justice sent some of the worst sinners the world ever saw to the "boothill" graveyards.

These "end-of-track" towns were followed by the "cow towns" in which morality stood on only a little higher plane. When the buffalo had been killed or frightened away cattle were fed upon the grass these animals had been munching time out of mind. The herds must be sent to market and were driven in to the most accessible shipping points on the new railways. At first they came to Abilene on the Kansas Pacific. In 1871 some 600,000 head, many of them from ranches as far away as Texas, were received in and sent east from this place. With the construction of the Santa Fé, 80 or 100 miles to the south, this line was preferred for use and a dubious fame came to Newton, Dodge City and a number of other towns thronged with saloons, brothels and gambling houses which throve upon the trade of the whooping cow boys who brought in the "long horns."[4]

The emigration agents of the railroad companies were covering Europe with enticing reports of the wealth of the new

[1] N. Y. Tribune, July 14, 1868, quoting Cincinnati Commercial; cf. W. A. Bell, New Tracks in North America, vol. i, pp. 17-18.
[2] Phila. Ledger, Feb. 1, 1869.
[3] For Benton see J. H. Beadle, The Undeveloped West, pp. 87-99.
[4] G. D. Bradley, The Story of the Santa Fé, chap. iv.

country, and in all directions settlers were erecting shanties, sod houses and in many places buildings of creditable proportions. The Santa Fé Railroad Company before March, 1873, had sold 250,000 acres of land.[1] Civilization was advancing. The railhead towns, unless the companies had established car shops in them, or had made them junction points for branch lines, were without qualities conducive to healthy existence. So, too, with the cattle towns—the rapid invasion of the pastures by men who were ready to turn up the soil and plant it with crops brought their notorious careers to an early end, unless they could be regenerated to serve some purpose in an orderly scheme of life.

Nebraska in 1870 had gathered within its boundaries a population of 125,000, Kansas nearly 400,000; Colorado, it was computed in 1873, was the home of not less than 100,000 people. Denver may then have had 15,000 inhabitants and Pueblo 4,000. Seven or eight railway lines already converged at Kansas City. Eastern Kansas was criss-crossed with rails leading out to the new prairie towns. Though no roads had been built in the state prior to 1865 2,500 miles were in operation in 1873.[2] There was not a mile of railway in Colorado in the spring of 1869; four years later 646 miles were finished and in use, while 671 more were in course of construction.[3] The railway mileage in the seven states of Kansas, Missouri, Iowa, Minnesota, Wisconsin, Illinois and Nebraska in the decade ending in 1870 had increased from 5,167 to more than 15,000—it had been multiplied by three.[4] The total for the whole country in 1870 was 53,000 miles of finished track; it was 67,000 in 1872.[5]

Some of the lines at once found lucrative trade in carrying in the emigrants and the household goods, tools, material for

---

[1] G. D. Bradley, The Story of the Santa Fé, pp. 113, 124; cf. W. A. Bell, New Tracks in North America, vol. i, p. 17.
[2] Westward March of Emigration in the United States, Lancaster, 1874.   [3] The Pueblo Colony, p. 7.
[4] Poor's Manual for 1871-2, p. xxxiii.   [5] Ibid. for 1873-4, p. xxix.

farm buildings and general supplies necessary to establish
them in their new homes. The seats, even the aisles of the
cars, on the long trains of the Kansas Pacific were filled with
passengers, so rapid was the influx of colonists in the territory
which it traversed.

Set on the high bluffs at the Great Bend of the Missouri,
just below the point at which it was joined by the Kansas
River, Kansas City had distanced Leavenworth as the metrop-
olis of the Missouri valley. It was the principal outfitting
station for settlers bound farther west, and the receiving point
for cattle. The city soon came to have large stock yards. A
tract covering 35 acres was acquired for this use. Packing
houses were located here; one firm established a plant with
a capacity of 50,000 beeves annually. At an exposition of the
products of the soil on the line of the Kansas Pacific, held in
Kansas City in 1871, visitors were shown sorghum from which
sugar could be made, Indian corn, broom corn, peanuts, wheat,
melons, beets, potatoes, pumpkins, and a large variety of
fruits, grains and vegetables, some of them grown 300 miles
west of the Missouri and without irrigation, in the very heart
of that region which a little while ago was declared to be unfit
for any agricultural use.[1] Kansas was sending fine fruits to
fairs in Philadelphia, Boston and other Eastern cities where
her orchardists were taking prizes for their products. Her
farmers laid claim to the honor of raising more wheat to the
acre than could be got out of the soil in any other state of the
Union.[2] A large body of Mennonites and other sectarians had
come from their adopted homes in Russia to settle on lands of
the Santa Fé. They turned their attention to the culture of
wheat, a crop with which they had had successful experience in
the Crimea.[3] Mills were built in Kansas City to grind the
grain into flour.

The treeless plains were being planted at many places with
timber for shade, for wood, for wind shields and for climatic

[1] St. Louis Democrat, Oct. 3, 1871, quoted in Weston's Guide to the
Kansas Pacific Railway, pp. 183-4.
[2] Weston's Guide, p. 186.   [3] Brown's Gazetteer, pp. 198-201.

effect. The Kansas Pacific employed an agent to superintend this work. Cottonwoods, elms, box elders, maples, osage oranges and willows were set in the ground and enjoyed rapid growth.[1]

A similar development was going forward in the fertile valley of the Platte. Many farmers came from the East to take up quarter sections and plant crops. Corn throve in the rich black soil and in summer time the green fields delighted the eyes of the "overland tourist." As in Kansas timber culture was receiving public care. Once a year an "Arbor Day" was set aside for afforesting the state, when even the children put young trees into the ground. In the course of a single spring season it was estimated that no less than 200,000, mostly cottonwoods, were planted to become in a few years a blessing to the commonwealth.[2]

Omaha, which had flourished on railway construction business, underwent a reaction after the completion of the road. But it soon began to advance along many lines, becoming an entrepôt for the cattle men who shipped in their live stock from the ranches, and then, after the frontier was pressed farther and farther west, for the enterprising agricultural population. As the home of manufacturers' agents, jobbers, cattle yards and packing houses Omaha, like Kansas City, soon became a substantial commercial centre with a future which was assured.

With the consciousness of their strength, gained by the remarkable progress and growth of the country, some Western men gave their active support to the plan to carry the national capital to the Mississippi Valley. A "Capital Removal Association" was formed in St. Louis where a wealthy man offered the government 5,000 acres of land upon which to erect a capitol and other Federal buildings. On October 20, 1869, a considerable body of delegates from various states and territories met in that city to give impulse to the movement. While one

---

[1] Weston's Guide, pp. 177-82.
[2] Williams, Pacific Tourist, p. 31.

orator advised them to let capitals alone and confine their
energies to the building of factories and railroads and the
development of the soil, the vast majority of those in attendance were of a different mind. They made speeches and
adopted resolutions. It was absurd to suppose, so they declared, that the handful of inhabitants which this country had
contained in 1789 possessed or desired to exercise the power
of permanently locating the national capital on the banks of
the Potomac, against the wishes of the millions who might
come after them. The people had endured the inconvenience
of its situation for three quarters of a century, but it was time
now for a change. The proper place for the capital was in
the heart of the Mississippi Valley, where it would be forever
safe from foreign foes and sectional seditions. The effort in
this direction would never cease until the end was attained.[1]

An address was sent out to the people. Petitions were circulated and signed; conventions, legislatures and city councils
passed resolutions. The Mississippi Valley Convention in session at Keokuk, Iowa, declared in favor of the idea.[2] So did
the constitutional convention of Illinois which instructed the
state's representatives in Congress to support the project.[3]
The movement was endorsed by the legislatures of Indiana,[4]
Missouri, Iowa, Kansas,[5] Nevada and some other states.[6]
Now, before authorizing further outlays of money for the enlargement of the public buildings and the erection of new
edifices in Washington, the nation's course should be made
plain.

In the East, when the suggestion was noticed at all, it was
discussed with ridicule. Plainly enthusiasm for the undertaking was not great even in the West, although the Chicago
Tribune and other newspapers espoused it. Communities vied

[1] Phila. Ledger, Aug. 16 and Oct. 21, 1869; N. Y. Tribune, Oct. 22,
1869; cf. W. A. Bell, New Tracks in North America, vol. i, pp. 9-10.
[2] Phila. Ledger, Sep. 10, 1869.
[3] Cong. Globe, 41st Cong. 2nd sess., p. 4470.
[4] House Mis. Doc., 41st Cong. 3rd sess., no. 100.
[5] Ibid., no. 91.
[6] Cf. House Reports, 41st Cong. 3rd sess., no. 52, p. 11.

with one another rather jealously for the site, and to gain larger support for the plan it was necessary to extend the area within which the honor might fall. The available locations came to include both banks of the Mississippi and finally the shores of the Ohio and the Missouri. A few Western members discussed the subject in Congress, but they spoke as men urged to their tasks by their constituencies.

"The power of empire" was advancing westward, said Jesse Moore, a representative from Illinois, and "as sure as God lives" the "seat of empire must go with it." No "rational living human being, except it may be some venerable old maiden lady or widow, who has from time immemorial kept boarding house in the city of Washington," he continued, who would not be "sensible enough to see and admit" that the idea of keeping the capital in a place which was "vitalized" only by the presence of government employees and the distribution of public money was "preposterous and absurd." [1]

John A. Logan drew upon the fountains of his rhetoric. He, too, would not have the nation's course on so important a subject shaped to please the pecuniary convenience of boarding house keepers. The cost of removal, men said, would prevent it. The investment in public buildings used in connection with the administration of the government in the District of Columbia was stated to be but $37,000,000, some found it to be as little as $25,000,000. Anyhow it was a paltry sum. If need be, said Logan, "when science and art are making such rapid strides, leaping over obstacles the preceding generation set down as impassable," the blocks of marble and granite could be floated out the Potomac and up the Mississippi, to be re-erected on the new site. But he would let the various edifices stand where they were. They were not large enough to satisfy the growing requirements of the government anyhow, and they could be turned over to Maryland for a capital. The Chicago Tribune would use them to house a great national university.[2]

[1] Cong. Globe, 41st Cong. 2nd sess., pp. 671-4.
[2] Phila. Ledger, Aug. 30, 1869.

"The place for the heart," Logan continued, "is the interior of the body from whence the arteries may convey the blood with uniform motion to the extremities. And as the heart in the human system is placed between the ribs, that it may be better protected from external danger, so in our national system it should be located between the mighty ribs, the Appalachian and Rocky Mountain chains."

"As the vanguard of empire," the ashes of the martyred Lincoln had gone into the West. "Let us follow them," Logan exclaimed. If Washington could rise from his tomb on the banks of the Potomac and "look abroad over the mighty empire which claims him as a father he would stand amazed. . . . His sense of justice would force him to say—'Carry it into the midst of the people, cherish, my children, a kind regard for the old homestead, but go forth to the glory that awaits you.' "[1]

Crebs, also from Illinois, offered a resolution asking the House Committee on Public Expenditures to inquire into the subject. A joint commission of five members from the House and two from the Senate should be appointed to select a site for the future location of the capital. The reference was made and the Western men awaited the report.[2]

Another convention which met in Cincinnati in October, 1870, brought Horace Greeley to the support of the enterprise. He and Joseph Medill of Chicago and three other men composed a committee to frame a memorial to be forwarded to Congress.[3] This document assumed such a form that Greeley would endorse it only to the extent of asking for a consideration of the question to set the agitation at rest before further sums of money should be expended upon public buildings in Washington. The capital of a government which embraces a continent, said the memorial, must itself be continental. "The geological strata, the configuration, the topography and the isothermal lines of North America"—all were proof that the Mississippi basin had been "designated by nature" to con-

[1] Cong. Globe, 41st Cong. 2nd sess., pp. 679-85.
[2] Ibid., p. 4470.
[3] N. Y. Tribune, Oct. 26, 1870.

tain the seat of government of the nation. Here in this valley in fifty years would be concentrated eight-tenths of all the population and wealth of the country. The removal of the capital had become a "public necessity." Washington was more remote from the Pacific states and territories than Constantinople was from Great Britain, or St. Petersburg from Spain or Morocco.[1]

On the last day of the Forty-first Congress, March 3, 1871, the committee to which the subject had been referred submitted an unfavorable report. Coburn of Indiana and Philetus Sawyer of Wisconsin dissented. Their argument followed familiar lines. Not only was Washington inaccessible to the people by reason of its great distance from an increasing number of them, and unsafe because of its location with reference to a foreign foe and to domestic traitors, as had been made so clear at a recent time, but it was set "in the midst of a barren region, incapable of sustaining a powerful and vigorous people" and had a bad climate. A pitiable object did Mr. Coburn and Mr. Sawyer make it out to be—"solitary, helpless, idle, in danger, friendless and a beggar." The capital of the country should be carried into the West.[2] The question was quickly disposed of by the House. It was laid on the table, in accordance with the recommendation of the majority of the Committee without a division, and the discussion soon came to an end.[3]

With the aid of the Pacific Railroad a man could go around the world in three months. Some day Benton declared, as long ago as in 1849, that the line would be "adorned" with a statue of Columbus, "hewn from the granite mass of a peak of the Rocky Mountains," pointing with outstretched arm to the western horizon and saying to "the flying passenger—'There is the East! There is India!'"[4] "Today you have made

[1] House Mis. Doc., 41st Cong. 3rd sess., no. 105.
[2] House Reports, 41st Cong. 3rd sess., no. 52.
[3] Cong. Globe, 41st Cong. 3rd sess., p. 1940.
[4] Speech in St. Louis in October, 1849. See J. P. Davis, The Union Pacific Railway, p. 136.

that prophecy a fact," said General Dodge, when the tracks were joined at Promontory Point. "This is the way to India."[1]

The locomotives had met. What they had said to each other, "pilots touching head to head," on that great day was recorded by Bret Harte:—

> "Said the Western engine 'Phew!'
> And a long, low whistle blew.
>
> You brag of your East! You do?
> Why, I bring the East to you!
> All the Orient, all Cathay,
> Find through me the shortest way."

In achieving so much it was satisfactory to realize that we had beaten all rivals, and the politicians and the newspapers rejoiced.[2] "Listening races" had heard the sound of the silver sledge at Promontory. A "pathway of nations," a great thoroughfare between 800 million people in Asia and 200 million in Europe, was open for use. They were to have "harmonious intercourse across this continent."[3]

> "Plunging through the mountains,
> Flying o'er the plains,"

the railway was bringing the treasures of the Orient to the Atlantic coast.[4] At New York the agents of mandarins and daimios would soon be assorting their silks and teas to meet the demands of the European markets.[5] The first day the road was open an invoice of tea left San Francisco for St. Louis to signalize the beginning of the overland trade with Asia.[6] England was forwarding mail for Australia across America, even before the railroad was finished, covering the

[1] E. L. Sabin, Building the Pacific Railway, p. 220.
[2] "John Bull must take a back seat,
    And Nap may rip and swear,
But Jonathan is wide awake,
    And for them does not care.
The road to China's open,
    Hurrah for Uncle Sam!"
                              —Phila. Press, May 15, 1869.
[3] John Covode of Pa. in Cong. Globe, 40th Cong. 3rd sess., p. 454.
[4] N. Y. Tribune, May 11, 1869.
[5] Ibid., April 15, 1868.   [6] Phila. Ledger, July 12, 1869.

gap which separated the track ends with the stage coaches. Now San Francisco was but 31 days from Auckland, 38 days from Melbourne. New Zealand could get letters out of England by way of San Francisco in 41 instead of 55 days over the East India route; telegrams via California might be received in 20 days.[1]

But this long-wished-for line of communication was scarcely open for use when the Suez Canal was completed, so that Europe, for a way to the East, might turn more conveniently to this artificial passage from the Mediterranean to the Red Sea which the French engineer, de Lesseps, had projected. Thousands of laborers had been at work for a decade making the excavations and in November, 1869, six months after the ceremonies at Promontory Point, Empress Eugénie of France, Emperor Francis Joseph of Austria and a large body of princes and other representatives of powers and dynasties were assembled in Egypt to witness ships sailing a course where dry land had been, with a saving of the thousands of miles which were involved in circumnavigating the continent of Africa.[2]

Seward's outreaching mind, with a comprehension of our destiny as a force in world politics far in advance of his age, had not been without a care for the proposal to cut a way for ships across the Isthmus of Darien. In 1868 Caleb Cushing was sent, as an agent of the State Department, to Bogota to assist our minister to Colombia in negotiating a treaty that the United States might have control of the canal which it was hoped might soon connect the waters of the Atlantic and the Pacific oceans. Secretary Seward and Attorney General Evarts proceeded to New York and a meeting with a number of New York capitalists was held at the home of Peter Cooper with a view to securing subscriptions in a sum approximating $100,000,000 to the stock of a company which would undertake the construction of the work. But the days of Johnson's administration were far spent, the treaty did not receive the

[1] Phila. Ledger, May 24, 1870, and Aug. 27, 1871.
[2] N. Y. Tribune, Nov. 17, 1869.

approval of the Senate, nor was it ratified by the government of Colombia, and the scheme fell by the way.[1]

With the beginning of the Grant administration negotiations with Colombia were resumed. Congress made the necessary appropriations for thorough surveys of the ground, based upon Admiral Davis's excellent report on the subject in 1866. There were 19, some said 26 proposed routes for an interoceanic ship canal in Mexico, Central America and on the isthmus proper.[2] In Darien the work was entrusted by the Navy Department to Commander Selfridge. The steam sloop *Nipsic* and the store ship *Guard* were designated for his use and he was to be served on the Pacific side by a vessel detached from the fleet at San Francisco. The party, composed of navigators, engineers and scientists, left New York in January, 1870, and was soon on the ground. "The Department," said Secretary Robeson in his letter of instructions to Selfridge, "has entrusted to you a duty connected with the greatest enterprise of the present age; and upon your zeal will depend whether your name is honorably identified with one of the facts of the future."[3]

The duty was assumed and discharged in a serious spirit. "The Pacific is naturally our domain," said Selfridge. "The one great commercial nation on its borders, any work that brings it within close communication to our eastern coast and avoids the long and tempestuous passage of Cape Horn, cannot be too highly appreciated, and no cost or labor should be spared to forward the undertaking. What the Suez Canal is proving to Europe in a far greater extent will a canal through the isthmus prove to America." While he accounted it a "gigantic task, the greatest the world has ever known," he expressed the opinion that such strides had been made in engineering knowledge that it was now possible to carry it forward to successful completion.[4]

[1] Seward at Washington, vol. iii, pp. 393-4.
[2] N. Y. Tribune, July 25, 1870.
[3] House Mis. Doc., 42nd Cong. 3rd sess., no. 113, p. 1.
[4] Ibid., p. 6.

Since it presented the largest difficulties Selfridge determined first, while his men were fresh and keen for adventure, to attack the so-called "Darien route" which ran over the isthmus from Caledonia Bay by way of the Sucubti and Savanna rivers, the path Balboa had used in 1513 when he discovered the Pacific, and the track of the Bucaneers in their incursions upon the Spanish settlements on the western coast. This route had been explored previously, but the data were accounted inconclusive. As the country was covered with a dense primeval growth it was difficult to penetrate, except along the streams, but the course was soon declared to be impracticable for use, as was the "Sassardi route" which was examined at the same time, whereupon the party turned to the "San Blas route," where there was greater promise of success. This, too, was found to be unavailable, and, as the rainy season was at hand, Selfridge came home with nothing of a favorable nature to report.[1]

Returning to the isthmus in the following year, 1871, he made explorations further south. Parties were detailed to examine the "Cacarica route," "De Puyt's route," the "Napipi route" and other lines which had been the subject of suggestion or recommendation by engineers and writers, who now, for long, had been dealing with the problem of a ship canal to join the two oceans. At the end of his investigations he was prepared to endorse the "Napipi route," which he said was "superior to any other upon the continent." At the most southern point on the isthmus, where it began to broaden out into the great body of territory known as South America, he had found a way from sea to sea. Utilizing the Atrato River, which could be navigated for 150 miles, the actual distance to be canalled was only 31 miles. The route involved the use of a tunnel more than five miles in length, and, necessarily, of great size of bore to admit the masts of sailing vessels. But with the Burleigh drill and nitroglycerine Selfridge declared that this

---

[1] Report of Sec. of the Navy for 1870, House Ex. Doc., 41st Cong. 3rd sess., no. 1, pt. 3, pp. 133 et seq.; cf. N. Y. Tribune, July 25, 1870.

part of his plan would offer no insuperable obstacle. The completion of the Mt. Cenis tunnel, eight miles in length in Switzerland, and the successful progress recorded on the Hoosac tunnel in Massachusetts were proofs of the entire feasibility of engineering feats of this character. Nine locks would be used to reach the summit level on the east side and thirteen locks on the west side. The harbor chosen for a terminus on the Pacific was Cupica Bay. The cost of construction, it was computed, would be about $123,000,000.[1]

Since other problems were to be worked out and better ways might be discovered in the valley of the Bojaya, lying to the south of the Napipi, Selfridge was sent out a third time in January, 1873. As a result of further explorations and surveys he was enabled to modify the original plan in a material way, especially on the Pacific side. The harbor now would be Chiri Chiri Bay instead of Cupica Bay. The tunnel would be but three miles in length. Using the labor of Chinamen, who could be employed at $16 a month, it was estimated that the cost of the completed work over this route would be not more than $60,000,000.[2]

Meantime, in September, 1870, Captain Shufeldt led an expedition to Tehuantepec in Mexico. Including navigation up the Coatzacoalcos River on the Atlantic side, supplemented by canals, the route led to Salina Cruz on the Pacific, a distance of about 172 miles. The obstacles to be overcome he found to be "of the most ordinary nature." Shufeldt, however, did not underrate the magnitude of the undertaking and hinted at the need of calling upon "national resources" for its completion. "A canal through the Isthmus of Tehuantepec," he said with enthusiasm, "is an extension of the Mississippi River to the Pacific Ocean. It converts the Gulf of Mexico into an American lake. In time of war it closes that gulf to all enemies. It is the only route which our government can

[1] Report of Sec. of the Navy for 1871, House Ex. Doc., 42nd Cong. 2nd sess., no. 1, pt. 3, pp. 9-10, 178 et seq.
[2] House Mis. Doc., 42nd Cong. 3rd sess., no. 113, pp. 75 et seq.; Report of Sec. of the Navy for 1873, pp. 164 et seq.

control. So to speak it renders our own territory circum-navigable. It brings New Orleans 1,400 nautical miles nearer to San Francisco than a canal via Darien, and such is the character of the intervening waters that it permits a canal boat to load in St. Louis and discharge her freight in California with but little more than the risk of inland navigation." [1]

Early in 1872 Commander Hatfield was ordered to proceed to Nicaragua to explore the route by way of the San Juan River and Lake Nicaragua. But his work was interrupted by the coming on of the rains, and, in December, Commander Lull, who had performed valuable services on the Selfridge expeditions, with the aid of A. G. Menocal, a Cuban, educated in engineering in the United States, continued the surveys. Their plans called for the construction of several dams in the river to render it navigable, canals totalling 61.74 miles in length, and the use of the lake. Thus could shipping be passed from Greytown on the Atlantic to Brito on the Pacific. Commander Lull concluded in his report that the line presented "by far a better combination of favorable conditions than any other route" which yet had been examined. [2]

Men said that the sickly climate would prevent the prosecution of the work. Commander Lull remarked that in a period of four years three expeditions had visited Darien, while two had been engaged in exploration in Nicaragua. As many as 300 persons, counting ships' companies, were in the service at one time, but not a single man had succumbed to climatic disease. [3]

In 1873 the Secretary of the Navy was able to report that in his belief little more need be done in the direction of surveys. Expert opinion supported the construction of an interoceanic canal on any one of three lines across the continent— along the Atrato valley in Darien, by way of Nicaragua Lake, or over the Isthmus of Tehuantepec. Private enterprise could

[1] Senate Ex. Doc., 42nd Cong. 2nd sess., no. 6, p. 20.
[2] Report of Sec. of the Navy, House Ex. Doc., 43rd Cong. 1st sess., no. 1, pt. 3, p. 207.
[3] Ibid., pp. 205-6.

now make its choice of routes. The government had pointed
the way to a successful connection of the two oceans.[1]

Pending the completion of the canal Marshall O. Roberts
and other capitalists in New York projected a railroad across
Florida from Fernandina to Cedar Keys, a distance of 140
miles, and another in Tehuantepec which, though involving
four transshipments of freight, would afford a route to China
2,000 miles shorter than that now taken over the isthmus at
Panama.[2]

The two cable lines which Cyrus W. Field had laid from
Ireland to Newfoundland were so fully employed in 1869 with
the transmission of messages to the British Islands, and every
part of the world reached by telegraph from London, that a
French company was on the point of entering the field. A
route was surveyed from Brest to St. Pierre, an islet belonging
to France, off the south coast of Newfoundland, and thence
to Duxbury, Mass., at the mouth of Cape Cod Bay, thirty
miles southeast of Boston. The distance was easily double
that which was covered by the older lines. But much had
been learned by recent experience. The services of the *Great
Eastern* were again employed and, in company with two
smaller vessels and some French frigates, she sailed west-
wardly from Brest in June, paying out the cable as she went.
The armored wires were landed at St. Pierre on July 15, to
be carried on by the smaller boats to Duxbury, which was
reached on July 23,[3] and came ashore, despite reports of the
opposition of our government at Washington to such a visitor
from France without the nation's consent.[4] On the 28th there
was a celebration which was participated in by the people of
Massachusetts. The prefect of Paris and the mayor of Boston
exchanged greetings. Speeches were made; a dinner was served
under a large tent; a wealthy man in the neighborhood opened

[1] Report of Sec. of the Navy, House Ex. Doc., 43rd Cong. 1st sess.,
no. 1, pt. 3, p. 9.
[2] Phila. Ledger, Sep. 3, 1869.
[3] Ibid., July 14, 17 and 26, 1869.
[4] N. Y. Nation, June 22 and 29, 1869.

his house at night for a levee.[1] The next day Napoleon cabled
his good wishes to General Grant who sent his salutations to
France in return.[2]

The completion of this line was a signal for a marked reduction in the charges for cablegrams. At first over the Ire-
land-to-Newfoundland route the rate between New York and
London had been $100 in gold for ten words of five letters;
it had fallen to $17, without restriction as to the length of the
words. The French cable company fixed a price of $7.50 in
gold and 75 cents for each additional word, and the English
companies met the rates of their competitor.

At the lower prices the business was still lucrative. The
French company was soon earning $5,000, $6,000, even $11,000
in gold a week, which for a total investment of $6,000,000
should yield the stockholders, it was computed, nine per cent.[3]
The lines, early in 1870, entered into an agreement to pool and
divide their profits to prevent a further cutting of rates.[4] The
shares of nearly all the submarine telegraph companies were
selling above par and the promoters of new lines were encouraged to go forward with their plans. England had just
established a direct service to Bombay via Falmouth, Lisbon,
Gibraltar and Malta,[5] and various schemes were in a more or
less advanced state with reference to China, Japan and Australia.[6] In this country a group of men were trying to form
the East India Telegraph Company with a capital of $5,000,-
000 to connect the seaports of China. A. G. Curtin, the "war
governor" of Pennsylvania and later for a time our minister
to Russia, was president of the corporation and its stock was
offered for sale through the largest American banking houses.[7]

[1] Phila. Ledger, July 28, 1869.
[2] Ibid., July 29, 1869.
[3] Ibid., Oct. 8, 1869, and Jan. 4, 1870.
[4] Ibid., Feb. 7, 1870.
[5] Edinburgh Review, July, 1870.
[6] Ibid.; cf. N. Y. Tribune, Dec. 14, 1869.
[7] N. Y. Tribune, Sep. 1 and 14, 1868, advertising columns. The reasons for supposing that the lines might be profitable were that China
contained at least 414,000,000 people, that they had no postal system,
that they were inquisitive and fond of news, that such as had come to
this country made much use of the telegraph in California, etc.

At the same time Field, now enjoying a high reputation because of the final triumph of his plans in reference to the Atlantic cable, proposed to cross the Pacific. He would "supply the only link remaining to be completed in order to make, in connection with lines now in operation and under contract, a chain of telegraphic communication around the globe." He asked for public aid. It had been offered Collins for his scheme to reach Asia by way of Behring's Strait in 1864. Foreign governments extended a helping hand to such enterprises and it could not well be withheld by the Congress of the United States from an undertaking "of large magnitude" and "encompassed by greater difficulties and hazards . . . than any line of telegraphic communication which has ever been set on foot." Mr. Field asked for incorporation under the name of the Pacific Submarine Telegraph Company which was to have a capital of $10,000,000. Upon the conclusion of the work within five years he and his associates were to be invested with a quantity of public lands "in full property." Naval vessels were to be assigned to the company's uses in surveying the route, while the government, in return for its favors, might transmit free of cost messages the tolls on which, at the regular rates, should amount to as much as $500,000 annually.[1]

Charles Sumner presented the memorial to the United States Senate,[2] and Field visited Grant at the White House with charts, plans and letters in proof of the feasibility of his enterprise. Should the line proceed along our coast to Alaska and to Asia by the Aleutian Islands, or should it, as Admiral Porter suggested, "boldly push across the ocean" by way of the Hawaiian Islands, through deep water, following the longest route (6,000 miles) over which a cable had yet been submerged in the sea?[3] The President expressed a lively interest in the success of the project.[4]

[1] Field's Memorial to Congress, House Mis. Doc., 41st Cong. 2nd sess., no. 126.
[2] Phila. Ledger, April 15, 1870.
[3] Ibid., May 12, 1870.
[4] Oberholtzer, Jay Cooke, vol. ii, p. 292.

The spirit of progress was astir in China and Japan and we were eager to give them the fullest encouragement in a realization of their design to come out from the mystery and darkness which so long had enveloped them. Seward's international mind gave him understanding of the part which we might play in bringing these ancient peoples into closer contact with the rest of the world. For the advancement of this cause in China he found a ready ally in Anson Burlingame. This man had been born on a farm in New York state. As a lad he was taken by his parents successively to Ohio and Michigan. He returned to the East to study law at Harvard and settled for practice in Boston, where, by his affable manners and an admired eloquence, he easily advanced himself in the counsels, first of the Whig and then of the Republican party. He served for several terms in Congress where he won distinction as an anti-slavery man; but, defeated for re-election in 1860, President Lincoln proffered him the mission to Austria. To the government of that country, however, he had rendered himself unacceptable as he learned upon reaching Paris on his way to Vienna to begin the performance of his duties, because of his having expressed his favor for the independence of Hungary and Sardinia, whereupon Motley was appointed in his stead and he was sent to China. There he displayed abilities of a peculiar order. He not only made himself a highly respected figure in the diplomatic corps at Pekin, but he earned the respect and confidence of the Chinese government to such a degree that he was able to exert a considerable influence upon the course of internal affairs in that country. He came home in 1865, intending not to return to his post, but he was dissuaded by Seward and his further residence at Pekin raised him still higher in the public estimation.

A Chinese sage had been banished some twenty years earlier for having set before the people in some historical works an account of the life of George Washington. With a happy prescience President Johnson, through Seward, had caused a copy of the Stuart portrait of Washington to be made by an artist in Boston and forwarded to Burlingame, to be presented

in the name of the American people to the venerable Chinaman, who but recently had been recalled to a place of honor
at Pekin. With this as his text Burlingame used the occasion
to bring the two countries into more cordial relations. China
was "the mother of inventions." From her came paper, printing, porcelain, the compass and gunpowder. For "your charm-
ing manners," said he, "your temperance, your habits of schol-
arship, your improvements in agriculture and your high culture of tea and silk" we could exchange "our modern sciences,
our steamboats, our railroads and telegraphs." The Golden
Rule had been framed by Confucius 500 years before it came
from the lips of Jesus—"We should not do to others what
we would not that others should do to us." Together we
could serve as exemplars to the world of the value of this
great moral law.[1]

In 1867 Burlingame again resolved to retire from his post.
At a farewell dinner tendered him in Pekin Prince Kung,
the Regent serving during the minority of the Emperor, made
a most unusual suggestion—Would he, upon leaving the diplomatic service of the United States, enter that of China? He
would be appointed, if he should consent, a minister pleni-
potentiary and envoy extraordinary to visit the United States
and a dozen powers of Europe to assure them of China's desire
for friendly international relationships, to be expressed in
treaties which he should be clothed with authority to negotiate.[2] He asked for a little time to consider the proposal,
and, seeing an opportunity for service which might assume a
very important form, he agreed to accept the mission. He left
Pekin on the morning of November 25, 1867, being escorted
to the gates of the city by all the foreign residents, reached
Shanghai in December and sailed for America in February,
1868. On the last day of March he arrived in San Francisco.
Accompanying him were two of the Chinese Emperor's ministers of the "second class," serving as associated high envoys,
Chih-Kang and Sun Chia-Ku, and a body of students, in-

[1] China corr. of N. Y. Tribune, March 30, 1868.
[2] Seward at Washington, vol. ii, p. 373.

terpreters, scriveners, a doctor and servants, numbering more than 30 in all.

Although Burlingame had assumed his unusual duties "in the interests of our country and of civilization," as he believed,[1] it was not without misgivings that he had entered the service of a foreign power. He was doubtful of the reception which might await him in the United States. Would it not seem that he had held his American citizenship but lightly—that he had exchanged allegiances, indeed, now that he bore a commission of a government not his own? Seeing the wharves in San Francisco crowded with people, as he stood upon the deck while the vessel advanced to her dock, he was very dubious as to their attitude toward him.

But he was not long to remain in uncertainty. The whole city had pressed into the streets for sight of him and his retinue, and to acclaim them with enthusiasm. Government officials and delegations of citizens called upon him at his headquarters at the Occidental Hotel. He was tendered a banquet at the Lick House which was attended by the governor of California, General Halleck, Admiral Thatcher, in command of the fleet in the harbor, and the most distinguished men of the city.[2] After six weeks in San Francisco the party embarked for the East by way of Panama. On May 22 the *Arizona*, bearing the interesting company, came up New York harbor with the Chinese Imperial dragon at her peak. Salutes were fired. The East like the West was prepared to accord Burlingame a warm welcome. The impeachment trial rendered the embassy's coming in some degree untimely, but in its despite preparations were made for their early visit to Washington and a formal reception by the President. Social attentions generally were declined until they had presented their credentials and had taken the initial steps toward the negotiation of a treaty, the principal business which had brought them across the Pacific. In Washington, on June 1, they first paid their respects to Mr. Seward at the State Department.

[1] Seward at Washington, vol. iii, p. 379.
[2] N. Y. Tribune, May 16, 1868.

A reception followed on June 5, in the Blue Room at the White House where the President made them a speech.[1] Their coming, said he, gave expectation "that the great empire, instead of remaining, as heretofore, merely passive will henceforth be induced to take an active part in the general progress of civilization." That our intercourse should be closer and more advantageous he urged the construction of the Darien ship canal and bade the ambassadors commend the project to the Chinese government, to the government of Colombia and to the several European states to which they were accredited.[2]

A state dinner, a party at Seward's home, where the decorations in the garden were Chinese lanterns, a reception in the House of Representatives, with an address by the Speaker and a response by Mr. Burlingame,[3] and many minor exchanges marked the visit of the embassy. The Chinese flag flying from the staff on their hotel on Pennsylvania Avenue, the mandarins in their flowered gowns and gay silken sashes, the strangely attired secretaries gave the city an Oriental air which curiously impressed everyone.

On June 23 they were again in New York for a banquet at Delmonico's, tendered them by a committee of prominent citizens. The governor of the state, the mayor, Mr. Evarts, Horace Greeley, David Dudley Field, Edwards Pierrepont and several others spoke. But here, as everywhere, Burlingame himself was the central figure, because of the strange credentials which he held and the manifest importance of his mission, which was not less than the voluntary proffer of the national good will and the commerce of more than 400,000,000 people hitherto shut off from our intercourse or understanding. "That East which men have sought since the days of Alexander," said Burlingame, "now itself seeks the West," and he was its herald and messenger.[4]

[1] N. Y. Tribune, June 6, 1868.
[2] Ibid.; Seward at Washington, vol. iii, p. 381.
[3] N. Y. Tribune, June 10, 1868.
[4] Banquet to Burlingame on June 23, 1868, in New York, a pamphlet; cf. N. Y. Tribune, June 24, 1868.

In due time a treaty was agreed upon at Washington. On July 4 it was signed. Concluded on the 28th of the month it was ratified and finally proclaimed in February, 1870. Comprising eight articles, supplementary to the treaty of 1858, it is usually and quite properly known as the "Burlingame treaty." Its provisions covered the use of the waters and tracts of land in China granted for purposes of trade or residence. The Emperor did not relinquish his dominion over such areas. In them no attack should originate against our citizens, nor should we, on our side, pursue war-like policies from such vantage points. Thus would an end be made to all foreign pretensions to concessions of territory in treaty ports. Chinese consuls might be appointed to act at American ports, where they should enjoy the privileges and immunities enjoyed by British and Russian consuls in the United States. There were mutual guarantees as to the exercise of liberty of conscience and worship in the two countries; pledges as to free immigration and emigration, when passage between the countries was voluntary. American citizens could visit or reside in China on the terms enjoyed "by the citizens or subjects of the most favored nation" with reciprocal rights for the Chinese people in the United States. Exchanges of students in educational institutions could proceed unhindered. No citizens of the United States should presume to interfere in the internal affairs of China in building railroads, telegraphs or the like until the Emperor had given his consent to the construction of these works. He reserved to himself "the right to decide the time and manner and circumstances of introducing such improvements within his dominions."[1]

Early in August Burlingame and the mandarins were ready to visit Seward at Auburn where they had a most amiable reception. They then proceeded to Buffalo and Niagara Falls. On the 21st they were tendered a reception in Fanueil Hall in Boston, which was followed by a banquet by the corporation. The governor of Massachusetts spoke, as did Caleb

---

[1] Haswell, Treaties and Conventions, pp. 179-82.

Cushing and E. P. Whipple. Oliver Wendell Holmes read
a poem—

> "Brothers whom we may not reach
> Through the veil of alien speech,
> Welcome! Welcome! Eyes can tell
> What the lips in vain would spell,
> Words that hearts can understand,
> Brothers from the flowery land."

Ralph Waldo Emerson gave expression to the "surprise
and pleasure" that he and all must feel "when the venerable
Oriental state, hitherto a romantic legend, suddenly steps into
the fellowship of nations," while Charles Sumner was at hand
in proof of his satisfaction at the unlocking of "these great
Chinese gates" which had been "bolted and barred for long
centuries." [1]

Returning to New York the embassy was soon ready to proceed on its way around the world. It sailed on September 9
on the *Java* for Liverpool, to be accorded similar receptions
in England, France, Prussia and other countries. Treaties
were made with most of the European powers, in spite of the
rumbling that preceded the outbreak of the war which Bismarck was meditating upon Louis Napoleon, and of news of
hideous atrocities committed upon foreigners in China, gravely
tending to cast discredit upon the friendly intentions of the
government which was seeking to take a place in the civilized
world, and its ability to execute pledges solemnly made by its
ministers. When Burlingame reached Russia he was suddenly
taken ill. He died in St. Petersburg on February 23, 1870,
while his laurels still were green, to be brought home to lie
in state in Fanueil Hall before being buried with high honors
in Mount Auburn in Boston. There was "more of the picturesque and romantic" about his enterprise than had fallen
to the lot of anybody in the western world, said the New
York Nation. [2] In the light of later events his achievement
does not seem large, but had he lived to return to Pekin and
had he remained in China to interpret the meaning of his

[1] N. Y. Tribune, Aug. 2, 1868.
[2] Issue of March 3, 1870.

treaties, results of lasting importance might have come out of his extraordinary adventure in diplomacy.

That he had done much to improve the relations between our own and the Chinese government was indicated a few months later when Seward visited Pekin while on a journey around the world, which he had undertaken upon relinquishing office with President Johnson. He was the recipient of many honors. It was the opportunity for him again to meet the two Chinese ministers who had accompanied Burlingame to the United States. The regent, Prince Kung, and a party of distinguished officers of the Empire visited him at the American legation.[1]

More came to pass in Japan. Only 18 years had elapsed since Commodore Perry had made a treaty with the Mikado and opened two ports to our shipping. A number of Japan's public men arrived in San Francisco in 1860; they proceeded by way of Panama to Washington and our Atlantic coast cities. Everywhere viewed with curiosity by reason of their unfamiliar faces, their strange dress and manners they, nevertheless, were received with real hospitality. Upon their return home the imitative faculties of their people were soon occupied in adapting what had been learned to the national needs.

Courtesies had since been exchanged with every evidence of sincere good will upon both sides. In April, 1867, two Japanese commissioners with their secretaries and interpreters arrived in New York by the Aspinwall steamer. They bore gifts for President Johnson, Secretary Seward and General Grant, which they presented in Washington and remained in the country for several weeks to acquaint themselves with our educational, military and industrial systems.[2]

In Japan as in China, Seward, during his travels, was the object of much friendly notice. Upon his arrival at Yokohama he was met with an invitation to an official feast to be presided over by the Prime Minister in the Imperial palace.

[1] W. H. Seward's Travels Around the World, pp. 143, 168-9, 199-203.
[2] N. Y. Herald, April 23, 1867, and later issues.

Six hundred of the highest dignitaries of the country were to attend. This courtesy Seward declined on account of his health, but he visited the Foreign Office and had conversations there and elsewhere with the ministers. Before his departure he, "as a special friend of Japan," was granted a private audience with the Mikado,[1] an unusual attention which was taken to contain further promise that the country would pursue an enlightened policy with reference to the outside world.[2]

In 1871 an Imperial prince headed a mission to the United States. The party included Arinori Mori, who was to act as Japan's chargé d'affaires at Washington, the first representative who yet had been despatched by the Emperor to reside with us, if he were not the first to be sent to any foreign country.[3]

But more important than any of the visiting embassies was that one which, in the middle of January, 1872, was led by Iwakura, vice-president of the Imperial ministry. With him were several other high ministers of state, who came as ambassadors and commissioners, and a retinue of 80 secretaries, interpreters, servants and students. They were accompanied by our minister to Japan, C. E. DeLong.[4]

Their entertainment in San Francisco at receptions and dinners and on sight-seeing excursions continued for many days.[5] Early in February they proceeded to Salt Lake City where, because of the snow storms which bound the Union Pacific Railroad east of that point, they were marooned. De Long said it would cost us millions of dollars. If the road were seen by them to be unfit for use in winter time the trade of Japan would take other routes. Men were despatched on sleds from frontier posts with supplies to save from starvation the unlucky persons who were imprisoned on the trains.

[1] W. H. Seward's Travels Around the World, pp. 49, 71-4.
[2] Appleton's Cyclopedia for 1870, article on Japan.
[3] Mori was presented to the President on March 2.—Phila. Ledger, March 3, 1871.
[4] Ibid., Jan. 16, 1872.
[5] Ibid., Jan. 22, 1872.

The *America,* which had brought the Japanese to San Francisco, was obliged to return to Yokohama and Hong Kong without the Eastern mails.[1]

While the snow sheds in the Sierras served very well those on the Union Pacific were inadequate in number; where they had been built they were ineffective. The greatest indignation was displayed on all sides, except, perhaps, by the promoters of other Pacific railway enterprises who always had prophesied that a central line at high altitudes would prove to be impracticable. Some declared that the Japanese should be taken back to San Francisco to be carried east by way of Panama. But finally the blockade was raised. On February 17 eight trains from the east reached Ogden, the first to come in in 28 days, and, in a little while, when danger of a recurrence of such conditions had passed, the embassy started for Chicago. The bridge at Omaha had just been finished and they crossed the Missouri without recourse to the ferry. Before leaving Chicago they gave the mayor $5,000 to be distributed among the poor of the city and on the last day of February they reached Washington, where an elaborate reception awaited them.[2]

On March 4 ten of the principal visitors, led by the envoy extraordinary, Iwakura, were presented to President Grant in the White House. High officers of the government, civil and military, were gathered in the East Room. Very shortly the Japanese, escorted by Chargé Mori, dressed in their odd and brilliant native costumes, appeared. They were welcomed officially by Secretary Fish, who presented them to the President. Their address was read. They had come from the Emperor of Japan in the interest of national development to study the customs and note the achievements of the West-

---

[1] There were 70 days in December, January, February and March of this severe winter of 1871-2 in which no mails were received in New York from San Francisco, and nearly all that did come in were late. There were 78 days in which San Francisco was without postal communication with New York.—Report of Postmaster General for 1872.

[2] Phila. Ledger, Feb. 5, 6, 9, 13, 15, 19, 22, 24, 27, 29 and March 1, 1872.

ern powers. Their object was the establishment of peaceful and friendly relations, and to promote and develop commerce with the world. Thus would they gain "fresh impulse in the paths of progress." They extended their "good wishes" to the President and to all the people of the United States.

Grant in reply recalled how we had been the pioneer among the nations in establishing diplomatic and commercial communication with Japan. No longer could any people "keep apart from others." One of the most ancient of organized communities was welcome to view and learn of the achievements of one of the most recent. He hoped that the abode of the ambassadors in this country would contribute to "a more intimate acquaintance and intercourse," and a strengthening of the bonds which united the two peoples.

Subsequently the President, with Iwakura on his arm, led the company to another room of the Executive Mansion to meet Mrs. Grant and a number of ladies who were assembled there to greet them.[1] This reception was followed by a round of festivities in honor of the visitors.[2] On March 6 they were guests of the House of Representatives. The galleries were crowded with distinguished persons. Speaker Blaine delivered the address of welcome in the name of the American people and Iwakura made a poetic response. In the future there would be an extended commerce uniting "our national interests in a thousand forms, as drops of water will commingle, flowing from our several rivers to that common ocean which divides our countries." He expressed the hope that "our national friendship" might be "as difficult to sunder or estrange as to divide the once blended drops" of that common sea.[3]

Various proposals for a new treaty were discussed at Washington. In a few weeks some members of the party returned home for further instructions.[4] Those who remained visited

[1] Phila. Ledger, March 5, 1872.
[2] Letters of Mrs. J. G. Blaine, vol. i, pp. 94-6, 103, 107.
[3] Phila. Ledger, March 7, 1872.
[4] American Annual Cyclopedia for 1872, article on Japan.

the coal regions of Pennsylvania and other industrial centres, enjoying the hospitality of cities and of organizations
and individuals who were eager to honor them.[1] At the end
of July Iwakura and his associates were guests in Philadelphia,[2] passing shortly to New York and to Boston, from
which port on August 6 they embarked for Europe to continue their observations in the interest of a new Japan.[3]

The regular monthly service of the Pacific Mail Steamship
Company, which was founded upon a government postal contract of 1866, had of itself given an appreciable impetus to
our trade with Asia. At first there were scarcely any exchanges of merchandise between the United States and Japan
and China, except in small degree with Hong Kong.[4] The
import and export trade of San Francisco with those countries had grown from $10,485,000 in 1866 to $14,814,000 in
1869.[5] The influence of the Pacific Railroad was seen immediately. In 1872 the incoming and outgoing commerce
with China through San Francisco had increased to $17,767,-
700, with Japan to $10,382,000, a total of $28,000,000.[6]

In the first ten months of the year 1870 the shipments of
tea from San Francisco east over the Central Pacific reached
a total of 1,712,271 pounds; for the corresponding ten months
in 1871 they aggregated 13,255,716 pounds. In the same time
the shipments of silk had increased nearly seven fold.[7]

The Pacific Mail steamers were large and comfortable;
passengers confined to the cabins, saloons and decks for the
twenty days, which were consumed on the voyage between
Yokohama and San Francisco, spoke highly of them. They
were "side wheelers," although the vessel of this type had
generally given way to the ship propelled by a screw. The
old form was preferred on this line because it admitted of

[1] A. Mori, Life and Resources in America, p. 404.
[2] Oberholtzer, Jay Cooke, vol. ii, pp. 456-8.
[3] Phila. Ledger, July 30, 1872.
[4] Senate Mis. Doc., 41st Cong. 2nd sess., no. 125, p. 2.
[5] Ibid.   [6] Commerce and Navigation for 1872.
[7] American Annual Cyclop. for 1871, p. 89.

larger steerage accommodations. On each eastwardly trip from 1,000 to 1,200 Chinamen were stowed below decks and not many fewer returned with the money they had earned and saved in this country.[1]

In like manner the postal traffic was increasing. Postmaster-General Randall and his successor, Mr. Creswell, repeatedly urged upon Congress the establishment of a semimonthly steamer line. In 1869 five times as much postage was collected on mail for China and Japan as in 1867.

The position of the Pacific Mail was not improved by the completion of the transcontinental railway. The Panama Railroad and the company's steamer service to and from San Francisco on the one side, and between Aspinwall and New York on the other, would soon be rendered nearly valueless. For a time an equal rate to Shanghai and Hong Kong of $300 was offered passengers, whether they bought their tickets at New York or San Francisco.[2] But such arrangements could not long continue. Passengers and the mails at once, and, in a little while, all the lighter kinds of freight took the overland route.

Undoubtedly the company, in spite of its subsidy, was operating its monthly line at a loss and no hope of its giving the country more frequent communication with Asia without further legislation could be entertained.[3] Finally, by act of Congress of June 1, 1872, the necessary provision was made for an extension of the service. A contract calling for two departures from and arrivals in San Francisco monthly was concluded with the Pacific Mail company,[4] and it instituted the service at once, though with boats of smaller tonnage than the government required, pending the construction of new steamers whose keels were being laid in yards on the

---

[1] C. C. Coffin, Our New Way Round the World, p. 446; W. H. Seward's Travels Around the World, pp. 4-5.

[2] C. C. Coffin, op. cit., p. 512.

[3] Senate Mis. Doc., 41st Cong. 2nd sess., no. 125; cf. Report of P. M. General for 1868, p. 20; ibid., for 1869, p. 13; ibid., for 1870, p. 13; ibid., for 1871, p. xiii.

[4] Report of P. M. General for 1872, p. 12.

Delaware River. Already, it was observed, this company
had built of American materials with American labor at a
cost of about $15,000,000 a fleet of thirty steamers, eight
of these taking rank among the largest and best equipped
wooden side-wheel boats of their time in the world. Now, in
consequence of the encouragement found in the act of 1872,
the construction of iron screw steamers was begun. Eleven
of these were built, several of the number being regarded as
in every way the equals of the best ships made in England.[1]

A company was formed to establish a steamer line connecting San Francisco and New Zealand and Australia by
way of the Sandwich Islands. For this enterprise the government was asked for a subsidy, which was recommended
unanimously by the Senate Committee on Post Offices.[2] But
Congress turned a deaf ear to this as to so many other
groups of men who now craved public aid for their commercial undertakings. New Zealand discerned the value of the
project and favored it by payments large enough to warrant the institution of a monthly service. Sailings began
in 1871; thus were our mails carried to and from the British
colonies in the southwest Pacific, though for want of support
the boats were withdrawn after a few months.[3]

Daily three mails left New York for San Francisco, one
in the morning and two in the afternoon, but there was only
one train a day west of the Missouri, which was held at
Omaha for the last mail from the east. The average time
required for conveying letters from coast to coast, barring the delays due to snow storms in winter and other causes,
was seven days. There was no service on Sundays until
January, 1871.[4]

The completion of the road from Omaha to Sacramento
gave no pause to the promoters who had centred their hopes

[1] Statement of John Roach to Congress of the United States, Feb. 11,
1875, in House Mis. Doc., 43rd Cong. 2nd sess., no. 78.
[2] Senate Reports, 42nd Cong. 2nd sess., no. 19.
[3] Report of P. M. General for 1871, pp. xii-xiv; ibid., for 1873, p. xvii.
[4] Ibid. for 1870, p. 81; ibid. for 1871, p. ix.

and interests in rival enterprises. The central line had been
a "compromise line," chosen at the sacrifice of better routes.
It had been selected without regard for the South on the one
hand, or of the Great Lakes and their connections on the
other. Anyhow one road would not suffice to meet the country's swiftly growing needs. Men confidently predicted that
before the centennial anniversary of American independence,
which was to be celebrated in Philadelphia in 1876, there
would be four railroads across the continent.[1]

The International Pacific Railroad, to run from Cairo,
Illinois, via Little Rock, Ark., and Jefferson and Rio Grande.
City, Texas, to San Blas on the Pacific coast of Mexico, asked
Congress for incorporation and a bond subsidy. It hoped to
receive aid from the Mexican government for such parts
of the line as lay in that country. The distance to the Mexican boundary was 1,000 miles, and it was 600 miles farther
to San Blas. By this route, New York, so it was said, would
be brought 1,000 miles nearer the Pacific Ocean than over
the Union and Central Pacific railways. Green Clay Smith
urged President Johnson to come to the support of the project
in his last annual message to Congress. "It is difficult,"
said Smith, "to overestimate the immediate and ultimate
value to the nation of this measure." While directly developing the resources of the South and the Southwest it would,
he averred, supply "indispensable commercial, industrial and
military facilities to the whole nation." The road could be
completed in two years. General Gordon Granger endorsed
the enterprise. He knew the country through which it would
pass and declared it to be "by far the best route" yet .pro-
posed for connecting the Atlantic and Pacific coasts.[2]

But no one took this suggestion very seriously. The roads
for which public interest was expressed would go to the coast
on American soil. In the South two lines were projected, one
to follow the 32nd parallel of latitude, running near the Mexican border and reaching the Pacific at San Diego, the other,

[1] Report of Sec. of Interior for 1870, p. 218.
[2] Johnson Papers.

the 35th parallel with San Francisco as its destination. These rivals were persistent claimants for popular favor and their promoters were seeking buyers for their bonds in the money markets of New York and Europe, and importuning Congress for bounties such as had been vouchsafed the central line.

For the honor of going to the Pacific on the 32nd parallel through Texas, southern New Mexico, Arizona and California several contenders appeared. In the north there was the Memphis and Little Rock, but not a rod of this road had been laid down beyond Little Rock. Farther south, the Memphis, El Paso and Pacific which had been chartered in Texas in 1856, and had been given certain grants of land by the legislature of that state, of doubtful validity because of the expiration of the time limit set for the completion of the work, was urgently claiming the right to go forward over the route. Before the war some fifty miles of the way had been graded from a place called Texarkana in the northeastern corner of Texas in the direction of Dallas. Recently twenty miles more had been made ready for the laying of rails, but the channel of the Red River had filled during a freshet, boats laden with material from New Orleans could not proceed beyond a point near Jefferson, fifty miles south, and the company had begun to build a branch from this place to Texarkana. About three miles of track had been finished and a pony engine and a few cars were set upon it. Here the promoters' achievements ended, though surveyors were at work in the West seeking passes through the mountains, and in California a route was being explored from San Diego to Fort Yuma near the Mexican boundary, the head of navigation for large boats on the Colorado River.

The road as it was projected had no eastern connections, and it was a mere hope on the prairie. Yet the enterprise was widely advertised as "transcontinental." John C. Frémont, the "pathfinder," whose name in many minds was still bound up with the romance of the West, earlier engaged in Pacific railway promotion in Missouri, had followed a man named Epperson as the president of the company, and the sale of a few millions of dollars worth of bonds in Paris, by· resort to the grossest misrepresentation, precipitated a great scandal.[1]

A road located farther south, called the Southern Pacific, passing through Marshall, also chartered before the war by the legislature of Texas, enlisted the sympathy and support of another group of promoters. It had leased certain lines, still unfinished, which gave it connections with Shreveport and Vicksburg, and was preferred over rivals by the people of Louisiana and the Gulf states. Though it had been sold out two or three times for debt, it now made strong claims for selection as the eastern end of the proposed trunk line on the 32nd parallel.[2]

The line on the 35th parallel, called at first the Southwest Branch of the Missouri Pacific, then the South Pacific, and now the Atlantic and Pacific was designed to give St. Louis direct communication with the coast. The tracks left the Missouri Pacific road some miles west of that city and proceeded southwest through Springfield. By act of Congress of July 27, 1866, it had received a land grant equal to that of the Northern Pacific, viz., alternate sections in a belt 40 miles wide in the states and 80 miles wide in the territories, through which it should pass. Before the end of the year 1872, 327 miles of the road had been completed. It had reached Vinita in the Indian Territory.[3]

This company found rivals in the Kansas Pacific, and later the Santa Fé. The Kansas Pacific had ambitious direction and even before its tracks had yet entered Denver it had employed engineers who were to hurry forward with surveys for a line to the coast.[4] Its railhead was farther west than any other company's. Making an "elbow" in Kan-

[1] Senate Mis. Doc., 41st Cong. 2nd sess., no. 121.
[2] Ibid.; cf. Report of Sec. of Interior for 1872, p. 19. The later career of this road can be followed under the name of the Texas Pacific.
[3] Report of Sec. of Interior for 1872, p. 20; House Ex. Doc., 41st Cong. 2nd sess., no. 195; J. H. Beadle, The Undeveloped West, p. 354; Appleton's Western Tour, p. 230.
[4] W. A. Bell, New Tracks in North America, vol. ii, pp. 258-62.

sas the tracks would cross the Rio Grande at or near Albuquerque, and, with government grants or without them, if these were not to be procured, go to the Pacific on the 35th parallel. State legislatures, chambers of commerce, boards of trade, city governments and individuals memorialized Congress in behalf of this scheme.[1]

While much of what proceeded on the subject of the southern lines was plan and promise it was not so in the north with reference to the road which had been projected to connect the Great Lakes and Puget Sound. The company had its land grant of 25,600 acres for each mile which it should complete and a charter—little more. But the promoters were presenting their cause to Jay Cooke and his sponsorship meant performance. He had declined the invitation to finance the Southern Pacific lines but gradually he was being brought to an appreciation of the large potentialities of the Northwest. In connection with the sale of the bonds of the Lake Superior and Mississippi Railroad, projected between St. Paul, the head of navigation on the Mississippi, and Duluth, a new town at the western end of Lake Superior, he visited the country and, moved by a patriotic sense as well as commercial considerations, became imbued with the importance of the undertaking. The timber, the minerals, the rich agricultural lands, the water power aroused his enthusiasm. With houses in New York, Philadelphia and Washington he had large agencies which he would be glad to employ in some useful field, and he was ready to give the project careful examination. The well known engineer, W. Milnor Roberts, accompanied by other men, was sent over the proposed route west of the Rocky Mountains, to inspect it and make a report for the guidance of the Philadelphia banker. Another party proceeded under cavalry escort west from St. Cloud into Minnesota and Dakota.

General Sherman had said that the road would pass through 500 miles of country in Dakota, lying between the

[1] Report of Sec. of Interior for 1870, p. 217; N. Y. Tribune, June 1, 1868.

Red and Missouri Rivers, which was "barren and worth-less." It was "as bad as God ever made, or any one could scare up this side of Africa." [1] Most men seemed to picture the territory to be traversed as bound in perpetual ice and snow.[2] To project a railway in such a latitude was folly too obvious to be discussed.

But Cooke's commissioners returned with glowing accounts of the land they had visited. Puget Sound, "well called the Mediterranean of the Northwest," the fine harbor of Seattle, the luxuriant timber and vegetable growth, the lakes and rivers beyond the Rocky Mountains were viewed with astonishment. Instead of icebergs and polar bears they had found a "tropical paradise." [3] The riches of Minnesota in the east were witnessed with no less enthusiasm.[4] Roberts found no engineering obstacles which could not be overcome. The passes in the mountains were lower than on the central line, and could be crossed without difficulty. He computed that the actual cost of construction of the road, which would have a length of about 2,000 miles, would be $70,000,000. Other expenses might increase the total to $85,000,000.[5] The settlement of the zone with emigrants from the East and from Europe, as the work proceeded, the development of a valuable commerce with Asia, which would vastly increase the population of the Pacific coast, the opening up of the wheat fields of the Red River Valley and an extensive area running far up into British America, would make the enterprise a commercial investment of great strength and complete security.[6] Moreover such a road would be of incalculable value to the government in reaching its forts and in dealing with the Indians.[7]

Finally, in December, 1869, Cooke took the step which identified his firms with the undertaking. He had hoped to

[1] Oberholtzer, Jay Cooke, vol. ii, p. 113.
[2] Pyle, Life of J. J. Hill, vol. i, pp. 103-5.
[3] Oberholtzer, Jay Cooke, vol. ii, p. 119.
[4] C. C. Coffin, The Seat of Empire.
[5] Oberholtzer, Jay Cooke, vol. ii, p. 154.
[6] Ibid., pp. 154-5.   [7] Ibid., p. 156.

ally the Rothschilds with him in the operation, and a partner visited the heads of the house in Europe. But no encouragement was received.[1] Cooke would go forward without them and, if he needed assistance, after he had appealed to the people of America, as he had done in the sale of the war loans, he would approach other banking houses in Europe in behalf of the enterprise. All else failing, he felt that, through his political connections, he could induce Congress to favor the road with a subvention. Five millions would be raised at once to construct the line to the Red River. Very attractive prospects in the way of bonuses were held out to subscribers. A large number of men of prominence and influence were brought into an inside ring, or "pool," the members of which were to reap enormous profits in case of success, which seemed to be in no kind of doubt.

Soon surveyors were in the field and when the snows melted in Minnesota in February, 1870, ground was broken and the actual work of construction was begun. By the end of 1871 the road had been laid to the east bank of Red River and a force of men, proceeding simultaneously on the Pacific coast, had succeeded in completing a few miles of track, extending from a place called Kalama on the Columbia River on the way to navigation on Puget Sound. When the road should enter Olympia Portland would be in touch with Seattle, and, after the completion of another section in Washington Territory, communication could be established, by the aid of the boats of the Oregon Steam Navigation Company on Lake Pend d'Oreille and the upper Columbia, with Montana, a service of much temporary value, pending better arrangements for reaching the growing settlements in that region.

As the difficulty of selling bonds to the public in this country and Europe increased the lobbyists of the roads congregated at Washington. Before Cooke had yet identified himself with the fortunes of the Northern Pacific, promoters in-

---

[1] Oberholtzer, Jay Cooke, vol. ii, pp. 147-9.

terested in that company struck hands at Washington with the Southern transcontinental railway men, the various schemes were pooled and, early in 1869, a bill was reported out of the Senate Pacific Railroad Committee. Its adoption was urged by six of the members,—four from the West, headed by Senator Stewart of Nevada, and two Southern carpetbaggers. The lines selected for government aid had a total length of nearly 5,000 miles. First came the Northern Pacific. Already Frémont's 32nd parallel line was discredited, so the Atlantic and Pacific, following the 35th parallel, was selected for favor. To give this line eastern connections the Little Rock and Fort Smith was to be subsidized. This would bring the road to Little Rock, from which place there was communication with Memphis. A branch was to be run down into Texas to join the road at Marshall, where there were connections with Vicksburg and New Orleans. The Kansas Pacific was to be aided in the work of extending its tracks southwest to join the Atlantic and Pacific at a point near Albuquerque in New Mexico, whence the two would go on together through New Mexico and Arizona as the United States Southern Pacific to meet the Southern Pacific Railroad of California. To connect the Union Pacific and the Northern Pacific lines a road would be run up the Humboldt Valley in Nevada to Portland, Oregon.

Many arguments were adduced by the committee in favor of the bill which would establish for the country this "general system of transcontinental railway." In the "highways of nations" was to be found "the measure of their civilization." Without roads, Mr. Stewart and his associates on the committee said, there could be no "society, government, commerce or intelligence." Indeed there was nothing else to which public money could be applied so profitably. The railroads, it was alleged, had increased the commerce of the country "2,000 fold"; every dollar invested in them "created five dollars yearly," on which account such enterprises "should take precedence over any and all other objects of legislative endowment." Immigration would follow the construction of the northern and southern lines to the Pacific. Already the Union Pacific had its agents in Europe seeking colonists for its lands. Likewise with the proposed new roads—they and the Homestead Law would go hand in hand across the continent, and "in less than ten years" it was predicted that "at least three millions of the best population of northern Europe—farmers, graziers, mechanics and miners"—would be established in homes in these new belts of settlement.

The Southern states must have "access to the Pacific on their parallels of latitude." They had been ruined by the war; they had "a right to their share of the transcontinental commerce between Asia and Europe." The people of Georgia, Alabama and Mississippi ought not to be compelled to go up to Nebraska to commence their journey to the Pacific. In the West Washington and Oregon objected with reason to travelling "700 miles south to get 1,700 miles east."

The two new lines were a necessity on other accounts. With but one road there would be a "monopoly," very disadvantageous to the public service. The "single track" from Omaha to San Francisco, within a year after it should be opened, would be "unequal to the traffic" certain to be "crowded upon it." The line would "clog." So much was easy to see, for in the East the single track line of the Pennsylvania Railroad between the Atlantic seaboard and the Ohio Valley had been doubled, of necessity, and this road had four vigorous rivals—the Erie Canal, and the New York Central, Erie and Baltimore and Ohio railways. There were such gradients and curves on the central road that in winter there must be "long and serious interruptions in the service" because of snow, an opinion which found impressive confirmation in 1871-2.

Furthermore these two new roads to the Pacific were "necessary to the government as a part of its military system," in moving troops and transporting supplies. We would be at war with the Indians "for years and years." Their "Parthian cavalry" came "unseen." They were "out of sight and beyond pursuit in a moment," said the report; "our warfare

upon them is a tardy pursuit of vanishing trails." They could
be "permanently conquered" only by the railroads. The locomotive was "the sole solution of the Indian question."

More than this the Northern Pacific would "seal the destiny of the British possessions west of the 91st meridian."
Their annexation would be "but a question of time." The
road in the South would bring us the northern states of Mexico. "Eventually" they would be "absorbed into our Union
without the cost of purchase, or the crime or expense of con-
quest."

In the case of the central road the government had made
an outright issue of bonds for the benefit of the companies.
The grant had taken the form of a bond subsidy. Now nothing was proposed but a government guarantee of six per cent
interest on issues to the extent of $30,000 a mile, which was
"perfectly safe." It was computed that the sum to be advanced would amount to only about $4,500,000 per annum for
the five years during which the roads would be in course of
construction; the earnings would meet the interest afterward.
It was little more than "the equivalent of the sum which for
the last few years has been yearly expended in making unavailing treaties and maintaining Indian agencies." [1]

A minority of the committee, made up of five senators of
much greater influence in Congress and in the country than
those who had signed the majority report—Henry Wilson, E.
D. Morgan, John Sherman, J M. Howard and James Harlan—
combatted the position taken by Mr. Stewart and his colleagues. It was a scheme, said they, to make the government
liable for the interest on $150,000,000 of bonds for thirty
years. This meant an outlay of $9,000,000 annually and in
the end would call for the expenditure of the "enormous sum"
of $270,000,000. There had been log rolling—a variety of
interests had joined their forces to present this "gigantic omnibus scheme." Already the government was burdened with
debt; the people were borne down by great taxes. It was

[1] Majority Report, Senate Reports, 40th Cong. 3rd sess., no. 219; cf.
W. A. Bell, New Tracks in North America, vol. ii, pp. 271-2.

a time to "cherish and fortify the credit of the nation," not to assume "new obligations." The people demanded of their agents and representatives "rigid economy" in expenditures. "A project so vast, in the present condition of the national credit, should be met by Congress with a peremptory and emphatic No."[1] The subject did not reach the stage of debate.

Cooke, when he took over the management of the Northern Pacific, aimed to keep entirely clear of entanglements with the lobbyists for other lines.[2] He would be satisfied with a larger land grant, and to this end his agents in Washington bent all their energies. The company would be authorized to build two roads from Montana to the coast, one to Puget Sound, and the other by a more southern route to Portland, thus doubling its claim upon the public domain. West of the mountains it would have the pick of the public lands in a belt 200 miles wide.[3] Congress passed the measure and Grant signed it on May 31, 1870.[4]

Upon such extensive agricultural and mineral areas it seemed not too much to hope that $100,000,000 could be borrowed in the United States or Europe. The campaign to sell the bonds proceeded in this country with all the vigor and zeal which Cooke's experience with popular loans could bring to the work. Circulars, pamphlets and books, newspaper advertisements and "write ups," lectures, exhibitions of the products of the country and of the barrow and spade used in breaking the ground in Minnesota, the general offering of the bonds in banking houses and by agents who personally appealed to the patriotism as well as the business sense of small investors in every part of the Union,—all were used with disappointing response. New and stronger efforts were

[1] Minority Report, Senate Reports, 40th Cong. 3rd sess., no. 219.
[2] Oberholtzer, Jay Cooke, vol. ii, pp. 174-5.
[3] The company was given the privilege of taking the odd numbered sections in a belt ten miles wide beyond earlier limits on each side of the tract to make up for the loss of tracts gone beyond the government's control since it had been chartered in 1864.
[4] Cong. Globe, 41st Cong. 2nd sess., app., pp. 742-3; Oberholtzer, Life of Jay Cooke, pp. 177-8, 181.

put forth in Europe. The bankers of London, Frankfort, Berlin, Brussels and Amsterdam were visited by Cooke's representatives and his new London house, with ex-Secretary Hugh McCulloch in charge, exerted its influences in the road's behalf. At the outbreak of the Franco-Prussian war a contract for a loan was on the point of being signed. But this event upset the proposed arrangement. The bringing to America of a party of European financiers to inspect the terminal points and traverse the route came to no practical result.

Cooke's furore-makers were, perhaps, too zealous. Their claims for the wealth of the country, though not far from the truth, sounded wild to some men. The great trees, the luxuriant vegetation, the products of the almost voluptuous climate of the Northwest fell upon incredulous ears and caused many derisively to call the strip, which was pictured on the company's maps, Jay Cooke's "Banana Belt." Duluth, to whose harbor all this country, 2,000,000 square miles in extent, was "tributary," was made the object of the wit of a Kentucky Congressman, J. Proctor Knott. Men laughed at the "zenith city of the unsalted seas."

But the road strode on into the West. Rumors of a Canadian Pacific Railroad to run still farther north were in the air and Cooke's active mind was busily employed in revolving plans for spurs to serve the Red River Valley and to bring the grain and peltry of British America to Duluth. Alliances with the Hudson's Bay company were sought. Cooke purchased the Lake Superior and Mississippi Railroad, which gave him a foothold in St. Paul, and the St. Paul and Pacific, which followed the Mississippi Valley north to St. Cloud, and would intersect the Northern Pacific line at Glyndon. West of the mountains he absorbed the Oregon Steam Navigation company with its boats and portages, and he had in his grasp a transportation system designed to cover and serve the entire Northwest.

Nothing less than the annexation of the adjoining British possessions was in Cooke's mind and he was ready to do all

in his power to cause so much to come to pass.[1] It was a
grand commercial and political dream which the disturbed
times did not befriend, but which remains a chapter of
notable planning in the financial and commercial history
of the United States.

Meanwhile the colonization of this region proceeded along
the new railway lines as it was going forward in Kansas
and Nebraska. The work of bringing in emigrants had
spirited direction. In New England, in Europe agents of
the company sought in a wide variety of ways to start migra-
tion to the company's lands in Minnesota, and new towns on
the prairie were a promise of what the future would yield
in the settlement of the zone through which the railway ran.
Particularly active was the work among the Germans and
the end-of-track in 1872, in spite of discouragements, was
approaching Bismarck,—thus named to propitiate this people
—at the crossing of the Missouri River, 450 miles west of
Duluth.

Duluth itself, a place of but six or seven frame buildings
in 1868,[2] before the end of 1872 had come to contain 2,500
houses. It had churches, schools and factories. To its docks
came many ships. In 1873 there were three newspapers in
the place, two of them dailies; one in Brainerd, one in Glyndon, one in Detroit Lake, one in Moorhead and one in Fargo
—all new towns on the new railroad. George Alfred Townsend estimated the number of persons settled on the company's lands at 30,000, mostly in the country lying between
the Missouri and Red Rivers, but there were "claim shanties,
barns and wagon camps" beyond, prophetic of future development.

The frontiers in eastern Minnesota and in Wisconsin were
advancing as rapidly as on the central and southwestern lines
of settlement. The prospect of profitable wheat growing in
this region drew to the country thousands of men not averse
to agricultural labor and waving fields of grain were seen,

[1] Oberholtzer, Jay Cooke, vol. ii, p. 296.
[2] Ibid., p. 106.

where but a short time since only grass and prairie flowers had been. Minnesota's crop in 1870 was 18,000,000 bushels;[1] Wisconsin's, 26,000,000 bushels.[2] The population of Minnesota which had been 172,000 in 1860 was 440,000 in 1870; in the decade Wisconsin had gained a quarter of a million. New railroads running in all directions served the farms and villages. At the end of 1872 there were nearly 4,000 miles of railway in the two northwestern states, more than twice what there had been four years before.[3]

Seattle, the probable western terminus of the road on Puget Sound, was a small settlement largely populated by Chinese and Indians when Jay Cooke's engineers visited it in 1868.[4] It still, in 1870, was a place of only 1,500 souls, but even the decision of the Northern Pacific managers to found a new city to be called Tacoma, in a forest of fir trees 25 miles south, as a western outlet for trade with Alaska, Japan, China and Australia, could not impede its growth.

That the end of subsidies for other private undertakings, as well as railroads, was near at hand was discovered by another ambitious character who had cast his lines in the West. Adolph Sutro was a German who had come to this country as a young man. He moved out to the Pacific coast with the gold miners in 1850 and appeared in Nevada ten years later, while crowds of excited men were rushing thither to make their fortunes on the Comstock Lode.[5] After a rather unfortunate experience with ore reduction works he conceived a plan for constructing an adit or horizontal tunnel to drain the mines, thus doing away with pumps; to furnish fresh air to the miners; to reduce the temperature in the shafts; to carry out the pay ore, now raised by expensive hoisting machinery; to remove the rock, and otherwise serve in the development of the important underground operations around

[1] Census of 1870, vol. on Industry and Wealth, p. 181; cf. Oberholtzer, Jay Cooke, vol. ii, p. 315.
[2] Census of 1870, loc. cit., p. 281.
[3] Poor's Manual for 1872-3, p. xxix.
[4] Oberholtzer, Jay Cooke, p. 118.
[5] House Reports, 42nd Cong. 2nd sess., no. 94, pp. 395-6.

Virginia City. In a short while, hereabouts, the yield of gold, and particularly of silver had been immense, and there was confident expectation of returns which might attain fabulous proportions, if exploration should be extended and deep mining were made possible. Sutro would begin to bore his tunnel in the foothills near the Carson River and pierce the mountain for a distance, including branch shafts, of about seven miles, until he struck the Comstock Lode, well below the level at which the mines were then being worked.

The value of the tunnel seemed tolerably obvious and the legislature of the new state of Nevada gave Sutro an exclusive right of way for fifty years.[1] A company was formed with Senator William M. Stewart as its president. The mine owners endorsed the project and entered into contracts for the use of the tunnel when it should be completed, agreeing to pay Sutro and his associates $2 a ton royalty in perpetuity for every ton of ore taken out of the Lode. They, furthermore, would pay 25 cents a ton a mile for hauling refuse rock from the mines, and 25 cents might be charged each passenger carried on the cars to or from the shafts. Proceeding to Washington Sutro persuaded Congress to give him land at the mouth of the tunnel, and rights to ore in veins which he might tap on his way to the Lode. At the same time they confirmed the contracts he had already made with the mining companies and authorized him to lay similar tribute upon other companies operating in this neighborhood which should be benefited by his enterprise. It was believed that the royalties which he would receive from the Lode, after it was connected with the tunnel, would yield an income of $2,000,000 annually. The act was approved on July 25, 1866.[2]

Armed with these valuable grants and privileges Sutro visited New York. He presented the subject to "Commodore" Vanderbilt, William B. Astor and other capitalists. They suggested that he should begin to take subscriptions at home.

[1] A. Sutro, Mineral Resources of the U. S. with Special Reference to the Comstock Lode and the Sutro Tunnel, pp. 171-2.
[2] Statutes at Large, vol. xlv, p. 242.

If the Pacific coast would express its confidence in the project he could the better hope to enlist the favor of investors in the East. He asked for this opinion in writing and some forty well known men appended their names to a statement to this effect. With this in hand he returned to San Francisco where he succeeded in getting pledges amounting to about $600,000.[1]

But at this point he somehow aroused the bitter hostility of the mine presidents and superintendents, who were in the clutches of what he called the "California Bank Ring." The men who dominated this strong financial institution in San Francisco were the governing influences on the Comstock Lode; they controlled the opinions of most of the Pacific coast's representatives in Congress, and all together now suddenly changed front. Some of the subscriptions to the stock of the company were cancelled. Success appearing slow and uncertain in the face of such opposition, Sutro determined to appeal to Congress. The legislature of Nevada asked for a loan of credit for the tunnel.[2] Thousands of miners and other men, residents on the Pacific coast, appended their names to memorials in the same behalf.[3] But Congress would not meet until December and Sutro, meantime, in the summer of 1867, went to Europe to visit bankers, statesmen, geologists and mining experts, many of whom endorsed the project, though he procured no capital to prosecute the undertaking. Returning to the United States he took up his residence in Washington. Full of confident energy he met and talked to nearly all the members of both houses of Congress, presenting each with a handsomely bound volume furnished with maps and illustrations descriptive of the undertaking.[4] He met with and frequently addressed the members of the House Committee on Mines and Mining who had under considera-

---

[1] House Reports, 42nd Cong. 2nd sess., no. 94, p. 399.
[2] A. Sutro, Mineral Resources, pp. xiii-xiv; House Reports, 42nd Cong. 2nd sess., no. 94, p. 63.
[3] Mineral Resources, op. cit., pp. 199-200.
[4] This book was the work already cited.—Mineral Resources, etc.; cf. House Reports, 42nd Cong. 2nd sess., no. 94, p. 66.

tion a bill to make the tunnel company an appropriation of
$5,000,000. In spite of the admitted "novelty of the pro-
posed legislation" six of the nine members of the committee,
under the influence of this tenacious and persuasive man,
united in a report expressing "a thorough conviction" that a
government loan to the tunnel would be "wise, judicious and
to the best interests of the country." An increase in the stock
of precious metals would increase the value of taxable property, thereby reducing the burdens bearing upon each individual citizen. Indeed, if the Comstock Lode could be made
available to greater depths it would pay off the national debt.
The mines here had produced over $80,000,000 of gold and
silver bullion in the last six years and their annual yield
now was $16,000,000. As the work proceeded other mineral
veins as rich as the Comstock Lode might be discovered.
Anyhow after the tunnel was cut the production of the mines
already open would be increased to $50,000,000, or, perhaps,
$100,000,000 a year. Public aid would take the form of
bonds to be issued at the rate of $15,000 for every 100 feet
completed and accepted by the government.[1]

But the impeachment proceedings supervened. Sutro's detractors never were so active. Senator Stewart, though he
had been the president of the tunnel company, now called the
scheme a "humbug"; Sutro was "tunnelling Congress and not
the mines." [2] There was no water in the shafts to be drained
off. So far from being hot, visitors when they were taken
down the shafts had to be cautioned against seating themselves on the rocks lest they catch cold. The draughts of air
blew out the candles of the miners.[3] It was all an "hallucina-
tion" of Sutro who somehow had persuaded himself into
thinking, whenever anyone doubted his scheme, that he was
being robbed of "a supposititious inheritance in the Comstock Lode." In the right which Congress had given him

---

[1] House Reports, 40th Cong. 2nd sess., no. 50; cf. House Mis. Doc.,
40th Cong. 2nd sess., no. 156.
[2] Cong. Globe, 41st Cong. 2nd sess., p. 3027.
[3] Ibid., p. 2031.

in 1866 to tax the output of the mines he had a "monstrous monopoly." [1] It was a "huge job" founded on the assumption that the miners did not know how to manage their own property.[2]

Sutro replied in a speech to his "fellow citizens" in Virginia City.[3] It was the "old fight of stage coaches against railroads." He minced no words in dealing with the "California Bank Ring" and he was received with great enthusiasm. He asked 5,000 men in western Nevada to save $10 a month out of their wages, and to invest it in the tunnel. Many of them subscribed at once.[4] With sums received from this source and money he had collected in California, he was able to begin work, which he did on October 19, 1869, proceeding nearly 500 feet before New Year's Day.

Sutro's enemies in the following year actually sought to induce Congress to take away his franchise, but their conversion had been too sudden. What all Nevada had prayed for in petition and resolution two or three years before could not be entirely iniquitous now, and the House by a vote of 124 to 42 on March 23, 1870, laid on the table a bill to repeal the act of 1866.[5]

Clearly there was water in the mines; clearly it impeded production; in 1868, 47 engines, which there was only wood to fire, were at work pumping it out. Some mines had been abandoned on this account. Clearly, too, the air in the shafts was hot and stagnant. At some places the rock seared the miners' hands. Everyone knew that 42 men had been caught in a fire in one of the shafts and had been burned to death because there was no exit, and the prospect of finding new lodes as rich as old Comstock's had proven to be was never absent from the public fancy. There was a suggestion

[1] Cong. Globe, 41st Cong. 2nd sess., p. 2137.
[2] House Reports, 42nd Cong. 3rd sess., no. 44.
[3] Ibid., 42nd Cong. 2nd sess., no. 94, pp. 58 et seq.
[4] Ibid., p. 405; cf. N. Y. Tribune, Nov. 19, 1869.
[5] Cong. Globe, 41st Cong. 2nd sess., pp. 2176-7; cf. House Reports, 41st Cong. 2nd sess., no. 40; House Reports, 41st Cong. 2nd sess., no. 94, p. 406.

that a loan of 15,000,000 francs might be obtained in Paris and in the summer of 1870 Sutro was on the point of sailing with Reverdy Johnson, who would use the friendships he had made while serving as our minister to England in behalf of the project. But news of the outbreak of the Franco-Prussian war halted them and nothing more could be done in this direction.[1]

Up to January 1, 1871, 1,750 feet of the tunnel had been finished and Sutro asked that a commission be appointed to report upon the scheme.[2] Congress authorized the President to name three men, two officers of engineers in the army and a civilian expert to perform the service. They visited Virginia City and each party made a stupendous effort to impress them with the merits of its side of the controversy. Naturally the three commissioners saw only what the mine·superintendents desired them to see in the more than 200 miles of drifts cut into the Comstock Lode.[3] In most particulars, therefore, they found against the project. The tunnel was not needed as an outlet for water or for ventilation. But as an engineering work it was regarded as entirely feasible for an expenditure of probably $5,000,000 in gold. The commission said guardedly, to the satisfaction of Mr. Sutro and his friends, that "as an exploring work for deep mining" it could "justly claim favorable consideration." [4]

The commissioners were brought before the House mining committee for cross examination by the members and by Mr. Sutro who submitted an exhaustive argument,[5] and in June, 1872, the committee with only one dissenting vote again recommended the subject to Congress on the grounds which had been taken in 1868, though the sum now to be loaned to the company was reduced to $2,000,000.[6] The bill was not

---

[1] House Reports, 41st Cong. 2nd sess., no. 94, p. 406.
[2] Ibid., p. 407.
[3] Ibid., pp. 407, 408-9.
[4] Report of Commission in House Reports, 42nd Cong. 2nd sess., no. 94, pp. 12-32, and Senate Ex. Doc., 42nd Cong. 2nd sess., no. 15.
[5] House Reports, 42nd Cong. 2nd sess., no. 94, pp. 395-434.
[6] Ibid., pp. 1-4.

reached at this session and when it was taken up in the following year little came of it except some discussion in which Sutro was called a "wild speculative adventurer" and the tunnel a "stock jobbing scheme" which was presented to Congress with "brazen effrontery," [1] though General Banks eloquently praised the indomitable pioneer.[2]

[1] Cong. Globe, 42nd Cong. 3rd sess., p. 1595.

[2] Ibid., app., pp. 83-6; cf. House Reports, 42nd Cong. 3rd sess., no. 44. Meanwhile Sutro went to Europe again. In London he somehow negotiated a loan of $650,000 in gold and with this sum in hand he could purchase improved machinery and go forward at a greater rate of speed. The controversy with the mine owners proceeded, he aiming to enforce his agreements with them and they to escape their obligations (Cf. Senate Reports, 43rd Cong. 1st sess., no. 422), but finally on September 1, 1878, the tunnel reached the Comstock Lode and connection was made with the Savage mine. Instantly the deep shafts were relieved of the noxious gases which had interfered with the work of the miners and the temperature at a level of 2,000 feet which had been 120 was reduced to 90 degrees Fahr. (American Annual Cyclopedia for 1878, pp. 288-9.) The tunnel was completed in 1882. The main adit measures more than 20,000 feet, while the lateral branches added 11,000 feet to the total length. A number of vertical shafts were cut to the surface to make the work still more serviceable. For the greater part of the way the opening was seven feet high and from eight to nine feet wide, and it was furnished with ditches to carry off the water and track rails for mule teams. The first royalty payments by the mine owners to the tunnel company were made in September, 1879, and up to March, 1887, the sums received on this account amounted to $773,000. (Theodore Sutro, Sutro Tunnel Co., Report to Stockholders under date of 1887.)

CHAPTER XVI

THE END OF THE ORGY

THE day when government subsidies could be sought, with hope of receiving them, had indeed come to an end. Men so rich that they knew not what to do with their plenty were seen on every hand. They strutted over the land. Bragging and insolent, vulgar and fat with their gains, flaunting themselves and their wives in other men's faces they were stared at in amazement and discussed without favor. How had they come by their wealth? Delving Adams and spinning Eves only a little while ago what methods had they employed to raise themselves so far above their fellows? Our democracy is sometimes on the point of forfeiting its character and passing over to another social and political form. But we invariably halt upon the verge of our transposition. A sense of humor it has been said, plus a sense of right come to our rescue. Soon we are grimly in earnest. We even exaggerate the wrong we are complaining about and in a moment there is a complete revulsion of popular feeling. The nation had had a great vision; it had surrendered to its imagination. Eager, bold, expansive minds, many of them constructive geniuses of the highest ability, had come to the fore during and after the war and we were being carried to a commanding national and international position. The people followed their leaders with confidence, giving freely of their admiration and faith and contributing their money, that great material ends might be attained. But the return in very many cases was not what had been promised and expected; the time had come for looking around to see with what judgment the trust had been bestowed.

Durant, living in exotic grandeur in New York, made rich

out of the Union Pacific;[1] a half dozen men who, as by a
magician's wand, were flourishing on the profits which came
from building the Central Pacific, now rearing themselves
splendid palaces in Sacramento and San Francisco;[2] "Commodore" Vanderbilt and Daniel Drew, who with so ·much
advertisement of their movements robbed each other and other
men in "corners" in Wall Street; James ·Fisk, Jr., and Jay
Gould whose morals in connection with the Erie Railway
were as low as any thief's;[3] William M. Tweed and his confederates in the Tammany "Ring" who were stealing the
whole city of New York under the very eyes of the population; the infamous nomads who under the name of "Reconstruction" were carrying booty out of the stricken South, and
a host who followed such example and whose only God was
Mammon, had come, so it appeared to control the life of the
country.

To so many persons the accumulation of wealth had become the one absorbing and all important object in life that
the methods by which the end was gained, no matter how
abominable, shocked nobody.[4] Falling into the general way
gradually, and long familiar with it, better men were
condoning such perverted moral standards. Many of sound
consciences were intimidated, or were brought to believe in
the hopelessness of protest. Public opinion seemed oppressed
and silenced by prolonged experience with wrong.

In New York and other cities holders of real estate, trades-
men and the propertied classes generally, were deterred from
complaining by fear of reprisal. For a word they might be
more highly assessed and taxed. Quiet submission was discretion, which has been said to be the better part of valor.[5]

[1] Cf. J. K. Medbery, Men and Mysteries of Wall Street, pp. 191-2.
[2] N. Y. Tribune, July 12, 1869.
[3] For accounts of these men and their like and the manner in which
their fortunes were made see J. K. Medbery, Men and Mysteries of
Wall Street, chap. ix.
[4] Cf. C. F. Adams and Henry Adams, Chapters of Erie, pp. 94-5;
North American Review, July, 1867, p. 172.
[5] Myers, History of Tammany Hall, pp. 217-8.

Offices were sold; men were nominated for what they could "put up." [1]

The board rooms of large corporations were too often mere plotting places for the spoliation of stockholders. The agents of these corporations found their way into legislatures and came to sit upon the bench. Law was prostituted and the judicial ermine was soiled to serve sordid ends. Men had places even in the United States Senate, because they were attorneys for railroads, mining companies and great banks. Leaders in Congress who were lawyers, while engaged in the performance of their public duties, were put upon the pay roll of a corporation ostensibly to act as its counsel. Plainly they were chosen not for their knowledge of the law but because they held places of political power. Yet worse was the position of advocates, some of them men of large abilities and deserved distinction, who hired themselves out for the business of defending officers of corporations against those who sought to bring these officers to book for their rascalities. One of the eminence of David Dudley Field, heedless of his own reputation and of the influence of his action upon the whole profession of the law, chose to identify himself in the most public way with the insolent operations of Fisk and Gould in return for $125,000 a year. [2] For legal principles while acting as counsel for this "band of robbers," [3] he substituted chicane and trickery, and in the sight of his colleagues at the bar, and of other men, made himself the partner of criminals. [4] His course, indeed, awakened such a revulsion of sentiment in the profession that impeachment charges were presented against him and he barely escaped expulsion from the Bar Association. [5]

[1] Myers, History of Tammany Hall, p. 220.

[2] The sum which Fisk told Tilden, when he tried to employ the latter in a cause, had been paid by the Erie managers to Field for acting in their behalf.—Bigelow, Letters and Memorials of S. J. Tilden, vol. i, p. 300.　　　　　　　　　 [3] North American Review, October, 1874.

[4] Adams, Chapters of Erie, pp. 34-9, 109-10, 152, 175-83; The Lawyer and His Clients, Correspondence between Field and Samuel Bowles, Springfield, 1871; North American Review, July, 1875, pp. 146-8.

[5] North American Review, July, 1875, pp. 148-9.

There had come about "a steady demoralization of the bar," a "debasement of its tone" under the influence of money.[1] The entire system of gaining your ends by fair argument, founded upon facts, rules and precedents, was being swept away in favor of what Mr. Tilden denominated "back door access to the judiciary."[2] A client would employ an advocate because he was known to have friendly influence with a judge, or some politician who swayed and controlled the opinions of that judge, and relied upon such a connection for the favorable outcome of his suit.[3]

As the bar lost its character and dignity the bench, which draws upon the general body of lawyers for its moral vitality, deteriorated also. Which of the two fell first, what was cause and what effect, it was difficult to determine. The "loathsome degradation" of the bench had begun with the introduction of a judiciary elected by popular vote.[4] Conditions in New York—they were evil elsewhere also—were infamous to the last degree. Lawyers themselves were alarmed on selfish grounds; right verdicts were so difficult to obtain that clients preferred to submit to pecuniary loss rather than commit their causes to litigation.[5]

A horde of newspaper writers with itching palms stood by like servants at a Saratoga hotel from which you were about to take your leave. Though they had the smallest connections, even with journals of insignificant influence, they, by their effrontery, often came to participate in the division of the spoil. The American press in general had never been so corrupt. Not before had newspaper owners been such creatures of the corporation financier and the politicians who were being fed from the rich man's hand. Bennett's opinions in the New York Herald, always loosely held, were to be had by the shrewdest person and that one who had the most to

---

[1] Henry Adams in Chapters of Erie, p. 109.
[2] Bigelow, op. cit., vol. i, p. 301; North American Review, October, 1874, p. 391. [3] North American Review, July, 1867, pp. 159-60.
[4] Ibid., July, 1875, p. 145; cf. article on New York Judiciary, ibid., July, 1867. [5] Ibid., July, 1875, p. 145.

give in flattery and attention if not in other kinds of gain.[1]
Many reporters of the Herald as well as of other New York
newspapers were quartered on the city by Tweed, drawing salaries they did not earn in return for such favorable
opinions as they might utter from day to day in print.[2]

In order to secure even fair consideration for Seymour as a
presidential candidate in 1868 an experienced man wrote Tilden that from $3,000 to $10,000 a month should be distributed
among about 30 newspaper reporters in New York City.
These fellows made the opinion of and gave the tone to every
"important newspaper in the country."[3] The money articles
in most of the journals were "admiring discussions," said Tilden, "of the relative dexterity" of men of colossal capital con-
tending with one another in feats which had a "moral aspect
about like cheating at cards."[4]

If the journalists were not paid outright in money, bankers,
promoters and the heads of corporations presented them with
stock and bonds, employed them as publicity agents for various
enterprises, gave them passes on railroads, conveyed them
and their families hither and thither on pleasant junkets in
return for expected "write ups." Jay Cooke carried speculative accounts for reporters and editors. They paid nothing
for the stock which he bought for them, assumed no responsibility for loss, but were made glad from time to time
by "turn overs" resulting in profit. His management of the
American press was more successful than any man's has ever
been.

Even the church swung loosely at its moorings, as it seemed,
in view of the part taken by its leaders on many occasions,
when it should have remained silent, as during the trial of
Andrew Johnson on the impeachment charges, and when, as

[1] Cf. F. P. and Montgomery Blair to S. J. Tilden in Bigelow, Letters
of Tilden, vol. i, pp. 240-2, 245-6.
[2] Myers, History of Tammany Hall, pp. 232-3; North American
Review, January, 1875, pp. 124-5; cf. A. B. Paine, Life of Nast, pp.
146, 161.
[3] Bigelow, Letters of Tilden, vol. i, p. 240.
[4] S. J. Tilden, N. Y. City Ring, pp. 51-2.

in other cases, it should have sounded a clear call back to wholesome life.

The young men born of this time were provided with models for emulation of which many of them could never rid their minds, and the influences of such example held the country in the toils of sordid fortune seeking for a generation.

In Congress were men who had sunk so low that they were ready to sell appointments to cadetships at West Point. It is true that two or three caught at this base traffic were compelled to resign their seats.[1] But contemptible as such a course might be it was only a degree or two worse than bartering lucrative Federal offices for contributions to campaign funds, or parcelling out these offices to men like Conkling in New York and Cameron in Pennsylvania in a full consciousness that the appointees would not competently or honestly perform their duties; billeting your unthrifty kindred upon the government; filling the entire civil service, indeed, with men who were not chosen because of their fitness, but to promote some selfish object. Yet it was just this policy which was habitually followed by President Grant, and was defended by those whom he gathered around him, and made responsible for the direction of the government.

Almost any senator or representative would take stock and bonds in railroad and other companies which were soliciting public lands, bond subventions and material advantages of this or that kind at the hands of Congress, or which might do this tomorrow. Grant himself was accepting pecuniary assistance calculated to put him under obligations from which a president of the United States ought always to be entirely clear. He and the members of his family were receiving loans of money from the banks of Jay Cooke, though it was well known that the Northern Pacific Railroad and other enterprises in which this financier was concerned were asking for public favors.[2] His accepting courtesies from several

[1] Cf. Cong. Globe, 41st Cong. 2nd sess., pp. 1547, 1617.
[2] Oberholtzer, Jay Cooke, vol. ii, p. 181.

rich men who hovered about him to flatter him and catch his attention would have been avoided by any to whom proper moral distinctions were known, and by whom they could be appreciated. That he should have made himself the companion publicly of such a one as James Fisk, Jr., passes the bounds of credulity.[1]

From the Atlantic seaboard to the Pacific coast few men of his day were more admired and trusted than Schuyler Colfax, long Speaker of the House of Representatives and now Vice President of the United States. The love in which he was held by large classes of the people had caused Samuel Bowles to call him "more than the Henry Clay of his generation." Unlike Clay's Colfax's friends knew no party lines.[2] His influence as an orator and a leader was so great that Jay Cooke offered him $25,000 a year if he would leave the Vice Presidency and espouse the cause of the Northern Pacific Railroad.[3] He declined. In spite of his eminent position he took a share in the Northern Pacific "pool" when he was invited to do so, though he was unable to carry it without loans,[4] and was involved in the Crédit Mobilier in a similar way.

Chief Justice Chase, a man more meticulously careful of his honor than any of his day, was so fond of money that he would have left his high office to become the president of a railroad company.[5] He was deterred from taking such a course, but he became a member of the Northern Pacific "pool," permitting his name to be put upon the list of stockholders on a mere understanding that he was to pay for the

---

[1] Grant himself, said the New York Sun, had done more than any "to destroy in the public mind all distinction between right and wrong, to make it appear that the great object of life and the chief purpose of official authority is to acquire riches and that it makes no difference by what means this object is attained."—Issue of Feb. 17, 1872; cf. J. H. Wilson, Life of C. A. Dana, chap. xxv, "Epoch of Public Corruption."

[2] Hollister, Life of Colfax, p. 343.

[3] Ibid., pp. 352-3; Oberholtzer, Jay Cooke, vol. ii, pp. 230-31.

[4] Oberholtzer, Jay Cooke, vol. ii, pp. 416-64.

[5] Ibid., p. 130.

investment out of the future profits of the road when they should be distributed.[1]

James G. Blaine, Speaker of the House of Representatives, occupying one of the highest positions as a leader of his party and as a statesman, allowed himself to be a borrower, without adequate security and without a feeling 'of obligation to meet his engagements, at Jay Cooke's banks. If he escaped the Crédit Mobilier it was not so with other railway enterprises which were seeking government grants. He offered almost any service in his public capacity to those who would give him money to aid the Fort Smith and Little Rock Railroad in the success of which he was pecuniarily concerned. The Cookes thought some of the demands which he made upon them in 1872 akin to blackmail.[2]

Few men in political life were more respected than James A. Garfield, William B. Allison and Henry Wilson, yet they thought it not unfitting, until their attention was drawn to the subject, to take stock in the Crédit Mobilier, when it was offered to them by Oakes Ames, though they had no money to pay for it, and would be carried along by the courtesy of the management until the sums were earned in dividends.

Robert C. Schenck, the able Republican leader in Congress from Ohio, who had been proffered a position as attorney at Washington for the Northern Pacific Railroad[3] and would have accepted it, probably, if he had not been induced to take Motley's place as minister to England, which no one could be found to fill, after going abroad, authorized a Nevada silver mining company, whose stock was being floated in London,[4] to use his name as a member of its board of directors. There were demands that he should be recalled.[5] He explained to Fish that he had paid for the stock "dollar for dollar" and he had not thought it wrong "to try to make

[1] Oberholtzer, Jay Cooke, vol. ii, pp. 164-5.   [2] Ibid., p. 354.
[3] Ibid., pp. 229-31.   [4] Ibid., pp. 290-91; Moran's Diary.
[5] As, e.g., in the N. Y. Evening Post. Cf. N. Y. Nation, Nov. 30, 1871.

something honestly for himself and his family."[1] But the
Secretary of State urged him to withdraw as a director of
the company, which he did at once. In due time his course
became the subject of a Congressional inquiry.[2]

If those who held eminent places in our public life dared
so much what were the conditions prevailing in the lower
ranks in Washington? From the top downward there was
something akin to moral blindness.

In 1871 the sums advanced by Jay Cooke to prominent
politicians and journalists to secure their good will amounted
to nearly one million dollars.[3] What must be done by the
Northern Pacific managers to bring its claims to the notice
of Congress was not left undone by the promoters of the
southern and southwestern lines to the Pacific, of every railroad however small, of nearly all enterprises of whatever
kind which came to a state legislature or to Congress for
bounties and advantages.[4] Countless lobbyists, largely recruited from the bar and the newspaper office, employed by
the corporations which were engaged in bringing their various
undertakings to public attention, swarmed Washington and
the state capitals to degrade political morality to a point it
had never touched before. Votes had their prices as clearly as
shares on the stock exchange. The nation, said the New York
Sun, was "passing through an epoch of public corruption
without precedent in its history and almost without precedent in the history of free governments."[5] "Corrupted
blood," said Samuel J. Tilden, "pervades our whole country."[6] By "speculation and gambling and jobbery and
corruption" it had come to "about the lowest point in the
great cycle" which it was obliged "occasionally to traverse."[7]

[1] Moran's Diary.
[2] House Reports, 44th Cong. 1st sess., no. 579, in case of "The Emma
Mine." By this time, in 1876, the House was in control of the Democratic party.
[3] Oberholtzer, Jay Cooke, vol. ii, p. 416.
[4] Cf. A. W. Dimock, Wall Street and the Wilds, pp. 225-6.
[5] N. Y. Sun, Feb. 17, 1872.
[6] New York City Ring, pp. 51-2.
[7] Bigelow, Letters of Tilden, vol. i, p. 301.

The "blackness of successful wrong" was overspreading "the whole heavens." [1]

No class of the population escaped the evil influences of the time. During the war nearly everyone was carrying some kind of stock on "margin," or was speculating in oil or gold. Encouraged to it by the sight of the petroleum and mining "kings," sons of Fortunatus by accident over night, who had come to take envied places in American society, workingmen and servant girls had put their savings into stocks, that they too might be rich. Business was changed into gambling and gambling became a business. [2] The purchases of diamonds, the consumption of wines and champagnes, the gorgeous finery carried about by women were noted on every side. Shopkeepers who dealt in silks, laces and precious stones were unable to supply the demand for what hitherto only a very few had had the means to buy. Dinners, which were called banquets, social entertainments, spectacles reached a degree of sumptuous display never seen before. So vulgar were the exhibitions of wealth that ladies of taste forebore wearing their jewels in public lest they be confused with the new rich who went about on the most inappropriate occasions bedizened with ornaments.

In November, 1871, the Grand Duke Alexis, third son of the Czar of Russia, arrived in New York. Such receptions, balls and parades as were arranged for him in all parts of the country were bewildering. The show and waste in which the people vied were indicative of nothing, as Harper's Weekly said, but a "comical" snobbery. Their outbursts came from a love, not so much of doing honor to Russia, about which few knew or cared, as of entertaining themselves. [3] The balls at the New York and Philadelphia Academies of Music were described as the most brilliant and elaborate which had ever been seen in America. [4] The wild extravagance evidenced in the

[1] New York City Ring, pp. 51-52.
[2] A. W. Dimock, Wall Street and the Wilds, p. 61.
[3] Harper's Weekly, Dec. 9, 1871.
[4] Ibid., Dec. 16, 1871; Phila. Ledger, Dec. 5, 1871; A. K. McClure, Old Time Notes of Pa., vol. ii, pp. 247-8.

decorations of the apartments, in the luxurious viands spread upon the tables, in the dress of the men and women who were present suggested national degeneracy. At Washington and other cities which the Prince visited, in Nebraska and Colorado whither he was taken to shoot buffalo,[1] there was proof of the same heedless spirit of a people who, blessed too much and too long, were riding for a fall.

The orgy had reached its limits. Gambling had exhausted itself by its excess, and it was being followed by defalcation, embezzlement and other breaches of trust in all parts of the country. It was not unusual for some poor victim to go mad or take his own life.[2]

All business had come to a standstill. Capital for new enterprises was not to be had. Those which had been undertaken so confidently at the end of the war were in the doldrums. Before the end of 1869 the $100 bonds of the Union Pacific had sold down to 85; in 1871 to 77½. Central Pacific bonds in 1870 were 94, Missouri Pacifics, 88. Various seven per cent railroad bonds bearing interest in gold could be had in the New York market or were for sale by the promoters of the companies at 85.[3]

Suddenly an end had come to the supply of money to carry forward the great schemes of material development which had been flourishing in so many minds, and which were coming to fruit on so many sides. Usurious rates of interest, enticing premiums and bonuses, inducements of unusual kinds must be offered, if capital were to be attracted to a railway or any other project, no matter how great its intrinsic worth.

To add to the difficulty of the problem public feeling had found expression in party platforms, and the suspicions which had been awakened were translated into legislative inquiries, and laws or projects of laws meant to restrict corporate activity. Not only were bond subventions denounced, but further giving away of the public lands to development com-

---

[1] Pacific Tourist, p. 37.

[2] Chapters of Erie, pp. 101-2.

[3] Oberholtzer, Jay Cooke, vol. ii, pp. 151, 225-6, 234.

panies was opposed, in many quarters in the most vehement terms. Men stood aghast at the enormous transfers of the national domain, tracts promised to single companies having an area equal to that of a dozen of the older states, as everyone knew, since the promoters were widely advertising their grants in order to sell their securities.

The country was in the condition of an overridden steed. Jaded, no longer would it respond to whip or spur. It was an inert mass of tired bone and fibre which could not be aroused to any new activity. The stock market was heavy and motionless. It had flashed up and down within a narrow range for months, running into years. It failed to heed news which at another time might have awakened enthusiasm, but it was extremely sensitive to any occurrence which could be construed to have evil omen. How prices could be shaken was seen on the memorable Friday, September 24, 1869, the "Black Friday" in Wall Street, of which more is soon to be related. As gold rose stocks fell. New York Central which had sold at 205¼ on September 1 was quoted as 145 on September 29; Harlem between those dates fell from 160 to 117, Chicago and Northwestern from 86¼ to 62, Michigan and Southern from 106¼ to 74½, Pacific Mail from 80¼ to 55.

Then came the burning of Chicago. The "miracle of the West" to which the enumerators in 1870 assigned a population of nearly 350,000 had just turned the waters of Lake Michigan into the Gulf of Mexico. As the city grew the slough which was called the Chicago River became a source of infinite vapors which hygienists said were heavy with pestilence. It was in truth a sewer in which the fetid matter of a great centre of population sluggishly moved about. Other devices for abolishing this grand nuisance failing, the Illinois and Michigan Canal, running down to Joliet on the Des Plaines River, was deepened and in the summer of 1871 was opened for use. The clear, sweet water of the lake sweeping through the city pushed the heavy mass before it to the great relief of the people.[1]

[1] Harper's Weekly, July 22, 1871.

But the Gethsemane of this wonderful urban community
which had so suddenly sprung out of the prairie was near
at hand. On the night of Saturday, October 7, 1871, a fire
broke out in a planing mill on the west side. A strong wind
fanned it and several blocks of buildings were destroyed before its progress could be arrested. The firemen were not
done with their task, when, on Sunday night, fresh alarms
were sounded. An Irish woman, Mrs. Leary—this is the
accepted account—in DeKoven Street, filled with squalid
wooden huts, carried a kerosene lamp to the barn behind the
house to draw milk from a cow which kicked the lamp and
scattered the oil upon the straw which, igniting, started one
of the greatest conflagrations of the age.[1]

The wind of Saturday night was now a gale, the firemen
wearied by their exertions were not very alert, and in a
little while were powerless to cope with the flames which swept
into the very heart of the city. Banks, theatres, churches,
hotels, newspaper offices, grain elevators, the chamber of
commerce, the court house were consumed like so much
stubble in a field. After the water works were burned the
outlook was still more hopeless. Whole blocks of buildings
were blown up with powder to stay the hand of devastation,
without effect. Brands, flying through the air, kindled new
fires and the flames roared on like some terrible hurricane.
In some places thousands of persons were hemmed in and
were in danger of perishing. Half dressed fugitives ran in all
directions to places of safety. The homeless and destitute
huddled together in camps on vacant lots, in parks, on the
lake shore and on farms far into the country. The light in the
sky was seen forty and sixty miles away.

The wood-block pavements saturated with tar, then an
experiment, were said to have contributed to the spread of

---

[1] Following John Hay's account in the New York Tribune of the
woman who came to the barn behind the house "to milk the cow with
the crumpled temper, that kicked the lamp that spilled the kerosene
that fired the straw that burned Chicago." (N. Y. Tribune, quoted in
Harper's Weekly, Nov. 11, 1871.) That this was the real origin of the
fire was denied at the time as it has been since. Cf. Harper's Weekly,
Nov. 11, 1871.

the flames, though this was denied as soon as the streets could be examined, and it was seen how well they had withstood destruction. However, the plank sidewalks, many of them laid on trestle work, served to extend the fire as did the prevalence of wooden buildings, and brick and stone buildings finished with cornices, parapets and other decorations, made from the lumber so cheaply procured by boat from the wooded shores of the lakes. Fortunately the wind diminished on Tuesday and rain began to fall. At last the flames were brought under control, but not before three and a half square miles had been reduced to a waste of ashes and crumbling masonry. This was about one-sixth of the area of the city, though upon it had stood edifices and other property valued at twice as much as those which occupied the remaining five-sixths of the municipal tract.

The news of the disaster awakened the profound sympathy of the whole country,[1] and of Canada and Europe. Succor came from all sides. Trains were laden with food and clothing and were forwarded with dispatch to the stricken people. Money was subscribed and made available for use. General Sheridan put the place under martial law and summarily executed two or three score scoundrels to restore order. The government sent tents to shelter the homeless and distributed army rations. But the gallant and generous response of the world to the city's needs was not surpassed by the spirit of its own people who set themselves with striking energy to the great tasks of the hour. Without recrimination of fate, or misgivings as to the future each man dedicated himself to the common purpose of raising upon the site of the old a new and better Chicago. A week later, when the embers were not yet cold, the cornerstone of a bank building was laid, and throughout the next following months wood, brick and granite, hammer and shovel, windlass and capstan made the place a hive of industry. With astounding rapidity the city rose again more marvelous than before.[2]

A panic almost as exciting as that which had swept Wall

[1] Cf. Letters of Mrs. J. G. Blaine, vol. i, pp. 45, 50, 53.
[2] Harper's Weekly, Oct. 21, 28, Nov. 4, 17, 1871.

Street on "Black Friday" overtook the stock market. The
rings and combinations which were engaged in holding up the
prices of railway shares were frightened by the prospect of
replacing such losses as were to be incurred by insurance
companies, merchants, mortgage holders and money lenders
generally in the East. Credit was on the point of crumbling
in every direction. But confronted by the evidences of the
city's remarkable recuperative power Wall Street was somewhat reassured and it soon resumed its accustomed, if turgid
and hopeless way.

The same gale which swept the flames through Chicago
spread fires in the wooded regions of Wisconsin and Michigan. Square miles of trees, and the saw mills and villages
which had been erected among them, on the shores of Lake
Michigan, Lake Huron, Saginaw Bay and Green Bay were
destroyed with considerable loss of life. Vast hardship was
visited upon the people settled there and engaged in the cutting and manufacture of pine lumber.[1]

In September, 1872, the bottom was again on the point of
falling out of the great structure of values, so wildly reared
in the ten past years. The presidential campaign was in
progress. Only the interposition of the banking interests
which were closely allied with the Republican party, and
the use of the government's strongest agencies prevented a
panic.[2]

On November 9, 1872, a fire, which originated in a granite
building in a business block in Boston, wrought great damage
in that city. It gained such headway that the fire companies
of other cities were summoned by telegraph. Before it could
be halted nearly 70 acres were burned over and a large
number of wholesale shoe and leather, dry goods and wool
warehouses were destroyed. The total loss was thought to be
at least $100,000,000. Here also the people exhibited a fine
spirit and soon employed themselves in rebuilding the wrecked

[1] N. Y. Nation, Oct. 19, 1871.
[2] Oberholtzer, Jay Cooke, vol. ii, pp. 355-6; Phila. Inquirer, Sep. 19,
1872; N. Y. Tribune, Sep. 19, 1872.

district.[1] Again the stock market was shaken, again it resumed its dull and heavy tone awaiting the excuse for complete disaster which it found in 1873.[2]

It was very certain that the European markets would absorb no more railway bonds. The length of the roads, their lands, their mighty prospects had been made the subject of so much panegyric in writing and speech that men wanted to hear no more about them, especially after the airing of the scandal in connection with the exploitation of Frémont's Memphis, El Paso and Pacific in France. The company's agent had been a certain Henry Probst. He, or others for him, inserted advertisements and articles in the news columns of the French newspapers, and placarded the city of Paris with statements that this was a great transcontinental line which connected at Chattanooga with practically all the railroads running west from the Atlantic coast. A terminus with wharves was to be built at Norfolk. Moreover, the road had received a subvention from Congress similar to the grants made to the Union Pacific and Central Pacific. On the strength of such falsehood a bond issue, which yielded the company about $5,000,000, was sold in 1869 to the prominent Paris banking house of Paradis for distribution to investors, who were the more likely to be attracted to the scheme by an announcement that the proceeds of the loan would be expended for locomotives and rails in French engineering works.

As a matter of fact a resolution granting a right of way to the promoters of the road through the territories had passed the House of Representatives, nothing more—and lobbyists were energetically engaged in the work of trying to secure favors for the company at Washington.[3] Its real assets were limited to three miles of track, a little machinery and some grants of dubious value from the state of Texas. When the deceived purchasers of the bonds learned the truth their wrath covered two continents. Some visited Minister

[1] Harper's Weekly, Nov. 30 and Dec. 7, 1872.
[2] Cf. N. Y. Tribune and Phila. Ledger, Nov. 12, 1872.
[3] Senate Ex. Doc., 41st Cong. 2nd sess., no. 59, pp. 18, 20.

Washburne who told them that the securities were "not worth the paper they were written on." [1]   He reported the matter to Secretary of State Fish. Congress asked for the correspondence.[2] The Senate Pacific Railroad Committee started an investigation of the fraud which Senator Howard, chairman of the sub-committee in charge, declared to be "one of the most infamous proceedings that ever took place." [3]

Probst, to cover his swindle, entered suit for libel, asking damages of a million francs, and indicted some of the men who had denounced him. Frémont denied the charges involving his integrity.[4] But to no avail. Irate Frenchmen came to this country to seek redress, employed skilful attorneys and sought to arrest Frémont in New York. He fled and escaped service.[5] Whatever his real personal responsibility may have been, over and above a natural incapacity for business operations, the scandal completely discredited him. Unable to proceed against him here the victims of the conspiracy later indicted him in the French courts. He was convicted and sentenced *in absentia* with great advertisement of his dishonor, and the experience ended his career, as well as that of the El Paso road.

A railway in the northwest, called the St. Paul and Pacific, which had visions of some day reaching the western coast, a rival of the Northern Pacific, had gone to Holland for money. In 1871 a loan of $15,000,000 was taken by Dutch capitalists through bankers in Amsterdam. The men who were manipulating the scheme—after remunerating themselves exorbitantly, reserved a part of the sum for use in paying interest for a time to their dupes. Less than 50 per cent of the sum which was subscribed found its way to Minnesota for the construction of the road.[6] There was little to show for the millions which the Hollanders had lent but some "odds and ends" of track on the prairie. They were "unrelated

[1] Senate Mis. Doc., 41st Cong. 2nd sess., no. 96.
[2] Senate Ex. Doc., 41st Cong. 2nd sess., no. 59.
[3] Senate Mis. Doc., 41st Cong. 2nd sess., no. 121, p. 53.
[4] Ibid., no. 96.
[5] Phila. Ledger, Aug. 11, 1870, quoting Newark Advertiser.
[6] Pyle, Life of James J. Hill, vol. i, p. 161.

scraps" which led no whither and soon fell into the hands of the Northern Pacific for consolidation with its great system which, however, had to relinquish the property as its own troubles accumulated. The bondholders in Holland eventually got four cents on the dollar for their investment. In a condition in which it could be described truthfully as "two streaks of rust and a right of way" the road finally came into the hands of James J. Hill, who was beginning his career as a railway financier in the Northwest, and upon this foundation he later developed that important line to the Pacific known as the Great Northern.[1]

Nearly $11,000,000 worth of bonds had been sold, principally in Germany, for the account of the Oregon and California Railroad to run from Portland to the California boundary. Ben Holladay, of the old overland stage line, was the chief figure in the management of this enterprise. When the German capitalists put their affairs into the hands of Henry Villard in 1873 it was discovered that, although 200 miles of the road had been built, it extended through a country which could yield no profitable traffic. Only about one-half of the whole sum subscribed in Europe ever reached the company. On another line against which $3,000,000 of bonds had been issued no work at all had been done.[2]

The general advertisement in the bourses and exchanges of Europe of such performances by our financiers relegated all American railway enterprises into a general nimbus of suspicion. The Chicago fire forcibly impressed the foreign mind with the crudeness of our country and the insecurity of investments in it. More than ever after this disaster were capitalists indisposed to send new sums across the sea. No one conducted a more thorough search of the money markets of England and the Continent than Jay Cooke. In the Northern Pacific he had the most attractive proposal for a railroad which the country afforded. His sponsorship of it was an assurance of skilful and honest management of the

[1] Pyle, Life of James J. Hill, vol. i, p. 164.
[2] Memoirs of Henry Villard, vol. ii, pp. 272-4.

undertaking. The industrious agents whom he sent abroad, and his own house in London with a respected ex-secretary of the treasury, Hugh McCulloch, at its head, gave the scheme the most favorable presentation. But two or three years of persistent labor to effect a loan for the assistance of the road ended only in total failure. An American in Frankfort-on-the-Main found the prejudice against our railway bonds so deep-founded that one would not sell, he said, if it were "signed by an angel in Heaven." [1]

We had forfeited our right to the world's respect in railway finance by not deserving it. Our achievements, if they had been large and rapid, were characterized by methods which took no account, on the one hand, of the rights of the public as travellers on and shippers over the roads, or, on the other hand, of their rights as owners or part owners of the property, as represented by the companies' stocks and bonds.

The lines were scarcely built and ready for use when they were combined into large systems. In the West the object of the railroad builders was the Pacific coast; in the East, control of the commerce between the Atlantic seaboard and the Great Lakes and the Mississippi Valley. Four great iron thoroughfares ran from the eastern coast to the interior of the continent—the New York Central, the Erie, the Pennsylvania and the Baltimore and Ohio. The New York Central had been chartered in 1853, and eleven distinct companies were merged to bring under one management a line extending from Albany to Buffalo. Its direction was dominated by Cornelius Vanderbilt who, born in the humblest circumstances, had begun life ferrying passengers and produce from Staten Island to New York City. Soon he navigated larger boats in New York harbor and on the Hudson River, and in a little while owned and managed lines of boats. At first called "captain," later, as his fleet increased, and his shipping interests extended, he came to be universally known as "Commodore" Vanderbilt.

[1] Phila. Ledger, Aug. 30, 1873.

From ferries and steamboats he passed to railroads, as soon as they were built and it was seen that they would supplant waterways.[1] The Harlem Railroad, the outgrowth of a line of stage coaches, ran from New York to Harlem village, and was being extended up the Harlem valley. By a coup in Wall Street in 1863 Vanderbilt gained control of this property. He drove a tunnel under Murray Hill and was enabled to take his trains down to the Battery.[2] In the north his tracks were reaching out toward Albany where he would find connection with the New York Central.

The Harlem was paralleled by a competing line, the Hudson River road. Shortly this, too, fell into Vanderbilt's hands under sensational circumstances,[3] and, in undisputed control of the situation at New York with reference to Albany, and the Western trade from New York by way of that city, he compelled the managers of the New York Central in the winter of 1866-7 to commit their road to his charge.[4] Then he combined the lines as the New York Central and Hudson River Railroad, with a trackage of about 1,000 miles and a capital of approximately $100,000,000.

But this was not enough: his vision carried him across the continent. In a little while he was in secure possession of the Lake Shore and Michigan Southern, a consolidation of lines connecting Buffalo with Chicago, and in May, 1870, of the Rock Island and the Chicago and Northwestern roads, so that he could run his trains from New York to Omaha. Here

[1] At first, according to Daniel Drew, Vanderbilt sneered at railroads as "them things that go on land." (B. White, The Book of Daniel Drew, p. 112.) Drew himself thought little better of them. To him locomotives were "steam buggies." (Ibid., p. 114.) Vanderbilt had few more literary sympathies than Drew, and Drew had none at all. —Henry Clews, Twenty-Eight Years in Wall Street, pp. 117-8.

[2] A. W. Dimock, Wall Street and the Wilds, pp. 62-3.

[3] Henry Clews, Twenty-Eight Years in Wall Street, chap. xvii; C. F. Carter, When Railroads Were New, p. 182.

[4] Navigation had closed, says C. F. Carter, and Vanderbilt had removed his station to the eastern bank of the Hudson, refusing to accept New York Central freights. Their communication with New York cut off, the price of the stock fell and Vanderbilt soon had millions of dollars worth of it in his possession.—When Railroads Were New, pp. 183-4.

was a vast corporation, or an alliance of corporations, in absolute control of 4,500 miles of railroad, representing a capital of not less than $250,000,000.[1]

Similarly, farther south, the Pennsylvania Railroad monopolized the traffic between Philadelphia and Pittsburgh. This corporation had made itself almost synonymous with the state government of Pennsylvania, directing elections, enacting and defeating legislation, determining the opinions of courts. Under the management of J. Edgar Thomson and Thomas A. Scott it leased roads reaching from Pittsburgh to Chicago, Cincinnati and St. Louis, while the ambitious men who controlled its destinies had personal connections with trans-Mississippi and Pacific railroad companies, to form a system, if all the projects should be realized, covering the continent. Near the end of the year 1870 it secured by lease lines which brought it to Jersey City on the shores of New York harbor. In this great combination were included more than 3,000 miles of track representing securities of a value of $175,000,-000.[2]

On all sides, as the companies were consolidated, their stock was "watered," [3] i.e., they were carried into the larger corporations at a valuation in excess of their building or purchase costs. For example, the stock issue of the Pittsburgh, Fort Wayne and Chicago Railroad which was $11,500,000 was increased when it was taken over by the Pennsylvania Railroad to nearly $20,000,000. It had debts of about $13,-600,000 more. A road which it was said had cost $24,000,000, therefore, was suddenly called upon to pay the interest on more than $33,000,000.[4]

More spectacular than anything which yet had been seen, however, were the performances of "Commodore" Vanderbilt

[1] Adams, Chapters of Erie, pp. 382-3.

[2] Ibid., pp. 383-7.

[3] A word ascribed to Daniel Drew, who came to New York as a drover. Before cattle were to be weighed for sale they were allowed to eat salt until they were thirsty. Then they were led to water so that the yield might be increased.—Cf. White, The Book of Daniel Drew, pp. 44, 59.

[4] Adams, Chapters of Erie, pp. 400-1.

in connection with the New York Central and Hudson River companies, and their western connections. The property lying between New York and Buffalo, which in 1866 appeared to have cost less than $50,000,000 and, indeed, had only $54,-000,000 of outstanding obligations, came to have a capital upon which interest was to be paid of $103,000,000. It was computed that the manipulation of the lines to Buffalo annually imposed upon the American people a charge of not less than $5,000,000 in excess of any rightful remuneration for services rendered by Vanderbilt and his associates as common carriers.[1] About $50,000 of "water" was poured out for each mile of road.[2] The lines west of Buffalo which were combined by Vanderbilt to give him a way into Chicago had a fictitious capital of $20,000,000.[3]

A leading financial newspaper said that 28 roads in a period of 22 months, from July 1, 1867, to May 1, 1869, had increased their capital stock issues from $287,000,000 to $400,000,000, or 40 per cent. Nine roads in less than four years had raised the total face value of their outstanding securities 150 per cent, nearly all of it "water."[4]

Not at all different from this principle in railway finance was the policy, invariably pursued by the promoters, of giving away stock of their companies as a gratuity to those who would purchase bonds. The actual cost of construction was represented by interest-bearing mortgages covering the property. Millions of stock, to receive dividends or not, according as business should develop in the future in the country penetrated by the lines, glutted the markets and the companies whose names they bore, as men of judgment well knew, were headed toward the bankruptcy courts and receiverships.

The railway man of the age was a freebooter at liberty to

[1] Adams, Chapters of Erie, p. 404.

[2] Ibid., pp. 402-3.

[3] Ibid., pp. 403-4. It was by such operations regardless of criticism that to Vanderbilt came to be ascribed the phrase that lived long after him—"The public be d—d!"

[4] Commercial and Financial Chronicle, May 15, 1869, quoted in C. F. Adams, Chapters of Erie, p. 409.

do what he might. He acted frequently under impulses which
had seemed patriotic. His services were greatly to the public advantage in connecting communities, putting populations
nearer to markets, stimulating the settlement of new lands.
But, with good reason, his movements came to be viewed with
distrust, and the reckoning day approached.

The extraordinary performances which marked the history
of the Erie Railway were designed in a particular way to
bring discredit upon American railroad management generally. A company to build this line had been chartered as
long ago as 1832. It had received loans from the state,
but it was 1851, nearly twenty years later, before its tracks
were down and trains could pass over them from Lake Erie
to tidewater.[1] "Uncle" Daniel Drew was to this road what
"Commodore" Vanderbilt was to the New York Central.
From gathering up and selling "bob calves" in the neighborhood in which he was born in Putnam County, N. Y., he
passed to the circus business in which he seems to have been
equally expert as canvas man, animal trainer and clown.
In a little while he was driving cattle into New York City,
at which pursuit he amassed a considerable sum of money,
the passion of his life. A drover and the associate of drovers
he soon established himself as keeper of the Bull's Head
Tavern on the "Boston Road," now Third Avenue, near the
present 26th Street in New York, then some miles out of town,
which under his management became the principal horse and
cattle exchange for the city. He emulated Vanderbilt
and in a short time was engaged in steamboating on the
Hudson River and Long Island Sound. A shrewd, wholly
unprincipled and most illiterate man he was soon "speckilat-
ing," as he spelled and pronounced the word, in railroads.[2]
He had set his eyes on the Erie Railway, pressed himself into
the board of directors through the tactics he had followed
in the management of his steamboat lines, and after a

[1] Cf. The Book of Daniel Drew, pp. 129-31.
[2] Cf. ibid., for proof of the man's singular want of the most rudimentary suggestions of literary culture; also Henry Clews, Twenty-
Eight Years in Wall Street.

diabolical campaign to destroy the company's credit, so that he would have it at his mercy and could offer to lend it money, he, during the panic of 1857, "got the sow by the ears," to use his own language in describing the feat, and put the road in his "breeches pocket." [1] He became the treasurer of the company and during the next ten years, in possession of all its secrets, he cunningly and unscrupulously used his high position for his own pecuniary advantage, manipulating the price of the stock at will.

Without a patriotic impulse to restrain his avarice he improved his financial position during the war by speculating upon his country's adversities and at its end, in 1866, was ready to wring another fortune out of "Erie." Now again in the company's need he lent it money, this time as much as $3,500,000 for which he took unissued shares, and bonds convertible into shares, as collateral. While the securities of the company were rising on the strength of its success in obtaining the aid which it sorely required, he was concluding contracts for the future delivery of stock. When he had caught the flies in his web he converted his bonds and poured 58,000 shares into Wall Street. The price soon fell from 95 to 50. It was "the finest scoop" he had ever made.[2]

Drew and Vanderbilt had been rivals for many years, at first in steamboating on the Hudson River and Long Island Sound.[3] They had met in the Harlem "corner" in 1863, when Drew lost a fortune because of Vanderbilt's prowess on that occasion.[4] Both now were men beyond 70; they had attained position and wealth by travelling rather similar paths. But while Drew was sombre, given to tearing down and despoiling, Vanderbilt was a buoyant, hopeful character, naturally as much of a "bull" as Drew was a "bear." [5] His mind

[1] The Book of Daniel Drew, pp. 139-45.
[2] Ibid., pp. 211-12; Chapters of Erie, pp. 6-7.
[3] The Book of Daniel Drew, pp. 96, 116.
[4] "Pretty much" all their lives they had been "fighting each other," said Drew.—Ibid., p. 207.
[5] "He was the dog, I the cat," said Drew. "A cat believes in going soft-footed, in keeping its claws hid till the time comes. A dog goes in with a big bow-wow; my plan has always been to go at a thing

inclined him to the purchase of the cheap stock of bankrupt roads which he sought to rehabilitate and render valuable.[1] He had bought a controlling interest in Harlem at a few dollars a share. If most of his money had been made in "corners" in 1863 and 1864 the stock, after he obtained possession of the property, was intrinsically valuable. When he had gained a dominating position in the Hudson River road, as a result of another "corner," that company's stock came to have substantial worth. Whatever might be thought of his motives and courses, which were plainly selfish, his was a constructive mind. He was the first of the American "railroad kings." He "earned dividends, created stock and invented wealth."[2] His reputation as a financier became national, if not international.

Having abolished competition between the two roads out of New York City by combining them he formed a similar design with reference to the trade across the state. He would control the Erie Railway as well as the New York Central and bring them into harmonious working agreement, an adventure in which he met Daniel Drew, and they were to lock horns again.

After some preliminary parleys, in which Drew's treachery and Vanderbilt's arrogance were disclosed, Vanderbilt began the purchase of Erie stock in preparation for the annual meeting in 1868. But while buying with one hand it was clearly necessary, having the experiences of 1866 in mind, to make certain, with the other, that new shares could not be printed and thrown upon the market. Recourse was had to the courts. Clever attorneys appeared before Supreme Court Justice Barnard, praying for an injunction against Drew and his fellow directors, who in turn, in Binghamton sought a

quieter." (Ibid., p. 207.) Vanderbilt was "a natural born hoper," said Drew again. "I have been more conservative—have never allowed myself to paint the picture in the bright colors." He was "by make-up a bullish fellow whereas most of my life I have been on the bear side of the market." (Ibid., p. 209; cf. J. K. Medbery, Men and Mysteries of Wall Street, p. 156.)

[1] Cf. C. F. Carter, When Railroads Were New, p. 185.
[2] Adams, Chapters of Erie, p. 11.

judge whom they thought that they could use for their purposes and from whom they succeeded in obtaining an injunction to restrain the Vanderbilt party. Thus was begun a contest which proceeded simultaneously in the stock exchange and in the courts for many months, in complete disregard of the rules of honor and at times of the commonest impulses of decency. Drew was "selling short," while Vanderbilt was on the bull side, executing plans that certainly on or about March 10 would lead to a "corner" from which the enemy would find it difficult to extricate himself. As there had been reason to anticipate, Drew and the "Erie ring" stood ready to issue $10,000,000 of bonds, convertible into new stock, which could be flung at the head of Vanderbilt, and this step was resolved upon without delay, in spite of every legal obstruction which could be placed in their way.

Drew had for his principal associates Jay Gould and James Fisk, Jr.,[1] stock brokers in New York and, like himself, Erie directors. Both were common desperadoes, not a whit better than the road agents of Montana who at the gun's point stopped stage wagons laden with gold dust coming down from the mines. Gould, a small, silent, scheming, spider-like man, with a touch of the Jew in his blood, had written a history of Delaware county, N. Y., owned a tannery in the wilds of Pennsylvania and had come to New York with a patent rat trap to sell. He now was a partner in the Wall Street brokerage firm of Smith, Gould, Martin and Co.

Unlike the sly and sphinx-like Gould Fisk was all bluster, noise and advertisement. He was the son of a peddler who had sold dry goods and gewgaws from town to town in the Connecticut Valley, a pursuit to which "Jim" turned at an early age. By the use of gaudily painted wagons, drawn by long teams of horses, hung with glittering harness, he soon distanced his father as an itinerant merchant of the countryside. His energy attracted the notice of a prominent Boston firm which took him into its employ and later into partner-

[1] They were "pupils" of Drew. They were "colts"; Drew "broke them in."—The Book of Daniel Drew, p. 122.

ship. He was able to withdraw from the connection with a small fortune as a result of profitable contracts with the government for army blankets. But in a dry goods shop of his own he soon lost all he had gained and was again "as flat as a nigger's nose." [1] In a little while he found a buyer for Drew's Stonington line of steamboats which led "Uncle Daniel" to start him on his career as a broker in Wall Street. Still the fat, florid, flashily dressed, gross, obstreperous fellow he had been when he drove the painted wagons in New England, and an unfailing talker in vivid though ungrammatical phrase, he was a picturesque figure for the pens of newspaper writers. Not without a sense of humor, and with unheard-of impudence, he was soon the most famous mountebank, as well as the frankest voluptuary, wastrel, and all-around outlaw in New York City.

The Erie stock which Drew and his apt young "pupils" ran through the printing press in their battle with Vanderbilt flooded the market. The "Commodore" bought it, the price fluctuating until at the end of the day no one knew which party had proven itself the stronger. Clear it was, however, that Vanderbilt's "corner" had been a failure and many expected him to go under.[2] But if he faltered he did not fall beneath his great burden and public attention was directed immediately to the coup of the Erie clique, as they tried to escape process for contempt and a journey to Ludlow Street jail. Filling their pockets and gripsacks with the assets and securities of the road, Drew, Gould, Fisk, and their confidants in iniquity fled headlong out of the company's offices in the direction of the New Jersey ferry house. One, in a hackney coach, had bales containing $6,000,000 in greenbacks. Drew crossed the Hudson at once. Gould and Fisk followed under cover of night, and, lest they be espied on the way, entrusted their lives to rowboats.

In Jersey City the fugitives assembled at Taylor's Hotel, an inn near the Erie Railway station which Drew had secured

---

[1] The Book of Daniel Drew, p. 204.
[2] Ibid., pp. 225-32.

for their use, safe from the attachments of Justice Barnard and comfortable in the possession of some $7,000,000 of Vanderbilt's money with which they had come out of the struggle.[1] The disputation in the courts proceeded and was marked by incidents which were a complete disgrace to the bench and bar of New York and, indeed, to the whole judicial system of America.[2]

The Erie exiles in Jersey City pretended to believe that Vanderbilt had designs upon their persons. Thugs, it was said, had been hired by the "Commodore" to cross the river, capture the hotel which was dubbed "Fort Taylor" and seize Drew and the other conspirators. So real did the danger of an outbreak seem to be that on March 19 Drew was secreted and a standing army of Erie employees was formed to guard his liberties, while Fish commanded an improvised navy of armed boats in the river. At night the stores were closed in fear of a riot and companies of militia were held in readiness. Throughout the month alarms continued to be sounded, but, whatever ruffians may have done on their own account, it was impossible to imagine that Vanderbilt had given any encouragement to such paltry strategy.

Soon the conflict was carried to Trenton and Albany. The legislature of New Jersey promptly made the Erie Railway company a corporation of that state. The governor signed the bill. What this move meant no one knew, but it presaged very little of importance, for the real contest was to be waged in the legislature of New York state. That money was to be used and members were to be corrupted, in view of the reputation of the body, was taken for granted from the first, and so it proved to be. Votes were for sale to Vanderbilt or Drew and the ruling quotations were high. At the outset the course of events seemed to be unfavorable to the Erie men and a

[1] The Book of Daniel Drew, pp. 233-41.

[2] The entire bar of New York City was corrupted by the enormous fees which these men were willing to pay to eminent lawyers for defending them in their rascalities.—S. J. Tilden, The New York City Ring, pp. 14-15, 49-50; Bigelow, Letters and Memorials of S. J. Tilden, vol. i, pp. 299-301, 307-10.

bill in their interest was adversely reported to the Assembly
on March 27. Jay Gould was despatched to the scene,
though he like the rest was in risk of being arrested and put
into a prison cell upon coming into ׳New York state. Immediately upon his arrival in Albany, he was confronted by
officers of the law but was released on a bail bond for a
half million dollars. When he was taken to New York for a
hearing, he escaped on a subterfuge and was soon back in
Albany to play his part as a corrupt lobbyist. The tide,
responding to Erie's secret service money, turned against
Vanderbilt, the bill was passed and the Governor signed it.[1]

Vanderbilt now was tired of the contest and Drew was tired
of Jersey City. The "Commodore" smuggled a note into
Drew's hands at "Fort Taylor," suggesting a conference,
whereupon "Uncle Daniel" made a Sunday journey to New
York and met Vanderbilt at his house in Washington Square.
They patched up a truce. But the terms of the agreement
were unsatisfactory to Gould and Fisk, who had not been
invited to places at the peace table and thought that they
had been too little regarded in the settlement. To reduce
them to quiet they were given the wrecked hulk of the Erie
Railroad and, discerning in that ruin still more opportunities for plunder, they accepted the situation and turned their
minds to new contrivings.

Their first step was to establish an alliance with Tammany
Hall, so that they would be spared further annoyance by
the courts, and would fare better at Albany. At the election
in October William M. Tweed and Peter B. Sweeny, leaders
of the corrupt political ring, which was governing New York
City, and now dominated the legislature at Albany, were
added to the list of Erie directors.[2] Drew, though he thought

[1] The New York Independent called this legislature of 1868 the
"worst assemblage of official thieves that ever disgraced the capital of
the Empire State." Drew said that they were as "slippery" as "wet
eels." He speaks of paying senators $15,000 each. (White, The Book
of Daniel Drew, pp. 263-4; G. Myers, History of Tammany Hall, pp.
222-3.) This festival of bribery was made the subject of a legislative
investigation.—See N. Y. Senate Doc., 1869, no. 52.

[2] How despicable and ominous an alliance this was both in New York
and at Albany may be gleaned from Myers, History of Tammany Hall,

he had left nothing to Gould and Fisk, found that they were making money "hand over fist." [1] The printing press had been started again. Indeed, it appeared upon investigation that the stock of the corporation had been increased by 235,000 shares in four months, or from $34,265,000 on July 1, 1868, when Drew retired, to $57,766,300 on October 24 following, and without consultation with the board.

The sight of others reaping profits which he could not share in this familiar field was disquieting to Drew and he made advances to Gould and Fisk, suggesting that they jointly should organize a great "bear campaign" in Erie. Secretary McCulloch had taken the first step toward the resumption of specie payments by calling in a few millions of dollars worth of greenbacks. It was clear that if Grant were elected to the Presidency, as now seemed certain, there would be further contraction with the same ends in view. It was now the fall of the year and the crops were to be "moved," a process annually requiring a large supply of currency. It was a propitious hour. If Drew and his young associates could make money "tight" they might bring about conditions in Wall Street very favorable to their operations.

Accordingly the three men made up a pool of $14,000,000 and deposited the money in various banks. Suddenly they called for it. The bankers asked for time, but it must be paid at once. It was not procurable immediately; lenders raised their rates when they were appealed to for money; speculators who were carrying stocks threw them upon the market in self defense, and when the smoke of conflict had cleared away it was seen that the conspirators in the course of the operation to enrich themselves, with the aid of Justice

pp. 223-4. "No such power so absolute in its sway, has elsewhere manifested itself on this continent," a writer has said, speaking of the Erie-Tammany combination. "Before it the legislative, the judiciary and the executive departments of the city and state bowed in unresisting submission. Governor, mayor, judge and legislator fell down before the golden image these men had set up."—W. Jones, Life of James Fisk, Jr., p. 50.

[1] "Although Erie seemed a badly waterlogged craft there was a lot of service in her yet."—White, The Book of Daniel Drew, p. 325.

Barnard, as ready now to serve the Erie men as he had been, a few months before, to forward Vanderbilt's plans, had ruined hundreds both in and out of Wall Street, had arrested the entire business of the country for nearly a fortnight, had brought banks to the verge of suspension and had severely shaken national credit.[1] The air around them was "fire and brimstone," said Drew. He was frightened. He had not supposed that "the thing would kick up such a rumpus," so he withdrew and left his "dare-devil" partners to escape in whatever way they might.[2]

Drew now resolved upon an operation in Erie on his own account. He was always fond of the revival and class meeting. For some time now he had been a "pillar" of the church, though in younger life he had been troubled with "backslidings." As godless as he was in every fiduciary relationship, betting on horses, gambling at Saratoga, playing cards and attending the theatre were to him things of the devil. In answer to the promptings of the religious side of his nature he had just promised some "brothers in the Lord" $250,000 for a theological seminary at Madison, N. J. But when the time came to pay over the sum he frankly disliked to part with it.

Since he had left Gould and Fisk in the lurch in the campaign "to lock up greenbacks" he had been on not very cordial terms with them. He would, therefore, "put out a line of shorts" on his own account. He fell on his knees and prayed laboriously that his new undertaking might prosper for the sake of his divinity school. But the "pupils" had led their

[1] N. Y. Nation, Nov. 26, 1868.

[2] How this nefarious scheme was developed and executed is told in The Book of Daniel Drew, pp. 325-32; cf. N. Y. Nation, Nov. 26, 1868. An "extraordinary army of free-booters," "organized robber gangs," "thieves," "conspirators," the Nation called them. The "perpetrators of these outrages" would be proceeded against in the criminal courts but for the "outrageous caricature of justice" in New York. "It makes but little difference," the writer continued, "whether the fortunes thus acquired are spent in social and literary dilettantism [Gould] or in boisterous festivities [Fisk] or in the building of churches and endowment of colleges [Drew]—all good men should unite in treating the owners as infamous."

"foster parent" astray. They had changed their tactics without giving him notice of their intentions or purposes. At this time they were acting as bulls with the result that they soon caught and "squeezed" him painfully. When he met them for a settlement of the account they were unrelenting. Again there were appeals to the Tammany judges, who in the face of an opportunity further "to disgrace themselves" grasped "at the infamy as if it were a distinction." [1] Again there was a flood of writs and injunctions. Wall Street was a bedlam until the crisis was passed. The experience cost Drew nearly a million dollars.[2]

Such operations were too outrageous even for the Wall Street of that day. Erie stock was stricken from the list of calls on the Brokers' Board, though the resourcefulness of Gould and Fisk was so great that they organized a board of their own and Erie soon was quoted, and bought and sold as before.[3]

To criticism by the press they usually were oblivious. Sometimes, however, their withers were wrung and for satisfaction they would call, not vainly, upon their friends, the Tammany judges. Justice Barnard, speaking from his place on the bench, told William Cullen Bryant, who had denounced some of that man's performances in the columns of the New York Evening Post, that he was "the most notorious liar in the United States," [4] and Samuel Bowles of the Springfield Republican, who in his useful journal had addressed remarks to the Erie men, was seized by a deputy sheriff, while at a hotel in New York, attending a dinner of the New England Society, and hustled off to Ludlow Street jail. There he remained over night; they had made certain that he could not be bailed out by his friends until morning.[5]

With incredible effrontery Gould declared to an investigating committee at Albany that his conception of his responsi-

[1] N. Y. Tribune, Nov. 19, 1868.
[2] White, The Book of Daniel Drew, p. 379.
[3] Chapters of Erie, p. 76.
[4] North American Review, July, 1867, p. 158.
[5] White, The Book of Daniel Drew, pp. 34-5.

bility as an officer of the Erie Railway was to issue, before
the time set for each election, as much new stock as might
be necessary to keep the road out of the hands of Vanderbilt.[1]
He and Fisk, through Tweed's aid and the grossest bribery,
even procured the enactment by the legislature of a bill continuing in office directors who had been elected for one year for
a term of five years, thus placing themselves entirely beyond
the reach of their stockholders.[2] After it had become entirely
clear that they were outside the pale of all law, either moral
or political, Vanderbilt abandoned the contest and left them
in possession of the field.

Securely entrenched in power they now leased other railroads, bought steamboats, ferries, rolling mills and a bank,
and built branch roads and side lines. They purchased a
huge building of white marble on Eighth Avenue at Twenty-
third Street in New York where they fitted up sumptuous
offices for themselves at the expense of the corporation. Here
in "Castle Erie," as it was called, they took their stand, surrounded by ruffians, their "Erie thugs," who could be sent
hither and thither on lawless missions.

The edifice contained a large theatre or opera house, which
Fisk personally directed. By a private way he could enter his
box. Many of the opera stars and ballet dancers were added
to his harem of debauchées.[3] His interests extended to other
theatres, travelling dramatic and opera companies which he
financed, a summer garden, splendid homes for his female
favorites and gaudy equipages (sometimes drawn by six
horses; three white ones to be viewed from one side of the
street, three black ones from the other) in whose cushioned

[1] Chapters of Erie, pp. 76-7.
[2] Myers, Hist. of Tammany Hall, p. 223.
[3] "The way he would carry on with women was something scandalous; he was very carnal," said Drew. They had free access to his offices
even during business hours, and when they came in his most important
conferences were brought to an end. These "wenching bouts" with
"lulus" and "cuddlesome" women, as Fisk called them, were very trying
to the religious sensibilities of Drew. Reverting to the Scriptures, he
likened the young man to "Solomon in all his glory."—White, The
Book of Daniel Drew, pp. 218, 340-5, 369.

seats he lolled in public sight with his women at his side. On his steamboats to Fall River, on which hundreds of canary birds sang, bands of music played and the finest meals were served, he himself would appear in the magnificent dress of an admiral, by which title he was glad to be addressed. In summer time he ran handsome boats to Long Branch. His money bought him a commission in the state militia and as a "colonel" he led his regiment about with great ostentation. In his splendid offices at his opera house he called himself "Prince Erie."

The next year, 1869, opened with a raid by Fisk upon the Union Pacific Railroad. His whole investment in the company, it was said, was only $240. He demanded $100,000; if it were not paid him he would "damage" them "a million." [1] Appealing to his friend Barnard on the Tammany bench, he was able to put the company in the hands of a receiver, no other than "Boss" Tweed's son, William M. Tweed, Jr. Directors of the company were arrested. The safe was broken open, bonds and other papers were taken out, and in the struggle between the "Erie thugs" and the clerks to get possession of them many securities were lost or stolen. What could be saved from the ruffians was carried by stealth to New Jersey. To preserve the organization of this great new government trunk line it was necessary for Congress to pass a law authorizing the company to remove its offices to another city and they were taken to Boston. [2]

Vanderbilt reduced charges for the carriage of freight upon the New York Central, hoping to compel the Erie to adopt the same course. Fisk sent agents into the West to purchase large numbers of cattle, sheep and hogs. They were shipped east over the New York Central lines, occupying Vanderbilt's rolling stock in an undesirable way. Meanwhile merchants and others, desiring early delivery of their goods on the Atlantic seaboard, must pay the higher rates of the Erie Rail-

[1] House Reports, 42nd Cong. 3rd sess., no. 77, p. 106.
[2] R. Hazard, Crédit Mobilier of America, p. 32; N. Y. Herald, April 3, 4, 5, 7, 1869.

way. Vanderbilt was operating his road at a loss, and the "war" soon came to an end.[1]

The United States Express Company had a contract with the Erie Railway. Fisk and Gould "went short" of the stock and then annulled the agreement. The price of the shares fell, whereupon they "covered" their sales and at once purchased heavily for a new operation. In a little while they renewed the contract with the corporation. The stock rose again, of course, and they made another "killing." [2]

Even more outrageous was a raid upon a small local railroad called the Albany and Susquehanna, built through a difficult region among the ridges and hills of central New York. It left the New York Central line at Albany, at which place there was valuable traffic in and out of New England, and ran some 140 miles to Binghamton, where it met the Erie. Strife for the possession of this road began in January, 1869, soon following its completion. Gould and Fisk had set their eyes upon it as a "feeder," and they laid their plans to seize it. Immediately they encountered the opposition of President Joseph H. Ramsey, to whose determination and energy the construction of the road could be ascribed. For seventeen years he had stood unflinchingly behind the undertaking, and he was in no mood to give over the line to buccaneers, whose chief interest in the property was founded on nothing less than a wish to obtain a monopoly in the traffic in anthracite coal to Boston, and to fix the price which the householders of New England should pay for their fuel.

Gould and Fisk began to buy the stock of the little railroad. But much of it was held by municipalities through whose boundaries it passed, and nothing could be done quietly. Apprised of their movements Ramsey resorted to the tactics of his enemies. He distributed unissued shares to his friends. Judicial orders and injunctions followed thick and fast, as a matter of course. Justice Barnard was asked to put the road in the hands of receivers. This extraordinary limb of the law was not then in New York, and his name seems to have

---

[1] W. Jones, Life of James Fisk, Jr., pp. 287-8.
[2] J. K. Medbery, Men and Mysteries of Wall Street, p. 168.

been forged to the order, which made Fisk and another the
legally qualified custodians of the property, by somebody at
the home of one of "Prince Erie's" mistresses, to be carried
thence to his opera house, and the two men started off with
body guard on a night train to assume their duties.

Meanwhile, a counter order had been procured in Albany,
and, in accordance with its terms, another receiver to act in
Ramsey's interest was designated. A collision of forces occurred in the offices of the company and Fisk and his "boys,"
as he called them, were soon sprawling in the street. More
writs followed and the notorious man chose next to attack the
subject at the other end of the line. He, accordingly, appeared
in Binghamton and, with the aid of sheriffs, seized locomotives
and trains, installed his men in the ticket offices and freight
stations, subsequently proceeding up the road to remove Ramsey's employees and put in his own at all stopping places as
far north as Afton, some 30 miles from Binghamton, where it
was learned that the Albany party, also supplied with sheriffs,
were in force at a point some six miles farther on. The men
from the north had attached to the main track a patent frog
with which they would slide Fisk into the ditch when he came
along. The trap was not discovered until after the Erie men
ran into it, at which moment the Albany train, which lay
on a siding, moved to Fisk's rear and cut off his retreat. It
was now long past midnight, and, as day broke, the Ramsey
party steamed down toward Binghamton, replacing their recently ejected men at the stations as they passed.

The real battle was to occur near a long tunnel about 15
miles out of Binghamton. When the Albany men reached this
place they met trains which were bringing up mechanics and
laborers from the Erie shops. Whatever their zeal may have
been it was surpassed by that of the force which opposed
them. Ramsey's men had a personal attachment for him,
formed and deepened by his long struggle to build the road.
Trains loaded with the rival mobs advanced on both sides
and the locomotives met head on. The damage resulting
from the collision was only slight, but it was a signal for a
riot. The two "armies" rushed at each other, and soon the

Erie people were in demoralized retreat, scattering in all directions for their return to Binghamton. They rallied before reaching that place. Defiant shouting, some clubbing and pistol shots marked the encounter, until the drums of a regiment of the state militia were heard. Thereupon the Albany party withdrew, blocking up the tunnel with a wrecked freight car as they passed, and breaking down some bridges to prevent, or at any rate delay the pursuit of the enemy.

All New York state was aroused by these lawless performances. The whole country was repelled by such exhibitions of corporate rapacity. The case was again in the hands of the lawyers and judges pending the annual meeting of the stockholders in September. In preparation for this event Fisk hired a party of roughs in New York and, each supplied with a proxy, they were taken in a herd for a show of force in the offices of the company. Meantime Ramsey and his friends were put under arrest by some sheriff on process begun by Fisk's lawyers, and the Erie men proceeded to vote themselves into possession of the property. Ramsey and his party, however, somehow made their escape from the toils of the writ-servers and organized a meeting of their own. The rival boards-elect faced each other in the directors' room. Both declared themselves in authority, and the road's affairs were again thrown into the confusion which may ensue upon the unscrupulous use of the law by cunning attorneys and a venal bench.

It was January, 1870, before the case was decided by Justice Darwin Smith at Rochester. He found in distinct terms against Fisk and Gould, and the band of conspirators whom these two men animated and led, and, after further legal scandals aimed at a stay of the entry of judgment, a vacation of judgment, and appeal, the contest came to an end. The Erie Railway men did not obtain their coveted prey and the Albany and Susquehanna was shortly thereafter leased by the Ramsey direction to the Delaware and Hudson Canal Company, a corporation strong enough to guard its future.[1]

[1] Chapters of Erie, pp. 135-91; W. Jones, Life of James Fisk, Jr., pp. 75-81; North American Review, article, "Lawyer and Client," April, 1871.

While the attempt to steal this railroad excited the amazement and disgust of all readers of the daily press Gould and Fisk were engaged in performances which still more widely advertised their moral obliquity. They staged and directed a conspiracy in the New York gold market which convulsed the entire country. A deep laid plan to depreciate the currency was nurtured in the silent and impenetrable recesses of the mind of Gould, who, already in April, by the purchase of $7,000,000 of gold, had raised its price from 132 to 140. During the summer others joined in the speculation. He had larger plans and, if he were to execute them without too much difficulty, he must find a way to keep the government's stock of gold under lock and key until his operation was completed. He would need, therefore, to enlist the sympathy of men occupying high positions in Washington. He spun a theory about the philanthropic service which it might be to agriculture to advance the gold premium. The price of grain in New York being determined by its price in London, and not by fluctuations in the value of the American paper currency, a speculative movement of the kind which he had in mind would help the farmer and start forward the large crops in the West for export to Europe.[1]

With charity for his mask he was ready to meet guileless persons who could be useful to him in the development of his wholly malign and selfish plot. It so happened that a sister of the President of the United States had lately married a pitiable old man named Abel Rathbone Corbin[2] who lived in New York in some degree of opulence. It was to Grant's brother-in-law that Gould addressed himself. A slight acquaintance was improved until, when the President was in New York on June 15 as a guest of Mr. and Mrs. Corbin, the master criminal of Erie was allowed to call. At this time he was able to present his plan for "moving the crops." So much might have been condoned, but the President, in full knowl-

[1] House Reports, 41st Cong. 2nd sess., no. 31, p. 132.
[2] "Old Mr. Corbin, better known as the Talleyrand of America."—A lady correspondent of Andrew Johnson, June 12, 1869, in Johnson Papers.

edge as he must have been of the character of his hosts, accepted an invitation to attend a performance in Fisk's theatre, where he was publicly seen in that sinner's private box, and the next day, going to Boston for the Peace Jubilee, he was a passenger with Fisk and Gould 'on one of their fine Bristol Line steamers, where Fisk appeared in his famous "admiral's" uniform covered with gold lace and silver stars, a diamond as large as a cherry flashing under his chin, surrounded by a retinue attired like their chief in livery fit for opera bouffe. The twin miscreants of Erie somehow gained such an influence over the President that shortly afterward, on Gould's recommendation, through Corbin, Grant appointed a tool of theirs, General Butterfield, to be assistant treasurer in New York, after those ingenious gentlemen had first suggested the name of Corbin's step-son-in-law, a man named Catherwood for the place.

Again on September 2 the President was in New York on his way to Saratoga Springs. At this time, though he seems not to have seen Gould, he announced to Corbin, at whose house he was once more a guest, that he had been converted to the Erie theory about helping the Western farmer and had written to Secretary Boutwell to urge that nothing be done on the subject of government sales of gold; it would be undesirable at this time to take any action tending to depress its price. At once orders were issued to this effect. Gould had got all he came for and he had knowledge, through Corbin, of what the government would do before any officer of the government yet had this knowledge.[1] A more scandalous breach of trust, cloaked though Grant's acts so often were by his ignorance, it would be difficult to find in the history of the presidential office. Corbin's reward was large purchases of gold for the account of Mrs. Corbin by Gould, who in three or four days carried the old man a cheque for $25,000 to cover profits which had accrued from the transaction. Some

[1] Chapters of Erie, p. 117; House Reports, 41st Cong. 2nd sess., no. 31, pp. 358, 359; cf. G. S. Boutwell, Sixty Years in Public Affairs, vol. ii, pp. 160, 171.

purchases were made, too, for Mrs. Grant, it was said, though the statement later was denied, and for General Butterfield.

For a few days all went well with the campaign, but some bears came Gould's way and his complete undoing seemed imminent. He sat at his desk in the opera house, brooding in his customary silence and nervously tearing paper into bits which he threw upon the floor. It was at this point that he felt impelled to invite Fisk into the speculation. Although such a step was against his better judgment there was no choice. Fisk carried his philanthropy a step farther than Gould. He must have freights from the West for the Erie Railway in order to stop the mouths of the starving wives and children of the company's employees.[1] So he entered the market making enormous purchases. More gold was bought for Corbin and Butterfield, while some was also put to the credit of one of Grant's secretaries, General Horace Porter, who at once, however, declined all connection with the operation.

From September 10 until the 13th the President was again a guest at Corbin's house, where Gould once more appeared, full of anxiety as to the policy to be pursued by the government. At this time Grant seems to have repeated his expressions of approval of Gould's crop theory.[2] Even after the President had left New York to continue his vacation in a little town in southwestern Pennsylvania Corbin was persuaded to send him by a messenger, supplied by Fisk, a despatch bearing upon the manipulation.

Fisk was purchasing on Monday, the 20th of September, and on Tuesday and Wednesday, until the price reached 140. "In order to frighten people into buying gold" he spread the report that practically everyone in authority, from President Grant down to the doorkeepers of Congress, were interested in the speculation.[3] The excitement was intense. The whole country looked on with astonishment. Legitimate trade was

[1] House Reports, 41st Cong. 2nd sess., no. 31, pp. 171, 177.
[2] Ibid., p. 15.   [3] Ibid., p. 8.

deranged. Business men read disaster in every bulletin from the Gold Room.

Thursday, the 23rd, found Gould and Fisk in Wall Street, one entirely uncommunicative as usual, the other as noisy as a fishwoman. While Fisk was buying through an "army" of brokers Gould laid his plans for escape. Secretly he was selling, though everyone believed him still to be a bull. Fisk's wild operations carried the price to 144.

Friday was the day of uproar. Gould was selling at any price he could get while Fisk's brokers were shouting their rising bids. The Gold Room was thronged with excited men. The Stock Exchange was in a panic. The telegraph offices were blocked with messages ordering purchases and sales. The streets outside were packed with people. No description could do justice to the scene, said the New York Tribune. Nothing like it had ever been witnessed in Wall Street.[1] Fisk swaggered around in the back office of a brokerage house, issuing his orders which sent the price up to 150, then to 160, and finally to 163½. But while he was still betting that it would reach 200 the bubble burst. His agents were literally swept out of the room; no one would any longer honor his engagements and the price sank quickly to 135. Meantime a telegram from Secretary Boutwell brought an order to sell $4,000,000 of gold for the account of the government.[2]

Gould had got from under the avalanche, but Fisk was in a very different position. As usual in emergencies armed ruffians were at his call. These came to his rescue and he, as well as Gould, made their way back to the Opera House, where under such guard any one would be content to let them remain undisturbed.[3] Hundreds of firms engaged in useful branches of commerce were seriously crippled, if not completely ruined on this "Black Friday." For days importers who needed gold had been at the mercy of the gamblers and

[1] N. Y. Tribune, Sep. 25, 1869; cf. J. K. Medbery, Men and Mysteries of Wall Street, pp. 261-72.

[2] G. S. Boutwell, Sixty Years in Public Affairs, vol. ii, p. 173.

[3] Cf. J. K. Medbery, Men and Mysteries of Wall Street, pp. 235, 263-71.

suffered great losses. For weeks and months the trade of the country had been in the grip of Jay Gould.

Further audacious efforts to involve the President in the speculation were made, and Corbin went to Washington to see Grant who, however, would have no more conversation on the subject. The mission failing, it was, said Fisk in his peculiar argot, "each man drag out his own corpse. Get out of it as well as you can." [1] In their usual manner he and Gould caused a variety of injunctions and judicial orders to be issued by their friends on the Tammany bench which put the Gold Clearing House in the hands of a receiver and made immediate settlements unnecessary. Fisk repudiated his contracts amounting to $70,000,000, laying the burden on his old partner, a worthless character named Belden, who was allowed to fail in return for some sum privately settled upon him. Adjustments came finally through the courts. [2]

The subject appeared in Congress and the Committee on Banking and Currency, with Garfield at its head, instituted an investigation. The principal figures were called as witnesses and were made to testify as to the parts they had played in the disgraceful affair. [3] In its report the committee set forth the grave offenses of Fisk, Gould, Corbin, and their confederates, while exonerating the President, Mrs. Grant and Horace Porter. The Committee on Ways and Means should be instructed to inquire into the expediency of preparing a bill to levy a regulatory tax on the transactions of the Gold Exchange and the Gold Exchange Clearing House; the Commit-

[1] House Reports, 41st Cong. 2nd sess., no. 31, p. 176.
[2] How the crash affected at least one gold operator who was caught by these "welchers" is told by A. W. Dimock, Wall Street and the Wilds, chap. x.
[3] It was in this investigation that Fisk, when asked by Garfield what had become of the money, made the observation that it had "gone where the woodbine twineth." What did that mean? "Well," said Fisk, "when I was a peddler in Vermont I used to notice that the woodbine was generally hanging on to the spout." It would have been "vulgar," he declared afterward, for him to have told Garfield what he really had in mind, which was that the money had "gone up the spout." —Romantic Incidents in the Life of Fisk, p. 16; Life of James Fisk, p. 455.

tee on the Judiciary should suggest needed laws to define and punish conspiracy against the credit of the United States; the Committee on Banking and Currency should give its care to legislation designed to prevent the improper use of certified checks by national banks.

Fisk came to his not unmerited end early in January, 1872. In his velvet and diamonds, with his famous coach at the door, he was shot down on the staircase of a New York hotel by another profligate named Stokes, a rival for the affections of one of the "Erie Prince's" strumpets, Josie Mansfield. He lingered until the next morning, with a dozen physicians at his bedside, and a hundred reporters outside the door of the room in which he lay ready to despatch the account of his death to a waiting world.[1]

In death, as in life, a natural showman, his funeral was a topic of popular interest for days until his remains were finally interred in Vermont, where he had begun his career as a peddler a few years earlier. Semi-laudatory pamphlet biographies of the man appeared on the news stands and were sold on the railway trains. A large subscription "Life" was prepared and hawked by agents over all the country. The lesson of his wasted life was eloquent, but the heedless age would not pause to take it to heart.

Fisk gone, Gould held fast to the Erie property with difficulty. Only a few weeks passed before he was deserted by many who earlier had been tied to him through fear,[2] and at a special meeting, called at the instance of the English stockholders, he was deposed and General Dix was elected president of the company. This result was not achieved, however, without a characteristic struggle with the 'Erie thugs" in the Opera House building and much serving of writs.[3] Nothing availed, though Gould remained a director. The New

---

[1] N. Y. Nation, Jan. 11, 1872; White, The Book of Daniel Drew, pp. 380-4; Romantic Incidents in the Life of Fisk.

[2] The men around him who had counted on "the patient submission of the American people to never-ending wrong" fled like rats on a sinking ship.—Phila. Ledger, March 13, 1872.

[3] Cf. Jones, Life of James Fisk, Jr., pp. 499-512.

York Nation wished to see him "lodged in the penitentiary,"
and it but voiced the general opinion of decent men.[1]

From his position as a director, also, Gould soon retired,
and, with the repeal of the law corruptly enacted at Albany,
the road was returned to the hands of its *bona fide* stockholders. How such gigantic robberies could possibly be executed was not clearly understood at the time, but it was plain
that proper laws and an honest judiciary would have done
much to save the country from this series of scandals. A
call went forth for an incorruptible and a competent bench
and legislation to prohibit railway financiers from issuing
bonds convertible into stock.[2]

With the fall of Gould and Fisk as powers in Erie came
the overthrow of their political allies. An abominable ring
had been formed in the Tammany Society. It acted with the
Democratic party. Indeed, the Tammany Society was the
Democratic party in New York City. Its leader for some
years now was William M. Tweed, physically a hulking man
about 45 years of age, whose trade after he had left off chair
making, in which he had failed disgracefully as a result of
outside stock speculations, was corrupt politics. His training
as a volunteer fireman and in ward management led him by
degrees to the responsible position of grand sachem of Tammany Hall.[3] It was very plain that the taxpayers were being
robbed on a great scale. In 1866 an intelligent observer said
that the government had "fallen into complete contempt." [4]
Its "disgraceful character" in 1867 was "notorious." That
"all honest men" were absolutely excluded from "any practical control of affairs" and that "pickpockets, prize-fighters,
emigrant runners, pimps and the lowest class of liquor dealers"
were supreme in the common council were facts admitting of
no question.[5] Here in the first city of the country in population and wealth, hideous forms of inefficiency and corruption

[1] N. Y. Nation, March 14, 1872.
[2] Ibid., March 22, 1872.
[3] Myers, Hist. of Tammany Hall, pp. 212-13.
[4] North American Review, October, 1866, p. 415.
[5] Ibid., July, 1867, p. 148.

marked every department of public administration. The streets were dirty, lighting and transit systems were bad, police regulations were loose. Thousands of criminals were at large. Money would buy punishment for the innocent and escape for the guilty. The income of the municipality was large and it was being misapplied, as every one knew, without hope of redress.

The responsibility was put upon the shoulders of four men—Tweed above all others as the "Boss" of the "Ring"; A. Oakly Hall, a debonair clubman and wit, mayor of the city; Peter B. Sweeny, a gloomy, taciturn, plotting character, a lawyer credited with some ability, treasurer of the city and the county, which were coextensive for administrative purposes; and Richard B. ("Slippery Dick") Connolly, with some early experience as an accountant, a cold, crafty and insinuating figure who served as comptroller.[1] In their private inner lives all were vicious and licentious.[2] Linked together "by self interest of the most sordid kind"[3] they held in their hands the whole fiduciary authority of the city and exercised it to serve their own ends.

The menace of the members of this despotic clique was the more clearly understood when it was seen that they had laid their hands upon the judiciary. Fisk had not corrupted the courts of New York; he found them reeking with corruption; they were on the streets offering decrees and writs to the highest bidder.[4] But he so boldly invaded the halls of justice and was so unfailingly successful in obtaining what he paid for, no matter how nefarious his enterprise, that public attention was powerfully directed toward the judges and the whole system of municipal government which kept them in place. At least two justices of the Supreme Court for the New York City district, Barnard and Cardozo, were the pliant tools of

---

[1] "Tweed was the bold burglar, Sweeny the dark plotter, Connolly, the sneak thief, Hall the dashing bandit of the gang."—A. B. Paine, Life of Nast, p. 143.

[2] North American Review, October, 1874, p. 378.

[3] Ibid., p. 361.

[4] W. Jones, Life of James Fisk, Jr., p. 52.

Tammany. Both displayed intolerable venality and many
other men seated on the bench in this and in the lower courts
were to an almost equal degree a public disgrace.[1]

The strength of the "Ring" was founded upon the manipulation of the lower classes of the population. Very genial in
his manners and voluble of speech Tweed was everywhere
hail fellow well met. He stood at the head of a paternal organization which gave work to the unemployed, aided the sick
and fed the hungry, and he early attached to himself the poor
and ignorant classes recruited constantly from the immigrant
ships which were discharging their cargoes into Castle Garden.
In the days preceding each election Irishmen were naturalized
in troops. The Tammany courts were mills to grind out citizens whom Tweed's henchmen herded and marched up to the
polls to vote for his candidates. Much of this naturalization
was plainly illegal. While not quite one-half of the whole
population was foreign born [2] three-fifths of the voters of the
city by dint of the activity of the naturalization courts were
natives of foreign countries.[3] There was false registration—
scores were accredited with residence in houses where their
names were unknown; men voted more than once at different
and even at the same polling places to increase the "Ring's"
majorities. .Tabulators of election returns cheated in the count.

The members of the legislature from New York City, who
were Tweed's men, distinctly and rapidly lowered the standards of public life at Albany. He himself came to hold a seat
in the senate and was reaching out over the state. In 1868 a

[1] For an excellent presentation of this phase of the subject see North
American Review, July, 1867. Tweed "not only controlled all the local
departments but swayed every court below the court of appeals. Judges
were nominated, partly with a view to the amount they could 'put up,'
and partly with a view to their future decisions on political questions."
(Myers, History of Tammany Hall, p. 220.) Barnard had served Vanderbilt. When it was made to his advantage to serve Fisk he changed
his master. He did "whatever Tweed directed him" to do. (Ibid., p.
223.) The "Boss," said Harper's Weekly, "held judges in pay like
hounds in a leash." (Issue of Dec. 2, 1871.)
[2] F. J. Goodnow in Bryce's American Commonwealth, 1st ed., vol. ii,
p. 339.
[3] North American Review, July, 1867, pp. 150-2.

governor was to be chosen and Tammany Hall again secured the Democratic nomination for John T. Hoffman, who had been defeated by Fenton in 1866, and who now for three years in the mayor's office had done the will of the "Ring." [1] He was elected only by the grossest dishonesty. The outrages perpetrated in the city as they affected the choice of presidential electors and representatives in Congress were made the subject of an investigation by a committee of the House. They declared the frauds to have been of "monstrous proportions" and of the "most dangerous character." [2]

In the following year, 1869, the Democratic party gained a majority in the legislature and Tweed determined to secure from that body a city charter which would give him larger opportunities for his knavery. It was alleged afterward that he had expended a million dollars at Albany, upon Republican and Democratic members alike, to gain the object which he had in view. Five senators were paid $40,000 each, six $10,000 each to vote for the measure, which was passed almost unanimously. But two votes were cast against it in the senate and five in the house.[3] Hoffman signed it, as a matter of course, and, like a chained slave, New York in 1870 was delivered over to Tweed and the thieves whom he allowed to share in the enjoyment of the loot. Tweed as commissioner of public works, Sweeny as president of the park commission, Connolly as comptroller and "Elegant Oakey" Hall as mayor were the members of a "Board of Apportionment," which had entire control of the expenditures of the city. An *ad interim* "Board of Audit," composed of Tweed, Connolly and Hall, was created and it was entrusted with special and supreme

[1] For facts concerning him see North American Review, October, 1874, pp. 397-8.

[2] House Reports, 40th Cong. 3rd sess., nos. 31 and 41. Cf. Goodnow in Bryce's American Commonwealth, 1st ed., vol. ii, p. 341; North American Review, October, 1874, pp. 400-4. Tweed held back the returns from New York and Kings County (Brooklyn) to which his influence extended until it was known how many votes would be needed to meet the Republican majorities "above the Bronx." Finally it was announced that Seymour had carried the state by 10,000 and Hoffman by 28,000 majority.—Myers, Hist. of Tammany Hall, pp. 217-18; North American Review, October, 1874, pp. 404-5.

[3] Myers, Hist. of Tammany Hall, p. 227.

powers with reference to indebtedness incurred by the city before 1870.

Now the bandits were firmly in place, ready for operations larger than any they had yet dared to undertake. Their authority was so uncontrolled that the crudest methods sufficed. If some one had performed services for the city which he accounted to be worth $5,000 he would be told by one of "Slippery Dick's" agents from the comptroller's office that the sum could not be paid. If, however, the bill should be raised to $55,000 he could have his money at once. Presented with the warrant he was asked to endorse it over to one of Tweed's stoolpigeons when he would receive five $1,000 bills, the members of the "Ring" dividing among themselves the $50,000 which remained.[1]

The stealing proceeded on an imperial scale. Armories for the state militia were held to have cost the city $3,200,000. A quarter of a million dollars covered the actual expenditure of money on this account.[2] Ten lofts, mostly located over old stables, had been rented for military purposes at a charge of $85,000 and, though they had not been used, an additional charge of $463,064 was made for keeping them in repair.[3] Enough chairs were paid for at $5 each to extend, if they were put in a line, for a distance of seventeen miles.[4]

Upon the county court house, $3,000,000 were expended; the "Ring" charged the taxpayers upwards of $11,000,000 and the building was still far from complete. A man named Garvey received $2,870,464.06 for his services in plastering the walls of this and other municipal edifices.[5] Carpets for the court house represented an outlay of $350,000. Forty old chairs and three tables had cost $179,929.60. In repairing fixtures through a firm headed by a man named Keyser, in league with the robbers, $1,149,874.50 had been expended. Within a period of a few days two liverymen were

[1] N. Y. Times, July 21, 1871.
[2] Report of Joint Committee, N. Y. Times, Oct. 28, 1871.
[3] A. B. Paine, Life of Nast, p. 170.
[4] N. Y. Times, July 26, 1871.
[5] Paine, Life of Nast, p. 175; N. Y. Times, July 24, 1871.

paid $50,000 for supplying carriages to aldermen wherein they might be driven to funerals.

Asylums, hospitals, dispensaries and other institutions of which no one had ever heard, and which never existed, were the objects of largess that found its way into the pockets of the brigands.[1] They bought real estate, and sold it to the city at exorbitant sums. They owned a small newspaper in which they could insert municipal advertising, a printing house, a manufacturing stationer's plant, chair and furniture factories, and drew profits from other business enterprises which they used to mulct the taxpayers.

City and county advertising and other printing cost the city in thirty months $7,168,212.23. Some of this was more or less cheerfully paid to the large journals to close the editorial eye to the enormities going around them,[2] much more to little papers which existed merely that they might be made beneficiaries in the distribution of patronage,[3] though the greatest sum reached the New York Printing Company, the name given to the "Ring's" own publishing house.[4] To this huge total on account of the press must be added a multitude of sinecures, created for and held by journalists, that the newspapers might be the more unlikely to engage in criticism.[5]

The three members of the "Board of Audit," created for no

---

[1] Myers, Hist. of Tammany Hall, p. 229.

[2] "There is not another government in the world," said the New York World on June 13, 1871, "which combines so much character, capacity, experience and energy as are to be found in the city government of New York under the new charter." (A. B. Paine, Life of Nast, p. 146.) The Herald found that the "crop" of "humbug reformers" which had sprung up in New York were mere selfish persons who had not had enough "city printing and advertising." The Times and Harper's Weekly were making "this parade of alleged extravagance, overtaxation and fraud" with the "intention of having their silence purchased by what they call the "Ring." (N. Y. Herald, July 4, 1871.) The Times had "sunk into a tedious monotony of slander, disregard of truth and blackguard vituperation," said the New York Sun.—Issues of Feb. 3 and 4, 1871.

[3] The "Ring's" Transcript, which three men had founded with a capital of $250, got more than three quarters of a million, while the New York Tribune's share in the same time was $54,000.—North American Review, January, 1875, p. 123.

[4] A. B. Paine, Life of Nast, p. 175.

[5] North American Review, January, 1875, p. 124.

purpose except *ex post facto* theft, signed orders for $6,000,000, representing value received by the city of barely $600,000. In this steal Tweed's share was 24 per cent, Connolly's 20 per cent, and Sweeny's 10 per cent, their confederates being assigned portions in accordance with a definite scale.[1]

Tweed was almost as famous a figure in New York as Fisk. His hands, it seemed, were "everywhere and wherever they were they were feeling for money."[2] His shirt front flashed with diamonds. His favorite retreat was the sumptuously furnished Americus Club whose members wore diamond badges. He removed from a small house to a large mansion on Fifth Avenue where he gave his daughter a wedding, the vulgar extravagance of which arrested the notice of the country. Upon his summer home at Greenwich, Conn., he expended a fortune. His stables, the stalls of which were built of the finest mahogany, were filled with blooded steeds. He boasted that soon he would be as rich as Vanderbilt.[3]

Unpleasant rumors were stilled during the campaign culminating in November, 1870, by calling upon a committee of wealthy men, including John Jacob Astor, Moses Taylor and Marshall O. Roberts, to visit Connolly's offices and examine his accounts. After six hours they went out ready to publish a statement that the city's financial affairs were being administered in "a correct and faithful manner."[4]

Aided by such devices Hall was re-elected mayor and Hoffman was re-elected governor. The "Ring" was now at the height of its power. Having advanced from New York to Albany the leaders fixed their eyes on Washington. Hoffman, it was seriously asserted and believed, would be the Democratic nominee for the presidency in 1872. Tweed, overworked and in need of a rest, was to be minister to England.[5]

---

[1] North American Review, October, 1876, p. 381; N. Y. City Ring, p. 24.   [2] Ibid., January, 1875, p. 130.
[3] See Harper's Weekly, Sep. 2, 1871, for illustrations of the summer homes of Tweed and other Tammany leaders.
[4] See, e.g., N. Y. Herald, Nov. 6, 1870. Cf. Myers, Hist. of Tammany Hall, pp. 231-2; North American Review, July, 1875, pp. 138-9.
[5] North American Review, January, 1875, p. 129. "These gusts of reform are all wind and clatter," said Oakey Hall, "next year we shall be in Washington."—Paine, Life of Nast, p. 164.

As a Christmas Day offering in 1870 Tweed gave $50,000 to the poor of his ward, and $1,000 to each of a number of aldermen to be used for the purchase of coal for needy families in their respective neighborhoods.[1] It was even proposed by the New York Sun that a statue of the man should be erected in commemoration of his services and benefactions, and an association was formed to sponsor the enterprise.[2] When this plan came to naught, through Tweed's declining the honor, the Sun suggested the erection and endowment of a "great monument of public charity" to be known as the "Tweed Hospital." [3]

But deep resentment at the sight of so much of Tweed's activities as could be seen and comprehended was surging in the breasts of several potential men. He boastfully and brazenly asked "What are you going to do about it?" but his downfall was not far away. The newspaper press had been stilled for the most part by public advertising; two voices could not be silenced by such bribery—the New York Times, now controlled by George Jones, whose editor was a fearless Englishman, Louis J. Jennings,[4] and Harper's Weekly which printed cartoons of telling force by Thomas Nast, with the

[1] Myers, Hist. of Tammany Hall, p. 230. By his "charities" Tweed like so many of his kind gained a high reputation. As he distributed what he had stolen he was hailed as a great philanthropist. Everywhere men said—"Well, if Tweed stole he was at least good to the poor." (Ibid., p. 230.) He had "a great, good heart." (Romantic Incidents in the Life of James Fisk, Jr., a contemporary pamphlet.) This virtue was also Fisk's at whose funeral Tweed was one of the chief mourners. "Fisk, sir, is an immense loss to New York," Tweed said to a reporter. "No other man can take his place. . . . He was generous as the day, always helping somebody, always giving some poor fellows work to support them when things were dull. . . . His money was always going."—Ibid.; cf. North American Review, October, 1876, p. 394.

[2] N. Y. Sun, March 14 and 15, 1871. The Sun called Tweed "the great New York philanthropist," a "noble benefactor of the people," etc. Here is to be found the measure of the moral quality of Mr. Dana even thus early in his career as a journalist.—Cf. Myers, Hist. of Tammany Hall, pp. 233-4; Paine, Life of Nast, pp. 159-60; N. Y. Nation, March 16 and 30, 1871.

[3] Issue of May 13, 1871; cf. Myers, Hist. of Tammany Hall, p. 234.

[4] Harper's Weekly, July 15, 1871.

support of Fletcher Harper of Harper and Brothers, the publishers of the periodical. Their criticism, running through 1870 and the first months of 1871, was felt, but they were acting in large degree upon evidence founded on mere suspicion. The rich men who had endorsed Tweed's government did so, it was said, because of a knowledge that if they reached any other conclusion the assessments on their real estate holdings would have been greatly increased. An emissary offered Jones $1,-000,000 for his silence.[1] Tweed sought to buy the Raymond interest in the Times which would have given him control of the journal; he was thwarted in the nick of time by Jones who by good fortune had learned of the scheme.[2] In revenge suit was begun by the Tammany Ring to eject the Times from its publication offices in Park Row on the ground of imperfect title to the property, but with no more success.[3] If Nast would go to Europe and cease caricaturing the robbers a half million dollars would be put at his disposal.[4] It was hoped that Fletcher Harper might be reached by Tweed giving orders to the Board of Education to purchase no more school books from the firm of publishers of which he was a member. Even those in hand, bearing the Harper imprint, valued at more than $50,000, were destroyed that they might be replaced by books manufactured by the "Ring's" printing company.[5] But of such fibre were these men that chicanery of this kind only increased their determination to pursue the subject to the end.

A train of circumstances favored those who were bent upon the exposure of the "Ring's" immeasurable villanies. The county auditor, a low wretch named Watson who had "crept into the City Hall out of Ludlow Street Jail," [6] was fatally

---

[1] Paine, Life of Nast, p. 153.
[2] North American Review, July, 1875, pp. 152-3.
[3] Harper's Weekly, Sep. 9, 1871.
[4] Paine, Life of Nast, pp. 181-2. "It is doubtful," says Paine, "if caricature in any nation had ever approached in public importance such work as this. Certainly America had never seen its like."—Ibid., p. 192.
[5] Ibid., p. 158.   [6] North American Review, July, 1875, p. 117.

injured while riding behind a span of his fine trotters in a
sleigh in Harlem Lane in January, 1871. As he lay on his
death bed his house was guarded by a band of Tammany
thugs lest at the last hour his conscience should lead him to
make compromising disclosures. He left his accounts, particularly with reference to the "Ring's" great job of widening
Broadway, in much confusion,[1] and the embarrassment of
Tweed and his confederates was so plain that still more men
were made to believe in the merit of the movement to un-
cover their rascalities and drive them from power.

These thieves, like others, were soon to fall out. The knowledge that there were newspapers which would give notoriety
to informers was a standing menace. A number of smaller
leaders had combined, calling themselves the "Young Democracy." Affront had been done them by Tweed, when under
pressure of public opinion, he had told the judges to visit
more severe punishment upon criminals,[2] and one of these,
named O'Brien, who earlier had been sheriff (acting on the
advice of Samuel J. Tilden, whose pathway the "Ring" had
most unwisely crossed in bringing forward Hoffman as their
presidential candidate, and who now, as a state and national
leader, though he had been in some degree in their confidence,
saw the immediate need of dissociating himself in the most
public manner from the whole Tammany organization)[3] visited Jennings in the office of the Times one night in the summer of 1871 with transcripts taken from Connolly's books.

Another man named O'Rourke came forward with material
of the same kind. Again Jones was tendered a bribe; this
time Connolly himself offered it—he would pay $5,000,000
for immunity from exposure [4]—but the Times on July 8, 1871,

---

[1] Cf. North American Review, January, 1875, pp. 144-6.

[2] Myers, Hist. of Tammany Hall, p. 225.

[3] Paine, Life of Nast, p. 166; North American Review, July, 1875,
pp. 131-2, and October, 1876, pp. 368-9. Tilden's account of his course
at this time in the pamphlet, The New York City Ring, 1873, indi-
cates clearly, however large and important his services may have been,
that he was acting as a Democrat for his party rather than as an
outraged citizen.

[4] Paine, Life of Nast, p. 170.

began the publication of the transcripts of the comptroller's books, enforcing its points with trenchant editorial articles, while Nast tirelessly continued to direct his accusatory drawings at the culprits, who now were seen for the unmitigated robbers which they were and long had been.

In the midst of this popular outburst Hall, to please the Hibernians, most stupidly forbade a parade of Orangemen. It was an attack upon the Protestant Irish to propitiate the more numerous Catholic Irish, and the "Ring" was set upon by newspapers which hitherto had defended it. Governor Hoffman at the last hour rescinded the mayor's order. The Orangemen were marching in Eighth Avenue on July 10, 1871, under the escort of a body of militia. Ruffians filled the streets. Missiles were flung in all directions. Arms were discharged promiscuously. The mob killed a woman who was waving a handkerchief in expression of her sympathy for the paraders, as well as a little girl who stood at her side. In a moment a soldier was shot down, whereupon the military opened fire. The ruffians fled, leaving nearly a hundred dead and wounded behind them.[1] It was a sorry day for Tweed; the storm was gathering fast.

A mass meeting was called for Cooper Institute on September 4, 1871. Not all who came could be packed into the hall. Another meeting must be organized in the street outside which was addressed by speakers who stood on the top of a hogshead. In Cooper Institute the venerable ex-Mayor W. F. Havemeyer presided. Scores of well known men were numbered among the vice presidents, some of them, including Edwards Pierrepont, Robert B. Roosevelt, and Oswald Ottendorfer, delivering addresses in angry and determined mood. Resolutions which were read by Joseph H. Choate were passed and the chairman, Havemeyer, was authorized to appoint a citizens' Committee of Seventy to wage unrelenting war upon the "Ring."[2]

Immediately Tweed, Sweeny and Hall took counsel to-

[1] Harper's Weekly, July 29, 1871.
[2] N. Y. Tribune, Sep. 5, 1871.

gether and decided that they would make Connolly the scape-goat. Mayor Hall would appoint a committee of eight city officials and sixteen taxpayers, usually called the "Joint Committee," or the "Booth Committee," to investigate the comptroller's accounts. But Connolly was not willing to be placed in such a position, and on the night prior to the day when the examination of the papers was to begin, September 11, 1871, some one cut a hole in a window pane of his office in City Hall large enough to admit the arm of a man who unfastened the catch, entered, took away the vouchers and burned them.[1] Hall, playing his part, asked Connolly to resign,[2] but, under the advice of Havemeyer and Tilden,[3] he refused, appointing a Democrat of high character, Andrew H. Green, as his deputy.

This turn in affairs was very alarming to Hall, Tweed and the rest. They sought to force Connolly from his office; if he should vacate it Mr. Green's functions as deputy would cease automatically. But he withstood their importunities. The examination of the records by both committees and also by the Democratic leaders, interested in clearing the party of such disgrace, proceeded actively. Tilden now came forward with some startling computations, made up in Green's office from the books of the Broadway Bank. It was alleged and substantiated in an unmistakable way that in accounts against the city totalling several millions two-thirds of the whole amount had stuck to the fingers of Tweed and his friends.[4] It appeared that in 1869, 66 per cent, and later 85 per cent of all the city's expenditures had found their way into the pockets of the members of the "Ring."[5] A private corporation with the same budget, it was said, if honest, business-like principles had been followed, would have been conducted for one-tenth of what had been spent to "govern" New York. The debt of the city had been increased from $36,000,000

[1] Myers, Hist. of Tammany Hall, p. 240.
[2] S. J. Tilden, N. Y. City Ring, pp. 42-3.
[3] Letters and Memorials of S. J. Tilden, vol. i, pp. 278-80; North American Review, October, 1876, pp. 376-8.
[4] S. J. Tilden, N. Y. City Ring, p. 46.
[5] Ibid., p. 25; Myers, History of Tammany Hall, p. 229.

in 1868, to more than $136,000,000 at the end of 1870.[1] The
total amount stolen by the "Ring" has been computed vari-
ously at from $45,000,000 to $200,000,000.[2]

The reformers, with the aid of Mr. Tilden and Charles
O'Conor, soon had enough evidence in hand for a series of
prosecutions. On October 27, at the height of the campaign
to redeem the city, led by the Committee of Seventy, Tweed
had been arrested, to be held in $1,000,000 bail, which was
provided largely by a son to whom he had transferred a considerable amount of property, and by his obliged friend Jay
Gould.[3] It was a desperate struggle between the good and
the evil forces of the community. Eminent preachers in their
churches besought the people to vote Tammany out of power.
On election day, November 7, the stores were closed, business was suspended, the streets were silent. The whole city
dedicated itself to the work at the polls and the "Ring" was
repudiated and condemned by sweeping majorities.

Sweeny instantly resigned from his place on the park commission; Connolly retired in favor of his deputy, Green; while
Tweed, who had held his legions together sufficiently to be
returned to his seat in the state senate, though he was out
of prison only by the grace of bondsmen, also saw the handwriting on the wall, and on December 28 relinquished his office as commissioner of public works. Oakey Hall, who always pretended to innocence and succeeded in deceiving a
number of gullible men, including Horace Greeley,[4] continued
to serve as mayor until the expiration of his term a year later.

A number of the rascals, beginning with the "plasterer,"
Garvey, boarded steamers for Europe or fled to Canada.[5]
Many indictments and trials ensued. Connolly was arrested
on November 25. His bail was $1,000,000. He offered to
settle for a large sum, but more, which he would not pay, was
demanded. He attempted flight, but he was caught and sent

[1] Myers, History of Tammany Hall, p. 237.
[2] Ibid., p. 297; Paine, p. 176; N. Y. Herald, Jan. 13, 1901.
[3] North American Review, October, 1876, p. 392.
[4] Ibid., p. 382; Harper's Weekly, Dec. 9, 1871.
[5] North American Review, October, 1876, p. 383.

to jail where he remained until January, 1872. Then he secured bail and joined the "Americans abroad," the number of
whom was increasing with the departure of each transatlantic
steamship, carrying away with him spoil enough to live in
luxury for the rest of his life. Sweeny also fled. He had
pocketed and saved enough to enable him a few years later [1]
to pay $400,000 for the satisfaction of claims upon him so
that he might return home. "Elegant Oakey" escaped a verdict, through the death of a juror on his first trial, and through
a disagreement of the twelve men selected to determine his
guilt on the second occasion in which his case came up in
court. He joined the expatriates in Europe. Returning to
New York he sought to be an actor, but, failing, he eked out
a living by a petty law practise and as a comic journalist.
The world was reminded of his continued existence in 1889
when he entered suit to protect his honor from animadversions
made upon it in the first edition of Bryce's American Commonwealth. That ruffian of the New York City bench, Justice
Barnard, with as infamous a name as American judge ever
bore, and Justice McCunn were impeached at Albany and
removed from office, while Cardozo, to escape a like fate, resigned.[2]

Some minor officials and contractors involved in the robberies were sent to prison, but of the "Ring's" leaders only
Tweed met his merited punishment. In December, 1871, he
was indicted, but his friend, Judge Barnard, whose downfall
had not yet been accomplished, released him on a trivial bond
of $5,000.[3] He was re-indicted and re-arrested at about the
time of Hall's acquittal. Twice in 1873 he was tried;[4] the
first time the jury disagreed, some of his friends having been
smuggled into the panel; the second time he was found guilty
and sentenced to twelve years in prison and the payment of
fines amounting to more than $12,000. At last he was in the
felon's garb in which Nast so long had shown him.

[1] In 1877. See Paine, Life of Nast, pp. 188-9, notes.
[2] Goodnow in Bryce's American Commonwealth, 1st ed., p. 350; cf.
North American Review, October, 1876, pp. 393-405.
[3] Harper's Weekly, Jan. 6, 1872.
[4] The Erie lawyer, David Dudley Field, very fittingly, defended him.

After a year on Blackwell's Island he was set free by a decision of the court of appeals, but was re-arrested to answer new suits, his bail being fixed on this occasion at $3,000,000. So large a sum was beyond the reach of such friends as remained to him, and he lay in prison until December, 1875, when he escaped. In hiding for a time in and around New York, he made his way on a schooner to Florida, whence he proceeded to Cuba. There he was recognized, and soon boarded a small sailing vessel, bound for Vigo in Spain. But his flight did not avail him for he fell into the hands of the authorities, who delivered him up to the officers of a United States war ship, which brought him back to New York on November 23, 1876. He was re-committed to prison. Further attempts to effect a settlement of the claims upon him and secure his release were futile and sixteen months later he died in Ludlow Street jail.[1]

The pursuit of men guilty of corrupt and criminal practices reached the state and Federal governments. What was going on in the South was ascribed to the unsettlement following the war and a mistaken policy with reference to reconstruction. But in some of the Northern states the conditions were not better. In Nebraska the gravest charges were preferred against the governor, the treasurer and some other officers. The governor was impeached, the accusations against him covering the collection of $17,000 of school money and the conversion of it to his own uses, the sale of appointive offices, the location and erection of public buildings with profit to himself, demands upon creditors of the state for commissions before he would agree to the payment of their claims. He was tried. On the charge that he had embezzled money collected for the schools he was convicted and removed from office.[2]

In 1872 the legislature of Kansas began the investigation of reports current for some time concerning the bribery which

[1] April 12, 1878. Cf. Myers, History of Tammany Hall, pp. 245-7. An excellent history of the "Ring" and its downfall is to be found in four articles in the North American Review for October, 1874, January and July, 1875, and October, 1876, by Charles F. Wingate.
[2] American Annual Cyclopedia for 1871, article on Nebraska.

had marked the election by that body of United States senators in 1867 and 1871. A joint committee was named and the testimony of such witnesses as had not fled the state was taken. It was found that money was corruptly used, that offices were bartered away and sold in the contest in 1867 which had resulted in the election of Samuel C. Pomeroy, and that when Alexander Caldwell was chosen to succeed Ross in 1871 the most infamous methods had been resorted to. Caldwell openly said, so the committee averred, that he had paid for his seat "twice as much as the salary of the office for the full term of six years would amount to, or about $60,000." [1]

While this scandal was still being discussed Pomeroy's term again expired, and he was again a candidate to succeed himself. A member of the state legislature, named York, alleged that the senator, whose record at Washington had been under a cloud for many years, had paid him (York) $7,000 in greenbacks for his vote. These and like revelations led to the unanimous choice in 1873 of John J. Ingalls in the place of Pomeroy, who in spite of various explanations and denials [2] left Washington in complete disgrace. His associate, Caldwell, resigned during the progress of proceedings which would have deprived him of his seat. [3]

The treasurer of Pennsylvania, William H. Kemble, later convicted of bribery and sentenced to prison, succinctly stated his rule for the public service in the phrase "addition, division and silence," which was echoed up and down the country for many years. [4] The code of official honor in a state which stood under the controlling influence of Simon Cameron was little if any higher than it had been shown to be in New York during the developments in connection with the Erie Railway scandals.

Such moral views in public life as they came to fruit in the Federal service led to a prolonged discussion in the Senate of

[1] American Annual Cyclopedia for 1872, article on Kansas.
[2] Senate Reports, 42nd Cong. 3rd sess., no. 523.
[3] American Annual Cyclopedia for 1872 and 1873, articles on Kansas; Senate Reports, 42nd Cong. 3rd sess., no. 451.
[4] J. H. Wilson, Life of C. A. Dana, p. 427.

the United States in December, 1871, by leaders like Trumbull
and Schurz. Senator Patterson, chairman of the Joint Committee on Retrenchment, had made a report with respect to
abuses and frauds in the New York custom house.[1] The taking of bribes by inspectors, weighers and other officers, and,
worse than all, the warehousing privileges bestowed upon political favorites, formed a setting for most unpleasant revelations.

It was clear enough that the custom house was a "party
engine." [2] It had as many as 1,500 employees, many of them
Republican henchmen who gave no services in return for the
salaries which were paid them. It sank deeper and deeper
into the mire of politics after Grant appointed Thomas Murphy to be its chief officer. A young man named Leet had
been on Grant's staff during the war. He messed in Washington with the President's private secretaries, Generals Porter
and Babcock, and had back stairs access to the Executive
Mansion. While he was still drawing pay as an officer of the
army he carried confidential information to Moses H. Grinnell who was to be appointed collector of the port of New
York, and of whom Leet sought privileges for himself and a
partner named Bixby in connection with the "general order"
business. There had grown up a mischievous custom by which
merchandise upon its arrival, if it were not claimed by the
importer almost at once, would be conveyed to private store
houses. In this event the consignee would be obliged to pay
the cartage and the storekeeper's charges for a month, though
the goods should remain on his premises for but a single day.

Grinnell thinking, as it appeared, that it was Grant's desire, gave all the business of this kind, arising out of merchandise shipments by the Cunard and Bremen lines, to Leet, who
after a while was not satisfied. He would have a larger share
of the trade and his not receiving it from Grinnell seems to
have been a factor in that officer's displacement in favor of
Murphy, in all probability as incompetent and as thoroughly

[1] Senate Reports, 41st Cong. 3rd sess., no. 380.
[2] Ibid., 42nd Cong. 2nd sess., no. 227, p. cxvi.

corrupt a man as ever held the office. With Murphy's favor pledged him Leet resigned from the army, availing himself of his right under the law to one year's pay as a lieutenant-colonel, and formed a partnership with another young man named Stocking, whereupon he extended his operations, until he was in possession of a practical monopoly of the North River "general order" business.

Their administration of the warehouses became "grossly exacting and oppressive to the merchants of New York." [1] The concession was supposed to be worth from $100,000 to $200,000 a year. It was held to be the most valuable perquisite in the gift of the President, barring, perhaps some of the Indian agencies. When Secretary Boutwell asked that the system be abolished his recommendations were disregarded. Grant was directly appealed to by A. T. Stewart and other merchants without avail. Each of two young upstarts was receiving an income at least double that of the President of the United States "for putting an obstruction in the pathway of lawful commerce." [2]

Just before the Patterson Committee made its report Murphy resigned to receive a most effusive letter of appreciation and regret from Grant,[3] and Chester A. Arthur was installed in his place. No change in the system being immediately in prospect, the Senate, as a result of the discussion of the Patterson report, appointed a special committee to investigate the subject. The hearing of witnesses in New York and Washington continued for months. Before it was ready to report the President was compelled to notice the scandal; as a result of the sensational exposures Arthur was directed to institute obviously necessary reforms and the careers of Leet and Stocking came to an end.[4]

Even before the trunk line between Omaha and Sacramento

[1] Senate Reports, 42nd Cong. 2nd sess., no. 227, p. xlix.
[2] Horace White, Life of Trumbull, p. 365.
[3] N. Y. Nation, Nov. 23, 1871; Senate Reports, 42nd Cong. 2nd sess., no. 227, pp. cxlii-cxliii.
[4] The testimony fills three large volumes, Senate Reports, 42nd Cong. 2nd sess., no. 227.

had been completed rumors affecting the honesty of its construction and management were put into circulation. The conviction that they were true deepened because of the unconcealed distrust which one of the companies expressed for the other. The Central Pacific, its vice president Collis P. Huntington averred, had been occupied in climbing the Sierras, which had required the construction of 15 tunnels at a cost on some portions of the route of $200,000 a mile. While he and his associates had been building 17 miles in the mountains the Union Pacific, with a smaller force of men, had laid down 400 miles on the plains.

It was complained that the company engaged in constructing the eastern end of the line had gone around obstacles to avoid tunnels, and had built temporary tracks in the interest of economy and speed, without regard to the location approved by the Secretary of the Interior. In a word they had skimped their work and were hurrying forward to gain the trade of Salt Lake City, coal mines in the Wahsatch Mountains and the subsidies which they would receive, if they should be able to reach an objective in advance of the other company. President Johnson was urgently asked by Mr. Huntington not to allow the Union Pacific to go west of Echo Summit.[1]

A government director, C. H. Snow, in February, 1869, wrote to President Johnson that the ties laid down by the Union Pacific company were of cottonwood and mountain pine, both unfit for the use. Since leaving Laramie a few days before four engines on his train had been disabled, mishaps which he attributed to the condition of the roadbed. At some places, he said, it was unsafe to run at a speed of twelve miles an hour. Not enough earth had been removed from the cuttings. Fillings were not brought to grade. Sections on which the levelling had not been finished, where, indeed, ties or rails had not yet been brought upon the ground, had been accepted by the commissioners and bonds had been issued.[2]

[1] Letter of C. P. Huntington, Jan. 19, 1869, in Johnson Papers; J. P. Davis, The Union Pacific Railway, p. 150.
[2] Johnson Papers.

Even before the road was completed the dispute as to the junction point of the two lines found its way into Congress with many expressions of suspicion touching the management of the companies and their relations with the government.[1]

The hints and charges particularly involved the Crédit Mobilier which had been engaged in building that part of the road assigned to the Union Pacific. It is likely that no more would have been heard of the sins of this corporation with the strange and mysterious syllables than of a company employed in a similar manner in laying the tracks of the Central Pacific,[2] but for a quarrel of Colonel H. S. McComb of Delaware, one of the stockholders, with his associates, particularly with Oakes Ames, who had made himself a commanding figure in the direction of the road's affairs.

This man and his brother Oliver were enterprising and wealthy manufacturers of shovels and other tools in Easton, Mass.[3] They had brought capital to the aid of the undertaking when it was sorely needed and had put to rout those men, from President Durant downward, who had been battening on the treasury of the company.[4] Oakes Ames was full of patriotic zeal for the work. No labor was too arduous, no sacrifice too great for him, and his initial investment was in excess of $1,000,000. Confident of a successful result he had risked everything he possessed to send the road striding westward over desolate wastes, through impenetrable mountains and across high cold tablelands on its way to the Pacific Ocean. At one time he had been compelled to suspend payments in his own business in Massachusetts and ask his creditors for an extension that he might execute his railroad contracts and bring to completion the great public improvement whose cause he had so energetically espoused.[5]

[1] J. P. Davis, The Union Pacific Railway, pp. 204-6.
[2] J. B. Crawford, Crédit Mobilier of America, p. 77.
[3] An old business inherited from their father. Their product was widely known. "The Ames shovel was legal tender in every part of the Mississippi Valley."—E. L. Sabin, Building the Pacific Railway, p. 71.
[4] Cf. Crawford, p. 91; Davis, Union Pacific Railway, p. 167.
[5] Crawford, p. 58.

McComb declared that he was entitled to $25,000 worth of Crédit Mobilier stock which he had not received. No one else thought so. It was a baseless claim. Indeed, there was a distinct understanding in writing that some shares still in the company's treasury should be confided to Durant and Ames. What Ames had received, he told McComb, he had put into the hands of influential men whose interest, if it could be elicited in the company's behalf, would give it strength. A direct, outspoken man he was unfortunate in the choice of his words, and when he wrote that the stock had been placed where it would "protect us" and "do most good," [1] and that he "wanted more friends in Congress," [2] McComb was in a position to act vindictively.

For some years Ames had held a seat in the House of Representatives for a Massachusetts district. It was in the closing months of 1867 that he had approached his friends in Washington, or they had approached him on the subject, as the case may have been,[3] and McComb's claim soon afterward appeared in the courts. A settlement was proposed by the lawyers. If this were not agreed to the letters would be published and the fame of many a man high in the counsels of the government would be smirched. Ames declared that he feared no exposure.[4] No idea of bribery had ever found lodgment in his mind; he would not be coerced into the payment of any sum which he did not fairly owe.

At last in 1872 the letters came out in the columns of the New York Šun under a caption—"The King of Frauds—How the Crédit Mobilier Bought its Way into Congress," etc.[5] The presidential canvass was at its height. Many of the accused were candidates before the people for re-election and they were thrown into a panic. For a certainty a reaction

---

[1] Crawford, pp. 104, 107.　　[2] Ibid., p. 110.
[3] Many most urgently besought him to let them have stock in the company as soon as it gave promise of showing profits and of advancing in price.—Ibid., pp. 103, 179.
[4] R. Hazard, Crédit Mobilier of America, p. 33.
[5] Issue of Sep. 4, 1872. Cf. Crawford, p. 101. For text of letters see ibid., pp. 104-10.

had set in against the war gambler, the promoter of railroads
and corporate wealth in all its shapes and guises. The trans-
gressions of the Crédit Mobilier were made to appear so fla-
grantly wicked that many, who a little while ago were glad to
have the friendship of Mr. Ames and were begging him for
favors, now fled from him as if he were contamination and
denied all knowledge of the company of which he was the head.
The presumption that in these denials they were not telling
the truth and that their and his misbehavior had taken the
most disgraceful forms spread like wild fire.[1]

Soon Congress gave its attention to the case. At the opening of the session in December, 1872, the Speaker, James G.
Blaine, whose name was being bandied about in connection
with the scandal, called S. S. Cox to the chair and moved
the appointment of a committee to find out whether any members of the House had been bribed by the corporation or its
officers and agents. Luke P. Poland of Vermont was made the
chairman of the committee, and it proceeded to hear witnesses
and take evidence. A few weeks later another committee,
under the chairmanship of J. M. Wilson of Indiana, was assigned the task of inquiring whether the government had been
in any way defrauded by the Crédit Mobilier. The two committees proceeded with their investigations simultaneously,
the country resounding with the disclosures day by day, as
soon as the injunction of secrecy which had but increased
popular suspicion was removed, and the doors were opened to
the reporters.

The testimony offered before the Poland Committee affected
Vice President Colfax, Speaker Blaine, John A. Logan, Roscoe Conkling, Henry Wilson, Henry L. Dawes, John A. Bingham, George S. Boutwell, James A. Bayard, William D. Kelley, James F. Wilson, William B. Allison, James Brooks,
James W. Patterson, B. M. Boyer and Glenni W. Scofield. Blaine, Conkling, Boutwell and Bayard were eliminated. No evidence was at hand to indicate that they had
had from Ames anything more than tenders of stock which they

[1] Crawford, p. 111.

had declined to receive. Senator Henry Wilson of Massachusetts had taken twenty shares for Mrs. Wilson and paid cash for it, but upon reflection he asked if he might return it. It was returned and thus had he escaped damage to his reputation. Henry L. Dawes of Massachusetts, who had had ten shares, also asked to be relieved of his obligations, and was reimbursed for his outlay. He returned such dividends as he had received, except ten per cent which was allowed him for the use of his money. Glenni W. Scofield, a representative in Congress from Pennsylvania, who, like Dawes, had taken ten shares, withdrew from the speculation in a somewhat similar way.

Logan was assigned ten shares and seems to have accepted them, without advancing any money and without delivery of the stock certificates into his hands, with the understanding that they were to be paid for from dividends. In due time he received a check on the sergeant-at-arms of the House for $329, a sum to his credit over and above the cost price. He cashed it. In a few days or weeks, doubtful about his position in the matter, he returned it to Ames. Garfield, Kelley and James F. Wilson similarly received checks for $329 on stock which Ames was carrying for them without risk on their parts. They also cashed the checks. To Kelley a further payment of $750 was made. Allison likewise received ten shares which cost him nothing. In June, 1868, Ames gave him a check for $600, a sum due him on account of dividends after deducting the purchase price. He cashed the check, but, in fear of the consequences, returned the money to Ames, though he had done this only after the commencement of the investigation.

B. M. Boyer, a representative from Pennsylvania, had taken 75 shares for his wife. It was "a legitimate stock operation," he said. He never denied making the investment which had "turned out to be profitable." His only regret was "that it was no larger in amount." What he had done was in his judgment "both honest and honorable."

Senator Patterson of New Hampshire held 30 shares for

which he paid Ames $3,000. He subsequently received considerable sums in cash and Union Pacific stock and bonds as dividends on his investment. James Brooks owned 100 shares of Crédit Mobilier, as well as some Union Pacific stock and bonds which he had demanded of Durant. He seems to have paid for them, but as he was a government director of the road, he chose to carry them in the name of his son-in-law, a man named Neilson. The dividends were forwarded to Neilson who immediately transferred them to the real owner. Subsequently Brooks had come to be the holder of 50 additional shares of Crédit Mobilier stock on the same terms.

Schuyler Colfax had 20 shares which were to be paid for out of dividends. When his indebtedness had been reduced to $534.72 the Speaker of the House, or the Vice President of the United States, as he may have been at the time, sent Ames a check for the amount, thus coming into ownership of the stock. To cover further dividend payments Ames testified that he had given Colfax a check for $1,200.

The Poland Committee found Ames "guilty of selling to members of Congress shares of stock in the Crédit Mobilier of America for prices much below the true value of such stock, with intent thereby to influence the votes and decisions of such members in matters to be brought before Congress for action." They recommended his expulsion from his seat in the House.[1] Brooks, whose eloquence as a leader of the opposition had so often resounded in the hall, was also to be expelled for procuring stock for his son-in-law, intended for and applied to his own use, and for his own benefit. As a government director he had been doubly culpable for his misconduct.[2]

For the consideration of the cases of such senators as might be involved in the scandal there was a committee in the upper branch of Congress under the chairmanship of Mr. Morrill of Maine. Its report recommended that Senator Patterson be expelled from his seat,[3] though what he had done that was

---

[1] House Reports, 42nd Cong. 3rd sess., no. 77, p. xix.
[2] Ibid.
[3] Senate Reports, 42nd Cong. 3rd sess., no. 519, p. ix.

in any manner more contumacious than the offenses of several other persons who were named in the disclosures, no judicious inquirer can discern. He dissembled and withheld facts. But his conduct in these respects was far less blameworthy than Garfield's, Colfax's or Kelley's.

Plainly Garfield testified falsely. Then when Ames did not come to his support with as much friendliness as had been expected, but in a blunt way proceeded to tell the truth, he lapsed into silence and as much as confessed his perjuries. Colfax, caught in the same web of falsehood, with far less sagacity made rejoinders. He interrogated and cross-examined Ames. But the more he tried to extricate himself from the quag the more deeply did he sink into it. Alleging that he had paid Ames $500, which after five years that man still owed him, without a suspicion that the sum had any connection with the Crédit Mobilier, was bad enough. But he countered as to the $1,200 directly given him on account of dividends by a complete failure of memory on the point. He had never received the money, though the sergeant-at-arms held the used check as a voucher, and, though there was evidence that he had deposited the sum in the First National Bank in Washington. When pressed further he reached the conclusion that the money he had put into the bank had come from a man named Nesbitt in New York, who had given it to him secretly to aid him in his campaign to become Vice President on the ticket with Grant in 1868. But it appeared that Nesbitt held a valuable contract from the Post Office Department for the manufacture of envelopes, and, as Colfax was chairman of the Post Office Committee in the House, his last state was worse than his first.[1]

Those who, like Bingham, Boyer and James F. Wilson, made no mystery of their connection with the company and frankly testified that they had taken the stock as an investment escaped censure. All who were involved in the investigation might much better have pursued this course. William B. Allison had been as culpable as Colfax. His course, perhaps, merited greater disapproval, yet he was but little con-

[1] Crawford, pp. 174-5, 182.

demned for it and he was destined like Garfield, Kelley, Dawes and Logan to enjoy many years of successful public life.

Very properly the whole impression of the investigation was disturbing. The Poland Committee was without discrimination in making up its judgments. Its members, like some of the accused, were unduly excited in the face of an aroused public opinion which, callous for years to public and private infamies, had suddenly become over-sensitive. Though Ames had spoken of assigning the shares [1] he did not give them away. His offense consisted in selling them to friends for par and interest, while in several cases he had agreed to keep open accounts with the purchasers and take his payments out of the dividends, none of which, however, had yet been declared. Indeed, at the time the stock was distributed it had no certain value.[2] No measure affecting the fortunes of the road was then pending in Congress; none was in prospect. No division of feeling existed, no distrust of the direction was expressed. Every department of the government was eagerly concerned that the work should be finished at the earliest possible day, and would have given its aid to this end freely and cheerfully.[3] Ames had had a long struggle to secure the co-operation of capitalists in the prosecution of the undertaking, and it would be of material assistance to him in this work, if he could say that a number of men whose names were favorably known in politics were connected with it.

Yet it is clear, though he performed a notable national service, that he acted tactlessly. Whether, when he had written his letters to McComb, he knew the finer meanings of words or not he was carrying stock for public men who should not have allowed him to do so. He was censurable for proposing the distribution; they were greatly to blame for receiving dividends on shares which had cost them nothing, and

---

[1] Crawford, p. 104.

[2] Hazard, p. 32; Crawford, p. 179.

[3] Crawford, p. 92. It was not until April 5, 1869, that the New York Herald found it feasible to say that the construction of the Pacific Railroad was "the most gigantic swindle ever perpetrated under the shadow of the law."

which they had never seen. But at this time the agents of other corporations in Washington were offering as much to Congressmen and the moral view of such transactions was plainly tolerant, when men so widely respected as Colfax, Garfield, Henry Wilson, James F. Wilson and Allison would stop to•listen to proposals of this kind. That Ames had had any corrupt purpose in selling the shares to his friends, or that their action was altered or influenced on this account was not proven at the time, nor is so much demonstrable in the light of later examination.

Denial of the power of the House to expel a member under such circumstances was expressed•by the Committee on the Judiciary [1] and the recommendations of the Poland Committee were not taken. It was resolved instead that the House should "absolutely condemn" •the conduct of Ames and Brooks. It was·a dramatic moment. Ames had listened to the excoriations of members who were seizing the opportunity for virtuous speech. His defence had been read from the clerk's desk.[2] He was a man nearing 70 years of age. His face was ashen as he awaited the decision of his associates. The vote was 182 to 36,[3] and immediately members who had known him for half a life time, and who in many cases were as guilty as he in transactions in reference to other corporate enterprises, crowded up to apologize for what they had just done. They had been constrained to their action against their judgment, in violation of the dictates of friendly hearts, by the clamor which had been raised by the disclosures. However indiscreet he may have been no man could be brought to sincere belief in any wilful intention of wrong-doing on the part of this public spirited and useful man.[4]

Brooks, for whom less sympathy could be felt, awaited his humiliation and disgrace, like Ames, in silence. The vote against him was 174 to 32.[5] Soon Congress adjourned. Both

[1] House Reports, 42nd Cong. 3rd sess., no. 81, pp. 8-13.
[2] Cong. Globe, 42nd Cong. 3rd sess., pp. 1723-7.
[3] Ibid., p. 1833.
[4] Crawford, p. 216; Hazard, pp. 39-41.
[5] Cong. Globe, 42nd Cong. 3rd sess., p. 1833.

men were broken by the fall and in a month or two died, Brooks at the end of April and Ames a week later in May, 1873.[1]

In the other branch of Congress Patterson whose term would expire in a few days was allowed to retire without a formal expression of the condemnation of the body of which he had been a member for six years. Not able to reply to his accusers in the Senate his defence was published afterward.[2]

Instead of the profits being enormous, as it pleased the public to believe, and, as the Wilson Committee, in order to be on the popular side, affirmed, it was clear from the evidence, if it had been studied, that they were not much larger than was justified by the labor and risk which attended this important national service.[3] The committee said that such frauds had been practised upon the government that the franchises of the company ought to be declared forfeited; or Congress might repeal the charter. Such action would lead to the government's operating the road, or forced sale in the market, and to either proceeding there would be "grave public objections." Moreover, judgment of forfeiture would do injustice to many innocent stockholders. The committee, therefore, recommended the passage of a bill instructing the Attorney General to institute a suit in equity against all who had ever received stock which had not been paid for, or dividends drawn from profits made in the construction of the road, with a view to recovery.[4]

[1] These two men were the "scapegoats." It was "a most miserable effort to appease public clamor by offering up to it the two most convenient victims."—J. P. Davis, The Union Pacific Railway, p. 202.
[2] Senate Reports, 42nd Cong. 3rd sess., no. 519.
[3] Hazard, pp. 26, 27-9; Crawford, p. 72; J. P. Davis, pp. 170-3.
[4] House Reports, 42nd Cong. 3rd sess., no. 78, p. xx. This proposed act was so amended, when the subject came into Congress, that it was made to include a direction to the Secretary of the Treasury to retain all of the money earned by the road in transportation for government account, a subject which it was supposed had been disposed of in 1871. The proceedings taken under the law at length reached the Supreme Court, which declared that no case had been made against the company. No fraud had been found in the progress of the work, and the government was ordered to pay the company the funds belonging to it which had been wrongfully withheld.—Crawford, pp. 118-20; Hazard, pp. 33-4, 38-40.

If Blaine could theatrically clear himself of connection with the Crédit Mobilier he, as many men knew, could not have done so had the accusation covered the affairs of other railroads. He was brought into the investigation concerning a line running from Dubuque to Sioux City, also in charge of the Poland Committee, which was dealing with the Crédit Mobilier scandal. The Dubuque and Sioux City Railroad was one of four lines projected through the state of Iowa from the Mississippi to the Missouri River. It was endowed with land before the war and the company succeeded in reaching Iowa Falls, 120 miles from Dubuque, in the ten years allowed it for completing the work. About 180 miles remained to be built. Unable to proceed the company transferred its franchise, its unused land grant and other rights to a new company of which John I. Blair of New Jersey was the controlling force.

But the life of the land grant had expired and it must be extended by act of Congress on March 2, 1868. Having secured the necessary legislation Blair began to sell the stock of a construction company, a small Crédit Mobilier to which various public men, including Oakes Ames (for a large sum), Samuel Hooper, William B. Allison and other Congressmen were subscribers. It was noised about that Blaine, who had had no money of his own, had brought in his friends, the Coburns, large capitalists in Maine, to the amount of $200,000. To what extent he personally was interested with them, what commissions he had received, if any, for securing their aid, no one found out, although he was "catechised," as he alleged, quite "impertinently." The committee when they were done, were without evidence of an incriminating kind against Blaine or any of his associates in Congress.[1] It was a further revelation, however, of the extent to which speculation was going on at Washington. Why, if not to gain their influence, were senators and representatives, many of them poor men, taken into schemes involving great issues of stock?

The truth is that Blaine's financial needs were much beyond what he was able to earn as a member of Congress. He spent

[1] House Reports, 42nd Cong. 3rd sess., no. 82.

freely and came in for not a little criticism by the opposition press for his "princely style of living." [1] His ambitions, socially and politically, were well known even now in the first years of his public career, and he turned to the speculation in which men generally were absorbed.

The enterprise which specially and most unfortunately occupied him was the Little Rock and Fort Smith Railroad, to which he had been introduced by a certain Warren Fisher, a business partner of one of Mrs. Blaine's brothers, Eben C. Stanwood, a merchant in Boston. Blaine and Fisher had been connected in speculative ventures while Blaine was still a newspaper editor in Augusta. The Little Rock road had received its land grant long before the outbreak of the war. No progress having been made under the first charter the company was re-incorporated, in 1866, by the legislature of Arkansas and the franchise in 1868 came into the hands of Josiah Caldwell, Fisher and a group of capitalists in Boston. Twenty miles of the road must be constructed within three years, or before July 28, 1869. An extension was obtained by act of Congress, while Blaine was Speaker of the House.[2] Soon afterward he was offered an opportunity for "participation" in the scheme on terms which he thought were "in every respect as generous" as he could "expect or desire." He did not feel that he would "prove a deadhead in the enterprise"; he saw "various channels" in which he knew that he could be "useful." [3] His reward would be large commissions in money and land grant bonds, if he would bring in his friends.

By September, 1869, he had sold bonds of the road to various persons yielding $130,000 in money,[4] and he was eagerly seeking more buyers. His attack upon Jay Cooke passed the limits, one could suppose, of delicacy, if not of honor. The construction of this road would lead "to a profit of many millions," he said. Through him bonds and preferred and common stock of a face value of $221,000 could

[1] Letters of Mrs. J. G. Blaine, vol. i, p. 22.
[2] Edward Stanwood, Life of Blaine, pp. 151-3.
[3] Ibid., p. 154.
[4] Ibid., pp. 155-6.

be had for $85,000. Not one but two Pacific.roads could be
Cooke's, if he should "make the contract now." Blaine, writing on the 10th, importunately asked for "a decided answer
by the 17th inst., Wednesday of next week." Bonaparte had
"lost his great and final battle by carelessly neglecting to secure the advanced position of Quatre Bras." Here was the
Quatre Bras of the "Southern continental railroad." If it
were secured the "field of Waterloo" would be won "without
a struggle." "And now in conclusion," Blaine continued, "a
few words personal and special. In the great enterprises
which lie before you I may say without egotism that my position will enable me to render you services of vital importance
and value,—services from which I cannot derive or accept
profit or gain to myself. I am willing, however, and ready
to do all for you in my power at any time you may desire. . . .
I am willing to serve you where I am absolutely debarred
from any participation in profits. Are you not willing to aid
me where you can do so with profit to yourself at the same
time?" How he himself would be aided by the subscription
Blaine said that he "need not explain." The letter was
"Strictly Private." [1]

Receiving no encouragement by course of mail Blaine soon
made his appearance in person. He would not take "no" for
an answer; but the offer was definitely declined early in
1870 with a promise to befriend the insistent man in other
ways. [2]

Others who were appealed to as eagerly did not display such power of resistance. Sales were made by some
one—Blaine or other person—to the Union Pacific Company,
the Atlantic and Pacific and the Missouri, Texas and Pacific,
without reason, so far as appears, except urgent appeal on the
one hand and a desire not to offend on the other. [3] The Little

[1] Oberholtzer, Jay Cooke, vol. ii, pp. 171-3.
[2] On Jan. 4, 1870, Jay Cooke wrote his brother Henry in charge of the
firm's offices in Washington, saying that they would "try and do everything that is right and kind and generous by him at the right time."
—Ibid., p. 173.
[3] Cf. Stanwood, Life of Blaine, pp. 145-7, 169; Cong. Record, 44th
Cong. 1st sess., pp. 2724-5.

Rock and Fort Smith road had been chosen from among a score for a bond subsidy in the "omnibus bill" which was reported out of the Senate Pacific Railroad committee in 1869.[1]

But the company was soon in sore straits. In December, 1870, Blaine was obliged to tell those to whom he had sold the bonds that the interest due in January could not be paid, and he was in a most unhappy situation. He and Fisher were involved in disputes about money matters which led to increasing friction between them. Now and then Blaine would mark his communications "Confidential," or "Private and Personal"; again he would write a postscript, "Burn this Letter," and some of the statements on both sides were equivocal. It was not until 1876 that it pleased Fisher to make the correspondence public through a clerk in his employ, one James Mulligan, who also believed himself to have a grievance against Blaine. The House of Representatives was now in Democratic hands and the Committee on the Judiciary on May 2, 1876,[2] was instructed to make an investigation of the case. Blaine was in doubt as to what course he should pursue[3] but he wavered only a short time. Whether for better or worse he visited Mulligan in a hotel, got hold of the letters, took them away with him and, carrying the package into the House, rose to a personal explanation. Waving them aloft, reading such parts as he chose with his comments, he appealed to the American people for a vindication. The effect of the performance, since the evidence contradicted what he had said in explanations only a few weeks before,[4] remains to be considered in a later place. But the offense belongs in the period under review, the loosest as to standards for men identified with our public life which we have ever known.

It has been said in Blaine's defence that his appeals to his

[1] Senate Reports, 40th Cong. 3rd sess., no. 219.
[2] Cong. Record, 44th Cong. 1st sess., p. 2884.
[3] Letters of Mrs. J. G. Blaine, vol. i, p. 136.
[4] He had said, e.g., on April 24 in the House that he had never had any of the bonds of the Little Rock company except what he had paid for "at precisely the same rate" at which they were sold to "other people in New England."—Cong. Record, 44th Cong. 1st sess., p. 2725.

friends for subscription to the bonds of the railroad were those of one business man to another.[1] They were not so regarded at the time. They were entertained in most instances, when they were entertained at all, because they came from an influential leader in Congress who could give much and take much away. When Henry D. Cooke in Washington wrote to his brother, Jay Cooke, in 1872—"Blaine is so persistent in this matter that I feel it is important that he should be conciliated—We are not yet through all our fights in Congress—He is a formidable power for good or evil and he has a wide future before him—However unreasonable in his demand he may appear to you to be my conviction is irresistible that he should in some manner be appeased," and so on,[2] it was not with any belief that the Speaker of the House of Representatives was acting as a business man.

When Caldwell wrote to Fisher concerning $25,000 which Blaine asked for to meet a note and said—"I hope you can help him—I would if it were in my power—Blaine is an important man for us to have feel all right toward us," there was an imputation that he might use his political influences in an unfriendly way if he were not satisfied.[3] Whether Blaine gained or lost pecuniarily as a result of his connection with the unfortunate railway enterprise in Arkansas is beside the mark. He was playing for high stakes without a scrupulous care for his own reputation or the honor of his high office.

Oakes Ames who was caught for examination, judgment and disgrace had done much less. He was preeminently a business man. He was inconspicuous in Congress. His offense consisted in carrying a few shares of stock for certain senators and representatives until they could pay for them. He was building a great railroad to the Pacific coast at much personal risk and sacrifice. It was a large, useful and patriotic service and he and his associates needed little further assistance from the government. Blaine, on the other hand, was

[1] Cf. e.g. Blaine's own statement, Cong. Record, 44th Cong. 1st sess., pp. 2124-5.

[2] Oberholtzer, Jay Cooke, vol. ii, p. 354.

[3] Stanwood, Life of Blaine, p. 159.

using his high position as Speaker of the House of Representatives to sell the worthless bonds of a little "stumptail" railroad in a Southern state, which came from nowhere and led no whither, simply that he might pocket the commissions from the promoters and increase his private income. That he escaped the reprobation which overtook others who blindly threaded their ways through this era of our history is one of the accidents of life.

INDEX

ADAMS, Charles Francis, Johnson appoints McClellan to succeed, as minister to England, 237; his arrival in England, 391, 392; treated discourteously, 404; his opinion of Queen's officers in Liverpool, 405; his representations to Russell concerning "Florida," 405; concerning the "Laird rams," 408; concerning municipal law and international law, 412; concerning destruction of American shipping, 413; concerning the Queen's proclamation, 414; demands reparation, 415; characterizes England's offense, 416; Russell tells him that escape of "Alabama" was a "scandal," 417; that British shipbuilding industry must be protected, 419; that England will take no responsibility for acts of rebel cruisers, 418, 419; suggests arbitration of the case, 420; again states the case, 422; his arrival in England anticipated, 436; appointed member of Geneva Tribunal, 450-51; disqualified as presiding officer, 452; his representations to English government recalled, 456; value of his influence in reaching a pacific settlement, 465-6; wishes damages for losses sustained through "Retribution," 468; his final statement, 468; recognition of his services by England, 470.

Adams, Charles Francis, Jr., his opinion of Bancroft Davis's "case," 455.

Adams, John, 122.

"Agrippina," 396.

Aiken, ex-Governor of South Carolina, 11.

Akerman, Amos T., appointed Attorney General, 311; visits South Carolina, 387.

Alabama, seeks white colonists, 3; cotton factories in, 8; apathy of

white voters in, 15, 20; gerrymandered, 20; negroes invited to sit with whites, 21; election for convention, 27; constitution of, completed, 37; divorces granted by convention of, 37-8; negroes in convention of, 39; convention of, denounced, 45-6, 48, 54; conservatives in convention of, 51; day of prayer in, 53; constitution submitted to people, 54; whites refuse to vote, 54-5; restored to place in Union, 59-61; freed from military control, 61; bill to admit to Union, 148; ratifies 15th Amendment, 266; restoration of, 258; corruption in, during reconstruction, 320-21, 328; carpetbaggers in, 324; legislators in, pay no taxes, 324-5; depredations of negroes in, 339; law to suppress Ku Klux in, 369-70.

"Alabama," cruiser, ordered of Lairds, 391; escape of, 396, 405-6; cruise of, 397; sunk, 397; depredations of, 399; friendly treatment of ship and crew, 402-3; English press applauds feats of, 403; loss of, deplored in England, 403-4; escape of, encourages rebels, 407; Russell fears consequences of escape of, 409; "a fraud on neutrality," 413; diplomatic protests, 415; escape of, a "scandal" Russell says, 417; Russell disclaims responsibility for acts of, 418, 419; proposed arbitration of dispute over, 420-21; King of Prussia to umpire dispute, 424; Stanley-Johnson convention to settle dispute, 425-6; Johnson-Clarendon convention, 427-8; damages sustained through acts of, 453; steps taken by England to detain, 456; England held liable for acts of, 468; court to distribute fund secured from England, 470.

Alaska, annexation of, 225, 235;

622 INDEX

124; supports candidacy of Grant, 151-2; votes for San Domingo treaty, 237; opposes repeal of tenure of office act, 253; votes with Democrats, 257; Murphy adjutant of, 308; corrupt leadership of, 313, 543; escapes Crédit Mobilier scandal, 602.

Connecticut, ratifies 15th Amendment, 266.

Conness, Senator John, of California, eager for conviction of Johnson, 124.

Connolly, Richard B. ("Slippery Dick"), member of Tammany "Ring," 582, 584, 585; his share of the loot, 587; books of, examined by leading citizens, 587; transcript of records taken to New York Times, 590; offers bribe to George Jones, 590; confederates aim to make him scapegoat, 592; asked to resign and refuses, 592; appoints A. H. Green deputy, 592; retires, 593; arrested and goes to jail, 593-4.

Conover, 64, 67.

Constitutional conventions, registration for elections on, in South, 9-21; conservatives oppose, 21-4; carpetbaggers and scalawags support, 24-6; result of elections for, 26-30; delegates to, to meet, 31; character of, 37-54.

"Constitutional Guards," 340.

Contraction of currency, 160, 285.

Conway, T. W., 40.

Cooke, Henry D., 613.

Cooke, Jay, cashier of bank of, 65; his sales of five-twenties, 160; political campaign demands on, 187; opens office in London, 278, 529; his organization of national banks, 279; forms syndicate, 278-80; makes further proposals for funding, 281; brought before Ways and Means Committee, 281; inspects route of Northern Pacific Railroad, 522; commissioners report to, 523; obtains larger land grant, 528; selling Northern Pacific bonds, 528; his "Banana Belt," 529; his plans to annex Canada, 528-9; settlement along line of road, 530; carries speculative accounts for journalists, 542; lends money to Grant, 543; offer to Colfax, 544; his advances to politicians, 546; searches money

markets of Europe, 555-6; Blaine's urgent assaults upon, 610-11; letter to, concerning Blaine, 613.

Cooper, Edmund, 145.

Cooper, Peter, 498.

Corbett, Senator, of Oregon, vote of, in impeachment court, 125.

Corbin, Abel Rathbone, used by Jay Gould, 575; Gould buys gold for, 576, 577; condemned by Garfield's committee, 579.

Corti, Count Louis, 471.

Council of Safety, in South Carolina, 340.

Covode, John, 72.

"Cow Towns," 489, 490.

Cowan, Edgar, 211.

Cox, Jacob D., appointed Secretary of Interior, 216; influences Grant concerning Cuba, 250; congratulates Fish, 252; opposes office-mongering, 309; cool toward San Domingo treaty, 310; resigns, 311-12; Grant will not support, 313.

Cox, S. S., nomination of, rejected by Senate, 198; defends conservatives in Virginia, 257; moves to investigate Cooke's syndicate, 281; on Ku Klux Committee, 378; takes chair at Blaine's request, 602.

Craig, J. B., charged with corruption, 144.

Cramer, Dr., Grant's brother-in-law, 152.

Crawford, Judge, of Louisiana, 42.

Crebs, Congressman, of Illinois, advocates capital removal, 495.

Crédit Mobilier, exposures in connection with, 544, 545, 600-609.

Creswell, J. A. J., nominated for Vice-President, 157; appointed Postmaster General, 216; urges semi-monthly steamer service to China, 517.

Crews, Joseph, South Carolina scalawag, 379.

Crocker, Central Pacific Railroad contractor, 476.

Cromwell, 89.

Cuba, Grant's plan to annex, 228; proposed recognition of, 229; insurrection in, 244-5; insurgents form Junta in New York, 245; proposed purchase of, 247; Fish controls Grant on subject of, 248; agitation for recognition of, continues, 249; Fish again directs Grant concerning, 249-51; out-

10; opposes Sheridan's removal, 31; revokes orders of Hancock, 33; Congress proposes enlargement of powers of, 37; witness in impeachment inquiry, 63; gives keys of office to Stanton, 69; reticence of, 151; his Radical sympathies, 151-2; "son of the soil," 154; nomination of, conceded, 154; nominated for President, 157; makes a speech, 158; accepts nomination, 159; contrasted with Chase, 167, 168; Seymour to run against, 181; traveling in West, 184-5; charged with drunkenness, 185; not a "show candidate," 186; put under obligations by campaign managers, 187; "Tanners" in campaign to elect, 187, 190; Sheridan supports, 191; election of, assured, 190-92; quietly remains in West, 194; decisive majorities for, 194; visits polls, 195; returns to Washington, 195; trust reposed in, 195-6; counting electoral votes for, 201-3; notified of election, 203; withholds names of members of Cabinet, 203-4; endorses 15th Amendment, 205; his antipathy to Johnson, 208-9; transfers command to Sherman, 212; inaugurated, 212-3; appoints Cabinet, 214-21; private secretaries of, 220-221; civil appointments by, 221-3, 305, 306-8; removes conservative commanders in South, 224-5; his scheme to annex San Domingo, 225-6; dismisses scheme to annex Danish West Indies, 227; his plan to invade Mexico, 228; favors annexation of Cuba, 228; urges Fish to stay in office, 230; sends Babcock to San Domingo, 229-31; visits Sumner, 231-2, 237; calls Schurz to White House, 232; his hostility to Sumner, 233-4; urges Senate to act on San Domingo, 235-6; public opposition to annexation, 236; appoints Motley minister to England, 238; demands Motley's resignation, 239; extravagant claims for San Domingo, 239; attacked by Sumner, 240; considers himself insulted, 242; sends report of San Domingo Commission to Senate, 244; end of his annexation scheme, 244; his interest in Cuban independ-

ence, 244, 247; orders Fish to issue proclamation, 248; guided by Fish, 248-9, 250, 251; thanks Fish, 253; on tenure of office act, 253-4; proclamation as to Virginia, Mississippi and Texas, 255; fixes date of election in Virginia, 255; approves bill restoring Virginia, 257; fixes date for election in Mississippi, 260; brother-in-law nominated for Governor, 260; approves bill restoring Mississippi, 261; befriends Davis faction in Texas, 261; approves bill restoring Texas, 261; on conditions in Georgia, 263; returns Georgia to military rule, 264; approves bill restoring Georgia, 266; message on 15th Amendment, 267; serenaded by negroes, 267; elected on an honest money platform, 272; signs bill to strengthen public credit, 275; takes credit for funding operation, 280; anxiety about his re-election, 281; appointments to Supreme Court, 287; signs Schenck bill, 303; movement hostile to, 304; Rawlins's influence over, 305-6; appoints Belknap, 306; nepotism of, 306-7; vindictiveness of, 308-9; refuses to support Hoar and Cox, 309; dismisses Hoar, 310; accepts resignation of Cox, 311-2; in hands of politicians, 313; his office brokers, 313-4; on task of filling offices, 316; appoints civil service commission, 317; promises to give rules a trial, 317; insincerity of, 317-8; informed of conditions in North Carolina, 374; sends accounts of Southern outrages to Senate, 376-7; addresses Congress concerning South Carolina, 380; his Ku Klux proclamations, 380, 382, 383; Democrats hold him responsible, 386; martial law in South Carolina, 387; opposed to Johnson-Clarendon convention, 428; in accord with Sumner, 431, 432; ignorance of international law, 437; favors invasion of Mexico and Canada, 437; acts in behalf of San Domingo and Cuba, 438, 439; under influence of Badeau, 441; hostile to Motley, 441; anger of, 442; awakens Motley's ire, 444; seeks a new minister to England.

Seymour, 188; on Ku Klux Klan, 357; appears before Ku Klux Committee, 383.

Hancock, General W. S., welcomed in New Orleans, 32; Radicals attack, 33; removed, 33, 35; difficulties confronting him in Louisiana, 36; mentioned for President, 166; nominated for President, 172; strength of, in convention, 174; sent to Dakota, 225; murders in Texas during administration of, 363.

Hanks, J. M., 378.

Harden, General, 11.

Harlan, James, witness in impeachment inquiry, 63; efforts to convict Johnson, 127-8; nominated for Vice-President, 157; favors annexation of San Domingo, 235; votes for treaty, 237; opposes railway subsidies, 527.

Harlem Railroad, Vanderbilt secures control of, 557, 561, 562.

Harper, Fletcher, 589.

Harris, ex-Governor Isham G., of Tennessee, 4.

Harris, a carpetbagger in Georgia, 264.

Harrison, William H., 66, 153.

Harte, Bret, 497.

Hastings, Warren, 92.

Hatch, imprisoned in San Domingo, 236.

Hatch, General, reports murders in Louisiana, 366.

Hatfield, Commander, 502.

Havana, base of supplies for South, 411.

Havemeyer, W. F., ex-mayor of New York, 591, 592.

Hawaii, Seward's plan to annex, 225; telegraph to, 505; steamer lines to, 518.

Hawley, General, presides over Chicago convention, 156; Grant writes to, 159; revenue reformer, 303.

Hayes, S. S., 290.

Hayti, Seward visits, 227; scheme to annex, 228; Grant using force against, 231; independence of, menaced, 233.

Hazen, General, protests slaughter of buffalo, 487.

Heffter, 454.

Henderson, Senator John B., on removal of Stanton, 71; independence of, 125; denounced by Rad-

icals, 126; pressed and pursued by Radicals, 128; votes "not guilty," 131; proscribed, 132-3, 136; Chase's influence over, 135; committee to investigate, 141; insulted, 142-3; characterizes Butler, 146; votes with Democrats, 150; end of term of, 211.

Hendricks, Senator Thomas A., supports Johnson in Stanton matter, 71; objects to Wade sitting in impeachment court, 86; mentioned for President, 166; votes cast for, 174; New York supports, 177; other states support, 179.

Henry, Patrick, 33.

Hepburn v. Griswold, 283-5.

"Heroes of America," 13.

Hibernians, parade in New York, 591.

Hill, Benjamin H., opposes reconstruction, 12, 23; delegate to New York convention, 171; supports Seymour, 188; deprecates Ku Klux Klan, 354; appears before Ku Klux Committee, 383.

Hill, J. J., secures control of St. Paul and Pacific, 555.

Hoar, E. Rockwood, appointed Attorney General, 216; helps to influence Grant, 250; congratulates Fish, 252; nominated as Justice of Supreme Court, 287; his defence of Supreme Court, 289; opposes office mongering, 309; nomination rejected, 309; dismissed, 310-11; public expressions of regret, 312; compliments Fish, 312; appointed member of Joint High Commission, 447.

Hoar, George F., witnesses Grant's exhibition of anger, 241; his estimate of Grant, 313.

Hodges, negro leader in Virginia, 41.

Hoffman, John T., Governor of New York, 584; reëlected Governor, 587; candidate for President, 587, 590; rescinds order of Hall, 591.

Holden, W. W., Governor of North Carolina, 319; impeached and convicted, 337-8; declares martial law, 373-4.

Holladay, Ben, 481, 555.

Holliday, Cyrus K., 485.

Holman, Wm. S., 74.

Holmes, Oliver Wendell, 511.

Holt, Joseph, Judge Advocate General, 63.

service commission, 317; favors removal of capital, 495-6.

Memphis and Little Rock Railroad, 520.

Memphis, El Paso and Pacific Railroad, construction of, 520; Frémont president of, 520; scandal affecting, 520-21, 553-4.

Menard, J. Willis, 325.

Mennonites, settled in Kansas, 491.

"Men of Justice," in Alabama, 340.

Menocal, A. G., in Nicaragua, 502.

Meredith, William M., 451.

Merriam, Congressman, of New York, 375.

Methodist Church, used against Johnson, 127-8.

Mexico, Southern emigration to, 1, 7; proposed invasion of, 56; Grant's plan to invade, 228, 437; recognizes Cuban insurgents, 249; Ku Klux flee to, 388; railroad through Tehuantepec in, 501-2; railroad through, to Pacific, 503, 519; annexation of, 527.

Michigan, ratifies 15th Amendment, 266; fires in forests of, 552.

Miller, shipbuilder in Liverpool, 393, 406.

Miller, Justice, opinion in legal tender case, 284.

Minnesota, ratifies 15th Amendment 266; fertility of, 523; settlement of, 530-31.

Mississippi, registration of voters in, 20; gerrymandered, 20-21; election for convention, 28; Ord's course in, 35; constitutional convention in, 37; foolish proposals in convention of, 51; constitution submitted to people in, 56; in hands of military governor, 61; does not vote for President in 1868, 201; Grant's proclamation as to, 255; final acts in reconstruction of, 258-61; restored to Union, 261; ignorance in legislature of, 321-2; ignorance of office-holders, 323; sends Revels to Senate, 325-6; high mileage charges in, 331; high taxes in, 335; reports murders in, 367; law to suppress Ku Klux, 370; Ku Klux trials in, 387; outrages in, 389.

Mississippi River, bridge over, at Omaha, 482, 514; bridge over, at St. Louis, 485.

Missouri, majority in, for Grant, 194; ratifies 15th Amendment, 254,

266; liberal movement in, 268-9, 303-4.

Missouri Pacific Railroad, 521, 548.

Missouri River, bridges over, 485.

Missouri, Texas and Pacific Railroad, sale of stock to, 611.

Monks, outlaw leader in Arkansas, 364-5.

Monroe, James, consul at Rio, 2.

Moore, Jesse, favors removal of capital, 494.

Moore, Col. W. G., Johnson's private secretary, witness in impeachment inquiry, 99; on President's composure, 121; bears President's message to Congress, 200.

Moorhead, J. Kennedy, 99, 300.

Moran, Benjamin, criticizes Motley, 440-41, 445; takes charge of legation in London, 446; complains of Schenck's delay, 459.

Morgan, Senator E. D., on removal of Stanton, 71; vote in trial of Johnson, 132; opposes subsidies to railroads, 527-8.

Mori, Arinori, 513, 514.

Mormons, construct section of Pacific Railroad, 475.

Morrill, Justin S., of Vermont, opposes readmission of Alabama, 60; probable vote of, in impeachment court, 125; speaks against annexation of San Domingo, 237; votes against treaty, 237; tariff act of, 292, 297.

Morrill, Lot M., of Maine, probable vote of, in impeachment court, 125; member of committee of inquiry, 147; votes against annexation of San Domingo, 237; votes with Democrats, 257; votes against civil rights bill, 271; heads Crédit Mobilier committee in Senate, 604; recommendations of his committee, 604-5.

Morrissey, John, 178.

Morton, Levi P., 278.

Morton, Oliver P., Senator, on committee to arrange for impeachment, 81; probable vote of, 125; testimony of, 145; favors paying debt in greenbacks, 162; on committee to notify Grant, 203; favors annexation of San Domingo, 233; changes ground on greenbacks, 274; nominated minister to England, 445.

Moss Troopers, 362.

Panama Railroad, 517.

Paradis, banking house in Paris, 553.

Parker v. Davis, 287.

Parsons, ex-Governor, 65, 100, 383.

Patterson, Mrs., daughter of President Johnson, 209.

Patterson, David T., Senator of Tennessee, 71.

Patterson, James W., Senator of New Hampshire, votes against San Domingo treaty, 237; makes report on New York custom house, 597, 598; involved in Crédit Mobilier scandal, 602, 603-4, 605, 608.

Patterson, John J., corrupt speculator in South, 330-31.

Pease, Governor E. M., on murders in Texas, 363.

Peck, Judge, impeachment of, 95.

Peirpoint, Governor, 25, 57.

Pendleton, George H., candidate for President, 145, 164-5; nominated, 172; votes cast for, 174; New York refuses to support, 176; friends of, in convention, 178; withdraws in favor of Seymour, 179; disliked by friends of Johnson, 184.

Penn, William, 190.

Pennsylvania, Republican majority in, 190-92, 194; ratifies 15th Amendment, 254, 266; strong support of protective tariff in, 300-301.

Pennsylvania Railroad, fast train to Chicago, 483; double tracks, 526, 556; political power of, 558; leases Western roads and enters New York City, 558.

Pensions for soldiers, 156, 289.

Perry, B. F., ex-Governor of South Carolina, 375.

Perry, Commodore M. C., 512.

Perry, Congressman, of Ohio, 375.

Perry, Mrs., 64-5.

Peru, recognizes Cuba, 249; ships armed to attack, 252.

Pettus, General, 383.

Phelps, Congressman, of Maryland, 74, 274.

Philadelphia, dishonesty in elections in, 191-2.

Pickering, Timothy, 122.

Pierce, Franklin, 240.

Pierrepont, Edwards, suggested for English mission, 445; speaks to Chinese envoys, 509; addresses Cooper Institute meeting, 591.

Pile, William A., Congressman of Missouri, denounces Johnson, 77; nominated to be minister to Brazil, 221-2.

Pinchback, negro leader in Louisiana, 41.

Pittsburgh, Fort Wayne and Chicago Railroad, 558.

Poland, Luke P., on Ku Klux Committee, 378; heads committee to investigate Crédit Mobilier, 602; report of committee, 602-4; want of discrimination of committee, 606; recommendations of, not taken, 607; investigation of Dubuque and Sioux City Railroad, 609.

Polk, President, 472.

Pomeroy, S. C., on committee to arrange for impeachment, 81; on committee to visit Chief Justice, 86; eager for conviction, 124, 127, 128, 143; disclosures reflecting on, 145; nominated for Vice-President, 157; charged with bribery in Kansas, 596.

Pool, John, Senator, 378.

Poor Whites, antipathy of, to negroes, 358.

Poor, Admiral, in San Domingo, 231.

Poore, Ben Perley, guest of Sumner, 231.

Pope, General, in command in Georgia, 9; appoints registrars, 11; offered assistance, 11; arbitrary action of, 22; criticism of, 31; removed, 34.

Porter, Admiral, in San Domingo, 227-8.

Porter, Horace, private secretary of Grant, 221; Gould buys gold for, 577; exonerated by Garfield's committee, 579; friend of Leet, 597.

Porto Rico, proposed purchase of, 247.

Portugal, minister to, 222.

Powers, Lieutenant Governor of Alabama, 320.

Pratt, Daniel D., Senator of Indiana, 378.

Press, low estate of, 541-2.

Prevost, Admiral, 472.

Price, Congressman, denounces Johnson, 77.

Price, General, of Missouri, in New York convention, 171.

Probst, Henry, 553-4.

Protection, through tariff acts, 292;

Carey's doctrines of, 293; Greeley's views about, 294; sentiment in West, 295; of wool growers, 295-6, 297-8; as a Republican party issue, 297; Democrats denounce, 297; David A. Wells reacts against, 298-300; bills providing additional, 300-301; demands for less, 301-5.

Prussia, advance of, upon Denmark, 410; King of, as arbitrator of "Alabama" case, 424; war of, with France, 444, 461; receives Burlingame, 511.

Pruyn, Congressman, 203.

Public Debt, repudiation of, a national crime, 156, 159; plan to pay it off, 160-79; plans to pay it in greenbacks, 272-4; Congress promises payment of, in gold, 274-5; proposed distribution of, in Europe, 277; taxes used to pay, 289.

Pullman cars, improvement of, 483-4.

QUESADA, Cuban leader, 244.

RAASLAFF, General, 226.

Railways, extension of, in West, 490; financial mismanagement of, 556; consolidation of, 557-8; watering stock of, 558-9; lawless performances in connection with, 560-81.

Ramsey, Joseph H., railway president, 572; his contest with Fisk and Gould, 572-4.

Randall, A. W., Postmaster General, witness in impeachment inquiry, 63; witness at trial of Johnson, 106; confident of acquittal, 122, 126; urges more frequent sailings for China, 517.

Rawlins, General John A., at headquarters in Washington, 197; companion of Grant, 219; appointed Secretary of War, 220; his interest in Cuba, 247, 248, 438; death of, 305; successor of, 306; influence over Grant, 305-6.

Raymond, Henry J., 589.

Ream, Vinnie, sculptress, 142.

Reconstruction, under Congressional plan in South, 9-62; Johnson denounces plan of Congress in last message, 198; of Virginia, Mississippi, Texas and Georgia, 254-66.

Red River Valley, 523, 529.

"Red Strings," 13.

Reed, Harrison, Governor of Florida, 320, 336.

Reed, Henry, 188.

Republican party, convention of, in Chicago in 1868, 143, 151, 154-8; in Indiana committed to payment of debt in greenbacks, 162; sweeping victory of, 194; tariff issue confronting, 297; corruption of, in South, 386.

"Retribution," losses sustained through, 453; claims for losses by, rejected, 468.

Revels, negro preacher, in United States Senate, 326.

Revolutionary clubs in South, 340.

Reynolds, General J. J., 34, 62, 225.

Rhett, R. B., 171.

Rhode Island, ratifies 15th Amendment, 266.

Rice, B. F., of Arkansas, 377, 378.

Richards, Radical leader in Florida, 48, 49.

Richardson, Wm. A., Assistant Secretary of Treasury, 280.

"Roaring Towns," 489.

Roberts, Marshall O., his connection with Tehuantepec Railroad, 503; his endorsement of Tammany, 587, 589.

Roberts, W. Milnor, inspects route of Northern Pacific Railroad, 522, 523.

"Robertson Family" in Mississippi, 340.

Robeson, George M., appointed Secretary of Navy, 220; asked to send ships to San Domingo, 229; helps to influence Grant, 250; congratulates Fish, 252; instructs Selfridge, 499.

Robinson, J. C., Congressman of Illinois, on Ku Klux Committee, 378.

Robinson, Wm. E., Congressman of New York, tries to clear Johnson's name, 447.

Rock Island Railroad, Vanderbilt secures control of, 557.

Rocky Mountains, Pacific Railroad reaches, 474.

Roebuck, friend of South in England, 423.

Roosevelt, Robert B., 591.

Rose, Sir John, connection with funding, 278; discusses "Alabama" question, 483; conferences with

10-11; commended for fairness, 35; his removals from office, 36; asked to be Secretary of War, 149; appointed and confirmed, 149; Grant talks to, about Johnson, 151; in charge of White House, 204; greets Grant, 212; succeeded by Rawlins, 219-20.

Schurz, Carl, temporary chairman Chicago convention, 156; opposed to greenback, 162; urged by Grant to support Jones, 221; asked by Grant to vote for San Domingo, 232; against San Domingo, 235, 237; leads Liberal movement in Missouri, 269; elected senator, 269; votes against civil rights bill, 271; punished by Grant, 309; civil service reformer, 315; opposes Ku Klux law, 381-2; his opinion of Sumner's speech on Johnson-Clarendon treaty, 431; a leader against public corruption, 597.

Scofield, Glenni W., member of Ku Klux Committee, 378; involved in Crédit Mobilier scandal, 602, 603.

Scott, John, Senator from Pennsylvania, votes against San Domingo, 237; votes with Democrats, 257; on North Carolina inquiry committee, 377; on Ku Klux Committee, 378.

Scott, General R. K., Governor of South Carolina, 320; pays no taxes, 324; railway speculations of, 330-31; gets rich, 333-4; enemies of, attempt to impeach, 337; enrolls negro troops, 374-5; insolence of his militia, 379.

Scott, Thomas A., 558.

"Sea King," see "Shenandoah."

Seattle, 523, 524, 531.

Selfridge, Commander, explores Isthmus of Darien, 499-500.

Semmes, Raphael, supports Seymour, 188; commander of "Sumter," 396; takes command of "Alabama," 397, 403; honored in England and her colonies, 403, 404; farcical prize courts of, 412.

Semple, conservative leader in Alabama, 42.

Seward, F. W., testifies in hearings as to impeachment, 106; sent to San Domingo, 227-8.

Seward, Wm. H., Secretary of State, appealed to in behalf of rebels in Brazil, 2; his circular on Chinese, 6; witness in impeachment inquiry, 63; objects to Field as counsel for Johnson, 90; suggests other names, 90; nominated by Evarts, 91; faithfulness to Johnson, 91; his clerks search records, 122; confident of acquittal of Johnson, 122; announces adoption of 14th Amendment, 197; dines Grant, 208; advises Johnson concerning course to be followed at Grant's inauguration, 209; ability of, 215; expansionist, 225; plans to annex Danish West Indies, 225-6; visits Hayti, 227; his policies in Cuba, 246; addresses England as war breaks out, 391; his apology for sinking of "Florida," 395; informed of unfriendliness of people in Liverpool, 401; hears of pro-Southern sentiment in Nassau, 402; England's view of, 404; protests England's course, 404-5; protests building of Laird rams, 408; informed of blockade running, 411; declares American commerce is "perishing," 413; denounces Queen's proclamation, 414; hears from Adams, 416; repels advances of Russell, 421; restates case, 422; in haste for settlement, 424-5; shapes Stanley-Johnson convention, 425-6; shapes Johnson-Clarendon convention, 427; leaves office, 428; Reverdy Johnson writes to, 433; visits California and Alaska, 481; welcomed in "Walrussia," 482; his plans for an isthmian canal, 498; persuades Burlingame to return to China, 506; sends portrait of Washington to China, 506; Chinese embassy pays respect to, 508; entertains embassy, 504; Japanese bring gifts to, 512; attentions accorded, in Japan, 512-3.

Seymour, Horatio, Jr., chairman of New York convention, 172; career of, 175-6; his attitude toward Chase, 177; nomination for Presidency forced on, 179-80; country receives his name coldly, 181; urged to withdraw, 183; Johnson's friends distrust, 184; supported by South, 188; disloyal to Chase, 188-9; Chase declines to support, 190; retirement of, urged, 192; sticks, 193; takes the stump, 193-4; elec-

sion of Alabama, 59-60; independent mind of, 125; denounced by Radicals, 126; votes Johnson "not guilty," 132; proscription of, 132-3, 136; disrespect shown, 155; suggests franchise for Chinamen, 206; thorn in side of Radicals, 211-2; opposes repeal of tenure of office act, 253; debate with Sumner, 257; supports conservatives in Mississippi, 261; denounces Radical course in Georgia, 265; aims to influence Sumner, 270; votes against civil rights bill, 271; opposes Ku Klux law, 381-2; offered English mission, 445; visits California, 481; leader against corruption in politics, 597.

Tucker, Beverly, 396.

Tugendbund, 362.

"Tuscaloosa,' losses sustained by acts of, 453.

Tweed, Wm. M., friend of Murphy, 308; wholesale robberies of, 539, 585-6, 592; quarters journalists on New York City, 542; ally of Gould and Fisk, 566, 570; son of, made receiver, 571; leader of Tammany "Ring," 581, 582; basis of his power, 583; secures new city charter, 584; in full control of city, 584; his share of loot, 587; extravagant life of, 587; public gifts of, 588; proposed statue of, 588; attacked by New York Times and Harper's Weekly, 588; tries to buy off Jones and Nast, 589; destroys Harper schoolbooks, 589; embarrassed by death of Watson, 589-90; affronts "Young Democracy," 590; frightened by Cooper Institute meeting, 591; attempts to make Connolly scapegoat, 592; arrest of, 593; resigns, 593; in felon's garb, 594; set free and rearrested, 595; death of, 595.

"Tycoon," "Alabama" burns, 397.

UNION LEAGUE, in South, 12-3.

Union Pacific Railroad, progress of work on, 474; passes 1,000th milepost, 475; end of, joined with Central Pacific, 476-8; congratulations induced by completion of, 478-9; high freight and passenger rates on, 482; reduction of rates on, 483; buffalo on line of, 486, 488; the way to India, 496-7; deep snows on, 513-4; hurts busi-

ness of Pacific Mail, 517; a compromise line, 519; seeks colonists for its lands, 526; predictions concerning, 526; subsidy for, 527; Durant's connection with, 538-9; low price of bonds of, 548; raid on, by Fisk, 571; dissensions of, with Central Pacific, 599; scandals affecting, 600-608; officers of, accused of fraud, 608; suits to recover dividends paid by, 608; sales of stock of Little Rock road to, 611.

United States Express Company, 572.

VALLANDIGHAM, Clement L., 171, 423.

Van Buren, John D., supports Chase for President, 169, 173, 177-8; urges Chase to support Seymour, 189; declines in behalf of Chase, 193.

Vance, Zebulon B., supports Seymour, 188.

Vanderbilt, "Commodore," asked by Sutro to help build tunnel, 532; his "corners" in Wall Street, 539; early career of, 556-7; secures control of Harlem, Hudson River, and New York Central railroads, 557; his Western connections, 557-8; "waters" stock, 558-9; buoyant character of, 561-2; seeks control of Erie, 562; meets Drew, 562-3; outwitted by Drew, Fisk and Gould, 563-4; accused of designs on person of Drew, 565; buying votes in New York legislature, 565-6; makes peace with Drew, 566; abandons contest for control of Erie, 570; in "rate war" with Fisk, 571-2.

Van Horn, Burt, 99.

Van Trump, Congressman, 378.

Van Winkle, Senator, of West Virginia, takes oath in impeachment court, 86; probable vote of, 125; votes "not guilty," 132; denounced and proscribed, 132, 136; Chase's influence on, 135; end of term of office of, 211.

Vermont, Republican majority in, 190; ratifies 15th Amendment, 266.

Vicksburg, battle of, 409.

Victoria, Queen, proclamation according belligerent rights to South, 391, 414, 418, 422, 430, 433, 440, 441, 453, 456; to choose members

DATE DUE

GAYLORD			PRINTED IN U.S.A.